Our Common History:
The Transformation of Europe

Our Common History:

The Transformation of Europe

Edited by Paul Thompson
with Natasha Burchardt

Humanities Press
Atlantic Highlands, N.J. 07716

First published in the USA in 1982 by
Humanities Press Inc., 171 First Avenue,
Atlantic Highlands, New Jersey 07716, USA and
simultaneously in Great Britain by
Pluto Press Limited, Unit 10 Spencer Court,
7 Chalcot Road, London NW1 8LH

Typeset by Red Lion Setters, 22 Brownlow Mews,
London WC1N 2LA
Printed and bound in the USA

Library of Congress Cataloging in Publication Data
Main entry under title:

Our common history.

1. Social history-20th century-addresses, essays, lectures.
2. Europe-Social conditions-20th century-Addresses, essays, lectures.
I. Thompson, Paul Richard, 1935- II. Burchardt, Natasha.
HN16.093   306'.09   82-1028
ISBN 0-391-02606-2   AACR2

309.14
093

Contents

6 CONTENTS

To
Esther
born
24 March 1979

Baker's boy on his rounds (Paris 1937). *Collection Viollet*

Introduction by Paul Thompson

Why 'Our Common History'? The truth is that as I look at it again, now ready for printing, I am still a little surprised myself. For this is a book which has claimed its title from its own intrinsic qualities: from its sense of common purpose and from the criss-crossing of themes and concerns which give it such overall coherence. In this it certainly far exceeds the hopes which I or – I imagine – most of the other contributors could have held before the weekend in March 1979 at which these twenty-one papers were presented.[1] Few of the authors had ever met before, or even knew of each other's work. They had written about the past of eight different countries in Europe, focussing on various different decades back to the beginning of the present century, and tackling problems which ranged from the political struggles against Fascism across Europe to the private loneliness of the Swedish bedchamber. Although most of them would call themselves historians, five currently work as sociologists and one as an ethnologist; one is an independent writer of international standing; while the professional academics run from young researchers to acknowledged leaders of scholarship. On the face of it, all they had in common was that in their own countries they had been pioneers of 'oral history': in some fashion or other they had discovered that history was not merely hidden away in documents, but was carried down to the present in the memories, words and life experience of the people who had witnessed it and still survived among them. And so, in describing and interpreting the past, they had begun to listen to the testimony of the living. Yet as anybody who has heard many life stories will know, it is a part of their fascination and challenge that each life has, as a whole, a unique shape and often locally rooted particularity. How could the use of such diverse and individual material lead, apparently without any consciously shared intention, to the writing of 'Our Common History'? I would suggest that there are strong reasons of two kinds.

The first is that we have much more of a shared European past than we can easily imagine. It is obscured from us in many ways: by barriers of language and contrasts in appearance, by the diversity of national politics, and especially by the traditional presentation of history itself as most of us first heard it at school and still hear it on the media or as tourists, a history which segments itself around political and national themes and the celebration of famous individuals. Yet it hardly needs to be argued that even at this level the grand themes are cross-continental: the rise of mass politics and socialism, the counter-thrust of Fascism, the Resistance and the two World Wars almost everywhere provided the turning points which divided period from period and the issues which united the victors and the defeated. And behind the surface conflicts lies the fundamental social transformation of Europe in the present century: the uprooting of the peasantry, the flight to the towns, the moulding of industrial working class consciousness, the changing position of women and the growth of the small, privatised family.

We have grouped the papers so that two sections focus on political issues: the first on working class consciousness in phases of both hope and despair, and the penultimate section on the destruction wrought by Fascism and the resistance to it. The papers in between are primarily concerned with social change. These divisions are inevitably arbitrary, for the subject-matter of the papers overlaps—so that there is more, for example, on the history of women and also on Fascism than the headings suggest; and one could have chosen to highlight some alternative recurrent themes, such as social change through migration and urbanisation (as in Bertaux-Wiame and Bertaux; Jalla, Scaraffia and Passerini). But we have stuck with this framework, not only because it is close to that in which the original papers were given, but also because we think that it serves to underline the dual concern of the papers as a whole with the impact of both political struggle and the changing social structure—of class, of space (as in Wilke and Elégoët), of sexual and age divisions: in short, with politics *and* everyday life. For this is in part what binds this book together. These grand themes emerge at the level of the lives of ordinary people as a shared experience right across the continent, from Scandinavia to the Mediterranean. The two papers on the roles played by women in the wartime resistance in Italy and Holland show this especially vividly. And the British social historian, too, will recognise again and again elements of our own two hundred years of industrialisation—some of it part of a past which has long receded beyond living witness in our own country; times, for example, when the land was still largely worked by the peasant family, or the early factories fed by child labour. But there are some regions of Europe where much the same process of social change has been compressed within a single lifetime, and the voice of that experience is still to be heard: which makes this book 'Our Common History' in yet another sense again.

*   *   *   *

The other reasons for its claim to this title spring from the special characteristics of oral history itself. This shows itself both in the vividness of human detail, and in the new originality possible when historians can cease to be 'captives of the pre-existing sources'.[2] For as soon as they realise that where written documents are unreliable or non-existent they can through interviews create the missing material which they need, historians can begin to turn their attention to the forgotten areas of history where some of the key dynamics of social change lie hidden, and in particular to daily life at work and in the home; and to those people most often missed by the records—the women and children of the household, and the labourers at the workplace. It is striking how often it is at this level – even in the more directly political papers – that new interpretations are reached. And closely linked to this is the radical potential of oral history. For in bringing ordinary people to the centre of the stage, it offers not only a new way of viewing the past, but a means of generating confidence and changing consciousness which could actively contribute to the reshaping of our future. As a hope this is shared, I believe, by all the contributors; but it rings clearest of all in Sven Lindqvist's powerful conclusion.

Scarcely ten years ago if you had asked any historian this side of the Atlantic what 'oral history' was, they would probably have never heard of the term. If they had, they would have thought of it as an Americanism coined to describe the tape recording of the memoirs of 'great men'. Since then a very different oral history movement has arisen in Europe, rediscovering in the process deep roots which go back to the early collectors of oral tradition in Britain and Germany, to the mid-19th century pioneers of systematic ethnology in Scandinavia or of the social interview like Henry Mayhew, and to founders of both popular national history and scholarship like Michelet in France. How far does this collection represent this new European oral history movement?

First of all, *Our Common History* has to be seen as complimentary to the British achievement in oral history. Here the Oral History Society and its twice-yearly journal *Oral History*[3] goes back to the early 1970s, and important articles using oral history methods have also been appearing for some years in other journals. Because of this, parallel with the present volume, we have also been able to plan a second volume of essays in oral history concerned entirely with Britain, under the title of *The Past Among Us*. The themes interweave closely with those of *Our Common History* and we expect that many of the readers of the one will be drawn to the other too. Besides such work there has also been a great variety of other publication: popular best-sellers like Ronald Blythe's semi-fictional *Akenfield*; scholarly books like Robert Moore's *Pitmen, Preachers and Politics* or George Ewart Evans' *Where Beards Wag All*; community booklets like those of Centreprise in East London, Queenspark in Brighton or Bristol Broadsides; and a full-scale discussion of the oral history method in practice, and its implications for the interpretation of history, in my own *The Voice of the Past*.[4] In Britain we had been finding our way alone for six years or more before we gradually began to discover, in country after country, another separate network of fellow-spirits stumbling in the same direction. And when we invited them to join us in the first International European Conference in Oral History – for the first has been followed by a second in Amsterdam, and a third is planned for Aix-en-Provence – we above all wanted to hear them, rather than ourselves. And we hoped too to learn not so much about the basic problems and traps in the method which we had already discovered through our own experiments (although the papers do, in fact, concern themselves to a considerable degree and with new insights on certain key methodological issues); but rather to share with them what oral history had enabled them to discover.

We were aware at the time of some of the gaps among those who came, and have come to realise others since. We had one participant only from Eastern Europe, from Hungary, but in the event none from Poland, although we had already made contact with the remarkable development of popular life history writing there. Hence the inclusion here of a paper of my own. During the discussion sessions at the conference we were also able to learn more about other pioneering work in Scandinavia, such as that of the Danish National Museum or of the ethnologist Ilmar Talve in Finland.[5] We clearly could have had many more contributors both from Italy and from France. There is lively oral history work in progress in many parts of Italy besides Turin: projects on popular culture and on the Resistance abound in the north, and the Amsterdam conference revealed a remarkable group of oral historians from Sardinia too. And Turin itself can also boast Nuto Revelli, author of *Il Mondo dei vinti* ('The World of the Defeated'), that extraordinarily moving and politically passionate account of the last generation of Piedmontese peasantry which has become Italy's oral history best-seller.[6] In France, too, there is much

more oral history happening, not only in Paris, but still more in the provinces. From Brittany, Revelli's achievement is matched in popularity by
the reflective memories of a landless farmworker's son, Pierre Jakez
Hélias, whose *Le Cheval d'Orgueil* (now translated into English as *The
Horse of Pride*) has sold over a million copies. And in the south there are
two especially notable circles of activity, one centred on the museum of
the old metal factory town of Le Creusot and the university of Lyon, the
other, the regional study of 'ethnotexts' – combining social history, oral
tradition and popular culture – launched by Philippe Joutard and his
colleagues from Provence.[7] Lastly, we lacked from Britain itself one of the
creators of oral history in Europe. Unknown to us, Ronald Fraser was
about to publish his masterly *Blood of Spain*[8]: a book which finally
demonstrates how it is possible to construct a new historical vision of
great events, of political crisis, civil war and social revolution, through the
memories and words of the common people.

To have included all this would of course have been far beyond the
scope of this single volume, yet notwithstanding the gaps, it does I believe
fairly reveal the overall shape of the contemporary oral history movement
in Europe. The four papers from Scandinavia represent the most continuous development, going back to the inter-war use of wire recorders and
further back still with written-down interviews, to the extent that Orvar
Löfgren can make good use in his own work of the material which earlier
ethnologists collected from the late 19th century peasant communities of
Sweden. Since the 1930s this Scandinavian ethnology has left its
influence in the British Isles too, with the work of the Irish Folklore
Commission, the School of Scottish Studies, and other centres studying
dialect and popular culture in Wales, Leeds and Sheffield. Subsequently
the growth in the 1970s of a new form of social history in Britain through
the use of interviews has, conversely, had its influence in Europe. This is
reflected most directly in the character of the two papers from the Netherlands—and indeed, for some time, experience has been shared through
the presence at British social history meetings of groups from the notably
student-based Dutch movement. There have also been personal links
with the much more recent spread of oral history activity in Spain and in
Germany. Both these countries have, however, shared a special obstacle:
for in Spain at least until the death of Franco, and in Germany still today,
it is hard to generate enthusiasm for unburying a past best forgotten,
memories of pain or shame. In Italy, by contrast, the oral history movement was itself born of the Liberation movement—even if (as Ellwood and
Brave, Lanzardo, and Passerini all indicate) this has had a parallel effect in
influencing the shapes and silences of popular memory, and provided one

of the particular challenges with which Italian oral historians have been concerned. Here – as in Britain, Holland and France – a second major stimulus has come from feminism. In their combination of sensitive historical detail with questions of both general theory and the practice of politics – socialist and feminist – the seven papers here well represent the special vitality and diversity of the Italian movement. Another separate current, again carried forward by the post-1945 political transformation, half grown out of American inter-war sociology but not yet quite oral history (partly just because the tape recorder remains a luxury in Eastern Europe), is found in the Polish life histories. And finally there is France, under-represented here, even if a relatively new movement, but again with a particular character of its own. This comes across especially in a sensitivity (as in Bertaux-Wiame) to not only what is stated through a life story, but also to the precise forms and words in which it is spoken, and a use of both in order to penetrate the layers of conscious and unconscious meaning which a testimony can convey.[9]

What has this diverse movement in common? It is certainly not identical methods or objectives, let alone the standards and procedures now formally adopted by the American Oral History Association, where the pace has been led by professional oral history archivists. Most European practitioners of oral history are not primarily 'oral historians' as such, but using the method, as one among many, for some particular purpose in a wider context. They are unlikely to be concerned in an exclusive way with spoken evidence. What holds them together is a belief that what other people have to tell about their own lives is profoundly important for understanding both our past and our present.

We have already observed that these papers were not intended to focus on discussions of method, which we have considered much more fully elsewhere. It is however worth picking out a few of the methodological issues which do arise in several of them.

The first is the relationship between the evidence of interviews and written documents. None of the contributors here has been working exclusively with oral evidence. Each would wish to see the two forms used in interaction, reinforcing or correcting, checking or setting limits to each other. One advantage of interviewing is in fact that it can lead to the discovery of new documents; or to seeing new points in documents which were already familiar. But in some fields it has been partly the inadequacies of written documentation which led initially to the use of interviews. Activities deliberately concealed, like Nazi concentration camp genocide or the underground organisation of the Partisans, leave few reliable documents. In the Netherlands indeed the *forging* of documentation was in itself a considerable activity by the Resistance. And more generally, written records inevitably concentrate on what their compilers thought was socially significant. Thus they have little to say about informal social activities or sentiments such as those within the family. And again and again they miss the significance of both women and children. There are no statistics to measure the extent of child labour in Italy, for example, while in Norway, where there were only two inspectors for the entire country appointed after child factory labour was forbidden in 1892, oral history inteviews reveal that the contemporary official reports were entirely wrong: for child labour – including nightwork – continued to be *normal* for at least twenty years afterwards. Similarly, Norwegian agricultural statistics provide a thoroughly inaccurate record both of farm wages, by missing out those lowest-paid farmhands who received no regular wages at all, or of the farm workforce, because they excluded farmers' wives despite the fact that, on account of the frequent absence of the men, these women performed the *greater* part of the labour on the farms. In these and many other fields oral history can provide an essential corrective to or substitute for the inadequacies of the written document. But its special potential goes beyond this, for it may be used particularly creatively in *linking* different kinds of information, some available in written records or statistics and some freshly uncovered, through the connecting thread of individual life stories, and using this combination to discover, for example, the differing migration objectives and patterns of men and women (Bertaux-Wiame); or the normally suppressed subconscious impulses of peasant women for social or sexual self-realisation, as they react to the changes in everyday life forced on them by the crisis of the war (Bravo).

Parallel with this has been a recognition that in any case no hard and fast line can be drawn between written and oral evidence. The great majority of documents, whether press reports or official statistics, derive originally from oral sources. Conversely, we normally work from oral evidence which has either been transcribed from recordings, or was noted down by hand in the first place. This two-way exchange between written and oral communication has in fact been normal for centuries. The regional group of oral historians in Provence, who are especially interested in tracing how this evolution effects the character of popular traditions, thus use 'ethno-texts' as a term to cover evidence in both forms.

The second issue which cannot be separated from this is the nature of the evidence provided through interviews. We have fortunately now put behind us the stage when the main issue was whether memories could be relied on at all. It is now accepted that they can provide a great deal of rich and reliable detail, especially about everyday life at work and in the home during childhood and early adulthood. Much more caution is required in the reconstruction of events, although with a sufficient cross-cutting of testimony this too may be possible: one example here is the account of the five-day insurrection of the Catalan miners in 1932 (Borderias and Vilanova): All memories, however, are subject not only to simple, gradual erosion over time, but also to conscious or unconscious suppression, distortion, mistakes, and even to a limited extent outright lies. This is because 'stories about the past are told from the present'; telling one's life story is 'an *encounter* with reality . . . It gives meaning to the past *in order to* give meaning to the present'.[10]

We should take comfort from this, rather than panic: for it is also an indication of the relevance that our efforts can have for the present. And it is important to emphasise too that acute suppression or distortion is rare except in two contexts. The first is in interviews with certain types of person, such as those with a public reputation they still think vital to protect, or hide—crooks, teachers, politicians, top people like those who produced such 'very purposeful V.I.P. memories' to Lutz Niethammer.[11] The second is with memories which are felt to be too shameful or embarrassing to be revealed. Here the problem will depend in part on the views which – maybe unconsciously – the interviewer conveys, but also on social attitudes which prevail more widely. Thus it is rare to find an old person who will talk at all readily about stealing as an adult, and most are likely to feel some reticence about sexual matters. The silences which have been noticed in both Italy and Germany about some forms of association with Fascism are clearly a problem of this kind.

The fact that such contexts are recognisable provides the means through which the difficulty may be overcome, or even turned to advantage. In part this must be through the development of more subtle approaches to interviewing: the use of a series of interviews which allow for the uncovering of different layers of memory, perhaps beginning with spontaneous recollections and then moving on in a second session to memories recalled in response to questions; using both direct and indirect types of question, and even the exchange of information—all in different situations helping to render 'the self-evident or trivial problematic . . . the invisible visible'.[12] It is possible to compare group discussion with individual memory; or to conduct an especially searching type of interview through having two interviewers, one an insider and the other an outsider.[13] It is also particularly important to seek evidence from different standpoints. This does not mean that a deeper exploration of a few or even a single life story cannot be rewarding: as one paper here shows, it can result in very interesting insights and suggestions. But to advance with any confidence it is clearly right that 'variety of the sample' is crucial.[14]

Most of the papers here suggest how, sometimes after painful early disillusionment, it has been found that even in the more treacherous fields – like the exploration of the impact of Fascism – the most rewarding material has tended to come from accounts of patterns and incidents of daily life. Clearly, in using such evidence, it is essential to recognise the dangers of romanticisation of the past and also to avoid placing too much emphasis on continuities in social patterns which may have been desperate strategies for maintaining some sense of personal stability in situations of overwhelmingly rapid change.[15] But the opinions, the distortions – even the silences – in interviews can also contribute to interpretation. For the essential point is that interviews carry two kinds of clue, firstly through the explicit information which is conveyed, and secondly, the form of its telling. 'The facts of the story will allow us to see *social relations in action*. The forms, on the other hand, reveal the shape of the mind, the cultural and ideological structures'. Isabelle Bertaux-Wiame indeed closely relates her conclusion, that while men migrate with the aid of the family to find work, migrant women should be seen as moving through job networks to found a family, to the distinctly different ways in which her informants speak. 'Men present their life as a series of self-conscious acts, a rational pursuit of well-defined goals . . . as the subjects of their own lives—as the actors . . . Their whole story revolves round the sequences of occupations they have had'. But women are not mainly interested in recalling self-conscious acts. 'Instead, they will talk at length about their *relationship* to such or such a person'. And this contrast goes as deep as the very grammatical structures which they choose: the women turning to the use of '*on*' ('one', 'we',), linking themselves with parents, husband or children, where the men would have been invariably 'I'.[16]

It follows that the kinds of new historical insight which may be gained from oral history may be similarly divided, even if the best work invariably tends to combine both. There is first of all the possibility of reconstruction and interpretation through the recovery of lost perspectives. One could pick out many instances of that here: in Fañch Elégoët's 'dense and fine' description of the moral economy of peasant Brittany, or Gerhard Wilke's demonstration of the character of space as a social dimension in itself through its changing use, or in Daniele Jalla's identification of two contrasting types of family within the Turinese working class, distinctive both in terms of economy and tradition in ways closely parallel to the chasm between labour aristocrat and casual labour in Victorian Britain. And just because the history of women has hitherto been so seriously neglected, the group of papers dealing with women at work, in marriage and in politics (Bakker and Talsma, Scaraffia, Bravo, Slettan, Bruzzone and Swegman) make a particularly strong contribution of this kind. Some of their conclusions especially should challenge accepted platitudes: the extent for example to which even in the wartime context of Resistance organisations, accepted sexual role divisions were maintained; and the post-war trend of social and technical change in actually undermining the position of women in Norwegian farm families. One is watching the scaffolding going up here for a whole new wing to history.

The second aspect is the interpretation of changing consciousness. Although this is inevitably much more difficult to grasp, many of the papers move towards this aim. Part of Anna Bravo's purpose, for example, is to take apart the social construction of the fixed image of women's 'nature', by relating roles and ideology, consciousness and subconscious impulses. Other papers are concerned with class consciousness in a number of very different groups ranging from peasants, and the master bakers of Paris and their journeymen, to workers on the assembly lines of the vast Fiat factories in Turin. There is in this case considerably less identity in method, partly because the research contexts vary, but also because the work is still more experimental. Three ways of approaching the interpretation of consciousness are suggested which could, I believe, be very interestingly developed. The first is to examine the recollections singled out by *spontaneous* memory to see whether, as Lutz Niethammer suggests, such moments may be 'the cross-roads of learning, through which consciousness is built up'.[17] The second, which is used by both Liliana Lanzardo and Luisa Passerini, is to look especially at the contradictions in people's ideas, for it is here that consciousness is revealed in its full complexity. The third is to find meaning not only in what people say, but in what they do *not* say. Why do Torinese workers so rarely recall their association with the Fascist trade unions and leisure organisations to which many of them must have belonged or their contacts with the state social security organisation under Mussolini's regime? This very self-censorship, Luisa Passerini concludes, 'must be understood as a scar, a violent annihilation of many years in human lives which bears witness to a profound wound in daily experience'.[18]

If people can feel so compelled to bury their own past, that is in itself a measure of the power of the messages that history carries in the present. The historians who write here are unusual in their awareness of that power of history: whether it be in using history to raise consciousness, here among a first Breton generation which has turned its back on the land, there among women's groups or after-work sessions of factory workers; or in seeking, through understanding its roots, to prevent the resurgence of the tragedy of racial genocide, to lay the ghost of 'that side of our history which haunts us all'.[19] If history does matter to this extent, it is all the more vital for it not to get diverted into the shallows of mere celebratory rhetoric and too immediate and short-term political use. The interpretations have to be right. That implies in some respects a long and challenging path for research.

But this is not all, for equally, it also means that history cannot fulfil its promise if it remains the exclusive preserve of professionals. And it is just for this reason that we end with two final papers which describe how, at least in two European countries, ways of writing history which are at the same time both communal and professional are taking shape. 'History is important because its results are still with us', writes Sven Lindqvist. The past still goes on giving power, generating money, causing death, in the present. That is why 'history is dangerous'. And that is why history has to be shared.

1   The first International European Oral History Conference was held at the University of Essex on 23 25 March 1979 by the Oral History Society, with support from the university's departments of sociology and history. It was preceded by a travelling seminar, held at the South Wales Miners' Library in Swansea, the Women's Research and Resources Centre, Centreprise and the Imperial War Museum in London, and Debenham village hall in Suffolk; this was funded by the Social Science Research Council. In addition to the contributors whose papers are printed here, the programme also included Ronald Grele of the New Jersey Historical Commission, whose paper on the in-depth analysis of two interviews, 'Listen to Their Voices', is published in *Oral History*, Volume 7 (1979) Number 1; pp. 33–42; George Rawick of the University of Missouri on 'Life Histories of Working Class People in the United States'; Eugenia Meyer of the University of Mexico and Claudia Canales on their work in the Mexican National Oral History Project; Trevor Lummis on oral history research and the archive at the University of Essex; Roberto Leydi of the University of Milan on work songs in north Italy; Anne-Marie Tröger of the Freie University of West Berlin, on 'A Berlin working class neighbourhood under Nazi rule', and Robert Manchin of the Institute of Sociology, Hungarian Academy of Sciences, on 'Understanding Social Change in Rural Hungary'. In the session on Democratic History there were also presentations by Carlo Poni of the University of Bologna on the Museo della Divilta' Contadina (Museum of Peasant Life) of S. Marino in Bentivoglio; by Jørgen Burchardt of the Danish museum service who subsequently has published a joint article with Carl Erik Andresen on 'Oral History, People's History and Social Change in Scandinavia', in *Oral History*, Volume 8 (1980) Number 2, pp. 25–9; and by Jim Kelly, whose report on 'Oral History in Spain and Catalonia' appeared in *Oral History*, Volume 7 (1979) Number Two, pp. 10–4. Papers were also presented for workshop discussions by Lothar Steinbach (Düsseldorf) on 'Socialisation and education in early 20th century industrial Mannheim'; by Carl Ryant of the University of Louisville, Kentucky, on 'Reconstruction of a Black Business District'; Don Bennett of University College,

Dublin, on 'Work and Childcare in the Woman's World of the Dublin Street Trader'; and in summary, by P. Natali and F. Sitti of the Centro Etnografico del Comune di Ferrara, Italy, on 'From Oral History to Political Participation', and by Anne Roche of the University of Provence (Aix-Marseille I) on 'Vie politique et syndicale à Marseille du début des années trente à la guerre'. The two hundred participants came from eleven European countries, including also Austria and Iceland.

2   Bull: p. 223

3   For all inquiries: Oral History Society, Department of Sociology, University of Essex, Colchester CO4 3SQ, England.

4   Ronald Blythe, *Akenfield: Portrait of an English Village*, Harmondsworth 1969; Robert Moore, *Pit-men, Preachers and Politics*, Cambridge 1974; George Ewart Evans, *Where Beards Wag All: the relevance of oral tradition*, London 1970; Paul Thompson, *The Voice of the Past*, Oxford 1978—which includes chapters on how to interview, project design, and problems of memory, as well as discussions of the origins of oral history, its achievements, and interpretation—'the making of history'.

5   See Jorgen Burchardt and Carl Erik Andresen, 'Oral History, People's History and Social Change in Scandinavia', *Oral History*, Volume 8 (1980), Number Two, pp. 25–9.

6   On oral history in Italy see Paul Thompson, 'The Bologna Conference', *Oral History* Volume 5 (1977) Number One, pp. 21–32. Nuto Revelli, *Il Mondo dei vinti*, Turin 1977.

7   See Paul Thompson, 'The New Oral History in France', *Oral History* Volume Eight (1980) Number One, pp. 14–20. Pierre Jakez Helias, *Le Cheval d'Orgueil*, Paris 1975; *The Horse of Pride*, Yale 1978.

8   Ronald Fraser, *Blood of Spain*, London 1979; also, *In Hiding*, London 1972 and *The Pueblo*, London 1973.

9   The influence of Foucault is one source here, but the cooperation of students of language and history in the 'ethnotext', and also the work of Yves Lequin in Lyon, show other parallel approaches (see special issue of *Annales* on oral history, 35° année (1980), no 1, with articles by Joutard and Lequin).

10 Bertaux, p. 98; Bertaux-Wiame, p. 194.

11 Niethammer, p. 24.

12 Löfgren, p. 234.

13 Niethammer, p. 29; Luchterhand, p. 259. The double interviewer technique was also used very effectively for an oral history investigation with top scientists: David Edge, *Astronomy Transformed: The Emergence of Radio Astronomy in Britain*, New York 1976.

14 Jalla; Bertaux, p. 98.

15 Tröger (see footnote 1) puts this well.

16 Bertaux-Wiame, pp. 192-95.

17 Niethammer, p. 32.

18 Passerini, p. 61.

19 Luchterhand, p. 270.

The Industrial Working Class
in Politics and Daily Life

Oral History as a Channel of Communication between Workers and Historians

Lutz Niethammer

The question I want to explore here is how oral history can be instrumental in bringing about innovations in working class history in Germany. I will try to do so by telling you about my own experience of using historical interviews and the experiences of some of my friends who have been working on a variety of projects over something like fifteen years. I have three reasons for choosing this unsystematic approach. First, I hope in this way to convey something of the changing cultural flavour of Western Germany and the approaches there to labour history. Second, because my thinking about it is still in the phase of digesting experiences and is not really systematic (and probably never will be)—and, after all, telling rambling stories should be a way of communication familiar to oral historians. Third, and most important, because I feel that oral history – at least within the German setting – can transform the relationship between historians and workers, and that this ought to be an on-going experiment.

When I first interviewed people in the course of my historical research it was neither workers nor was it oral history. In the context of a study on American denazification policies in Bavaria,[1] for which a wealth of archival sources were available, I went to see politicians and military people who had been involved on both sides of the Atlantic, to get a feel of their personalities, and to fill very specific gaps in my archival documentation. This was in the mid-sixties, and I was a liberal student who approached these famous personalities with due respect, taking notes on my knees. Most of them seemed to be even less at ease than me, but for very different reasons. The student population at that time was drifting to the left: the issue of Nazism and the lack of a real post-war purge, revolution or major reform was one of the influences which politicised a movement which had originated more or less as a conflict of generations within the upper and lower middle classes. But it was at that same time that the German Chancellor had, with a sigh of relief, proclaimed the end of the post-war period with the slogan, 'We are somebody in the world again'.[2] This did not create enough confidence for me to be able to find anyone who had been denazified to interview, but it carried enough weight to hinder those who had carried through the purge from recalling any of their more vigorous actions. However, it was not only the devaluation of their experience but also its complexity which brought about this dislocation of memory: for example, German politicians found themselves in a multinational system of government, first as a kind of privileged underdog and then changing rapidly to the status of privileged partner; and whereas most of them did not really understand their function in the former position, they tended to interpret it subsequently in the light of the latter. As interview followed interview, I became more and more suspicious of these very purposeful V.I.P. memories. In my naïvety I had approached these people in all good faith. But what they poured out was an unanalysable mass of bits of information, together with apologies, misrepresentations and a lot of redundant material covering up conflicting values which they had accumulated during the course of their careers, in a society marked by a series of more or less abrupt political discontinuities. Once my trust in them was dispelled, the shape of my interviews with political insiders degenerated to the level of a detective with suspects. And so I finally ended up collecting five substantially different versions of one and the same story about a major event all by one and the same author, a very highly placed American: recorded in his files, in his memoirs, and in three oral history interviews with me and others[3] over a time span of twenty years.

These experiences left me deeply sceptical about the usefulness of autobiographical memoir as a 'voice of the past', because it was so much blurred by more recent voices. My impression was that interviewing historical witnesses could only be useful in a project where the interviewer already knew quite a lot from archival or similar sources, could single out the information needed and could check it for probability against these sources. The other lesson these interviews taught me was that the content was not just a reflection of the reliability of memory but that, to a large extent, it was shaped by the present situation of the informant: and with the more reflective and honest individuals, these two dimensions combined to produce a third—a point to which I will return at the end of my paper.

My second encounter with the possibilities and limitations of oral history came in the aftermath of the student movement, when many of my generation turned to the labour movement which we saw as the key to the driving forces of historical change. Most of us did not know any workers, but I had the good fortune to belong, not to one of the more theoretical of the revolutionary factions, but to a group of a dozen young historians who had discovered that post-war German history began with working-class liberation committees in almost every major German city. The Antifa,[4] as they were named, were quickly repressed by the occupying powers, whether capitalist or not; and most of the source material about them had been seized and lost in America. So had any trace of the existence of the Antifa in German historiography. It was obvious that this collective initiative on a local basis was an excellent topic for an alternative history, and interviews seemed the only way of collecting evidence. Some of my colleagues had had experiences as frustrating as mine with V.I.P. interviews. But this time, we thought, it was not to practised manipulators but to honest workers, to heroes of spontaneity and local democracy, that we were going to put our questions.

It came as something of a shock that with these local working class functionaries, many of them Communists, we again faced almost impenetrable barriers. This was not only because many of them thought that we were disguised secret service agents – for they had never previously encountered German academics who asked them, as comrades, to recall their experiences – but also because it quickly emerged that the political discontinuities since that time are by no means a special privilege of the privileged. This point has been emphasised by the sociologists of the symbolic interactionist school, so I will only give two examples here.

After a long exchange of letters, telephone calls and the presentation of credentials from other anti-fascists, I managed to contact a Communist who had fought in the Spanish Civil War, was arrested later by the Nazis and held in Dachau, was one of the leading heroes of the liberation of that camp, and was also instrumental in setting up of the local Antifa committee. Later he had remained loyal to the party through the Cold War, the party purges of emigrées to the West after the Slansky affair, and the outlawing of the party by the West German High court. He was now a local official of the new Communist Party, Moscow line. We did not work with tapes for this project—we had decided we could retreat to our notebooks because we found the tape recorder usually increased suspicion of us academics. On this occasion I was received very formally by my informant, my host, in his house: he had borrowed a tape recorder to preserve a record of our talk for his party, so that he could clear himself if I misrepresented him later in my quotations. So we began what at first looked as if it would turn out to be a very awkward interview, with the informant arranging the microphone and asking me to begin with my name and address. It turned out that we liked each other and, as often in these talks, after the first hesitant steps, we got down to a very open and fascinating account of his experience lasting more than two hours—until he discovered that his cassette had run out after twenty-five minutes, and nearly had a heart attack.

The second example is of my visit to see the leading shop steward of the public service workers of a major German city, now a Social Democrat, holding the sort of post which in Germany today would typically entitle him to a company car and secretary. Before the war he had been in various Communist front organisations and after it he was one of the leading Communists in the local Antifa—by virtue of which he was able in 1945 to climb to the leading position which he still held almost thirty years later. But to keep it he had had to become a convert to Social Democracy in the heyday of the Cold War. We sat in his kitchen and, sweetly, he told me what I knew from other sources to be one outrageous lie after another; and there was no way I could bring him back to anything of the political reality of his pre-conversion life. He had brainwashed himself and rethought his earlier life to conform with what he thought was necessary to live up to a standard biography of his position.

I do not want to overstress this point, because quite a few rank-and-file workers whom we approached were very helpful and open, and even allowed us to feel a kind of partnership with them in reconstructing a moment in German popular history that had been completely ignored, and in which they had played a major role. Many of them gave us papers and information or opened other doors. But here again there were limits to the oral evidence they provided. I will mention only a few.

Firstly, these Antifa committees had undertaken collective action in a very fluid situation. Usually we were only able to speak to one person at a time, and besides, many of the committee members were no longer alive. When we pieced together the information we had gathered, we could see that quite a lot of the factual recollection was just plain wrong, or else it only represented one perspective. If we had not found corroborating archival sources (mostly in the papers of the American Secret Service[5]), we might well have fitted together the information in quite misleading ways.

Secondly, when Antifa activists had later on become working class party officials, they tended to devalue and minimise their former spontaneous activity, and were unable to recover their political outlook of 1945. The others could often provide structural or personal information, but they had lost – or never had – a sense of the dating and sequence of events, because it didn't matter to their 'circular experience of time' – as it has been called – in everyday life.

A third set of limitations arose from the fact that the most articulate story-tellers were not necessarily the most important and active members, nor had they necessarily been at the centre of things. Conversely, some of the men of action were very unforthcoming. Indeed most of the people who talked a lot had the least to say, and tended, moreover, to overrate their own importance.

Finally, many of the people we talked to conveyed their messages through metaphors, anecdotes or personal allusions. This proved a tough code for many of us to decipher: some of us dismissed them as merely stories, while others could sometimes find hardly any meaning in them.

In the end we decided that no definitive statement in our book[6] should be made on the basis of interview evidence alone. Yet in spite of all the difficulties, not to mention the problem of simple lapse of memory, these talks proved an essential aid to our study. This was because they guided us to the location of sources, and still more important, opened our eyes to how these sources might be interpreted. Through these interviews abstract categories were transformed for us into real men whose biographies, experiences, capabilities and environments varied greatly. Through the interviews we were introduced to new ways of thinking and acting, often anathema to our own petit-bourgeois habits and style: to prosaic creativity, collective initiative, spontaneity in response to practical need; and to a language full of images and metaphors, but at the same time direct and challenging, and relying on a basis of non-verbal communication. The interviews provided clues and those little pieces of additional knowledge that made other information meaningful, rather than basic documentation. We began to appreciate sources that we knew already or discovered later in a new light. In spite of some really appalling experiences of the distorting influences of power structures, which had no less impact on these men because they were working at a lower level and within a smaller world than the V.I.Ps., most of our talks with them were warm, open and helpful, bringing respect and sometimes even leading to friendship. What I want to emphasise is that oral history taught us how to ask new questions and proved to be a training ground for imaginative interpretation, rather than an alternative to archives which were missing. It may be that this experience is particular to Germany, where the labour movement and academics (especially historians) have traditionally existed in two separate worlds—a separation which was very much reinforced by Fascism, survived through the Cold War period and was only challenged in the wake of our small cultural revolution of the later sixties. At that time students and scholars turned towards the workers. Thus it was not – as in England – on the basis of a broader cultural tradition of the common people, but for political reasons and in search of the politics of the labour movement, that oral history in Germany became a channel for the communication of experience.

Maybe what I have said is still as ambivalent and confused as were our experiences with interviews on this project. Looking back, I think we learned a lot, but also that we missed an opportunity. We met a great many of the more active working class anti-fascists, many of whom are now dead, and we asked them the wrong questions. Sticking determinedly to our project's aims, we recorded what they had to say about two or three months of social and political activity twenty-five years back in 1945, and we found their reports heavily burdened with distorting factors, as nearly any recollection of political and similarly marginal events in workers' lives is almost bound to be. This is especially so when the memory has to overcome the barriers of political discontinuity and cross the desert of a working class culture which has now disappeared. But along with this not very satisfactory information, these workers conveyed to us parts of their wider life experience, and insights into their ways of everyday thinking and acting, that we did not record—stories now lost, from which we, but only we, learned by abstraction.

The conclusions which I drew from this experience became rather clearer through participation and association with three projects of friends of mine. Detlev Peukert, one of my friends in our history group at Essen, has been working during the last few years on a dissertation, now completed, on Communist resistance against Nazism in the Ruhr area.[7] In common with many of the more enthusiastic young intellectuals of the seventies in West Germany, he wanted to harness his intellectual work to his political engagement; and as he had come through students' groups to the new Communist Party, he decided to research into its more heroic period, a project which suggested the use of both archive material and direct testimony. But his experience of interviewing surviving party veterans was very similar to ours with a politically less aligned group: though useful for locating sources and also for adding bits of missing information, the oral evidence often proved incorrect when compared with the archival fragments left behind by those two great bureaucratic systems, on the one hand the Fascist police and on the other the Communist Party —bureaucratic even in resistance. I choose the word 'incorrect' deliberately, for what often emerged was not the 'other side' of the story, as against that of the written document, as no story at all, or else mere false recollection or false information. Two distorting factors were paramount: individual rationalisation of an experience that had broken many a militant's backbone, at least when set against the exaggerated standards of

heroism within his own political milieu; and, secondly, a streamlining of
the resistance record of the Communists, which cut out any analysis of
the catastrophic bloodshed resulting from the party's tragic misjudge-
ment of fascism in the first place, and its insufficient coordination of anti-
fascist activities subsequently. The realities of day-to-day underground or
camp-life resistance had been polished out of the memoir, or at least from
the interview, by party discipline, the effects of which were further
emphasised by a series of disrupting purges and changes of party line, and
by the continued McCarthyism of the German political climate even long
after the Cold War. What remained were only dull and unconvincing
formulas.

This extremely defensive attitude to its own history, which robs it of
much of its well-merited popular interest, is not unique to the German
Communist Party, although it is perhaps seen most blatantly there. It is
the attitude most commonly held among all working class organisations
in West Germany. They had lost their cultural environment under
Fascism and could only succeed in reconstituting themselves in the Cold
War period at the cost of either repressing the past or of reformulating it,
in either case putting a severe strain on a relaxed approach to their historical identity and, consequently, on their relations with intellectuals. So it
is all the more important that opportunities to bridge this gap are taken. I
would therefore like to tell you briefly about a workshop that took place
earlier this year.

*   *   *   *

Ulrich Borsdorf and Hans-Otto Hemmer are two young intellectuals
on the central staff of the German trades union headquarters. They are
both historians by training and they are constantly engaged in bringing
trade union history to life and building bridges between university and
trade union people.[8] Recently, they held a workshop for twelve trade
union leaders, formerly prominent in the movement and now retired, and
some historians, as an experiment in the reconstruction of collective
memory, and in the hope of making a breakthrough towards the acceptance of oral history interviews in the trade union machine—a formidable
task in the German context. All the veterans had held high office in post-
war Germany and were born (with one or two exceptions) before the First
World War. The workshop was divided into three sessions: the first on
their early lives and how they became trade unionists; the second on their
experiences at the end of the Weimar republic and under Fascism; and the
third on the post-war reconstruction of labour organisations. Everything
was taped, even videotaped; the historians only intervened with a few very

general questions and the atmosphere gradually became more and more comradely over the last two days.[9] The outcome of each of the three sessions was very different: the last, on post-war Germany – the one to which everybody thought the veterans would have the most to contribute – was a failure, because they rarely said anything new; instead they made generalisations about themselves and offered few spontaneous recollections. It was apparent that political routine in responsible positions had left them with a defensive attitude, with few experiences that had affected them deeply, and with at best scattered factual memories that could only be tapped or reconstructed in a project approach. But the other two sessions were quite memorable.

The second session, on trade unions and Fascism, began with a statement by the eldest of the veterans – a Jewish emigré who had later become secretary of the international trade union federation – that the intellectuals had failed to support the Weimar republic, while the trade unions had done everything possible to prevent Hitler's rise to power. Though our veterans now all called themselves social democrats, at the end of the Weimar republic they had belonged to almost every political faction of the German labour movement. One of the former left-wingers reacted sharply, saying that the labour movement was itself guilty of not having launched a major battle to defend democracy at an early enough point in time. We then witnessed a very long and heated debate and also a very instructive example of the influences of generation, faction and group dynamics on the reconstruction of collective memory. The debate turned quickly to 20 July 1932 when the conservative German Chancellor, von Papen, who paved the way for Hitler, dissolved the government of Prussia, the stronghold of the Social Democrats. This blow removed the biggest remaining block of institutional resistance. Ever since, leftist intellectuals have been asking why the labour movement accepted this decimation without responding with a general strike— a possibility that was actually debated in the trade union headquarters of that time. And ever since, that decision not to strike has been defended by trade union leaders, including our veterans, because support for the strike was as uncertain as its outcome, given widespread unemployment and the pull of radicalising influences from left and right, and because the leaders were afraid to start what they thought was almost bound to lead to civil war.

Now, in fact, it turned out that our veterans, most of them shop stewards in 1932, were all waiting on the night of 20 July 1932 with their comrades for the order from Berlin calling them out on general strike and that when this order did not come they were frustrated and failed to take further action. Nobody in the session protested at all when, finally, a former Communist proclaimed the central leadership of the German trade unions guilty of having missed this last opportunity for organised resistance against Fascism when faced with a membership eager to fight. Now two or three things should not be forgotten about this debate which many of us leftist historians would be only too willing to quote as proof. Everybody in that room was on the side of the angels, because the scapegoat was long-since dead. During their active careers two thirds of our veterans would not have endured such a statement without a vigorous protest against that sort of Communist lie which labelled the Social Democratic leadership with the general guilt of the German people and was blind to the doubts and risks in making a responsible decision. And somehow, some rather important questions had slipped from the debate. How many rank-and-file members could tell the same story as our political activists? What does the fact that they went home after midnight in frustration tell us of the fighting spirit of our rank and file and of the level of their understanding of the decisive character of the situation? And so on.

Though this attempt at reconstructing collective memory produced a most notable debate, I have a feeling that the tape would lose much of its content if edited in the American way, giving the informants an opportunity for afterthought out of the context of group testimony.[10] This experience certainly renewed my scepticism about the use of oral history transcripts at face value for political history. Had they really produced a document representative of a generation of German shop stewards, or had they simply bridged their factional disagreements by consigning their predecessors to the wilderness as scapegoats? I believe that the complexities involved in such a collective enterprise in reconstructing memory are such that it would have needed an extremely critical and comradely historian to control and evaluate the debate; and though, in this particular case, I know quite a lot about the people involved and the circumstances of the group interview of which most readers of the transcript would not be aware, I feel unable to reach a conclusive judgement.

The first session, however, was much less ambivalent and it produced a very different dimension of oral history. Without our side asking any specific questions, each person spoke of what he thought was important about his childhood, his first experiences of work and the early steps of his political socialisation. In most cases this produced excellent results: a chain of stories, images and evaluations that were all very concrete and personal in depicting individual experience: moments and situations that were significant and formative. Many of us will have heard similar autobiographical accounts, especially of childhood and the period leading up to a career. They seem to me to be of prime importance for two reasons. First, they destroy intellectual assumptions about the homogeneity of the working class, breaking these assumptions down and providing ways of reconstructing a more complex, more dynamic and more sympathetic framework for understanding. Half our casually picked veterans had been, so to speak, born into the union, coming from the families of qualified and unionised workers. The others ranged widely: from the boy from a miner's family in a small and isolated rural pit, whose kinsfolk formed the major part of the workforce and themselves constituted the local union for which he was appointed cashier, to the poor Catholic choir-boy who had to give lessons to his richer classmates to finance his education, and was shocked into socialism by being offered chocolate by their parents instead of a wage, through to the middle class youngster alienated by the religious superstition and militaristic attitude of his public school teachers, who ran away to become a porter in Hamburg harbour. This is the sort of experience we hope will now be more widely documented in Germany, by a society just being launched by historians and trade union veterans, which will probably be called 'Memoir Workshop'. It will produce practical advice for research and especially for trade union educational programmes.

A second reason for its importance is that this sort of recollection singles out those moments that generated lasting experience, moments which come to mind through spontaneous memory before any more ambitious two-way or collective reconstruction takes place. I believe that such moments are the cross-roads of learning, through which consciousness is built up; and it is precisely the leap-frogging and anecdotal character of this sort of memoir that I think makes it preferable to any polished autobiography which has been filled out by follow-up questions put by a representative of a different culture. If the true problem of working-class history today centres on the question of the roots of cultural identity (not to use the narrow concept of class consciousness) and action, my belief is that through a systematic evaluation of this sort of memory, we could hope to penetrate beyond the inadequacies of crude economic reflection on the one hand, and abstract theoretical deduction on the other.[11]

*   *   *   *

The third project which I should like to mention also uses oral history in an encouraging way. This is the dissertation by Franz Brüggemeier at Essen, on the sources of radicalism among the Ruhr miners from 1889 to 1920. He started his research some years ago, intending to record the stages of political socialisation of the rank and file in a miners' union in Bottrop, using an oral history survey. But as a result of the evidence from the first interviews and his simultaneous research into explanations for miners' protest during that period, he changed focus. There had been a sudden explosion in mining in the Ruhr from 1880: up to then the workforce had been largely traditional, but afterwards it was swamped by massive immigration from the surrounding regions and eastern Germany which within a short time outnumbered it, bringing a rise from 80,000 miners in 1880 to some 400,000 on the eve of the First World War. These were the workers who staged the first massive strike in 1889 and who again, in 1905, came out almost unanimously. They formed the backbone of the radical movement after the First World War, and only succumbed to the large-scale military forces sent in by the Social Democratic government after a veritable civil war. Most of these strikes and similar activities were launched without or against the union, which usually only joined in some time afterwards in order not to lose contact with its mass following. But in some places that contact was indeed severed, with the result that the one and only anarcho-syndicalist centre of any size in Germany was created in the western Ruhr region.

Bourgeois historians have explained this phenomenon – in accordance with the well-established motto, that wild protest must be due to maladaptation – as being due to the coincidence of miserable conditions and repression in the mines, and the uprooting of a rural population that was unaccustomed to industrial discipline and town life. Spokesmen of the major working class organisations, including Communists, have joined with them to condemn this immaturity, which they too saw as the reason for the miners' resort to irrational spontaneity. But when Franz interviewed old miners, he was led to a very different view of the matter. Not that he asked them bluntly why they had been radical or anti-unionist, or similar political questions which they would probably have flatly denied in the current very pro-unionist and moderate environment. He listened to what they had to say to him about their work before the First World War, especially about how work in the pit was organised in relatively independent teams. They were all semi-skilled, working in teams which, given the technological level of that time, could only be controlled by their output of coal. The result was cooperative multi-functional workgroups, egalitarian in spirit, notable both for their interdependence and independence, and for their hostility to a management that sternly controlled them by judging their product, in terms of its quantity and quality, in a very authoritarian and arbitrary manner. He also gained the old miners' confidence sufficiently for them to speak to him about their private lives too – as against their public work lives – about which they rarely volunteered information. And he found a parallel structure of independence, cooperation, mobility and collective opposition to exploitation from outside, in what they told him of their living conditions, drinking habits and family life. A prominent feature of their living conditions was that it was a regular practice for almost all young miners to be lodgers in families of work comrades, thus economising on expenditure on both sides, and opening up families to a dimension of class solidarity as a socializing factor for children and lodgers alike.[12] This living structure allowed them to combat high rents in the housing market, and to evade the restraints imposed by the employers' paternalistic social policy in the miners' colony; and it encouraged a mobility that could fight repression in the work place by evasive tactics. Put in relation to this new structural information, the political action of the time can be seen as rooted in this miners' culture over a period of more than thirty years, as a form of action at the same time collective and independent; and it then clearly takes on a very different meaning from the 'lack of adaptability' which earlier interpretation had given it.[13]

But Franz has also asked me to tell you about the limitations of his oral history approach. Similarly, but perhaps rather less compellingly than in my own experience in the Antifa project, he has found the interviews principally a source of inspiration rather than a means of documentation. Making generalisations from the long accounts of work, and piecing together the more fragmentary information on family living conditions and attitudes proved not wholly convincing, so he turned to other sources, such as archival reports and statistics. But looking at them with new ideas in his mind, he found all sorts of things in those files which others who had read them before had not seen: and in this way he could more easily arrive at really useful generalisations.

In this sense our experience is, I believe, not unique. The conditions of everyday life are held firmly in the memory and hardly distorted at all by later experiences or changes in attitude. Maybe this is the only field where oral history can be regarded as a direct way of tapping the past, although it still requires an interviewer who can open up informants' minds to those areas that they may otherwise take for granted and neglect. But oral histories of everyday life also have a tendency to swamp the oral historian, producing no more than a meaningless literature of nostalgia. As far as I know, this research example I have reported is outstanding in the way in which it structures the information, so generating a new explanation, which restores to workers a true estimation of their own creativity and gives back to them a sense of their importance as a motive force in history.

* * * *

Summing up, I would like to draw three conclusions from this rather personal account,[14] and I shall end with some remarks which attempt to put it into perspective.

First, in the German experience, oral history has provided a great opportunity for bringing intellectuals and workers together and bridging the gulf in the long-divided culture of the left.

Secondly, in political labour history its usefulness as a technique for documentation is very much in doubt. It is important to stress this point especially in the context of the splits and discontinuities of the German left.

Thirdly, interviews by themselves cannot provide a direct understanding of working class cultures: a very careful exploration of the function of memoir and of intercultural interview situations is needed. Within a project approach, however, accounts of everyday life and unstructured autobiographical memories, especially of a person's formative years, are very useful raw material—though I think that the major intellectual task is in evaluating them and situating them within a historical interpretation if this channel of communication is to work both ways.

There is, however, a danger that this research technique, with its great potential – for instance for labour history – in bringing together the actors of history and historians, may be seen as a new division in the department store of history, producing interviews out of context and with little consideration for their value or use—drawing leftist historians to dying cultures, almost as once the blue flower attracted the romantic poet.[15] I would not wish to discredit the task of getting as much interview material on record as we can; but I sense in these nostalgic implications a possible and alarming analogy with the romantic intellectuals of the last century who produced academic folklore. They turned initially, with the best of progressive intentions, to the experience of the people, and generally recorded it through using what we would now call oral history techniques: but, in doing so, they escaped from the intellectual challenge of their own dynamic society. They allowed their research to stagnate, dwelling with relish on the habits, tools and traditions of rural people and transforming them into a 'natural' alternative, selling them in the end as a conservative utopia.

Our general lack of theoretical understanding of the complexities of our own societies, and more particularly of the behaviour of much of the industrial working class, may be sufficient to warn us against repeating the mistake of constructing such empirical nostalgia—in which perhaps this time the progressive impoverishment and radicalisation of the working class might be the natural image projected. Hence I believe it is important to keep open the channel of communication, and to explore popular experience in post-war society, not just as one of a decline of class or class-consciousness, but as fundamental in the formative experience of individuals who are moving through the conflicts generated by the supplanting of one cultural pattern by another, and who in the course of their everyday lives may be creating new possibilities for independent action and collective creativity. At the moment in Essen we are designing a joint research project on life experience and the restructuring of work, social conditions and popular culture in the Ruhr from the thirties to the fifties, including of course the war experience. Through this project it is our hope that we may extend the usefulness of oral history as a means of communication with members of the working class in the Ruhr—a working class which does not find much difficulty in resisting the intellectual's weakness for nostalgia.

1   See my *Entnazifizierung in Bayern*, Frankfurt 1972.
2   The German '*Wir sind wieder wer*' is much more impressive with its mix of understatement and dramatising alliterations. The phrase was coined by Ludwig Erhard when this symbol of the economic 'miracle' of the '50s (he was Minister of Economics at that time) succeeded Adenauer as West German Chancellor in 1963 to lead the Federal Republic into its first major slump. The phrase became a very widespread ironic formula when Erhard tried to manage the crisis by preaching austerity (*Maßhalten*) and corporate discipline (*Formierte Gemeinschaft*) before he was brought down by his own party in 1966.
3   I could have quoted parts of a major oral history undertaking by the American High Commission in Germany to put on record their own part within the framework of the histories of the occupying armies of the period 1949—52, which I came across while editing the papers of a historian and one-time special adviser to the American intelligence service OSS on German affairs and to the Military Governor (Walter L. Dorn, *Inspektionsreisen in der US-Zone*, Stuttgart 1973), including excerpts from this oral history: but the example quoted is not his.
4   Some of the relevant monographs by members of our group include: Peter Brandt; *Antifaschismus und Arbeiterbewegung*, Hamburg 1976 (on Bremen); Holger Christier, *Sozialdemokratie und Kommunismus*, Hamburg 1975 (on Hamburg); Albrecht Lein, *Antifaschistische Aktion 1945*, Göttingen 1978 (on Braunschweig); Harmut Pietsch, *Militärregierung, Bürokratie und Sozialisierung*, Duisburg 1978 (on the Ruhr cities); Horst W. Schmollinger, 'Entstehung und Zerfall der antifascistischen Aktionseinheit in Leipzig' (unpub. Diss. FU Berlin 1976); Arnold Sywottek, *Deutsche Volksdemokratie*, Düsseldorf 1971. Other members of our research group were Ulrich Borsdorf, Hajo Dröll, Inge Linke-Marssolek, Ulrich Schröder and Alfred Weinrich.

5 Some of the more analytical reports were edited by Ulrich Borsdorf and Lutz Niethammer in *Zwischen Befreiung und Besatzung*, Wuppertal 1976.
6 *Arbeiterinitiative 1945*, edited by Lutz Niethammer, Ulrich Borsdorf and Peter Brandt, Wuppertal 1976. Our study has provoked considerable discussion, not least in the GDR, see: Günter Benser, 'Antifa-Ausschüsse – Staatsorgane – Partei-organisationen', *Zeitschrift für Geschichtswissenschaft*, vol. 26, 1978, pp. 785–802.
7 Detlev Peukert, *Die KPD im Widerstand*, Wuppertal 1980; see also his documentary report *Ruhrarbeiter gegen den Faschismus*, Frankfurt 1974.
8 They co-edited two festschrifts on trade union history: Heinz Oskar Vetter (Ed.), *Vom Sozialistengesetz zur Mitbestimmung*, Köln 1975; Ulrich Borsdorf et al. (Eds.), *Gewerkschaftliche Politik – Reform aus Solidarität*, Köln 1977, engineered the establishment of a historical advisory council to the President of the German Trade Union Federation and prepared on his behalf a major conference of trade unionists and historians, the first cooperative venture of this type and size in Germany, to celebrate the 30th anniversary of the Deutsche Gewerkschaftsbund. (Meanwhile the proceedings have been published: *Aus der Geschichte lernen – die Zukunft gestalten*, Cologne 1980).
9 See also the conference report by Ulrich Borsdorf in *Gewerkschaftliche Monatshefte*, vol. 30, 1979, pp. 250–253.
10 The tapes have been transcribed, but it comes as no surprise that the first impulse to edit them for publication has by now almost faded away. But it is very likely that parts of the audio-visual tapes will be used for trade union rank-and-file education.
11 I have made some more suggestions along these lines in my report 'Oral History in USA', *Archiv für Sozialgeschichte*, vol. 18, 1978, pp. 457–501, especially pp. 474 ff.
12 Franz Brueggemeier has elaborated on his idea about a 'semi-open proletarian family', which is based both on these oral histories and a systematic evaluation of printed autobiographies of workers, in two articles, on which we collaborated: 'Wie wohnten Arbeiter im Kaiserreich?', *Archiv für Sozialgeschichte*, vol. 16, 1976, pp. 61–134; 'Schlafgänger, Schnapskasinos und schwerindustrielle Kolonie', in Jürgen Reulecke and Wolfhard Weber (Eds.), *Fabrik, Familie, Feierabend*, Wuppertal 1978, pp. 135–175.
13 See also his 'Bedürfnisse, gesellschaftliche Erfahrung und politisches Verhalten', *Sozialwissenschaftliche Informationen für Unterricht und Studium*, vol. 6, 1977, pp. 152–160. His argument is now more fully developed in 'Soziale Vagabondage oder revolutionärer Heros?', in: Lutz Niethammer (Ed.), *Lebenserfahrung und kollektives Gedächtnis*, Frankfurt 1980, pp. 193–213.
14 This experience should not be generalised to the whole German oral history scene which is currently developing, since there has been to date no deeper analysis of trends and results. We have, however, prepared a survey of current projects and archival material in oral history in the Federal Republic to ease contacts. The result is a small catalogue including a bibliography (as of 1979) that can be ordered from Fach Geschichte, Universität Essen, Universitätsstrasse 12, D 4300 Essen 1.
15 This refers to the theme of *Heinrich von Offterdingen*, the well-known German romantic novel by Novalis (i.e. Friedrich von Hardenberg) whose hero searches eternally for the blue flower, rather as King Arthur and his knights sought for the Holy Grail.

Memories of Hope and Defeat: Catalan Miners and Fishermen under the Second Spanish Republic, 1931–9

Cristina Borderias and Mercedes Vilanova

In constructing the recent history of Catalonia it is essential to take into account the social strength of libertarian communism because of the decisive influence which the anarchists exercised through the CNT (the National Confederation of Labour). Several thousands of workers belonged to this trade union federation under the Second Spanish Republic. And in an account of anarchist strength during the thirties, the period of 'dual power' between the state and revolutionary local communities in the crisis summer of 1936 – the first phase of the Civil War – was clearly critical, both for the wider class struggle, and for the CNT itself.

We wanted to uncover through local studies the mechanisms through which Popular Committees were constituted, and to follow the unfolding of their collectivist programmes. We also wanted to explore two different, rather simpler, phenomena: firstly, the significance of electoral abstentionism, to see how far the masses of the population responded to the anarchist slogan, 'Do not vote'; and secondly, the relationship between insurrectionism and repression, so as to estimate the degree of Centistes (CNT) influence among miners in the face of a distant possibility of launching libertarian communism. We decided to focus our research on L'Escala[1] and L'Alt Llobregat[2] two small and relatively accessible municipalities, a coastal village, and an inland mining settlement. L'Alt Llobregat experienced an insurrection in 1932, while in L'Escala we knew that before the period of the Republic some libertarian groups had already existed. In both places there had been Popular Committees, and some collectivisation was started after July 1936. Because of the kind of questions we were asking, it was difficult to find any relevant written material. At the end of the Civil War many documents were burnt in fear; other archives were removed, or were ravaged by Franco's troops to erase the vestiges of evidence for a truer interpretation of history. So we had to turn to oral memory.

The questions we wanted to explore were vague, partly due to their local character. From bibliographies produced during the Republic or afterwards and from the newspapers, we found accounts of various tendencies which, in general, coincided with the official standpoints of the political parties or trade unions. But we were less interested in the opinions of leading militants or politicians, because they were well enough known already. Many of them had written their memoirs and have been repeatedly interviewed by both historians and journalists. We did not want to know the incidence of libertarian ideas in a minority of famous people. We wanted the story of what happened in the villages, told by the people.

Through our interviews it became possible for us to understand the fundamental impact of the long years of Francoist repression. Even today the emotive power of memory brings people to tears at what they have lost. Many are still afraid to say things which they may never have spoken of before: to express the loss of hope, or condemnation of a neighbour. Such reactions show clearly how the burden of the republican period still weighs on them, a heavy backcloth to the freedom of memory for those who survived. This extraordinary, lasting sensitivity, even so many years after, means that the oral history of the Second Republic almost inevitably highlights the blackest, most negative aspects of the subsequent political regime. It uncovers, perhaps all the more strikingly because this was not our aim, the naked reality of what the Franco regime meant for the great majority of those who were adolescent or young during the thirties.

When we interviewed people we tried to find out what their main areas of concern were, and from this to go on to listen to what they could tell us through direct experience of particular critical moments.[3] So we had to seek out the protagonists, and build up the chronology of personal events day by day, almost hour by hour. We also had to be careful to explore certain questions which from our own perspective were crucial. For example we wanted to know whether the insurrection of L'Alt Llobregat in 1932 was purely local or part of a wider movement, and whether there had been important last minute changes of plan and, if so, how these had come about. We wanted to know too if the sudden, unexpected possibility of achieving communism produced fear or hope; whether people were willing to arm and fight for it, or had just waited for the night to come so as to be able to hide in the forest. We wanted to understand the significance of this 1932 insurrection for the people of the region—and for the people of Spain. We were also interested in who voted in the elections, and who they voted for; and also in examining the deeper motivations of the abstentionists, and why most radicals did not even put up candidates in their villages.[4] We also wanted to know what the people who went into the streets on 18 July 1936 – the day after the Spanish Army in Africa had risen against the Popular Front government of the Republic – saw or did.

This method of interviewing has produced stories with very different perspectives, frequently distinctive to a particular narrator. There are small entrepreneurs, for example, who were so attached to their property that some pretended to be just workers, and covered up assassinations, or allowed executions; while others would not share property so that 'afterwards' nobody could claim it, or because they felt that property belonged to others. We have also listened to the silence or fear of people who in the first moments of enthusiasm took to the streets with guns to preserve the new revolutionary order, men who, when Franco's troops approached, had to disappear into hiding, run away to the mountains or escape into exile.

Oral history has also helped us to interpret certain written documents. The actions of local committees, the formation of militias, the requisitioning of property, revolutionary taxes, the black market, cooperatives, revolutionary bonds, the local significance of certain decrees like obligatory affiliation to the trade union federations, collectivisation, municipal government, public order, the identification and characterisation

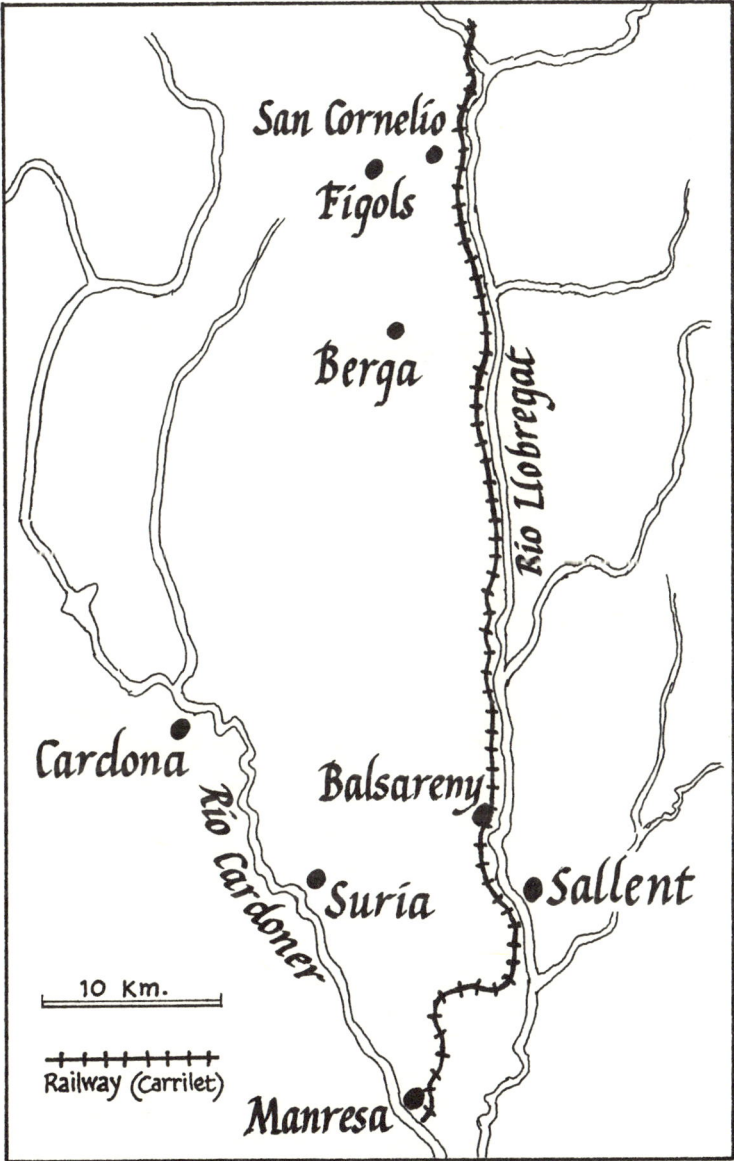

San Cornelio

Figols

Berga

Rio Llobregat

Cardona

Rio Cardoner

Balsareny

Suria

Sallent

10 Km.

Railway (carrilet)

Manresa

of those who were always or sometimes abstentionists: none of this could have been adequately investigated without the direct aid of the people who had experienced the events we wanted to analyse.

In particular, we developed a technique of cumulative oral documentation in order to understand how local collectivisation started and went on. We found that one person can give different versions of the same event in successive interviews. We discovered unconscious or conscious untruths, unwillingnesses to tell certain things, and lapses of memory. But through these repeated interviews, the interpretation could be deepened as the earlier arguments and conclusions were discarded and new ones established, and the informant had the chance to remember, correct or enlarge his or her version.

Interviewing has produced some problems which we are not yet able to answer. To a considerable extent it presupposes the content of answers, and neglects aspects for which no questions are formulated. It is also difficult to limit it to the period under question. Certainly we found that if we were investigating a key social question, each individual would refer to it not as a collective fact, but as a part of his or her direct personal experience which gave answers of a precise and vital significance. At the same time the interview can give a broad description of the past, an image of yesterday from the present. But it is also obviously easy to give quick, stereotyped partial answers, agreeing neatly with inner wishes and the lesson of subsequent events. Whether intentionally or not, people tell untruths, and oral history has to recognise this fact and learn how to interpret it.[5] Interview technique needs developing, because untruths have to be spotted during the interview, in order to penetrate their significance.

The use of the interviews has also to be looked at. The tension between interpretation and description, between preserving the integrity of the story and the need to analyse it, has yet to be resolved. The interviews have given us material that we have used in different ways: both as direct selections from the transcriptions, arranged by themes or chronologically; and also as part of a story – some of it new – that we have tried to narrate ourselves. The two brief interpretations which follow are of the latter kind.

Certainly in our work oral history has helped to answer very specific questions. Three years of a civil war presupposes many questions and unless one limits the scope, confusion easily arises. Indeed to reconstruct and interpret the vicissitudes of the masses during the period of dual power entirely through oral history would be very difficult: for ideally the history of critical periods requires a witness living with them just as William Hinton did in China during the forties.[6] But five days of an insurrection may be followed more or less in its whole drama. And we are in no doubt of the special value of oral history as a technique for recording and analysing the more recent past.

L'Alt Llobregat: hopes of an insurrection

Just five days: but in the closed valleys of the Llobregat and Cardoner rivers they served to focus simple wishes and revolutionary hopes, to liberate feeling, to unleash creativity. The oral history of the people from these valleys uncovers a situation of successive hope, oppression and repression. The insurrection at San Cornelio, a mining barracks high up near the top of the mountain – one of many worker colonies[7] set up near the coal and potash mines – was the beginning of a brief revolt which spread in one way or another into all the villages in or near the valleys: Balsareny, Sallent, Figols, Suria, Cardona. But it was precisely in the atmosphere of "apartheid" which so many people remember of the mining colonies, that the insurrection was strongest. They were colonies of *pijos*,[8] of outsiders, people who came to the mine from Murcia, Andalucia, Extremadura, Aragon. They were known as the rebels; and they had the hardest work, the worst possible places, the lowest salaries. Out of all the work in the region they had to choose the mine; and at the mine, they had to go underground into the pit, where the language was always "Castilian".[9]

The work was hard, inhuman, piecework. Stripped naked to endure a heat of 40 to 45 degrees centigrade, blisters on their shoulders from the coal sacks, they worked long days in constant danger. Life was little valued down the pit; the mine killed, and killed quickly. Because of this it was a job for the young. The firm did not take on workers over 25. At 14 children would go to their first day's work in tears because they knew what awaited them. Yet these very facts explain how underground, any differences between the workers disappeared; ideology, place of origin or any other disagreement ceased to count. The menace of death imposed solidarity. The Alt Llobregat was justly known as an 'explosive place'. The insurrection of one of the mines meant the insurrection of the whole valley.

It was a group of anarchist miners from the colonies of Figols who decided to start the insurrection. This was the second moment of hope. The first took place when the Republic was established on 14 April, 1931. To the miners it meant a promise of justice and freedom. They had hoped to finish with the all-powerful Conde de Olano; but this did not happen. The Count was the proprietor of the mines, and he decided wages and salaries, prices of food, houses and work. He controlled the Civil Guards too, and forbade meetings and public assemblies. The people of the valleys had hoped that the Republic would end the need for clandestine organisation and activities. The miners wanted to have their own trade union, to be able to meet, to express and discuss their ideas. Nevertheless what was permitted in other places was not allowed in Figols. Views on these questions differed: some were altogether disillusioned with the Republic, while others saw the Count as the negation of the regime, standing in the way of freedom. They wanted to attract the attention of the Government, and hoped that other regions of Spain would join the movement. Maybe even the realisation of libertarian communism was not so utopian a hope. But, be that as it may, life was inhuman—they could not wait anymore. For them it sufficed to establish contacts with some comrades in Berga and other nearby villages.

In the early hours of 18 January, a Revolutionary Committee was formed, with its headquarters at the top of the mountain in a building called 'Casablanca'. Some hours before work was to be started in the mine, a small group of men spread the news that 'Communism has arrived'. They went from house to house calling the comrades onto the streets with their guns. For most it was a surprise, something unexpected, news received without much faith because nobody thought that it could be so easy. The idea of Communism itself was not new. There was an extensive tradition of anarchist groups in the valleys; popular athenaeums, readings, underground meetings in the forest. And a revolutionary wish had certainly grown, a spontaneous identification with the libertarians and the CNT, because these were the most determined, the best fighters. Communism was a familiar word, although difficult to define, but to all it implied arms, justice and freedom. And because of this, most people agreed with the insurrection: 'Yes, there everybody agreed, everybody wanted it ... Communism—this had to be done ... and everybody did it'.

Armed groups of men patrolled to control strategic points. The arms of the *somaten*, the civil armed corps, were confiscated; and similarly the arms of those few who did not agree with the movement, or people who had a good position or would often be seen in the company of the civil guards ... and the Revolutionary Committee seized the Food Cooperative of the mining enterprise, because maybe food would be needed in order to resist. The news spread quickly from Figols to the nearby villages, and to the whole countryside; and by the 20th, two days later, miners from neighbouring Cardona, Suria, Sallent, Balsareny, had all stopped work in the pits. This was a spontaneous reaction, out of solidarity and companionship.

Anarchist groups saw the insurrection as the signal to start the revolution. Convinced that they would be supported by the working class of Spain as a whole, they designated Popular Committees, seized the town hall, substituted for the republican flag the black and red, and distributed publications announcing that the era of libertarian communism had started. And as in Figols they seized the arms belonging to the priest and the *somaten* functionaries, patrolled the streets, and closed the shops. Everything was paralysed; and the streets became a feast. Some people stayed indoors, not trusting what they saw even though they agreed with the movement, fearing what would happen in case of defeat. Others feared what might happen in the case of victory by the poor and downtrodden, who only knew how to revolt and make a noise; these people waited for the government to re-establish public order.

Attention was fixed on Figols; and in Figols everybody looked to the rest of Spain, because they knew that the decisive battle would be fought beyond their mountains. When the insurrection was started, some people went to the railway station. They knew that revolution was not easily accomplished, that everybody must be prepared to resist, and above all that it meant that all activities must be completely paralysed. Hence the continuing functioning of the Carrilet railway,[10] was, from the very beginning, a symbol of defeat, because it was a sign of normality beyond the valleys. It was a tremendous blow to accept that theirs was an isolated action. So before accepting this crucial fact, they looked for other explanations: 'If the Carrilet is functioning, it is to transport armed companions'; 'If the government says that only Figols has revolted, the leaflets show that it's the whole of Spain'. Thus for some hours people were able to maintain their hope, and started to put into practice what they had thought and discussed so often. They went to the Co-operative store, owned by the Count of Olano, to distribute what in fact 'belonged to them', and the Committee was forced to give it to the miners, although even so some did not take anything, because 'this was to steal'. Nevertheless small property was respected, and the small shopkeepers kept their shops. The slogan of the revolutionary bands was: 'Money the symbol of legal power has been abolished'. Money was not needed; the miners had the arms, the civil guard remained shut up in their headquarters, the engineers did not give orders; certainly all the signs there confirmed the existence of communism. The Committee looked for support from the workers' national organisation. Representatives and leaders arrived in Figols. From the villages came hope, determination, commitment to utopia; but in return the Regional and National Committee of the CNT could offer only astonishment, confusion, weakness. Eventually after three or four days of meetings and talks the CNT decided to call a strike. But by this stage military troops already occupied almost the whole zone, and in Barcelona the best-known anarchists had been arrested. Nevertheless, in the Llobregat and Cardoner valleys the situation had reached a point which allowed people to forget the world outside, perhaps because as they said later on, 'It is better to die living like that'. The depth of their anarchist belief and the hardness of their ordinary life gave them little to lose.

On the 22nd troops from Zaragoza, Lérida, Gerona and Barbastro reached Manresa and immediately went on to the villages, with Figols and Cardona as their objective. Because they felt isolated and knew that all was lost, the rebels did not put up much resistance. Some took refuge in their homes, others escaped to the mountains. Women threw salt at the soldiers as they arrived. The troops occupied the villages as they passed through them and arrested people. In Berga and Cardona some men resisted in the town hall, but the army soon defeated them. In Figols, when the soldiers were near, people were uncertain whether to escape or to fight. They had few arms and the army didn't want a dialogue. There remained a last gesture—the *polvorin*.[11]

Some who had been against the insurrection from the start decided at the last moment, to abandon Figols for the mountain, fearing army reprisals and fighting. And a thorough reprisal was indeed the government's answer to the insurrection. Hundreds of men were arrested and thrown into the prisons of Manresa and Barcelona. And because it was argued that the insurrection was part of a general movement against the Republic, the vital centres of working class organisation were destroyed: the CNT trade union federations of Catalonia and other parts of Spain were shut down.

The anarchist and communist leaders in the region itself and from many other cities were imprisoned. There was a spectacular demonstration of strength by the same army in order to avoid, it was argued, a worse fate for the Republic. The arrested men of Alto Llobregat and also of Barcelona, Valencia, Andalucia were to be deported to Africa, and for almost two months to remain at sea without a fixed destination, on board the *Buenos Aires*. Meanwhile in Figols they suffered one of the hardest aspects of the reprisal. All the miners lost their jobs, and were only taken on again one by one. The fighters, the old and the sick were all sacked. The government wanted to destroy the workers' vitality; and the Count of Olano was backed in the enjoyment of his possessions.

L'Escala: the defeat of a revolution

L'Escala is a Mediterranean village of fishermen, peasants and day labourers. Situated in the Ampurdan, close to the ruins of old Ampurias, it is a place known for its anarchist tradition. Fishing boats used to catch sardines and anchovies are beached along the sand. It is a municipality with no big enterprises, and although there are very large farms, most families possess a small piece of land, a vineyard, a boat or a house. These factors may have helped to create an egalitarian atmosphere far from landlordism. As in so many other places, the Republic brought the possibility of new hope. The reformist left had always won elections and the anarchists sometimes voted and sometimes did not vote, according to the political situation of the moment. There was quite a group of militant workers, mainly belonging to the CNT but also from FAI, POUM, the Unió de Rabassaires.[12] They never wanted to put up their own representatives for election, not so much for ideological reasons, but because they assumed they could not get sufficient votes; and anyway the changes they wanted could not have come through the ballot box. This simple and lucid pragmatism allowed a varied political life. With its open landscape, plentiful sun and north wind – the *tramontana* – between the Pyrenees and the Mediterranean, very close to France, L'Escala is a place of strong individualism shaped by the life of the vineyards, and by the fishing or smuggling, the solitude and freedom of the sea.

As in many other places, the village of L'Escala experienced the start of the civil war through radio news bulletins. Thus it was learnt that high army officers had attempted a coup d'etat, and that Franco at the head of the best troops was crossing the Straits of Gibraltar. Once the victory of the republicans in Madrid and Barcelona was confirmed, L'Escala started its own attempt to realise a different political and social organisation. The village set up a Popular Committee with militants from the workers' organisations, and ignored the legal authorities, even though the mayor was an independent socialist who belonged to the village committee for some days. At first it was thought that the success of the revolution would depend on the ability to administer the social life of the municipality. The committee's most important programme was the collectivisation of all economic sectors: construction, housing, transportation, agriculture, and so on. . . . This project brought out the difficulties inherent in the property structure of the village, especially since the Catalan government supported property of all kinds, and also maintained the means of repression. Collectivisation was legalised, but only in order to control it; and partly because of this the Popular Committees in most villages were abolished, and subsequently the revolution was defeated. But meanwhile two powers co-existed: the municipal Popular Committees, and the official government of the State.

At all levels there were difficulties and contradictions. Those who had no fear of sharing – the young – were mobilised and the more able were promoted to positions in distant workers' organisations. But an active group remained in the village wanting to make the Committee into an instrument to organise municipal life. And the *Generalitat* (Government of Catalonia) fought against these men. There was not only a war at the front, but also another war in each village. The arms of the government were juridical—to legalise and to penalise: and economic—to control raw materials and, as far as possible, the market. But even so, L'Escala resisted when the *Generalitat* decreed the abolition of the Popular Committees and their replacement by legal authorities. The men on the committee expressed their attitude clearly by locking up the town hall bulding and taking everything off with them including the secretary and all the files. They wanted a new, unofficial civil life. They had little respect for the law, or the orders given to them on matters like the harvest.

In L'Escala all these events were lived through with passion. If the politicians in the government wanted to legalise, control and govern, the aim of the local committee was to collectivise the village. Power was in the hands of Cenetistes (CNT) or POUM, and they planned to put into effect their ideas for solving old social problems. So they tried to collectivise everything: bakeries, barber's shops, garages, etc. . . . but there were many opinions and many economic sectors, and everybody understood the advantages and disadvantages of the new situation through personal experience. The Agricultural Collectivisation was an interesting case of this. Tensions relating to property and respect for small owners forced the Committee to accept transactions with each sector, almost with each individual. Thus all the fishermen who cultivated a small piece of land in their spare time, or families that lived off the land without the need of extra labour, were allowed to remain individual free peasants, and even families that would sometimes need extra help were allowed to keep their piece of land if they gave the collective the portion of the land that they were unable to cultivate themselves. As a result only the great farms of absentee owners were confiscated, and the only people who joined the collective were day labourers who had never before had access to any ownership. Those who lost most were the rural tenants, who ceased to run the large farms and lost all their advantages.

The Committee wanted to collectivise everybody with the maximum acquiescence. The great obstacle which they could not overcome was that of different types of ownership. People felt a great reluctance in giving and also, and maybe even more strongly, in accepting what was thought to belong to others. Nor were there only difficulties in distributing the land. Something very similar happened with respect to housing. The construction collective wanted to collectivise the houses of the families that wanted to join it. In theory all the houses belonged to the collective, and therefore it should have been possible to proceed to a better distribution of the houses according to needs. In practice, as with the peasants who did not want to abandon their own land, the families of L'Escala did not want to leave their family houses, even to change to a better and bigger one. But they did accept, and even demanded, that the collective should take responsibility for the buildings, and the village was modernised with w.c.s, running water, electricity, and so on: a lasting material gain from the revolution.

The great mass of independent fishermen who belonged to the construction collective was nevertheless unwilling to collectivise the fishing. Nobody wanted to give away their boat, nets, or repair work, and each had their own knowledge of where and when to fish. To collectivise these small boats, with so little need for capital investment in equipment, made no sense, and would have only created additional bureaucracy. And the bigger ships for sardine fishing were not allowed to fish because their strong lights could have alerted the enemy.

During the war, for many people, work remained the same old work, because the Committee kept the same salary policy, even though it abolished the use of money in the village. Only the master—they said—had changed. They continued to work by the day even though the wages were paid in revolutionary bonds, given as an advance payment of possible benefits. But this advance payment was experienced as a wage. They occupied the same house, cultivated the same land, worked at the same bakery or drove the same truck. Certainly there existed some local rich people who were afraid at first, and paid some fines as a revolutionary tax when money for transactions outside the village were scarce. With time the fines were paid less willingly, and finally they ceased to pay them because they said they had no more money left. But soon, with the support of the Republican government, the rich – people whom we found especially tense during our interviews – began to act, even legally, and started to denounce everything and everybody, because in L'Escala nothing was legal. And when the war was almost over and the troops very near, it was not enough to return the wheat-sack, the piece of land, or the truck. People had to hide at home or in caves, or in the mountains and fields, or leave for exile or face the possibility of prison and concentration camps. Some died. Others had to wait months, years, even decades to return.

Conclusion

Through these studies, oral history has brought unknown facts to light, modified some conclusions and brought us closer to the roots of working class consciousness. Thus we were able to discover that the anarchist groups in Alto Llobregat had actively resisted the Republic mainly because landlordism did not allow the development of an open workers' movement in the mines. When the government's prestige fell in 1932, because of its repression of workers and peasants and its failure to touch the main social problems, the miners considered the moment suitable to revolt. The insurrection was, nevertheless, isolated and localised. The government's repeated assertion that there was a combined revolt of all the non-parliamentary left against the Republic must be understood as an ideological justification for the brutal repression, with no real factual basis. In fact the insurrection came as a surprise to the workers' organisations. Six days passed before the Executive Committee of the CNT decided to call a general strike, after being informed of the insurrection and after hearing the decisions of the local, regional and national Committees. The strike was only partial and took place only when the army had already occupied the whole zone.

The government, through what, even at the time, was thought an excessive reprisal, skillfully avoided summary military courts, which might have created serious political difficulties, and so avoided public declarations, testimonies, and explanations. Silence covered up the truth. Denunciation, dismissals, the banning of trade unionism, meant hard and lasting consequences, because it left the working class without the means to make an immediate response.

The study of electoral returns when combined with oral evidence showed how a significant part of the constant abstentionists during the Republic were Marxists, independent libertarians or members of the CNT or the anarchist FAI. But we also found other independent and organised libertarians who had voted. In practice, the electoral profile of the anarchist population is lost within the whole electorate, so that we have reached the following conclusion: 'at a municipal or provincial level the ideological abstentionism, whether libertarian or cenetistes, can in no case explain total abstentionism, nor can it be correlated with political strength'.[13] This drastically alters the view that people during the Republic – and historians since – have had of Spanish elections. Our conclusion is that the absence of a working class party was not due in Catalonia to the libertarian watchword, 'Do not vote'; there must have been other causes for this failure.

Collectivisation during the Civil War had neither the time, the means nor, indeed, the intention to change the production process. Legalised for less than two months, prohibited after less than two years, starved of sufficient raw materials, and with the State against them, the collectives were nevertheless the testimony of a will for change. Certainly in Catalonia the masses were able to show their ability to organise and govern themselves, to negotiate and to avoid unnecessary violence. Yet this lesson has been silenced. Collectivisations were the other face of power and justice, closely related to the vicissitudes of the Popular Committees. The Committees were not formed spontaneously in response to army aggression: they took root where anarchist groups existed, in villages with libertarian traditions, and in places where the absence of big landowners made an initial confiscation of land easier.

All three inquiries – insurrection, electoral returns and collectivisation – produce a parallel image of hope, dialogue and final failure. First there is hope for the possibility of change: hope and struggle in spite of repression. The fight continues into prison or deportation, or with a forbidden trade union. Electoral returns, even in the sectors strongly influenced by libertarian ideas, show how easily the masses could be led. They voted even though nothing could be gained from the ballot boxes. They voted to lose less, to protect their own anonymity. And, as all over the world, so in Catalonia, people voted sporadically because the process of parliamentary democracy is only sporadically alive.[14] And when the war started the trajectory immediately prior to it was decisive. Committees were formed by men who belonged to organisations. In the villages it was the most prepared who provided the ideas on how to collectivise. But at this critical moment the State was neither destroyed nor conquered. The war at the front confused the war behind it, and consequently the defeat was a lasting failure. Because of the long military dictatorship which followed, the Republic remains, in the memories and feelings of the working class, a parenthesis of human life and hope.

1   Mercedes Vilanova, 'Estructura demográfica y económica en la Escala (Provincia de Gerona) en 1930-1940', *Estudis 2*, University of Valencia 1973, pp. 259–305; and 'La propiedad territorial en dos pueblos de la provincia de Gerona (1930–1940):

Posibilidades de la ficha perforada manual', *Actas de las I Jornadas de Metodología aplicada de las Ciencias Históricas*, University of Santiago de Compostela, 1973, v. IV, pp. 121–138.

2 Cristina Borderias, 'La insurrecci'on del Alto Llobregat. Enero 1932. Un estudio de historia oral', Master's thesis, University of Barcelona, September 1977, and 'Causas origines y lucha de una insurrecion: Figols, 1932' a paper presented to the Internacional Coloquio sobre la Guerra Civil de España, April 1979, Barcelona.

3 For our work a decisive influence has been Ronald Fraser, *Tajos, The story of a village on the Costa del Sol*, New York 1973. As he here rightly observes (p. 7): 'In attempting to make articulate the experience of people who historically speaking, would otherwise remain inarticulate, the writer is midwife to another's history. It is truth, not *the* truth that is his material. However, it is also the truth as he sees it which guides his investigation, orientates the questions he asks and provides the basis for the selection he finally makes . . .

4 Mercedes, Vilanova, 'El abstencionismo electoral y su relación con las fuerzas políticas en la provincia de Gerona durante la Segunda República: Un ejemplo: L'Escala', *Homenaje a Joàn Reglà*, University of Valencia 1975, Vol. II, pp. 491–503.

5 But as Paul Thompson says in *The Voice of the Past*, p. 96: 'Social statistics, in short, no more represent absolute facts than newspaper reports, private letters, or published biographies. Like recorded interview material, they all represent, either from individual standpoints or aggregated, the *social perception* of facts; and are all in addition subject to social pressures from the context in which they are obtained. With these forms of evidence, what we receive is *social meaning*, and it is this which must be evaluated.' The problem is not unique to oral history.

6 William Hinton, *Fanshen, A documentary of Revolution in a Chinese village*, 1966.

7 The colonies were blocks of houses, owned by the mining enterprises, built near the mines and manufactures for immigrant workers. Thus the marginality of these men began in the house.

8 This was the derogative nickname given to the immigrants as they arrived at L'Alt Llobregat.

9 The original inhabitants of the zone were Catalans and spoke Catalan, and usually had better jobs. The hard work in the pits was left to the immigrants who spoke Castilian; and in this way they expressed their separation and marginality.

10 The Carrilet was a small railway which came to Figols from Manresa through the mining villages. It was the usual means of transportation.

11 *Polvorin*: dynamite and explosives deposit of the mine.

12 FAI: Federacion Anarquista Iberica (a militant federation of anarchists formed in 1927); POUM: Partito Obrero de Unificacion Marxista (a party of dissident communists formed by the fusion of two previous groups in 1935); Unío de Rabassaires: Peasants Union of Catalonia.

13 Mercedes Vilanova, 'Un estudio de geografia electoral: la provincia de Gerona en Noviembre 1932', *Revista de Geografia*, University of Barcelona 1974, Vol. II, pp. 159–202.

14 Mercedes Vilanova, 'L'estabilité de l'electorat Catalan a la province de Gerona 1931–1936', *Tijdschrift voor Geschiedenis*, Groningen, The Netherlands, 1979, Vol. 92, pp. 473-91

Work Ideology and Working Class Attitudes to Fascism

Luisa Passerini

The promise of oral history lies in part in the challenge which oral sources present to the conventional interpretative categories of history and the social sciences.[1] For oral sources certainly belong to the sphere of subjectivity—provided one eliminates the sense of second-rate reality which this word can often convey. I would wish to include within subjectivity the whole range of cultural and psychological activities and expressions of consciousness – individual and collective – which can be embodied in language and behaviour, as well as expressed in more 'spiritual' forms, like speculative thought. The interpretative schemes of history and social science, on the other hand, almost invariably assume that 'society' is to be conceived of as a series of pre-given facts which only have to be discovered and described (though they might be 'spiritual' facts). It is one of the great merits of oral sources that they can clearly reveal the poverty and inadequacy of such a crudely positivistic interpretative framework.

However, if we are to reach beyond this towards a more satisfactory and subtle approach, recognising that reality is many-sided and that our own interventions may alter the character of the 'truth' to be discovered, we must take care to avoid certain pitfalls. These are firstly to use oral sources in a mainly or entirely factual way, simply to convey or confirm evidence on particular events: and secondly, to evade discussion of the problems which they pose in relation to wider historical interpretation, protecting but at the same time stifling oral history within a ghetto of its own. It is no longer enough for oral historians to demand the opening up of new frontiers of historical research. The priority now is to question the validity of the concepts which history has borrowed from the social sciences and of our own intellectual methods as historians. If we fail to do this, we cannot hope to receive any satisfying answer to our questions— and I am not referring to the questions we may put to informants in interviews. I mean the questions which emerge when we analyse interview material. There are certain kinds of questions which oral sources refuse to answer. Seemingly loquacious, they prove finally reticent or enigmatic; and like the Sphynx, force us to reformulate the problems we pose, and reflect on our fundamental habits of thought.

These considerations arise from research I am conducting on the working class in Turin between the wars. I realise now that for a long time I was asking questions of my sources which I had taken from the present Italian debate about Fascism. I had also inferred them from existing labour history, but to a lesser extent. This was because most studies of the Italian working class refer to the pre- and post-Fascist periods, and very few deal with the interwar period.

What statistics we have show that the working class remained less numerous than the agricultural wage labourers until the end of the 1930s, and limited to a few urban zones of north and central Italy. The history of the pre-Fascist period has created the image of a working class which, because of the unequal development and general relative backwardness of Italian industry, was markedly divided—between skilled and unskilled workers, and between different regions: but was nevertheless a militant working class, politically well developed despite its structural weaknesses. Following the First World War the trade union movement made rapid strides and the majority of urban workers became organised in unions with a socialist outlook.

For the Fascist period a social history of the working class is almost totally lacking. On the one hand, traditional sources on the workers' movement are missing, since Fascism outlawed existing working class forms of organisation, substituting its own and suppressing all those that had been in any way socialist, communist or anarchist. On the other, documentation based on available statistics and police archives (covering strikes, disturbances, etc.) requires particularly careful evaluation in view of the control and manipulation to which such data were subjected in this period of political dictatorship. The only substantial published evidence on the interwar Italian working class is composed of memoirs, mostly written by political militants, who usually belonged to the higher strata of the working class. This literature conveys a picture of a spontaneously anti-fascist working class, reflecting the image fostered by militant historians and by the left in general.

This, however, leads to a second kind of difficulty, for there are major problems of conceptualisation too. According to such images, the Italian working class has remained throughout antagonistic to the system. All its struggles and demands have been immediately political if not revolutionary; for its culture and consciousness could not – and cannot – help being

independent and alternative to bourgeois culture. But can such a stereo-
type be really adequate to deal with the problem of a working class which
was denied for twenty years all its traditional forms of organisation and
struggle? British labour historians, for all their experience, have not faced
such a difficulty—and indeed they have perhaps tended to err in the opposite direction, in underplaying those aspirations to overthrow or challenge
the dominant culture, which surely must be basic to the concept of class-
consciousness.

Much post-Second-World-War Italian historical writing, by contrast,
has tended to remain faithful to the image of a spontaneously anti-fascist
working class, unquestioningly loyal to the worker's traditions handed
down from generation to generation and unchanged by the dictatorship.
And this is particularly noticeable as far as the working class of Turin is
concerned, with its political heritage of factory occupations, the experience of workers' councils, and the relationship with Gramsci's newspaper, *Ordine Nuovo*. From such accounts one received the impression of
an uninterrupted core of anti-fascism within the working class, witnessed
both by an irreducible opposition and refusal to participate in Fascism and
also a tireless capacity to give shelter to the militant anti-fascist organisations of those in exile. A more promising approach has been emerging
through recent discussion by historians of working class acquiescence in
Fascism, and the degree to which consensus was achieved during the
Fascist era. Even in this debate, however, there has, to my mind, been an
insufficient consciousness of some of the underlying issues.

For our present purpose, it will be enough to summarise the principal
and most recent issues of this debate on the question of consensus
through looking at the positions taken by Renzo De Felice and Guido
Quazza. De Felice maintains that there was a limited period, between
1929 and 1934 or 1936, during which the working class, like other
social classes, participated in the general consensus created by the Fascist
regime. He accounts for this in terms of what he calls the 'material'
components of consensus. Compared with the *biennio rosso*, the two
years of struggle and chaos – including the Turin factory occupations – in
1919–20, workers' conditions under the subsequent Fascist regime did
not deteriorate much in real wage terms: arbitration through the
Tribunale del Lavoro (industrial tribunals) and the activities in their
defence of the Fascist trade unions gave more security to the employed,
while the unemployed received benefits and assistance and appreciated
the efforts made by the government to create new jobs. De Felice's view is
that these elements of material security were more crucial than either
police repression or Fascist influence on the new generations entering the

factories during those years, in accounting for 'the lack of political consciousness in an anti-fascist sense' which characterised the economic demands put forward by workers in demonstrations and agitations. He considers this to be a sign of a substantial consensus, more widespread and totalitarian in character than the enthusiastic support later achieved by the regime during the Ethiopian war. De Felice also proposes that there was a 'moral' component of consensus, particularly among the younger generations, 'a wishful aspiration for a change', 'a revolutionary spirit . . . aiming at building something new'. This moral component distinguished Fascism as a movement from Fascism as a regime.[2]

Guido Quazza has argued in reply that it is contradictory to suggest a moral consensus for the years during which the Fascist regime in practice destroyed the Fascist movement. According to Quazza, in the early thirties the struggles in the factories showed 'a capacity of active protest — for this same reason ''political'' — opposed to the regime'. In his opinion, active consensus must not be confused with one which is 'extorted or endured'. He differentiates between consensus 'from above' and consensus 'from below'. The latter cannot be considered active: 'the less so, if we add that it was extorted with prevarication and harassing methods of ''social control''.

This second position has the advantage of reminding us that constraint must be included within our conception of consensus, for Quazza introduces the concept of social control. He also takes into consideration some sort of *subjective* constraint, like the coercion exerted by means of propaganda and the 'seduction', as he puts it, of leisure organisations. De Felice indeed goes still further, in admitting that Fascism did answer some existing needs of a 'non-material' character. Such needs may perhaps exist in a wider and more fundamental sense than he suspects—in the need for full human self-realisation: and it does not occur to him that these needs might have been met in another way than under Fascism.[4] Nor, as Stedman-Jones has cogently pointed out, can the problem be solved simply by introducing the notion of social control.[5] The image of a working class switching from a revolutionary state of nature, very much like a good savage, to regimentation and integration, leaves something out. How was it possible to extort or to impose consensus—that is, control extended to the sphere of subjectivity? If consensus means anything, it must be that somebody not only was defeated, but accepted defeat and rationalized it. And might not this happen again?

There is one old and rather simple way of averting this threatening question: to assert that working class consciousness is embodied only in its traditional organizations, while individual subjectivity is altogether irrelevant. This argument leads straight to Stalinism, although it was already lurking with Lukács's *History and Class Consciousness*.[6] Yet ironically there are striking similarities between such viewpoints and the present workerist version of the Italian new left, according to which all struggles are expressions of class consciousness. The oversimplifications on both sides are spectacular: either the working class without a party is only capable of economic demands, incapable of true self-consciousness or subjectivity and therefore of conscious political action; or by the simple act of protesting, the working class is immediately political and so has no need of subjectivity. Again we are left with a highly mechanistic vision of the tensions existing in the working class between revolutionary capacity and historical determination.

The problem of consensus under Fascism is not merely a historical question: it is clearly also of contemporary political relevance. The central question to be answered is: how and how far can constraint be exerted in the sphere of subjectivity? Even if we accept that constraint always has a material basis, what makes the oppressed internalize the acceptance of their dependence? What leads them to accept their oppression in cultural and psychological terms, to the point of even praising it and preferring it to any struggle for change? Thanks in part to the various movements which have developed since the 1960s among women, youth, racial and linguistic minorities – all of which have helped to extend the idea of free-dom to the spheres of ideas and of personal life – the problem has now been recognised as important. But we are a long way from full under-standing. We know very little, for example, about the impact of the manipulation of information and of emotion, or how and why particular social stratum such as youth can shift from apathy to violence and terror-ism. I therefore see the need to face the issue of subjectivity as one of polit-ical urgency.

As historians, our task must be to point out that subjectivity and consciousness also have a history and undergo change—and that their changing forms and expressions are never neutral, but part of the struggle: for ideas take side with or against institutional power. We need to find a place in history for examining subjective attitudes towards authority: to construct a specific element within our framework of inter-pretation for a subjectivity or consciousness which is not to be considered a mere reflection of economic conditions, or to be simply reduced to matters such as collective security or collective protest. In my opinion, it is precisely the lack of any effective conceptualisation of subjectivity which has made a travesty of the debate on consensus. For if the specific character of subjectivity is overlooked, oral sources can only be seen as a series of statements about 'what really happened'. All one would need to do would be to interview those who were there and ask them about it: this was more or less what I tried to do myself at the start of my research on the Turin working class under Fascism; and I now see that it was the principal obstacle to my understanding the sources I had collected, and to ordering them systematically.

I originally attributed the difficulties mainly to the discrepancy between local and national history, and between the individual and his or her epoch. The problems have been accentuated by the fact that my research is still incomplete, so that the samples I give here cannot be fully representative of the Italian working class in the interwar period. I have drawn in this paper on the life-stories of some 60 working class men and women: in all some 100 hours of tape-recorded interviews that I have compared with about 110 published life-stories of workers. My informants are divided into two generations, those born before 1910, and those both between 1910 and 1925 who did not start work until the Fascist era. Most of them were either born in Turin or had immigrated there by the early 1930s. A small number lived and worked in small towns near Turin (Asti, Pinerolo). The life-stories have been collected in two stages: the first, free narration – sometimes very short, according to the informant's wishes, the second conducted on the basis of general questions concerning daily activities. Other more general questions were also asked like 'What do you remember of the period before the last war?'[7]

This method of procedure, seeking to obtain from informants the most spontaneous type of reply by reducing direct questions to a minimum, has produced primary source material which is by no means easy to interpret. Certainly it has elicited replies with scant significance for any history which is predominantly concerned with establishing 'what really happened'. And at first reading my sources offered little help on the question of consensus. It was clear that I did not know how to read them – in the sense of interpreting their message – and that I did not understand them. For by posing the wrong questions of the material I had gathered, I could only get what I deserved: what, to my ears, seemed either irrelevant or inconsistent answers.

'Irrelevant' answers are mainly of two sorts: silences and jokes. Anecdotes and jokes would deserve a special study. The general meaning which they convey is that there was an irreverent attitude towards the regime, and that this attitude was usually brutally curbed.[8] There are two types of silences. Firstly, whole lifestories are told without any direct reference to Fascism, only casual asides while talking about other events considered more essential for a life story. For instance, one woman

told how she used to meet her boyfriend who was in a prison for teen-
agers:

> They used to come to Via Passo Buole – there was Fascism then, you see, and they
> were put through their gym drills – they used to come to Via Passo Buole, those
> boys, they'd come out all regimented for the drills, and so we'd go straight across
> to them. 'Cause we'd got to know who they were, looking out from our windows.[9]

This seems to be characteristic of informants with few or no political
interests. But a second type of silence can be found in interviews with
people who had some understanding of the encroachment of institutional
power on their lives. In their life stories one can often pick out a striking
chronological gap between 1922–23 (1925 at the latest) and the outbreak of the Second World War. Beppino, born in 1897, a Lancia worker
who later became a manager in a smaller factory, narrates his life up until
his military service and his return to work after the Great War:

> Then there was the occupation of the factories, and at that point they (the workers
> on strike) came in there, into the Lancia, and kicked us out and made us leave. In
> those days there weren't all those buildings there, but fields, real fields, and so we
> fled into them, split up and then went back to our homes. When all that was over,
> we went back to work and we worked normally again. Well, of course life was full
> of fear and anxiety because inside the factory there were always all these Fascists
> who could point their fingers at any Tom, Dick or Harry. And then when you left
> in the evening there were always groups of Fascists waiting and they'd beat some-
> body up, so we were always worried. There was one bloke who worked near me,
> who was the personnel manager's son and always had a gun in the drawer and as
> we were in the same team, I had this gun in the drawer near to me and it was none
> too pleasant; in any case we went on like this. Then the bombing started, and
> when the bombs started here, in Via Di Nanni we got bombed too, in the house
> where I lived.[10]

The extraordinary thing about this testimony is that it refers, with the
exception of the last sentence, entirely to a period no later than 1925.
With the last sentence the story suddenly jumps to the Second World
War. Then afterwards Beppino goes on to talk about the post-war period.

Up to now I have been referring to the spontaneous part of the interviews. When questioned more directly, the interviewees can usually
recall the period of Fascism's rise to power with all its atrocities – sometimes by hearsay, if they were then too young – and the Second World
War. Their memory reaches its highest pitch about 1943–45: resistance, war and liberation have left distinct marks, even if sometimes negative, of disapproval or of fear, as in this example:

On the 25th of July when Fascism fell I was in bed and heard people shouting. I went to the window to see the people in the streets: they were shouting, destroying the emblems and pulling down the Fascist headquarters, then I went back to bed because it was better to keep clear of them; they are all hypocrites, they'd all been on the Fascists' side before, and then they were all against them.[11]

But a question mark still remains for those fifteen to twenty years between 1922–25 and 1941–43. And whatever the reasons for it may be, this self-censorship must be understood as a scar, a violent annihilation of many years in human lives which bears witness to a profound wound in daily experience.

Answers may be 'inconsistent' in the sense that they show discrepancies with the accepted picture of main historical events and processes. Informants speak very little about any form of organised leisure, scarcely ever mention Fascist trade unions, seem to remember nothing about assistance and social security, and so on. By and large they speak about their jobs, their marriage and their children, recounting a story of a daily life apparently insulated from Fascism.[12] It has been suggested that even the traditional concept of anti-Fascism is too narrow, if compared with the issues emerging from the oral sources.[13] But can such discrepancies be interpreted solely as signs of the estrangement of the common people from Fascism? Not really, for this, in my opinion, would be to proceed from an incorrect formulation of the problem.

Irrelevancies and discrepancies must not be denied, but they should be taken to indicate in the first place that some important operation has been forgotten by the historian. History, like other social sciences, must 'transform the concepts which it brings, as it were, from outside, into those which the object has of itself, into what the object, left to itself, seeks to be'.[14] It may sometimes be necessary, in order to do that, to make a detour and try to consider the object from a wider point of view. Oral sources need to be taken as forms of culture and testimonies of that culture's changes over time. But we must strive to develop a concept of culture which can embrace the reality of daily life. Oral sources start to speak more clearly, even on the difficult problem of consensus, in relation to day-to-day attitudes and responses to the family, to religion, and to work. It is this last on which I want to concentrate here.[15] The acceptance of alienated work relations, of the apparently free and equal exchange between worker and employer, involves internalized acceptance of social hierarchies. Ideologies of work, whether expressed in thought or in behaviour, can be considered one of the main channels of the acceptance

of authority, by individuals, and a channel which was already in existence
in the period of the Liberal state.

*   *   *   *

Work ideology is an expression covering a wide range of meanings, even
when applied to the working class only and not to other important social
groups, like the peasants or the upper and middle classes. At the present
stage of research we can indicate two poles within this vast range. Working class pre-fascist [16] culture encompassed a spectrum of attitudes which
ranged from valuing work as a social and moral duty – so that stigma and
shame would be cast on those who did not fulfil it – to extolling craft work
as a proof of special skill, implying not only manual ability but also some
sort of creative style. This second attitude was that of an elite, though it
fitted perfectly with the first one, which can be considered as its matrix.
The first attitude could be shared by anyone: men, women, children,
labourers and skilled. It was a basic principle of education, informing the
whole personality, and a guide through life. It was a principle held among
all classes, strongly rooted in a common land and language, or rather – in
the Italian case – in a common region and dialect. But the upper classes
could avoid most of the negative implications of work undertaken in a
context of compulsion and driven to the point at which it threatened to
annihilate other activities and personal relations. So the benefits of labour
were praised, but not practised, by everybody. In certain respects working
class culture remained subordinated, in so far as it made a virtue of necessity in taking up those values. Of course it was not just passive: it re-
elaborated them, developing techniques, inventions, a special pride in
manual abilities. But only exceptionally could working class culture
transform needs originally tied to the ascending bourgeoisie and change
their role into the opposite one—from confirmation of the established
order into the prefiguration of a freer future.

    I shall first consider one of the most elaborate forms of pre-fascist
work ideology, that shared by the rank-and-file Socialists belonging to the
group around the newspaper founded by Gramsci in 1919, *Ordine
Nuovo*. [17] This ideology combined the idea of work as moral and social
duty, the pride of being a professional worker, with the social-democratic
conception of continuity between work and political activity. But it also
tried to add something new, as we shall see from the words of an old
member of the group. Giovanni was born in 1886. He was a worker and
political commissar at Fiat up to 1921, and, as well, an actor and player of
comedies in socialist associations. He was then one of the Red Guards
who defended *Ordine Nuovo* from Fascist attacks, and one of the founding

members of the Communist Party of Italy. In the early 1930s Giovanni was not involved in any clandestine anti-fascism, but his past and the Depression made it very difficult for him to find a job. At last he was introduced to an engineer, manager of a mechanical engineering workshop, who hired him:

The first morning I go to work he says to me: 'There's this job to be done here – piece-work'. And I says to him: 'Well, look, I've never done any piece-work! Never done any. It's not my way. If I don't do enough work, you just have to tell me: ''You haven't done enough''. Don't think about it twice, just tell me, I won't take offence.' Well, there was this job, you see, and I had to do it, bore holes into a small iron key. At the end of the month, when I got my wages, he put an extra 10 lira bonus in my pay packet. Well I'm damned (I) – 'If I earn it, I want the money, but if I don't I won't take it.' And I marched into the office.

I had this foreman, a good man, I remember him, he really deserved the job of foreman: he was a master, a master of mechanics. And then he fell ill, he did. The engineer told me to take his place. 'But I've only been here one month!' I had to take his place, the foreman's I mean. That engineer had taken a liking to me and I got him to hire a lot of people, 'cause they'd been sent away from the RIV (a local firm) and couldn't find any job anywhere. 'Cause he'd say: 'You go and ask Giovanni'. And I'd say: 'Well, look, engineer, I can't take no one on without asking you.' 'Well, Giovanni, ask me and I come and ask you.' You got that?

I used to go and we were ninety in the shop I'd go to his office and he'd keep me there for hours, half a day to show me the map of Italy. Thirty he was – young – but he knew everything down to the last screw we had in the warehouse. He always had this notebook on him and when you said: 'The stock is so much', he'd say: 'No'. Mind you, he couldn't make head or tail of mechanics, but was he a bright one for the accounts!

And then we caught one chap stealing! A poor devil, a Tuscan, a widower, good at his job he was. He was a labourer, and he'd take away a glass of lathe chips every shift. And they told the engineer! If only they'd come to me: but they didn't tell me. They went straight to the engineer and told him. And so he came – it was three minutes to noon – and he says to me: 'Listen, this and that happened, now you – ' 'Now look, I'm no guard, no, not me. It's not my job, that isn't'. That poor man! They called him into the office and he pulled out what he'd got in his pockets – a bit of chips from the turning. They'd give him a glass of wine in exchange for it at the place where he went to eat. He was sent away. 'Look, engineer, he's a good man, works a lot: a labourer, but one you like to see working'. 'It's theft and it's a question of principle'.

So I says – you see, the one who told the engineer used to be a cobbler once, red-haired he was. Well I went to get him in the afternoon as soon as I get to work, he worked in the warehouse. 'What did you go and tell the engineer for?' 'But, no, I . . . ' 'You, you, your job was to come and tell me! And I had to go to the engineer, not you. And now I'm giving you the sack. You did something that was my privilege. I'm the foreman and I want to be foreman. Now I'm sending you away. You took my privilege and I'm sending you away in exchange.' When the engineer arrived, I talked to him for two hours, I did: 'If he does not go, I go.' And they sent him away. 'Why must he? ...'

It was a bit like a family, you see, all nice good people. Some were fond of a drink...(One of Giovanni's friends chips in with a story about how nobody worked on Mondays because of drinking – not only on Sunday but 'getting drunk again on Monday, then go to work half-drunk'. Giovanni continues:) But once I lost a 50 lira coin, think of that, 50 lira. We had a stack of supplies in the work-shop, two meters of them. Two labourers! they worked in their lunch hour for three or four days, going through it all to find my 50 lira. Well, that's saying something. 'Cause you see I'd take eight or ten of them home with me to eat when there was overtime working, like working on Sundays, well, in the evening I'd take them home with me to eat...'[18]

I should like to underline the following points in this interview. First, the refusal of piece-work is based on the idea of work as ability and honesty, which allow self-regulation. Secondly, hierarchy is based on merit, both in the foreman's and in the engineer's case. The same is true for Giovanni himself. This means that work is at the same time the found-ation and the limitation to all forms of authority. Thirdly, there is a moral value attached to the word *job*: 'It's not my job, I'm no guard', 'Your job was to come and tell me'. Lastly, there is the emphasis laid on an attitude of independence and irreverence, well exemplified by the international myth of the merry Monday.

The ideology revealed in Giovanni's behaviour expressed faithfully the main aspects of a body of beliefs common to skilled workers, whatever their political affiliation: their pride in the quality of their products, but also carefulness as to the quantity of work they carried out; self-regulation of productivity; mutual respect and esteem between workers and bosses, though this reciprocal relationship always conveyed a touch of paternal-ism on the owner's side; an attitude of superiority towards labourers or the unskilled; an awareness of their share in the power of decision-making in the factory; and a touch of scorn for the young ones and the office workers. Into this common set of beliefs socialist ideology introduced further elements which moderated the most brutal characteristics of capitalist order and authority. It did not eliminate inequalities—in fact it accepted them, postponing their abolition to a far-distant future. But nevertheless it somehow enabled the idea of equality to be effective through the recognition of a solidarity independent of the division of labour and the roles which individuals had within the work hierarchy created by it (foreman/labourer; engineer/foreman).

Ordine Nuovo went further, introducing more clearly the idea of a sudden and complete change, a break with present conditions, in contrast to the social democratic notion of a progressive evolution, and thus substantial continuity, between the present and the future. In this sense *Ordine Nuovo*'s theory broke with the dominant work ideologies. But it retained a strong link with the diffused idea of work as moral and social duty. The double meaning was well expressed by Gramsci in his justification of the right of workers to transfer their labour effort from the factory machines to a strike: 'Why should the workers not employ their "property", their wealth-labour, and divert it from the process of production to an action aiming at stopping waste and destruction?'[19] This argument is not only materialistic – in referring to the material source of surplus value, that is living labour power – but also psychologically effective. 'It requires an immense psychic effort to leave the old way of life and to adopt a new one, especially if the latter demands increased rational activity'.[20] Producers, whether labourers or skilled workers, have both the moral right and the psychological force to interrupt the existing social order and to create a new one, with the sanction of a shared ethic. But *Ordine Nuovo* did not solve two important problems. Firstly, a balance had to be kept between an appeal to contemporary values and the need to overthrow the existing order. In the case of work ideology, this resulted in a failure to challenge 'that vulgar metaphysic of labour . . . present in the old Social Democratic movement, which consists in celebrating labour as the bringer of redemption, with no questions asked about the particular effects it has on the labourer'.[21] Secondly, *Ordine Nuovo* failed to expand the concept of producer beyond that of the skilled worker, and thus to meet the needs of the increasing masses of the unskilled.[22]

But we are concerned here not with the failures and strengths of *Ordine Nuovo* (although one important direction of research could be to confront its political theory with popular attitudes). Our aim here is rather to see how a politicised version of labour ideology functioned through rank-and-file members' daily activities, and what results the impact of Fascism had on its inherent contradictions. Certainly, work ideology had an important role in anti-fascism. Even complicity between workers and bosses could become an alliance of anti-fascist relevance. We have seen in the case of Giovanni how the factory hierarchy could be bent to save victims and fight against injustices. Many other informants who were young in the 1930s told how they avoided pre-military-service drills (instituted and made compulsory by Fascism), thanks to agreements with their bosses. The latter proved ready to declare that the young workers had to work on Saturdays, even when this was not the case. But work ideology was especially embodied in the behaviour of 'old' workers—by which I mean workers belonging to the generation adult before the 1930s. The

Communists principally – for they were the backbone of working class anti-fascism – but also the anarchists and socialists, rooted their identity in the certain belief that they were at the same time both producers and representatives of a coming social order. Mussolini was referring to them in his famous speech of Ascension Day in 1927, when he spoke of the 'generation of the indomitable' (*la generazione degli irreducibili*). And again in 1928, addressing 10,000 Milanese workers on a visit to Rome, he warned them when they got back to Milan, to remind 'those at the same bench, in the workshop and at home' that roles had now reversed: 'We are the Revolution; they are the counter-revolution'.[23] For although Fascism made it impossible for earlier working class ideologies to be openly expressed or developed, there were still channels for them. Old values were preserved through day-to-day action, protected and handed down through the strength and personality of individual workers: and younger workers received the message, even if not grasping its full meaning. Antonio T., born in 1924, a foundry worker, was a young Fascist:

I believed in the power of the musket and bayonet and had a great spirit of adventure...

But he also remembers that:

Because the reaction against the bosses was not collective, it depended on each individual's personality and on his physical strength, the men who were strong and resolute got respect. We couldn't defend ourselves collectively because the Fascist trade unions were just a farce.
I used to listen to political discussions we had in our shop. Even then, the old socialists, like the foreman who's now retired, always used to say: 'You'll see, they'll have a war and they'll end up like Napoleon'. I would have liked to react because I was Fascist, but I ended up by understanding he was right.[24]

The old working class culture had provided some defences from the harshness of a capitalist labour market which meant wild competition among individual workers. When Fascism confined the old ideologies to ghettoes, besides destroying the workers' political and trade union organizations, relations among workers almost returned to a state of nature—a state of free competition. In the following interview, two workers, Domenico, born in 1924, and Armando, born in 1916, illustrate how this point has become symbolised in their own memories. Domenico speaks first:

My father managed to get me a job in a workshop, people we knew, it was wire-drawing and I worked as a labourer. Well, I went there as a boy, I'd go and work at the furnaces. Well, in those days when you were a boy in the small factories, however big they were, and this one was big, you were badly treated. Well, not really ill-treated, apart from the boss laughing at you, but the workers did too. It was the sort of mentality they had in those days, and since you were a young lad you'd always be under everyone else, and the jokes, all sorts of things. I remember, we were six or seven young lads in Lingotto, the tongs came out from the press, and I got home at night with a hard spot of corny skin. And lots of times they slipped, the tongs slipped or jets of fire came out and burned you. They laughed, they did, because that's it, I'm just telling you, that was the metal worker's attitude in those days... ... And nobody would teach you a skill. No, you had to steal it; and more than that, the ones who were the so-called experts, you see, their idea was that a skill was money.

And Armando:

Well, I wanted to tell you about the ignorance there was in those days. If you saw a horse falling, they'd all be saying: 'The poor animal!'; but if anyone fell off a bike and broke his head – mind you, I'm referring to things like, well, behaviour in the workshop – there would be a loud laugh: 'What a big fool, he fell off his bike!' At work you got the same reactions as you got in the streets, you know—when your boss told you off, you could see the others liked it. Fascism had created this type of feeling, because in the socialist days these things had already been disappearing. You know what I mean, I heard my old folks talking about it, and read something too—but it was mostly my old folks who told me about it. [25]

If the ruthless violence of earlier capitalist work relations had been largely restored under the Fascist regime, this had not been achieved only through political repression. There had also been major socio-economic changes in progress. Technological innovation linked with a massive entry of the unskilled into the factories had already taken place in the years around the First World War. [26] During the interwar period, internal labour migration, although officially prohibited, continued and increased, [27] modifying the working class's local linguistic unity and sense of common belonging. In the thirties, efforts were made to pursue the entrepreneurs' policy of isolating factories from surrounding society, [28] while transforming the organization of production. [29] The Bedaux system was introduced which greatly accelerated work rhythms. Other important changes were increases in schooling, which reached more children and raised the school-leaving age, [30] and increases in formal technical training. This reduced the possibility of handing down skills – with their attendant ideas and values – from worker to apprentice. And finally, in the early thirties, came unemployment, in contrast to the twenties when it had usually been quite easy to find a job, and mobility between factories had been high. It is of course very relevant, given our subject, that these socio-economic changes were accomplished under a Fascist regime which either wholly repressed social conflict or regimented it within rigid channels. Certain processes of modernisation therefore took on different forms than they would have done in a capitalist system with other kinds of institutional and state organisation. The nature of the Fascist regime made it impossible for the working class to develop cultural defences of its own to keep pace with the socio-economic changes.

These changes certainly undermined the material bases of work ideologies, both as a skill and as a universal duty. But we must exercise great caution in transferring interpretations from one field to another. Cultural expressions can never be mechanically deduced from socio-economic changes. Nor have historians yet explained to what extent these social changes resulted in real day-to-day differences when compared with earlier times. There is a risk of antedating modernisation and mistaking the extent of a process which – at least in Italy – was just in embryo at that time, and was to develop fully only after the Second World War. Moreover, the process of taking away intelligence and skill from men and incorporating it into machines is a long-term one, which capitalism develops continually. Far too often what are in the long run small changes appear in a medium or short-term perspective as fundamental turning points. For our purposes here, we can assume that a partial modernisation[31] had taken place, which did not completely eliminate the material base for the old work ideologies, but tended to give them a different value.

Consensus, in the form of acquiescence to the established order and authority, had always been present in those ideologies. Now it could emerge and acquire a new force. Earlier acceptance of work as something to be done properly and with care tended in the changing conditions to turn into mere acceptance of working whenever possible. The appeal of a well done job was less and less meaningful to the younger generations. So was an ethic based essentially on labour. The new characteristics of work beginning to emerge were subordination, acceptance of control, time-tables and hierarchies—no longer justified by personal ability and merits. Many life stories are examples of how the old idea of skill became a basis for consensus, in spite of the anti-fascist personal feelings of the informants (whom I believe speak in good faith, although they are thus self-contradictory). But we do not have the space to pursue this here, and it is more important to see what happened to the more general and widely held ideas, such as the one we have called the matrix of other work ideologies: the idea of labour as a principal moral duty. Their fate was similar, for

Fascist authority was, to a certain extent, a reinforcement of the previous social order. It based its power on compromising – in spite of occasional conflicts – with the old authorities: the army, the king, the Catholic Church.[32] A basis for consensus was already there, broader for those who had never challenged such authorities, but existing for everyone in so far as certain areas of common consensus had never been in dispute.

The extracts which follow are from an interview with a woman, Aurelia, born in Asti in 1912, who entered a local engineering factory at sixteen and worked there for 38 years. She married, and had a child in 1934. Her story is permeated by work: at the factory, in the house, in the form of extra hours to supplement her income:

When I was young, we really worked, we did then, 'cause there was nothing else. We went to work and we had to melt the ice in the containers, while now – the factory's gone to ruin now, because there were a lot who got their wages and didn't work.

What did you make in your factory?
At one time we made bolts. A long time ago we used to make bolts and we worked hard, I can tell you, and we made bits for bikes, bike chains and those sort of things. Later on we made other things, but we were always near the machines, round them, setting them, and they worked alone. We always had to stand, I got pains in my legs and couldn't work any longer, so they made me sit. I used to sit on a bench near there.

What about the times of unemployment? Were you ever out of work?
I can't remember really—no, I think we always had work, because it was a small factory, not big as it is now. Only four or five shops and they hadn't even a proper roof. There were more, later on, but at the beginning when I started, there were only two or three, three or four shops, all without windows – we used to jump out of the windows. Cold, and full of smoke it was, because we used wet cloths, we'd go and dip them in petrol, smoke all the time. We'd be black when we got home, like a bunch of maskers.

And what did you do in your free time? Did you get holidays?
If there'd been any, some would have gone to work just the same to earn something, the wages were so low. Not enough, see. Things aren't so good again now, I mean there is unemployment now, isn't there? But in those days you worked all week in the factory, and in the afternoon sometimes – sometimes I'd go as a cleaning woman, to earn a bit more money. And on Sunday we had the dirty washing because we hadn't too many clothes and couldn't change and they had to dry, in front of the stove in winter, so we could iron them on the following day, so we hadn't all that much time to go out. Then things started to get better – they got worse again – that's how it went. In our block of flats, for instance, there were five or six families and if we did anything we'd all get together, maybe cook some *bugie*

(carnival cakes), when it was the season, or roast chestnuts. All together one time in your own house, another in somebody else's, and did something like that, you know, at times. But going out for treats or spending money, we couldn't do that, really.

What about parades, or gymnastic displays, do you remember any of those? On Saturday, there was the Fascist Saturday, didn't you join in? Didn't you have to go to any demonstration?

Yes, they often went, but I never did. No, they didn't make me. When I could, I went to work for the market gardeners on Saturdays. They gave me some vegetables, some fruit. They gave me food instead of money. I couldn't go to those things. When I got home, the others went to demonstrations.

Were there ever any strikes or anything like that?

Well, sometimes, but rarely. We didn't go on strike that often in those days, people needed to work. Then people started wanting only to have fun, go wandering, and they don't work any more. Eh, you've got to say the truth, haven't you? When people were used to hard work, they really worked. Because me, when there were strikes, I didn't like it, and going into the streets, there would always be someone who used bad language—and I was afraid, because sometimes there were fights.

Were there any such things here in Asti?

Yes, there were. They would beat each other up, for the party as well. One was for the Christian Democrats, the other for the Communists, and another was for something else. It's always been like that.

When Mussolini came to power, do you remember anything about what happened then?

Eh, I remember I was wearing a ribbon in my hair, it was red, and they pulled it off! (laughs) I'll always remember that. My mother was a washerwoman and she had sent me to carry some clothes people needed. And then these two came holding these truncheons and got hold of me, and I must have been 10 or 12, and they got hold of me, and took − ripped the ribbon off − red, it was, and they ripped it off my hair. I cried my eyes out! You know, they'd got those truncheons. I ran up the stairs and didn't say a word—a child I was, and in those days we weren't as quick as children are now.

So there was much trouble.

Yes, there was, and the Muti[33] were here, when B. was here. Oh, and I got two medals from my factory. Would you like to see them? (Interruption in order to show the medals.)

And who was B?

He was one of those against us, on the *Duce*'s side he was... Once I opened the door, just a beam of light coming, and he came in, pointing that bayonet, like this − he said to me: 'Where is your husband?' 'My husband is at war, I don't even know where he is. You should know where he is, not me'.[34]

Aurelia's interview presents the simplest and most widely spread ideology of labour. The worker expresses no love or interest for the product or for the machine, but on the contrary, indifference and estrangement towards both. No relationship seems to exist with the bosses, no feeling of equality with them at any level: rather a sense of impotence and resignation prevails. But we find a pride in having been worthy of the work-medals, and an absolute certainty that work is indispensable to keep the world going. According to Aurelia, it was lack of the will to work that ruined her factory (which actually was incorporated by a multi-national during the 1960s): and the same lack is ruining society now. Work is also, to her, a justification for pacifism and indifference, two attitudes which both help to maintain oppression. However, Aurelia does not idealise work, which, for her, includes hard labour, tiredness, health hazard, loneliness, and the anxiety caused by pressing economic necessity. The consciousness of all this makes, at least partially, her conception more materialistic than the refined and sophisticated ideology of the skilled workers.

This more popular idea of work did, in fact, have some real anti fascist potential in and of itself.[35] Fascists were often labelled as 'maccheroni', 'young ones who don't want to work, layabouts'.[36] As one woman put it:

I was against Fascism, but not because I had something else clearly in mind. I used to see the Fascists who lived near us, all loafers, without any skills, out of work, good for nothing, didn't like to work, layabouts in the true sense of the word. I couldn't stand them.[37]

It was certainly easy for Fascism to incorporate and use these ideas to its own advantage. The Fascist ideology of work cannot by any means be confused with the popular idea expressed by Aurelia that work is a curse, an idea devoid of all optimism, heavy with bitterness and complaint. Yet such an idea helped to discourage Aurelia and people like her from rejecting Fascist propaganda on work. Threatening placards hung in many workplaces: WORK – FUNDAMENTAL TO EVERY SOCIAL ORDER – IS AND WILL BE IN ALL TIMES NECESSARY. While denying any hope of real emancipation in the future, Fascist mystifications pretended that alienated work conditions were a form of present emancipation. By making people accept this, and not merely respond to the charisma of a leader, Fascism could succeed in imposing its regime. In 1936 Horkheimer had clearly seen this:

It is a mistake to try to identify the authority structure of the present period with the relations between leaders and followers and to regard the acceptance of such hierarchies as fundamental. On the contrary, the new authority relationship, a more everyday but also a deeper reality, has not yet lost its power. The political leadership is effective because great masses of men consciously and unconsciously accept their economic dependence as necessary or at least do not yet fully realise it, and this situation is in turn consolidated by the political relationship.[38]

Coming closer to the issue of consensus, I think that we must reject any interpretation tending to make people like Aurelia appear irrespons-ible or 'natural' beings. Such would be the assertion that common people are separated from politics, and therefore spontaneously anti-fascist. But I also disagree with interpretations which consider the latent anti-fascism, which emerges anecdotally from the interviws, as simply the product of a more recent adjustment to the present-day ideology of anti-fascism. The isolation of common people from politics cannot be interpreted in such simplistic ways. Their words are evidence of contradictions within their own attitudes and thoughts. We must recognise that they partly accepted and adhered to the order imposed by Fascism, certainly in the sense that Fascism was to them in many ways the continuation of the past. And they also realised and accepted some of the changes a regime like that implied: an increase of oppression and of security, both in material and moral fields. But the colonisation was not complete. For if Fascism did satisfy some of the basic needs of the people, a potential rebellion was also rooted in their embryonic dissatisfaction. We find its signs: again, scars, more than anything else, since consciousness can emerge only in a critical and not in a positive form. The clear recollection of the injustices these people had to suffer can be interpreted as the sign of a potential consciousness, showing not only that the dissatisfaction had material bases (and not merely of an economic kind), but also how they experienced more than a mechanical reaction to a bad situation. The two anecdotes told by Aurelia describing her direct encounters with Fascism express well an underlying feeling of revolt against arrogance and violence. The recognition of such potentialities confirms that the hope Horkheimer expressed in 1941 was not unfounded: 'One day we may learn that in the depths of their hearts, the masses, even in the Fascist countries, secretly knew the truth and disbelieved the lie, like catatonic patients who make known only at the end of their trance that nothing has escaped them'.[39] The patients had really been catatonic, and had suffered because of this, although they preferred this suffering to the risk of rebellion. But their apathy cannot have been total, if they are now able to denounce the injustices they underwent.

By the thirties the old working class ideologies, both in their sophisticated and in their more popular forms, had become fragile and distorted; partly even a basis for consensus. To become once again an effective antifascist inspiration, their cultural points of reference needed to change completely. In what form could a new and updated political consciousness emerge? The following is an interview with Martino, born in Turin in 1912, a Fiat worker in the thirties and in the post-war period, now a member of the Italian Communist Party. He explains the reactions to the introduction of the Bedaux system:

I've not mentioned so far the system we worked by. It comes back to me now. I'd really like to talk about it, so that you can realise what it meant, working at Fiat before the war. I'm saying this just to explain how you could earn your bread. Well when you worked there, you see it was piece-work for us, it was called Bedaux, and this Bedaux system meant that a bloke called the time-checker would look at you working once, ten – twenty – thirty times, what you did, how you did it, how you made your piece, I mean the job you were doing. Sometimes he'd do this openly, but other times he'd hide to see if you'd use a faster method. Finally, when he'd found the quickest possible way to do that job, he'd check the time you'd taken to do that job with his stop-watch. And they'd fix the price on that.

Once the price had been fixed, that was fixed and for each job a price was calculated according to man's ability. Now ability meant that since you were fifth, fourth, third, second or first category, the job and not the man was classified. Then there was a minimum. If in the time fixed for the job, the worker couldn't make it – you know, there is the quick one, and the one who is not so quick, the one who is a bit brighter and the other one who isn't as bright and couldn't make it – and so we had a minimum. Those who were at that level were still tolerated. But there were some who were a bit slower and they couldn't manage the minimum and it was easy for them to get the sack. There were lots of these—sort of rope round your neck of checking your speed. And they worked all day, they had families and wept and you could see them working with tears in their eyes. They counted every single piece they made, they looked at the time, the time was over and they hadn't made it, they hadn't managed to keep within the limit and could be sacked.

When I entered Fiat, I found I had no choice. I squashed my brains on that. I was quick at work, and could understand these things and how they were getting money out of us, like money-lenders. Let's say one chap took ten minutes to do a certain job, and me, let's say I took five minutes.

That left me time to help the weaker ones. There was a book and I'd write down how much production I had done – and so you had to find a way to help the others. So, at a certain point I started to – the two or three, shall I say sleepy ones – I'd write down how much they'd done on their books, and put some of the work I'd done, I wrote it down on theirs, so they could earn their bit of bread.

Now, to manage, I used the same tricks Fiat used against us. We worked with metal sheets, and there was one heading I could make use of in the book: 'Other eventualities'. I'd take a hammer and go and ruin the body work. And by ruining the body, when they came to – they'd call a tester. 'Look' – I'd say – 'if you want to send it off like that'. 'Oh no, this has got to be repaired'. So it goes under 'Other eventualities'. 'Write it down and give me the money!' By the end of the month or week, I'd found a lot of money I could share out in our work-team and give it to these people who couldn't manage otherwise. This was one of the ways to reach the minimum indispensable to have enough bread to feed the family.[40]

Evidence of the dissatisfaction generated by the Bedaux system can be found in many written contemporary sources. But the interview, in addition, tells us much more about political consciousness and how this related to the cultural attitudes of the time, which were evidently undergoing a change. Martino found himself obliged to leave the old values behind in his resistance, while in other parts of the interview he refers to them and to his father who had handed them down to him. Could we imagine Giovanni ruining the metal sheets? Or Aurelia performing a similar act of insubordination? Resistance to the Bedaux system could no longer be based on skill and honesty, but on different qualities, like manual and mental quickness: 'I was quick and understood these things'. No space was left for a refusal of piece-work, so that the objective had become to get it based on collective rather than individual effort. The bosses' authority was no longer softened by mutual respect, and there had ceased to be any limits to the foreman's requests. Resistance could thus only take the form of boycott and clandestine rebellion. Hence the new forms of protest bore the signs of having originated from a dispossession of skills and a destruction of traditions. But for the same reason, the new egalitarianism had a wider and more concrete basis: for compared with previous ideas, it came closer to the labourers' mentality than to the skilled workers' ideology.

The new forms of rebellion, sabotage and violence were in some way a straightforward response to new work conditions, in that they were imposed by the new organisation of factories and society. Martino does not praise them: he presents his revolt as part of the terrible oppression that was forced upon the working class. In his case, factory violence and sabotage did subsequently evolve into armed Resistance: this gave these earlier acts a richer and deeper significance, transforming them into open, organised, collective violence aimed directly at liberation. But Martino is also conscious, as other parts of his interview testify, of the problems implicit in his action. It is difficult to develop a vision on the basis of an impoverishment of culture.

We end therefore with a paradox. I believe that there must be, at the level of subjectivity, a coexistence of coercion and freedom, of inheritance and critique. A new form of consciousness can only establish itself through an act of critique, of detachment, of opposition to the existing ideas and attitudes. Yet it could not exist without them. In other words class consciousness in the 1920s could not help taking into account and criticising – not accepting – the existing forms of approval of wage labour. Insofar as this was done, the denial of the present prefigured the future: in this sense daily forms of struggle against alienated work relationships anticipated formally, if not substantially, freer relations between human beings and between them and nature. Today the struggle towards consciousness has to take account of different elements, among which there is a range of attitudes which have come to be known collectively as the refusal of work. Neither of these two basic work ideologies – whether that of praise or rejection – intrinsically contains a greater truth than the other, and both have been contained from the beginning within the capitalist relations of labour. The predominance of one or the other at different moments in history is mainly due, on the one hand, to technological and economic changes (organization of work, mechanisation, organization of the firm, etc.), and, on the other, to a relationship with the general culture of the epoch. But neither of the two contains anything closer to a socialist consciousness than the other, except in a negative sense: for instance, it may appear nowadays that the appeal to a way of working characterised by dedication and sacrifice corrects the crudest implications of the refusal of work. Actually the appeal to 'work well done' is just an antidote and cannot help but be nostalgic.

Compared with these spontaneous ideologies, consciousness is a problematic potentiality, never guaranteed, yet nevertheless possible. Here is the clue to the ambivalence of 'needs', which always combine both a reference to the full potential in human nature and, on the other hand, a partial acceptance of the existing order which denies their realisation. The problem posed by an ideology of work which rejects the existing conditions imposed by an unequal division of labour, yet fails to link up with contemporary cultural and psychological aspirations and attitudes, remains of central importance today. The underlying connections between work ideologies and attitudes to authority – from totally passive acceptance to unlimited rebellion – need to be further investigated: for, as we have seen, there have been forms of consensus and acceptance containing within themselves a potential *dissent* even greater than that displayed in the more narrowly conceived political sense. To explore them may throw some light on the chances of achieving, in the future, freedom in the sphere of subjectivity and consciousness. In this perspective it becomes meaningful, through history, to do partial justice to those who suffered in that cause in the past.

1   This article is a revised version of the original paper presented at the International Oral History Conference, University of Essex, March 1979. In the interim a different, longer version has been published in *History Workshop Journal*, number 8. The present paper owes its smooth English to the help of Paul Thompson. I should also like to thank all those who have so generously told me the stories of their lives – without whom of course this work would not have been possible – and in particular, Lorenzo Anselmo, Arturo Gunetti, Giuseppe Ivaldi, Angelico Pavone, Carola Pennasso and Angelo Sargian. The translations of the interviews are by Victoria Franzinetti.
2   R. De Felice, *Mussolini il duce. Gli anni del consenso 1929–36*, Torino 1974, particularly pp. 54–95; R. De Felice, *Intervista sul fascismo*, Bari 1975, p. 29.
3   G. Quazza, 'Consenso e violenza nel regime,' in *Resistenza e storia d'Italia*, Milano 1976, particularly pp. 71–75.
4   As had indeed been pointed out at the time by Wilhelm Reich in his *Zur Anwendung der Psychoanalyse in der Geschichtsforschung*, "Zeitschrift für politische Psychologie und Sexualökonomie", Kopenhagen 1934.
5   G. Stedman Jones, 'Class Expression versus Social Control?', *History Workshop Journal*; 1977, No. 4, p. 168.
6   Cf. F. Cerutti, D. Claussen, H.-J. Krahl, O. Negt, A. Schmidt, *Geschichte und Klassenbewusstsein heute*, Amsterdam 1971.
7   The original tapes are part of two collections: one at the Istituto di Storia, Facoltà di Magistero, Università di Torino (tapes belonging to that collection will be referred to with the abbreviation ISM, followed by numbers and letters indicating the position in that archive), and the other at the Galleria d'Arte Moderna of Turin (GAM; this archive is in the process of being newly catalogued).
     Male informants had all been factory workers for at least part of their lives; this was the case also for some of the women. A number of them however were daughters, wives, sisters, mothers of workers and/or had been involved in the putting-out system, working for the factory at home.
     I have compared these sources with about 110 published life-stories of workers, included in the following books:

E. Vallini, *Operai del nord*, Bari 1957;
A. Pizzorno, *Comunità e razionalizzazione*, Turin 1960;
D. Montaldi, *Militanti politici di base*, Turin 1971;
P. Crespi, *Esperienze operaie*, Milan 1974
A.M. Bruzzone/R. Farina, *La Resistenza taciuta*, Milan 1976;
B. Guidetti-Serra, *Compagne*, 2 vol., Turin 1977.

The resulting sample cannot be considered as representative of the Italian working class between the wars. My observations in this paper are therefore to be taken as hypotheses more than anything else. In this sense I think this work bears some resemblances to anthropology, although the ambition is to place working class culture in a historical perspective. This is also why I have given preference, in the choice of interviews to be quoted at length, to the ones I could conduct myself, which included some sort of participant observation. In order to preserve confidentiality, some of the informants' names used here are pseudonyms.

8 So far jokes have been considered simply as symbolic compensations for impotence: e.g. E.R. Tannenbaum; *The Fascist Experience. Italian Society and Culture 1922–45*, New York 1972, Ch. IX. They might be studied as a specific part of a culture and of its reactions and changes under Fascism.

9 GAM. The interview is A.M., born in 1919, in Veneto, immigrated to Turin in 1930; she subsequently worked in three small factories.

10 ISM, TO/SP/10.

11 Antonio T., born in Turin in 1911, in E. Vallini, *op. cit.*, p. 254.

12 Such a discrepancy has been shown by the documents collected for the exhibition on 'working class culture and daily life in Borgo San Paolo' (a district of Turin) between the wars: see the essay by G. Levi, D. Pianciola, B. Bianco, A. Frisa, M. Gribaudi, S. Cavallo, E. Gennuso, C. Savio, 'Cultura operaia e vita quotidiana in borgo San Paolo', in the exhibition catalogue, *Torino tra le due guerre*, Turin 1978, pp. 2–45.

13 Cf. G. Miccoli, 'Contadini del cuneese e storia delle classi subalterne', *Bollettino dell'Istituto Regionale per la storia del movimento di liberazione nel Friuli-Venezia Giulia* V, 2–3, 1977, pp. 66–71; and N. Isnenghi, 'Valori popolari e valori "ufficiali" nella mentalità del soldato tra de due guerre mondiali', *Quaderni storici*, 38, 1978, pp. 701–9.

14 Adorno in, T.W. Adorno, K.R. Popper, R. Dahrendorf, J. Habermas, H. Albert, H. Pilot, *The Positivist Dispute in German Sociology*, London 1976.

15 I hope to deal with other aspects (forms of irreverence; authority in the family; relationships between daily life and politics) in a more general study on which I am now working.

16 I use 'pre-fascist' not in a strictly chronological sense, but in a sense similar to 'pre-colonial', which can refer to societies contemporary with colonialism, but generated by previous social relations.

17 I refer to the first series of *L'Ordine Nuovo*, Rassegna settimanale di cultura socialista, 1° maggio 1919–24 dicembre 1920. Writings by Gramsci of that period can be found in A. Gramsci, *L'Ordine Nuovo 1919–20*, Turin 1970.

18 ISM, TO/LI/13.

19 A. Gramsci, *op. cit.*, p. 49.

20 M. Horkheimer, *Critical Theory*, New York 1972, p. 67.

21 A. Schmidt, *The Concept of Nature in Marx*, London 1971, p. 144.

22 Cf. S. Bologna, 'Composizione di classe e teoria del partito alle origine del movimento consiliare', in S. Bologna, G.P. Rawick, M. Gobbini, A. Negri, L. Ferrari Bravo, F. Gambino, *Operai e stato*, Milano.

23 B. Mussolini, *Opera Omnia*, Florence 1957, vol. XXIII, pp. 137–8. The Ascension speech is in col. XXII, pp. 360–389.

24 Vallini, *op. cit.*, pp. 100–101.

25 ISM, TO/LI/6.

26 Cf. S. Musso, 'L'operaio dell'auto a Torino. Struttura e lotte dal periodo giolittiano alla fine della prima guerra mondiale, *Classe*, IX, 14, 1977, pp. 87-143.

27 Cf. A. Treves, *Le Migrazioni interne nell'Italia fascista*, Torino 1976.

28 Cf. G. Sapelli, *Organizzazione lavoro e innovazione industriale nell'Italia tra le due guerre*, Turin 1978.

30 Cf. G. Ricuperati, *La scuola italiana e il fascismo*, Bologna 1976.

31 Cf. N. Tranfaglia, *Sul regime fascista negli anni Trenta*, in N. Tranfaglia (ed.), *Fascismo e capitalismo*, Milan 1976.

32 Cf. the essays by G. Rochat, G. Neppi Modona, G. Miccoli, in G. Quazza (ed.), *Fascismo e società italiana*, Turin 1973.

33 She refers to the Fascist squads active in Asti in 1943–45.

34 ISM, AT/CO/2.

35 G. Germani has written about the correctness of the popular image of fascists as 'displaced' persons: 'the human basis of Fascism was provided by a process of "displacement", basically caused by the deterioration of the capitalist system but nonetheless accentuated by the particular upsetting conditions of the war' – 'Fascism and Class', in Stuart Woolf (ed.), *The Nature of Fascism*, London 1968, p. 72.
36 Crespi, *op. cit.*, p. 44.
37 Guidetti Serra, *op. cit.*, p. 192.
38 M. Horkheimer, *op. cit.*, p. 89.
39 *Ibid*, p. 290.
40 ISM, TO/LI/2.

Class Consciousness and the Fiat Workers of Turin since 1943

Liliana Lanzardo

Over the last twenty years my research has developed as an attempt, while maintaining a Marxist perspective, to overcome the limitations imposed by conventional Communist Party approaches to history. It has also been distinguished from traditional historiography by the use, from the earliest stage, of oral evidence as a principal source.

I carried out my first two inquiries along with *Quaderni Rossi* groups in 1960–1 and 1964–8, interviewing two groups of about 100 Fiat workers each, in order to analyse the new forms of conflict between labour and capital which were then emerging, and the relationship between workers' patterns of behaviour and their awareness of socialist values. Both are partly described in *Quaderni Rossi* no. 5. By 1967 I had begun historical research into the earlier period from 1943 until 1950, in order to discover whether during the post-war phase of less organised and more spontaneous conflict the workers had been aiming for more radical social changes than those proposed by the left wing parties. I used some fifty of these interviews in my book, *Classe operaia e partito comunista alla Fiat*, published in 1971. In each of these earlier inquiries I was using the direct testimony of protagonists to reach a new analysis of class consciousness, which challenged the official versions offered by the parties and trade unions. Subsequently I have become interested in exploring how class consciousness is formed, and for this purpose in using oral sources in a less descriptive or 'factual' way—in an approach which might be described as a type of Marxist anthropology.

In this current research I am aiming to reconstruct with the help of about 150 interviews the events of the Resistance and the post-war period in the city of Turin, with a special focus on Fiat, contrasting the perspectives of rank and file political militants in the factory with those of the Marxist and Catholic parties and union organisations. In order to justify decisions whose consequences are still with us the parties have often used misleading versions of the facts of their own past: for example, a party seeking a 'democratic' image will not admit to having earlier used violence. But the testimonies of the rank and file have sharply revealed the omissions and distortions of this official history, yielding frequent instances of forgotten episodes, such as revolutionary plans involving the use of weapons, or violent struggles in the factory, using force against the Fiat management and their foremen. Interviews have also brought to light documents such as photographs, letters, and company papers, which would probably have otherwise been lost, especially in view of the line which they conveyed. And beyond this, oral evidence has allowed a special insight into the general and political culture of the workers, and the way in which they themselves understood the events of the period.

These revelations led me to the ambitious aim of writing a history founded on the viewpoint of the protagonists, rather than on the political or socio-economic frameworks of traditional history. I wanted this to be independent, but the basis for a new, wider reinterpretation rather than simply a separate 'alternative' history. With this purpose I organised history courses for workers at Magneti Marelli and Autobianchi in Milan and Fiat in Turin, and through the discussions which ensued I acquired a lot of ideas and was able to establish a new basis for the relationship between the historical researcher and the protagonist. Firstly, through being called on to tell their own stories, the protagonists immediately assume a more central place; and secondly, since these accounts are then discussed and evaluated by the whole group, the historian has to descend from the pedestal of neutrality and make his or her present-day political beliefs and perspectives clear through this participation. The Marxist historian can in this sense become a participant and protagonist in working class struggle too: but at the same time is protected, by this direct contact, from romanticising, building a myth about the ideal worker, and assuming a total identification with the protagonists – a kind of 'proletarianisation of the intellectual – in the name of the common cause; and conversely, is able to see more clearly a particular role for the historian, both in politics and the academic world.

For both sides, historian and protagonist, the return to the past is seen as a means to explain the present. And it is this confrontation which *produces history*. It is certainly a partisan form of history, indeed, doubly so, since the perspective of the protagonist is reinforced by that of the historian as interviewer. To some extent this can be checked by the number of interviews: in this case already more than 150, as well as group discussions which yield further information. Thus the mosaic has many pieces and allows multiple points of view which can be used in reconstructing a wider reality. In eliciting and interpreting all this interview evidence, I have obviously played a leading role as a professional historian and a Marxist intellectual with my own vision of the history of class. I have in effect been actively participating in *the construction of my own sources.*

The part which I have played has varied, however, with different types of informant. With the less politically sophisticated who do not realise how tangled the historical implications are, I think one should rely on one's own honesty as a researcher rather than impose an immediate discussion of the implications of information which they have given in good faith. I took this approach, for example, when Communist or Catholic militants revealed how arms had been kept concealed in expectation of a political clash, up to 1948 and even later. Thus the memory of Felice Orsi, Communist Party (PCI) worker—'We'd got an arsenal under the factory . . . The guns weren't given up, a lot were kept . . . We kept them oiled. We didn't give them all up, even after '48'— is in this way paralleled by that of a Catholic woman worker and Christian Democrat (DC) activist, Giuseppina Fiandra: 'We kept the guns after the Liberation, even after '48. We even brought them here when we moved house, but then we gave them up.'

I felt a similar reticence was most appropriate when such people revealed unedifying episodes of party life which would have discredited some of their political leaders who – maybe in a book of the period – had given a different version of the facts. An example of this was the local Communist leadership's involvement in locking up the Fiat managers in the 'pre-revolutionary' factory occupation of 1948 which was their response to the assassination attempt on their national leader, Togliatti. Many PCI activists could remember this:

In '48 I shut the managers up in a room for three days . . . We'd got everything under control with the guns . . . I shut them up 'cause if I hadn't, the workers'd have done for 'em. (Ezio Roi)
They even took the managers to the lavatory with a machine gun. (Francesco Loiacono)
The workers said to the managers, 'You pray Togliatti doesn't die, because if Togliatti dies, you're going to die too!' (Patria Giovanni)
He got a telling off from I know who; he didn't tell you he put the blame on Fabbri after . . . (Vergnano Severino)

This version of the facts, which was denied in the subsequent trial, still does not appear in official party literature.

There are also other cases in which innocence itself bears witness of a particular political perspective, like that of a woman partisan who was the only woman I have so far interviewed from a Catholic background who took part in armed combat. She expressed the widespread view that the Communist partisans were thieves, because they forced the peasants to give them provisions. But she then described the excellent meals which were made possible by Allied air-drops of supplies—as a result of which her group had no need to requisition food; and even said that it was her own group, the Autonomi themselves, which helped the Communist bands because they were in such need. A much more common form of ingenuousness emerges from the discrepancy between a professed ideology, such as the Catholic belief in the virtue of humility, and a wish to bring out their own party faithfully in the historical recounting of facts. As Anna Fanton put it:

> More ought to be written about the women, because the men have written something, but not a word about the women . . . The mountains of papers I had! I threw them all away because I thought, 'It's all pride, to make a show of what you've done!'

Much more common, however, than testimony of this kind, is the very opposite: that of the highly aware militant, still politically committed, who determines what is to be told and discussed, and even deliberately uses the historian as a voice for his or her experience. Indeed, in the *Quaderni Rossi* inquiries, when a lot was said about 'co-research' (in fact the later inquiries came much closer to it), it was in practice the militants who imposed this through their own high degree of self-awareness, their historical sense, and their ability to identify the importance of matters that the researcher would probably have missed. Such informants are often vividly aware of the critical part which an individual such as themselves can play in the most notable historical events. As Lauro Morra, a Catholic worker, summed it up:

> We weren't in touch with intellectual circles, we were men of action . . . We were the ones that made history day by day, we ourselves . . . You don't make history in the abstract. History's something each of us makes by doing his bit. *We* made this history!

Another splendid example of a similar attitude comes from a 76-year-old Communist worker, Arturo Ferraris who, since I interviewed him, has written a book called 'The Workforce of Anti-fascism', published in 1981. In it he sets out to demonstrate the essential part played by individual workers and their slightest day-to-day political acts in the success of the struggle against Fascism: a greater part, in his view, than that played by the political leaders.

In this respect, men are more likely to take their own contributions seriously than women, whether their official function within the party or union was an important one or not. In detail, however, the versions given by the party official, the factory committee representative, the union activist, and so on, will differ from each other, in ways which reflect their various functions. And frequently differences of opinion and past motives are sincerely revealed. The question of motive is interesting, for militants will rarely attempt to prove their own innocence. On the contrary, they present themselves as informed witnesses, carefully selecting what to tell one and explicitly weighing its significance. When, for example, they say, 'Turn the tape recorder off!', this means that what they are about to say is important from the point of view of historical truth, but something they do not wish to become public knowledge—for the present.[1]

One of the most serious dangers when a historian is politically committed lies in the confusion of immediate political objectives and those of the research. I have seen from my own direct experience how this can bring undeniable harm to the gathering and development of information. Because their concerns are too closely tied to the immediate struggle, projects are often too soon abandoned. This was the case with the two *Quaderni Rossi* inquiries. They were successful in contradicting the then current view that the mass of workers was integrated into the production system (Fiat, 'the happy isle'), while only the old Communist avant-garde retained a revolutionary class consciousness. The interviews with workers showed how it was less rationally articulated attitudes which were more likely to spark off conflict within the factory; and equally that the workers had by no means fully absorbed the ethos of intensive productive rationality held by the Fiat firm. But ironically, at the very moment when the correctness of this interpretation was confirmed by the outbreak of industrial action at Fiat in 1962 – for it had been alone in forecasting that large-scale strike – this led to the abandoning of the inquiry in favour of immediate political action. The second inquiry disappeared with the 1968 student movement. Both inquiries, moreover, were limited in scope by the political assumptions of the researchers. Because we assumed the independent role of the working class in class conflict, and that such conflict centred on the militant industrial struggle, we focussed exclusively on the factory. We did not take full life histories, and treated the details of daily life outside the factory as of minor significance. Hence we missed certain key elements of working class conditions, such as housing, transport and the difficulties brought about by recent immigration from the South, which were in fact to prove explosive factors in 1968. This was despite the fact that we had found the most revealing informants were not the Communist party militants, but less politicised workers, included almost accidentally in the survey through the Catholic trade unions. We should perhaps have anticipated this, for these unions had grown as a result of advantages granted to them by management (such as being able to take summer holidays with their children), while on the other hand the Communist presence had been much reduced by this date, after thousands of activists had been dismissed or deliberately isolated from the mass of the workers. It was thus the less politicised informants who most helped us to understand the contradictory and ambiguous attitudes towards industrial conflict of the ordinary worker. They also, significantly enough, spoke much more freely about the problems of their social and private lives outside the factory; but we did not see the importance of this.

In some ways one should see this restriction to political questions, in retrospect, as a product of the period. In the years immediately after the war, class conflict was openly expressed. This was in contrast to the years of Fascist repression, when daily life had become the only remaining sphere for expressing political opposition, or the more recent phase from the sixties, when the mass media have attempted to reduce everything to the private sphere. The Communist workers saw daily life as subsumed in the political: they failed to understand it as a sphere for choice. Yet it was in precisely this sphere, through the family, the school and social welfare, that the Catholic sector launched its counter-attack in building alternative values. Communists concerned themselves with such areas only when they saw them as electorally important: for example, because many of the Turinese workers' wives were Catholic, they feared the women's vote— itself newly-granted in 1946. This fear was shared by women Communist militants like Lia Corinaldi of the Teachers' Union:

We realised that giving the vote to women would be very dangerous because the women were influenced by their parish priests...When Togliatti came to the Federation in Turin I said to him, 'Don't you see what a risk it is?' He said to me, 'It's a risk, but they'll learn from it; they'll get to know something about politics and become capable of choosing.

But despite these new electoral concerns, Communist activists saw social changes such as nurseries and sharing the housekeeping, which could have led to the liberation of these women and their active political commitment, in a merely negative light, as taking away energy from the political work of the men. The family and the women were expected to bear the whole material weight and cost of male militancy. Thus the omission of questions of daily life and culture from working class history reflects the priorities established by the militants themselves. Thus, when the militant worker's wife is not politically active, at the interview it is she who will introduce precise observations about their life conditions, their poverty, the difficulties in bringing up children, and the burden which militancy has imposed on their family regarding entertainment, relationships and neighbourhood life. On the other hand, for politically committed women, the concerns of politics would always come first, as two Catholic (DC) activists, Rosa Gallesio and Anna Fanton remember:

We in the DC spoke up against divorce. The Communist women spoke in favour of divorce, from political necessity mostly: they always added, 'But I should never divorce myself' . . . When the Liberation came, they suggested in Rome that the mass organizations should not be united. We were on friendly terms with them and we were rather sorry; however, party instructions were more important . . .

We've always kept completely apart from the PCI women . . . You couldn't act on your own initiative. We just ignored each other, because we were Catholics and they were Communists.

The male party activist may have been unaware of his family's problems. He may have regarded them as a necessary sacrifice, a price required by the family's commitment to the class struggle. Or he may have simply resented them as a constraint on the full dedication to political activity which he considered ought to have been his liberty and right. As one Communist worker, Cordone Piero, summed it up:

More than anything the women were what held us back. The big trouble in the families was the wife . . . At home the worker was subjected to all the conditioning influences of the family . . . so the worker had to free himself of this burden; from being conditioned so heavily . . . My trouble for example was my wife; she was anti-fascist, but she was a church-woman.

Sometimes during an interview such a militant may turn to events in the family to pinpoint a political event, such as dating a strike by the birth of a child; but he will rarely – as Catholics quite often do – reverse these values, to trace the internal process of becoming aware within the family, before the political event.

In a similar way, it took me a long time to realise the importance of the Catholics just because they had not seemed important to the Communist militants. Indeed, in the immediate post-war period in Turin they had not seemed to carry much political weight. During these years the Communists, who controlled the city council, effectively ignored the problem of the Catholics and the Church. Similarly, in the power structure of the factory, the Christian Democrat Party and the Catholics counted for very little indeed. If they tried to raise their voices, they were forced to desist. It seemed at the time that the problem had been solved. Why speak about it? And the interviews reflect this attitude. There were no more than scanty allusions to these questions. Cordero Piero summed up the Communist attitude:

The Christian Democrats never intervened outside the parish... What they did was even childish, but they were there—Our Lady the Pilgrim, processions without end. The DC didn't exist, it was the Church. The DC didn't have an office; and where was it, this DC?... The business about chaplains in the factory doesn't count. They didn't have any effect. What did they do? All trifling stuff!

The acceptance of such estimates was a serious shortcoming of the earlier research. It was only later, when I had realised how significant the Catholic organisations were to become in the power structure, that I began to put questions on these points, and deliberately to extend the scope of my interviewing to include the Catholics themselves. In retrospect, too, it has become much easier to see how the Christian Democrat victory in the 1948 elections, which relegated the Communists to permanent opposition – a victory unexpected by the Catholics themselves which brought deep consternation to the Communists in the factory – was all but inevitable. Ironically, it was the very particular character of the Christian Democrats in Turin, as revealed through my interviews, which made the Communists less aware of their significance. Rather than being allied with the landowners as in the south, in Turin, the Christian Democrats were also on the left, so that they were not harassing the Communists in local politics. In the factory the Communists exercised their power forcefully over the Catholic minority, taking a clear anti-clerical and anti-Christian Democrat stand—trying to stop their political and union activities in the factory, impeding their meetings and denying them the chance of addressing the workforce *en masse*:

We saw to it that the Catholics got the push...
They couldn't hold any meetings... They were afraid. (Arturo Ferraris)
    Folk were afraid then... We had only to whistle and there was a strike on...
The sly ones had a bad time of it, if they didn't keep quiet. (Giovale Carlo)

Later on, of course, the Catholics, in their turn, were to be equally repressive towards the Communists in Fiat; and even at this time, they had the advantage of the legalised violence of the governing Christian Democrat party in Rome on their side. But the party has since tried to hide or belittle the violent actions which such interviews reveal, for it cannot afford a resumption of such intolerance by Communist militants at Fiat towards the Christian Democrats.

These militants in their own accounts make the same omissions, but for different reasons: they do not wish to deny the truth of such episodes, but they still judge them unimportant, holding on to the attitudes they had then. Here the problem is less in the evidence than in its interpretation: for with the advantage of hindsight both historian and narrator can see the centrality of events which were not felt to be so at the time.

In a similar way, I have found myself re-evaluating the part played by the ordinary worker. During the early post-war years the Communist militants often judged the mass of workers with a certain condescension—a 'them and us' attitude which varied according to the support which they gave to the party line. Any behaviour in conflict with political objectives was regarded as invalid. Thus they criticised the ordinary workers for their reluctance to work harder when the party was calling for 'order and productivity', and for the need to use force to make strikes effective because of the lack of active backing for them; while at the same time they took the massive electoral support for the left as a sign of agreement with their policies. They assumed that it was right for the party to determine what were the 'needs' of the masses. Nor indeed was their 'vanguard' role in this period based simply on political theory. The more highly skilled workers were the more involved politically. Fiat workers had been the political avant-garde ever since the factory occupations of 1920 (led by Gramsci and the Factory Soviets), both because of the part they played in the strikes of 1943 and later against the Fascist regime, and in the fight for the Liberation. Besides, at that stage of industrial development the factory could be said to lie objectively at the centre of things. The dominance of the skilled men rested firmly on their earnings and qualifications, on the importance of industrial production within the whole economy, and above all on the central place of the factory within the neighbourhood. It could determine the life of an entire quarter—and this was especially true of Fiat. It would be no exaggeration to say of a sector like Fiat Grandi Motori which made ships' engines and other such large installations, that the life of the working class area around it beat with the heart of the factory. And this was reflected in politics. At the end of the war it was to the factory committees set up in Grandi Motori, that the surrounding

population denounced local Fascists, requesting the workers to purge and
try these people:

> We took some prisoners—for a week: they had been reported by the people, some
> were Fascists, one from the railway police, one a Fascist union official, another had
> been reported by a Jew because he had stolen things from his house... There was
> no written charge—they brought a spoken charge against them at the factory and
> we went and fetched them and took them to the Grandi Motori. (Becutti
> Armando)

And in subsequent years, whenever there was a political crisis, it was
always the workers who responded openly, leaving the factory to occupy
the streets and squares of the city as a tangible demonstration of their
presence and controlling power. As one Communist woman worker, Elsa
Zago, recalled:

> The difference between then and now is that the working class masses really
> existed then. Every time there was conflict they left the factory on lorries or on
> foot and set out downtown. Who was going to keep them back? Like a high tide
> they were, in their overalls, with their tools on their backs... The bosses were
> trembling in their shoes...

And the population of Turin accepted the factory working class as its
political expression.

All this led to assumptions, which I have gradually come to question.
It no longer seems to me that it can be taken for granted that because
ordinary workers fought against capitalistic rationalisation, the factory
power hierarchy, or other forms of repression at work, this was an expression of their political awareness—or of a fundamental class consciousness
and antagonism. Nor, even if this were true, would I now hold that
moments of open conflict – like that of 1948 – are 'more noble' than the
less dramatic but more continuous effort needed to maintain any political
ideals in day-to-day life. Instead, by seeking to understand the basis for
such continuities, I have found myself constructing a new picture of the
internal, subjective mechanisms of class consciousness and patterns of
behaviour.

For both Communist and Catholic militants to a certain extent
shared a common ideology, which was moulded by the conjunction of
official party views and organisational pressures (including the militant's
own party status) with the experience of personal life, work in the factory,
and political vicissitudes. By ideology I mean overall social and political
vision: and even for those most politically active, such a vision was

distinctively independent of official party standpoints. The Communists, especially, saw the world of the factory as to some extent separate, in a dialectical relationship with the party and the unions—just as the workers themselves were a recognised power, a separate force, in relation to the government and other external organisations. Hence it is false to attempt to explain the behaviour of the factory workforce in the post-war years simply in relation to the perspectives of the Communist party leadership. Communist class consciousness was rather the product of the fusion of twin perspectives: of working class power in the factory, and the party's role in national government, carrying with them the contradictory implications of class rule and national unity. These were held together by the ultimate hope of an electoral victory, which would allow the working class alternative vision, the socialist transformation of society, to be set in motion: so that these two projects were not seen as conflicting alternatives. Catholic class consciousness was also very contradictory. For it has become clear through my research that in every head-on clash since the war, one important ingredient has been a working class utopian vision of the future. This revolutionary utopianism has been one of the foundations of the whole way of life of the Communist worker. But ironically it has also permeated every action of the Catholic workers in their struggle against Communism. Mario Gedda, Catholic trade unionist, explains:

I think it was the radicalisation of the struggle that made people throw themselves into things like that. The Catholics, too, were bent on emancipation for the workers then ... In the post-war years people had two great aspirations—to get enough to eat ... and a new world with less injustice. Up to '48 you were either on one side or the other. I'm speaking as an anti-communist of those days, even though, Catholic or not, I vote PCI now. People felt the PCI as a dictatorial force.

Such complexities are by no means easy to grasp, yet I believe that through interviews with protagonists, both militants and ordinary workers, by observing the relations between the political and the private, and the many inconsistencies which a worker's utopian vision brings out in daily life, it is possible to reach towards a deeper understanding of the roots of working class consciousness. Here a vast field still waits to be explored.

1   At that time party members were all the more willing to grant interviews to outsiders, even though this was forbidden, because the PCI had not yet realised the need of its militants to put their experiences on record. Party historians like Amendola and Ragionieri have since helped to correct this.

The Journeyman and the
Small Master

A typical French bakery between the wars. The actual bakery would be downstairs from the shop itself. *Seeberger* © *Arch. Photo. Paris/S.P.A.D.E.M.*

Stories as Clues to Sociological Understanding: the Bakers of Paris

Daniel Bertaux

For me one of the most striking features of European oral history today – leaving aside the exceptional conviviality of its gatherings – is the way in which it draws people trained in different 'disciplines' into genuine encounters and exchanges with each other. This success springs, I suspect, from the conviction which all of us have reached in wrestling with our material, that it demands to be approached from a variety of distinctly different perspectives if we are to have any chance of finally grasping its inner core. We have to penetrate the tangle of facts, customs and attitudes to discover the hidden social structures which underlie them; and then to pick out the contradictions which cut across these structures in order to identify the dynamics of social change; and further still, to know the dynamics of a particular social group or formation from its own experience, 'from within', if we are to know how history was made in the past, and is still being made today.

It is perhaps easier to move into such a 'pluridisciplinary' approach from some backgrounds than others. Thus, it is a relatively short step for an ethnologist, already familiar with fieldwork and working with concepts and objectives very close to those of social history, to become an 'ethno-historian'. But it is a much longer journey for a sociologist to travel, from the typical concerns of mainstream academic sociology, with its emphasis on large-scale, quantitative statistical data and timeless transhistorical theorising, to the concrete 'fieldwork' of social history. In my view, this is because the very institutional success of sociology is probably based on a deep misconception. The founders of the discipline, desperate to endow it with academic legitimacy, tried to build it into a kind of *'physique sociale'*, a science which would be to social forms what physics, the paragon of scientific legitimacy, is to Nature. But as the laws of Nature are unaffected by time and space, so these founding fathers were led to propose the existence of social laws which would be at work in all human societies throughout time and space: and the task of the new discipline was to search out these laws. The pattern which they thus set has led generations of sociologists to focus almost exclusively on those parts of societies which are the most regular and stable, that is to say, its institutions of one kind or another, and to remain blind to most of the contradictions either within institutions or between them. Similarly, other sociologists have fallen for the equally serious mistake of trying to reduce human action – or praxis – to mere coded behaviour, in the belief that in order to appear to be objective as scholars, they had to objectify human beings. It is out of this socially, highly successful – but intellectually hopeless – quest for legitimacy, that has come the protracted divorce between history and sociology which has been so much to our cost.[1]

It was in search of a way out of this maze that I found myself involved, first of all, with the bakers of Paris, and then, with oral history. Ten years ago I was studying social mobility and class structure[2]—a classic theme in sociology. Tired with the aridity of statistics and surveys, I made up my mind to identify some particular set of class relationships on which I could carry out a small piece of empirical research myself—if only as a kind of personal hobby. From the influence of structuralist theory I had grasped the idea that classes had to be understood not in themselves, but in their relationships to each other; while from Marxism I took my emphasis on the relations of production. My idea thus became to choose a particular sector of material production for observation, and from analysing its structuring of the relationships of production to go on to study the consequences of this on the overall lives and everyday experiences of the men and women – workers, owners and managers – embedded in them. I wanted to choose something basic. First of all I thought of motor cars. But to grasp the complex totality of their production was clearly beyond the scope of the simple project I wanted. This was how I ended up with bread: with the 'real' bread which is still made, in Paris as everywhere in France, by small artisan bakers.

Next I had to decide how I ought to study bread-making. My wish to work with life histories went back to reading Oscar Lewis's *The Children of Sanchez*. But in 1970 no French sociologist of any standing would have even considered collecting life stories. At that time they were dismissed as valueless, 'soft stuff': 'hard' quantitative facts were the fashion. All the same I decided to experiment with collecting some life stories for the bakery project in my spare time with the help of a co-worker, Jacqueline Bessette-Dufrêne; and our first interviews with old bakery workers proved so interesting that before long I was seeking out research support for a funded project that was eventually to last for several years. By the end, Jacqueline, Isabelle Bertaux-Wiame, Renée Colin and I had collected a hundred life stories: thirty from bakery workers, thirty from master bakers, twenty-five from bakers' wives and fifteen from apprentices. Meanwhile we gathered together all the historical, economic and demographic information we could find on artisan bakery.

I had begun as a structuralist with a specific blindness to history, and an even worse blindness to the historicity of contemporary social life. But as soon as we began to listen to these old workers' stories it became obvious that we had to deal with history as well as with structure. Some features of the bakery system had changed over the years: this would have to be explained. Other features, so it seemed, had remained identical—and we should need to explain *this too*: for what was functional in the twenties, such as the sixty-hour week, seemed wholly anachronistic in the seventies, yet nevertheless remained the rule rather than the exception.

The historical aspect of the research took on momentum when Isabelle Bertaux-Wiame who is a historian by training joined me on the project. In order to build up a general frame within which to situate and integrate the individual life stories she started to look for existing studies of the bakery trade during the interwar period. They proved to be very few, and superficial. Investigations of conventional archive sources also yielded little of much value. Although there was at that time no oral history as such in France to help us tease through this problem, we eventually came to realise that we already had the historical data which we were seeking—*in the life stories themselves*. For example, before 1936, apprentices were literally outside the law: there were no written contracts, very few visits by factory inspectors (and a very obvious complicity between them and the master bakers), and hence no reliable written sources were to be found; while on the other hand, in our own interviews we had very detailed accounts, from old bakery workers, of the extremely harsh conditions of work and life during apprenticeship; indeed, including accounts of how heavily biased were the few official documents which were supposed to provide 'evidence' of its conditions.[3]

What I learnt from this venture into history was not just the necessity of studying the past if one is to understand the present. I also came to understand how the present itself is historical. This may be less naive than it sounds. Artisan bakery accounts for more than 90% of bread production in France so that it looks like a very strong social force, almost a national institution. But we soon discovered that in fact huge economic interests were lying in wait for the right moment to wipe it out of existence and conquer the whole market for bread, just as has already happened in the majority of other industrial countries. The discovery of this invisible but permanent threat transformed our perspective. From our original conception of a set of socio-structural relationships with the consistency and stability of an institution, we moved to the idea of a living social form threatened from outside, regenerating itself daily through the strenuous efforts of the 200,000 people who worked in one of its 40,000 'cells', the artisan bakeries. True enough, several direct 'causes' could be picked out to 'explain' why all of them, from bakers and bakers' wives to workers and apprentices, were working such incredible work-weeks: one could point to the constraints of commercial competition, the need to reimburse huge loans (many bakers are former bakery workers), the quest for a rapid accumulation in order to retire early – or, for the workers, the strongly internalised project of themselves becoming self-employed masters – '*Quand tu seras patron*'. But in view of the unusual strains of the way of life which follow from it, strains which become much harder to accept in the midst of a 'consumer society', all of these 'causes', even if each is bound up in a total structure to which they contribute and within which they make sense, are only of limited explanatory power. They can enable us to explain—or rather to describe in depth—just how artisan bakery functions in France: but they cannot tell us why it still exists here and not elsewhere. For if conversely the flow of dissatisfied apprentices, bakery workers and bakers' couples dropping out of the trade became a haemorrhage so severe that collapse ensued, *this* could be retrospectively 'explained' equally easily through picking out other structural features and calling them 'causes' in a similar way. We need to get beyond a purely structural analysis and accept that the evolution of social forms is not predetermined: in short to conceive of these forms in their *historicity*, perpetually threatened with sudden disappearance and only remaining alive and strong through the conscious human struggle of their agents— through the praxis of their individual lives. While one can understand this point in abstract theory, I do not know of any sociological technique other than the life history which has the capacity to make it concretely perceptible.

In allowing us to penetrate behind the appearance of the present as static, of the social as structural, of the world as given, in reintroducing the crucial role of human action, of praxis, within a present which is also history-in-the-making, in all these ways life histories constitute powerful tools for a historicisation of the way sociologists conceive of the present.[4]

*   *   *   *

One must not think of life stories as just dead strings of factual beads waiting to be taken apart and sorted back into different piles—hard and soft. The stories are themselves part of a living, if in some respects fleeting, social relationship: between teller and listener, past and present. So far from being a drawback, this is a great strength: for as we discovered, the telling of the story may give as many clues as what is told.

In the first place, there may be something to be learnt from one's own impact as a researcher. For example, at first I found that with master bakers, in contrast to bakery workers, it was practically impossible to obtain an interview. I would no sooner introduce myself as a state-paid research worker investigating artisan bakery than a kind of invisible iron curtain seemed to drop between us. Long experience has in fact taught shopkeepers that State investigations, whatever their original purpose, can only have one end result: more taxes. Silence is their weapon. After the warm welcome of the bakery workers this coldness from the master bakers was especially disconcerting. We found the solution to it by accident, one day on holiday in the Pyrenees, when Isabelle and I decided to go along together to see the village baker. First, of course, we met the baker's wife in the shop, and we asked for an interview. She was somewhat surprised and she got her husband to come up. 'What are you doing this research for?' he asked—as they all had. So we explained that being husband and wife, we worked for . . . 'Husband and wife?' he interrupted. 'So you are working like us—*en couple*. Only we are making bread, and you are making . . . research? You are some kind of artisans like us, is it that?' Both couples looked at each other and some process of mutual identification, some non-verbal, human communication happened. And it solved our problem. After that, we either conducted the interview as a couple, or if Isabelle went alone, she was careful to mention that this research, although financed by the State, was a family thing. . . .

More obviously, it matters a great deal who you get your stories from, even if the hard facts in them follow a similar pattern. For example, Isabelle interviewed fifteen old men specifically for information about apprenticeship. Eight of them had subsequently become master bakers, by going self-employed; while the other seven had remained bakery workers throughout their whole life. Not one of them was a baker's son—all but one came from poor peasant or working class backgrounds. They all had started as apprentices in their teens – usually at 14 – with small bakers in villages or small towns. We can safely say that all experienced more or less the same patterns of work and living, the same processes, the same hardships. What is interesting is that their accounts were so different.

The *facts* they described were the same: night work, twelve to fifteen hours each day, lack of sleep, and so on and so on—but the presentation of these facts, their interpretation, the overall tone of the account differed strikingly. This depended on whether the narrator was still a bakery worker at the end of his life or whether he had become self-employed *and, in his turn, had trained apprentices.* Those who still remained workers could bitterly recall every pan of cold water thrown in their face, every kick up their arse, every blow, every act of pressure which was exerted on them to drive them to *work*—and all for no pay. But on the other hand those who were now themselves master bakers seemed to have forgotten all this. If, after some probing by Isabelle, they did remember some act of brutality, they simply laughed about it. To a man, they justified the hard work and constant pressure by explaining that there could be only one way to learn the trade, and this was it. Their *relationship* to their own past has been drastically altered.

Do we need to go further? The point we want to make is well-known: stories about the past are told from the present, from a situation which may have changed over the years and defines a new relationship to the past. It is *this relationship* which underlies the whole story, defines the meaning which it is supposed to convey: for one never tells a story in itself, but in order to convey some meaning. Telling a story about the past is a way of expressing indirectly a meaning about the present; in most cases this – often unconscious – goal of meaning-construction prevails over the faithful reconstruction of the past.

This is why variety of the sample and good questioning are so crucial. The variety of informants helps to break a consistency of recollections of the past which may be due more to consistency of ulterior life trajectories and situations than to the past itself. Questioning focusing on *facts* (working conditions, living patterns, time schedules, health problems, money matters) will also help, within the interview itself, to reach beyond the veil of reconstructed meaning and discover power relations, repressed desires, frustrated projects. To develop reflexions along such lines seems to us a good deal more likely to prove fruitful for the future methodology of oral history and life history research than to allow ourselves to be side-tracked by the artificial experimental studies of memory designed by behavioural psychologists.

*   *   *   *

From time to time in the field, one picks up a story which is about history in the more familiar sense: about collective events of a local or national past. It is tempting to treat stories of this kind as 'oral documents' and try to use them to reconstruct the way 'things really happened'. All too often this will yield equivocal or disappointing results. Yet, rather than discarding such apparently worthless stories, one can sometimes find in them the first stepping stones which lead towards new paths of under-standing.

In a conversation with a former leader of the *Syndicat Patronal de la Boulangerie Parisienne* (not to be confused with the *Syndicat Ouvrier!*) we came to mention our interest in the past history of this union which stands for the interests of Parisian master bakers as against the workers' union and, most of all, against the State which (up to August 1978) decided the price of bread. This man advised us to contact a Mr. T., retired baker, who had been the leader of this Union 'some time ago'. 'He may have interesting things to say', he added without further qualifica-tion. We therefore telephoned this Mr. T. and explained briefly the aim of our research; he agreed to meet us, and an appointment was made.

He lived about 80 kilometres from Paris. When the day came we drove in our old 2 CV to his village and finally stopped the car in front of a cottage, built on the edge of a dark forest. Two fierce barking dogs preven-ted us from getting into the garden. We rang the bell: a woman came out of the cottage and yelled that her husband had changed his mind and did not want to meet us. Our long ride in the bumping car gave us the strength to insist. Finally, the man came out reluctantly, and standing behind his dogs, said we had misunderstood him: he did not want to be interviewed. Well, would he care to *talk* to us at least—without being recorded? The dogs would not keep quiet, so that he had to come up to the front door. After a short discussion, he seemed to change his mind. He came out; we shook hands at last. Then he led us to his Mercedes, and invited us to get in: 'We'll drive around', he said.

And so we did for half an hour, circling through the forest. We asked questions more or less as if blind-fold, vainly trying to fish out some inter-esting topic. He also questioned us. Who was in charge of this inquiry? Who was paying for it? What was going to come out of it? Meanwhile he was driving around on minor tracks, and soon we had completely lost our sense of direction as well as control of the conversation. Then the car turned once more and the cottage appeared at the end of the road. We were back to square one . . .

But suddenly the man seemed to reach a decision; he pulled the car to the side of the road and stopped. Turning in his seat and looking straight at us he said:

—Well, do you know exactly *when* I was in charge of the Syndicat?
—*Well, yes: it must have been in the early fifties, or was it the late forties?*
—No. C'était pendant l'Occupation [that is—during the Second World War, while the German troops were occupying France].

We remained silent and shocked. What the man had just said meant that he had been 'collaborating' with the Germans, that he certainly had had some trouble at the end of the war ... We did not know what to say. Nevertheless, he went on:

Tout ça c'est du passé, [All this is past now—and we won't come back to it] But I'll tell you one story, which may be of interest for your research.

Well, after the Allied troops had landed in Normandy, when it became clear that they would eventually reach Paris, the Germans decided to retreat back to Germany. Off they went one morning, and because they were a long way from home, they took away with them all the fuel they could find. You see what it meant?

We did not see anything, and it must have shown on our faces, for he went on:

—No more fuel: this meant, no more bread. Without fuel, you cannot bake bread anymore, can you? Do you understand now?
—*Well ... the Allied troops were bringing fuel with them, I suppose, and ...*
—No, no you don't understand. But you are too young of course. It took them one whole week to reach Paris. Meanwhile, streetfighting had begun. The *Résistants* (partisans) came out from underground. They were sniping at the German rearguard. They were all Communists: they wanted to take power *before* the Allies reached Paris. They were trying to subvert the whole situation.
—*What does this have to do with the fuel shortage?*
—No fuel, no bread; *et quand il n'y pas de pain, c'est l'émeute!* [When there's no bread, you get a riot.] This is what the Communists wanted: riots. To have a revolution. See?

So, you know what I did? I knew that in many bakeries, the ovens were quite old and could still be operated with wood, as before. But, it was almost impossible to find wood; imagine, we were in August, and there were no stocks.

So I organised brigades to go into the Bois de Vincennes [a forest on the edge of Paris], cut the trees, and bring the wood back to Paris on hand-carts. This wood was distributed to all the bakeries which could make use of it. I explained the situation to everybody, and everybody in the profession gave a hand. Oh, it was hard work, because the wood was not dry! It did not burn well; it made a lot of smoke. We spent several nights coughing in front of the ovens. And during the day, instead of sleeping we would go back and cut more wood. It was a hell of a job for one whole week, I tell you. *Mais Paris n'a pas manqué de pain!* [But Paris didn't go without bread!]

Having finished his story, he started the engine and dropped us in front of our car; and we drove away, carrying with us the message this man had wanted us to pass on: that he had saved Paris, and hence the whole of France, from Communism. This was in his eyes the part he had played in Fench history.

If our focus had been an historical one, we would have tried to check this story from other sources. Being occupied with other questions we failed to do so. But the sociological meaning of the story remained with us. Thus far we had focused on the inner structure of the artisan bakery, and had almost forgotten that bread is also a *political* matter. We began to consider this question seriously, and discovered a number of interesting facts. Not only that most major upheavals in France did start with bread riots in Paris, including the French Revolution of 1789 and the Paris Commune of 1871; but also that conversely, during the events of May-June 1968, while most workers were on strike all over France, the bakery workers were among the very few who carried on working. Their Communist-led union had asked them to do so (for, as is well known, the Communist Party was very much frightened by the May movement and especially by its possible consequence, counter-revolution: so they feared rioting even more than the government).

The recurring association, throughout history, of shortage of (cheap) bread in Paris (and other big cities) and riots led us to the assumption that the availability of cheap bread, being a necessary condition of public order, was a close concern of the authorities. Once on this trail we indeed discovered several ways by which the authorities kept a close watch on the stocks of flour, the price and quality of bread, the possibilities of strikes among bakery workers or bakers. Even the secret police (*Renseignements Généraux*) has bread on its task-list. Thus, whether true or half-true or even one-tenth true (but which tenth?), this man's story helped us deepen our understanding of some key social workings.

*   *   *   *

Another story was told to Jacqueline Bessette-Dufrêne, our first co-worker, by a truckdriver of the biggest Parisian flourmills, who was himself an experienced union activist. So far we have not succeeded in checking this story either; but in the meantime it has provided us with some especially precious clues.

In 1966, he said, the *Grand Moulins* tried to take over the bread market for the whole Paris area. They had prepared their coup for a long time. They had secretly drawn up plans for a large factory for industrial bread to be built next to their mills on the banks of the Seine. They had negotiated government approval. The only remaining obstacle was the existence of the 5,000 small bakers in Paris: for all previous attempts to sell industrial bread in competition with artisan bread had failed. The big combine knew they had to break the back of the small bakers *before* building the factory.

The Grands Moulins had a lever on the bakers: they had the *de facto* monopoly of flour delivery. So one day, without warning, they informed the bakers that they would not deliver flour anymore except by full truck-loads. Most of the bakers could not accept this: they lacked storage space, and could not use that much flour. For a few days a panic swept through the trade.

Then some of the bakers found a solution. They made contact with some of the small mills which were still functioning at a low cost in rural areas, around a hundred miles from Paris. These mills were only too happy to take orders from Parisian bakers, and so to work to their full capacity. Convoys of trucks started to bring flour to Paris by night and day; the Grands Moulins were losing their customers one after the other. They soon realised that bakers could live without them. They withdrew their dictate, lowered the price of their flour to win back the market, and decided to wait for better times.

What this story taught us was extremely important. So far we had tended, like everybody else, to take the existence of the small bakeries for granted: after all they control more than 90% of the bread market. Suddenly we realised how precarious was their situation, how strong was the latent threat of agro-industrial business. Seen in this light, the harsh pace of work of artisans took on a new meaning: it was not only competition between themselves which led them to such crazy rhythms of life, we began to perceive, but also this threat, this silent shadow behind their shoulder: the covetousness of big business lusting for a profitable market. Whether bakers are conscious of it or not (none ever mentioned it to us spontaneously), certainly it is only because they are accustomed to working so hard individually that collectively they can succeed in keeping industrial bread off their territory. Like the previous story about the bakers at the end of the German occupation, the account of the defeat of the Grands Moulins lacks the status of a 'reliable' source. Nevertheless, both stories have conveyed to us important messages for our main task, that of sociological understanding. For it is not only for traditional history that *historical crises*, such as the ones they claim to describe, are of interest; crises also reveal inner workings whose efficacy in daily life remains hidden, although their effects are everywhere.

*   *   *   *

It is one thing to reestablish the structure of power relations, the laws and customs governing some sector of social life in the past, another to imagine its consequences on the lives of people. Direct testimonies help to chart these consequences.

For instance, in our investigation we had been told several times that until the thirties, there was no day off in the baker's trade. We also had been able to check this partially by referring to documents. (A day off was imposed in some of the 90 *départements* in the early thirties, but it was not until the *Front Populaire* of 1936 that it became general all over France.) What we had failed to understand was the meaning it had for the people in the trade.

Talking with a widow, a former rich baker's wife in a small town, we came to ask her if she had ever travelled outside the town. She stared at us as if we had asked a most irrelevant question (which we had):

—Don't you know that there was no day off until very recently? When could I have found the opportunity to travel?
—*But after 1936, there was a day off...*
—For workers! Only for workers, and for salesgirls! That day was the worst for me: I didn't have anybody to help in the shop!
—*But you could have closed the shop...*
—Close the shop! And let the other bakers take up our customers! No, no, it was impossible.
—*Then, maybe on holidays...*
—But we had no holidays! We could never close, never close: I have just told you why.
—*So, do you mean to say you spent* every *day of your life behind the counter and...*
—Yes of course, every day, until we sold the shop two years ago. Everyday, even before my marriage [she was a baker's daughter and helped in the family shop]. Every day, yes; that is the way things were in those days. We did not know what leisure meant, we had no idea of... Work, that's all there was. *J'ai travaillé tous les jours de ma vie.* (I worked every single day of my life.)

Later, when Isabelle interviewed old bakery workers to learn about apprenticeship in the twenties, she was able to check that there was, indeed, no day off. But knowing that workers would usually work twelve hours per night and sleep in the afternoon, one might well wonder how they even found the time to meet their wife, or simply had time for living. To this question which we had not yet asked ourselves, the answer came as Mr. G., born in 1900, told his life story. Having described, at Isabelle's usual request, one day's work, he added:

I was working from midnight to noon, seven days a week: $7 \times 12 = 84$ hours. Never a single religious feast day. It's in '34 that I began working the six-day week, which means that, for twenty years, I worked seven days a week. So, we used to work as long as we could and, when we couldn't go on anymore, after five, six, seven months, we would stop. The expression in the bakery, was, '*je découche!'* (I'm sleeping out!) When we stopped working, we said: *je découche!* That was the usual word.

So, he [i.e. the baker] would hire a substitute. And, when you wanted to get back, you came to see the boss, you just said: 'I'm coming back to-morrow'. It worked, it was all understood. The substitute, he would go to the labour office to get taken on elsewhere.

The origin of the term 'je découche' is easy to imagine. As they were working by night, the young, single workers (and the apprentices) were usually given a bed in the bakery itself, especially those in the country-side.

In Paris, single workers used to live in one of those cheap 'hôtels garnis' (lodgings) whose function was to provide room and board for young men of provincial origin (as were most bakery workers and, in fact, a very sizeable part of the capital's working class). Mr. D., who lived in one of these 'garnis' as a young man, had a nice way of warning his boss when he would not be coming to work. This would happen most often in springtime; he would just telephone him and say:

Look, I won't come to-day; *je vais aux jonquilles* (I'm going to pick wild daffodils).

These pretty flowers blossom in the forests surrounding Paris, and it has long been a popular custom on sunny Sundays to ride there by train or bicycle, spend the day in the woods and get back with an armful of them—the secret of the whole thing being, of course, that it is more fun to go there in company . . .

Another bakery worker, Mr. B., who lived a happy life in one of these lodgings during his bachelor years, tells a similar story. His friends (who as industrial workers had their Sunday free) pressed him to come with them for a picnic in the woods; they brought with them their girl-friends, who brought other girls. '*Alors tu viens, la boulange?*' ('So, will you come, baker-boy?'). Quite often Mr. B. did not resist the invitation. When he came back on Sunday evening, he would know he had lost his job.

Unlike provincial bakers, the Parisian ones very much disliked being the only ones left out when it was a sunny Sunday. But it did not matter, for there were plenty of bakeries, and a chronic shortage of labour. He knew, like Mr. D. coming back from 'the jonquils', that he would find another place quite soon.

Once married, things changed a lot. Usually the wife did not work, there was a baby around and money was needed. Still it was impossible to work day after day after day, with never a break. Many had difficulties with their sleep; as one of them told us: 'When you are too tired, you can't sleep; then you're really fucked up'. To restore their capacity to work, many bakery workers went as far as taking two weeks' holiday each summer, at their own expense. In doing so they were pioneers of a kind, for it was only in 1936 that, thanks to the victory of the *Front Populaire*, holidaying became usual for workers: they won the right to two weeks' holiday paid by the boss. The bakery workers had done this for years at their own cost. They would take the train with the family to their, or their wife's native village and *rest*. They needed it, too.

*   *   *   *

The problem does not end with understanding a given social process. How, as a sociologist, does one convey such an understanding in words? Pop sociology in the Vance Packard mode has rediscovered, under the influence of American journalism, the oldest solution to this problem, easily enough observable among the most 'primitive' cultures—the use of an anecdote which 'puts it in a nutshell'. More high-minded social theorists dismiss such a solution as vulgar. Even if – as is very often the case – they got their initial idea precisely from such an anecdote, they will do their utmost to erase its down-to-earth origin and present it in a purely theoretical form, regarding this as the only legitimate one. The outcome is a curious paradox: for the layman will be unable to recognise what has been written, even if it was he or she who told the story in the first place.

We find this most unfortunate. Social theory should be of easy access, and a balance should be sought between the ideal of generality and the necessity for communicability. Oral history research provides particularly good opportunities for experimenting in this direction: for it produces much concrete data, yet also aims at some degree of generalisation.

As an example of this, let us take the particular character of traditional apprenticeship. Old bakers will describe it by saying, quite appropriately:

On apprenait par voir-faire. (We learned by looking-and-doing.) [Note that the expression 'voir-faire' cannot be found in any dictionary; it is a popular creation.]

What this means has many implications which are not immediately perceptible to us, because we have all been brought up in a different system of learning, a system in which knowledge has been objectified in books, pedagogic sequences, institutions, and so on. In the master-apprentice relationship, none of this exists. For instance, the apprentice

can only learn what the master knows (which is why it was common practice for young workers to complete their apprenticeship by moving from
one baker to another, from countryside to town where the techniques
were different). Moreover, the master might keep some secrets for himself
so long as the apprentice had not tried and failed, and understood the
reasons for his failure. Until then he would remain an apprentice, that is,
an unpaid, dependent worker. The master bakers commonly forbad the
young lads to put the bread into the oven: a skilled task. They did so under
the pretext of not wasting the dough, but in fact the aim was to keep the
youth in a relationship of dependency for as long as possible. Apprentices
had to learn it for themselves, by practising secretly with pieces of wood,
for instance, instead of bread.

We could develop the analysis further here, as Isabelle has done in
her report; and certainly no series of anecdotes could replace such an
analysis. On the other hand, however, no theoretical discourse could put
across the very nature of traditional learning better than the following
anecdote, told to us by Mr. Bailly. (The blade he refers to is used to draw
three very slight cuts on the top of each loaf of dough, in order to let the
bread develop fully in the oven.)

—Once, the boss looks at me, and says to me:
—What, you're left-handed then?
—Why, no, I say.
—So, why are you holding the blade in your left hand?
—Well, I am doing it like you do!
—Yes, but, I *am* left-handed!

By quoting this anecdote and briefly commenting on it, by arguing
that it carries within it an implicit but quite conscious cognitive meaning
which is comparable if not equivalent to the cognitive meaning made
explicit by sociological analysis, I want to suggest that sociological thinking is not the monopoly of social scientists. The layman also makes investigations, and tries to discover the 'rules of the game', the logic of that
part of the social world which is relevant to him. This is done through
personal experience, through discussions with friends and more experienced people; it becomes a collective process. Whatever conclusions are
reached make the core of, for instance, a work culture. They are not put
in written form; neither are they expressed through theoretical concepts,
but rather through sayings, proverbs, or telling examples—what we have
called 'nutshell anecdotes' here.

The very existence of social science tends to devalue such

'commonsense' wisdom—which does not come from spontaneous. unreflective opinion as the word 'commonsense' seems to imply, but grows out of accumulated experience and reflective communication. But while social science devalues commonsense knowledge, it itself amounts, more often than not, to the very same—to nothing more than just such knowledge dressed up in the guise of social-scientific discourse. How many sociological concepts remain obscure to sociologists themselves, until they are 'exemplified' through precisely the same everyday example which gave rise to the concept in the first place?

Everytime this happens, it means that a process of *symbolic exploitation* has taken place. Exploitation, in Marx's sense, refers to the process by which the surplus value taken from the workers is converted into capital and subsequently faces them as an unrecognisable, alien force. It is not limited to profit-making. By proposing the term 'symbolic exploitation', I mean to suggest that a similar process is at work in the symbolic realm: commonsense knowledge, carrying a cognitive value, is being taken from laymen and converted into social-scientific discourse which can eventually face them as an alien force, exposing them to all kinds of sinister manipulations.

While transferring knowledge through social space and changing its form, the social-scientific process at the same time erases its footprints. Eventually, what is thus created artificially is a *'lieu'*, (a place) outside society, from which society is to be analysed scientifically; a 'metasocial' place where one has to stand if one is to speak the Truth. Economists have succeeded in convincing almost everybody that there is such a place, with far-reaching political consequences: political decisions are given legitimacy through reference to an economic 'rationality' which stands beyond the reach of the layman. Economics function as the metaphysics of our time. Other social sciences seem eager to clamber up in their turn and seize a similar position 'above society': for sociology, this hope is the driving inspiration of the positivist project. Life history and oral history work, on the other hand, suggest that we might do a great deal better to look for another kind of way forward. For in allowing the possibility of openly recognising the cognitive value of so-called commonsense, they indicate how we might instead build up social knowledge through real exchange: and this would indeed put genuine social research back on its feet.

1   Daniel Bertaux, 'The Life Course Approach as Challenge to the Social Sciences', in Tamara Hareven (ed), *Ageing and the Life Course*, Guilford Press, forthcoming.

2   Daniel Bertaux, *Destins personnels et structure de classe*, Paris, Presses Universitaires de France, 1977.

3   Isabelle Bertaux-Wiame, *L'apprentissage en boulangerie dans les années '20 et 30*, xerox 126 pp, 1976. This is probably the first explicit 'oral history' study completed in France. It comprises an historical analysis of the legislation and a sociological analysis of some of the features of apprenticeship: its length, conditions, the relations of production, the cycle of learning, the meaning of the frequent shouting and hitting, the control over the whole life of the apprentice, etc. Five accounts of childhood and apprenticeship are also included. The monograph will be sent on request from the author, Groupe Sociologie du Travail, Université Paris VII, 2 Place Jussieu, 75005 Paris.

4   On the life history approach, see also Daniel Bertaux, (ed.), *Biography and Society, the Life History Approach in the Social Sciences*, London, Sage Publications, 1981; and the special issue of *Cahiers Internationaux de Sociologie*, vol. LXIX, December 1980.

I should like to offer my warm thanks to Paul Thompson for his contribution to the revision of an earlier version of this text.

The Peasantry

110

Hay-making on the Trøndelag coast, Norway, c.1920. All generations had their functions. The children took out drinks to the adults. Only the larger farms on the coast had a harvesting machine. On smaller farms the hay was cut by scythe. Photo: *J. B. Brevold, Aafjord.*

The Peasant Economy of Léon, Brittany

Fañch Elégoët

Oral History

Oral history deals with matters which are taken from the past, but, being from the relatively recent past, are still accessible through oral inquiry, held in the memory of informants who can explain the society which they themselves experienced. Oral history can provide a substitute for direct social observation which through the passing of time has become impossible, and thus can mitigate the limitations of written archival information for peasant societies.

In contrast to written information, which is finished, definitive and limited, the material of oral history has very different qualities. It is quantitatively almost limitless. Questioning can go on almost indefinitely, as long as the informant is alive and memory still viable. And it allows a continual shifting of the focus of inquiry: for oral information springs directly from the social actors themselves. Thus it allows a society to be investigated from within, even though it is historical.

In this spirit we have set about collecting life histories of old men and women from a Breton village,[1] who held different social positions in peasant society. We now have about two hundred hours of interview, recorded in Breton, the ordinary language of that generation of peasants. We are systematically transcribing all this material and reconstructing it into life history form, limiting our own intervention to a thematical reconstruction.[2] The object of our enterprise is the writing of a dense and fine history of our peasant society in the 20th century, a history captured from within, the history which these peasants lived.

This brief note constitutes a summary of our preliminary findings on the peasant economy, such as we report in our biographies.[3] It indicates one of the directions of analysis which we are pursuing with this material.

I. Social and Economic Structures: Social Class, Kinship & the Peasant Economy

The economic process of the peasantry was moulded by the structures of the society within which it operated. And two principles of social organisation bore a critical influence on the structuring of the economy: those of kinship, and of social hierarchy.

The basic economic form within this society was the domestic household, which was founded on kinship, whether in the shape of the nuclear or of the extended family. The normal manner of social regeneration ensured that it evolved and changed primarily through inheritance within the stem family:

> Of course, it didn't have to be the eldest who took over the farm. You see, there were eight of us kids and I was the sixth—I only had two sisters younger than me. I think that was what the parents who stayed on the farm liked best. I dunno . . . But it wasn't the eldest.
>
> If the eldest married onto the farm, the other children could find themselves chased out of the house—if it did come to that!
>
> You couldn't say who would marry onto the farm. It wasn't just a matter of age. Some mothers liked a married daughter at home better than a married son—I don't know why. Maybe they thought a daughter'd respect them more than a daughter-in-law . . .

As the basic unit of this economy, the domestic household constituted at one and the same time the unit of production, of consumption, and the dwelling.

The second principle of social organisation which shaped the peasant economy was the organization of society in classes, so that economic circumstances were distributed according to social standing. The class structure was founded on the unequal distribution of landownership and unequal provision of land. This divided the peasants up into rent-receiving landowners (*moc'heilh* or *moundian*), peasant owner-occupiers (*en e leve*), tenant farmers (*merour* and *forsal*), living-in servants, and living-out labourers. By the beginning of this century beggars no longer formed more than a residual population. The hierarchical organisation of peasant society on the basis of landownership was modified by the actual distribution of access to the soil. It was clearly preferable to be the farmer of an important piece of land than the proprietor of a minute patch, even if the farmer might owe rent to the proprietor and, in this, be his subordinate:

The rich were the masters of the community. If someone fell out with the land-owners, he'd had it. He couldn't expect no help from nowhere, not from the council or nowhere else. Old Ronvel, he was the councillor, you see ... You could be chucked off your farm for less than nothing, it was that easy, at the end of the lease —and they could make you run fast all right to find another one!

Land constituted the most precious capital in this economy of mixed cultivation and stock rearing. In a society whose population had swollen, it was a rarely transferred, immobile asset. According to the land at its disposal, the household would either hire labour from outside, or have to resign itself to selling its own surplus labour in order to compensate for its insufficient income:

Everyone had to earn the bread to feed their own children. My father never got any share of the family land, so he had to work every day. And we looked glum enough many a day, you can be sure.
    If you had a small farm, you had to pack your kids off to work somewhere before they'd hardly left school – when they were just thirteen, had made their first Easter Communion – sometimes even before.
    Yes, you had to go off and work somewhere, when you'd only two or three hectares of your own. And a good many had less. As soon as you'd weaned a child, more or less, you had to look for a place for it on a farm.

II. The Process of Production

An economy of mixed farming
    The peasant economy of Léon depended on both arable farming and stock raising. The agricultural space was divided between moorland, natural meadow pasture, and cultivable arable land. The arable carried a variety of crops for human and arable consumption and also cash crops aimed at the market. The peasantry raised horses, both as draught animals and for sale; cattle, for milk and for meat; pigs, and to a small extent poultry. It was a highly diversified mixed arable-pasture economy.

Productive labour
    The process of peasant production consequently appears remarkably complex. This complexity came partly from the great diversity of productive methods, and partly from the numerous transformations which were carried out by the unit of production, the peasant household, on its own products. This explains the great range of productive tasks which were carried out within this single basic economic cell.

Around an annual cycle of production, the processes demanded various tasks which were daily, weekly or seasonal. With crops, the tasks changed largely according to the season, while with stock raising the work generally ran to a daily pattern. So the day's work included repetitive tasks – daily or even two or three times a day – and variable tasks, weekly or seasonal, for example. But the times, rhythm and intensity of work varied only with the seasons. The bustle and anxiety of summer and the harvest – long, exhausting days would be succeeded by a winter which was less demanding, and its days shorter too:

You had to work so much, but you stayed poor all the same! Because people *were* poor. Yes, they really knew what poverty was then. When I think what we suffered ...Mornings, you'd to be up by half past four—sometimes we'd hardly got to bed afore one or half past one that night, and by half past four we'd be already up again. We'd be off to cut a cartful of clover for the horses – or to be at the harvesting. It was always like that at harvest time. You had to bring a jug of water to the field so when you were thirsty you just went to the jug for a drink!

The religious and moral order maintained within this society also affected the pattern of work tasks. On Sundays all work was strictly forbidden, except for attending to animals (*ar servichou*). But work was given a very high social value in the peasant society of Léon. The peasantry provided an enormous productive investment. The demands of work weighed unceasingly on every individual, except during a few socially accepted times of rest, mostly of religious origin. Here was a severe and unchanging ethical principle:

It was bad luck – when I was thirteen and a half, I was going to pass my school certificate – but then there I was, that very Easter, forced to stay at home! I wasn't able to pass it: it was just a stroke of bad luck—my father fell ill, and there was nobody left to do the farm work. I was just the lad for it—and there was my certificate down the drain! But the schoolmaster, M. Le Gall, he came several times to Kernevez to see my father and ask him to let me go on. But father said it wasn't possible.

Economic inactivity could not be tolerated: even though one must remember that the application of the rule was modified according to the varying intensity and difficulty of the different work tasks required.

Economic topography

Peasant productive labour was spatially distributed between field work (*labour park*), work in or adjacent to the farm buildings (*labour tro'r gear*) and work in the house (*labour an ti*). This was the topography of the peasant's everyday life: a localised space, restricted, but densely occupied by a numerous population. The fields were for cultivation; the farm buildings and yard for production (stock raising), and for transforming and preserving products. The house was the place for human consumption, and for the preparation of this food supply, but it also functioned as a place for the transformation and preservation of cereal crops, for example, and even for production (domestic industry). Corresponding to the distribution of work tasks over time, these various spaces were occupied, and made their own, by the different members of the work force.

Sex, age, class and the distribution of productive tasks

Spaces and tasks were allocated according to the principles by which the society was structured, that is to say by sex and class, further varied by the physiologically and socially defined attribute of age. Thus tasks were defined as either masculine or feminine. The house was a place strictly reserved to the women, while the fields belonged to the men. Thus each sex had its space of power.

However, the women also took part in the fieldwork, at least during certain seasonal tasks. And the activities carried out in the yard and the farm buildings were distributed between both sexes, so that this intermediate space was taken up in turn as either masculine or feminine space.

The allocation of tasks within the workforce was also by age, that is to say, by strength, or by competence. On the other hand the employment of servants and labourers, like the enjoyment of an income from rent, could very exceptionally permit rent-receiving landowners to enjoy total idleness, or more commonly, at least a reduced personal investment in the productive process:

There were those who worked, and those who didn't. Pronost didn't work, but Ronvel and Loaëc did. The Deputy never worked, never at all! You had to be a big landlord, not to have to work...The biggest landowners didn't work, but the others did...
Marie Pronost would have had five or six maids and three or four manservants. At that time of day there were a lot of folk on the farms. At Ronvel's, I've seen – as many as three maids and two manservants as well as the family, that's Jean-Marie, Kaour, Pierre and the two girls – they had a family of five, and three maids and two manservants as well.

Internal transformations and self-provisioning

The complexity of the peasant economy was primarily due to the

Village women washing clothes

diversity of crops and stock raised within the productive unit. But it was further accentuated by the multiple transformations which the peasantry wrought on its own products. It transformed primary products which it had created itself, and once transformed, these were suitable for yet further transformations. Through such productive chains the peasant household was able to obtain products which it consumed itself (bread, flat-cakes, butter, milk), or which it sent to market, products which were immediately consumable (butter) or which were to undergo transformations in the external economy (corn, animals for the butchers, etc.). The techniques of stock raising yet further elongated the internal chains of production and transformation, for the crops grown were largely intended for animal fodder. Thus the peasant economy supplied itself through a very large number of products which were transformed internally within the basic household unit.

External services

It would however be inappropriate to think of this economy in terms of self-regulation or self-sufficiency. Despite the importance of self-provisioning and internal consumption, the peasant production unit had to call on external services, both technical and commercial. Equipment had to be obtained and kept in repair, and for this the peasant relied on various artisans in the community as well as industry beyond it:

You hardly bought anything . . . Just coffee, sugar, chicory, soap . . . That's all you ever bought.
When the plough was finished, you had to buy another one, or a new *défonceuse* (deep action plough) when that wasn't any good any more. And you needed to get the ploughshares sharpened too . . . There were all sorts of little things like that you had to get done.

The peasant economy has also to be seen in terms of the numerous economic transformations which took place on its own territory.

Work and Sociability

If this economy was not either self-regulating or self-sufficient, it would be equally misleading to regard it as the work of solitary individuals isolated in the depths of the country. Each productive unit required a substantial number of workers. As a heavy consumer of labour, in compensation for its low level of mechanisation, productive activity engendered multiple social relationships, imposing and organising an important circulation of people on the local terrain. Mutual help held an especially important place in peasant society. The economy thus contributed to the high degree of sociability which characterised this peasant society:

> That time of day, people used to help each other much more than nowadays. Much more! People have changed. It's not like it once was when people were glad to help – though for my own part, I've had nothing to complain about – even if I kept him all night, Job Le Page hasn't said no to me. On that basis, he's had nothing to be ashamed of and nor have I, I've never said no to him—I've even passed whole nights long at his place.

An intensive economy, but at a low level of productivity

To conclude these brief notes on the productive process, we may observe that as economic agents, the peasants showed a wish to mobilise the maximum labour force which the space at their disposal would allow. The economy thus carried within itself a drive towards intensification, with – and despite – the means of production, which included a backward technology. But as a result, while intensive at the level of labour mobilisation and the use of territorial space, it remained an economy with a low level of productivity, despite the massive investment to which the need to maximise products and surplus drove it.

III. The Appropriation of Products and Financial Strategies

The appropriation of products: self-provisioning and surplus

The unit of production, the domestic household, also constituted the unit of consumption in peasant society. The household directly consumed a part of its own produce, and its need to aim for as much self-provisioning as possible, and to minimise external purchases, was explicitly recognised. The diet of the peasantry was based on cereals (wheat, buckwheat, oats) and dairy produce (milk, butter). Consumption by the household marked the final link in the long technical chain which existed within the peasant economic unit. We should note that the level of consumption – and self-provisioning – clearly varied according to social position:

> The daymen didn't eat like they belonged to the family – oh no, no, no! Now they do. They have done a long time. But those days, there was no question of it. It wasn't so long ago, what's more, in some of the farms, that they got fed separately. The family ate in the living room and the servants in the kitchen. They didn't eat together. Or maybe there were two tables in the same room, the owner and his family ate at one table and the servants at another. That was even more rotten of them!

But here again, in respect of internal consumption the peasant unit could not achieve self-sufficiency; external purchasing was forced on it. The household would perhaps have been better able to supply itself in isolation, had it not also needed to realise a surplus from its production, in order to furnish a means for providing the money payments which it had to meet. The surplus could come from crops (corn, flax, etc.) or from the stock raised (horses, cattle, pigs, butter, etc.). Peasant households had very deliberately to force themselves to maximise their surplus, partly through raising production as far as they could, and partly through reducing their own consumption to the lowest possible level:

In the morning, you ate soup. There was only soup, no question of coffee. At midday, oat gruel. Followed by soup, and a dinner of potatoes, a big pot of potatoes—but still no meat! Other times, there'd be 'pouloud' – girdle-cakes ...

We lived basically on buckwheat. So we'd often have soup twice a day. Wednesdays and Sundays we'd have 'kig ha farz' (buckwheat dough with pork and vegetables in soup) at midday. You only ate meat when you had 'kig ha farz'.

You drank water and milk, that was all. There were three bowls of water on the table, and if you were thirsty, you drank. To fill them, we used an earthenware jug—it had a handle above a kind of mouth for pouring the water. You had to put the jug in a hole in the wall, near the window, and when you were sitting on that side you'd never get a chance to eat at all, because they were always asking you to fill up the jug.

The ethic of thrift and saving was ever present in the economic decision-making of the peasantry. The extraordinary ability of peasants to reduce their domestic consumption explains their astonishing capacity for economic survival. Their surplus produce, somehow extracted, was delivered to the markets and fairs, and through it they were assured of the means to make the money payments vital in this economy, which were all the more demanding because so infrequent.

As the key-stone to the articulation between the peasant economy and the dominant economy of the wider society, the market held a critical place in the peasant's strategy. It was here that the dominant society bought the power of peasant labour, and the terms of exchange between the two societies were defined. These exchanges were made through money. Considering the enormous work effort made by the peasantry and the very small amount of money at their disposal, they had little choice but to sell their labour power cheaply to provide low-cost nourishment for the non-peasant population.

Not all the peasant surplus went, by the way of the market, to money. A part, although much smaller, was kept by the household for its own enjoyment in consumption. This was on festive occasions, chiefly at marriages, and for the richer peasants also at family feasts. Such were the occasions when the surplus of the productive units was consumed in kind:

> For the family feast, we had to put tables in the barn to fit everyone in. I've seen tables right down the whole length of our big barn at Kernevez. The pig would be killed one of the days before, and that night, there was nothing of it left at all! They ate up the whole lot! The head and leftovers were cut up into little bits to make tripe. That was good! The roast was cooked in the breadoven in a pan, with potatoes round it . . . And they'd put wheat-cakes in the oven too . . . We used to eat well that day all right!

Financial strategies

The peasants entered into many economic transactions which were non-monetary, such as mutual help and barter (the exchange of equipment, work, etc.). Nevertheless, through its very rarity, money held a key place in the economy, because of the need to provide for unavoidable expenses, and also, as we shall see, because of its fundamental place in the mechanism of social reproduction. In a situation of short supply even if not absolute poverty, it was essential to maximise incomings and cut back expenses wherever possible.

Maximising incomings

The peasants used a variety of strategies in order to raise the money receipts of the household. They produced crops like flax explicitly for the market, or raised horses for the same purpose. They reduced their own consumption in order to be able to market more of their produce. Or else, where the household's workforce exceeded the needs of its own land, they would look for additional earnings – 'complimentaires' – outside:

> Where they had a big family, they'd go to school up to ten. By the time they were twelve, school was over. There was only one thing you could do: become a servant for the rest of your days, to earn your bread. You had to, because parents hadn't the means to feed their children—so you'd no choice but to go out to work.

In this way an important circulation of the workforce was stimulated within the peasant economy. Manual labour had to be mobile just because the hierarchical structure of the society and its land distribution was so rigid. Earnings could be had by paid agricultural work by the day or for the season, or through some specialised craft work (butcher, thatcher, etc.). All this work took place within a situation of scarcity, in which any activity likely to result in additional income, however small, would be undertaken.

Minimising outgoings

The same logic of thrift and saving was applied to outgoings. They deliberately and expressly tried to reduce any money payments. This strategy took varying forms, from the cutting back of every kind of external purchase – such as food and clothing – to an absolute parsimony in individual expenses like the Sunday church collection:

> With twenty francs in your pocket, you were rich! What's twenty francs worth now? A seat in church, that cost twenty francs for a start . . . If you hadn't twenty francs, you couldn't hope for a seat! How much would you spend on Sunday? Maybe four or five sous . . . You would have one drink—although there were some who had one too many. You would buy a little tobacco . . . Some smoked it and some chewed it, but they all wanted their 'baccy.

A very strict administration of money and a draconian restriction of expenses were essential because money was scarce, certain expenses were unavoidable, and hence saving was vital to the household's security.

The power of money

Cash would be needed first of all to cover essential expenses for human provision (food, clothing, etc.). Other expenses, which might be reduced, would remain not wholly avoidable. Operating costs had also to be covered: charges for equipment, for repairing implements, fees for livestock transactions, etc. Here were expenses which, however slight, mounted up and made for inevitable cash outlays. A further monetary payment still more vital for the peasant unit of production was the rental due to the landowners, a sum which had to be met in cash. This represented a heavy charge on the peasant budget, and it could not be postponed without risking eviction from the farm:

> Our farm, at Kernevez, was worth 25 days labour and we had to find 1270 francs to pay each year in rent. How much could you sell a horse for in those days? Five or six hundred francs? . . .
> You would sell off animals when you had too many of them. Sometimes, you had no choice. When there was nothing else to pay the rent, you just had to sell some of the stock . . . We raised bulls – we always had some bulls and we usually sold them around Michaelmas. We had two or three of them to sell each year. So that had to be put out on offer. They had to be sold one by one. That's how we managed to pay the rent.

State taxation was by contrast a very small matter. The state kept its distance; it took little, and it redistributed less.

One other especially heavy burden on the peasant budget was the expense of social reproduction. In Breton society the transmission of inheritance followed a strictly egalitarian form. Each child received an equal portion of the family property. As a result the child who was to carry on the farm had to repurchase other parts of the family inheritance from brothers and sisters in order to preserve its unity and integrity. Each generation of peasants was obliged to buy back its own land and patrimony. This egalitarian system of inheritance therefore caused an enormous monetary drain from peasant incomes, each time forcing their economies into at least temporary debt:

The parents kept half the farm, because they had nowhere else to go and no other income. When they died, the children who had left would come to take their share of the inheritance. Those who stayed on the land would have to buy back their own parents' share.

Cash reserves were therefore necessary to re-purchase the patrimony; and also as an insurance against the risks and uncertainties of the society and its economy.

There was uncertainty in the yield of their enterprise, both from crops and from stock. The loss of an animal was always possible, while a wet summer could ruin a crop. Fires were a real danger too. The household's cash provided the only protection against such misfortunes. Beyond this, there was always uncertainty about what the produce would fetch, as agricultural prices rose and fell:

I remember the horse fair ... Once I went to the Folgoat fair to sell a three-year old mare – there were six or seven of us, one after the other, with three-year old mares, and nobody came to ask to buy a single one of those mares – nobody at all! We had to lead the whole lot of them home!

There was further uncertainty regarding the health of the members of the family. Although medical care was very ineffective, the cost of illness and attendance were a real disaster for the household. The state stood apart and the family had to assume the entire burden of such charges.

All these factors forced a self-protective thrift on the peasant economy. The uncertainties and insecurities of this society had to be guarded against. The money receipts of the household were partly regular – weekly, for example – partly seasonal; but most commonly irregular, and moreover often unpredictable. All cash went into the household's single, common purse. Money matters, whether incomings or outgoings, were treated from a strictly collective standpoint. An absolute family communism was the rule. Within peasant society there was no place whatever for financial autonomy of the individual.

Conclusion: structures and dislocation

Social crises and social dislocation can only occur at particular points within the complex structures of social economy.

The transformations of the Breton peasant world and the break with its past brought about by the new rural generation of today, heirs to the last generation to carry on the old peasant economic system, have been shaped largely in direct reaction to the structure of that peasant social economy. For example, free time is demanded—countering the demand for incessant productive activity; financial autonomy—as opposed to absolute family communism; a separate place to live—parting with the family of origin; and, as the final rejection of an economy of scarcity, migration.

During the first half of the twentieth century the peasant economy has become progressively penetrated and overwhelmed by the dominant wider society. In the collision between a peasant and an industrial society, the former has been smashed. Hence the peasant population has poured into the towns and industry. Peasant society, dominated and kept down, could only offer scarcity and poverty. As an economy of low productivity, it could not possibly allow room for the dominance of consumption; it had, in short, no room for the realisation of what had become the dominating social ideal and symbol.

1   Le Grouanec, (Plouguerneau), in Léon, about 30 km north of Brest.
2   See especially, *Mémoires d'un paysan du Léon—Nous ne savions que le breton et il fallait parler français*, Editions Kendalc'h, La Baule 1978—from which all the interview extracts in this paper are taken; and also *Tud Ha Bro, sociétés bretonnes*, a review publishing life history material from Brittany, ed. F. Elégoët, B.P. 25, 29232 Plouguerneau, Brittany. Already published, nos. 1 (*L'homme et la mer*), ·2 (les paysans parlent), 3–4 (Paysannes du Léon).
3   See also, *Mémoires d'un village breton*, Multigr 1977.

Threshing

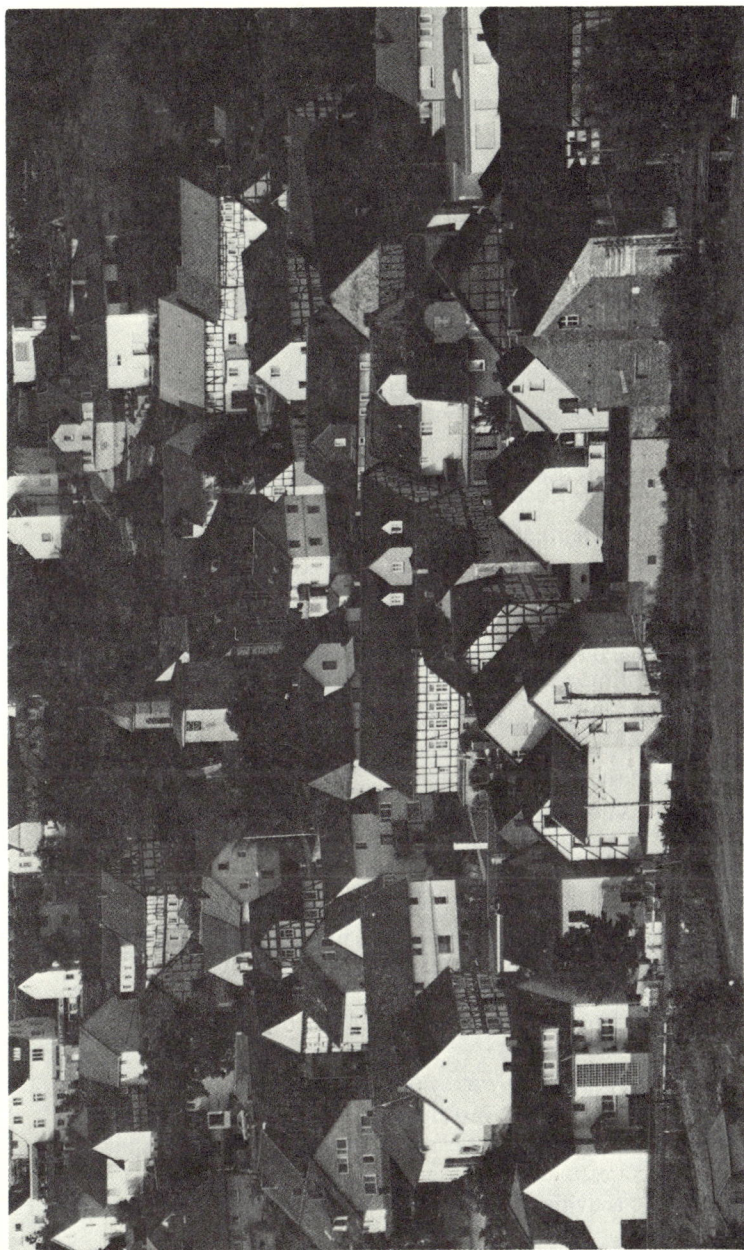

Typical houses in the German village discussed by Gerhard Wilke in the article that follows.

Houses and People in a Village in interwar Germany

Gerhard Wilke

People were born in the house and they died in the house.
Hardly anyone is born or dies at home today.[1]

My research is essentially based on oral interviews. These range from formal interviews to conversations which arise out of social and work situations. Although I regard the close examination of available statistical and official records as necessary in order to verify the material which I collect, I would nevertheless suggest that the method of participant observation is more important in an attempt to reconstruct the living conditions of different people in a village earlier this century. Housing statistics can give us an adequate impression of the number of houses being built over a given period of time, and can also offer an insight into the state of the housing market, but it is virtually impossible to reconstruct the spatial organisation of the houses and the role the houses, rooms and various objects played in the lives of different social groups.

The village is situated in the northern part of Hessen, approximately 20 kilometers south of Kassel. The old village centre is dominated by a Lutheran church which stands above on a little hill. Spread around it are the 86 houses which constituted the village in 1864. The house design was, without exception, traditional. The size of the houses depended on the relative wealth of the family and reflected the basic function they have had right up to the 1960s: they served as living quarters for a household rather than a single nuclear family, and they were the base from which this household earned a living.

Although more and more people had to look for industrial employment in the twenties and thirties, agriculture remained an essential part of the household economy. A survey of agriculture by the Prussian State in 1929 revealed that with the exception of a cobbler every household had land and raised animals. Only the twelve bigger farmers (cultivating more than 12.5 hectares) made a living out of agriculture alone; the rest followed a multitude of activities to scrape together the income required to keep everybody alive.

Although some migration and emigration occurred in the 19th century the construction of a railway prevented significant depopulation. In fact, the population increased steadily from the middle of the last century. The arable land, on the other hand, did not and as it became more difficult to make a living on the land, opportunities opened up for industrial employment in Kassel, since the railway enabled the villagers to commute. A railway station was opened in the village in 1892 and by about 1900, fifty to sixty out of altogether just over 600 inhabitants travelled to and from work every day.

Throughout the interwar period the number of full–time farmers shrank and the number of people who were absorbed into the industrial world increased. Men were most affected in the 1920s, but more and more women took up non-agricultural employment after about 1934. (This date coincides with the introduction of milking machines and other technical innovations in agriculture.) However, the new industrial workers did not regard themselves as being a separate group within the village during the period with which we are concerned. The occupational differentiation was absorbed into the traditional way of categorising status groups within the village: horse farmers, cow farmers and goat farmers, in that order of importance.

Horse farmers were essentially people who made a living from agriculture and employed other people as agricultural or seasonal labourers (*Mägde, Knechte* and *Dienstleute*).[2] Cow farmers were farmers with a supplementary income, self-employed artisans, skilled workers and in a few cases unskilled workers who increased their incomes by agriculture. Goat farmers were, on the whole, first and second generation skilled and unskilled industrial workers who did not earn enough to provide for a 'whole household'. They therefore kept and owned or rented little plots of land. Being without draught animals, they hired their own and their family's labour out to big farmers when extra manpower was needed. In return, their fields were ploughed by the big farmers.

The increasing social differentiation did not lead to open conflict in the work sphere within the village. The clash of real social and economic interests simmered permanently but was never allowed to threaten the solidarity of belonging to *the village*. This is no romantic nostalgia but reflects the interests of the people as they perceived them then. Almost without exception people felt that the world inside and outside the village was unjust: they had a very deep mistrust of industrial society which they associated with turbulence and insecurity. Their incomes were inadequate, and the balance of the household's budget was upset by the slightest misfortune of accident. Against this background they believed that they were ultimately dependent on each other and regarded the house, family, land, neighbours and other villagers as their only real social insurance policy.

The traditional model of the breakdown of the household economy under the influence of industrialisation does not adequately describe either residence patterns or family structures in the village in the interwar years. Since kinship ties were important in determining inheritance and seniority, but did not decide exclusively who was considered part of the household, I will avoid the use of the loaded and ill-defined term 'family' in this context and substitute for it the terms 'household' or '*das ganze Haus*' (the whole house).[3] The details of construction, spatial organisation and design in housing only make sense against this general background of relative poverty for many, a deep fear of suffering misfortune, and a refusal to give up links with agriculture and the household economy.

Up to the early 1920s houses were constructed at a rate of one or two per decade and the village centre was dominated by the large farms. Most of these had a large yard adjoining the main road, at the back of which stood the farm buildings and the farmhouse. Off the main roads, along the side streets, stood the houses of the smaller farmers which sometimes had a small yard. Their houses consisted of living quarters, a barn, a stable, a cellar and a grain and hay loft.

Throughout the '20s and '30s the overall picture of the centre of the village did not change, but some of the houses were put to different use and the functions of certain rooms were modified as living conditions changed and technical innovations were introduced. The open hearth in the kitchens gave way to iron stoves and closed chimneys. Subsequently kitchens became parlours rather than merely rooms for cooking in.[4] Some of the traditional farms were inherited or bought by people who opened up businesses and converted the houses into bakeries, slaughterhouses and workshops. However, people always retained some storage space for their agricultural produce and stables for their animals.

The period between the two wars also witnessed the first real expansion in housing and construction of other buildings. Just before the First World War the parish council had subsidised the construction of a shunting station and had hoped that, as a consequence, industrial employment would be attracted. Between 1922 and 1924 a saw mill and a basalt works were built and started production. Both offered employment to a considerable number of villagers and also attracted workers from surrounding villages and three families from Thuringia. These families lived in three houses that were constructed by the company when the factory was built. But even these houses, like all others which were built before the early 1960s, accommodated more than one generation under one roof, had a plot of land and allowed the occupants to keep pigs, goats, rabbits, geese, ducks and hens.

At the opposite end of the village, towards Kassel, houses were built between 1921 and 1923, 1929 and 1931, and 1937 to 1938. In the twenties the increase in house building went along with the formation of a pressure group demanding more land from the state and the church. Essentially it was the same group who built the new houses and demanded the land for cultivation to replace their own which had been used for building. Here again, we are dealing with skilled and unskilled workers seeking extra insurance against the insecurities they associated with their factory jobs. The *Landhunger* and the fact that some people plucked up the courage to build a new house reflected not only this need for security but also worries about an ever faster depreciating currency. From 1921 to 1923 seven houses were commissioned and built and from 1929 to 1931 eight houses.

Most aspects of village life were charged with moral significance. There were therefore definite ideas and rules about the way in which a house could be built. Although today, in a period of prosperity, a substantial proportion of the new houses are built by self-help, this was unthinkable in the 1920s. In what was essentially still a 'moral economy', the household which was building a house undertook not only a personal commitment, but also entered into a whole series of moral obligations.

Total self-help in the construction of the house was frowned upon during the '20s and people were expected to offer the work to local builders and craftsmen. Once the artisans had been hired, family members and relatives helped as labourers in order to reduce costs. It was in nobody's interest to inflate construction prices unduly since this would have prevented the whole project from being viable. Personal savings were never enough to finance the whole house. The remaining money was raised outside the village at the Kreissparkasse or from the Jewish tradesmen who regularly visited the village. Often the parish council was asked to act as guarantor. This behaviour was consistent with the belief that 'you never borrow from relatives or neighbours'. I also know of two successful attempts to play the inflation game and pay the remaining mortgage on the house for the equivalent of a basketful of eggs!

The major design and construction innovation of these houses was that they were no longer built with beams, wattle and daub, but had concrete foundations and brick walls. As to the basic design and the function of these houses, little changed. They still had a hay and grain loft and a potato cellar. At the back, most workers had rabbit cages and a vegetable garden. This basic design did not change until around 1965 when the inhabitants started to convert the stables into garages and the lofts into extra rooms.

The houses in the next expansion in 1937 and 1938 were again built for industrial workers, but this time under the auspices of the Nazi parish council and Nazi housing association (*Die Siedlungsgemeinschaft*). The villagers joined the association as members, but it was organised from a regional office in Kassel. Most people regarded the selling of land, for whatever purpose, as a sacrilege. To encourage others to make their land available for building purposes the Nazi *Bürgermeister*, a forest worker and farmer, set an example by offering some of his own for sale. The centrally led association also introduced the idea of offering work to the cheapest bidder. Consequently, the village 'gave work away' for the first time. Additionally, the future owners were persuaded to minimise the costs of their own home by doing as much of the work as possible themselves. For the actual construction of the house this advice seems to have been followed and relatives, workmates and neighbours were drafted in to help in the construction. This help was not paid for with money, but repaid by the equivalent number of working hours. In some cases the debts were not repaid until the 1950s and 1960s. For interior decorating, carpentry and plumbing jobs it was still considered 'immoral' not to call in the local craftsman.

The workmen associated with the construction of the basic frame (the *Rohbau*) of the house had evolved rituals which underline the moral and ideological implications of building a house. These rituals existed long before the First World War, and they are still observed today. *Richtfest* was celebrated when the Rohbau was finished. It marked the end of the first stage in the construction of a house and signified a transition: after the appropriate people had been hired and the house frame completed, the Rohbau had to be blessed before the house could be transformed into a home. Interestingly enough, the ritual resembled the Christian *Abendmahl* (the communion or Last Supper) which is celebrated to mark the transition from childhood to adulthood and transforms an ungracious state into a gracious one. In this sense, Richtfeste were a rite of passage and involved a redefinition of territory and status and relieved one group of people from their association with this social space and bound another group to it. As in most similar rituals, it was associated with feasting, merry-making and, in the case of non-observance, with spell-casting and cursing. The future owner of the house had to foot the bill. In exchange he received a blessed house. All those who had so far been involved with the construction of the house were invited. Everybody knew the financial position of the owner and expectations of what would be offered during the celebration were adjusted accordingly. The celebration itself usually took place at the owner's local or in his family home. Beer, schnaps, fresh mince meat, onions and dry bread were the traditional food and drink offered.

Before the feasting, however, owner, employer, workers and helpers, dressed in their best assembled outside the Rohbau to witness the ceremony. The senior carpenter and bricklayer fixed a small pine tree decorated with coloured paper, to the top of the – as yet – unslated roof. Afterwards, they descended to one of the windows on the first floor which faced the street and looked down on those who had gathered below. The bricklayer held up a bottle of schnaps in his left hand and a new glass in his right. The carpenter then proceeded to recite a rhyme praising all those who had worked on the house and wishing the building and its inhabitants safety and protection from all misfortune and ill will. As soon as the verse finished the bricklayer proceeded to drink a schnapps and pronounced the words: 'I drink for you all!' He then pretended to pour himself another schnaps and a mock battle ensued between the bricklayer and the carpenter who complained that the schnaps belonged to everyone who had worked on the house. The bricklayer then repented and handed over the bottle and glass to the carpenter who, when he had finished drinking, threw the glass down and smashed it at the feet of his fellow workers. He then repeated a blessing on the house and invited everyone to celebrate.

When a house owner refused to pay for the celebrations, the ritual took place away from the house, at a site selected by the carpenters and bricklayers. They fixed a comical object on the roof, ate the same food, observed all other details of the ritual and cursed the house ('Das Haus wurde verflucht'). I know of one example where this is supposed to have happened. Three out of the last five owners either went bankrupt or were unable to pass their farm or business on to the *third male heir* ('nicht an den dritten Erben gekommen'). I leave the reader to ponder on the meaning of this example. Locally, the 'failure' by a household to 'produce a third heir' was and still is regarded by many as a direct result of an open or secret curse and an actual moral transgression.

It is important to emphasise that *traditions* like the Richtfest appear to those who celebrate them as timeless customs. In reality, however, their meanings and functions do change. As house construction became increasingly commercialised after the Second World War, house builders occasionally refused to hold a Richtfest. In most cases, this was done as a protest against bad workmanship. Although the workmen would still celebrate their own Richtfest and curse both the Rohbau and its owners, public opinion would be divided. Both the refusal to hold a Richtfest and shoddy work were perceived as an offence, compensation for which was paid in kind at a future date, the amount being agreed by local discussion. The whole household would share the responsibility for this debt.

There are several points relating to the structure and symbolism of the Richtfest which need explaining. It is essentially a *Rite of Passage*, structured in several stages which serves the purpose of publicly confirming the changed status of one or several members of the community. The Richtfest ritual helped people in the village to 'know where they were' in relationship to property and social position. Property was perceived in relationship to people who owned it and they were judged by their proficiency in maintaining the property and inheritance. The Rohbau was associated with the workman and the home with its owners. The transition from one social category to another involved a process of clarification. In the first stage of the ritual the workmen were in charge of the proceedings; the nominal owner was not allowed onto the site. As the ritual progressed both 'parties' were separated from their initial role and status; the definitions of 'normality' and 'abnormality' were juxtaposed and acted out. Finally, the actors were returned to normality and acceptability during the celebration. The model for the ritual itself was, as I have mentioned, the Last Supper. The bricklayers' phrase 'I drink for all' is Catholic; however the performers were, without exception, staunch Protestants. Perhaps this was an attempt to maintain a distinction between the *sacred* and the *profane*. The pine tree could be seen in a similar light. It obviously was a symbol for the Christmas tree which represented the time of grace and invoked protection and new life. The tree which was fixed to the house-top was decorated with coloured paper and not with the normal Christmas decorations. The smashing of the glass signified the builders' actual point of dissociation from the house and symbolised the sacrifice of the owner—an act which finalised and represented the price for a lucky house. Consequently, after that, the party which celebrated the Richtfest left the site and celebrated elsewhere. The celebration was remembered long after the hard work was forgotten—the celebration not the work made the association of the workers with each house special.

The Richtfest ritual again confirms that almost all actions were interpreted by the villagers as having moral significance. Observance and transgression of conventions and the established moral code did not necessarily modify the behaviour of those individual inhabitants. Although there was room for individualistic behaviour, the household was expected to take the responsibility for containing it. Most houses and the households in them were associated by name and reputation with households who had lived in them for many generations before the present occupants.

Everything people did had implications for and reflected on the whole household. Naughtiness in children reflected equally on the ability of their elders to bring them up. The whole household was obliged to repay debts in cases of neglect, illness or death. This arrangement was consistent with the material basis of life for most people in the village: nobody counted as a wage earner in his or her own right; everybody was seen as being part of a producing, earning and consuming household. As I hear again and again in my interviews: 'My whole wage was handed over to my mother who put it in the kitty'.[5]

If we are to look at household organisation we must consider the relationships within the house, and between the members of a particular household and the village. Both sets of relationships served a multiplicity of functions and were charged with an equally complex set of meanings. A change in the use of space inside the house usually went hand in hand with a redefinition of the social relationships. Houses were not empty shells but reflected principles of social organization and a particular household's way of life. The transition from one social category to another – heir apparent to owner – involved a territorial passage.

People were very observant and noticed when the *wrong* person occupied a particular space. If a young and healthy man was seen looking out of the living room window people interpreted this as a transgression: only somebody who was 'no good' and 'idling away his day' could afford to waste time in this way. If, on the other hand, an old and immobile man was seen at the same window people interpreted it positively: here was a man who still took an active interest in the outside world. The window for him represented a socially defined space which enabled him to take part in village life. It also demonstrated publically that those who were obliged to take care of him were doing so. The window-panes weren't neutral either. They, like the stairs leading into the house, demonstrated to the outside world the standard of cleanliness and orderliness which a visitor could expect inside. The organisation of space inside the house allowed its inhabitants to define their relative social status, and, as power was not distributed equally, social space wasn't either. In the same way there were clear ideas of organisation for the division of labour and occupation of space outside the house and in the fields.[6]

*   *   *   *

I will now try to give you an impression of the inside of two representative houses, one belonging to a big farmer, the other to a tailor. There were twelve big farmers in the village between the wars and their farms all had the same basic design. Farms needed storage space and large stables and had to provide additional accommodation for the *Knechte* (farm hands) and *Mägde* (maids). *Knechte* were the only group of people, as far as I know, who did not sleep in what was considered a *proper house*. On ten of the farms their rooms were above the stables for the horses, and on two they had, until 1932, a bed and a cupboard in the stables itself. In this way, the farmers drew a social distinction between themselves and the workers; the rest of the village thought of the *Knechte* as part of the farm's inventory and belonging to its household.

Farm (1914)

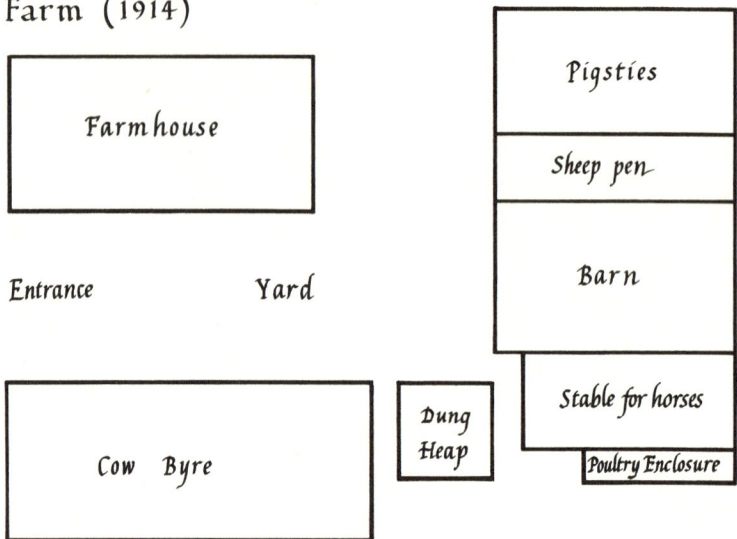

Entering the farmyard the farmhouse stood on the left; on the right was the cowshed and the dung-heap and straight ahead from left to right were the pigsties, sheep pen, barn, the horses' stables and, in a corner, the hen, geese and duck enclosure. The cowshed had been added in 1914, changing the farm from an L to a U shape. Most of the farms changed from L to U shapes before the First World War. Rebuilding had been encouraged when villagers stopped using water wells in 1906. Before the installation of a mains water supply the wells were in the cowshed which was attached to the farmhouse in those days.

After this modification, the basic design of the farm did not change until 1960. The house had three storeys, a cellar for potatoes, turnips and preserves and a dairy. The entrance to the cellar was to the right of the stairs leading into the house. In front of the cellar was the wash-house where the women washed every two weeks, where fruit was dried on drying racks, bread was baked, the pigs were slaughtered and sausages made. In fact all the major household jobs were regularly performed in this ante-room.

On entering the house one stood in a largish hall with a tiled floor. On the right a stair-case led to the second and third floor. The first door on the left on the ground floor led into the *Gute Stube*, the main sitting room. This room contained the most prestigious family furniture and a *Kachelofen* (tiled stove). During the summer the room was only used by the farmer and his immediate family for receiving guests or for concluding business deals. Being warm and larger than the kitchen it was used every day in winter for mending and sewing grain and potato sacks and holding *Spinnstuben* (spinning bees). Adjoining it was the bedroom of the *Häre* and *Froche*—the owner and his wife.

Opposite the front door, at the other end of the hall, was the kitchen. The kitchen was the centre of most of the daytime activities inside the house. Weather permitting, most meals except morning coffee and the evening meal were eaten in the fields during the spring, summer and autumn. The food was prepared by the farmer's wife and brought to the field by one of the seasonal helpers. The evening and Sunday meals and all the meals during winter were eaten in the adjoining dining room. This room was simply furnished with a long table with benches along each side and a chair at either end for the farmer and his wife. Cooking itself was the prerogative of the farmer's wife. The Mägde lit the fire in the morning and helped with washing, mending and cleaning. Otherwise they grew vetegables in the garden and worked in the fields, cowsheds and pigsties. For major household jobs like preserving vegetables and cooking jam, seasonal help was recruited from families within the village.

The *Knechte* only came into the house to eat or carry sacks to and from the grain and flour loft. Their domain was the farmyard. Their duties included feeding, training and caring for the draught animals, and ploughing, sowing and transporting the farm produce. On one farm the farmer and the family ate in the dining room, while the labourers and helpers had to eat in the kitchen. Naturally, they also ate different food – 'each to their own'. As one ex-worker on that farm told me: 'One day I had had enough of this monotonous stuff and I threw it over his head and yelled that he should eat the dogshit himself. I left the same day.'[7] On

Farmhouse

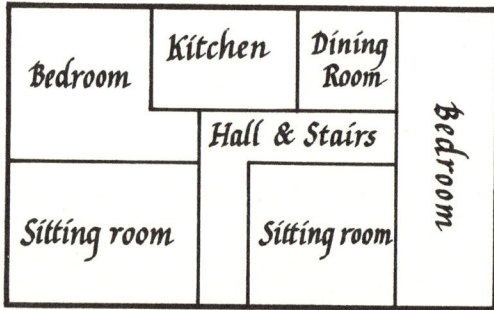

Bedroom | Kitchen | Dining Room | Bedroom

Hall & Stairs

Sitting room | Sitting room

Ground Floor

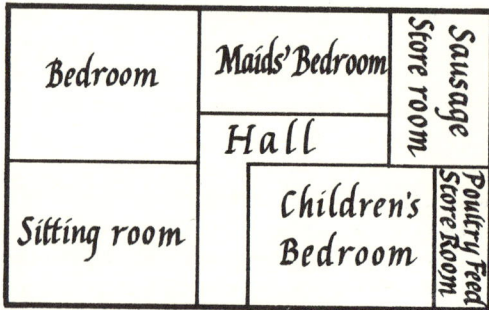

Bedroom | Maids' Bedroom | Sausage Store room

Hall

Sitting room | Children's Bedroom | Poultry Feed Store Room

First Floor

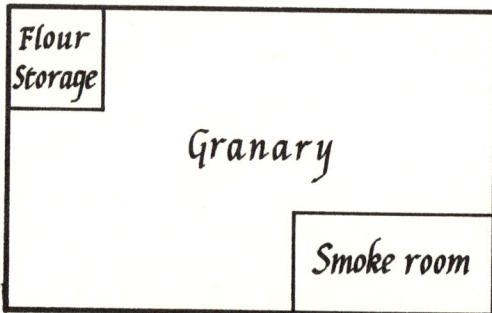

Flour Storage

Granary

Smoke room

Second Floor

another farm the farmer and his immediate family shared the same table with their workers but made them eat inferior food. These were, however, the exceptions. On most of the farms, the farmer's family and workers ate the four daily meals together. Sharing food often created the illusion that people were not really all that unequal.

Adjoining the dining room were another little sitting room and bedroom. These two rooms were occupied by the unmarried brother of the farmer. Each of the big farms made provision for a *Sitz im Haus*, a room or rooms used by relatives who had been granted rights in a will or by parents who had handed the farm over to their children. Those brothers and sisters who had a right to an inheritance but had left home were 'bought out' (*ausbezahlt*). This could be expensive and often meant that the older generation remained the official owners of the farm whilst a designated heir managed it. The older generation held on to their security through this arrangement and the delayed legal hand-over of the farm often reduced the cost of buying out other relatives. The son managed this particular farm from about 1925, but only took it over legally in the late 1940s. Another way of cutting costs was the so-called *Tauschheirat* (exchange marriage). A daughter from one farm was exchanged for a son from another. Both lost their claims to the family farm but gained a farm of their own. This arrangement, of course, was only possible if one family had only daughters and another only sons.

The space on the left-hand side of the second floor was divided into a bedroom and sitting room for the family of the son or daughter who was to inherit the farm. The sitting room was rarely used and served to store the dowry and furniture. When the farm was handed over the son and his wife moved down and the parents moved upstairs according to custom. The change in residence signified to the rest of the village that the change in status had occurred. 'These things were done in secret and not bragged about. By and by people learnt that the farm had been handed over'.[8] If the parents were too old or immobile to live upstairs they moved into the *Sitz im Haus*.

Territorial division was of extreme importance in terms of the relative and absolute standing of members of the farmer's family inside the house and in the village. The aunt or uncle with a room in the house could not be deprived of residency, but had to be content if this space was redefined if the need arose. They could not rise in the hierarchy, were expected to be loyal to the famiy, and could not rise to public prominence in the village. They were often more approachable than the farmer and had a reputation for being good with children.

Next to the bedroom of the young farmer's family was the room of the Mägde which differed from the family's bedroom in that it had no heating and no furniture apart from beds, sometimes shared, and a cupboard. Adjoining this chamber was the sausage room—*Wurstekammer*. The key for this room was kept by the young farmer's wife and it was her responsibility to ensure that the contents lasted from one year to the next. A farm of this size consumed about four to five 'heavy pigs' and one or two cows each year. The sausage rooms of particularly mean farmers were occasionally robbed. This was, on the whole, a legitimate sport until the 1960s and had the function of revenge or public ridicule which was designed to modify the victim's social behaviour. 'Almost everybody approved of *Streiche* (pranks). Those who didn't and became most upset about them became the first victims. Most young people, both boys and girls, took part in them'.[9] Of course the victim did not play the game and became even meaner after being robbed; meanwhile the 'thieves' had a full belly as well as winning the public esteem of most people.

Opposite the living room on the second floor was the children's bedroom and at the far end there was a little storage room for keeping the poultry feed. Essentially the whole design of the second floor was such that it enabled the young farmer's wife to rule over her domain: children, household goods and provisions and the *Mägde* – in that order. On the third floor the bread flour and grain were kept. There were also two smoking rooms for curing sausages and bacon; both the farmer and his wife had a key.

In contrast to the big farms all other houses incorporated all the different functions of a household economy in one building. Depending on the size of the landholding and the animals which were kept, they had a barn or hay loft, a cellar and stables. Usually there was a door which connected the entrance hall and the stables. The living quarters were strictly functional and reflected the fact that the house was a place for living and working and that people were poor. I have chosen to describe as an example a small house which belonged to a tailor. Here the entrance to the house was in the middle, to the left of the stable and barn. The foundation and cellar reached to about a man's height, so the main living room on the ground floor could only be reached from the hall by a wooden staircase. Opposite the door at the other end of the small hall was the kitchen.

The living room was exactly that: except during meal times, when people sat in the kitchen, this was the only room used during the day. 'The sitting room (*gute Stube*) in our house was also our workshop'.[10] The room had painted floorboards which were scrubbed every Saturday by the mother and covered in white sand. This sand had been fetched on the previous day by the son, and was swept out of the room on Sunday by

Tailor's house

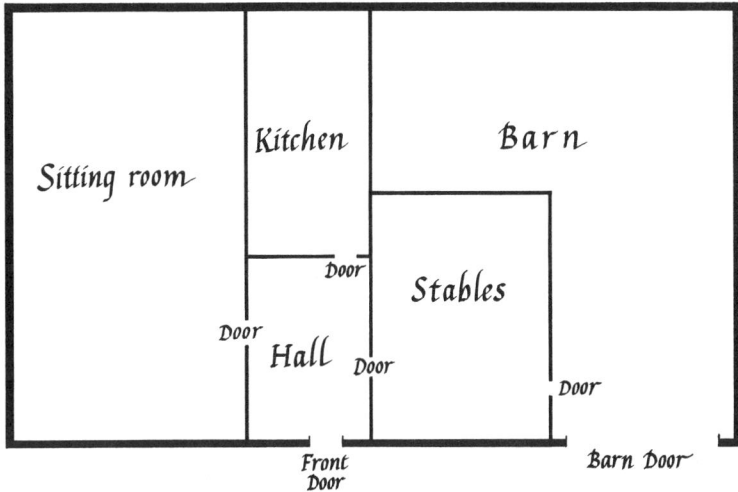

the daughters. This practice continued until 1936. Each household had a right to a bucket of sand each week from the communal sandpit. The walls of the room were wallpapered. A sewing machine stood to the left of the door. At the far end of the room on adjacent walls there were two windows under which stood two wooden benches with room to sit four or five children or guests. The mother usually sat on a chair by the sewing machine and the father sat at a large work table. To the right of the door stood a tiled stove (*Kachelofen*); during the day one or two chairs stood next to it which were used by the grandparents, and the area around the oven was reserved for them. After the chairs had been used in the evening, they were moved to the back of the room which was separated off by a curtain and served as a bedroom for a number of people. The chairs were used for hanging the clothes on, since the family had no cupboard. This bedroom within the living room was typical of most houses during this time, although from around 1935 those who had saved some money began to alter arrangements; although the double function of the room was not completely abolished until the fifties. In this particular house the bedroom contained two beds which stood at opposite walls. In one of them the grandmother and two, sometimes three, children slept; in the other the parents. The windows of the room had no curtains and when people changed and washed they hung up a kitchen apron to cover them.

In 1928 the family bought its first dresser which was placed at the far end of the room, between the work table and the bedroom partition, so as to be noticed by visitors immediately they entered.

The kitchen was strictly a workroom for the women of the house. Most of the housework was done by the grandmother and the daughters, while the wife helped the husband sew trousers for the railway company, worked in the fields with him or helped farmers in order to supplement the income. The kitchen contained a table, two chairs, a bench, one cupboard, a copper for washing, a sink and a stove. The ceiling and walls were blackened by soot from the open chimney. In 1929 the family built itself a closed stove out of brick and heat-resistant stones. The kitchen became warmer and was increasingly used as a living room.

In contrast to the big farmhouses there was just one bedroom upstairs. In addition there was a sausage room and a room for grain, preserves and flour. The hay and straw loft above could be reached from the house itself and by ladder from the barn. Until 1936 the bedroom upstairs had a clay floor because the family could not afford floor boards. The three eldest siblings shared the double bed in this room. This was considered perfectly normal up to the age of confirmation, usually fourteen. Only if brothers and sisters were still sharing the same bed after this age would rumours of incest start. Usually by this age the boys had begun an apprenticeship and the girls had moved away from home to work on farms. As far as possible the parents saw to it that these young adults took up lodgings with their employers. The eldest son of this house served an apprenticeship as a bricklayer from 1930 to 1933. After working for three years as a journeyman he had accumulated enough cash to make some improvements to the house—an extra bedroom and floor boards upstairs.

*   *   *   *

Technical innovations had begun to influence living conditions and life styles before the First World War. Water supply was first brought to the houses in 1906, electricity came in 1921 and street lamps were introduced towards the end of the 1920s. Old habits die hard. Every household which could afford one bought a lamp shade at an auction in 1921, but continued to use oil lamps for at least another decade for fear of running up large bills. Until the 1930s people kept up the tradition of opening the oven door on winter evenings for warmth and light. Electrically driven machinery was first used by farmers and businessmen from about 1934— by this time enough people had overcome their suspicions and convinced themselves that these contraptions were not really as dangerous as they had assumed. The first radio was bought in 1929 for a blind boy by his parents. By about 1935 there was a set in every neighbourhood and people who owned them had to open their doors to listeners from round and about. The first car was bought by a cattle dealer in 1934.

The interwar period was marked by relative poverty. By the end of the thirties the majority of the village bread-winners were working in industry but they continued to have a deep mistrust of industrial employment. Almost without exception they insisted on cultivating some land and keeping some form of the extended family together. They looked upon the family house, its land, relatives, neighbours and the village itself as their real insurance policy.

This continued involvement of the whole household in the upkeep of the house and provision of food for the family influenced the design of houses built between the wars and well into the 1960s. The design of the house itself incorporated the ideology of 'how each villager ought to live' and determined how the available space within the house should be classified and used. Both the physical structure and the social organisation of the house helped to maintain the division of labour within a household which had links to both the industrial and agricultural economy and also preserved a hierarchy of seniority which, in the villagers' view, was a prerequisite for the co-existence of several generations under the same roof. Neither physical nor social space within the house, therefore, was neutral, indeed its use had to be negotiated between the members of the household, and its occupation and allocation were as much subject to moral judgements as any other social act. The division of labour, based on the organisation principles of role differentiation and social inequality, implied that certain individuals were associated with very definite spatial domains within the house and village at large. Social status distinctions became meaningful and legitimate through spatial boundaries which, in the process of everyday social interaction, were made explicit and demonstrated the different categories to those people who had to learn or needed to be reminded of them.

This 'imperative' of clear social and spatial boundaries was, in my view, not entirely related to an 'innate' human need to classify, stratify and order the environment, which is the essentially unprovable thesis of Structural Anthropologists, but was more immediately linked to the maintenance of property and a particular life-style in the context of an 'acute' shortage of land resources and living space.[11] The social and spatial classification system of these villagers can only be fully understood in terms of the specific and, from the villagers' point of view, 'rational' adaptation of life-style which they had developed in the face of rapid industrial changes.[12]

1 From an interview with a local woman in 1978.
2 *Mägde* were female agricultural labourers; *Knechte* male agricultural labourers; *Dienstleute* casual labourers or domestics.
3 Otto Brunner, 'Das "Ganze Haus" und die alteuropäische "Ökonomik"', in a collection of essays edited by the same author, *Neue Wege der Verfassungs-und Sozialgeschichte*, Göttingen 1968.
4 Interview with a local man in 1978.
5 For a good summary of the general principles underlying Rites of Passage, see Edmund Leach, *Culture and Communication*, Cambridge 1976.
6 Similar findings are discussed in, P. Bourdieu, 'The Berber House', in Mary Douglas (ed.), *Rules and Meanings*, Hammondsworth 1973.
7 Interview with an ex-farm labourer in 1976.
8 Interview with a retired farmer in 1978.
9 Interview with a local man in 1978.
10 *Ibid*
11 Claude Lévi-Strauss, *The Savage Mind*, London 1966.
12 E.P. Thompson, 'Folklore, Anthropology and Social history', in, *The Indian Historical Review* 3, pp. 247–266.

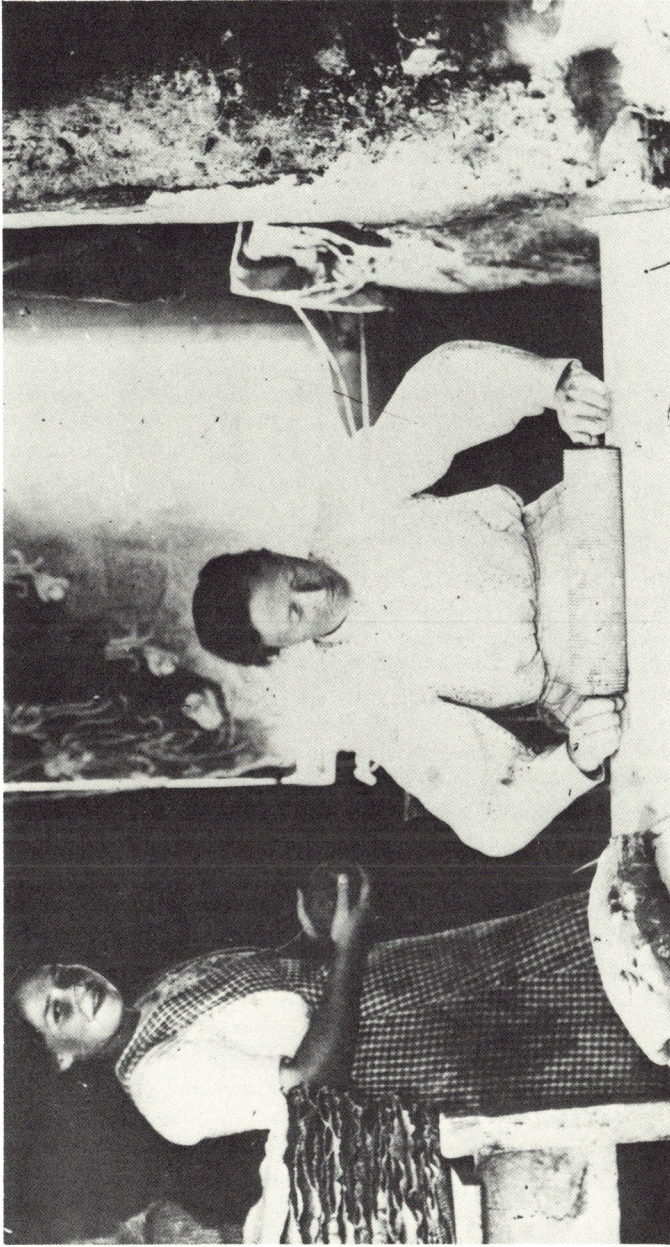

Flatbread-making in Trøndelag, Norway. 1920. Flatbread (very thin, crisp, unleavened bread) was an important item of diet for the farming community of Norway. Normally, baking was done for two days, twice a year. The bread was baked in large round sheets on a griddle over the fire. It was dry and crisp and could be stored for a long time. Photo. *J. B. Brevold Aafjord.*

Farmwives, Farm Hands and the Changing Rural Community in Trøndelag, Norway

Dagfinn Slettan

Norwegian historians have long been interested in the profound changes which Norwegian rural society underwent from the end of the 19th century onwards. The development from a static, self-sufficient society to a rapidly changing, mechanised agricultural society had far-reaching economic, social and cultural consequences. Research in this field at first concentrated on the period before the First World War, but in recent years it has been considered desirable to view the changes over a longer time period, to view the development over the last hundred years continuously. Both the onset and rate of change show considerable regional variation. In central farming areas in Østlandet (South East Norway) the transformation occurred about the turn of the century or earlier, whereas in many mountain and coastal areas and the greater part of North Norway this did not happen until about half a century later.

Historians who have studied this subject have concentrated largely on general economic developments, on economic and technological change. For social historical questions most of the work remains yet to be done, and in particular for some groups which have been largely overlooked. This is obviously the case for groups who have left behind them few traditional written sources and figure little in official statistics—such as women, old people, day labourers, or children. It is a challenge to those who work in the field of oral history to redress this balance; and it has been one of the principal aims in the collecting work which over the past few years we have been carrying out from the history department of Trondheim University in the Trøndelag, the region within which the university lies.[1]

Trøndelag is in many ways a miniature Norway. There are mountain settlements where dairying and outfield activities are important, valley settlements where lumbering is an important subsidiary occupation, more open country where corn growing is dominant, and coastal and fjord settlements where fishing and farming are combined. There has also been considerable variation within the region in the rate of change. Whereas the open country round Trondheimsfjord was well on the way to mechanisation and commercial agriculture even before the turn of the century, there are mountain and coastal settlements where the transformation did not take place until between the two World Wars or after the Second World War.

The period between the two World Wars was a time of crisis for Norwegian agriculture. Although again there were considerable regional differences, few people were not affected by the crisis in some way or another. In Trøndelag many experienced forced sale and foreclosure, while the clearest memory of the majority is the fear that such a fate would also befall them—the fear of not being able to meet their obligations to banks, firms and the administration. The path to poor relief was not lightly trod, and hung as a threat over many of them. It is therefore a rural society simultaneously in transformation and crisis that we were wishing to reconstruct when travelling round the country with pen and tape-recorder. Through the study of statistics and protocols, local and national archives, we can sketch the main lines of development. But how did people experience this period? Statistics count isolated items; a life history interview can link the individual environmental components together in a natural way.

I will limit myself to illustrating this through just two occupational categories, both examples of groups which historians have neglected in rural society. One of these is women in agriculture: we will concentrate on the farmer's wife. Another group are the farm hands, those who did not own land, but had their labour to offer.

The Farmer's Wife

In official statistics it is the men who are entered as farmers. The women are entered under 'housewives', which includes both farmers' wives and other housewives. Investigation has shown, however, that it is the women who contribute most to the work of the farm if one includes work inside the house. Between the two World Wars women partook in work both outside and in the cowshed as well as doing the housework and looking after the children, and it was not unusual on smallholdings that at times the wife went out to work for wages as well as working at home. We have no figures to tell us exactly how widespread this kind of additional work was amongst farmers' wives, but it was certainly quite common. For many families the kroner which this work brought in must have been very important at times when many people were feeling the lack of cash for necessary expenses.

The farmer's wife not only had many tasks; she was also responsible for seeing that her part of the 'concern' worked efficiently. Her working day could be both long and strenuous, and the husband took advantage of the privileges the male-dominated society afforded him. However, it would be hardly correct to maintain that the women accepted subordination. What they accepted was the division of labour. The women had their particular jobs and the men likewise. Often the women were worst off as regards working hours and income, but it nevertheless seems fair to point out that the farmer's wife had a high degree of independence and took part in decision making. Perhaps this is most clearly illustrated in coastal settlements where the fishing and farming combination was still dominant between the two World Wars. The men were away fishing for long periods – maybe up to three or four months at a time – and sole responsibility for running the smallholding then fell on the women who, together with the children, did all the farm work. And there were many tasks, as a fisherman's daughter born in 1903 remembers of her childhood on the family farm:

We were seven brothers and sisters where my parents fished and ran their small-holding. We had a good home and never lacked anything. But mother had a lot to do. Grandmother lived with us and she was bed-ridden for thirty years. She lay quite stiff with arthritis and couldn't feed herself; mother did everything for her. Besides that, she had us children to look after and did all the housework, and father was away fishing for long periods at a time and mother had to do all the farm work together with us children. We didn't have water in the house, but carried it from a nearby stream. In the winter, when father was away fishing, there was no water in the stream, so mother carried it from the river, and had then to go down a steep hill to get there. She often had to hack steps in the snow and ice to get up again with the buckets. She had to go many times a day; we had lots of cows so we used lots of water both in and out. As well as this, there was fodder collecting. We didn't have enough hay, so we fetched seaweed from the sea and birch twigs from the woods which we fed to the animals.

Another woman born in 1896 recalled:

There was a fireplace in the kitchen where we cooked all our food. We baked bread in it too. We didn't get a wood-stove until us children were nearly grown-up. We had water laid on about the same time. Before that we carried all our water, using a yoke, both to the house and the cow-shed. If it was a dry year and the well ran dry, it happened we had to fetch water from quite a way away.

We made *lye*[2] from ashes for washing the clothes. We boiled the clothes over the fire in the kitchen and rinsed them by the well. Drew up buckets and rinsed. After rinsing we laid the clothes over a stone and beat them with a paddle to get out the lye. Afterwards we rinsed and beat again. All clothes were home-made, so they could stand the treatment. The washing-up was done in a tub in the kitchen, there was no sink. Water had to be carried in and out.

Did the children help with this work?

Us children helped with everything. We wove, span, knitted and carried water, scrubbed and washed, helped with minding the animals and worked in the cow-shed.

Was work in the cow-shed for women and children only?

Yes, it was. There were *never* men in the cow-shed.

Not for clearing out the muck either?

On no! We were lucky, we had a muck cellar underneath the cow-shed; some people had to throw the muck up through a hatch in the wall. That was much heavier work.

The women also took part in outside work at harvest time. It was a long time before we got a mowing machine. Then all the hay was cut with a scythe, and the women spread it out to dry. In the evenings we gathered it into piles, and in the mornings spread it out again. Also, us children worked for day-wages on other farms round about as soon as we were old enough. Us girls got 50 øre a day for this work. The boys weren't as quick at taking up potatoes as we were, but they got 80 øre. No wonder it's International Woman's Year!

We have only just touched on the woman's daily tasks; many, like looking after the children, are not taken up here. Nevertheless, one can get an impression of how diverse the farmer's wife's work was. When in addition, one considers that she was often pregnant over a period of several years, a further dimension is added to her life. But this picture began to alter in the period between the two World Wars and the result can be seen most clearly after the Second World War, beginning with the settlements in the open country. The use of machinery made her super-fluous in the fields, and eventually in the cow-shed as well. There were fewer children, and the first technical aids appeared inside the house. The woman's work became more limited in range and lighter, but her inde-pendent role as farmer's wife was at the same time weakened. The daily running of the farm became gradually less dependent on her contribution. She lost responsibility and was forced back on her house and children. The situation was similar for the smallholder's wife on the coast, even though her situation changed more slowly. Combined fishing and farm-ing continued well into the post-war period in many places, not least along the Trøndelag coast. But as this combination also disappeared, the same dramatic changes in the housewife's role occurred. The smallholding was entirely dependent on her and the children's contribution. She ran the smallholding almost by herself, and if often provided her with an essential part of the family's income. In the course of two or three decades, specialization and structural changes in fishing have made the combination uneconomic. The result has been specialization in either fishing or farming. In each case the consequence is that the women and children have had to move aside and have lost responsibility and tasks. While other sources are of little help on all this, through interviews we have been able both to bring out the diverse and specialised tasks and the extent of responsibility which the farmer's wife had, and also to learn how the women themselves considered their role and how they experienced the structural changes in farming which so deeply affected their social position.

The Farm Hand

Another of the 'silent' groups is the farm hands. This section of the lower rural classes has played an important part in the farming community for centuries. As far as earlier centuries are concerned, we do know something, not least because their position was precisely laid down by law. They provided essential labour for the farmers, and the laws aimed at ensuring that this labour was stable by binding the hands to their place of residence and work. Even if the laws did not always work as intended, all those in the rural community who did not own land were bound to contract themselves out as hands. They had to seek regular work, and this bound them more completely to the farm than was the case for day-labourers. Conversely, the farmer felt greater responsibility towards his hand who formed part of the farm's household the year round, ate and slept there, was provided with clothes and worked daily alongside the farmer. In addition, the hands were tied to the farmer by earnest money and their contracts could only be broken at fixed dates. Both these formed part of the labour contract.

The hands were thus a part of the farm community. But their position was quite different from that of the farmer. The majority had little chance of financial independence. They came from the farming community's bottom ranks and had no one with power or money to support them. Social barriers were very difficult to overcome in most parts of the country. Nor, partly because of their particular living and work situation, did the farm hands ever manage to band together as the industrial workers did early on to make their demands heard.

From the end of the 19th century, the situation of the farm hands and other landless in the rural community began to be transformed for a number of reasons. The path over the sea to the New World was opened, and gradually the supply of jobs in industry and construction work increased. The old laws which bound the farm hand to one place and situation disappeared. The mechanisation of agriculture also meant that the farmer became less dependent on the hands, so that the occupation gradually died out during the first part of this century.

The number of hands declined sharply up to the First World War. But then a change occurred. The crises between the two World Wars delayed the disappearance of this occupational group. The restructuring of agriculture was slowed down, finding markets became difficult, and farming experienced a price crisis. At the same time there was high unemployment, so it was therefore possible for farmers to take on hands whilst other employers were reducing their labour force. The root cause seems to be clear. It was more profitable for the farmer to use his products to pay his hands in kind than to sell them at rock-bottom prices. And for many young people in the country farm work was the only possibility in these hard times. For bed and board in addition to a small wage in cash they could at least be saved from unemployment and public assistance.

Farm hands as an occupational group were in a quite special situation in the period between the two World Wars which makes them of particular interest. Whilst Norway had in most respects become an industrial nation, and the majority of workers had long been paid wages in cash, the number of farm hands who received most of their wages in the form of bed and board was maintained. Whilst the patriarchal relationship between those who sell and those who buy labour began to be replaced by conflict and unionism, the farm hand was still part of the household and bound to the farmer during both working and leisure hours. Whilst large groups of workers'had regulated working hours and an eight-hour day and paid holidays were beginning to be introduced in industry, there were scarcely any farm hands who had fixed hours or holidays. The hand was released from the laws which had bound him to service, but at the same time his situation had much in common with earlier times. Here, too, there exists a two-fold challenge for oral history research. We know too little about the farm hand's daily tasks, his working hours, his responsibilities and social position, and we know even less about how he himself experienced his occupation and considered his future prospects.

Even for wages, official statistics and archive sources can only be of limited use. The archives of the local tax offices can provide some information, and we find that even when one includes bed and board, farm hands are clearly in a low-wages category when compared with industrial workers. But this material on its own gives an incomplete picture. During the course of the field work, it became clear that it was not unusual for the youngest hands to receive no cash wages at all or to receive so little that they paid no tax. They therefore do not get included in any statistics. A farm hand born in 1912 reported:

I was 22 years old when I began receiving wages. Before that I worked many years as a hand for bed and board.
Didn't you receive wages in cash?
Maybe I got 5 kroner once in a while, but a regular wage was out of the question. We had to count ourselves lucky to get food.

It was not unusual for boys and girls to be sent out to regular work after confirmation at 14 or 15, and it was in particular such youngsters who would not receive wages in cash. They usually came from families who were badly off, and one mouth less to feed meant much. But children began some kinds of work long before confirmation, at haymaking, minding other children, and, not least, minding animals. Children as young as eight or nine could be away from home the whole summer at this kind of work. Yet such cases are unrecorded in any statistics: A farm hand born in 1897 remembers:

I worked many summers on the farm while I went to school. Sometimes I worked during the school year too, when there was no teaching. There were a lot of animals on the farm, and since they had no children of their own I spent a lot of time in the cow-shed.
Did you get paid?
No, only food and clothes. That was usual before confirmation, also for the first year afterwards. I worked there a year after I was confirmed, and didn't get wages in cash then, either. It was the custom that you worked one year without wages for those who had fitted you out for confirmation.

How were wages determined? Since farm hands were not organised, and wage agreements were usually verbal, this is not easy to discover. In the interviews certain guidelines which the farmers followed emerged, but it was also easy to lower wages, particularly those of the weakest. Whereas organised workers (those of them that had work) were able to maintain the level of real wages through wage disputes, it is clear that the farm hands' real wages sank in the period between the two World Wars. The farmer held a strong hand, as a farm hand born in 1914 recalled:

I tried to get work for the winter (of 1931), but there was none to be found. At last I heard of a farmer who was looking for a boy for the winter, so I tried there. He asked me what wages I wanted, so I said he should make an offer. 'There's enough unemployed labour about, I don't need to make an offer,' was the reply. So I asked for 20 kroner a month, and the farmer said I would hear from him later. I never did. Someone else got the job. So I was unemployed. There weren't any other possibilities besides farm work.

The farm hand had neither an 8 nor a 10 hour day. Such statistics of their working hours and leisure time as are available are difficult to use: they were compiled from information given by farmers, and in any case, in the period between the two World Wars it was still not usual to distinguish between work and leisure time in farming. It was the work that determined the hours, not the clock. The statistics assume that the weekends were 'leisure' time. The accounts of farm hands give a different impression. The men had their tasks at weekends too, but this is even more true of the women. For them work at weekends was little different from during the week: in the cow-shed, food preparation, washing up, looking after the children. Moreover, food preparation was even more demanding at weekends since the food had to be extra good. One woman farm hand – born in 1900 – was asked:

> *Did you have any agreement about time off?*
> There was no question of time off on the farms then. The work in the cow-shed had to be done, the food made, etc.
> *Did you never go home at weekends?*
> Yes, but I had to ask for leave each time. And it had to be quite certain that there was someone else to do my work while I was away.

There was no legislation on time off for farm workers. There was no regular summer holiday either. It was not uncommon for the hands to get some days off during the summer, but it was the farmer who decided such matters.

In the 1930s some hands began to organise themselves, and gradually fixed agreements about working hours became more common, but by this time the farm hand as an occupational category was disappearing.

Such details of the farm hand's situation illustrate how the material from oral sources can supplement and correct the picture available from existing evidence. But, more important than such correction, is the possibility through interviews of linking together the various aspects of each informant's circumstances and reconstructing attitudes and feelings. Thus the evidence of long hours and low wages seen in isolation, might lead us to believe that the occupation of farm hand was disliked, and that farm hands felt dissatisfied. But the interviews do not give this impression.

This might partly be due to the time lapse between experience and account. Perhaps the darker sides get forgotten. But there is little indication that the accounts suffer from this sort of bias to any great extent. A clear majority emphasise that there was a good relationship between the farmer and his hands, that the food was good, and the working conditions good: the main explanation would seem to lie in the feeling of community on the farm. In Trøndelag it was usual for the farmer and his hands to live in the same house and eat at the same table of the same food. They worked together on the farm and spent much of their leisure time together as well. It was only in the exceptional case that the hands were treated differently from others on the farm. In spite of low wages and lack of future prospects, the descriptions in the interviews are repeatedly positive in tone, both as regards the work and in their evaluation of the farmer and his wife. The key to this harmony where one might have expected conflict and frustration, lies in a communal spirit of work and household with which farm hands could identify more easily than with a working class with whom they still had little in common.

1   The project, which started in 1974, was initiated by Professor Edvard Bull, who between 1950 and 1962 had directed the collection of Norwegian industrial workers' autobiographies, sponsored by the Norwegian Folk Museum. This archive has been transferred to the University of Trondheim, and the Trøndelag project is in many respects a regional continuation of it, but occupationally widened, to include broad groups such as farmers, fishermen, industrial workers, white-collar workers, house-wives and farm hands. Our primary aim is to collect life histories from people who lived through the interwar period and to systematise this material for research and publication. There are abundant sources for this period in general, but not for the conditions and experience of ordinary people who do not normally leave any written records. It is the main purpose of our project to throw some light into this void.

Both the written answers and the taped interviews are based on questionnaires which are specific to the different occupational categories. These questionnaires attempt to cover some central areas in as much detail as possible. This is the case for standards of living and social welfare, conditions of work and career. Other central questions concern the affiliation to and activities within social and political groups, and aspects of a more ethnological or folkloristic character, such as customs, feast days and work routines. It is a particular aim of the project to chart the effect of the economic crisis on the life of the ordinary person. In this context it will be interesting but difficult to interpret how people experienced their situation. It is important that the questionnaires do not tie the subject or the interviewer too much, and thereby hinder the process of free association or fruitful dialogue. About 750 narratives have so far been collected. Some of these are written, but the majority are taped interviews. In just a few cases the narratives have been based on rapidly written notes taken by the interviewers because the informant objected to the recorder.

Strong emphasis has been laid on recording conditions of life, rather than customs and traditions, and also on using life histories as the general framework for the questionnaire. This is of crucial importance. It gives the informant the opportunity, in the course of his or her story, to choose the context in which specific information is given. One may object that this method, based on unstructured interviews, will make comparative, systematic work difficult and time-consuming, and there is certainly truth in this. Nevertheless, we consider that the value of the data as source material is infinitely enhanced by a method which is based on continuous and essentially free narratives by the respondents and, in our opinion, this is sufficient justification for it. Information which is given in the narrator's own context has greater historical value, and it is in any case the only way in which we can come near to the respondent's subjective experience. If the term 'history from below' is to have any concrete meaning, this type of source is essential. We have to get to know the story at first hand, from the actors themselves.

Some of this material has been used in the preparation of theses. Furthermore, when it has been adequately transcribed, registered and indexed, it will be available to all those working in the field of modern social history and to local historians—to whom it will of course be of particular value. The publication of three or four volumes of extracts is also planned, and a first volume concentrating on Trøndelag's coastal districts, was published in 1979. Lastly, though the current project is restricted to a few selected areas within Trøndelag, it is our hope that similar projects may be initiated in other places.

2   'Lye', or in Norwegian, 'lut', was a form of soap produced by leaching wood ashes.

An Amsterdam tailoring sweatshop, probably of NV Hollandia-Fabrieken Kattenburg & Co., c.1919

Women

Italian Peasant Women and the First World War

Anna Bravo

The topic of this paper – part of a larger research project on the role and identity of peasant and working-class women[1] – is the transformation of women's social conditions in the countryside during the First World War. At the same time I shall be looking at the processes of adaptation and the elements of conflict present in the way in which women experienced these changes. In this way we shall be examining a specific example of the broader problem of the relationship between women's conditions and external historical moments—between women's history and 'great' history.

Among the various significant events which have affected Italian peasant society, the First World War appears as a moment of primary importance. Indeed, the war's importance as representing one of the central elements of popular memory has recently been re-emphasised in Nuto Revelli's great collection of life stories from the countryside around Cuneo, south of Turin, *Il Mondo dei vinti*. However, until now research has been primarily focused on the figure of the peasant soldier and the conflictual relationship between resignation and dissent which characterise his behaviour.[2] Much less attention has been given to analysing the impact of the war on the rural communities themselves, whose life was thrown into disorder by the massive call-to-arms, by material difficulties, and by the increased interference of state authorities in the fabric of daily life.

As for women, while some attention has been given to female workers in their role as labour power, which was of primary importance in this period, and as the subjects of a significant process of social activation, peasant women have been considered only as silent victims of poverty or as protagonists of sporadic and spontaneous outbursts of struggle against the war.[3]

Between these two extremes, which represent the two sides of an existence of radical oppression and exclusion, there is nothing: these women have a past, but not a history.

In a similar way the researcher, whose interest is women's social conditions, faces a central problem: the risk of oscillating between a narrowly specialised and 'ghettoised' understanding, and an understanding that results in a subsidiary inclusion of women with a larger predetermined framework of interpretation. We do not want to create a separate history which makes no sense of history as a whole, nor do we wish to see ourselves relegated to a small women's section – no more important than many other sub-sections – in 'great' history.

The current interest in the use of oral sources – linked to a growing attention now being given to the methodological and analytical categories of social science disciplines like anthropology, sociology and psychoanalysis – can bring a significant contribution to the redefinition of this problem. New areas of research, new keys to interpretation, different measures of social changes and continuities are now all suggested to the historian. Furthermore, the political and cultural presence of feminism has contributed to a better understanding of the theoretical and methodological complexities of research, and has made clear the inadequacy of some of the conceptual systems now used in social science: for example, the inadequacy of concepts of the social division of labour which deny the social and ideological relevance of the condition of women, or of a history seen as the development of Reason, which entails a radical exclusion of women, identified as irrational, subjective, 'different.'

To overcome this exclusion, it is necessary to reaffirm the specific centrality of women in any attempt to reach an understanding of social structures and social and political processes. Thus, the analysis of the workings of mature capitalist societies remains not only incomplete, but also profoundly falsified, if the importance of the economic and social role and the cultural significance of women's condition is not considered. But even this approach still risks establishing the centrality of women simply in their old role as symbols of the particular cultural level reached by society—as the passive 'stepping stones' which mark the stages of historical development: restored to the centre of attention, but of a broadened, all-encompassing 'great' history, rather than a history of women.

Although we still lack the fully-developed theory and concepts which such a true history of women demands, we can at least attempt to penetrate behind the fixed image of women's 'nature' which culture has produced and history documented. We can try to see how at different times this 'nature' of women is socially constructed, by examining the connections between women's roles and ideology, the elements of consciousness and false consciousness, the non-rational aspects and subconscious impulses. In other words, we can interpret consciousness and subjectivity as a historically determined reality—but with stages of development and causal processes of its own.[4]

Within this perspective, oral sources become essential, precisely for the very specific richness they offer for an understanding, not only of daily experience, but also of processes of adaptation and resistance to social and structural transformations. In other words, oral sources can contribute to a project of women's history which lays the foundation for the recovery of different times and spaces, of different and hidden historical facts.

* * * *

The territory which we have been studying, the Langhe, is a hilly region of extremely poor countryside to the south of Turin, with a great predominance of small, or extremely small, family-run farms. Only marginally influenced by industrialisation, these communities have been marked by a sense of exclusion and a close-knit defensiveness towards the outside world. Inside the communities, life has been dominated by the struggle for survival, by the hunger for land and the conflict to possess it. Land is what unites but can also divide the community and the family.[5]

The women work both in the house and in the fields. Their existence is characterised, on the one hand, by the centrality of their family and work roles which makes their presence indispensable, and, on the other hand, by the delimited nature of their recognised rights.

The hereditary system excludes them from land ownership; the dowry consists exclusively of items of clothes and furniture. Therefore, women have value, in the matrimonial market and the social life of the community alike, only as labour power and reproductive power; and, along with this, to fulfil the demand for a psychological and moral force which guarantees the cohesion of the family. The space for women's social life is severely restricted both by the characteristics of their role and by the moral rigidity of the community. Sexual alienation is generalised and brutal. Their identity is marked by the contradiction between the image of strength and indispensability which they hold of themselves, and their acceptance of the weakness of their social conditions.[6]

The intervention of the war made its mark, first, on the women's relationship to both agricultural and domestic work. The delicate balance between consumers and producers upon which the present family is based was disrupted by the disappearance of the most active section of the male labour force. The women found their work cycle expanded even more: small baby girls and old women now had to work; the work day grew longer; and the variety of their tasks increased until it included all of those formerly held by men.

This meant the end of the traditional division of labour in which the men performed the heavier and, in some ways, more exacting jobs, such as manoeuvering the threshing machines. All of the oral accounts insist on this point:

—I had to do all the tasks the men used to do. I even had to unload the wheat, spread the wheatsheaves, help to thresh when the machine came around. And then, I was always looking after the animals. We even took the hoes and weeded the corn, the beans, everything.[7]

—They didn't give me any easy jobs just because I was a girl. I hoed, watered the vines, cleaned the stalls, looked after the animals.[8]

The marks that this excessive exertion left on the women's bodies are emphasised, and so is the women's capacity to resist and adapt:

—I had to do everything that a man does. My brothers were in the war. We watered the fields bare-foot. It was bad for our health. We ate badly, but we would have eaten anything...I got married when I was twenty; no doctor had ever touched me.[9]

—The hired boy was in front watering the vines. I came behind spreading the sulphur. When I came home in the evening my eyes were burning. I washed and washed. But when I went to bed I didn't even want to sleep any more because if I closed my eyes they watered all night long...I weighed only 45 kilograms. (My brother) always said: 'You look like the living death'...Well, I'm still here; I've always been healthy.[10]

When this redistribution of work was not sufficient to ensure the family's survival and the continued possession of the land, the women returned temporarily to the nearby factories or to some other type of work outside the family, including, in some cases, semi-clandestine seasonal emigration to France. This migratory work even involved married women with children, and thus disrupted the tradition whereby such experiences ended at marriage.

Beyond these cases of forced absence, there was also a reorganisation of family life and domestic activity. Mothers devoted themselves almost entirely to work in the fields, while the weight of the house and the care of the children fell on the daughters who were often only slightly older. In some cases a daughter looked after the children from several families, so that the other girls could work in the factories or as servants. In any case, daily household tasks – cleaning, cooking – were reduced to a minimum. There was a parallel growth in the time devoted to the tasks which external changes imposed, in particular to those imposed by rationing and by intensified forms of immediate family consumption of production:

—We made oil by crushing the nuts and sunflower seeds in the wine press.[11]
—We dealt with the problems ourselves. We milked the cows to make butter because what they gave out for the rations was meagre and awful. We made our own bread.[12]
—We had rationing cards, but we made a type of bread mixed with potatoes.[13]

In spite of the quantity of these efforts, the situation of certain families became so desperate that some were forced to eat animal feed and others even to stealing. Two women openly admit it:

—We stole... Well, if you wanted to eat...[14]
—My mother, your grandmother Antonietta, Carolina, eight or ten women altogether, you know what they did? They stole at night; potatoes, onions; they stole firewood together. They did all these things just to keep going.[15]

These women justify these small-scale thefts and other illegal activities by their families' need to survive. But the unambiguous social and cultural rejection of these women by others is a stark confirmation of community disapproval:

The wife would take a large apron, roll it up, and walk around the streets. In one place, potatoes, in another, beans. She stole a little here, a little there, and came home with the apron full. That woman was looked down on.[16]

In all oral accounts, the women's acceptance of such a vast array of responsibilities appears both as out of the ordinary and also as a duty: almost as if it were natural for women to make themselves responsible for exceptional tasks, tasks which were accepted as the utmost expansion of a multiform and never-ending role.

This attitude seems accurately to reflect the meaning of matrimonial exchange in the community, and the conditions which had to be endured in order to be accepted in the new family. The man brought the land, which was a quantifiable good, always equal to itself; the woman brought a subjective capacity to work which was indeterminate. This capacity of hers had to be adapted to the family's life cycle and needs. The woman realised that she was accepted – and could feel her own value – only through her own capability and this willingness to adapt. Hence, there were no special compensations envisaged for her efforts. The few attempts to rebalance the family relationship in her favour tended primarily to improve her own condition only within the traditional family structure. The situation was perhaps slightly different for unmarried girls who worked within their original families, where the promise of some small rewards in exchange for longer and heavier work [17] was not merely a sign of consideration for their youth as such, but also an indication that their obligation to show unconditional willingness to work was less institutionalised and less general.

*   *   *   *

In the life of these communities, the war manifested itself above all through an increase in the presence and power of the state: in inspections, requisitions, forced hoarding, rationing; and the introduction of difficult procedures for obtaining benefits, exemptions from the draft, and military leave. This new relationship with authority fell on the women, as the only remaining young section of the population. But the new responsibility was also asked of them by their husbands at the war-front. [18] The women's lives, previously restricted to the house and community, were now filled with new tasks: going to government offices, discussing with local administrators and officials, travelling as far as provincial capitals to follow through these extended chores. Thus greater contact was established with the outside world, with new places, with a new environment of different experiences, with the public sphere of life. The women now had a direct relationship with the activities of a state authority which they also identified as responsible for the war. When the oral accounts deal with these themes, they are given great emphasis:

—When my husband was a soldier, they sent a letter to my mother-in-law saying that she had to pay a certain amount because he was unfit for war duty. The poor old woman paid, and then wanted me to pay her back. 'I'm not paying. He may be unfit for war, but he sure isn't at home, he's off in the army.' I said it to the police too. I went to talk to the city officer. Other notices of payment due arrived. They told me to go to the tax office here in Caraglio. There they told me to pay and then to sue to get back my mother-in-law's and my money. 'Thanks, I have my money in my pocket and I'm keeping it. My mother-in-law paid her own money. I don't want it.' [19]

—I was in bed with the six-year-old baby, and I caught the Spanish 'flu too. One day the marshal comes; I was in bed. He wanted me to give some hay to the government. I told him: 'Doesn't it seem disgraceful to you that they ask me for hay; me, here in bed, with my husband a soldier, and young as he is they've never given him an hour's leave; and I'm here in bed with nobody to help me. Aren't you ashamed?' Finally they sent my husband a telegram and gave him a ten-day leave.[20]

Attitudes of this type were an integral part of a more general estrangement from the state and of peasant society's opposition to the war. Furthermore, the encounter with the state occurred with the woman acting as representative and defender of the family, and this role appeared as a necessary extension of her function as guardian of the common interests. There are, however, other elements which suggest additional interpretative keys. It would be reasonable to expect that these women's behaviour would be marked by a combination of both insecurity and aggressiveness. The oral account, however, emphasises only the latter aspect, often presenting a kind of drama in which the woman actively sets herself against arrogance and arbitrariness. This strong element of self-affirmation suggests the hypothesis that we are also dealing with the dynamics of a more general conflict with authority. Repressed and forbidden expression inside the family, these dynamics of conflict were shifted outside against a socially shared enemy, against an authority experienced as pure abuse of power, against an authority which could not, therefore, kindle processes of identification and complicity.

Furthermore, if we examine the special emphasis given in the oral accounts to other war-imposed encounters with the external world – the purchase of a pair of oxen, buying and selling at the market in the husband's absence – we discover that each of these episodes, beyond the particularities of the conflict with authority, is also experienced as a moment of self-realisation, of individualisation in the social world and the public sphere. The women seem only partially conscious of this stimulus, but as they tell their stories, one senses resonances of emotional involvement, not only in the goal they had in each encounter, but of a hidden ability and quiescent desire which they had at last found acceptable ways of realising.

*   *   *   *

The war affected relations between the sexes in contradictory ways. It opened – as we shall see – spaces for a less restricted and less orthodox sexuality. However, given that the peasant models of morality and the power relationships did not undergo any change, the position of women, already structurally fragile, appears to have been further weakened. In this society the women were not only productive and reproductive power, but were also sexual objects to be used as freely and brutally as the weakness of their social and personal position permitted. Their only defence was the family's control or protection. When this was lacking – something which coincided with extreme poverty or internal disintegration – violence, incest, the cheap sale of children and child prostitution, and persecution endured as farm hands and servants, were not uncommon.

The departure of husbands and brothers left the women weaker and more exposed. Furthermore, with the war women had increased contact with the external world; they needed masculine help for certain agricultural operations; local officials and police entered their houses to identify animals and goods to be requisitioned; deserters and draft-dodgers sought refuge in their barns. Certain oral accounts – only a few, probably because of a form of self-censure – document the spread of a threatening and predatory attitude. The man takes it for granted that the woman is suffering from male absence and aggressively proposes himself. The accounts speak of cases of rape and murder. [21]

In most of the accounts it appears that the women experienced this situation by a strong denial of their own sexuality: those accounts that deal with the problem do so only in order to reject its existence, and, at the same time, to re-confirm their own adherence to the model of wife and mother:

My head was filled with other things. I swear that I never even thought about 'that' because I had so many other worries. I thought about him off in the war, and the children, the animals, the land, everything, and the debts to pay. [22]

Male sexual proposals were experienced without gratification, and the only emotional agitation was in the expression of harsh disapproval for an initiative considered 'shameful.' The women's refusals never betray an effort to control themselves, never show anything like the rejection of 'temptation'. The episodes take on the character of simply dealing successfully with a difficult moment, with a dangerous or socially embarrassing situation. Only the male has sexual impulses—and those that chase women are *lurdun* – good-for-nothings and pigs—because women have more important things to do.

Only through the women's references to deviants – from whom they rigidly distinguish themselves – do they let us see that the war had introduced specific kinds of disturbance in their sexual behaviour:

—There was one ... The marshal always went to see her ... I wasn't one of those that they could go to bed with. [23]

—There are women who had a hard life. And there were those who used their husband's absence, but you certainly had to have a lot of courage! [24]

—The woman wanted to enjoy herself, and neglected the house, or else gave up the land and everything, and when the husband came back he didn't find anything.[25]

Certainly, this subject is influenced by the demands of social and self-respect and the need to reaffirm the values of their own past against the greater permissiveness attributed to the present. However, when evaluating this model of behaviour it is necessary to keep in mind that the acceptance of a subordinate and restricted sexuality in marriage is a 'natural' fact of these women's experience, and is closely linked to the other aspects of their roles. It is not a coincidence that sexual transgression is associated with the spectre of the loss of the land and the ruin of the household. Since the husband's absence created new material problems of solidarity and respect, the women had an even stronger stimulus to hold on to the models they had been socialised to accept. This stimulus was further strengthened both by the intensified control or protection exercised by the community and neighbourhood, and by the woman's understanding of the weakness of her social position, a weakness based on her exclusion from land ownership. This understanding makes the risk of destroying the marriage unthinkable.

In this situation – in which the stimulus to maintain the established order went hand in hand with increased opportunities to violate it – the traditionally marginal dimension of sexuality in women's lives and self-identity presumably favoured the mechanism of self-repression and, beyond that, of total denial, which controlled the woman's sexual behaviour and judgement.

*   *   *   *

The changes that the war created in social life are seen with particular prominence in the social life of women which was, until then, tied to very rigidly traditional and limited relationships. The time and space for the old forms of social life became even more restricted with the war:

Life changed a lot during the war . . . To think that I hardly learned how to dance. Before the war people often danced during the festivals. But we didn't dance very much. People were worried. We still spent the evenings together in the barns, but we laughed and joked a lot less.[26]

In this exceptional situation, new, infrequent and 'unorthodox' parallel forms of social life began to develop. Many were directly linked both to the reorganisation of agricultural and domestic work, and to the new solidarity created among the peasants:

—In Rivera, I remember, we were all women who threshed the wheat. There were a few machinists ... but we did everything else ourselves: some of us spread the sheaves, others cut the wheat. We were all young girls and we enjoyed ourselves. There was a steam engine we called the 'black locomotive' because it seemed like the old train locomotives you had to feed with coal.[27]

—In Albaretto, everyone who lives in that farmhouse there is still called 'oilman', 'cause we all used to take our walnuts up there to be pressed.[28]

—In the evening we would help the women who had small babies. We did some of their work for them ... One of them had her husband off in the war. She wasn't very quick, so we went and did her sewing and knitting. She made us a plate of fritters, and we ate![29]

New relationships were also formed as a result of those created at the war-front:

I had all the addresses of his companions: one from Mondovi, another from Garessio, and many more. Afterwards, they all came by to see me and bring me the war news.[30]

But the most significant element for understanding the transform-ation of both the women's daily social life and their subjective attitudes is the presence of small bands of deserters and draft-dodgers who moved from one hillside to another. This extremely important development was dependent on a conspiracy of silence and on the solidarity of the peasants.[31]

The subject is often discussed in the oral accounts. This presence of so many unknown young men, who lived clandestinely and suddenly appeared – perhaps in the middle of the night – in the barns or courtyards of a farmhouse, became a part of daily life, and enlivened it. For women, stuck to the old-established system of relationships it was an entirely new experience:

They wandered around at night and came to ask for something to eat ... then others came on Sunday. They slept wherever they could, in hay-lofts, under the porch. Sometimes we'd see one come down from the loft, and we hadn't even real-ised he was up there. Once I got frightened: my father sent me to throw down some hay from the loft, and I uncovered one who was half asleep.[32]

In this extremely closed and suspicious society, the new situation was experienced with a tolerance and sympathy that cannot be fully explained, either by the fact that some of the deserters came from the villages under discussion, or by the generally exceptional situation. The young men helped the women with their field chores, and, although their lives were semi-clandestine, in some cases they became so integrated into the peasant family's life that they were allowed to organise football matches, festivals, and barn dances:

—They said to my father: 'Bastiano, let us dance a little.' He replied: 'Oh sure! If I let you dance, the police will arrive tomorrow!' Meanwhile, one of them began to play the accordion, and we started dancing.[33]

—Sometimes they sent around trying to find a house they could dance in, and then invited everybody. They always did the organising. I remember that there were some who could really dance!![34]

The opinion of the women is explicitly positive, and contains none of the rumours of rape and other forms of violence which are present in some of the men's oral accounts.[35] On the contrary, the women's opinion emphasises that the deserters were good people, who worked, who moved from one hillside to another in order not to weigh too heavily on the peasants, who never did anyone any wrong, and with whom it was perhaps even pleasant to talk and dance.

This evaluation is clearly influenced by the implicit comparison with the partisans of 1943–45 who are remembered in this region in a more conflictual manner.[36] However, the approval and emotional involvement are too strong to be tied only to this negative comparison: the personalities, the nicknames – one is found in a number of different accounts – are recalled with precision; the dangers faced to give them hospitality are emphasised; their courage is exalted:

They sure were courageous! They weren't scared of anything; played football in San Sabastiano village. One always kept guard in case someone arrived. We helped them, but if the police found us with deserters in the house, we were in for a lot of trouble. But the police weren't in any hurry to come to this region, because there were a lot of deserters, even if they weren't armed. I never saw them armed.[37]

The accounts emphasise the continuous cycle of escapes and arrests in the life of the deserters. They are recalled as the protagonists of an unfought war with the 'carabinieri' which in reality was probably less intense than this would suggest. The regret that some relative who died in the war did not follow their example is present in almost all of the oral accounts.

The role of positive hero given to the deserter springs above all from the tradition of peasant estrangement from the state and opposition to the war already mentioned. The deserter incarnates the most explicit opposition to the war which was achieved within this culture. But for the women there were probably additional aspects to the question: not so much elements of specific sexual and emotional tension – hinted at in the male accounts – which would have set off conflictual dynamics among the women; but rather, the presence of a desire for a less restricted social life, for a way out of daily routine, for affection. This gives the entire experience more complex emotional content and significance.

The deserter became a part of daily life and brought with him new, less 'orthodox' relationships; at the same time, however, he did not violently disrupt this existence. It was a parenthesis that was, at any rate, destined to end. It was danger, adventure, disorder, but it was also the denial of a rule imposed by the outside world. It was a transgression which could be identified with, a symbol of a conflict of values in which everybody was involved. The deserter was a young man, courageous but needing protection, afraid of nothing, but evoking pity.

The relationship was at the same time both completely internal to the experience and culture of these women, and completely external, suspended in a temporary time-slot and in imaginary spaces. In the oral accounts, the relationship crops up as a central element of the war experience and as a subject for many recollections; it is on the one hand escape, on the other a confirmation of the women's own existence.

It is no coincidence that only at this point do the women's oral accounts reveal a recuperation and recollection of the war. In all other parts of the accounts this is entirely absent. While in the men's accounts, the experience of the war-front is revisited 'with a certain level of immediate identification, and often even with a reserved form of pride and nostalgia,'[38] the women's accounts express a total rejection. Forced to endure the entire weight of the war, yet at the same time excluded from those 'heroic' aspects worth re-evoking, the women respond by denying them:

I tell him: 'Drop it; you're boring; by now we are all tired of hearing the same stories over and over again.' But him? Never. Onward with Monte Grappa, the Neapolitans, the Germans, his colonels. I've heard about the war so many times it comes in one ear and goes out the other.[39]

And the women counter the four-year war with one that lasts a lifetime: with the fact that 'the war was out there, but here we had to eat every day'[40].

For when the war was over and the men had come back home, apart from a few wives whose husbands returned seriously disabled, or went off abroad for work, the women had to retreat to their earlier confines, and forget most of the wider responsibility they had briefly borne. A venthole had been opened, which could not be wholly closed; and a good many wives continued to exercise their new-found expertise in dealing with state officials, now on behalf of their husbands. But, within the community, old roles were resumed, and the women forced back into traditional peasant silence, leaving the men to monopolise the claim to war honours. Yet the fight to feed the family had to continue without respite in the new circumstances. And the weight of that still fell primarily on the women: a seemingly timeless, immutable labour – a fate without history – moulding their consciousness of both past and present.

1   This is a research project on which I am working together with Lucetta Scaraffia. We are using the biographies of Piedmontese peasant women, born around the turn of the century, all married with children, and all from the same social stratum, and the biographies of Turinese working class women. Altogether, we have carried out 40 interviews.

   The peasant witnesses all belong to families of small or very small farmers. Some of them had short experiences as domestic servants in the city before marrying; a very few of them worked for some time in small industries; and others migrated as young girls to France for seasonal work. All of them married farmers and spent most of their lifetime in the country, where some of them still work, although now very old. On the whole their response to being interviewed was positive, as was their interest in a research project on women's conditions in the past. In fact, several of them told us that they saw this as a chance to re-evaluate their own life experience and to communicate it to the outside world.

2   N. Revelli, *Il Mondo dei vinti*, Turin 1977; E. Forcella and A. Monticone, *Plotone di esecuzione: i processi della prima guerra mondiale*, Bari 1968.

3   See R. De Felice, 'Ordine pubblico e orientamento delle masse populari italiane nella prima metà del 1917', in *Rivista storica del socialismo*, Vol VI, no 20, 1963.

4   Among contributions to the study of consciousness and psychology, see especially, A. Besançon, *Storia e psicanalisi*, Naples 1975; and for women's consciousness, U. Prokop, *Realtà e desiderio. L'ambivalenza femminile*, Milan 1978.

5   Revelli, *Il mondo dei vinti.*

6   See A. Bravo and L. Scaraffia, 'Ruolo femminile e identità nelle contadine delle Langhe: un'ipotesi di storia orale', in *Rivista di storia contemporanea*, 1979(1).

7   Oral account of Nina Rinaldi (b 1893).
8   ,,   ,,   Luisa Nebbia (b 1901).
9   ,,   ,,   Maria Civalleri (b 1900).
10 ,,   ,,   Nina Rinaldi.
11 ,,   ,,   Maria Chiavarino (b 1894).
12 ,,   ,,   Nina Rinaldi.
13 ,,   ,,   Domenica Bertaina (b 1901).
14 ,,   ,,   Maria Bernardino (b 1893).
15 ,,   ,,   Rita (b 1902). In 1917, the worsening of living conditions in the region was such that there was a protest demonstration with insults, rocks, and

vegetables thrown against the 'carabinieri', with the workers hidden in a tannery, the railroad station, and the grain warehouse: see Forcella & Monticone, *Plotone di esecucuzione*, op. cit. p. 124−6. This event does not often appear in the oral accounts, perhaps because it occurred in a nearby village and not in that of the women interviewed.

16 Oral account of Spirita Arneodo (b 1891).
17 Oral account of Maria Bonetti (b 1903).
18 See the correspondence of the soldier Sabino Traversa with his wife in A. Bandand 'Problemi e aspetti della participazione dei contadini delle Langhe alla prima guerra mondiale', University of Turin, 1979, unpublished dissertation supervised by Anna Bravo.
19 Oral account of Spirita Arneodo.
20   ,,   ,,   Spirita Arneodo.
21   ,,   ,,   Maria Domini (b 1896).
22   ,,   ,,   Spirita Arneodo.
23   ,,   ,,   Spirita Arneodo.
24   ,,   ,,   Lucia Cravero (b 1892).
25   ,,   ,,   Carolina Arneodo (b 1902).
26   ,,   ,,   Angiolina Boschis (b 1893).
27   ,,   ,,   Maria Cagnasso (b 1893).
28   ,,   ,,   Maria Chiavarino.
29   ,,   ,,   Lucia Cravero.
30   ,,   ,,   Nina Rinaldi.
31 On the phenomenon of desertion, see Revelli, *Il mondo dei vinti*, Vol II, Le Langhe and Introduction.
32 Oral account of Nina Rinaldi.
33   ,,   ,,   Maria Domini.
34   ,,   ,,   Nina Rinaldi.
35 See Revelli, *Il Mondo dei vinti*, Vol II, Le Langhe.
36 *Ibid*; and N. Gallerano, '*Il Mondo dei vinti*', in *Rivista di storia contemporanea*, 1978(4).
37 Oral account of Nina Rinaldi.
38 M. Isnenghi, 'Valori populari e valori ''ufficali'' nella mentalità del soldato fra le due guerre mondiali', in *Quaderni storici*, no 38, 1978, p. 704.
39 Oral account of Luisa Nebbia.
40 Oral account of Angiolina Boschis.

Women and work between the World Wars: the Amsterdam seamstresses

Nelleke Bakker and Jaap Talsma

Female labour in the Netherlands was only widely recognised as a social problem for the first time in the 1880s. Of course, women in this country too, have always done a lot of work besides their housekeeping duties. But until well into the 19th century, family labour dominated the economy in the agrarian as well as in the industrial sector, and, compared with other countries, relatively few women worked outside their homes. Women never entered factories in large numbers. This can at least partially be explained by the late start of industrialisation in the Netherlands: in recent publications the 'take-off' is dated in the nineties, when there were enough men to supply the demand for labour.[1] But in the 20th century female employment outside the home still lagged behind by comparison with other European countries.[2]

The advocates of special protection for female workers, who took their arguments mainly from situations abroad, were the first to start the debate on female labour. Standpoints in this debate were defined by attitudes towards the social position of women in general: in the predominant bourgeois ideology, women were seen first and foremost as housewives and mothers. Their principal task was to take care of the family—an unmarried girl being doomed to this future task. The impact of this ideology was strengthened further by the position of church-based groups in the Dutch socio-political system. Catholics as well as orthodox Calvinists considered the nuclear family to be the divine cornerstone of society. Basing their policy on this view, coalition governments of denominational political parties from the beginning of the 19th to the mid-20th century repeatedly attempted to restrict, or even to forbid, the employment of married women. Through the churches, and more particularly through the not unimportant, denominational labour movement, this ruling ideology had a manifest and direct influence on the consciousness of particular sections of the working class. But it was an ideology that was widespread in other parts of the working class too.

About the turn of the century, two groups challenged the ruling ideas about women's place in society. The bourgeois feminists demanded equal rights for men and women in every respect. One of the rights they claimed for women was the right to waged work. Some of them therefore completely rejected the idea of special protection for employed women. For example they opposed the *Arbeidswet* (Labour Law) of 1889 which restricted working hours for women to eleven hours a day. On the other hand, Marxist intellectuals considered participation in the production process a necessary condition for the liberation of women: in their opinion this condition could only be fulfilled after a socialist revolution, but meanwhile women's double burden could be lightened to some extent by welfare provisions and labour protection. However, they condemned as reactionary every attempt to prevent female labour. On this point not everybody in the socialist movement agreed with the Marxists: in the trade unions and among the reformists in the Social Democratic Party – *SDAP (Sociaal-Democratische Arbeiders Partij)* – many men took their stand with the ruling bourgeois ideology in their prejudices against women. For example, the Social Democratic leadership hesitated to claim universal suffrage for women along with universal suffrage for men; and within the socialist labour movement, the proponents of prohibition of employment for married women had to be checked repeatedly by the action of the socialist women's propaganda clubs *BSDVC (Bond van Sociaal-Democratische Vrouwen propaganda clubs).*[3]

In the 1920s, after the achievement of universal suffrage for women in 1919, the bourgeois feminist movement fell rapidly into decay. The BSDVC was also changing in character at this time. As a result, the active counterbalance to the ruling 'mother-cult' faded away. At the same time, as a consequence of a slowly rising standard of living in the working class, a growing proportion of married women could afford the luxury of not doing any waged labour. It must be mentioned at this point that the rate of female employment in the Netherlands did not rise substantially during the First World War. Because of the neutrality of this country, there was no need to force women to enter the labour market in large numbers, as there was in the countries which were at war. Subsequently the number of female employees, especially married women and widows, remained very low in comparison with other European countries.[4] Between the World Wars, more and more women took it for granted that their work outside the home was *supplementary* and *temporary*. The interdependent relationship between this attitude and 'external' circumstances is the subject of this paper.

According to the existing literature, female labour has been in many respects characterised by marginality, at least from the 19th century until the Second World War.[5] Low wages are characteristic of all female labour. Girls tend to accept low wages more readily than boys because they regard their work as temporary and their wages as a supplement to the wages of their fathers. Expecting their employment to be temporary, they are less inclined to value a professional education. Consequently they mainly get the less-skilled and low-paid jobs. Failure to acquire sufficient professional skills is also disadvantageous to the few older wage-labouring women and these women, whether married, unmarried or widows, are faced with the wage-depressing influence of the large number of low-paid girls as well. In general women do not resist low pay with much energy, rarely following the example of male trade unionism. Difficulties in organising young girls are mainly due to the way in which they regard their work as temporary. Adult and especially married women predominantly work in 'domestic industry' as home workers or outworkers: a form of industry notorious for its low rate of organisation. For the employer, female labour is attractive in those areas where labour costs constitute the greater part of production costs and this is part of the explanation for the concentration of workers in particular sectors and occupations; the other attraction is that female occupations are commonly connected with the traditional idea of the 'good housewife' and her tasks.

We will now try to give a more concrete form to this general picture by focussing on women working in the clothing trades. A variety of statistical sources show the dominant position of female labour in these trades. Women constituted three quarters of the labour force in them as a whole.[6] In some branches (ladies' clothes, underwear) the proportion of women employed approached 90%. Between the wars the majority of these women – and even more than the statistics can show – were still working in small workshops, as outworkers in their homes, or as independent homeworkers. In this context it should be noted that married women and widows mostly worked in their homes, while girls and younger women worked predominantly in workshops and factories. In the workshops and factories there was a trend towards concentration and rationalisation. In larger workshops, division of labour became normal, and in some workshops the assembly line was introduced at the height of the great depression. In this kind of business the workers were mainly unmarried girls. Though the total number of registered employed women in the clothing trades was declining slightly (the number of women homeworkers is systematically underrated), the proportion of young girls was rising. In spite of concentration, wages in this whole sector still formed a major part of production costs. Capital investment was relatively low and mechanisation was limited chiefly to sewing machines. As we have seen, all these points are considered to be characteristic of a branch of industry where female labour predominates. The same can be said of another aspect: the work of seamstresses can be seen to be an extension of traditional female tasks. In pre-industrial times tailors only made clothes for a small section of society; ladies' and children's clothes were nearly all made at home by women. Until recently girls were given instruction at school in *nuttige handwerken* (useful needlework), for proficiency in needlework would do credit to a good housewife.

The skill required by a seamstress distinguished her job from other typically female occupations such as servant or worker in the textile or food industry. Certainly, the introduction of the assembly line and increased division of labour reduced the need for skill, but in most workshops a strong strain of the handicraft origin lingered in the work. In this context we should notice the importance of skill and experience in opening up some possibilities for careers in this trade for women.

Another difference between seamstresses and other women workers was their social background. The majority of the fathers and husbands of the seamstresses can be classified as skilled labourers. Seamstresses, possibly with shop girls, seem to have taken an intermediate position between the typically unskilled women workers, on the one hand, and the office girls, nurses and teachers, on the other.[7] Until the last World War, however, these latter occupations were only open to girls of middle-class origin.

It follows from all these data that the wage-labour of seamstresses fits into the general pattern by being objectively *temporary* and *supplementary*. But how did seamstresses themselves experience their work and lives? Because written sources could tell us little apart from providing some general data we decided to use oral evidence. By using interviews we trust to have changed dead figures into living women.[8] Behind the collective behaviour known from statistics, there are lots of different individual motivations which can only be known by interviewing. Moreover, interviewing deepened our understanding of certain infrastructural aspects of the clothing trades, especially of the 'domestic industry'.

Mainly because in our period about 25% of all Dutch seamstresses worked and lived in the capital city, we decided to do our interviewing among (former) Amsterdam seamstresses. An appeal in the local press produced nearly 300 replies from women willing to co-operate. From these we selected a quota sample of sixty women to be interviewed, using the following criteria: place of work (factory, large or small workshop, at home); kind of work (ready-mades, bespoke tailoring, underwear, etc.); and age group. We also requested and received additional written inform-ation from over a hundred women we did not interview. This is the story all these women together told us.

*   *   *   *

At thirteen, or later on at fourteen, a girl left school. A working class family could not afford a girl's education to be extended beyond school-leaving age.

> It was out of the question that they could get me a good education. There was no money for that.[9]

The women we interviewed nearly all had the choice of two jobs: becoming a servant girl or a seamstress. These jobs were valued above factory worker or charwoman by their parents because, especially at the workshop, the skilled worker's daughters — marriage being their destiny — would learn a real job with skills that would always be useful in their future households. These skills were also welcomed by their mothers to whom they could immediately become a great help in making clothes for the often large families.

> Mum used to say: 'If you learn to sew, you'll make some money and later on you can make your own clothes and you can help me too.'[10]

The possibility that a girl would have to support herself some day was part of the argument.

> Then I had to learn a job, sewing. It was mum, who told me so: 'You'll never know what life will bring, but seamstresses will always be needed.'[11]

After her 48 hour week in the workshop, a girl had many duties in the family. Usually her mother did not work outside the home, and her father never worked in it. Housekeeping was the second job a girl had to learn. Added to that, she had to do needlework in the evening—altogether a heavy weight on young shoulders. Still, most seamstresses had some real leisure: dancing or going to the cinema on Saturday nights and walking and bicycling excursions at the week-ends, often together with friends from the workshop. Eight women we interviewed were members of the Social Democratic youth organisation *AJC (Arbeiders Jeugd Centrale)* and took part in its activities. A still smaller number of women had no time at all for themselves, like the one who always had to help her father, a homeworking tailor:

I did all the handwork: making seams and buttonholes. There were no fixed hours; often we worked till midnight. And then up early in the morning to finish the lot. [12]

A girl started as an apprentice: she had to learn her trade on the job. During her apprenticeship she was an aid, sitting next to an accomplished seamstress. She earned an apprentice wage and one after another she had to learn all the stages of making coats and dresses. Because of greater division of labour the apprenticeship was only three to four months in the larger ready-mades' factories. In the smaller workshops the apprenticeship was longer, especially in those where ladies' fashions were manufactured, because there the seamstresses still made complete coats and dresses. It took a few years to become an accomplished seamstress in these workshops and the women themselves really had the feeling of learning a trade.

In the old days you could take pleasure in having made something good, you could be proud of knowing your trade well. [13]

In the shops where underwear, blouses, shirts and linenware were manufactured it was the same: one seamstress made a whole piece and the apprenticeship was two years. This was fine and delicate work but was paid much less well than outer-clothes' manufacture. Only in the bespoke tailoring shops were there a relatively large number of men working beside the women. But the number of these shops was rapidly declining while the number of ready-mades' shops and factories was increasing. In the bespoke tailoring shops, the highly skilled work was done by men while the women did the routine jobs.

With progressive rationalisation of production and increasing mechanisation which brought the assembly-line into the larger ready-mades' factories in the second half of the thirties, there was a certain decline in skilled labour. Mass production made it less important to learn the skills of the job and, accordingly, pleasure faded away. Skilled workers despised working on the assembly line. The women we interviewed called it 'boring', 'awful' or 'nerve-racking'. In general only the unskilled younger girls worked on the assembly line where most women did not last long.

Then we all had to make small parts. There were marks on the belt, the sewing-machines were standing beside. When your mark came up you picked off the stuff. When your next mark came up you had to be ready and put the stuff back on the belt. At times every one was behind; it got on your nerves.[14]

Women's wages were low—in any case insufficient for them to support themselves. At home the girls had to hand over their wages in return for a little pocket money. Even when women and men were doing the same job, unions and employers still agreed on lower wages for women in their contracts. Such contracts only applied to a small number of shops and it was easy to get round them. Piece-wages were the rule: only women in higher positions, like those who made the samples for the ready-mades, or did the cutting, and also department managers, got fixed weekly wages—later, the girls on the assembly line too. A seamstress could improve her wage by extra effort, but an employer had several cunning ways of keeping wages down. During sickness, holidays and often also during the slack season, no wages were paid, and quite often there was no extra pay for overtime. As a result of this the actual wage varied substantially from week to week and from season to season. Nevertheless, resistance against low wages was exceptional. Resistance was generally spontaneous and defensive: against wage-cuts, sackings, unreasonable fines and more time-consuming work for the same pay:

If we got underpaid for a coat . . . we protested. We said: 'That's not enough, we must have more for such a coat.' So we got five or ten cents more.[15]

*　　　*　　　*　　　*

The phase as a workshop seamstress ended for most women with marriage. Like most Dutch women at this time, the women we interviewed generally married when they were about twenty five. Like their mothers, they married skilled labourers: masons, typographers, steel-workers, carpenters or tailors. They met their husbands in their free time: in the neighbourhood, at dances or in the youth movement. Most of the seamstresses left the workshop and lost contact with their colleagues when they got married—to give up outside employment was the accepted thing to do. Women explaining this in the interviews used expressions like: 'When you married you left the workshop like you left your family'; or, 'That was the way it was. You didn't really have a choice.' Sometimes the woman's husband urged her to stop: 'Yes, my husband didn't want me to work in the workshop any longer.'

Some worked on for a while, usually until the birth of the first child.

This is not surprising because their whole education had been geared to the idea of future marriage and motherhood. The members of the Social Democratic youth organisation were no exception; even they thought it self-evident that marriage meant the end of their wage-labour, at least in the workshop. Five women we interviewed never married, but they still had been influenced by this ideology ever since they were girls.

Marriage in combination with the birth of the first child meant a turning-point for the majority of the women we interviewed. Only five continued their work in the workshop for any length of time after marriage, and they recognised that their situation was exceptional because their husbands were unemployed or away at sea. Especially when they had a child, the shortage of crèches or other welfare provisions made them conscious of their special position. It is easy enough to imagine the arduous duties of a woman who was both working in the factory and having to take care of her little daughter at the same time:

Up at six to make breakfast, I washed my child and at seven left the house. First I brought my daughter to the crèche, where I would pick her up again at half past five. On my way home I bought bread. Then cooking, putting the child to bed and preparing the food for the next day—I always did that for two days. Friday evenings I had a charwoman, with whom I cleaned up the mess. Saturdays I came home from work around one o'clock and did my shopping for the whole week. On weekday-evenings I only fetched bread and milk—you could do that then because the shops were open till eight. Saturday evenings I bathed my daughter and then put her to bed. Then I put the clothes in to soak and next morning I'd wash them out.[17]

This same woman also illustrates the opportunity that just a few women had to make a career. Because of her skill and experience, she had a more responsible position in a ready-made clothing factory. She inspected the work of the younger girls and earned a higher wage, a so-called 'man's wage', which enabled her to pay for the crèche and a charwoman. Not only her wage but also the satisfaction she got from her work allowed her to enjoy it, in sharp contrast to the girls who had more routine jobs.

Although marriage meant leaving the workshop, in many cases it did not however mean being relieved of wage labour. Almost all women who left the workshop on marriage or at the birth of the first child exchanged wage labour out of doors for wage labour within the walls of their own home. Either regularly or occasionally they took on sewing for some manufacturer or on their own for relatives and acquaintances—in one case for a husband, who was himself a homeworking tailor. The women, in common with the census enumerators, did not think of this work as professional labour and they do not therefore usually appear in the occupational statistics: so that here oral evidence fills a gap in the written information. To keep this labour hidden was also profitable for the employer, because it enabled him to evade labour legislation. One woman literally worked behind close curtains to hide what she was doing from the neighbours.

Of course, behind closed curtains in those days. What would people say? You could use the money.[18]

In the better working class quarters, wage labour for married women was not acceptable in any case: 'That was something you didn't do. A working wife was the last step to poverty.'[19] But homework was accepted more easily than employment outside the home, because it enabled a woman to keep her house tidy and an eye on the children at the same time. It was scarcely ever recognised that the two tasks might be incompatible.

The earnings of homeworking women were usually a necessary supplement to the husband's wage or, for two of the women interviewed, to the insufficient unemployment benefit.

Remembering their former homework, many women tend to underestimate the importance of their earnings, pretending it was only a small contribution to the family income—for special expenses, for example.

Sometimes I did work a while and then sometimes I didn't. For instance, when we'd bought something special, then I did. And after that I did nothing for a couple of weeks—just the house and the child.[20]

Some women also stress the pleasure they got out of this work; they did not want to be at a loose end. One woman mentions the importance of keeping her professional knowledge up to the mark.

Homeworking actually had undeniable advantages over the workshop for women with children. The freedom to organise their own time-schedule and the possibility of contact with women neighbours compensated for the loss of workshop friends and persuaded them to take the never-ending character of homework for granted—just as they were accustomed to assume their household duties. So their mothers *had* been right: the skills of a seamstress were always needed.

Whatever she did, paid work or not, the first task of a married woman was housekeeping. It was taken for granted that she would sew clothes for the children and herself. In this way a good seamstress could save substantially on the family budget. Husbands almost never helped in the house, so the responsibility for the household rested completely on her shoulders. Tidiness during those years had become the most valued quality in housekeeping, even among skilled labourers. Consequently the burden of housekeeping was heavier than today, and more so as modern household equipment had not yet been invented or was too expensive for working class families. Looking back most of the women regret all that scrubbing.

Always scrubbing and scrubbing and working. It was madness. I don't do that no more. But it all had to be clean, the windows, everything – madness.[21]

Though wage-labour meant a heavy burden for these women, they still spent much of their time on household duties. Normally these repetitive household tasks had priority, but there were situations when wage-labour took precedence: when the lot had to be finished in time or a client was waiting for a coat or a dress. 'When I worked I had little time for housekeeping. I still did the cooking, but it was a quick and easy meal.'[22]

There was hardly any free time. Except for visiting relatives on Sundays there was little opportunity for social life. And the little free time a seamstress had was not her own; she was expected to use it to amuse or take extra care of her family. The task of a woman who had to look after her children, as well as the household duties and her paid work, was extremely heavy. It is no wonder that most of the seamstresses we interviewed had only one or two children and sometimes none at all. Although contraceptives were fairly unreliable, their use was quite widespread. The relatively late birth of the first child – in many cases one and a half to two years after marriage – appears as evidence of this. And women with their double burden had every reason to take responsibility for the decisions in family planning. One of the women told us – and we do not think she was exceptional – that it was not *her* desire to have another child.

My husband would have wanted another one. But I said, only if you make more money. It all came down on me. I had to take care of everything and even more.[23]

Despite their incredibly heavy daily work the women we interviewed spoke positively about their lives, contrasting them with those of their mothers 'My mother had six children and I had only two. Besides, housekeeping has become much easier.'[24] As for them, they only did two jobs, seven days a week!

*   *   *   *

We assumed at the start an increasing impact on the working class of the ruling ideology of female labour. So far it appears to us that the attitudes and behaviour of seamstresses in Amsterdam can be explained partly by the internalisation of elements of bourgeois ideology, made possible by the rising standard of living of some parts of the working class. Marriage for almost all of them was much more important than wage labour, but the gap between material circumstances and the ideals in which they believed had to be bridged by homework. The ideas of *temporary* and *supplementary* employment thus not only influenced the treatment of women workers by employers, but also the behaviour of the seamstresses themselves. [25]

As a result, the rate of union membership among the seamstresses was very low. Several women we interviewed had never heard of the existence of a union in the clothing sector and this is the more striking in that almost all of them once they were adults voted – like their husbands – for the Social Democrats. A seamstress with an explicit socialist background told us that her father gave strong encouragement to her brothers to join the union, but he did not think it urgent for his daughter. 'Yes, now I could say, yes, I was a member. But at that time, no, I was not a member. In those days women did not meddle with politics.' [26]

For the mass of women workers an additional factor should be mentioned here: in many cases pocket money was insufficient for payment of the union subscription. For married women active union membership was difficult because of their double burden. Moreover, as we have seen, most of them worked isolated from each other in the domestic industry, a form of production the unions were continuously campaigning against. This shows the unions were quite oblivious of the special positions of women workers: and other examples of this blindness could be mentioned. The unions apparently did not realise the advantages which married women themselves could find in domestic industry. It was not that the demands which they made on behalf of homeworkers were wholly irrelevant: indeed the unions did denounce the enormous wage differences between men and women. But they failed to make any consistent claim for equal pay. Their principal objective was to safeguard the work and wages of the organised tailors—that is to say, the men. In this context working women sometimes appeared as competitors rather than comrades of the men. It is no wonder that women were not very union-minded. [27]

As we have seen, action by the seamstresses to gain improvements in their conditions of employment was infrequent and usually spontaneous. and defensive. Because union membership was uncommon, they could not depend on the unions. Spontaneous action seldom led to more permanent organisation. Certainly the unions sometimes tried to take over the action but they hardly ever succeeded in consolidating the ground gained. Since they regarded their work in the shop as temporary and they had no ambitions for careers, the seamstresses saw no sense in taking the trouble.

They thought it all mighty fine. Yes, that was caused by well—they were all young girls, weren't they, not people who had to take care of a family? So they thought – well, only a couple of years, you know, till – then I'll get married, that'll be it—well you don't get a good fighting-spirit that way, do you? [28]

The possibility of collective action was also hampered by the hierarchical relations and competitive atmosphere which characterised work organisation in the workshops and factories.

Most seamstresses reconciled themselves to their situation. From whom else might they have expected help in changing the deep-rooted sexual division of labour? We have already mentioned the diminishing interest in women's affairs of the Social Democrats; and the weakening feminist movement could be of little practical help. In 1935 a committee for the defence of working women was formed by the joint efforts of all the women's organisations with a non-denominational background, (*Comite tot Verdediging van de Vrijheid van Arbeid voor de Vrouw*). But the main objective of this agitation was to stop the government policy of discharging married women staff from the public services and the restriction by law of the employment of married women in general. [29] As far as the everyday, working conditions of the mass of women workers was concerned, the campaign had little significance.

So traditional role patterns and a corresponding ideology conditioned the position of women workers in the Amsterdam clothing trades. In the years between the wars the strength of this ideology was increasing rather than waning. The web of temporary work and supplementary, hence low wages remained intact. Female labour continued to offer extra profits to the employers who could keep a cheap labour force of very flexible size at their disposal, and in the clothing trades it retained this economic function until after the Second World War. But when by the end of the sixties traditional role patterns at last began to crack, a lot of sewing machines were already on the move to southern Europe or to countries in the Third World.

This paper is based on material collected by the participants of the seminars in women's history in the History department of the University of Amsterdam in 1976/77 and 1977/78 by:

Wietske van Agtmaal (1)
Nelleke Bakker (2)
Martje Bartel (2)
Anne de Boer
Frank Galesloot (2)
Janny Gerrits (1)
Lia de Graaff
Wilfried van Hal (2)

Rina Korporaal
Frank Maas (2)
Suzanne van Norden (1)
Jaap Talsma (3)
Carla Verberk (1)
Marijke Weisglas (2)
Liesbeth Wiewel

(1) These four participants, together with Marja ter Schegget and Jeroen Strengers have written a report on the seamstresses in the period 1870–1914. This report was published in March 1979 as an internal publication of the History Department of the University of Amsterdam.
(2) These six participants are together preparing a report on the period 1914–1940. This report is available in manuscript at the History Department.
(3) Supervisor.

Most of the above-mentioned participants commented on the draft of this paper, although only the two authors can be held responsible for the present text.

We owe a great debt to George Welling for helping us to translate this paper.

Notes

1 J.A. de Jonge, 'Industrial growth in the Netherlands, 1850–1914', *Acta Historiae Neerlandica*, V (1971), pp. 159–212.
2 In 1938 Mrs W. Posthumus-van der Goot collected and published statistical data about the employment of married women in the Netherlands as compared with other countries:

Number of employed (agriculture excluded)

	Total	Women		Married women only	
		number	%	number	%
The Netherlands	2.546.790	658.261	25,8	55.578	2,2
Sweden	1.851.531	654.214	35,1	82.313	4,4
Great Britain	17.654.095	5.550.280	31,4	888.150	5,0
Switzerland	1.529.290	559.973	36,6	132.121	8,6
Belgium	3.115.253	851.805	27,3	315.338	10,1
France	13.907.655	4.706.615	33,8	1.856.964	13,4

(These data are based on the 1930 censuses. Those concerning Great Britain and France on the 1931 censuses)

Source: Annet Schoot Uiterkamp, 'Terug naar het paradijs? Akties tegen de beperking van vrouwenarbeid in de jaren dertig', *Jaarboek vor de geschiedenis van socialisme en arbeidersbeweging* (1978), p. 190.

3 W.N. Schilstra, *Vrouwenarbeid in landbouw en industrie in Nederland in de tweede helft van de negetniende eeuw*, Reprint (Nijmegen, 1976), pp. 99–102.
4 See note 2 above.
5 For example: Schilstra, *Vrouwenarbeid*, pp. 27–28.
6 This section is mainly based on census returns. Censuses were taken in 1920 and 1930. The next census was not taken until 1947.

7   See also Selma Leydesdorff, 'Vrouwen dragen geen witte boorden maar schone jurken' *Socialisties-feministiese teksten* 1 (1978), pp. 204–221.
8   The interviewing was done by the persons mentioned above (see acknowledgements). For the sake of convenience we simply use the words 'we interviewed', whenever we mean 'one of the participants in the seminar interviewed'.
9   Interview no. 15; for the sake of confidentiality we refer to our interviews by number. The original interview reports can be consulted at the Historisch Seminarium of the University of Amsterdam.
10 Interview no 15.
11 Interview no 37
12 Interview no 10
13 Interview no 54
14 Interview no 11
15 Interview no 19
16 Interview no 17
17 Interview no 20
18 Interview no 56
19 Interview no 56
20 Interview no 17
21 Interview no 3
22 Interview no 45
23 Interview no 20
24 Interview no 44
25 Other factors conditioning the behaviour and attitude of the seamstresses fall outside the scope of the paper.
26 Interview no 18.
27 This paragraph is mainly based on union periodicals: Het Kleeding-bedrijf (Bond in de Kleedingindustrie); Nederlandsche Roomsch-Katholieke Naaisters- en Kleedermakerscourant (Nederlandsche Roomsch-Katholieke Naaisters- en Kleedermakersbond Sint Gerardus Majella); Onze Klaroen (Nederlandsche Christelijke Bond in de Kleedingindustrie).
28 Interview no 1.
29 *Van moeder op dochter. Het aandeel van de vrouw in een veranderende wereld*, Onder redactie van W.H. Posthumus-van der Goot (Leiden 1948), pp. 418–434.

An Auvergnat wood merchant's shop-sign showing the characteristic mixture of merchandise sold by immigrants to Paris from the Auvergne. *Cliché Musée des arts et traditions populaires, Paris.*

The Life History Approach to the Study of Internal Migration: how Women and Men Came to Paris Between the Wars[1]

Isabelle Bertaux-Wiame

France is unique in Europe: a country whose people stayed on. In the age of the great inter-continental migrations which populated the New Worlds – the Americas, Australia, New Zealand – all the other nations of Europe bled themselves to swell the immense migratory currents. Only the French because of their particular history, and helped by the richness of their own land, chose instead to bear fewer children, and remain confined within their own frontiers.

Yet this immobility is deceptive, for during the same period *internal migration* was growing very significantly. And this movement was not just drawing country-dwellers into industrial towns, commercial centres and the ports, but still more, and above all, into the industrial, commercial, administrative, political and cultural metropolis: to Paris.

Migration of the French population towards Paris and its suburbs goes back centuries. During the 19th and especially the 20th century it accelerated—so much so that today ten million out of a total French population of fifty two millions live in the Paris area. Yet this long-standing movement has been surprisingly little studied. The best studies have been carried out by demographic historians (like Louis Chevalier[2]), demographers[3] and geographers[4] and are consequently based on *statistics*. They provide us with a picture of the growth of the Parisian population, but not of its geographical origins, because the information collected by the censuses about the birthplaces of Parisians has not been included in the available statistics. As for the *sociology* of internal migration, it is still less developed, and has largely focussed on the problem of rural depopulation, the desertion of the villages: French sociologists have shown much less interest in the arrival of migrants in the city.

Statistically based studies are certainly essential. Where they are available, they set out the human flows of migration, regionally and between sexes, and their evolution over time. But it is beyond their purpose to allow a deeper, sociological understanding of the nature of population movements. It is no accident that while in the 19th century demographers were solely concerned with the 'biological' attributes of population (numbers, sex, age, mortality, fertility), they have now extended their interest to 'economic' characteristics (profession, occupation, unemployment, level of education): demography is not a 'pure' science, but rather the scientific eye of the state counting its flock. Population was considered first as a biological mass; but it is more and more seen as a potential source of labour power, an economic resource.

Some demographers such as Guy Pourcher or Yves Tugault have felt the need to complement demographic studies with a sociological approach. They have tended to focus, however, on the question of the *motives of migrants*. Such a question is more psychosocial than sociological. If sociology is correct in seeing people as caught up in webs of social relations, then we should aim at uncovering the structures of these webs, and the movements of these structures which have produced the migratory flows. Furthermore, migrations have not only causes; they also have consequences. An urban population which is predominantly from a rural background ought not to 'function' in the same way as a population which has been urbanised for generations. But precisely what kind of differences does this make? If we knew, we might be able to reinterpret some of the cultural differences which distinguish, say, Londoners from Parisians, or English from French, as differences between populations with an urban or a rural background.

In the work of contemporary demographers, the lack of a sociological perspective is to a certain extent concealed by the presentation of individual case-histories as illustrations of general social processes. But this leads to an oscillation between statistical and psychological modes of thought, an oscillation which revolves around a truly sociological viewpoint without ever coming face to face with it.

While these studies cover an important field and enable the historical evolution of emigration to be established, they remain incapable of identifying the *social relations* which lie behind emigration or, to be more precise, behind the different currents of emigration. A new methodological approach is essential in order to reveal these relationships, and to separate out the principal types of population flow.

A historian approaches the somewhat abstract, a-historical categories of demographers with scepticism. A 'permanent' migration may not have the same sociological cause or social meaning in two different periods; nor, similarly, may a 'seasonal' migration. I suspected that a critical transformation in the traditional character of migration might have occurred around the period of the First World War. The growth of large-scale industry in the Paris region, already started before 1914 and continuing through the 1920s, created a very important new labour market. Basic changes in the rural world forced a large part of the population to reassess its situation and consider a transfer to industrial work. The social upheavals brought about by the war set going a migration of women and this *female* migration established new general currents. Women's migration stimulated men's migration, for it forced farm workers who wanted to marry to look further afield.

The period between the two world wars thus looked as if it might be crucial. But the true reason why I chose to start my work there was that those informants who themselves participated in the migrations are now disappearing.[5] This was therefore the starting-point of my research which, for the moment, focusses simply on Paris and its region. I have been collecting *life stories* from elderly Parisians who were born in other regions of France, and came to Paris as young men and women.

The first task was to find them. One possible source of contact seemed to be the voluntarily formed, regional associations known as Amicales, which reunite migrants coming from a given region—e.g., the Auvergnats of Paris, the Bretons, the Creusois, etc. I was soon to discover, however, that these Amicales give access to a *particular* category of migrants only: those who have succeeded in life. Some of them are self-made men: they started from little or nothing, and they 'made it big'; they are at the heads of the Amicales, their example is very often quoted, they are the most *visible* of all migrants. Others came to Paris already well-equipped, either with some capital and a clear career plan, or with some educational qualification, or with some security through a recommendation to a 'notable'. As for the migrants whose life experience has not been a success story – the vast majority, probably – the managers of the Amicales not merely pretended to ignore their existence, after having attempted to conceal it, but they even tried to prevent me from contacting them. Yet, in effect, through this they helped me to understand their true nature. Their fundamental belief is not, as they profess, in the value of 'keeping alive the community of people born in —— region', but rather in maintaining in Paris itself the kind of social relations which existed in rural society—relations of patronage, the influence of charismatic leaders, and so on. An exception to this is the Amicale des Bretons, which is led by communist activists; but again it proved impossible to use the Amicales network to contact 'unsuccessful' migrants, this time because of the mistrust of politically-conscious leaders towards any external inquiry.

To contact the hidden part of the great iceberg of immigration thus required another approach. Consequently I started visiting old people's homes and clubs. These homes and clubs were primarily concerned with women.

Old men stick much more tenaciously to living at home, so that for them neighbourhood cafés provide the usual place for the regular reunions with which they break their solitude. I also went to the reunions organised for retired members by some trade union branches, like bakers and taxi-drivers. These reunions provide not only for social contact, but also information and mutual help in dealing with the red-tape of bureaucracy.

In novels, two contrasting images are offered of the migrant to Paris. There is the young man, courageous and enterprising, leaving his village to seek his fortune in the big city, eager to succeed; and there is the adult migrant, alone in the metropolis, helplessly pitted against the twists of the labour market and the traps of city life. From what I have been able to observe, both images are caricatures, which means they are at the same time false *and* revealing. The image of the free-willed hero, fully conscious of his goal, his strategy, his acts, does not depict real life, but may be a model that some young men (and even women?) do indeed have in their heads. The image of the proletarian burdened by his fate, with no hold left on his life's path, also depicts a certain reality, but one which is not particular to migrants. However, it may well be that it is among migrants that the *fear* of such a fate is strongest.

What is certainly wrong about both images is that they are images of *individuals, lone men*, like all characters in novels; and both, of course, are images of men. It is understandable that novelists should project themselves in the characters they create, and that they should conceive of people as autonomous individuals: this is one of the basic rules of the novel as a literary form. But in reality, migrants are never alone. They are always located in some *network of social relations* which both guides them and sustains them, provides them with opportunities and protects them from threatening risks: in short, which *controls* them.

These networks, it would seem, are thus all-important. But they grow, develop, and fade, in the wake of the concrete activity of migrants: at work, with friends, with parents; they are networks of *relations between people* which leave no written trace behind them. None of their dealings were formally established, so that they can only be known through being recorded at source. These networks, moreover, were of crucial importance to people who came to Paris without either capital or qualifications. They provided not only a supportive social circle; it was through these same networks that migrants would seek out a better job, a better place to live, even a wife or husband. Hence the relevance of an oral history approach.

                    *   *   *   *

When I started my research, I considered that the so-called 'pull' factor, that is, the drawing-power of the region of arrival, with its work and other opportunities, would be the critical factor, more important than 'push' from the region of departure, through unemployment, a low standard of living and so on. If the economic theory of 'migration as result of the two factors of push and pull' is rather mechanical, at least when Paris is the target, it deserves the label of 'pulling factor'. Paris, the city of bright lights! What a pole of attraction for the young provincial butterflies! I imagined already, probably as the result of my own literary readings as an adolescent, how the images of Paris penetrated into the depths of the countryside, reaching particular young men and women and awakening in them a desire, a longing for the famous city. I had in mind Balzac's novels, or the passionate, pathetic cry of Checkov's *Three Sisters:* 'To Moscow!'.

But in as far as I expected, somehow unconsciously, to find in the life stories indications, descriptions, allusions revealing the strength of the attraction which Paris exercised on the provincial, I was to be disappointed. Paris and its lights had no place in their stories. No homages to the Eiffel Tower. Not the slightest allusion to the magnetism of that great crowd in which the young immigrant is supposed to lose himself. Novels had affected me but not, so it seems, my informants.

On the contràry, what seemed to them essential was not where they were going, but what they were leaving, what they found hard to stand: farm life, village life, and sometimes their family too. Many had reached a breaking point; so, they left. Some went to the nearest city, others to Paris, but the important matter was to leave, not where to go.

First it had been necessary to find a means of going and, very often, this meant finding access to a network, however tenuous. Next they had to decide to follow one lead rather than another. The importance of opportunities in Paris played in the capital's favour. But its very large and diversified labour market remained an abstraction: for once a particular lead from this great world was chosen, it was usually followed to its end, with little attention given to alternative possibilities. It was as if there was not so much one labour market offering a multiplicity of choices, as a series of sectional markets each offering jobs of a certain type, reached through particular leads.

From this point of view the historical evolution of the Auvergnats is characteristic. The fact that in certain periods it was the Auvergne rather than the regions adjacent to Paris that produced the strongest flow of emigrants was not a mere accident. 19th century Paris was a great devourer of firewood, charcoal and coal. The heavily-wooded Auvergne, over 200 miles from Paris but linked to the capital by a navigable river, began to supply the city from the 18th century. On their way the Auvergnats passed by the rich vineyards of Burgundy; and before long the Auvergnat wood-merchant (the famous Paris 'bougnat') began to install some wine barrels in his cellar. It was down this well-established commercial path that the rural population of Auvergne found its way towards Paris, rather than to the much closer big towns of Lyons, Toulouse or Marseilles. The logic of this historical process may still be read in a nutshell on the shopfronts of the last remaining ''bougnats'': VINS-BOIS-CHARBONS.

Not all migrants, however, came from regions with such strong traditions of emigration. Most of them either had to find existing networks or more likely create new ones, which would fall apart almost as quickly as they were constructed. For example, during a break in the workshop, workers would be talking. One would mention his hopes of emigrating to earn more. A fellow worker would know somebody in just the next workshop who also wanted to leave. He would try to put both men in touch. It was only on the day of departure, on the station platform, that one of my informants met up with the person who was to take him away to Paris. It does not seem that these contacts were taken over by some people who were more generally involved than others. Each person was a link in a chain and the person best placed locally helped the next. At its very simplest this help might be no more than taking the same train and getting off for the same Hotel-Café-Restaurant. And there it would be necessary very quickly to make other relationships in order to find work somewhere. Generally, the migrant would only be out of work for one or two days. It was the very shifting character of these contacts which ensured their effectiveness. There was a constant adaptation to the needs of a particular situation. Yet behind the dealings recalled in each story, one can see the essential structure of the migratory path.

Among the networks of relationships, one took a principal role: that of the extended family. This was the only one whose structure was pre-established through parental connections. However, the links were often remarkably tenuous. The last-born of the family did not always know the eldest, who might have left before they were born; the eldest son had gone away to work, an emigrant who never came back and rarely, if ever, wrote. Once the parents died, the thin thread linking the siblings would be broken, and they might lose each other; all the more so if there was no inheritance to share.

For still more distant cousins, aunts, uncles, the bond was still more fragile. But on the other hand, it was precisely these weak ties which might provide a lead into a network extending as far as the big city. And if daily life separated the extended family, there were some special occasions which brought it together: baptisms, and especially marriages and funerals. These last ceremonies brought together the largest number of relatives, and allowed information to be circulated; news and inter-personal relations would be updated by encounters; the young ones could review the field of possible moves, and the adults who had already migrated, if they had set up a small business, could look for a young 'cousin' who was willing to come to the city and could be used as an unpaid 'family hand' for some time. The more extended the family net-work, the weaker, but also the better for reaching out towards something else.

So far we have been implicitly concerned with migrant *men*. All too often in this type of study women are left aside, almost ignored. For this reason I have been especially concerned to learn about women who had emigrated to Paris in order to *work* there—as distinguished from those who came to marry a man from their village who had already migrated. Step by step, thanks to the life-history approach, it became clear to me that despite apparent similarities (women, like men, emigrate to earn more) the method, conditions and significance of their migration were different. At its simplest, I would say the difference is that, while men move through the family network to find work, women move through job networks to find a family.

The difference between men and women, respecting the social logic underlying their lives, shows up both in their life stories, *and* in the way they tell them.

From what men say about their work, it seems that it gave them the feeling of 'who they were': a social identity. This is true of those who have succeeded, but also (to a lesser degree) of the others; in the second case more emphasis will be put on sociability in the workplace than on self-expression through work itself. Men seldom talk spontaneously about their family life—as if it was not really part of their life. *Their* life: men consider the life they have lived as *their own*; this is perhaps the key differ-ence from women. Men present their life as a series of self-conscious acts, a rational pursuit of well-defined goals—be it success, or simply '*la tranquillité*', quietness and security. Their whole story revolves around the sequence of *occupations* they have had, as if they insisted on jobs because work is the area where they are active. They present themselves as the subjects of their own lives—as the actors.

Women do not insist on this. Self-conscious acts are not their main interest. Instead, they will talk at length about their *relationship* to such or such a person. Their own life stories will include parts of the life stories of others. They bring into view the people around them, and their relations with these people. In contrast with men's accounts, women will not insist on what they have done; but rather on what relationships existed between themselves and persons close to them, what Mead has called their 'significant others'.

These differences are echoed in the very expressions and speech forms that men and women use. Men will use the 'I' much more often than women. The masculine 'I' definitely points to the subject of an action. The feminine 'I' often has a different meaning. It does not designate the narrator as subject, but as one pole of a relationship; it is the 'I' in relation to another person. And very often, women preferred to use 'we' or 'one' (*on* in French), thus denoting the particular relationship which underlay this part of their life: 'we' as 'my parents and us', or as 'my husband and me', or as 'me and my children'.

In an interview with a couple, one can see these deep differences brought out in the clashes which sometimes arise between the husband and wife in their accounts of the past. The man may tell the story of his life with a concern for chronological accuracy; but he will be constantly turning to his wife for help. For it is she, rather than him, who holds the family memory for dates—a memory nourished by innumerable stimulants in familiar objects and surroundings, faces, photographs and so on. And with the backing of this knowledge, she will keep on trying to intervene to correct her husband's account. Her corrections will always be in the same direction—*to subdue the 'I'*. The husband recounts an incident with himself as actor. She will retrieve a web of contradictory influences from the surrounding environment within which to place it, and her interventions will quite obviously frustrate her husband in his attempt to reconstruct his life story as the biography of a self-willed individual.

The life stories told by people from different social classes can be analysed in a similar way. Not only do they have different stories to tell, but they have a different relation to their life and, hence, to the *act* of telling it.[6]

It should not be forgotten that every biographical account takes place in the present time, and *in relation to the present*. For the person who tells his or her life-story, the first purpose is *not* to describe the past 'as it was', or even as it was experienced (*vécu*), but to confer to the past experience a certain *meaning*; a meaning which will contribute to the meaning of the present (and even to the 'future' whose image lies in the present under the form of projects, and projections onto the children). To tell one's life story is not only to talk or to remember; it is an act, an *encounter* with reality. If this encounter seems to limit itself to an account of the past, its orientation is in fact determined by the present, in two ways: first it reconstructs the meaning of the past from the present point of view; second, and more deeply, it gives meaning to the past *in order to* give meaning to the present, to the present life of the person. And this last meaning cannot be the same for all social groups.

Let me give an example. I was trying to discover what apprenticeship was like in artisan bakeries in the early 20th century. Because of the almost total absence of written sources I decided to collect information through interviews with retired bakers, both masters and workmen.[7] All my informants had had an almost identical experience of severe exploitation as apprentices. Now those who have remained workmen all their lives still remember apprenticeship today as a very tough period of their life; they remember how, from the age of 12 to 15, they would be woken up at midnight to work for 12 to 15 hours at a stretch, six and even seven days a week; and how, whenever they felt sleepy during nightwork, they would be hit and beaten by the master (who was himself made tense by the lack of sleep).

But those who, by contrast, later on became independent bakers, and in turn employed apprentices, seem to have forgotten all this. They remember the long hours of work, the learning of the various ways of the trade; but they have forgotten the pressure of the master. They instinctively connect every oppressive aspect of apprenticeship to the *technical* demands of bread-making. They consider the relations of work, the relations of master and apprentice in the workplace, not as authority relations, but as the necessary result of a kind of natural order deriving from technical necessities. Their descriptions of concrete situations are factually correct, yet all the same if one were to trust them entirely, one would get a very biased picture, because they have wholly reconstructed the *meaning* of the facts.

In my study on migrants, I put the emphasis on the first days and weeks of arrival in Paris. I wanted to know what it was like to turn up in a metropolis straight from a village, what it was like to look for a job, a place to stay, company. I thought it must have been pretty difficult, and was looking for accounts of hard times; and I expected to find such accounts in the life stories of those who had stayed workers or servants all their life. I expected that the other ones, the ones who had succeeded, would have forgotten this part of their life—like my master-bakers.

But it was just the reverse which had happened. Migrants who had been socially successful, looking back from the position they have now reached, can speak of the unhappiness of their childhood, their difficult start in the metropolis, the dreary lodgings they had for home then. But they can talk about it because they have left it all behind them. Some will talk complacently; others will point out – as if to justify their subsequent social climb – how much courage they must have had. I have found, by contrast, that migrants who cannot take such a distanced pride in themselves can be very reluctant to recall the miseries of their past. For them, to talk about the unhappiness of the past is to talk about the present, too. When this reluctance is overcome, not so much through my prompting, but spontaneously from within themselves, sometimes quite different sides are recaptured: an account of an impoverished childhood is suddenly lit up with memories of precious moments of happiness, of brioches on Sunday morning, of the family gathered round the fire at night, of the love of an affectionate parent.

*   *   *   *

The forms of life stories are therefore as important as the facts which they contain. And because of this, freedom of self-expression is all important. If it is true that we can learn not only from the facts of a life story but also from the way in which these are expressed, it is essential to ensure that informants organise their own stories in their own way. The facts of the story will allow us to see *social relations in action*. The forms, on the other hand, reveal the shape of the mind, the *cultural and ideological structures*, for it is through ideology and culture that interpretations are given to the real conditions of existence. Of course these cultural and ideological structures are more often than not unconscious. For instance, women do not intentionally choose to tell their lives in terms of personal relationships rather than as accounts of what they have themselves done; the form of their story only reflects the form of their real life, that is to say, the condition of women in French society. And if many individual men really believe they have been the subject of their life course—which is highly doubtful—it is simply because this is the way men are supposed to live their lives. When people tell their life stories, culture speaks through their mouths. There are several ways of listening to a life story. The way of the sociologist or the social historian implies 'listening beyond'—trying to hear, beyond the words of a given person, the speech of a social culture.

What made me conscious of the differences between men's and women's accounts was the life story of a 90-year-old woman. This woman had told me her story in the first person, just like a man; but this

had not caught my attention because I had just ended a series of interviews with men. But on relistening to her account, I realised that she had
spoken very little about the time when she was married. In fact the death
of her husband, which had given her the responsibility of head of the
family at the age of thirty, had been for her the start of a successful professional career. She had chosen not to remarry. When I had asked her if she
ever thought of looking for a second husband, she had burst out laughing
and answered frankly: 'Oh no, why should one? I hadn't to answer to
anyone!' And when I went back to her recollections of the phase when
she was married, I was struck by how the tone and style differed from the
rest of her story. Events arising out of her own life seemed to give way to
those connected with her husband. Her own personality, which up to this
point had been strongly affirmed, became overshadowed by the narrative
of her conjugal life—that is to say, the main point of the story became her
husband's life. These varying forms within the same life story precisely
corresponded to the successive stages through which she had lived, as a
wife and then as a *woman on her own* with the responsibility of head of the
family. Because the shift had come early in her life, when she was only
thirty, she had been able to identify herself completely with her role as
family head, to the extent of speaking in a way which normally I found
only with men.

   If men and women tell their life stories differently because their lives
follow differently shaped courses, these courses, in turn, depend upon
distinctive *social* – rather than sexual – positions. Men relate their search
for work. For women the search is to establish the family context in which
they can produce what society has defined as their proper product: children. For children are 'produced', and not just biologically, but also culturally. And it is because they are placed within this domestic sphere that
women are almost invisible in studies focussing on the economy of
material production by the wage-earning workforce.[8]

   It is within this context that women themselves see the reality which
shapes their lives. But one must be careful. Here is what one woman told
me of how she left a small village in Corrèze at about the age of twenty
(she has lived in Paris ever since):

I was in a bakery—my employers were very nice, but there was only me to deliver
the bread to the farms round about, with the horse van. It was hard work. And
then, one day, it was getting late, it was almost dark, there was a corner in the
road, and the horse took fright and bolted. I was that frightened that the very next
day, I left the job. I decided to come to Paris to look up an old childhood friend,
whose parents had a hotel. I sent on word to her and without even waiting for a
reply, I set out.

Here was the actual incident which gave the young girl a reason for leaving. It presented her with an opportunity for realising an already strong wish for a change in her life. It was only later on that she mentioned in a whisper that she had had a fiancé, but the engagement had been broken off: 'I had to go, I had known a young man'.

Now, what would have been the situation of a formerly engaged young woman in a small village? The 'objective' – that is to say, the *social* – reality of her situation would surely have been a diminished chance of marriage as a result of her fruitless 'association'. And if it is marriage which gives peasant women their social standing, did she not face the possibility of a future without any standing, any social identity? One can see through life-stories how social relations permeate private life, and how each person in their own way internalises them as part of their own self consciousness. As sociologists and social historians it is our task to detect the play of these social relations when they are hinted at, in implicit ways, in life stories; it is also our task to make them visible to everybody.

'Society', social relations, bear upon each of us, but as an invisible atmosphere; and we are no more conscious of social relations and culture than we are of the air we breathe. It takes an accident, a particular event, to reveal to our consciousness what has been around us and in us for so long. Thus it takes a keen observation of the particular to show us the way to the universal.

But it takes even more. The pressure of the village 'marriage market' bears upon all village girls. It shapes all their lives. It shapes all their sexuality. But it does so in a kind of natural way. In the life of this girl, something went wrong; she could have stayed, ending as a spinster, and letting her 'fault' determine her whole life; it would have appeared as a mere accident particular to one person. But she left. It was probably very difficult to leave, but 'the horse took fright', and that did it. She left, and by leaving she rejected the whole logic of the marriage market, thus making it visible to everybody. The point I want to make is that social relations become visible not by mere accidents, but by wilful acts of persons *reacting* to their pressure.

To end this short presentation, I would like to discuss the most obvious concept of internal migration: the concept of 'region of origin', and of 'regional identity'. All statistics are constructed on the basis of this concept, used as a statistical category: one tries to determine how many Bretons, Auvergnats, Creusois, Alsatians, and so on live in Paris. In common speech, it is also a very common theme; there is no doubt that the recurrent voicing of one's regional origins ('Me, I'm from Creuse'—a region of central France) has a social function. It seems to fulfil a need for self-identification.

But in Creuse itself, nobody considers him or herself a Creusois. People belong to a given village, or a clan, or a family. It is only in Paris that they discover that they are 'Creusois'. And this is a very necessary discovery for the young migrant who has just arrived in a place where he or she knows nobody, and where – much worse – nobody knows him or her. Who is he, who is she? To belong to a given village or family is now utterly irrelevant. In this situation regional identity will confer a new identity. 'That is who I am—I am from Creuse'. But this identity, which seems so obvious remains problematic—for the migrant who in Paris is a Creusois, on returning to Creuse becomes 'the Parisian'.

Nevertheless, when one looks more closely one can see that attachment to the home region takes many different forms. At its simplest, it would seem that attachment grows stronger with those who own a house, or still more, who own land. The importance of this connection with property is not so much due to its influence on self-perception, as to the practical opportunities which it opens up. First of all, property gives someone a standing within the highly stratified, little social world of the Amicales. But this standing does not have just a static significance. When the young migrant to Paris is welcomed by the Amicales, he is evaluated by his seniors not only for his family background and his personal qualities, but also for the financial resources which he is capable of raising. If he is able to raise the necessary money for a mortgate on a house or some land with the backing of a business, this immediately raises his standing with his elders. If he cannot it is – believe me – a very different matter.

Those who come the best-endowed are also those most likely to succeed socially, and to return to their home region to display the signs of their success. For them, attachment to their birthplace is connected with an experience of social mobility, of drastic change of class position. These are the people one finds as leaders of the Amicales, and they perpetuate the ideology of the regional affiliation of migrants. But, for those who came with nothing, the relationship with the region is quite different. Many of them told me: 'I haven't been back for twenty years. Anyway, I've nobody left there'. If the region is remembered, it is not so much geographically, as a place, but rather as part of their memories of childhood. For them, attachment to the home region will be nothing other than a nostalgia for their own childhood.

So, behind the different regional origins, one can also distinguish *class* origins. Indeed, ultimately, these seem to be the most important of all. Our interviews showed that there was more in common between the life paths and even the social values of 'proletarians' of different regions (people without property), than between migrants from the same region but with different resources. Thus the perspective which we finally reached was very different from the type of analysis familiar in demographic statistics, which categorises migrations according to region of origin.[9]

The life history method, in short, shows itself as much capable of analytical objectivity as statistics. But it works at another level. Statistics provide us with an indispensable *quantitative* knowledge of the human flows of migration. Sociological research endeavours to show the *social relations* which historically produce these human flows. For this purpose, conventional questionnaire surveys, which give much room for the exploration of 'motives', seem to me much less productive than a biographical approach using life stories, which make it possible to look at actual decisions and actions, and to perceive behind these practices the network of social relations which allowed them to take place.

But to do this, it is essential for the researcher first of all to listen to those who have lived, and who therefore know. Certainly their knowledge is not presented in a theoretical, or even in a written form, and quite often it does not even emerge explicitly in an oral form either. This is because their knowledge is entirely focussed on real life choices, on day to day activity. Social investigation is not a matter reserved to sociologists. *Everyone* is investigating, all the time. But the results of these 'investigations' are not construed into ideas, concepts or discussion; they materialise, as *acts*.

Hence it is necessary to listen, but this is not enough. The individual researcher has to put together bits of social and human knowledge, and beyond this also to find ways of making the results of social research more easily accessible to everybody: above all to those who could make use of it. Our ultimate goal, our dream, is to contribute to the collective writing of an alternative social history.

1   This paper was first presented at the Ninth World Congress of Sociology, Uppsala, Sweden, 14–18 August 1978, to Ad Hoc Group 20, 'The Life History Method'. It is based on research supported by D.G.R.S.T., Action Concertée, 'Europe du Temps présent'.
2   Louis Chevalier, *La formation de la population parisienne au XIXe siècle*, University of Paris thesis, 1950.
3   Guy Pourcher, *Le Peuplement de Paris*, Paris, P.U.F., 1964 (Travaux et Documents de l'I.N.E.D., cahier no 43); Yves Tugault, *La mesure de la mobilité*, Paris, P.U.F., 1973 (Travaux et Documents de l'I.N.E.D., cahier no 67).
4   Jean Bastié, *La croissance de la banlieue parisienne*, thesis, 1964.

5   The first longitudinal research on retired Parisians was carried out by Françoise Cribier. She was able to reconstitute several hundred complete occupational histories. The sample for her questionnaire survey included many migrants. See Françoise Cribier, 'Description d'une cohorte de retraités: Une étude de l'inegalité sociale' in *L'analyse démographique et ses applications* (Colloque CNRS no 934), Editions du CNRS, 1975; and her numerous research reports to the Laboratoire de Géographie Humaine, Paris.

6   Daniel and Isabelle Bertaux, 'Mémoires autobiographiques et mémoire collective', paper presented to the conference on 'Mémoire Collective Ouvrière', at the Ecomusée of Le Creusot.

7   Isabelle Bertaux-Wiame, 'L'apprentissage en Boulangerie dans l'entre deux-guerres: une enquête d'histoire orale', M.A. dissertation, University of Paris VII, roneograph, 1976.

8   Daniel Bertaux, *Destins personnels et structures de classes*, Paris, P.U.F., 1977.

9   Francois Cribier has shown how family origin determines the whole occupational career right through to retirement, fifty years later (note 5); see also Daniel Bertaux, *Destins* . . . , chapters 1, 5 and 6.

Marriage, Death and Nature

Lucetta Scaraffia

Women have always been denied their true place in history, their independent consciousness and action: for, confined to the house and oppressed by a rigid division of labour, they could not make their presence felt. Because we reject a history which simply echoes and legitimates this power relationship, we have chosen oral history as a principal means in our research.[1] Through it we can find out about the patterns of everyday life whch were the basis of each generation of women's experience. It was this day-to-day experience which moulded their consciousness, and even after material conditions had changed, the memory of it remained as symbols of a woman's experience of life to be handed down from one generation to the next. We have been collecting life stories from two groups of women born around the turn of this century, the first from Piedmontese peasant families around Cuneo, a hilly area to the south of Turin, characterised by small-holdings, and the second from working class families from the city of Turin itself.

The study of daily life can enable us to see the relationship between the individual life story and historical events, and between changes in attitudes and feelings and changes in the social and economic structure. Our principal aim has been to examine such relationships, rather than to create a parallel alternative history through life stories, filling the gaps without questioning the conclusions of traditional history.

This is a particular danger in the case of the history of women. Man has the power to define Woman, and has done so throughout history, meeting his own needs as they vary over time. At its simplest, this definition of a woman is as a body, able to provide for sex and reproduction. As modern anthropologists have clearly shown, it was originally based on two principles: firstly the definition of women as tradeable goods in marriage which was necessary to provide the basis for social life and exchange in the group; and secondly, of women as a symbol of nature in male culture.

Both principles inhibit women from developing a consciousness of themselves as individuals, for this would bring them into an independent relationship with social reality and with men. Clearly a history of women, taking their private lives into consideration, which simply creates another parallel history without challenging such male definitions, cannot be sufficient. When writing about women one must never forget the roots of their dependence. Social values and patterns of behaviour are shaped by the need to organise the exchange of women, and it is through this long-standing process that 'a woman is reduced to an object, seen as a tradeable good or means of exchange, with all the psychological and social implications which the words ''trade'' and ''exchange'' carry with them'.[2]

In listening to their life stories it proved particularly interesting to follow the changes which had occurred in the basic conditions under which women decided to marry, and the implications this had for them. In most non-industrial societies and rural communities, attitudes to marriage are normally practical and positive, with family needs and economic considerations brought into the open.[3] Among the peasant women whom we interviewed, the decision to get married followed what we would call 'negotiable' criteria.[4] The men, who owned the land, made the choice, and they generally picked women who offered the best assurance of moral and physical strength; that is, to work the land and bear children, the labour force of the future. If a woman had more than one suitor, she could enquire about her future living conditions, how much work she would have to do, whether any other woman would be living in the house. There were ambivalent feelings about this, for the presence of mothers and sisters-in-law might be a great help, but they could result in conflicts too. Women would also enquire about their would-be-husband's attitude towards his wife's future freedom. One old peasant told us about how she cross-questioned one of her suitors, trying to judge what treatment she might have expected from him:

Then along comes this fellow from Dronero, he comes to the house, and I don't like him, see. Do you know why I didn't like him? It makes me laugh when I think of it, he comes and says: 'Me mum's dead, there's only me dad and me left, so I think I'd like to get married'.

In the course of the conversation she was told that her arrival was looked upon as an answer to a lot of the tedious and heavy chores, and that she would have to wait on the two men. Her suitor was against all innovations, however small, in the way in which she dressed, and disapproved of a cloak which was then fashionable. In the end she said:

I don't want you, see, 'cause if you're already telling me all this now, think what it'll be like in the future![5]

Marriages were often arranged by match-makers who went round looking for rich girls. 'Put a 500 lira ticket on your daughters' arse—and you'll see, they'll get married at once!'[6] one matchmaker used to say when talking to poor peasants with large families. Parents would intervene to make sure their daughters married into a family with adequate means. As a result those who wanted to get married but didn't own any land often resorted to 'kidnapping' or 'elopements'. But whatever the reason may have been for such strategies, they evoked more shame than love. Another peasant told us about her arrival at the village after she had eloped:

The people were saying: 'Here she comes, here she comes, he stole his bride, here comes the bride', and I was ashamed and hid under the blanket in the cart, so they couldn't see me. We hadn't even got a bed, so we put two benches side by side, got a bit of hay and slept in the cow-shed.[7]

Marriage was a 'must', for there was no place in the community for a woman with no land and it was accepted with little joy, more often with actual fear.

I accepted marriage with a feeling I was going in for trouble and pain, but I thought I had to live the way others did, a little at least.[8]

After the marriage exchange had taken place, a new pattern of social relationships emerged, providing new possibilities of accumulating riches, though in very limited amounts. Provided they were not struck by illness, war or crop failures, and they had the right number of children – neither too many nor too few – a peasant family could build up its standard of living, buy more land and more livestock.

Women were conscious of this unequal exchange in which they gave their bodies – as labour power and for childbearing – and the men gave the land. In such a situation it was rare to find any feeling which corresponds to our idea of romantic love.[9] The women got married without any illusions, and without expecting marriage to be anything but what it, in fact, is; they therefore suffered less disillusionment.

Their resignation can be seen in the judgement they gave of their past marriages—for most of them are now widows. They protested only when they thought the rights adhering to their status had not been respected, but they never questioned the fundamental rules. Some would complain when forced to have an abortion, or to carry out heavy jobs when their baby was due. And they pointed to the end of their youth, as represented by their wedding day with regret: 'I was only twenty after all! I still had time! I was still young'.[10] But they completely accepted being regarded as a tradeable good by the men who owned the land, without any ideological adornments, except for the pride in having done their duty, and properly too. Pride for their working capacity in the fields, for the number of children they had and nursed.

This consciousness of their importance to the family did not however prevent them from understanding the nature of their general condition, and they did this with great bitterness:

A woman was worse off than the animals; they'd let them out, but a woman never had a moment's peace.[11]

*   *   *   *

Marriage was different for urban working class women during the same years. Without the bond of the land and with the weakened social ties of the cities, men and women, at long last, seemed free to choose their partner according to their own wishes. Spontaneity was at last appearing in interpersonal relations, and marriage beginning to take place between individuals rather than social groups. But even though the chance of meeting the 'ideal partner' – the twin soul – existed, they had a limited and foreseeable number of acquaintances in the family circle. They rarely met a man at work, for jobs were mostly sexually segregated. The city-dwellers would tell us about their first meeting with their future husbands in romantic terms; they remembered where it was, how and why they met, and often even the first words they said:

He was stationed in Turin, I worked in a shop, see, and he'd always come and buy his food, 'cause he'd leave the barracks without permission to go and help his parents. In the morning and then again in the evening, he'd come to the shop and buy. That was when he was going back to the barracks. After a while he says to me: 'Excuse me, Miss, would you come out with me once, 'cause I've got something to say to you....'[12]

The meeting usually took place in public, at dance-halls or on family outings, but the girls would later be granted permission to see their fiancés on their own, and so they were able to build up expectations of future married happiness on the basis of the emotions and thrills which these contacts had given them.

Life was much harder after the wedding, and in most cases beset by economic difficulty: 'We'd married but we hadn't got a penny:

we'd managed to get married on debts, everything still had to be paid for'.[13]

Thus women already had two jobs in their new lives; and soon would follow the burden of the children. Their husbands gave them no help and relationships often became antagonistic, even to the extent, as one woman confided – and she was not the only one – '...and then I was lucky, my husband died'.[14]

Poverty, drink and illness made life for a city couple more difficult, so that their conditions seem to have been no better than those among the peasants. What had changed was the woman's attitude towards her husband.

On the one hand the romantic expectations before the wedding had created illusions of hope for a good relationship with the husband which for cultural and economic reasons were not to be fulfilled. On the other hand, the men were no longer the sole economic foundation of the family, as they had been when they owned the land. Women worked as well now to earn, even though underpaid. One can feel the first potential rebellions against male authority – first against the fathers, then against the husbands – developing. Women were entering the labour market under grossly discriminatory conditions which made their economic insecurity apparent. Furthermore the development of institutions such as hospitals and schools, and the end of homework by women in 'domestic industry', did make housework lighter, but at the same time progressively undermined their function in the family which no longer seemed so essential and irreplaceable. A woman was now weaker at home, as well as discriminated against at work, so that her decision to get married was only superficially a free choice. She still had to sell her body, which was now no longer chosen for its physical strength and fitness, but for its looks. A woman was not exchanged on the basis of criteria as severe as the previous ones, but according to more variable and uncertain principles. The pride in her working capacity was now replaced by beauty, which could only last for a few years. It thus still proved impossible to have a relationship with a man which was not merely functional to survival, but rich in emotions and communication. The first mass media had encouraged deceptive new hopes in women, who were disillusioned, but did not always either accept or realise what had happened.

A woman could no longer be proud of her special domestic skills, for those activities which needed to be learnt – like making pasta and bread, preserving, or weaving, sewing and mending – had been gradually eliminated from the housewife's work. Commonsense and thrift had now become the qualities most appreciated in women, rather than the crafts of the past. None were more important than knowing how to 'make do' and 'put by'. One informant remembered her mother's domestic qualities:

I can only tell you that when peaches were in season, she'd take the bruised ones, then clean them out and say, 'It's all right, there, see'. Oh! She'd come back home tramping with her big bags full of this sort of fruit. Now me, you don't know what I do when I go shopping. I go round the whole market, look at the prices, then go and buy the stuff where it's a penny cheaper than the others.[15]

So while housework became a less laborious task and left more free time, the sense of a professional self-identity on which the countrywomen relied was now lost.

Events in national history – the First World War and Fascism – had a deep impact on relationships between men and women during this period of change. During the war, the important roles which women took up, both as workers in the productive sector and also in the handling of family affairs and social relationships in their men's absence, made them more aware of their own physical and moral abilities and strength, offering the basis for a possibly less dependent relationship to their husbands, fathers and brothers. But this new beginning was not recognised either in legislation or in the traditions of everyday life, and it was to be swept aside by Fascism which pushed women back into their subordinate role as wives and mothers.

The women were often aware of this defeat, which in some respects, like the battle to raise the birth-rate, took place on the terrain of their own bodies. And they answered with conscious resistance: 'I've had only two sons, in spite of Mussolini!', a peasant woman told us defiantly.[16]

'   *   *   *   *

Women have not only been seen as goods to be traded. Another cultural image now deeply rooted in psychological structures has been forced on them. A woman's body cycle and her reproductive function make her a powerful and frightening symbol of nature.

A woman's opening is an opening into Nature, to the fundamental mysteries of the universe, an opening into what lies beyond the natural rhythms of life: to death and life after death.[17]

Most of the peasant women we interviewed were conscious of such a power. It might have been due to surviving superstitions, confirmed by religion, which characterise particular moments in their lives –

menstruation and childbearing for example. Women were said to have magic powers, and both good and evil witchcraft existed.

Prohibitions during the menstrual period were considered natural, like not being allowed to touch plants because they would die, or food because it would decay. So were the necessary purifications after confinement, such as keeping a lamp burning until an offering had been made to the parish priest. Sexual intercourse was also forbidden during this period, reinforced by the fear of a new pregnancy which would certainly mean more work for the mother, but might even spell her death.

A woman's body, good for work and reproduction, could also be dangerous, 'pregnant' with threatening meanings, however meek and subdued the woman might be. There were in every community some women who consciously took on this role, this power given by the relationship with death and illness. They used it both to harm and to protect people. A less extreme form of it was represented by the older women whose duty it was to help with deliveries and lay out the dead. But the more explicit form was that represented by the *masche* or *desmentioure* (witches) who could kill and heal and were said to have relationships with the devil and the dead.

Women were an irreplaceable presence because of the mysterious echo which could be heard in 'a series of critical moments, of fundamental importance in their culture, because they represent rites of passage from the world of the living to the world of the dead'.[18]

Although my research is still in its early stages these hypotheses have already emerged. I shall however need further evidence to clarify them, and in particular, the relationship between the use of witchcraft and women's more widespread social function as far as births and deaths are concerned.

There is also the question as to how far a woman can remain such a clear symbol of nature in an urbanised industrial society. Births and deaths mainly take place in hospitals under scientific control and the rites of passage seem to be disappearing, although the Roman Catholic Church still insists on a woman making a specific request before being re-admitted into Church after confinement. More evidence is needed to analyse women's role in these fundamental moments and to understand what their presence and the rites of passage meant. Perhaps one revealing clue in this respect is to be found in the large number of older, working class women from the Turinese suburbs who, when asked, said they had gone to the fortune-teller to get news about a member of the family. One old worker told us that in 1947 she had been without news of her husband for three years:

Then, one day she comes along – she did Miss, it's a bit like a fairy tale. Well, me sister-in-law comes and says to me: 'Listen, I've been to a fortune-teller' – I didn't believe in those things then – 'I've been and she says, do you know what she says? We must go to Rome, 'cause Gino is a prisoner in some place he can't get out of, and he's ill.'[19]

The woman too went to the fortune teller's, who confirmed the news. She left for Rome, where she managed to get news of her husband who was a prisoner of war in Africa. She eventually succeeding in getting him back to Italy.

This would suggest that in a family crisis, or when a member of the family was in danger due to war or illness, it was the woman who set about getting news. She would often go to someone, usually another woman, who it was thought could help. Once more it fell upon the woman to face the fear of death, and to act as intermediary between the living family and the world after death.

1 The interviews, roughly forty in number, have been collected in the course of teaching by myself and Anna Bravo at the Istituto di Storia, Facolta di Magistero, University of Turin, where they are now deposited. Those with peasant women in the Langhe have been collected by Margherita Bortello for a student project under the supervision of Anna Bravo, and those of Turin women workers by the students of a seminar which I held during the academic year 1979–80.

In view of their limited number and the lack of parallel work on statistical sources which would be needed to establish how representative they are, I confine myself here to presenting some hypotheses. These were suggested by my initial reading and analysis of the interviews, and will require verification and correction by subsequent work on a larger scale.
2 I. Magli, *La donna, un problema aperto*, Vallecchi, Florence 1978, p. 39.
3 L. Mair, *Marriage*, Penguin Books, Harmondsworth 1971.
4 A. Bravo and L. Scaraffia, 'Ruolo femminile e identità nelle contadine delle Langhe: un'ipotesi di storia orale', in *Rivista di storia contemporanea*, 1980 (1).
5 Interview CA/TD/4.
6 Nuto Revelli, *Il mondo dei vinti*, Einaudi, Turin 1977, vol 1, p. 144.
7 Revelli, op. cit, vol II, p. 41.
8 A. Bruzzone and R. Farina, *La Resistenza taciuta*, La Pietra, Milan 1976, p. 232.
9 On this theme see E. Shorter, *Famiglia e civiltà*, Rizzoli, Milan 1978.
10 Interview CA/TD/11.
11 *Ibid.*
12 B. Guidetti Serra, *Compagne*, Einaudi, Turin 1977, vol 1, p. 33.
13 *Ibid*, vol 1, p. 64.
14 Interview, in the archive of the Galleria D'Arte Moderna, Torino, collected for the exhibition *Torino fra le due Guerre*.
15 *Ibid.*
16 Interview TO/SD/2.
17 Magli, op. cit, p. 52.

18 E. De Martino, 'Crisi della presenza e reintegrazione religiosa', in *Aut Aut*, no 31, 1956, p. 31.
19 TO/SD/19.

'Morning reveille in Orsa': an artist's impression of a peasant living room dating from 1893. The sharing of not only the same room but also the same bed by an entire family was regarded as a shocking lack of propriety and privacy by urban gentlefolk who travelled in the countryside during the 19th century. *Nordiska Museet*

The Family

The Working Class Family in Turin: Traditional Values and the Economy

Daniele Jalla

One of the most visible gaps in Italian social history is our lack of empirical studies of the family; and especially an analysis of the characteristics and development of working class families, which we need in order to test the – mainly sociological – assumptions which underlie attempts to explain present family patterns, by resorting to the past.[1]

Such explanations have too often been partial and schematic when compared with the complexity of real historical processes. In particular, the great number of differences within the working class make it impossible for us to talk about one pattern, a sole type of working class family, even for single moments or phases in history. Let us consider the period from the turn of the century to the First World War. Not only were the living and working conditions, wages and expenditure of the Italian working class very diverse, but so was their culture and consciousness: for it was a working class then only recently urbanised, unevenly integrated into the new industrial society, and still without any solid tradition of political and industrial struggle and organisation.[2]

All these factors contributed to the co-existence of many types of family pattern even though the various strata and sectors of the working class lived and worked in close contact. These distinctions begin to come out more clearly when we analyse testimony which, indeed, tends to highlight the variety and dissimilarity of the patterns of behaviour, ideas and values to be found in particular families. While we have not yet sufficient evidence to reach general and definitive conclusions, by observing the evidence and noting the significance which interviews give to these questions, we have been enabled to refine our own understanding of how to approach them.

This is an initial analysis, drawn from a wider research project which is being carried out in Turin in the department of history of the university's Facolta di Magistero. I shall focus on two interviews in particular.

The two women informants lived in the same community and were of nearly the same age, and they were both working class: yet their living conditions and culture were widely different.

Corinna Lanzetto, who was born in 1898 in Turin, belonged to the lower working class. Her father had no regular job, was often out of work and on three occasions had migrated overseas during the harvest-time. Her mother was thus the chief breadwinner, though her earnings were sometimes supplemented by charity. Corinna had to leave school at the age of eight and immediately began working at home as a seamstress, which she has continued to do ever since.

Maria Martino's father, by contrast, was a skilled man. From Valle Lomellina, the small agricultural town near Pavia where she was born in 1903, the family had come to Turin where he was a skilled railway worker. Maria's mother worked at home as a dressmaker. Their income and social position puts them into that skilled working class élite which formed the vanguard and aristocracy of the Turinese proletariat. Her father was a Socialist and her brothers were Communist (then, P.C.d'I. – Communist Party of Italy) militants. She has always worked as a dressmaker, specialising in underwear and shirts: and in the end she managed to open a little workshop run from her home.[3]

Though both grew up in the same community, the Borgo San Paolo in Turin, their childhoods were not at all similar, either in the kind of lives they led, or in terms of their standard of living. Above all, their patterns of family life and the structures of the families they were brought up in were very, very different, though both were proletarian. What were seen as the family functions and duties in each case? And still more important, what position did family values have in their *Weltanschauung*? The answers to these questions can enable us to reconstruct these two women's family ideals and how these ideals related to reality.

To give such answers, only certain of the elements in their two life histories are taken as indicators of family values. These are the family tradition, its attitude to housing, to housekeeping and to the management of the family budget. Between them they reflect both the (objective) material conditions and the (subjective) ideals of family life. And they also combine this to a varying degree with evidence on a cultural and an emotional level. The choice of these particular elements was not made because of their accuracy in conveying the 'facts' of the past, but because of their interpretative significance. For the truth is that both those memories which relate to the economic organisation of the family (wages, expenses, consumption, etc), and also those referring to emotional life (relationships between parents and children, the degree of solidarity of the domestic nucleus, etc), emerge equally through a distorting filter of a personal and social character.

It is still difficult to construct an order of reliability for the various elements which can be picked out from life histories, let alone from oral sources in general. Rather than attempting this, it is much more fruitful to return to a more fundamental point. For to use oral evidence correctly, we must first refuse to seek what testimonies cannot provide: the 'reality' of the past, facts 'as they happened'. We can best exploit oral sources if we ask from them – with the caution and critical care which all historical documents demand – what they can best (and in many cases only) provide: an insight into the mental world and culture of the lower classes.

*   *   *   *

Let us begin with family tradition. Corinna Lanzetto barely remembers where her mother and father came from.

My mother was from Parma, I dunno if my father was from Chieri, or some place. I don't know. Can't remember.

Maria Martino can easily work back to her great grandfather whose life story represents a background which helps both in explaining and in justifying the present:

My father complained when my brother started going to the Socialist Club. He said: 'You're too young, wait till you get to the age of discretion'. And my Granny says: 'Listen, I'm just going to say one thing, if I think of me Dad, him and another two or three young men from the village crossing the Po river and coming to Piedmont rather than serve as soldiers under the Austrians. It runs in our blood...'

Family history passed on by word of mouth from one generation to the next is important for reinforcing a sense of identity, family feeling and ties. In this way the family not only exists in the present but puts its roots back into the past and grows forward into the future. Each family nucleus becomes a fragment of a vaster system which, in its turn, is formed by similar nuclei and extends into time and space through its ties with the past and with present kin.

Thus the importance of the family is heightened and it takes on the meaning of a 'natural' structure in people's lives; it comes to be seen as the main setting for individual development, a moral and emotional community, as well as a material one. Where memory of this kind is absent or truncated, this indicates that the links with the past have been severed by a sudden change or by social transformation – as in this case moving to the city – which at the same time reduces the significance of the family itself: so that each individual now sees it as a more unstable, transient reality, based on meeting specific material needs and therefore less able to give its members a feeling of identity in belonging to the family.

The absence of tradition is also a symptom of decreased family unity and cohesion, of more or less latent conflict within it, and of the failure of cultural transmission from one generation to the next. And, indeed, we find in Corinna Lanzetto's family conflict between her parents, a gulf between parents and children and little chance for education within the family.

The contrasts with Maria Martino's story emerge still more clearly if we look at economic behaviour in relation to family life, that is to say, at the material basis of internal family relationships.

At the beginning of this century, living conditions for most of the Turin working class did not greatly differ from those described by Engels in Great Britain nearly 60 years earlier.[4] Working class houses were over-crowded, lacking in facilities, unhealthy and in very poor condition. The investment policy of Turin's wealthier classes did result in the expansion of the building industry, but it was mainly directed towards the upper working class who were the only sector able to put a significant share of their earnings towards housing. The city's bourgeoisie were also concerned to maintain the work capacity of the skilled workers for they were the hardest to replace.[5]

The size, amenities and external appearance of the house provided the clearest demonstration of the different levels of earnings between workers. Indeed, housing influenced living conditions to such an extent that it became the most evident symbol of the importance workers attached to their families and to family relationships. Corinna Lanzetto:

We lived there in Corso Vittorio, near the gaol, at number 108. Two attics packed with black beetles and mice. Nothing could be done. Well the kids, that's us, we didn't care too much, but the grown-ups, you know . . . we was little and couldn't understand these things—we couldn't understand what was wrong in the house which we didn't agree about, nothing, nothing, nothing. . . .

But Maria Martino remembers:

My Dad said: 'We sacrifice ourselves a lot, we all work, why must we live like animals?' Oh yes! He was really keen on it; not that he cared a lot about the furniture, and you can see, 'cause the house is just as it used to be when he was alive!

But he did care for the house. He'd say: 'There's lots of them one on top of the other: that's no good!'

Both considered the house as an essential condition for the development of a family life with positive relationships. They also relate these material factors to their own specific and individual family situations.

In the case of Maria Martino's family, this is a more conscious attitude which proves that the choice of a house was explicitly shaped by the need to protect and develop a family. Money for the house was the first and most important item in the household budget. They moved to a larger house soon after the family began to grow bigger. They also refused to take in lodgers, though this could have brought them extra money. In this their motivation was definitely moral and ideological, rather than economic:

All the railwaymen, all of them, always had a lodger, but your Dad never wanted one! Your Mum worked, your Granny worked, we all worked, but never had a lodger.

The presence of a lodger, of a stranger within the domestic walls, would in fact have threatened their intimacy and the integrity of the family. Even more than an external status symbol, the house served as a symbol of the family community, as a place of shelter from the pressures of external society. The house stood as counter to the factory and city; but it could not defend against their destructive powers when they were forced to live 'like animals', 'one on top of the other'.

*   *   *   *

These contrasts are again clear when we turn to the organisation of the household economy, and the part which the children played in it. There was a particular kind of child labour which played an important part in the balance of the family structure. It never appears in statistics. Some of these children's jobs were regular, some irregular; they might receive wages or be paid in kind; and the child could work in the family or be employed outside it. From a very early age parents or other adults would give children errands and odd jobs, and these turned into real jobs as they grew older. The significance of these jobs varied, not only according to age, but also according to the type of family. Corinna Lanzetto:

Now, when we lived in Corso Vittorio, we used to go and get half a litre of wine at the co-operative they had there, in Via San Paolo . . . and we had to go through the customs to get half a litre of wine and those who sent us gave us a penny or two. When we had a penny in our pocket we'd run and buy a penny's worth of cheese or salami, the posh food. And had a good eat.

Maria Martino similarly remembers how at home:

We always gave a hand: a little ... As I've said we'd go to the Rotificio to look for timber bark and then to the road on the other side where there used to be a foundry, and that's where they threw out the charcoal when they cleaned the furnaces. There was lots of people there! My brother Giovanni and I'd go there looking for charcoal. We was never cold at home. Never. We all took all of it home: the charcoal, the bark and the woodshavings, all of it, we did. But there was sacks of them and we couldn't carry them, so my Dad'd go there and pick the sacks up.

But for Corinna the odd jobs were a semi-independent activity, a means whereby the children could liberate themselves and provide for basic needs which were not being satisfied through the family. They certainly brought only a limited amount of autonomy to the child, but it signalled a deeper conflict, for their independence was less a choice than a necessity, a practical way to escape from hunger and family oppression.

In Maria Martino's case, on the other hand, the children's work was an activity which the parents guided and kept check on, and through saving on fuel costs, it was intended to contribute to the well being of the whole family. It was also an occasion for education; by helping the children learn how important and central work was to be in their lives and to appreciate its moral value. They were at the same time internalising as one of their own inner values a cornerstone of the ideology of the aristocracy of labour: the concept of work as the basis of its privileges, its authority, its prestige and dignity.

In this way, they were also taught from childhood to consider work, economic contributions and practical help as the main foundation for family unity and belonging. In this sense, as far as ideas were concerned, their position was closer to those of children in a productive family unit, like peasants' or craftsmens' children.

These differences become more evident if we examine the economic relationships between individual members of the family in the handling of the family budget. In the Martino family, we find a single system aiming at common objectives, but in the Lanzetto family we find a pattern of weaker, if not openly conflicting, emotional relationships, dominated by the need to provide for immediate necessities:

My Dad was always out, and my Mum worked for us, so we could eat and all the rest of it.

Here on the one hand were the parents, clearly antagonistic: the father 'was always out' 'eating and drinking', leaving the mother faced with the responsibility of keeping the family all on her own. But on the other side, were the children, in Corinna's memory as 'we', clearly opposed to the 'grown ups'.

Maria Martino's family situation was radically different. This was symbolised by the regular handing over of pay packets to the mother, always preceded by a collective discussion on how the money is to be spent.

Oh, I remember: he'd bring the month's pay back home. I was a very little girl and I was pushing the chair round, on my knees and looking ... and my Dad – there wasn't any gas then, it's a long time ago now – he'd say to my Mum: 'Well, what do we need?' And she'd say, 'Well, Giovanni needs a pair of shoes ...' He'd look at the accounts and say: 'We can manage, we can ...' First came the rent, then the coal and that sort of thing. And then he'd say: 'And now, Missus, do the accounts for the food—But no debts, never!'

This was a ceremony, a rite which embodied the family unity and gave a periodical demonstration of its material and emotional solidarity. The collective administration of their earnings was not only essential to survival, but also to improve their living conditions. It was the visible and verifiable cement and symbol of all the relationships within the family.

The working class family was divided by work, for if we except house-work and children's jobs, it was no longer a productive unit. It had become simply a unit of consumption. But in Maria Martino's family, consumption was organised in a way which echoed the peasant family structure, imported to the town by her parents and adapted to the new situation. The ties with the past were a guarantee for the future; social promotion and better economic conditions were to be won on the basis of a pattern of relationships, typical of a traditional peasant or artisan family. This pattern did not altogether correspond to actual economic circum-stances, but an effort was made to adapt them.

This becomes apparent when we look at the different roles within the family. The father's power, control and authority, reduced by the absence of any unified productive moment when the others would work under his direction had now acquired a basically moral significance. The mother's importance had grown proportionately, and though the role she had gained through paid work and her domestic activity remained subordinated, it had become more independent and distinctive. The separation of production from consumption defined and increased the significance of the role of women within the family, even if it also laid down the conditions for new forms of oppression. The children's position was changed too. With a job they could leave their father's home earlier and with more security than peasants' children; and even if they did not choose to leave they could become economically independent.

The disintegration which these changes could bring were resisted in a double way. There was first the practical function of the family. In the Martino family this meant that cohesion was not merely a guarantee for survival, but also necessary for social advance. Hence for Maria, separation from her family of origin was not in her interest and her aspirations for autonomy and independence were thus limited. But for Corinna Lanzetto, by contrast, they were essential for her to have any chance of improving her personal and social position. The second means of resistance came in laying a greater stress on the moral and emotional functions of the family. This was conveyed through the importance given to its tradition and to collaboration among its members, and also through the self-discipline and strict habits which were instilled by what amounted to a kind of lay family-centred religion.

*   *   *   *

The study of many other aspects of the life and culture of these two families has confirmed our initial hypothesis, that not only do they represent two opposite situations, but they are also 'extreme' cases within the working class as a whole. This probably means there are other types of family patterns which could be considered in between them, combining elements from both to form new and different patterns. But if this is so, it also creates some problems for historical interpretation.

The labour aristocracy, though numerically limited, has played a major role in working class politics and culture. Skilled workers enjoy a prestige from their relatively privileged situation which makes them a practical and personal model for wider working class social aspirations. This is reinforced by their dominant role in working class struggles; they have been the vanguard of its political and organisational development. The family pattern of skilled workers is a secondary but, as we have seen, not unimportant element in maintaining their status and at the same time bringing about their own social advance. The question is whether this family pattern also tends to become a cultural model for the class as a whole.

We have already referred to the peasant or artisan origin of these family patterns which enable the family to provide a haven of escape from the pressures of capitalism and the social relationships it imposes. This certainly also has a great importance in the early stages of capitalistic development and for first-generation city dwellers; but the question is to what extent and for how long do such traditional bases for behaviour remain explicit, and when do they lose importance and turn into something totally different?

The answers to these questions, and to the second in particular, are particularly important in Italy where agriculture and rural culture remained widespread right up to the fifties. What type of family did the left-wing parties have in mind when, for example, Tasca wrote that 'the factory kills the family' in Gramsci's *Ordine Nuovo?*[6]

Was not their inspiration the family ideal of the labour aristocrats, which alone seemed to offer an opposition to capitalism—but whose ambiguities and mixed origins we have attempted here, in part, to unravel? And what of the Fascists, for example in their campaign to raise the birth rate, or Roman Catholic culture, and 'populist' literary traditions—did they not all in different ways draw inspiration from the old myths of the peasant family? The historian, in short, faces a double task: first to establish the reality of differing family patterns and structures over particular periods in various sectors of the working class, and then to weigh how far the influence of some of these forms may outlast their own time.

1   See in particular C. Saraceno, *Anatomia della famiglia*, Bari 1976, and L. Balbo, *Stato di Famiglia*, Milan 1976.
2   See S. Merli, *Proletariato di fabbrica e capitalismo industriale*, Florence 1972, and G. Procacci, *La lotta di classe in Italia agli inizi del XX secolo*, Rome 1970. For Turin in particular see S. Musso, 'L'operaio dell'auto a Torino', in *Classe*, no. 14/IX, 1977.
3   These interviews were carried out between 1976 and 1977 in Turin, in the Borgo San Paolo. The tapes and transcriptions are deposited at the History Dept, Facolta di Magistero, classified as TO/SP/I-9.
4   F. Engels, *The Condition of the Working Class in England*, London 1969.
5   See E. Magrini, 'Inchiesta sulle abitazioni popolari in Torino', in *La Riforma Sociale*, Anno XII, Vol XVI, and *ibid*, Anno XV, Vol XIX 'Il problema delle abitazioni popolari a Torino'; and G. Consonni and G. Tonon, 'Casa e lavoro nell'area milanese', in *Classe* 14/IX/77.
6   A. Tasca, 'La casa', in *Ordine Nuovo*, AI, 6, 14, 6, 1919 p.1.

222

A saw-mill outside Drammen in eastern Norway. No other Norweigian industry employed so many boy workers. (*Norsk Folkemuseum, Oslo*)

Industrial Boy Labour in Norway

Edvard Bull

The important thing about oral history, of course, is not the orality and, even less, the mechanics of the tape recorder. The point is that we as historians are no longer necessarily the captives of the pre-existing sources. For the period still within reach of the memory of living people, we can contribute to the creation of new sources for our own purposes. Whether we do it with the use of a tape recorder, shorthand or other rapid note-taking, or simply by inducing informants to write down their reminiscences themselves—all these are minor matters.

To my mind it seems evident that the main point about these sources which the historian creates is the possibility of giving voice to those people who seldom express themselves in writing—to the working class, to children, and to women. This is all the more important since people living today have experienced more rapid and far-reaching changes than any earlier generations in human history.

If we take industrialisation as the key to those rapid changes, the early phases in Britain have, of course, long since faded from living memory. Many other regions of the world are still only in the early stages. Norway lies somewhere in the middle, with important developments taking place in the decades before and after 1900. (Steam engines for sawing and planing machinery were introduced from 1860, and paper and pulp industry began from the 1880s and '90s; while large-scale hydro-electric plants, and the electro-chemical and electro-metallurgical industries started from around 1900.)

The first Norwegian project which may be called 'oral history' dates back to 1950. (At the time I don't think we knew the term.) One of the purposes of that project was to enrich our knowledge of how the workers experienced the early phases of industrialisation.[1]

The first Norwegian Factory Act was passed in 1892 and came into effect in the following year. From then on it was categorically forbidden for children under the age of 12 to work in factories, and working hours and other conditions were specially regulated for those between 12 and 18. (The law, of course, also contained regulations concerning dangerous machinery, hygienic conditions, etc.)

It is easy to voice the suspicion that the law was perhaps not always very rigorously enforced—since we all know that there may be a great discrepancy between a law and the realities of life. The annual reports from the factory inspectors often disclose grave neglect of the regulations concerning dangerous machines. Sometimes they also reported on dirty and unventilated workrooms, etc. But they have very little to tell about child labour.

In the 1950s, however, it was still easy to find people with working experience from the period both before and after the passing of the Factory Act. The interviews did not specifically aim at getting information on the functioning of the Act. But when we got the old workers to tell their life stories from early childhood onwards, child labour inevitably proved to have been an important part of their total experience. Some of them could tell about factory law problems. But the main result was a quite new knowledge of what it was like for boys[2] to be wage earners for many years before they attended confirmation class, thereby (at the age of 14 or 15) passing the traditional *rite de passage* into adult status.

We did not ask direct questions about our informants' attitudes to child labour. And precisely because we asked no such questions, we got not only factual information about child labour, but were also able to learn about the attitudes of the child labourers themselves: how they had felt and thought about their own life situation.

*   *   *   *

We don't know the full extent of industrial boy labour. Statistics from 1875 quote 3,370 children under 15 years working in industrial establishments. That would mean about 8% of the entire workforce. But the figure is certainly a good deal too low. Many boys were not directly employed by the firm. They helped their parents or other adult piece workers and got their pay from them—if they were paid. Such children did not easily get into the statistics. In addition, the statistics were in principle meant to refer to the situation at the end of the year, in mid-winter. At that time, most sawmills were not operating—and that was exactly the industry with the largest number of child workers. So I don't think it is possible to say much about the numbers. Only this: in the communities around the sawing and planing mills, the pulp mills, the match and tobacco factories and some other plants, almost all working class boys had work experience long before the age of confirmation. This is supported by censuses, reports from school authorities and by the reminiscences of the old workers.

Why industrial child labour? Probably most adults felt it to be a matter of curse. In agriculture, fisheries, and old-fashioned crafts, children had always worked as much as they possibly could. Industrial work was definitely neither more dangerous nor more strenuous than, for example, lumbering or rowing a fishing boat. So, why should the children of industrial workers be spared?

We have one contemporary source apparently expressing the attitudes of a group of mineworkers. This is a letter to the Storting signed by 144 fathers at the Røros copper mines in 1893, protesting against the new Factory Act forbidding their children's work. They stressed the economic side: in large families the law would be 'ruinous'. But they emphasised also that the work did absolutely no harm to the eight- or ten-year-old boys. 'On the contrary, the children accustomed themselves at the right time to spending their days in a good way, instead of lying at home in idleness'. In fact, the work in question included night shifts, starting at 3 a.m. in the open air, 2500 or 3000 feet above sea level, in all sorts of weather—although not during the winter.

It is easy to explain away a letter of this kind. The workers might have been forced, persuaded or bribed by their superiors. It is, however, impossible to explain away the fact that scores and scores of old workers give the same impression: child work was not regarded as harmful, and the boy workers did not come merely from the largest or poorest families.

One informant, the son of a poor widow, explains with some bitterness that sawmill workers with high earnings exploited their good relationship with the foremen to get good jobs for their sons early. 'So only the worst jobs were open to those who were compelled by necessity to work'. Another informant sings the praises of the foreman who took him on as a shift worker when he was ten years old. Again and again to get work at an early age appears as a favour, even if it implied night shifts—as it often did for example in the large and 'modern' saw and planing mills. The boy who needed some extra money to pay for his confirmation suit felt himself especially lucky to get three extra shifts during one week. It meant a working week of 108 hours—but, no doubt, he might be able to find a hideaway and get a couple of hours' sleep during the nights.

Not only the parents, but also the children themselves often looked forward to the day when they could start work. It was a step in the process of growing up, just as you felt when you started school, when you left school or when you earned your first wage.

One informant who started working at the age of 12 had a 12 hour day, three days a week (the other days he attended school) and he says 'We felt we had become somebody, then. When we started working, we thought we were manly'. Another man in the same saw-mill community commented: 'It was fine, you see. All the youth here at Lillestrømmen went to the saw-mill, there was no way around that. And we had no other entertainment, so we hung around the mill every evening. We already knew the job when we started working'.

There are dissenting voices, however. Again from Lillestrømmen: 'I did *not* like it! But there was no question about it. You *had* to go. Earn money'. Or, it might be like this: 'I wanted to begin at the mill myself. But the wish soon passed away. I had to get up at five in the morning and walk from Strømmen to Lillestrømmen, no matter how cold it was'. On that road they would see ghosts in the dark, and one of our informants vividly remembers how scared he was to go home alone in the dark.

Nonetheless, the conclusion seems to be clear: most workers' families did nothing to avoid sending their boys to the factories, from the age of about ten, or sometimes earlier. In the children's labour market, supply usually exceeded demand. In that sense, there was a kind of semi-permanent unemployment, and consequently the children were often unable to get work until they were twelve or thirteen.

Compulsory schooling did restrict child labour to some extent. However, most Norwegian factories were situated outside the cities and towns, in districts where school usually was held only two or three days a week. So the children could work full-time the other days and during the long holidays. They often worked six hours on school days as well. In other cases, where school attendance was expected every day, the teachers might have to adapt to industry, for example by taking one group of children during the mornings and another in the afternoons; so the children went to the factory in relays.

In the 1870s the school authorities took the initiative in bringing about more serious restrictions. Obviously they noted that the factory children were often absent from school, or very tired when they attended. Children from the tobacco factories might even show strong signs of nicotine poisoning.

One of our informants described the snoring of those children who came to school after twelve hours' night shifts in the saw-mills. The other boys – he was one of them himself – had this experience:

When the school day began at eight in the morning, we had to rise at five, get some food to bring with us for breakfast and go to our work. We carried our school books with us. A few minutes to eight we took them out and ran to school. There we stayed till eleven. Then we had to go to the mill again and take up our work. . . . It was the same for the children beginning school at eleven. They also carried their school things with them to work, went to school some minutes before eleven and came back to work at 2.30 p.m., just before the afternoon meal. In this way the whole day was spent; and there were no bright pupils quick to learn among those who worked. You would rather fall asleep, far away from homework and mental effort.

The ban on industrial child work from 1893 was the result of the efforts of educationalists and philanthropic politicians. But the directly interested parties – the children, their parents and the employers – often felt that the law was contrary to their immediate needs. The radical politician Gunnar Knudsen (later to become Prime Minister) stated in the Storting: 'Experience from all other countries tells us that when the exploitation of child labour is curtailed the parents are the first to object. And this is natural, I would be the last to blame them, because it is a question of money, a question of food'.

The law *was* undoubtedly enforced in some cases. In a pulp mill the boys were happy when their work-day was shortened 'because then we got time to go skiing in the winter'. A boy who had started working in a nail factory about 1890 at the age of seven or eight was eleven when the new law came into effect.

As a result I got one year's leave, in the sense that I didn't have to work in the nail factory during that year. I don't remember how many we were, but there was certainly jubilation among those few who experienced that event. We boys thought it a good law. For just think of it: up at six in the morning, work until twelve, and then in school from one o'clock till five. And if we had plenty of nails in stock we often had to work overtime to get them packed. You ask what the parents felt about the new law. Most of them thought it a grand and just law, for they thought about their children's future.

It seems, nonetheless, that the new law was more honoured in the breach than in the observance. The two factory inspectors appointed by the government – merely two for the whole country – could not possibly exert effective control even if they had wanted to. Both of them were civil engineers and evidently more interested in improving dangerous machines than in chasing illegal child workers. Local, unpaid factory inspection boards depended wholly on the individual qualities of the chairman, usually a medical doctor.

Very often nothing was done to implement the new regulations concerning children. Five years after the passing of the act boys of ten or

eleven years still worked from 6 a.m. to 6 p.m. with two hours' break—
for instance at a saw mill in Trøndelag:

We didn't notice any effect of the Factory Act or the inspection board. Boys below
confirmation worked night shifts—and even three consecutive shifts if someone
was absent from the job. The boys also worked with dangerous machines like
crosscut saws, circular saws and the like. There were many accidents with fingers
or hands cut off, but it didn't happen often to boys.

Another boy began when he was fifteen years old with shift work in a
pulp mill: 'I saw the inspection board only once and nobody asked me
how old I was'.

But even if the authorities did attempt some sort of control it was
easy to evade. 'Usually they called on the telephone before they came.
Then we boys had to leave the machines and get hold of a brush. So we
brushed until they had left. This was in day-time. During nights they
were safe of course'. (Cleaning in day-time was not banned even if working with dangerous machines, and night shifts were illegal up to the age of
16. From 16 to 18 the boys were supposed to have a doctor's certificate to
prove that the work in question would do them no harm.) A man born in
1884 reported:

The difficulties came when we under sixteen had to work night shifts, because a
doctor who was leader of the inspection board would come to the mill to inspect. It
spread like wildfire throughout the mill: the doctor is coming! Then we went off
into the lumber yard and disappeared until the doctor had left. It was, in effect,
quite good to work at night, because then we might get some time for school as
well, and those who prepared for confirmation could attend class without missing
work. The general opinion was that one ought to get a job as early as possible.
There was some illness also, here and there, especially in the large families. Well,
not only the boys started work early, the girls also. My sisters began around the
age of thirteen, as maids in houses.

It seems to have been quite normal to lie about one's age, even to the
doctor. A fifteen-year-old boy starting as a shift worker one year too
young got his doctor's certificate to witness that night work would not
harm him. 'When I went to see the doctor I was terrified of being turned
down! Up to 18 it was tense, I was always afraid of being sacked'.
Another man related:

I had to lie to add two years to my age, to get permission for night work. Such was
the custom at the time. When you got that kind of work, you could help a little at
home [with the money]. And we *got* the money when it was time for it. With the

farmers you often had to wait for months before you got a little. Sometimes there might be an inspection to see if anyone was too young for shift work. If someone was very small, we had to hide him away for a while. I once went to the doctor to have some teeth drawn. As a factory worker I should have had free medical aid, but I didn't dare say that I worked at the pulp mill, because I was too young. So I paid my *krone* and said nothing.

Boys and foremen often collaborated to swindle the inspectors: 'Since I was too young, the foreman said that we had to lie and say I was one year older than I was'. 'I worked at a (dangerous) machine, and one day the master came and asked me how old I was. I was 17. "Well, there is nothing to do about it. I expect nobody will believe you are less than eighteen".'

*   *   *   *

Is it possible to get reliable information about attitudes, thoughts and feelings 50 or 60 years back by means of oral history interviewing?

If you ask directly: 'What did you feel about the ban on child labour?' or 'what did your parents feel?', you may get answers such as this: 'Most of them thought it a grand and just law, for they thought about their children's future'. It is, however, impossible to say whether such statements reflect the feelings of the 1950s or of the 1890s. But when you get the scores and scores of reminiscences about how boys strived to get jobs or to avoid being sacked, even in contravention of the law, I can see no reason why they should tell those stories if they were not simply the truth. And I can see no explanation of such behaviour if it is not that it reflects an attitude, namely: that the work and life in the mills might be interesting or boring, light or all too strenuous, but that it was in most cases *desirable*—first and foremost to earn money, but also as a means of winning higher status. No initiative to ban child labour came from the boys or their parents; no weighty support for the ban came from that side.

It is perhaps reasonable to interpret this situation as a sign of how far the working class in the 1890s accepted the existing capitalist system. Trade unions were only in their beginnings—and hardly even that in those industrial branches which employed the greatest number of children. The Labour Party – founded in 1887 – had as yet made little headway. So the workers had to make the best out of life on their own. The means nearest at hand was to get more family members out to work as breadwinners.

In the years from the turn of the century to the First World War, most of the illegal child labour seems to have disappeared. Several influences worked in that direction, in addition to the legislative ban. New machines supplanted some children's work. The schools claimed more of their time. Their fathers' real wages rose and the boys' earnings were probably felt to be less necessary. The labour movement inspired new visions of what life ought to be like.

It is, however, difficult to say whether the experiences of the boy workers themselves hampered or hastened the growth of the labour movement. Doubtless the boys were socialised into following in their fathers' footsteps to factory jobs, getting used to their status as wage workers. But some of them experienced class differences and conflicts very early. Some of them took part in strikes as children. Or, they might have experienced social realities in this way:

I went to confirmation class at the same time as the son of the mill manager, and that boy used to ride a horse to the parsonage. To get back to my work at the mill more quickly and easily, I was allowed to hang on to the rider: I clung to the horse-tail from the parsonage to the mill, and because of the pull I got from the horse it was easier to run the long way.

That *might* have been an experience to inspire radical politics!

It is, however, important to be careful with rash generalisations. Very few of our informants look back on their first working years with bitterness. But some do. And the nuances of their feelings are as many as they themselves are. The working class was never as massive a collectivity as it sometimes appears in history books. After all, this is perhaps the most important result of this kind of oral history: it compels us to see the working class as a very large number of individual men, women and children. All too often historical study has made readers identify merely with top people in the past. Oral history makes it possible for us – and, I hope, for our readers – to identify with ordinary people. It may enrich and even, to some extent, transform history as an element in general education.

1   Another purpose was determined by the needs of the folk museums – first, the Nordic Museum in Stockholm, and later, the Norwegian Folk Museum in Oslo: to illustrate the past of the working classes they could not follow the same method as they had used to describe the traditional peasant societies or the urban upper classes. Exhibitions of nice old houses, furniture and clothing could not give an adequate picture of people who were better characterised by their lack of such things. So the traditional museum collection had to be supplemented by oral history—to meet the wishes of a social democratic society.
    Other articles in English on the oral history project from the 1950s are:

Edvard Bull, 'Autobiographies of Industrial Workers', *International Review of Social History*, Volume 1 (1956), pp. 203–209.

Edvard Bull, 'Industrial Workers and their Employers in Norway around 1900', *Scandinavian Economic History Review*, Volume III (1955), pp. 64–84.

The project was organised by the Norwegian Folk Museum, Oslo, but the interviews are now kept at the University of Trondheim, Department of History.

2 Very few girls worked in factories, so that this paper concerns only the boys' experiences. Girls were usually expected to work as hard as boys, but at different kinds of work.

232

'The family gathered around the evening lamp': a favourite childhood memory in many middle-class families. This ritual moment often symbolised an idealised togetherness—the way a 'real' family ought to function. Usually, however, the relations between parents and children were more distant. *Nordiska Museet*

The Swedish Family: a Study of Privatisation and Social Change since 1880

Orvar Löfgren

This paper about changes in family patterns is based on a wider study of social and cultural change in Swedish society during the last hundred years which is being carried out by a group of us at the University of Lund in southern Sweden.[1] Our project is based partly on written sources and partly on oral evidence, collected either through our own fieldwork, or as a result of the work of earlier Swedish collectors going back into the 19th century. As European ethnologists we work within a discipline which to the unfamiliar may seem a somewhat strange mixture of anthropology, sociology and social history. We see our subject as the study of Swedish culture, past and present; and in it fieldwork and oral history techniques have from the beginning played an important role.

Earlier generations of Swedish ethnologists were chiefly concerned with salvaging evidence of a rapidly disintegrating peasant culture. Their work resulted in large collections of material on peasant traditions, mainly in the form of interviews, life histories and answers to questionnaires.[2] These ethnological archives provided the starting point for our own project on 'Cultural and class boundaries' since 1880. Our aim is to turn the focus onto the two newly-emerging social classes, the middle class and the working class, which have dominated the social scene in Sweden during the last hundred years. We have concentrated particularly on two themes underlying the changing experience of daily life: on the one hand the polarisation of work and leisure, and on the other the separation of the family and the outside world, which is my concern here.

Industrialisation and urbanisation occurred rather late in Sweden, considerably later than in Great Britain. This gives us a good chance of following how traditional patterns of peasant life were replaced by new life styles and subcultures in modern Sweden. We have drawn on a variety of different methods for our research. For the period up to 1910 we are relying heavily on written documentation and the earlier collections of oral history. There is of course an abundance of written material from the upper strata of society, such as memoirs, collections of letters, manuals of etiquette and so on; so that here interviewing simply plays a complementary role. But early working class life in Sweden left far fewer written traces, and this aspect of our study has thus called for more intensive field-work. So far we have concentrated our interviewing in two communities close to Lund: Svedala, a country town; and Landskrona, a town dominated by heavy industry with a largely working class population.

In comparing middle class and working class culture our object has been to discover how value systems and world views are generated and structured. This has led us to research on basic themes like the use and perception of time and space, the conception of the social landscape which surrounds the individual, the view of 'the good life', attitudes towards sex roles and sexuality, and concepts of hierarchy and solidarity. Through using a historical perspective we believe it becomes possible to show how such core values are generated by social and economic change, and how individuals learn to accept them as part of the natural order of things during childhood and through everyday activities later on in life.

Many of the phenomena which earlier sociologists viewed as part of human nature have turned out to be historical products. Gradually we have come to realise that words like family, home, career, childhood, love, intimacy and individualism have had other meanings during earlier times or that some of them are recent cultural innovations. By anchoring concepts like these in history and society instead of in human nature or biology we may get new insights into the workings of the modern family. In this way social history can provide a forceful tool for a better understanding of the present, and provoke new insights.

The problem is, of course, that many aspects of family life are difficult to reconstruct. A study of changes in parenthood, home-making or relations between family members calls for new types of historical knowledge. We often deal with activities and sentiments which are rarely verbalised, or even consciously present, let alone written down in traditional types of historical records. The family historian thus has the hard task of making the self-evident or trivial problematic. Here the techniques of oral history may become a powerful aid. And we have found a deepened historical perspective more generally a great help in this process. Thus the peculiarities of present-day culture, and the patterns of change, at once stand out more clearly if we contrast our contemporary middle class patterns of family life and ideology with the very different life styles of the 19th century Swedish peasantry.

*   *   *   *

Upper class travellers in the 19th century Swedish countryside were often shocked by peasant attitudes towards marriage, family life and sex roles. Their complaints were many. Children were not given a proper upbringing, and women behaved without modesty; love of home was lacking, and the virtues of privacy and propriety were not respected. Such comments may tell us more about the family ideology of the urban bourgeoisie than about peasant culture, but they also speak of a widening cultural gap in 19th century Swedish society. One country doctor brings out this sense of difference especially vividly in his recollections of journeys in remote peasant areas around the turn of this century:

For them (the peasants) there is no dividing line between public and private, all is public. Locks are never used in the isolated villages – night or day – and you never knock when entering a house.
   One light summer night I came to a farm where they used to take visitors in. The main door of the farm entrance was open as well as the door of main building, but not a person was in sight. I had to walk through the whole house until I found the family sleeping soundly in the innermost room. The mistress of the house woke up – and I told her who I was and asked for a bed for the night. Well, that was no problem! She just got up and made me a bed.
   We normal middle class people don't want to have strangers coming into the room where we are having a meal. The real old fashioned peasants never worry about that . . .
   We don't like to dress in the presence of strangers. That never bothers the peasants I am talking about here. And they just can't understand that type of feeling in others.

One particular memory of this especially stuck in his mind:

During the famine year of 1902 an unusually tall woman travelled up to Northern Lappland to help organising relief. It was autumn, so it was already dark when she came to the farm where she was going to stay. She was tired from her travels and went to bed immediately. But on the farm they had never seen such a tall woman before; and this sensation had to be shared with others. So the message was sent round. From all corners of the village one family after the other came along: father, mother, servants and children. For every new bunch of visitors the last piece of candle stuck in a bottleneck was lit and people walked over to the bed in the corner to look at the resting wonder. At midnight the lady had to say sharply that this had to be the end of the day's demonstration.

When visitors to peasant homes complained of the lack of privacy and the intolerable extent of communal living, with the whole household (including guests) sleeping, dressing, eating and working in the same room, it is clear that this complaint must be seen against the background of a rising cult of intimacy and privacy among the new middle class.

This cult of privacy was part of a cultural programme launched by the bourgeoisie in order to secure their position as the vanguard and elite of the new industrial society. The rising class of tradesmen, administrators and industrial managers needed a cultural charter to make their social ambitions legitimate. The old nobility never faced the same problem. Their position at the top of the social hierarchy was a matter of fact. They were simply born to rule.

The new and heterogeneous class of social climbers had to resort to other types of argument. So they created an ideology based upon personal ability. They asserted that their right to power and influence rested on moral superiority, on qualities like rationality and initiative, diligence, prudence and sobriety. And in developing this world view, the new urban bourgeoisie had to contrast themselves not only with the grey mass of workers and peasants, but also with the old gentry, whose life of extravagance and immoderation was now declared to be inferior to the thriftiness and moral superiority of the new class.

Through this social and economic process emerged the 'middle class culture' we know today; and it proved a powerful tool in shaping and maintaining a new social structure in late 19th and early 20th century Sweden. It was characterised by an obsessive need for boundaries, for taboos and rituals of avoidance and hierarchy. New types of dividing lines were created between public and private life, between work and leisure, between male and female, and between class and class. The sum was a new cultural framework for society; a totally novel organisation of both productive and social relationships.

This process has been documented and discussed in many European settings, and the withdrawal into the privacy of the home has been traced back into the 17th century. But because the process started late in Sweden, and thanks to the earlier collections of oral history, it is possible to reconstruct this process of privatisation in our own society in great detail. We can see how seemingly trivial changes in everyday life in fact signal a radical transformation of social relationships in the local community and between the family and the outside world. Let me illustrate this by indicating some of the signs of the changing social landscape in the late 19th century Swedish village.

The 19th century had been a period of growing social stratification in Swedish peasant society. The landowning farmer was emerging as a member of a much more distinct social class, increasingly anxious to disassociate himself from the rest of the villagers and eagr to adopt a number of traits of the life style of the urban bourgeoisie.

The testimonies of country people who grew up during this period show, through their contrasting experiences, how sharpening class conflicts could take on cultural forms and new social boundaries could be created in village life. As a starting point we may take on the example of one old peasant woman who recalled the village life in her youth when all the young people were called 'lads and maids':

there was never any difference between the sons of farmers and the farm servant boys, the same with farm girls and maids. It was like they were all one stock.

Such childhood memories may well present an idealised picture of a harmonious and egalitarian village life in the past. But perhaps more significant is that while other pictures of village life in the same period also depict free socialising across class boundaries, the limits to such contact are also recalled:

Master and mistsress, children and servants, they all sat at the same table and ate off the same plate. They did the same jobs, and the daughters of the farmer shared the bed with the maids, just like the sons with the male hands. But if the question of marriage between servant and 'free' arose, then the boundary appeared so sharp and so high that it couldn't be crossed, at least among more prosperous families.

The withdrawal of the farm family from the company of servants – who increasingly were recruited from landless peasants – was a step by step process. Gradually, the two groups within the household would cease to eat the same food at the same table. New sleeping quarters would be arranged for the servants. The division of labour on the farm would come to be rearranged, and the farmer's children withdraw from easy socialising with the farm servants or the families of cotters. The formerly open village feasts would become segregated. One farm hand recalls how at the beginning of this century in his district two new and adjoining dance floors were constructed for the village youth. But the entrance fees were not the same now:

The entrances were kept apart and the dancers were divided into two classes… On the ten öre (twopenny) dance floor danced farmers' sons and daughters, while the servants had to use the cheaper alternative.

Such spatial manifestations of new class boundaries had an important socialising effect: you soon learned your station in the local hierarchy.

We have found an equally marked process of change in perceptions of marriage and the family, again following urban middle class example. Here, the triple foundations of family life were now the concept of the loving and romantic couple, the moral importance of parenthood, and the sanctity of home. Elsewhere I have discussed how these concepts became part of the culture-building of the Victorian bourgeoisie in Sweden. Here I would like to illustrate the type of cultural confrontation which occurred when the new family ideology was introduced in 19th century peasant settings, where a totally different conception of marriage, family and home still existed.

Ideas of romantic love and the emotional intimacy of the married couple were alien to peasant culture. Not that intimacy between man and wife did not exist; but it was based upon the fact that the married couple was a tight-knit production unit. This fact was drummed into young peasant boys' and girls' heads, often in the form of stereotyped sayings. In those days preference and liking had to give way to money. Mothers used to say, 'The liking will have to come later'. The old men used to give the boys this advice: 'Never look at the lassies in the church door, but when they're (working) in the dunghill.' Even when married, men and women both remained firmly anchored in the peer groups of the same sex, which formed an important part of village life. Both women and men had a social life of their own, and there was, for example, a marked female solidarity. A married woman could always count on the support of other women, both emotionally and economically. Here we can hardly speak of a tight-knit dyad of man and wife united on an island of love against the world.

This was underlined by the fact that married couples were not supposed to show any tenderness towards each other in public. Swedish peasant society was on the whole anti-tactile. You did not, express emotions or love by touching others. Man and wife were not supposed to walk arm in arm, or embrace or kiss in public and the same went for boys and girls who were courting. 'Tenderness should only be shown between four eyes' was the rule one peasant remembered from his youth. In the same spirit another recalled: 'It was not proper for a woman to show affection—unless it was to her child. Because then it was real and natural.'

Against this background we can understand the sharp reaction against the 'improper' behaviour of upper or middle-class couples which was observed by the peasants. Strange stories about people seen actually kissing each other in public were circulated; and the local comment was: 'they must be fashionable people, or they'd be ashamed to be kissing when other people are looking'.

Nevertheless, the idea of the married couple as the basic unit of intimacy did slowly gain ground in the late 19th century Swedish countryside. This is revealed through what might otherwise seem unimportant changes in the seating arrangements in the parish churches. Earlier men and women were separated, and this pattern communicated a solidarity within each sex which cut across boundaries of kith and kin. Among the new urban bourgeoisie this arrangement was abandoned for a new one: the wife left the other women and came to sit by the side of her husband. The first instances of this rearrangement which occurred in country churches provoked reactions of strong hostility from the peasants. Usually it was urban visitors or local upper class couples who introduced the pattern: 'It was the fine folks who started this, like gentlefolk, no one else would be bothered by seating herself aside a man, but it caught on', one peasant woman recollects. Another remembered the angry reaction when visiting couples from the nearby town seated together: the older people really took offence and said, 'Those fine folks just fancy themselves with their manners'.

Many women felt it was a betrayal of the female solidarity when this practice slowly reached the ranks of farmers and farm labourers. It signalled the withdrawal of the married couple into the new intimacy of the family. We find the same development again at village feasts, where married couples began to sit together, rather than keeping to the traditional arrangement of separate seating for each sex.

It is interesting to note at this point that the sharp social division between the sexes which characterised the peasant world was carried over into the new working class culture of late 19th and early 20th century Sweden. A more family-centred culture did not evolve in these social strata, especially in the lower working class groups, until the 1930s and 1940s. But first let us turn back to the apostles of change, the middle class.

*   *   *   **

The notion of romantic love in the family ideology of the Victorian bourgeoisie was based upon a fictional definition of two equals, in love with each other. There was in fact a marked sexual division of labour in this love game. Victorian marriage, it has been observed, was based upon the two being united into one—the one being the man.

As in other European settings, marriages among the Swedish bourgeoisie were asymmetric alliances. First of all, we often find a great age difference between man and wife. A man could only marry if he had an income large enough to finance an adequate home and support a wife, children and at least one servant. As an optician who married in the 1880s recalled, 'In those days, you had to be able to offer your wife a flat and all the furniture too, before there was even talk of marriage.'

Ideally it was felt that a man should wait until he was firmly established in his career. This frequently meant that he would be five to ten years older than his wife: already a man of the world, who had usually lived by himself for some time, and was firmly integrated into public life. Very often, in accordance with the prevailing double standard, he would have had premarital sexual experience. The wife, on the other hand, was often taken directly from the protected life of her parental home or a finishing school. An upper class woman who grew up just before the turn of the century reflected: 'I was so totally ignorant. House-cleaning or bed-making were tasks I'd had nothing to do with at all. Before I got married I'd never scrubbed a floor and I'd no idea how to make a bed.'

A girl's knowledge of public life was often equally slight, and she would have had few opportunities to develop an independent identity of her own. She would indeed have been still a girl rather than an adult woman when she became a wife. This could make marriage into a kind of parent-child relationship, in which the man saw himself as provider and protector of a wife whom he regarded as a fragile creature, to be sheltered against the ugly realities of public life, like politics or economics. The woman, on the other hand, had been brought up to fulfil the role of emotional supporter, as loving wife, nurse and mother. She was expected to find complete fulfilment in a life committed to love and home-making.

The new view of marriage and the family had made home-making in particular a much more important matter. The home had become the scene for the new intimate family life, so that to build a home was not only a practical project; it became a *moral* one, too. If the ideal Victorian man had to be the provider, his wife ought to be the guardian of home and the virtues of homeliness. During this period notions of home and womanhood, privacy and sentiment became strongly interwoven. To understand the new definition of sex roles we can take a closer look at the concept of home and the kinds of qualities it came to stand for.

Why did the Victorians choose to invest so much time, energy and money in homemaking? Apart from the simple fact that they enjoyed far better material conditions for this project than earlier generations, it is important to understand that for the rising bourgeoisie the home was both a show-case to and a shelter against the outside world. The family home had become the setting where the family demonstrated its wealth and social standing. In this period of unstable class boundaries, the communication of status and social ambitions was of especial importance, and it was this which increased the representative function of the home.

At the same time there had been a development which stressed the significance of the home as a private sphere and haven. For the same economic class who administered the new production system under capitalism, also created a compensatory world of intimacy, a refuge of cosiness and warmth. The Victorian home became an antipole to the growing anonymity, rationality and effectivity of the outside world. In this dialectical process the sweetness of home increased, as the outside world became more complex and problematic.

The very plan of the Victorian home in Sweden bears witness to this dual function of the home as scene and shelter. A number of spatial boundaries were drawn with the help of entrances, passages, doors and sequences of rooms to separate public from private, servants from family, children from parents, as well as sorting out visitors of varying standing.

The history of the bedroom is a good example of this rearrangement of social space. The notion of a private and secluded room for sleeping was more or less unknown in early 19th century Sweden. Even in upper class settings the bedchamber was used for social entertaining. With the growing emphasis on the privacy and intimacy of the married couple, the bedchamber was transformed into the *sleeping* room. During the Victorian era it was usually located as far away from the entrance of the house as possible, and it became the most private sphere of the home, open only to the married couple. It was often furnished in a different way from other rooms. The whiteness of the walls, the polished brass or mahogany of the big double bed, underlined the new symbolic qualities of the room, a sanctum for the most intimate of all relations, that between man and wife: the territory in which the only form of legitimate sexuality could be performed in total seclusion and privacy, and a room where the married couple could withdraw at night to discuss the happenings of the day.

Such spatial rearrangements communicated new boundaries and rituals of transition and seclusion. Children were taught to respect these boundaries, never to enter their parents' bedroom or father's study without permission. They could also see how differently life was organised in the public and private spheres: how when Father came home from the office, he would always change out of his dark black suit into a cosy velvet smoking jacket, and remove his polished leather boots for a pair of soft slippers. Every evening the Victorian child could witness this *rite de passage* which transformed the efficient business man into 'Father', the family man.

Any child growing up in such a home inevitably learnt a great deal about social relationships. The actual physical arrangements became part of the silent and unconscious socialisation. It was as if the walls almost spoke to the children. And indeed we have found that many middle- and upper class children remember their childhood homes as filled with forbidden territories and significantly mysterious boundaries. The various rooms each had their different atmosphere. And some, as a boy from a town merchant's home recalls, were especially compelling just because forbidden:

I loved to sneak into the drawing room, where we were never allowed on ordinary days, and I used to place myself between the two mirrors and watch how my picture was reflected and distorted, becoming smaller and smaller as it reached the edges. I guess I understood why, but it still seemed eerie.

He also described the contrasts which he noticed between the neat furniture of the girls' room, all in blue, and the more casual decoration of the boys' room. Just a small detail like the fact that there was a spittoon in every room, but the girls' became part of the silent communication of sex roles.

For an industrial manager's daughter, too, it is the image of a room which sums up home:

Most strongly I remember the evening hours around the dining table with silent or loud reading ... The light from the singing paraffin lamp was concentrated on the table, further away there were shadows, and through the open door to the best room you could see the darkness. Whew! When you had to pass through that room ...

Her strong memories of the family gathered around the table in the evenings is fairly typical. For many Victorians these situations became very emotionally loaded, a symbolic manifestation of family unity and intimacy. They helped to represent things that one wanted to remember and often to conceal what was missing. For the truth was that contact with parents was very often both restricted and formal. For many Swedish children of this time the parents' bedroom was a forbidden territory. 'Behind the dining room was a world I never entered, but where I guessed my parents had their rooms', recollects one Victorian boy. And he also remembered his father, the judge, visiting the nursery only once during his whole childhood. Another described how he shared rooms with the servants above his parents' apartment, and had only the shadiest ideas about what went on downstairs.

This difference between the ideals and the realities of family life is a recurring problem when one wants to reconstruct Victorian everyday life with help of memoirs and oral history material. In my attempts to analyse patterns of fatherhood and motherhood, I soon came to realise that child-hood memories were filtered through cultural stereotypes of the ideal mother or father. Fathers were often described by phrases like 'strict but fair', 'charming but irascible', 'strong sense of duty and admirable'; and relationships with a father were seldom presented as uncomplicated. But memories of the mother seem quite different, so much so that they often take on a sacred flavour in which she stands suffused with light and warmth and radiance. Stereotypes like 'our sunshine', 'filled with good-ness', 'the good spirit of the house', are commonplace—and they tell us something about the Victorian division of labour in parenthood. But then occasionally one gets glimpses of another reality, such as the fact that many Victorian mothers were rather distant and above all that bodily contact and warmth could be very restricted. In that light, many pictures of Mother speak more of a longing for a mother with whom one wished to have closer contact, than of an actual relationship.

*   *   *   *

In retrospect the family rituals of the Victorians in their over-decorated homes, attended by slaving servants, may seem both distant and exotic. On the other hand, it is striking how much we have inherited in terms of values and habits from this subculture. We only have to look back on our own upbringing to realise how powerful this cultural influence has been during the 20th century.

Our attitudes towards sexuality and love, home and privacy, male and female are still perhaps more influenced by this Victorian ideology than we care to admit. So effectively can these notions be internalised that many people still take them for granted and as natural, and may find it hard indeed to understand cultures or historical settings where inter-personal relations are structured in a different way.

How did this Victorian middle class ideology of the family and the home come to attain such a marked cultural dominance in the whole of Swedish society during the early 20th century? How could it be so successfully transplanted to working class life, where the same material conditions did not exist and where quite different traditions of family life had developed?

We cannot, as sometimes is done, explain this cultural influence in terms of new ideals, or a wave of cultural innovation sweeping over the country and through the classes. Neither can we reduce the problem to the rather trivial statement that it is only a question of a new economic and political elite imposing their ideology on a helpless working class. We need to take a closer look at the manifold ways in which these new ideals were communicated and how they were turned into dreams and aspirations among the working people.

The last decades of the 19th century were in general a period of unrest and polarisation in Sweden. The old social structure was crumbling and traditional rules of hierarchy, loyalty and social control no longer seemed to function. Preindustrial society had been based upon a powerful notion of stability and a lack of mobility. Now new social groups were forming, and a rapidly growing working class was seen as a menace to the old social stability. There was an atmosphere of tension, of clashing values, which left those at the top frightened. If the old order could not be rebuilt, certainly a new moral cement seemed to be needed if a disintegrating society was to be kept together. And from this alarming situation a new answer emerged. If only the working classes could be disciplined or raised to middle class values, if only their unrest and ambitions could be turned inwards, towards the home and the family, many problems would be solved. The change should be moral rather than economic.

Arguments like these were not uncommon within the social and political establishment of the period, although they could be more or less consciously formulated. The virtues of a stable home life and a 'happy family' life style were not only echoed in parliamentary debates, in newspaper articles and pamphlets: they started to spread through many channels, such as housing and educational reform programmes, and campaigns for good housekeeping and homemaking. By the turn of the century we can find the ideal of the happy nuclear family extolled almost everywhere. It appears in the popular press and the penny novels, in advertisements, in popular oleographs and so on. Even in zoological illustrations the animals start to appear in family groups according to the Victorian model rather than to actual biological patterns.

An important part of this cultural campaign was directed towards working class women. A number of welfare associations were set up which had the reform of motherhood and housewifery among the lower classes as their chief aim. For many middle class women this missionary quest became an important calling.

It would be wrong, however, to talk in terms of a well planned attack with the explicit goal of pacifying or domesticating the unruly working class. Many of the social reformers saw themselves as missionaries of 'the good life', of modernisation and social development. They wanted to improve housing and food habits, or introduce more sophisticated methods of child care and hygiene. Many of them were not aware of the fact that their reforming activities had heavy moral overtones.

We are still, however, faced with the question of why these new ideals were so readily accepted in many working class settings. One important answer lies in the fact that they were part of another important message, that of social mobility through individual improvement. The dream of a better future for oneself or for one's children came to mean aspirations to the type of respectability and prestige which was linked with middle class values. To rise in the world one had to master the cultural language of the middle class. For many working class men mobility and social prestige meant having a 'proper' housewife tending a 'nice' home, well-behaved children, and a 'decent' social life. This longing for respectability led many working class families to set aside one room to be used as parlour on special occasions only, even if it meant that the family members had to sleep in the kitchen. It could also mean that they avoided the informal socialising which characterised many working class communities, and instead tried to 'keep themselves to themselves'.

During the first decades of the 20th century there was a return to the home and to the role of housewife for many working class women, who earlier had worked outside home, and with the new definitions of housekeeping there was much for a wife to do if she wanted to keep up with middle class standards of cleanliness. The middle class obsession with order and hygiene could easily turn housekeeping into a labour of Sisyphus: there was simply no limit to the amount of energy you could invest in cleaning and tidying. And the spread of the new housewife ideal must also have been encouraged by the important fact that the most common occupation for young working class girls was to work as domestic helps in middle class homes. And, indeed, working class reminiscences from the period around the First World War quite often confirm the spread of these new attitudes, with their insistence that it was, above all, Mother who struggled to keep them 'clean and decent' as children, and who shouldered the responsibility for the social facade of the family and the home.

*   *   *   *

If we want to explain the success of the new ideology of home and family we have to see it as not merely imposed through fear of the middle class, but also as a positive response to dreams of mobility and aspirations for respectability. And with rising standards of living, life at home could indeed become more attractive. Working class couples started to devote more planning and energy to creating an atmosphere of cosiness and intimacy in the home. They spent more and more time at home with the family. And when times got bad and the outside world seemed harsher, they too could find in home a sheltered refuge. So the working class family likewise began to retire into itself.

Nevertheless, a note of caveat must be introduced into this account of the *embourgeoisement* of working class family life: for it was never a simple process of cultural indoctrination. Cultural forms were certainly borrowed, but again and again they were transformed in the process, and given quite a different meaning and function. For the working class had its own aims, independent of those of the middle class, even if the rising organised labour movement often seemed to share the language and objectives of the middle class in many of its own campaigns. This process of culture-building and transformation is one of the key concerns of our research project.[4]

But what abut privatisation? During the 20th century the boundaries between private and public have been changing rapidly. We can follow how public activities have become private and social life more formal and family-centred. The invisible bubble of privacy surrounding the individual has grown rapidly and, today, Sweden stands as one of the most privatised cultures in the Western World.

I think this makes it even more important to take a closer look at the social history of this evasive phenomenon. Again, oral history becomes an important research tool.

In many interviews with working class people a clear pattern emerges. During the 1920s and 1930s social life in working class neighbourhoods was still public and informal. Older people frequently seem bewildered by the scale of the change which they have witnessed. Our interviews from the factory town of Landskrona often take up this theme:

Well, talking about neighbours then and nowadays—there's a great difference. Then, you never had to press the doorbell, you just walked in and out like one big family, and had so much in common...
There was six families for each entrance and you had parties together and nice times, playing cards. Now it's arrived, that great monster standing on four legs in the corner—the telly...

Or another:

I miss the old togetherness. There was more friendship then. Now everybody's got their own to think of.... And then there's the telly... People say, 'We've got to be at home tonight, there's this or that on the telly'. Earlier on you went out to watch telly with the others. It was years before we bought one for ourselves. But before that we used to play cards, and if someone had a birthday, we'd play and sing. But all that's gone now... Yes, that's what I mean, coming together was freer and more simple then.

And again:

People are more reserved nowadays. They kind of lock themselves in and have their TV set, of course. That's the way things are now. You don't get together now, time was you'd visit your brother and so on, but that's not done very much now. It's just the way things go.

Statements like these are very typical. People will often talk nostalgically of the solidarity and informality which characterised social life during earlier periods and then sigh: 'things are so different nowadays... I don't really know why...' To some extent this has to do with changes in the life cycle and ageing, but that is only part of the truth. The transformation is usually seen as a mysterious process which just happened to them. Quite often people see the advent of television as a specific cause of this change. But again this can only be part of the truth and is often an attempt to rationalise something much more complex.

To come to grips with this change we need to place the phenomenon of privatisation, both in our contemporary cultural life, and in that of earlier periods. How was isolation and togetherness defined in 1930 and in 1970, how were the boundaries between the individual and the collective experienced during different eras and in different social classes? Why is it that the same individual can talk about the need to 'keep oneself to oneself', and later start lamenting the loss of togetherness? The culturally defined need for privacy and individual freedom is combined with longing for less isolation and more social contacts.

The important point here is that we have to start dismantling this diffuse social change, and learn to understand that what we call privatisation is a complex phenomenon with totally different meanings in different settings. It is just not enough to rush out and start interviewing. Our oral history work must be combined with considerable theoretical reflection. In our project we have just started this work; but maybe our probing into the social history of privatisation, isolation and loneliness may help us to answer the question: 'What is it exactly you try to shut out or shut in when you close the door of your suburban home?'

---

1 For our project, see a short description in *International Journal of Oral History*, Vol 1 no 1, pp. 75–77. A fuller treatment of the themes presented in this paper is contained in our first report on the project, Jonas Frykman and Orvar Löfgren, *Den kultiverade människan*, 1980, pp. 74–131. In order not to burden this short paper with references all quotations are taken from the book.

2   For a presentation of this work see my survey, 'Historical perspectives on Scandinavian peasantries', in *Annual Review of Anthropology*, 1980, pp. 187–216.
3   The interviews have been carried out by members of our research team and by students on fieldwork training.
4   See the discussion in Löfgren, 'On the anatomy of culture', *Ethnologia Europea*, 1981.

Fascism and Resistance

250

A woman courier (*staffetta*) with other partisans (from Partigiane della libertà (Women Freedom Fighters), ed. Sezione Stampa of the PCI, 1973, p.139). See Anna Maria Bruzzone's article on pp. 273–83 below.

Knowing and Not Knowing: Involvement in Nazi Genocide[1]

Elmer Luchterhand

In current reappraisals of Fascism much theoretical interest revolves around the vastly greater destructiveness of Nazism than of other manifestations of Fascism. Certainly the most distinctive product of the German variant was the Nazi concentration camp (NCC) system with its complex genocidal outcomes.[2] It is my conviction that unless we confront and understand this question, and related ones from the past, we have much less hope of preventing a recurrence. Underlying the research described here is the assumption that detailed study of the development, operation and effects of selected units of the NCC system can significantly improve our conceptualisation of genocidal processes in a developed society.

As Martin Broszat put it in his scholarly submission on the history of the NCCs to the court in the Auschwitz trial in 1965: 'a strange contradiction remains: although the National Socialist concentration camps have become a familiar concept to those seeking to shape historical and political opinion, little reliable information on them exists.'[3] Particularly little is known about the catastrophic expansion of the system in the last years of the war. West German scholars have identified over one thousand *Kommandos*, of which some five hundred were large enough to justify classification as concentration camps,[4] which are commonly referred to as outlying camps, or out-camps (*Aussenlager*) of the base camps. This was the final phase of what Kogon perceptively called a 'veritable concentration camp boom' (*einen wahren 'KL-Gründer-Boom'*) during the last years of the war.[5]

The immediate aim of the research is to construct a detailed case history of a genocidal episode, and to include in it the fullest possible range of individual and group involvements. We needed to find a situation in which the everyday activities of perpetrators, victims and co-presents[6] could be reconstructed with reasonable accuracy. For this, the population studied had to be, *firstly*, small enough to make it possible to interview people in all social strata and representative roles; *secondly*, no different in any special way, from other communities in the region in its support for, or opposition to the Nazi movement; *thirdly*, one that had not provided respondents previously in any related study;' and *fourthly*, that had substantial knowledge about events from direct involvement or observation.

Exploratory field work showed that the episode-and-site which had been under consideration from the outset met these criteria well. The area is a compact one in the northern (Franconian) part of Bavaria (see map), consisting of the market town of Hersbruck, the villages of Happurg and Förrenbach, and half a dozen hamlets, some thirty kilometres east of Nuremberg. The present population of Hersbruck of around 9,000, and that of Happurg, the focal village, of about 1,000, represent modest increases since the 1940s.

It has been estimated that around 5,000 concentration camp prisoners lost their lives in ten months under the conditions and treatment received in Hersbruck concentration camp, and on the construction project to be described later. (This estimate includes unregistered deaths of Slavic and Jewish prisoners of various national origins. Also included is a sizable number of prisoners who were transported by lorry or otherwise, back to the base camp, Flossenbürg, as no longer fit for work, and who died soon after arrival. Also included is an undetermined but relatively small number of prisoners who were shot when they fell behind, or died otherwise, on the evacuation march to Dachau and beyond.)

In the study-site area there had been generally strong support for the Nazi movement. However, the Social Democratic party also won in many local elections in the Weimar years, and regularly participated in town and village governments. Research possibilities were not affected by notable attention of any kind, and the genocidal episode completely escaped scholarly notice, even though various SS men, minor corporation officials and concentration camp prisoners of rank were tried in 1949–50 for crimes against common prisoners of Hersbruck concentration camp. Indeed, a small but important part of the study site is now obscured by an artificial lake (part of a hydro-electric development finished in 1960) which is now a centre for local water sports. The first monument, a non-sectarian one, erected by survivor groups on the spot where the crematorium stood, is covered by the lake. A substitute, in the form of a Christian cross, stands on an adjoining hillside. It too has been damaged, but by a blast from a machine pistol, presumably fired by some local fascist primitive.

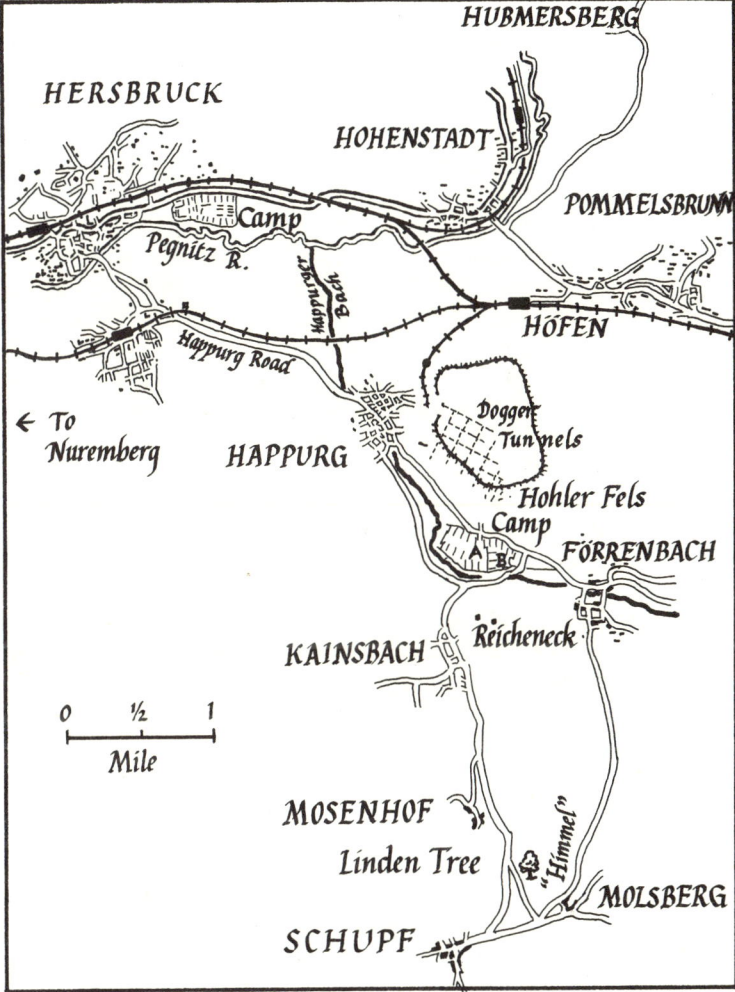

HUBMERSBERG

HERSBRUCK

HOHENSTADT

POMMELSBRUNN

Camp

Pegnitz R.

Happurg Road

HÖFEN

To
Nuremberg

HAPPURG

Doggen
Tunnels

Hohler Fels
Camp

FÖRRENBACH

KAINSBACH

Reicheneck

0   ½   1
Mile

MOSENHOF
Linden Tree

"Himmel"

MOLSBERG

SCHUPF

The general situation and nature of events important for the study were readily observable by the villagers and townspeople. Two compounds for prisoners existed temporarily in the centre of the village of Happurg. In the second of these, containing around 550 prisoners, the daily routine was a replica of that in the NCCs.

The NCC prisoners worked on a construction project for an underground armaments plant. This involved tunnelling into the side of a low mountain that dominates the valley in which Happurg and Förrenbach are situated, three kilometres apart. The project – one of many in the spring of 1944 to protect the German aircraft industry from Allied air raids[7] – was a desperate effort by a consortium of major German firms, aided by some fifty smaller ones. Concentration camp prisoners made up the largest component of the work force, which also included foreign 'slave labourers', around 500 SS convicts, and a fluctuating contingent of civilian tradesmen. The code word for this enterprise controlled by the SS, was Dogger, or Doggerwerk, meaning Dogger project.

Midway between the two villages was a special camp which was labelled Förrenbach *Konzentrationslager* (that is, concentration camp, here referred to as Förrenbach Camp) on the only engineering drawing known to have survived the destruction of records by the SS. This camp was never finished, and no part of it was ever occupied by concentration camp prisoners. Some 40% of the completed barracks space was occupied by SS men imprisoned for various code violations, and assigned to construction duty to work off their sentences. The rest of the space was occupied by foreign male and female 'slave labourers' rounded up in East European countries in the dragnet campaigns of Sauckel.[8] Many of these foreign conscripts were detailed, not to the construction project, but to the villagers as field hands and domestic workers, to make up for the shortage of labour caused by military operations on the Eastern Front.

Also midway between the two villages, and attached to Förrenbach Camp, was a crematorium used for disposal of corpses from Hersbruck concentration camp. The chimney stood clear of obstructing terrain features and was therefore visible from both villages and elsewhere, and to all who travelled the two valley roads leading to the market town of Hersbruck from the south. Two outdoor pyres were also set up for corpse disposal. The first, on low ground close to the road into Hubmersberg, was used only briefly because of complaints by leading citizens of Hersbruck about the smoke. Mrs. Mörtel, manager of an inn in Hubmersberg, could remember

...only one burning of prisoner bodies. On that day all roads in the area were closed by the SS. The official explanation was that an Allied plane had crashed there. People from around here watched two or three lorries stop at the roadside where the monument now stands. Clouds of smoke rose quickly and drifted over the area. In a few hours the burning was over. Sometime later the SS resodded the place where the grass was destroyed.

For the second pyre, a hilltop site near Schupf, and midway between the hamlets Mosenhof and Molsberg, was chosen. This pyre was in regular use to the end, with wood being requisitioned from farmers living in Molsberg and Schupf, and under some weather conditions the smoke pall hung for days in connected valleys.

On the eastern outskirts of Hersbruck, beside the road to Nurem-berg, was Hersbruck Concentration Camp. An outcamp of Flossenbürg, it had at its height nearly 6,000 prisoners crowded into its twenty barracks. They were divided into three shifts for round-the-clock work, digging tunnels for the underground armaments plant in the mountain at the edge of Happurg. Although the shifts were sometimes transported by train, more often they marched under SS guard, sometimes assisted by dogs, to and from work in their 'zebra uniforms' and clogs, through resi-dential streets of Hersbruck, and the full length of Happurg. The *Geister-zug* (processions of ghosts), was what local people called these prisoner formations travelling their streets, six times in a day and night.

In one way or another, in workplace or street, local residents were thrown into contact with concentration camp prisoners, foreign con-scripts, or SS convicts, all of whom worked on the Dogger project. Misery was experienced by all, but immersion in mass death was the lot of the concentration camp prisoners only. How did local citizens live from day to day with the sights and sounds and smells related to mass death? Did they know what went on?

Of course. We all knew about it. The bodies were usually hauled by lorries ... (People) said, 'They are coming again!' or 'They are bringing some again!' ('*Sie kommen wieder!*' oder '*Sie bringen wieder welche!*'). When one was returning from shopping in Happurg and saw the smoke, one knew what was afoot (*Man hat gewusst, was los war*). Up there (pointing to the high ground) they cremated them ...We were glad when there was nothing more to see or hear. One did not have to be concerned with it anymore.[9]

Just how did they respond? What did they do? How could parents explain such things to their children? What did these events do to their assump-tions about the reality and 'justice' of their life-worlds? How did they account to intimates for their own inaction when events brought them face to face with ultimate evil? To explore such seemingly unapproach-able matters, oral history techniques are indispensable.

*   *   *   *

An SS Control Staff (*SS-Führungsstab*) was installed in the centre of Happurg in an inn. It was responsible for the progress of Doggerwerk as a whole. It was responsible for the procurement of materials, management decisions affecting the construction timetable, and housing for the work force, including the concentration camp prisoners. Under it were two distinct bureaucratic structures whose activities were kept separate, but which it coordinated.

The supervision of the prisoners at work sites was under the command of camp officials who, like the commander, were housed on the premises of Hersbruck Camp. Because of this, they were effectively invisible to the local population. Their presence was signalled by the brutalities of SS guards toward prisoners, and by the guards' threats against local residents for all acts of compassion toward the prisoners.

On the other hand, almost all of the construction bureaucracy heads resided in Happurg and Hersbruck, and had offices in a common headquarters in Happurg. Their movements were readily seen. As a rule they made themselves quite inaccessible to the native population, and the villagers accordingly saw them as the keepers of extremely important secrets.

Except for the critically important fact of employing prisoners, the operating procedures of the construction bureaucracy were not altogether dissimilar from those of modern private enterprise in wartime elsewhere. On the other hand, the camp-system bureaucracy was a special type. In mode of operation it was a military bureaucracy superimposed on a system of penal slavery of the most extreme kind. In slightly more than nine months, this dual bureaucracy managed the production of more than nine kilometres of tunnels, either finished or in an advanced stage of completion.[10]

Since the manifest function of Hersbruck Camp was to supply labour for digging tunnels, the applicability of the terms genocide and genocidal processes might be questioned. In mode of operation the differences between centres such as those in Poland that were exclusively exterminative, such as Chelmno, Belzec, Sobibor and Treblinka on the one hand, and camps such as Hersbruck on the other, were enormous. In the former, genocidal action was unitary; there was no ambiguity of intent, and no ambiguity as to means, location, or the identity of the *immediate* perpetrators. The victims too, in the racist terms of the perpetrators, were of 'one kind': Jews.

Genocide, as manifested in Doggerwerk, was not a unitary phenomenon, but a decidedly complex one. The complexity of intent, means, locations, participation, and of victim categories was in fact reflective of the complexity of 'modern,' technologically developed society. Despite the enormous differences in operation between camps such as Hersbruck and Treblinka, it would nevertheless be fatuous to deny their kinship. In the Third Reich, Hersbruck-type camps were way stations on the road to destruction of all those that the regime classified and imprisoned as unwanted life.

The genocidal nature of the outcamp-industry relationship has been only poorly understood. The emergence of the outcamp network was a response to two developments of technological warfare: *firstly*, to its extreme material demands; and *secondly*, to the partial cancelling of the age-old distinction between battle-front and rear. At the same time, two conflicting aims were operative within the camp system: one was to serve as labour arsenal; the other, to exterminate. Out of the 'wild improvisations' to meet the demands of the military came an 'invention' of sorts to minimise the strains on the administration of Hersbruck Camp. In a word, this was the '*return* transport' of physically incapacitated prisoners back to the base camp. The rationale, of course, was the improvement of productive capacity by making room for incoming transports of people with supposedly greater capacities. Besides the rock fragments that had to be strewn, for reasons of camouflage, over the mountainside, there was the other awkward byproduct of tunnelling, the corpse pile. None of the four means of disposal – use of the crematory in a Nuremberg cemetery, an outdoor pyre near Hubmersberg, the Förrenbach Camp crematory, or the hilltop pyre near Schupf – was satisfactory. The *return* transport was an important aid to local administration. The visible condition of the returnees helped to explain to the SS command and control personnel the failures in meeting production deadlines. The space-problem chaos created by incoming transports was lessened, and so were the chores of local corpse disposal. Flossenbürg had better facilities, of course, and they needed them, for the mistreatment and fears connected with return almost certainly speeded up the dying. Insofar as the *return* transport was a general pattern in the outcamps, it helped to solve an administrative problem of the system as a whole. Accurate record keeping was operationally essential to efficient management in both parts of the dual bureaucracy of Doggerwerk, as the endless roll calls bear witness. In conflict with this was the ceaseless need to obfuscate, if not to obliterate all records of the terrible death toll. The *return* transport in no way interfered with the necessary keeping of accurate records, and it assisted in concealing the evidence of mass death.

My own discovery of the return-transport practice came from interviews with a former head nurse and a nurse assistant of the Doggerwerk *Lazarett* (hospital). They described the brutal loading of gravely ill prisoners onto a lorry, that was parked beside a barn being used as a collecting point for prisoners who collapsed at work. Nothing is known about the frequency of such transports.

At the highest level, certainly, the question of genocidal intent in administering the camp system is resolved by the Hitler order in 1945 that no concentration camp prisoners were to be allowed to fall into Allied hands alive. And at the lowest operating level, such destructive intent was routinely shown. It effectively dominated the behaviour of camp personnel until the final weeks of the war. For the SS heads of the camp bureaucracy, Doggerwerk meant productive extermination (*'produktive Vernichtung'*); for the hardened SS types among the constructors, it meant exterminative production (*'vernichtende Produktion'*).

*   *   *   *

There are of course many problems and pitfalls on the way to a valid reconstruction of events that occurred long in the past, and in an atmosphere of threats made credible by highly visible acts of violence. How does one know whether one is succeeding or not? In this regard, the focused life histories have a special function to perform. They permit a more detailed, finer grained consideration of lines of evidence for particular events. The shorter interviews provide evidence from many more and different sources. Finally, and very important, over 250 documents set limits on errors of fact and interpretation, even though some contain errors of fact, and others, poorly substantiated opinion. Included are several drawings, hastily written depositions by victims, some two dozen fold-and-seal letters with original postmarks, dated strength reports of Hersbruck Camp, dated transport figures, financial statements referring to prisoner work details allotted to Hersbruck business firms, etc.[11] Insofar as the evidence, cutting across a variety of sources, converges in support of the account of an event, or an interpretation, one is entitled to have confidence in its validity.[12]

The many-sided research attack is reflected in selection of respondents from the widest possible range of social classes and occupations in the study-site communities, and roles specific to the events under study. As indicated in Table 1, 73 persons were interviewed. They included eleven former prisoners of Hersbruck Camp. Of these one was a physician who worked in the sickbay of the camp.

The fourteen persons classified under 'Administrative and Other

Table 1. Social Class, and Role of 73 Respondents interviewed

	Survivors of Hersbruck Concentration Camp	Administrative & Other Personnel: Doggerwerk and Camp Complex	Members of SS Penal Detachments	Co-Presents: Town, Village and Hamlet Residents	TOTALS
Solidly Middle Class or Above	3	6	1	20	30
Lower Middle Class	4	8	1	17	30
Working Class	4	–	1	8	13
TOTALS	11	14	3	45	73

Personnel of the two bureaucratic complexes included: the secretary in turn to all three Hersbruck Camp commanders; three SS guards from the same camp; the director, head nurse and one assistant nurse of the Doggerwerk *Lazarett*, one general accountant; and six engineers. These were an engineer attached to the SS Control Staff, an engineer-architect who initially directed the planning and designing of the underground plant, and all other technical aspects of construction; three technically trained engineers who had been employed by different major firms; one 'practical' engineer (without diploma) who had been on general assignment. Of the three 'Members of SS Penal Detachments', one was commander of one of the two SS penal companies.

The 45 'co-presents' of Table 1 are included in Table 2 by major occupation only. Among these local residents were twelve farmers (men and women), six village officials, five teachers, four housewives, and a variety of others. Altogether eight of them were from working class backgrounds.

Many respondents were interviewed two or more times; in one case, initial interviews were followed by a special series of twelve. Each interview was developed individually without a standard guide. However, a list of general subject-areas was formulated at the start, and used throughout. Most interviews were conducted in tandem with one of two German-born assistants, a sociologist and a teacher in a local school. Usually we

Table 2.   Occupations of 45 Co-Presents

12 farmers (men and women)	1 *Landrat* (retired)
6 officials of villages	1 court official (retired)
6 innkeepers	1 district school official
5 teachers, including retired ones	1 police inspector
4 housewives	1 petrol station operator
2 public employees	1 newsdealer (retired)
1 newspaper publisher	1 musician (retired)
1 book publisher, Nuremberg	1 car mechanic (retired)

prepared for the interview together, which then tended to take on the quality of a three-party conversation, with active direction minimised. Note-taking was casual; and we did not use tape recorders. For the respondent, three-way talk avoided the occasional awkwardness of the one-to-one interview, and thereby made it less difficult for the interviewers to ease the discussion forward. At the same time the more 'passive' interviewer could observe gestures, take special note of words and phrases, grasp meanings that otherwise might have been lost.

Several people tried to avoid being interviewed. One person initially refused, but later cooperated. Only one man, through his wife and son, persisted in outright refusal. This was Professor Doctor Herbert Rimpl, an engineer-architect who had general direction of all technical aspects of construction, beginning in Autumn, 1944. The higher the interviewing reached in the class structure, the greater was the reluctance to give information. The villagers talked. They were deeply curious about the doings inside their mountain. We explained that the purpose of the research was to develop a history of the community in the last year of the war and the succeeding months. Everyone sensed at once that the focus was on Doggerwerk, but no one had heard that codeword for it. Early in the interviews, discussion was guided toward some 'objective element' in the episode that puzzled people. As our work progressed and we acquired bits of technical information, these were shared with respondents. Thus, even when highly sensitive areas were touched, the interview relationship continued as an exchange in areas of mutual interest.

*   *   *   *

For interpreting attitudes, we found some of the most revealing clues in accounts of everyday incidents. Mr Reiss told us of how, as a boy, he and his mother sometimes passed the *Geisterzug* on their bicycles on the way to shop in Happurg. One time, just as they were passing the procession of prisoners, he saw his mother let her bicycle wobble, and saw a hand dart out, to the saddle bag. 'She had some turnips and other vegetables tied to the back . . . ' He added, 'I noticed that when my mother went alone to Happurg that she always put something on the back of the bicycle or held it on the handle bars. When I went alone, usually right after breakfast, she sometimes gave me food to take along, but nothing was said about what was to be done with it.' [13]

The following exchange occurred with a more reluctant woman respondent:

What proportion of the village population would you say tried in some way to give the prisoners food?
Nearly all of the residents put small food items in the street at some time. (*Fast alle Einwohner stellten manchmal Nahrungsmittel auf die Straße.*) There were two kinds of guards, those who pretended not to see the food, and the brutal ones. Many guards kicked the food away.[14]

Many people do not feel they are entitled to say: 'I did this or that for the prisoners.' They may not claim virtue for themselves, but rather claim it for others. Yet practically all willingly cooperated with the research.

Typically, no we-relationship could develop between a villager and a prisoner, even though the villager somehow, sometime, put out food for the prisoners, or purposefully allowed something to be snatched from a bicycle when encountering a prisoner procession. True, a relationship of a mechanical, truncated sort was momentarily effected, but it instantly died. There was never a relationship with an identifiable person, except under remarkable and exceedingly rare circumstances in Hersbruck. In the technical usage of social science, no true interaction really occurred. There was no meeting of glances, no partnership, however fleeting, with a particular prisoner. There was only the occasional furtive passing, somehow, of a tiny morsel to the anonymous outline of a human figure in an endless procession of starving men. Such contact was almost as empty as though the supplier of a potato, a turnip or a piece of bread was an unseen vending machine that delivered once, twice or even three times, and then no more.

*   *   *   *

Among those with whom we talked, some were children during the war.

One, Dietrich Riess, the son of an evangelical minister, was troop leader (*Jugendschaftsführer*) of the *Jungvolk* (Young People) of Förrenbach:

As troop leader of the Jungvolk, I often went to meetings in Hersbruck and in Lauf. I thoroughly enjoyed all of the activities, but my father repeatedly cautioned me not to do too much. However, he was not opposed to my being a member of the *Jungvolk*...

I attended the *Oberrealschule* (nonclassical secondary school) in Hersbruck. I left my home on my bicycle between seven and eight o'clock in the morning. Sometimes I met columns of prisoners. I did not know what the insignia on their uniforms meant. I was aware that they were not really criminals, but I could not believe they were non-criminals. I concluded that they were not prisoners of war. I supposed that if they had been, they would not have had to work so hard. It did not occur to me that the columns of prisoners might be related in some way to things the Nazi party stood for. I only saw prisoners who looked starved and weak. I never saw any corpses. I had not yet heard about concentration camps.

I asked my father about the low brick building with the tall chimney. He did not want to talk about it. He turned my questions aside by saying, 'We do not know for sure what is going on. We only hear rumours.' When I asked my father who the prisoners were and why they were treated so badly, he said 'We cannot say for sure about these things. You have to be careful. You must not give anything to the prisoners. When people give, you know what the guards do.' [15]

Mr Goldner, now a postal clerk in Happurg, was a fourteen-year-old at Doggerwerk time, and the first hints had come to him earlier:

In 1941, when Germany invaded Russia, my mother, the village postmistress, said, 'Now we will be beaten.' A man from the village who heard this remark while collecting his mail, said, 'If you say such a thing, I will see that you go to a concentration camp.'

By 1944 Goldner was a troop leader of the *Hitler Jugend* (Hitler Youth) in Happurg:

In 1944, Göring visited the project. Although he had a castle in Velden, he arrived wearing *Lederhosen* (leather breeches). In the party were some engineers and various prominent people in civilian clothes. The word went around quickly that Göring was visiting the village, and members of the Hitler Youth troop collected at the Black Eagle where the cars stood. I managed to get a Göring handshake...

I was involved in every possible way in the Hitler Youth. I especially liked camping. There we were introduced to scouting and quasi-military training. Each morning we got up early. We had to run two kilometres over dewy fields before breakfast. We also spent a lot of time listening to radio news from the Eastern Front.

When the concentration camp prisoners were put into two special compounds in Happurg, I and four or five others from the Hitler Youth played a secret game. We stole vegetables from nearby fields, and threw them over the camp fence; in return we sometimes got Russian cigarettes, called Machorkas, which we secretly tried.

One day I was watching a prisoner detail lay a telephone cable to the headquarters of the SS Control staff. I was standing in front of our house eating a slice of bread when a prisoner begged for it. I gave him the bread. The guard saw this and beat the prisoner with his gun butt. My father watched the situation from an upper window. He shouted to the guard: 'Aren't you ashamed of yourself? Can't you see that these people are hungry?' The guard continued his beating, and proceeded to threaten my father.

I think it was only after people in the village actually saw prisoners that they became aware of what the words ''concentration camp'' meant. Neighbours talked with each other about the difference between those who wore green triangles and those who wore red ones. They observed that it was usually the greens who were the Kapos and who beat the other prisoners.

I got to know four SS men very well. They were very good people. They took care of four Alsatian dogs used on the march to and from work. The SS men trained them in a special field behind the barracks of the SS Control Staff. One man would put on a prisoner's striped uniform, and an arm protector. The other man would set the dogs at him.

Other children disliked the SS men but liked the regular soldiers. Riess told us:

At that time I went around with three other boys of my age. We often rode our bicycles from Schupf to Happurg. The road passed within about 35 metres of the place where corpses of prisoners were burned. Sometimes we were stopped by SS guards who stood on the road and shouted at us to go away. We were usually allowed to continue, but we were told to turn our heads to one side. We always gave some kind of excuse such as going to market for our mothers. All of us liked the regular soldiers we saw, but not the SS. Whenever SS men came to the village something bad happened.

There were other respondents who had rather special vantage points from which to observe events. Mrs. Högner, now some eighty years old, still lives on the family farm close to where the pyre was. We began talking with her by the roadside where she was filling two large farm baskets with dandelion greens for her rabbits. She responded to our questions freely, and at times with intense feeling, tears in her eyes:

Once when I was working in the field close to the pyre, an SS guard came out of the woods and into the field. He looked so thin and hungry that I asked if he wanted something to eat.

Another time, coming home from shopping at the grocery store in Happurg,

I met another SS guard who seemed to be very hungry. He saw bread in my bundle and asked for some. I told him that I did not have a knife. He took out his own knife and I cut some bread for him . . .
   The people here call that hilltop *Himmel* (heaven).

Why do they call it Himmel?
I don't know. Perhaps one reason was the reddish glow that lit up the sky above the woods. Maybe the people thought that the prisoners' souls went to heaven . . .
   One evening one of my sons came running into the house and shouted, 'Mama the woods are on fire.' Sometimes the flames were so high that it looked as if the trees were burning. Whenever they were burning bodies the smell was awful, and when the wind brought the smoke toward Molsberg it was terrible.
   The prisoners had to burn other prisoners. Other people from around here saw prisoners working there. One of the guards who was there from time to time, but not the one to whom I gave food, told me the same thing. He also said that prisoners were offered extra food for this work. After a fire had been going for quite a while, one could sometimes hear shots. People say that the officials did not want any prisoner witnesses, so they shot them . . .
   Before the war my husband had a job in Hersbruck. He used to take a short-cut through the woods. When he was home on leave he tried to take the same shortcut. He was stopped by a guard who said, 'I'll shoot you if you try to go farther.'
   Another soldier home on leave from the East was coming from Happurg by bicycle. To get up the long steep hill on the way to Schupf, he grabbed the back of a passing truck. The front end was covered with a tarpaulin. On the steepest part of the road, corpses started to slide out from under the canvass. The soldier said he was horrified . . .
   Once when I went to Happurg to buy food, a long column of prisoners came through the village. One prisoner suddenly fell to the ground. The column kept going, and the prisoner was left lying where he fell. No one did anything about him.
   One day when I came out of a store in Happurg, a long line of prisoners was going by. They looked hungrily at the bread I was carrying and I gave them part of the loaf. The guard in front of the column must have heard enough to realise that regulations were being violated. He turned around suddenly and shouted: 'What's going on? Get away! You are not to give them food.'
   When anyone is hungry, I have to give them food. If I give them something to eat, God will see that my children also get something from other people. ('*Wenn ich ihnen was zum essen gebe, so wird Gott dafür sorgen daß meine Kinder von anderen Leuten auch bekommen.*')

We drove Mrs. Högner to the family farm now managed by her daughter and son-in-law, Mr Träumer. They belong to the Evangelical Congregation of Förrenbach. Mrs. Träumer was seven years old at the time of Doggerwerk. She told us, 'My playmates and I knew that dead prisoners were burned in the woods. We also heard the shooting that sometimes followed, and we knew that it meant the death of more prisoners. I cannot remember how we came to know these things, but probably we learned about them through something our parents said. They did not let us go near the site of the pyre.'

Others whose social position might seem to have made it possible to understand clearly what was going on, remained astonishingly ignorant of events. Mrs Hagendorn is the widow of the Evangelical minister of Förrenbach. As a young woman she had been a teacher of English. She worked as interpreter for an American officer at the beginning of the occupation. She was a very willing, helpful and forthright respondent:

From our house one had a view down the valley to Happurg and beyond. One could see smoke pouring out the chimney on a low brick building. Often when I opened the door in the morning there would be an awful smell. It was always the same. At different times I said to my husband, 'There's that terrible smell again.' He told me 'There are rumours, but we really do not know what is going on.'

When did you first find out what the low brick building with the tall chimney was used for?
I did not know until the Americans came.

How could she not know? In such a field-work situation an American sociologist needs the wisdom of a German one from a small-town minister's family, to clarify the special social isolation of ministers' wives in the Third Reich.

Mr. Eichenmüller, another farmer of Molsberg, had been away fighting, first in France and then on the Russian front. His unit advanced to within 18 kilometres of Moscow. But by the summer of 1944 he had been recalled to work the farm. He described in meticulous detail the grillwork construction of the pyre, the position of the SS guards, and the place by the great linden tree where the farmers had to put the wood requisitioned for the pyre:

In all, I saw three or four trucks loaded with corpses. Each truck was hauling from 50 to 100 bodies. Cremating was not done on a regular schedule. After each burning a sickening, sweetish smell hung in the valley for days. Everyone knew what was going on. The women were more disturbed by the smell than the men. Many of the men were hardened by war experience.
   Once when I stopped to talk with the guard who stood near the linden tree, he said the dead prisoners had murdered German soldiers. 'They were partisans,' he said. Everyone among them had at least one German soldier on his conscience (*'Von denen hat jeder mindestens einen deutschen Soldat auf dem Gewissen.'*).

The innkeepers also had a close view of events. Hans Haberstumpf was later to become the first mayor of Happurg elected after the war, ousting a Social Democrat who had been appointed by the Americans. It was he who owned the barn which was used as the second prisoner compound:

At times I pushed some bread and potatoes under the fence. I told the guards to look the other way . . . I never saw any of the guards who had been transferred from the Wehrmacht beat a prisoner, but the Kapos were terrible. Once I bawled at a Kapo who was beating a prisoner—so sick he could hardly walk. The Kapo shouted back, 'If you don't shut up you will be in here too. I will report you to the SS.'

In the autumn after the prisoners had all been transferred to the Hersbruck Camp, I asked a guard how many bodies the crematorium could burn in a day. He answered, 'It does not work very well. It only burns three or four bodies a day'. Later, after some changes were made it burned about eight a day. Once when the Gestapo chief stopped at the Inn and I knew he would be staying long enough, I went over to the crematorium to have a look. I saw how prisoners were used to put the bodies in. They were so thin that the flesh had fallen away to the bone.

Anna Espenschied and her husband now run the Happurg inn which was her father's in the war, and which was the first prisoner compound. Anna was then a teenage girl:

Some SS officers regularly ate at the inn. One had a beautiful Doberman dog which I liked very much. In April 1945 when the Americans were approaching, the construction people and prisoners were ready to head south. My father asked the officer to leave the dog behind, and said that I would take care of it in the last days of the war. The officer refused . . .

We lived on the ground floor, directly under the prisoners' quarters. Fleas were everywhere. I was disturbed by them. I could not sleep. I was afraid I would be infected with the diseases many prisoners had.

When there were leftovers of food from the family kitchen I used to put them in the yard for the prisoners when the guard wasn't looking. I then went over and talked with him until I was certain the food had been picked up . . .

If you had a soft heart, it was terrible to look at the prisoners. There were times when I lay awake all night and cried. One day a guard saw me giving turnips to prisoners. He told me that if I did it again he would report me to the Commander, and that I would then be put in a concentration camp. I was terribly scared. When my father heard about it he became terribly angry. He told the guard, 'If you inform on my daughter I will kill you myself. Then we will have to go to the concentration camp, but maybe the prisoner will survive.'

In the rear of our quarters there were several windows. Through these I could see what went on, and sometimes talk with prisoners . . .

One of the prisoners I could talk with was a Russian. I also gave him food. He did not have to go to the mountain to work because he was a medical doctor. One day he took his wedding ring which was sewn in his collar and gave it to me. He said I had kept him alive, but that he would not live much longer. He told me about his wife and two children.

When I saw him again, I told him the trouble I was having with a tooth. It had to be crowned but it was almost impossible to get gold for a crown. I said I would like to use the ring. I am still wearing his ring in my mouth.

Those who probably came closest of all to the prisoners were the staff of the camp medical facilities. At Happurg a small *Lazarett* (hospital) was set up, primarily for the civilian tradesmen employed on the construction project, but some concentration camp prisoners – apparently those with special skills – were brought in by SS guards for minor disorders and injuries affecting work output. The guards prevented non-essential talk between the staff and prisoners. The staff consisted of six or seven nurses, usually, but not in all instances, without professional training.

A sickbay existed in Förrenbach Camp, where at least one physician, captured in eastern Europe, seems to have been available until his execution near the end of the war. A sickbay also existed in Hersbruck Camp, where almost all of the treatment available was provided by a prisoner-physician from Poland. Such medical facilities within the Nazi concentration camps have always been a source of some puzzlement. They existed, in the literal medieval sense, in limbo—'(a region) on the border (of hell)'.

Mrs. Haberzett, then in her forties, was head nurse in the Doggerwerk *Lazarett* at Happurg. She remembers some of the SS guards as 'nice' in allowing her and other nurses to drop bread on the streets where the marching prisoners could pick it up. But others were openly sadistic:

At noon one day, an SS guard brought in a Russian prisoner about seventeen years old, who had an enormous wound on his neck. It was caked with dried blood. The wound appeared to have been made by a rifle butt. The guard ordered me to bandage the wound saying, 'There is no need to take special pains in doing so. This man will be hanged tomorrow.' Then he said something frightening: 'Before that, I'll take him to my room and play my little game with him.' Dr. Vogel, another nurse and I begged the guard to leave the boy alone, especially since he was to be hanged anyway, but the guard said 'Why shouldn't I have my little fun?' Dr. Vogel asked what the boy had done, and the guard said, 'He stepped out of the column and begged for bread. It's against orders for prisoners to leave the column.' While this was going on the boy was saying over and over, 'Mother, mother, mother...' With the bandaging done, the guard shoved his victim out the door, and the other nurse and Dr. Vogel and I became genuinely ill.

Mr. Kreissel, who organised and managed the Happurg *Lazarett*, was never to forgert what he too witnessed during those few months:

Most prisoners who tried to escape were not just killed. Many were tortured to death. One prisoner who got away, but was caught, is an example. They hand-cuffed his hands behind his back and beat him terribly. It was winter and the guards left him in the open air at night. They threw cold water over him. During the night he froze to death.

Most of the time the prisoners marched the six and a half kilometres from the Hersbruck camp to the foot of the mountain. Then they still had a steep climb on treacherous polewood stairways to the level at which the tunnels had been dug. Many were so utterly weak and exhausted that they faltered and fell. Every day a number of prisoners were beaten, and then shoved down the slope beside the stair-ways.

Once when prisoners were marching up *Siedlungsstraße*, a trailer containing turnips stood by the side of the road. One prisoner took a single turnip. The guards with the active help of a Kapo beat the prisoner to death on the spot.

My greatest wish in life has been, that all men should be humane in their dealings with others. The members of the SS lacked any kind of humanity. It was as if they had come directly out of hell. They were real devils. (*'Es war, als wären sie direkt aus der Hölle gekommen. Sie waren richtige Teufel.'*)

*   *   *   *

With some of our respondents who had particularly close relation-ships to events in different ways, we developed fuller life-history material focused on the Doggerwerk experience. Among them were survivors of Hersbruck Concentration Camp, the commander of one of the two companies of SS convicts, and the two owners of property used as com-pounds for concentration camp prisoners in the first months of Dogger-werk. Another was the secretary, in turn, to the three SS officers, assigned as commander to Hersbruck Concentration Camp. This was *Dekan* (Dean) Hans-Friedrich Lenz, who at the time had already long been an ordained Evangelical minister.

As a young theology student during the disastrous years following the First World War, Lenz had briefly belonged to the Viking Bund (*Wiking-Bund*), a rightist military organisation headed by Captain Hermann Ehrhardt, leader of the *Freikorps* forces in the Kapp-Lüttwitz Putsch to overthrow the Weimar Republic. Lenz entered the ministry in 1926, and states that: 'For its sake, I refrained from political activity.' [16] Nevertheless he decided in 1930 to join the Nazi party, although know-ledge of his membership was kept from the local party unit. After Hitler's appointment as chancellor, Lenz joined the SA Reserve. He was also transferred into the local party organisation.

This however was just at the time when the *Gleichschaltung* – the whirlwind drive of the Nazis to consolidate their new power – was exten-ded to the institutions of religion. The party's instrument for this was the so-called German Christians (*Deutsche Christen*, or DC), an auxiliary movement of the Nazis organised in the pre-power years. Lenz found himself in the same theological position as Martin Niemöller and Karl Barth, who emerged as leaders of the opposition to the DC. 'Very quickly the NSDAP (Nazi party) indicated its disapproval of services that Lenz had been conducting in a local castle; it transferred complete control over them to the DC.

'Within the Evangelical Church, most of whose leaders had earlier come to accept the idea of a reborn Reich, a counterfront to the DC known as the Confessional Church (*Bekennende Kirche* or BK) began to take shape toward the latter part of 1933. It was not a movement of political resistance aimed at the regime. Rather its concern was to oppose the regime's encroachments on the autonomy of the religious institutions...'[17] While these objectives were narrowly defensive ones, the struggle that developed was socially important. Lenz joined the BK wing of the Church in 1934 and induced both of his parishes to do so. In the same year he was appointed to the BK's regional central body, the District Brethren's Council (*Landesbruderrat*) and became the leading BK organiser in his district.

Continuous friction between Lenz and local and regional Nazi heads consequently developed, leading to Lenz's expulsion from the SA Reserve in 1935, to his arrest, repeated interrogations and searches of his home, confiscation of his car, and withholding for five months of his salary. The regional leader (*Gauleiter*) of the Nazi party expelled him in 1939. Through all of the manoeuvres and local public uproar, Lenz's congregations stood by him, and resisted the DC to an extent that was not common in Germany.

After the Second World War had begun, Lenz found himself drafted into the military and assigned to a communications unit of the air force (*Luftwaffe*) a year prior to the call-up of his age group. In 1944, the then Sergeant (*Feldwebel*) Lenz, and 47 other air force men from various locations were transferred to Hersbruck Concentration Camp, mainly as reinforcements for the existing, sizable organisation of prisoner guards. In keeping with concentration camp procedures, all of the transferred men were inducted into the SS-Death's Head Formation (*Totenkopf-SS*). However, Lenz requested, and was allowed to remain away from the formal induction ceremony. Despite this dissent from the usual practice, he was picked to handle clerical work for the commander, and he served as secretary to the two subsequent commanders.

The evidence from surviving prisoners leaves no doubt about Lenz's commitment to their defence within the limits of the extreme conditions

270 FASCISM AND RESISTANCE

in the camp. Being a member of the camp administration, he was automatically cast in the role of official instrument of SS policy. From time to time, however, he was able to use his special position to intervene against murderous treatment of individual prisoners. There were also occasions when he took on interrogation "duties" in efforts to prevent executions. After the war he appeared repeatedly as a prosecution witness in court proceedings against persons who had belonged to the Hersbruck Camp administration accused of special brutalities against concentration camp prisoners there or elsewhere. In the meantime he generally maintained the demeanour of a camp administrator; simultaneously, he sought situations where he could perform the duties of the Protestant minister, Lenz.

*   *   *   *

Oral history techniques and the development of life histories are among the most useful means available to explore human doings in Nazi genocide, particularly if respondents are chosen with attention to the range of local occupations, social classes, and types of involvement. Reasonable accuracy in such reconstructions requires sources inside the Nazi movement, and outside of it. In an unusually close up, view of events, Lenz's account provides both. Its scope and complexity, and that of the other life-history material and shorter interviews, has permitted only a brief introduction to a study that is still in progress.[18]

There are events from which one cannot break free unless one understands them—unless one surmounts them with knowledge. For the surviving victims of genocide no such escape is possible, but gains in public understanding, however small, can help them by adding meaning to otherwise meaningless deaths. There still seem to be widespread doubts about the possibility of ever clearing up the mysteries of that peculiar destructiveness. The Doggerwerk study was begun, and continues with the conviction that the social sciences – and the arts – can greatly help us to begin to break free from that side of our histories that haunts us all.

1   The study on which this paper is based has been supported by grants numbered 0180E and 10120 of the Faculty Research Award Program of the City University of New York, and subsequently, by a grant from the Harry Frank Guggenheim Foundation. The encouragement and help of John Kneller and Donald Reich, formerly President and Vice President respectively of Brooklyn College at critical points in the work is hereby gratefully acknowledged. The understanding and help of Dr Werner Röder of the Institut für Zeitgeschichte, Munich, has been invaluable throughout the field work. The editorial suggestions of Paul Thompson and Natasha Burckhardt to an earlier edition of this paper are much appreciated. To those who live within the study area, who have helped and continue to help, special gratitude is due. The proper acknowledgement of their work, and that of many others, must await the final report.

2 Here the term, NCC system, is taken to include the first camps modelled on Dachau, which was begun in March, 1933; the 'euthanasia' centres; the special Jewish ghettos; the extermination centres for Jews, and also for other categories of victims marked for destruction; and finally the vast network of wartime *Kommandos* and outlying campts which were administratively linked to the great base camps.

3 Helmut Krausnick, Hans Buchheim, Martin Broszat and Hans-Adolf Jacobsen, *Anatomy of the SS State*, Walker and Co., New York, 1968, p. 399. Although much has been published since Broszat's long chapter in this work, the development of a body of reliable information on the camps is occurring haphazardly and slowly. Broszat's court submission (pp. 399–504) still serves as a very useful framework for a social science investigation.

4 Walter Bartel and Klaus Drobisch, 'Der Aufgabenbereich des Leiters des Amtes D IV des Wirtschafts-Verwaltungshauptamtes der SS,' *Zeitschrift für Geschucthswissenschaft*, 14 (1966), pp. 944–956. The fairly general *research* silence on the outcamp component of the NCC system has been broken by Herwart Vorländer, with the assistance of his students, in *Nationalsozialistische Konzentrationslager im Dienst der totalen Kriegsführung*, Stuttgart, 1978. This tends to support the judgement of many survivors that the erratic and arbitrary violence, and the hunger and chaotic conditions in the outcamps was very often more deadly than the hunger and somewhat more routinised violence of the older base camps. This comparison does not apply to those camps that specialised in extermination.

5 Eugen Kogon, *Der SS Staat*, Berlin, 1947, p. 46.

6 This term refers mainly to local residents whose normal activities made them frequent observers of extreme acts of aggression that are presumed to have had fatal outcomes. Except in rare instances, less awkward terms such as *witness* and *bystander* do not really apply.

7 A Fighter Aircraft Staff (*Jägerstab*) was formed in February 1944, pooling the skills of the Ministry of Armaments and the Air Ministry. Dr. Hans Kammler, engineer and SS-General (*SS-Obergruppenführer*), was put in charge of underground construction. He had been overall director of SS construction enterprises since 1941. (Enno Georg, *Die wirtschaftlichen Unternehmungen der SS*, Stuttgart, 1963, p. 67.)

8 Edward L. Homze, *Foreign Labor in Nazi Germany*, Princeton, 1967.

9 Mrs. M. is the wife of a Mosenhof farmer who was a Russian prisoner-of-war during Doggerwerk.

10 The figure of 18 kilometres has appeared in press references. This figure includes roughhewn, short tunnel borings, not much larger than human crawl space.

11 Documents were sought in eight archives, including three in the U.S. Among the most productive was the International Tracing Service (Internationaler Suchdienst) in Arolsen, West Germany, which also supplied almost all of the names of the prisoner-survivors who were interviewed. A modest supply of valuable material was also found in village and town offices.

12 In a different context, but with similar reasoning, LeVine has called this convergent validity. Robert A. LeVine, *Culture, Behavior, and Personality*, Chicago, 1973, p. 195.

13 Dietrich Riess holds an administrative position in the regional school system. During Doggerwerk he reached the age of ten.

14 Mrs. N. of Happurg was the supervisor of a group of three Polish conscript labourers engaged in cleaning the Doggerwerk construction headquarters.

15 From Mr. R. H., who is now manager of a publishing firm in a large German city.

16 Translated from Lenz's extended notes on a series of interviews conducted by Norbert Wieland, a German psychologist who had previously been a theology student. See Elmer Luchterhand and Norbert Wieland, 'The Focused Life History in Studying

Involvement in a Genocidal Situation in Nazi Germany,' in Daniel Bertaux, ed., *Biography and Society: The Life History Approach in the Social Sciences*, London, 1981, p. 276.

17 *Ibid*, p. 277.

18 This will appear under the title, *Doggerwerk: A Field Inquiry Into Human Destructiveness and Response in a Rural German Community, 1944–45.*

Women in the Italian Resistance

Anna Maria Bruzzone

'Women in the Italian Resistance': by this I understand both the tasks that many women undertook in the Resistance, and also the situations other women lived through in that period. The sources which could be used may be divided into various groups. One way of dividing them would be between, firstly, written sources: apart from textbooks and mono-graphs, we could consider narrative books, newspapers, letters and many other documents; and, secondly, oral sources. Another way would be to distinguish between sources (whether written or spoken),whose author was a man, and sources whose author was a woman. But either way, we should note that written sources have generally been created by men. For it was men who gained a monopoly of scientific knowledge, as well as of literary culture. Oral sources, by contrast – at least for the Resistance – come mainly from women: women speaking, and women carrying out the interviews.[1]

Among books of oral testimony on the Resistance published in Italy, there are a few collections of lives of men. These men, however, speak of themselves only, or mainly, in relation to the war or the Resistance.[2] But if we were to look for oral stories told by people who, having taken part in the Resistance, do not confine themselves to the Resistance but speak of their whole life experience, we would to all intents and purposes find only books about women.[3]

There are still very few texts in which we find women telling the story of the Resistance in the recent past in Italy within the context of their whole lives, and thus providing an account not only of their own problems and conditions of life during the War itself, but also of the prob-lems and conditions of all women. The present report is based on the three following works:

—Anna Maria Bruzzone and Rachele Farina, *La Resistenza taciuta,*

Dodici vite di partigiane piemontesi, ('The Unspoken Resistance, Twelve Lives of Piedmontese Women Partisans');[4]
—Bianca Guidetta Serra, *Compagne – Testimonianze di partecipazione politica femminile*, ('Women – Comrades – Testimonies of Women Political Militants');[5]
—Lidia Beccaria Rolfi and Anna Maria Bruzzone, *Le donne di Ravensbrück, Testimonianze di deportate politiche italiane* ('Women of Ravensbrück, Testimonies of Italian Women Political Prisoners in Germany').[6][7]

I shall leave out of my account the way in which women are represented by most written sources: in these women usually play a role of minor importance.[8]

With these three books in mind I should like to ask some questions. How are we to explain the fact that stories related by these women are full life stories? That was the kind of interview chosen by the interviewers; but the women interviewed were happy to accept it. Empathy was immediately established between them. Why? That type of interview obviously answered certain deep needs in all these women. What needs?

Although I have decided to make use of only three books, the subject 'Women in the Italian Resistance' covers a very extensive field. So I will select only a few facets of their work, those that seem to me most meaningful, because they sum up many others. They are, firstly, the causes and objectives – motives and expectations – inducing women to take part in Resistance struggles; secondly, the tasks they undertook; thirdly, their opinions about whether their expectations were fulfilled or not; and lastly, their judgement of themselves, as it changed with time, and through this, indirectly, their common consciousness of the situation of women in society.

At the same time a few other more or less obvious points need to be considered. First of all, these stories have been told directly by the protagonists, and therefore their memories may not be entirely correct. Moreover, each person has their own way of living, remembering and explaining events. As editors we[9] always examined the actual events as recorded in other sources and testimonies: this is shown by the footnotes we felt obliged to add to those pages, at least, where we thought an explanation was needed for the ordinary reader. We also recognise our work as just a very small sample of the enormous effort still needing to be undertaken in collecting and editing all the testimonies about women partisans. These testimonies will also be socially, ideologically, politically and geographically very various. Lastly, we must understand that each record is a fragment of real life in itself, reflecting the atmosphere of the meeting between interviewer and narrator, of public and private history, and sometimes, too, the particular moment of the interview—even though every talk was followed up by others.

Nevertheless I believe that these women accurately represent the struggles undertaken by women coming mainly from the Piedmontese working-classes who held to a Marxist ideology; all women who, after the liberation, had to live withdrawn, keeping their past to themselves.

*   *   *   *

In considering the subject 'Women in the Italian Resistance' it is also necessary to look more closely at certain facts, and especially at the number of women who really participated in these experiences. To summarise on this point, despite the difficulty in reckoning, even approximately, after such a long time, the exact number of women who in various ways took part in the struggles against Fascists and Nazi soldiers, it seems indisputable that not only were women no less numerous than men, but they probably outnumbered them.[10]

Perhaps Nazi Fascism was most hated and opposed in those very places where it ruled most directly, that is in the towns. In the remoter countryside and in the mountains where the groups[11] of armed rebels were more numerous, they were made up, in the beginning at least and in their vanguards, of young men born in the towns, surrounded by a generally helpful but sometimes antagonised population: antagonised by reason of the requisitioning of victuals the partisans were forced to carry out; the fright and danger that weighed on normal people where partisans operated, and the ancient peasant attitude, relic of a subordination which had lasted for centuries, of keeping themselves uninvolved in all events, so as to 'let the waters go downstream'.[12]

As a matter of fact, it is probable that this local population only just tolerated the partisans. Looking at the mass of people, it is difficult to argue that there was much difference between men's and women's attitudes. Perhaps women were quicker to help in a maternal way, to provide clothing, to give refreshments, to harbour partisans: but not only to partisans, but also to the Italian soldiers disbanded immediately after the armistice of 8 September 1943, to allied prisoners just escaped from prisoner of war camps and Jews, with all the attendant risks that everybody knew: destruction of the home, transportation and execution by shooting, and so on.

Thus we must limit ourselves, in approaching the problem, to considering the number of the women who, in different ways, undertook well-defined and precise tasks; therefore to particular groups of people who struggled against Nazi Fascism.

But even in this respect we find ourselves in the dark. In 1974 the Piedmontese Regional Council in a publication entitled *Il contributo delle donne alla lotta di Liberazione* ('Women's Contribution to the Liberation Struggle') reported for Piedmont the same figures which had been assumed by Ada Gobetti in 1953:

   99 women partisans fallen in the field
   185 women imprisoned in camps
   36 women fallen among civilians

Such figures must surely be far below the real ones. For instance, through the very limited inquiries made by Rachele Farina and myself for *La Resistenza taciuta*, two women were found whose names do not appear listed in the publications.[13] [14]

                    *   *   *   *

I will turn now to the first main question: causes and aims; that is, the motives and expectations relating to the actions these women undertook. The so-called 'awakened consciousness' that brought them to Marxism or at least to oppose Fascism[15] and to undertake important tasks in the Resistance in fact generally dates back to before the war.[16]

Some of them, coming from very poor families, had an anti-fascist upbringing, and found a model either in their father[17] or mother, or in both parents[18], or, generically, in the family atmosphere[19]. Some of them grew to maturity alone in the vast, terrible school of poverty[20]. Sometimes their poverty was made worse by that species of racism with which north Italians mock people from southern Italy[21]; whilst others found some support and confirmation for their changing attitudes in an elder brother.[22] Some of them were brought up by their mothers to hate injustice, and afterwards met and followed a male partner in his open political activity[23]. Others, early bereft of their families, whose opposition to Fascism they still remembered, also met and loved a militant Communist.[24]

Another woman focussed her youthful passion for struggle – and adventure – either in the direction suggested by poverty, or by the persecutions Fascists inflicted on her father and brothers[25]. In other cases, the same passion for struggle found its outlet at first in nationalism – these women having been educated in a Fascist school or by a Fascist family – but later turned to anti-fascism and eventually took on, sometimes quite casually, a Marxist colouring.[26]

Other women came originally from a healthy peasant family which did not oppose Fascism but took no part in it, until war upset its way of life. And lastly, but by no means least as a motive, there was mere chance. For example, one woman was sent as a teacher to an area controlled by partisan formations and this led to the start of her partisan activity.[27] For some it may have been an earlier education imbued with the best values of Catholicism and liberty, handed down by a mother of admirable strength in a solid and stable family and which led to struggle, almost as a matter of course[28]; on the other hand, for others, oppression suffered as a woman in the original family in childhood, or brutality suffered after marriage created an intense and deep loneliness which, when the moment came, made them ready to go into service for the sake of 'healthy things'.[29] In looking back at their past, they often connect that moment of choice with some traumatic event, like imprisonment or violence suffered by relatives during the Fascist period, or persecution by the police.

Therefore, it was not in the world of culture, of study or of books that these women found their stimulus to action – and of course that is hardly surprising, since they were almost all proletarians – but mainly through two aspects of life. The first was the tough experience of the daily struggle for survival, living day by day in a context of injustice and inequality. And the second was the world of feeling, for all the ideals they conceived in this poverty were embodied in some beloved person – either man or woman – who represented a model for imitation. This was true especially of feeling within the family, for the family still is in certain social situations the primary nucleus for influence and action.[20]

That does not mean that their choices and decisions were not autonomous. On the contrary, it is clear that independence and autonomy – for men as well as for women – had to be gained, for each of them was born, not into nothingness, but into a network of relations with other people. But autonomy showed itself in individual development, in performing small or great tasks neither too selfishly nor too humbly; in being able to stand up against their own partners in the fight, when that was necessary. As evidence of these women's independence I will take just one example out of many. From January 1944 Rita Cuniberti Martini was a member of the PCI[31] Federal Committee for the Province of Cuneo and of the Provincial Committee of the Women's Defence Groups. She was responsible for the Committee in the District of Mondovi, a member of the local CLN[32] and a promoter of one Garibaldi brigade; and in addition to all these jobs she was able to direct the struggles of her local comrades, including her own husband.

All the aspirations of these women are summed up in the words of one of them: to fight against Fascism was, as she says: 'a response to all our struggles, all our sacrifices, and, let us say it, to all our misery, the will to change, to change! Because I understood that there were two societies: a society of the rich and a society of those who possessed nothing'.[33]

The desire for freedom alone was the motivating force only for the Catholic middle-class woman who was imprisoned in the Ravensbrück concentration camp: for the others, there was a yearning not so much for freedom of speech and thought, as for freedom from poverty, exploitation, and inequality. Lenin might have said that these women were interested not in formal and juridical but in actual democracy.

*   *   *   *

And now to the second question: the tasks they fulfilled in the struggle.

In November 1943, in Milan, a few women who were members of the parties of CLN, created an organisation, the 'Women's Defence Group' in support of the freedom fighters which became larger and larger, co-ordinating and assisting activities of anti-fascist women from every class and ideology, including even those unenrolled in any party.

Almost all the women partisans we interviewed belonged to these groups. The tasks other women fulfilled spontaneously, when occasion arose, were helping, sheltering and supporting partisans or people wanted by Fascist and Nazi soldiers; the care of the sick and the wounded; and the burial of the dead and the care of their graves.

As for the members of the Women's Defence Groups, they fulfilled these same tasks as part of a programme of action. This could also mean, for working women, secretly introducing weapons into the factories (to be used at the moment of insurrection); acts of sabotage of war production; and for others, cutting the means of communication, assaulting stores or trains filled with food and fuel, getting money for people suffering from Fascist or Nazi persecution, or from bombings by the Allies; organising strikes and protests to demand food distributions or increased rations, and all kinds of possible agitation.[34]

These actions were often decided on by women, and then authorised, but at the same time almost disavowed, by male comrades. That is, they preferred to ignore them, fearing that women would throw themselves too much into the struggle, would get caught and speak under torture— although maybe there were other unconfessed fears too. But these women of ours never did speak. Six of them were captured and suffered both inter- rogations and tortures of various degrees; two were also raped[35]. None of them spoke.

The Women's Defence Groups accounted for the greatest number of women. An extremely wide range of tasks, however, was fulfilled by women partisans in the narrowest sense of the word. One essential task was performed by women who were called 'staffette' (couriers).[36] They linked together party and fighting organisations: they brought help, orders and news, everywhere that patriots could be found, in the towns, factories, offices, villages, and so on. Sometimes using unusual means of transport, sometimes by bicycle, sometimes on foot, they had to run for miles to carry perhaps just one envelope. Sometimes they had to carry heavy cases or bags containing, for instance, newspapers or propaganda materials, which were written by groups of women or by mixed groups or as was most usually the case, by groups of men, and then typed and printed by women.[37] Sometimes they carried weapons, too. To get about they used, as women always did in their exploits, extraordinary gifts of dissimulation (they pretended to be pregnant or fiancées or mothers, using the weapons of smiles and charm to pass through blocks and controls), exploiting the male habit of ascribing specific roles to women.

But from arms, and especially from using arms, they generally shrank: men kept those tasks where arms were needed for themselves[38] and women seldom laid claim to them. An age-old habit, a feminine peculiarity, or both? We do not know—we can simply state it as a fact. Only two of the women we interviewed used weapons: Elsa Oliva, who was the leader of a *Volante* (flying column), and Nelia Benissone, who trained both 'Gappisti'[39] and 'Sappisti'[40] and took part in many actions using Molotov bombs. We know there were armed squads, made up of women only, but we had no time to look for these women. However, in *Compagne* the writer included a woman Gappista from Turin who had a share in almost all the bomb attempts which were made in Turin.[41]

On the other hand, women did not shy from tasks far more risky than those connected with arms, although in their restrained testimonies they often confess they were frightened (and with the same lack of rhetoric they assure us that they could have, and indeed should have, done much more).

A few other tasks should also be mentioned: those of party organisers and of CLN members. In most cases, however, the tasks women fulfilled were executive rather than directive ones, in accordance with the generally subordinate position imposed on women at the time. In our introduction to *La Resistenza taciuta* we quote a document on the constitution of popular committees. It reads: 'If possible and if all the relevant necessary qualifications are at hand, *one* female element *can* become a member of the above-mentioned committee'.[42]

*   *   *   *

And now to the third and the fourth questions. All these women express a deep disillusion because their objectives, social equality and justice, remain unrealised. Many made statements like these: 'I am sorry that I did not die then and there, with the hope that the world would change', or 'That was the happiest period of my life'. Those who are still political militants, mainly in the Italian Communist Party, express this disillusion less dramatically, but even if they word it differently, the substance is more or less the same.

But none of them has retired, like Voltaire's Candide, to till their own small garden; on the contrary, they all continue to participate as much as possible, and to live according to their previous ideals. This shows not only the necessity they felt and still feel – as is normal after such experiences – not to lose their sense of identity but to stand by the fundamental events of their lives; but also the impact of such moments in life, the deep gratification they had felt then, the sense that the Resistance had given them a new life.

During the Resistance they were seldom given tasks formally equal to men's, but they knew very well that their tasks were effectively on the same level, mainly because they were able to exercise their own skills and often to prove that they were superior to men's. And in addition this was the first time they had emerged from the narrow family horizon, with its fixed, limited, suffocating duties and roles, into the midst of the wider social reality, as protagonists; they acted freely, autonomously, responsibly, and therefore they felt fully realised, as persons and as women.

They did not bring to the struggle a feminist consciousness, since in the years before Fascism left-wing parties had expressed very limited views on this matter, and in Italy, moreover, there had never been a strong and widespread feminist movement.[43] However, they almost unconsciously brought into the struggle against oppression the struggle against women's oppression too. When the revolutionary experience ended, therefore, they were much less ready than men to accept the more or less inevitable disillusion which always follows a period of struggle (and the Italian experience was among the most humiliating in its complete Restoration). They had greater difficulty than men in accepting the need to go on with the struggle in different ways and circumstances, and they could not – or refused to – find alternative rewards elsewhere.

There are two reasons for this: on the one hand in practice, since 1945, most of them have been isolated. On this it will suffice to recall the tragic rebuffs which the political women-deportees met with when they came back to Italy.[44] And they have paid for the Restoration and for today's crisis too, more dearly than men have. But on the other hand they cannot forget that in those past days they were able, however partially and briefly, to break their chains. The effect of all this is that they have, painfully and laboriously, become more and more consciously feminists.

1 This is not true in other cases. There are now in Italy many collections of oral testimonies and the first were made by men—by authors such as Danilo Dolci, Danilo Montaldi, and Nuto Revelli.

2 For example: *Il prezzo di una capra marcia* ('The Price of a rotten Goat') edited by Paolo Bologna, Giovannacci, Domodossola 1969; *Più in là, Ventritè partigiani sulla lotta nel Mugello* ('Onwards, Twentythree Partisans in Mugello'), edited by 'La Comune', of Mugello and the Centre for the Collection of Partisan Literature in Florence, La Pietra, Milano 1975; *Il coro della guerra* ('Chorus of War') edited by Alfonso Gatto, Laterza, Bari 1963; in this last the interviews were with women and men, but the subject was the war, rather than the Resistance.

3 And not even all the women who have said something sometime or other. There is a collection of short fragments, *Mille volte no* ('A Thousand Times No'), Editori Riuniti, Roma, 1975: women's voices relate some of the events here. Fragments of women's voices are also to be found in other publications (*I Divisione d'assalto Garibaldi Leo Lanfranco*, published by Anpi, Torino, 1974). Maria Rovano, who appears in *La Resistenza taciuta*, also recounts a brief episode in that book.

4 Edited by Anna Maria Bruzzone & Rachele Farina, La Pietra, Milano, 1976.

5 Edited by Bianca Guidetti Serra, Einaudi, Torino, 1977.

6 Edited by Lidia Beccaria Rolfi and Anna Maria Bruzzone, Einaudi, Torino, 1978.

7 Note that references (with one exception) are limited to the first and the third of these books, in order to avoid excessively long notes: in fact *Compagne* covers two volumes. Quotations from *La Resistenza taciuta* are given one asterisk; quotations from *Le donne di Ravensbrück* have two. (The first testimony in the last book is a written one, but it was preceded by several days of interview).

   Oral documents of this kind have challenged the common opinion that women's participation in the Liberation Struggle was no more than 'a precious contribution to the struggle' and have put forward a different hypothesis: that on the contrary, women's participation was 'the necessary condition on which that struggle came into being' (see *La Resistenza taciuta*, Introduction, p. 10).

8 The picture of woman directly or indirectly resulting from works written by women is quite different. It is worth while mentioning here one of the most significant publications created by women: *La Compagna* ('Woman Comrade'), a periodical for women published by the Italian Socialist Party of Proletarian Unity, some issues of which came out during the Resistance. The first number (25.7.1944, Lombardese issue) says that women are used outside the family when and as long as they are needed and – addressing women themselves – it continues: ' . . . at a certain point you will be told that women must stay home, be angels about the house, bear lots of children, bring them up; they will remove you from your jobs telling you they are not ''feminine'' ones, and force you back into a condition of dependence on a male, be he your father, brother, or husband, if you have one; and if you do not, you will have to look for one to escape starvation: they will then tell you ''today's women are incapable of behaving honestly''. This is what our future will look like, comrades, if the bourgeois outlook, the bourgeois family, and the bourgeois way of life is to survive'.

9 When I say 'we', I mean *La Resistenza taciuta* and/or *Le donne di Ravensbrück.*

10 As Arrigo Boldrini explains, in a regular war, for every soldier there are seven people

employed in various services who help him in some way; while during the partisan war every fighter needs thirteen or fourteen people, mostly women [from *Partigiane della liberta*, ed. by Sezione Stampa of PCI, 1973, p. 27] ('Women Freedom Fighters').

11   The smallest nucleus of the partisan organisation both in the country and on the mountains was the 'detachment' ('distaccamento'), which consisted of 17 or 18 men; ten detachments made up a brigade; three or four brigades made up a division (about 700 men); two or three divisions a 'group' ('raggruppamento'). This was the structure for the Garibaldini (mainly Marxists), who operated in the Piedmontese hills called Langhe. 'Formation' ('formazione') was a general term.
     Elsewhere this structure might be slightly modified.

12   Nuto Revelli, *Il mondo dei vinti* ('The World of the Defeated') Einaudi, Torino, 1977, p. CXIV.
     See also * Tersilla Fenoglio Oppedisano, p. 151.

13   Giovanna Prato and her daughter Marcella, who was responsible for the Women's Defence Group in Vicoforte Mondovi.

14   The text we have already quoted, *Partigiane della liberta* ('Women Freedom Fighters') gives the following figures for Italy:

Women members of the Women's Defence Groups	70,000
Women partisans	35,000
Arrested, condemned, tortured	4,653
Convicted in Germany	2,750
Women War Commissaries	512
Women patriots	20,000
Golden medals	15
Women executed, or fallen in the field	623

But these figures have been added up from publications like the one we quoted for Piedmont, and therefore need further checking.

15   One of them, *Elsa Oliva, became a Marxist after the War. Another, **Bianca Paganini Mori, was a Catholic middle-class woman.

16   About half the women of *La Resistenza taciuta* and of *Le donne di Ravensbrück* at the beginning of the war of liberation – that is in 1943 – were over 30 years old.

17   *Teresa Cirio, *Rosanna Rolando, **Livia Borsi Rossi.

18   *Nelia Benissone Costa.

19   **Lina and Nella Baroncini, sisters.

20   *Lucia Canova, *Albina Caviglione Lusso, *Anna Cinnani

21   *Anna Cinnani

22   *Rita Cuniberti Martini, *Anna Cinnani

23   *Maria Martini Rustichelli

24   *Lidia Fontana

25   *Elsa Oliva

26   *Tersilla Fenoglio Oppedisano

27   **Lidia Beccaria Rolfi

28   **Bianca Paganini Mori

29   *Maria Rovano. She said 'I was lucky enough to find in the partisan war an opportunity for healthy things'. (p. 230)

30   Family was, however, the most important element even for those who studied in secondary school – Licei or Institutes for teachers – and even for those who attended University. (**Bianca Paganini Mori, **Lidia Beccaria Rolfi, *Lidia Fontana).

31   PCI: Italian Communist Party

32   CLN: National Liberation Committee

33   *Lucia Canova, p. 213. These words refer to her youth, when she joined the Socialist Party in 1919, but they embody 'the aims and meaning of her whole life struggle.

34 I shall cite only the women's strike in Turin after the murder of the Arduino sisters (see *Teresa Cirio, pp. 87−8; *Nelia Benissone Costa, pp. 48−50).
    (a) See *Nelia Benissone Costa, p. 40
    (b) **Bianca Paganini Mori, **the Baroncini sisters, **Lidia Beccaria Rolfi, *Elsa Oliva, *Anna Cinanni
35 *Rosanna Rolando, *Lidia Fontana
36 For instance, *Tersilla Fenoglio Oppedisano, *Lidia Fontana
37 **The Baroncini sisters, *Teresa Cirio, *Anna Cinanni
38 It was also because many of them had become partisans after having been soldiers, since at the time of the armistice on 8 September 1943, they had escaped from the Germans who were militarily occupying Italy, and had started a clandestine armed movement; others had escaped forced conscription in the Fascist Republic of Salò, and therefore felt themselves already soldiers. Moreover it was impossible to start a new deep reassessment of roles in this matter.
39 The so-called GAP (Groups for Patriotic Action) were established by the headquarters of the Garibaldi brigades at the end of September 1943, and appointed to fight in the cities. They attacked German officers, Fascist leaders, military head offices, stores and columns of soldiers on the march, with very small bands of commandoes; Gappists in Turin were always about ten in number.
40 The so-called SAP (Squads for Patriotic Action) were formed with armed elements to control factories and to support mass demonstrations militarily. In Turin there were about 700 men.
41 Irene Castagneris Caudera (*Compagne*, pp. 284−309).
42 The underlining is ours, p. 12 (from *I Divisione d'Assalto Garibaldi Leo Lanfranco*, already mentioned).
43 From 1912 until the Fascist period, a Milan newspaper *La difesa delle Lavoratrice* ('Defending Working Women'), written from a socialist standpoint, had gathered around it a few women of resolute and modern feminist outlook (Anna Maria Mozzoni, Abigaille Zanetta, Clelia Montagnana, etc.) It was, however, a mainly intellectual movement, and had no roots in the population.
44 People said, for instance: 'If you had not meddled with politics, you would not have been convicted!'
    It must be emphasised that the experiences of these women were different from those of other women partisans. They were only able for a short time to enjoy the rewards which other women partisans had drawn from their militancy. They were soon imprisoned, transported to Germany, and shut up in one of the most dreadful 'total institutions' that has ever existed. So they cannot say—'That was the happiest period of my life'; at the most they claim to have learnt something even at the terrible school of Lager, to have tried even in Lager to react and to resist (**Bianca Paganini Mori, pp. 188−9; **Lidia Beccari Rolfi, pp. 116−8).

Oral History and Resistance History in Italy

David Ellwood and Anna Bravo

Italian contemporary history is currently passing through one of its periodic phases of soul-searching and crisis. In a field dominated by left-wing approaches of one sort or another, it feels profoundly the present wave of doubt and scepticism – now seen as long term – about the effective validity of Marxist and Marxist-derived methods of historical explanation. And in the short term it suffers also from the ebb of left-wing political energy and consensus which set in four or five years ago.

The context of this crisis is Italy's sophisticated, longstanding political culture – not only leftist – of which contemporary historiography forms a vital part. To show how the connections work between the world of historiography and the world of politics in Italy, one could in fact hardly choose a better subject than the Resistance. It was this episode in recent Italian history which – supposedly – gave rise to a new set of political institutions, on the one hand (i.e. to the present Republic); and on the other, brought forth a new range of popular values, reputedly enshrined in the Constitution of 1948. Since then a great deal has been written on the institutions and the values, and historiography has made its own contribution with an intense study of the crucial formative period between 1943 and 1945, that is, between the fall of Fascism in July 1943 and the emergence of Christian Democrat hegemony in November 1945. (The armed Resistance began in September 1943 after the Italian surrender and ended in April 1945 with the final defeat of the German forces in the north.)

Resistance historiography can be seen to have passed through three fairly distinct phases. The first, roughly from 1945–55, saw the emergence of the first 'official', that is party, histories and above all a rapid diffusion of personal memoirs, diaries, autobiographies and souvenirs of this kind. Written soon after, or even during these events, these lively, sometimes emotional accounts do convey something of the atmosphere, especially the moral tension of the struggle. Their defects are simplification, a certain rhetorical tendency and of course, lionisation of the protagonists and their movement. When debunking came in with the new generation of the 1960s, this type of literature was a favourite target, and is no longer produced. But, as we shall see, as a variety of oral testimony its relevance is not to be completely ignored.

In the second phase, approximately from 1955−65, a more detached attitude emerges. Methodological questions receive systematic attention for the first time and we see serious attempts to collate and examine the various types of documentation available, using an approach which examines general questions through their local expression. At the same time the international dimension begins to be added, usually by British or American academics who participated at some relevant level in the Allied armies. It is in this phase however, after 1960, that the first signs of a completely new approach appear, in the form of pioneer studies by representatives of the post-war generation. For them the Resistance was already past history, but past history with an immediate relevance, specifically as a source of legitimacy for criticism of the existing political class. These works, distinguished by their close attention to the internal life of the Resistance groups, as well as by the use of new sources ranging from fascist documents to oral testimony, made an immediate impact, opening the way to the third distinctive phase of Resistance history.

The new phase coincides − not by accident − with the start of the wave of student protest in 1967, inspired by anti-imperialist struggles in places like Greece, Vietnam and Latin America, as well as by a renewal of working class opposition in the northern Italian factories. As far as Resistance history is concerned, as G. Quazza has written, we see 'local or sectorial analyses which pay more attention to relations between partisans and people, to the links between military action on the one hand and social and political struggle on the other; and at the same time we see attempts to arrive at a general synthesis, moving beyond the events of the Resistance period as such to the longer period and to the international context.' Significantly, a key moment in this phase was the open attack by the new opposition on the so-called revolutionary parties, allegedly guilty, in the words of Quazza, 'of having "betrayed" the working classes by their incapacity to stop the Resistance in 1945 from becoming restoration instead of revolution.' In other words, after 1967 the history of the Resistance became once again directly involved in an open struggle in the world of political confrontation.[1]

As an alternative to the earlier types of approach, the post-1968 historians proposed to place the Resistance within a broader view of the class struggle in Italy in the 20th century. In particular this meant measuring the people, the programmes, the political and military actions of the Resistance against the range of social forces operating throughout the period from the rise of Fascism to the Cold War, that is to say against the Church, big business, the landowners and the State, as well as against the international political and economic forces acting in Italy. If then we look at books like those on 'Workers and Peasants in the Crisis of 1944' or 'Rural Society and Resistance in the Veneto Region' we find chapters on 'The Crisis of the Regime and the Social Crisis', 'The Big Estate in the Venice Region Between Fascism and Restitution', 'Priests and Peasants in the Padova area', 'Church and Resistance in the North Eastern Border Zone'.[2]

As expressions of the post-1968 generation of intellectuals, these works, and others like them, contained effectively a strong undercurrent of criticism against the whole course of post-fascist Italian history. In particular they attacked the very idea that the Italian Republic as it had developed in real terms had anything to do with the Resistance struggle, as conventional apologists of both the left and the right had always maintained. By demonstrating the continuity of men and institutions from fascist to post-fascist Italy, the left opposition contested the attempt by the traditional left to present the results of the Resistance as the most that was attainable at that time. In addition, they insisted on the autonomous *class* content of the most advanced sectors of the Resistance struggle. Hence specific attention began to be paid to ideology, to attitudes and values. The risks in this approach were on the one hand those of constructing new over-simplified ideological schemes, and on the other of giving too much weight to the economic context.

Unfortunately this new line of attack has especially suffered from the current mood of self-doubt and crisis, partly due to the collapse of the post-1968 forms of political expression and culture as a viable alternative to those of the traditional left: but also to a crisis of method, of the fundamental definition of the categories used by historians and social scientists to explain such phenomena as Fascism and the Resistance, which is directly linked to the political confusion within which Italian contemporary history now operates. This crisis has had a direct bearing too on the development of oral history.

*   *   *   *

'Politique d'abord' then, we might say, with a certain evolution of method of the history of the Resistance and the use of oral testimony for this purpose, concealed by the substantial take-over by the institutions and above all by the political parties. All the various ways in which history can be used by ruling groups or would-be ruling groups to legitimise their activities can be seen in the historiography of the Resistance, and the use made of oral testimony in these efforts only confirms this claim. First, let us take a closer look at the testimony itself, then at the uses made of it.

Right from the start Resistance history made use of interviews, oral testimony and other autobiographical material. This was perhaps inevitable given the gaps in the documentary sources. Documents were often destroyed or hidden before and after the liberation for political reasons or to avoid personal incrimination. Many were simply lost due to lack of suitable places to deposit them locally or nationally, though much has, in fact, remained in the hands of the original partisan authors. This is material in any case of a special kind, usually consisting of reports, notes or messages from people such as commanders or country priests: individuals in special positions. In spite of these limitations, papers from these sources constituted the raw material for much of the early phase of Resistance history.

They were not the only sources. Alongside these, there also flourished all kinds of biography and memoir, from the politico-military diary of the intellectual to the 'naive' account of the ordinary partisan. What links all this kind of writing is the awareness of the authors of having somehow 'made history'. Hence the common attempt to recapture the atmosphere of the struggle, to convey the moral tension, through the personal choices of individuals. In these works the first elements of an oral tradition of the Resistance make their appearance, the first expressions of a 'collective memory' of those activist minorities present in the struggle.

The type of oral interview conventionally used by Resistance historiography is similar to these autobiographic forms. The witnesses tend to be similar too; often intellectuals, or at least people of a certain level of education, but above all *leading protagonists*—almost always commanders, political commissioners, party men; not necessarily the most visible, but key figures in their own surroundings. The kind of testimony they offer and the use made of it also resembles the written autobiography: atmosphere plus detailed reconstruction of events. For instance in Tamarri Gasparri's book on the Resistance in Siena, a local witness describes a demonstration against the bread ration, then adds:

Chiurco (a Fascist official) understood the importance and the clear political meaning of the demonstration so well that the next day he sent out to Abbadia all the armed bastards he could find under the command of the infamous Rinaldi, to 'bring order'. They occupied the town militarily. Many of the women comrades were taken into the offices of the Commune and manhandled, and two of them, Adalgisa Sabatini Bisconti and Olga Fabbrini Flori were arrested and taken off to the San Spirito prison in Siena. The same happened to Pietro Sbrilli's father and Glacomo Sabatini's brother, the father and brother of two comrades sought by the Fascists.[3]

In the second post-heroic phase of Resistance history, this preference for detailed reconstruction of the facts tends to be reinforced, as an anti-dote to the swelling Resistance rhetoric. As a way of capturing elusive, fragmentary bits of history, its usefulness can hardly be doubted: but this is not the same as writing interpretative history of general validity, nor of developing the full potentialities of oral testimony.

Nevertheless it is the type of oral evidence which is most frequently used by Resistance historians, following a methodology which has changed little over the years (a recent edition of a Piedmontese Resistance history printed unchanged testimony first published twenty seven years previously).[4] In other words, oral evidence is treated just like any other historical document in reconstructing the facts, with increasing evidence, however, being put on the necessity to corroborate the statements made, with documents: so the specific nature of oral sources tends to be ignored, especially the specific nature of oral testimony on the Resistance, the product of a situation of clandestinity, strongly coloured by the protagon-ists' awareness of their own historic role and by their personal ideological commitment. There is plenty of reference to popular participation and mass support but far less effort to gather the oral expression of this experience *now*. Quantitative data, documents, professional interpreters are still the favoured reference points and there is little awareness that an oral source is always the product of *two* individualities, each with their own baggage of culture and experience.

Such then are the limitations of the sorts of oral testimony that have been used up to now. We must now give some attention to the political use of Resistance testimony and its relation to the institutional 'take over' of Resistance history. There have in fact been three dominant political uses made of oral evidence in Resistance historiography. We may take them in turn. The first one we might call the reconstruction of party history. The long-term effort to understand the achievements and consol-idate the traditions of the political parties has, since the early post-war period, often made use of direct testimony of one sort or another. Any form of enquiry directed towards questions such as how the Resistance was organised, or how its leaders emerged, invariably leads back to focus-sing on the parties, and especially on the Communist Party, whose domi-nation in terms of real contribution to the Resistance cannot be doubted. The point of books such as those of Longo and Secchia is not simply to reconstruct the facts at all levels.[5] It is also to offer concrete evidence from life of the meaning of the Party's existence in this period of struggle; to demonstrate the links existing between daily reality as experienced by the masses and the strategy of the Party; and to illustrate the role of the Party in organising, stimulating and encouraging opposition. This sort of history can, of course, be used by any party, though it is undoubtedly the Communist Party which has made most use of it, for example with Ferretti's 'Communist Profiles'. However its limitations are obvious; and it is now attacked as 'justificationist' even by party members: hence a book like Bermani's 'Pages of Guerrilla Warfare', based almost entirely on oral testimony, which depicts local communists taking the lead of a mass movement *spontaneously, not* as party representatives.[6]

The second way in which oral evidence on the Resistance is used politically is evocative. Three titles from the Emilia Romagna region, 'The Night is Darkest Just Before Dawn', 'When We Were Rebels' and 'The Ones Who Refused to Surrender' illustrate well how emotional links can be used to bind the past and the present.[7] This is nostalgia with a purpose. It aims to show values in action, men mobilised and conscious, a society – or parts of a society – in arms. In contrast with the alienation and apathy of the contemporary world, it shows people committed to a cause, united in struggle and, in the end, successful. There is no reason of course why people should not look back with regret to a time of exceptional hope and solidarity, at least in those zones where Resistance took place effectively. Nor of course is nostalgia for the Second World War period limited to particular parts of Italy (though it's harder to find in places such as Greece and Yugoslavia). But it is the *organisation* of memory by official and semi-official bodies of all kinds which distinguishes the Italian situation. The results are seen in books like 'The Second and Third Forms Tell the Story', published by the local branch of the national partisans' association. Here oral testimony collected by schoolchildren is coupled to a direct political message: 'These are the values of the Resistance, they have been betrayed; each one of us must be active, conscious and vigilant; as they were in the fight for democracy, so we must be in its defence.'[8] This pamphlet and others like it reflect the problems of communicating the Resistance experience from one generation to another. In spite of the high level of politicisation in Italian schools, there is considerable difficulty in understanding how the Republic, officially born from the Resistance, can have become so woebegone. The State, as such, discourages the study of contemporary history in schools, so local authorities, trade unions, partisan organisations and so on inevitably try to fill the gap with books, articles, collections of testimony. Although official patronage of evocation might seem to render it suspect, there is no slackening in this effort.

The third political use is celebratory. By far the largest quantity of material published on the Resistance and using oral testimony comes under this heading. It involves a veritable avalanche of printed paper released every ten years (not counting material produced for the annual remembrance days), by official committees at the regional, provincial and municipal levels who clearly see in it an indestructible monument to their efforts. A recent partial survey of the products of the 30th anniversary committees in Emilia Romagna, carried out by Luciano Casali, revealed 40 titles sponsored by the Regional Committee, 48 by provincial committees and 22 sponsored by outside agencies such as parties, trade unions and other organisations—and this is by no means all. Either directly or indirectly, the great majority of this material employs oral testimony of some sort, using it sometimes to provide a historical source, sometimes as a sign of authenticity and immediacy, sometimes to answer questions. The quality, says Casali, varies enormously, but the most crucial question, of course, is what possible purpose this massive flood of pages can serve. To the tons of pamphlets, discourses and articles produced in previous years we now have added volume upon volume of more or less serious local history. The general superficiality of these works, their second-rate ideology of popular unity and their tendency to read things in present-day terms, all give rise, says Casali, to the most serious doubts about the real value of the '30th anniversary operation' in contributing to popular awareness and political education. What sort of picture does this type of writing and testimony present? 'A golden vision of a people unanimously anti-fascist in the era of the regime and guerillas to the last man in the Resistance', says Casali.[9]

Just how oral testimony can be fitted into an anniversary operation is illustrated well by the programme for the 30th anniversary in one of the provinces of Piedmont. On the morning of the day itself a mass of remembrance is celebrated; in the evening a procession is formed in the main square which moves on to the Resistance memorial where a partisan offers *una testimonianza*—the choice of this word indicating that he will not make a speech, which is the task of the mayor shortly afterwards. In the permanent exhibition inaugurated the same weekend, alongside souvenirs, documents and photos, there is a written undertaking to 'collect oral and written testimony from partisans, peasants, women, deportees etc.', for use in schools and for general educational purposes. The overall objective, says the mayor in an accompanying pamphlet, is to 'underline the popular struggle embodied in the armed Resistance, emphasise the anti-fascist unity of the committee of liberation (and) recall the reaction of the local people to the ferocity of the Nazis.' [10]

Although no one has ever attempted a serious study of the rhetoric of the Resistance – in spite of its existence being acknowledged by everyone – it is not hard to pick out the main strains: the Resistance movement was *popular, national*, and above all *united*, fighting not only a war of liberation but also a struggle for social reconstruction. Of course these themes *are* based on certain aspects of Resistance reality, and it is important to remember that they belonged to a persecuted minority for many years after the war and still face strong conservative opposition, even neo-fascist at times. But the opportunistic, sloganeering use of Resistance values, especially that of anti-fascist unity, is all too clear. Town and country, workers and middle classes, socialists, liberals and catholics were all apparently as one then, and the need felt by certain left-wing parties to connect this past experience with their own current alliance strategy has led to some strange distortions of official memory.

*　　*　　*　　*

What has all this to do with oral history? Two things: first we see witnesses, usually of the 'professional politician' type, lending their recollections to the kind of celebration and exhortation tactic just mentioned. This is an old trick common in Italian politics, which may or may not permit the use of a piece of testimony by the historian depending on the case. But alongside it we now see a new development, destined possibly to do something to crack the old myths. If there is one aspect of human life which oral investigation reveals time and time again, it is the *non-uniformity* of experience, the extraordinary variety of links between individuals and their environment, no matter how limited that environment might be. And this is true whether we look at perceptions or objective reality, at social situations or historical ones. Thus it is not surprising that some of the most recent books published on the Resistance, or some of the work now being done in using oral history, refer repeatedly to this non-uniformity of experience and make attempts to come to terms with it. In the work of G. Verni, a communist militant, on the history of the Communist Party in Tuscany, [11] the differences in the levels of political awareness and participation during the Resistance from village to village represents the first important result of the research. In the book of Viviana Pierloni and Maria Rosa Pancaldi on the formation of a 'collective mentality' in the Bologna area during and after the war, non-uniformity constitutes a background to the whole study; and the same is true for the image of the first Resistance bands in Piedmont built up by

Paolo Gobetti's video interviews; as one of the witnesses says, they were
'disorganised little organisations.'[12]

The point is that findings of this sort inevitably clash with the old
rhetoric of popular unity and general participation. They bring into relief
in a new way precisely who participated and who did not, how they participated or why they didn't. Although it is too early to say how this
confrontation between new results and old myths will work out, it seems
inevitable that some sort of adaptation will have to be made.

Other themes exposed to this kind of alternative vision include the
constitution of the committees of liberation throughout the north, the
real impact of so-called Resistance values and morality in the armed
struggle and the nature of mass support. But the gap between conventional documentation and what individuals recall from experience is so
wide that opposition is almost certain to develop from the established
authorities. Some years ago Cesare Bermani described the uneasiness of
the Communist Party structures when faced with the tape recorder in his
pioneer work on Resistance in a sub-alpine valley: 'Pages of Guerilla Warfare', which we have already referred to. As for a concrete example of the
gap between documents and facts, an episode from the area of the partisan
'republic' of Montefiorino is extremely revealing. According to official
sources, municipal elections were held throughout the areas held by the
partisans and returns – which can be consulted – eventually filed. What
really happened? The economic commissioner of the leading band told
Luciano Casali recently: 'Elections? What elections? What was the name
of that fellow I made mayor? Pellesi! We made him mayor because he was
the first to bring into our granary, on his shoulders – he was enormous – a
bag of wheat. It was important because it was the first or second day of our
occupation. It was decisive for us, that first bag. . . . ' As far as the rigour
of Resistance values is concerned, we have, for example, the testimony of
women partisans, such as those interviewed by Anna Maria Bruzzone
and Rachele Farina, who recall the presence right after the war of ex-
fascists in the front ranks of the women's defence groups of the left-wing
parties.[13]

These examples demonstrate how a new approach *is* emerging in
Resistance history, capable of introducing voices from outside the established frames of reference into the historical debate. Interviewing people
such as women or peasants means reaching people who automatically see
the Resistance period within a general view of their own past, and thus
help to illuminate the roots and the consequences of that moment. And
the variety of subcultures and individualities one meets in this kind of
research immediately provides authenticity for explanations beyond

officialdom. To approach this variety however it is necessary to design questions which come from *inside* the reality one is trying to analyse; only in this way can keys be found to the 'view from below' of the crucial historical episodes.

To see how this can be done, we might take some of the new studies in women's history, such as those of Anna Maria Bruzzone and Rachele Farina or Bianca Guidetti Serra's book 'Women Comrades'.[14] The starting point is a desire to get rid of the Resistance rhetoric which always pays a token tribute to the role of women but never asks just how crucial it was. So in the case of 'The Unspoken Resistance' the questions bring into relief the underlying conflicts between men and women, and do not hesitate to talk of the 'betrayal' of socialist values by the left forces, and the men in particular, at the time of the Resistance. In 'Women Comrades' the questions tend to bring out the significance of their political commitment, in those circumstances, of the women in the rank and file. Similarly Nuto Revelli's work in *Il Mondo dei Vinti* ('The World of the Defeated') seeks out a *general* view from below to confront the essential general problem of that world: in short, the destruction of the rural peasant world, by the dominant modes of life of contemporary society. This is a way to stimulate collective memory and to recapture a subculture which is at risk of total extinction in present circumstances.[15]

It is important to note that these projects have been produced by researchers working on their own initiative outside the normal network of university departments and institutes of political culture. And although stimulated by the post-1968 debate on marginal classes and groups, they have succeeded in avoiding the excessive ideologisation common in much recent analysis of the working class and the 'disinherited'. Feminism *has* acted as a stimulus to works such as 'The Unspoken Resistance'; but the important point has been to seek out the *specific* modes and characteristics of womens' participation in the armed struggle. The debate on continuity from Fascism to post-fascism is relevant to the discussion of the role of women in the political parties during the Resistance, but it is the examination of the role of women that comes first, not the debate.

So far, however, it is probably Revelli's 'The World of the Defeated' which goes furthest beyond established historiography. 'We made mistakes when we were fighting, we made mistakes when we were on the run, we always made mistakes', writes Revelli in his introduction; and this is his starting point for his attempt at a different approach to the relations between the Resistance and the peasants. Revelli's two volumes are based on the corrected transcripts of more than 270 three-hour interviews. They convey directly the conflicts, the difficulties and the inconsistency of experience in this exceptional Resistance province of Cuneo in West Piedmont. Peasant solidarity emerges as far from total, with constant hesitation and lapses. The early forms of support to refugees, and the first bands, wither under the pressure of government search-and-destroy operations, massacres and reprisals. The solidarity which remains is always precarious, subject to the fear of reprisals and to resentment against the requisitions necessary to keep the bands alive. The only people the peasants support unflinchingly are the deserters, the youths who refuse to answer the call up of the neo-fascist puppet government. 'They were the ones seen as the real patriots', says Revelli, 'while the partisans were seen as individualists and hotheads, the troublemakers who only made things more difficult.' The partisans were in one way 'our people', but the general judgement on them today from the peasants who remember is harsh: 'it would have been better if they had never existed. They were like gypsies, constantly moving. *We* never ran away ... ' 'If they'd just kept out of things. People who interfere have to pay the consequences'. It is the voice of a closed, self-defensive culture, of a poverty-ridden rural world concerned above all to hang on to what little it possesses. Revelli goes as far as to comment: 'they have forgiven the Germans and Fascists who carried off their sons, but they've never forgiven the partisans who carried off their calves'.[16]

The embitterment is not just a product of the politicians' neglect of the rural world in the post-war years. It comes out of a historical condition of passivity, of constantly being subject to political action from outside. The Resistance too was in many ways another imposition to be lived through, making the choice of those hundreds of peasants who did take up arms all the more exceptional. But the gap between politics and rural society was destined to remain as wide as ever, no matter how hard the party men try to ignore it or to cancel it out.

Revelli's work is a starting point. Besides suggesting different parallel projects, perhaps more scientific, less literary, the interviews published are accessible to different methods of interpretation. Linguistics, psycho-analysis, anthropology are just some of the disciplines which could usefully be applied. Inevitably such approaches focus attention on the individual and the individual's relationship with history, and if we look a bit more closely at the full range of current historical research in Italy, we find all kinds of large and small projects, local and general, which convey the experience of factory workers, and housewives, printers and shop-keepers, the protagonists often of 'minor' episodes, or at the lowest level of the 'big' episodes. Hence, it seems certain that in the rediscovery of local history underway at the moment, oral history is bound to play an important part. This is a rediscovery not limited to full-time researchers; it is also, in its emphasis on *transmitting* the experience of the past, particularly relevant to work in schools. In this area special mention might be made of Paolo Gobetti's work on the participation of Italian volunteers in the Spanish Civil War and on the Resistance, using video interviews.[17]

Gobetti's projects began with the aim of using film and video material as a means of communicating aspects of the anti-fascist experience in schools. But as interviews were collected and analysed – without any outside models or reference points – it became apparent that the video medium was also a subtle research tool with a language of its own, a tool applicable to the whole problem area of the individual and historical experience, of personality and circumstance, consciousness and action. Hence the projects became research not just into the specific theme of anti-fascism but into the potentialities of the medium itself. Video interviews convey personality in full, as well as giving a glimpse of the context in which people have lived and acted. In the case of the Turin material, the principal problem has been to evolve, unaided, criteria for effective analysis *and use* of the interviews: it seems as though each occasion requires its own montage of video testimony and film—there is never a finished product.

Like the others cited, this video project offers not only new ways of looking at the Resistance and its consequences, but at Italian contemporary history in general. Discussions and conferences being organised this year on oral history, local history and other topics reflect the extent of the current interest in renewal; and the fact that they are being organised by agencies such as the Resistance history institutes, shows that at least part of the historical establishment is beginning to sit up and take notice. Novelties *do* have a way of being absorbed in Italy, of being taken over and turned inside out to make new conventional wisdom and set phrases. This is a risk: but it seems worth running if we are to have a new phase of Resistance history.

1 Guido Quazza, *Resistenza e storia d'Italia*, Milan, 1976, introduzione.
2 Bertolo et al, *Operai e contadini nella crisi italiana del 1943/1944*, Milano, 1974; *Società rurale e Resistenza nelle Venezie. Atti del convegno di Belluno, Ottobre, 1975*, Milan, 1978.
3 Tamaro Gasparri, *La resistenza in provincia di Siena, 8 settembre, 1943–3 luglio, 1944*, Florence, 1976, p. 135.
4 Istituto storico della Resistenza in Piemonte, *Aspetti della Resistenza in Piemonte*, Turin, 1950 and 1977.
5 Luigi Longo, *I centri dirigenti del PCI nella Resistenza*, Rome, 1973; Pietro Secchia, *I comunisti e l'insurrezione, 1943–45*, Rome, 1973.

6   A. Ferretti, *Profili di communisti*, Massenzatico, 1976; C. Bermani, *Pagine di guerriglia, l'esperienza dei garibaldini della Valsesia*, Milan, 1971.

7   P. Scalini, *La notte più buia è prima dell'alba (Ravenna 1944–45)*, Imola, 1975; S. Prati, G. Rinaldi, *"Quando eravamo i ribelli"*. *La valle del Panaro nella Resistenza*, ANPI, Modena, 1978; L. Bergonzoni, *Quelli che non si arresero*, Rome, 1957.

8   ANPI, Valleggia e Quiliano, *I ragazzi della 2 e 3 A raccontano: 1915–1945, il paese in quegli anni*, Albisola, 1975.

9   Luciano Casali, 'Poteri locali e celebrazioni della Resistenza: insufficienze della pubblicistica del XXX in Emilia Romagna', in *Italia contemporanea*, aprile-giugno, 1978, pp. 81–87.

10 Comune di Asti, *Celebrazioni per il conferimento della Medaglia d'argento al Valore militare alla Repubblica partigiana del Alto Monferrato*, Asti, 1977.

11 Conversation with G. Verni, Istituto storico della Resistenaz in Toscana, Florence, 13/2/79.

12 V. Pierloni, M.R. Pancaldi, *La formazione della mentalità "collettiva" nelle campagna bolognesi, 1943–47*, Bologna, 1978, conversation with Paolo Gobetti, Archivio nazionale cinematografico della Resistenza, Turin, 13/1/79.

13 Testimony on Montefiorino by Gianni Vandelli collected by L. Casali 21/2/70; conversation with Casali, 3/12/78, Bologna; A.M. Bruzzone, R. Farina, *La Resistenza taciuta*, Milan, 1976.

14 B. Guidetti Serra, *Compagne*, Turin, 1978.

15 Nuto Revelli, *Il mondo dei vinti*, Turin, 1978.

16 Ibid., introduction.

17 See *Il nuovo spettatore*, journal of the Archivio nazionale cinematografico della Resistenza, Turin, n.1, April, 1980.

Women in Resistance Organisations in the Netherlands

Marjan Schwegman

The Resistance movement and the Second World War in general are favourite topics in present-day Dutch historiography[1]. Most authors, however, have concentrated on the *exploits* of *individual* resisters (most of them men), rather than approaching the Resistance as being a complex network of organisations partly overlapping each other. Consequently little attention has been paid to women, for women were not commonly involved *directly* in Resistance actions which could have attracted publicity. It seems that women usually played a part in the background. Without their work, however, the more spectacular actions would not have been possible. So now it seems right to turn the spotlight onto the part which women played.

In this paper I will leave aside the question of whether Resistance groups can be considered to be *organisations* (of an informal kind). I will take it for granted that they are and will deal with two questions: first, how did women fit into Resistance organisations? And as a corollary: how were Resistance organisations structured? Secondly, did women's presence in Resistance organisations break the pre-war division of roles between the sexes? (For the sake of brevity, I will not consider the question of whether the involvement of women in the Resistance movement had any impact on possible changes in the prevalent ideas among women themselves, for example—about the position of women in society after 1945[2].)

Because it was impossible for me to study *all* Dutch Resistance organisations, I singled out some of them on the basis of their functions. This is an artificial move, because most organisations had multiple functions which partly overlapped each other, so that they cannot be sharply distinguished from each other now. I chose the following organisations:

1 *The 'Vrije Groepen'* (Independent Groups) in Amsterdam.

These groups were mainly engaged in helping *onderduikers* (people in hiding). I concentrated on *'Groep 2000'* and on a group that saved many Jewish children.

2 *The 'PersoonsBewijzen Centrale'*, abbreviated PBC (Identity Papers Agency). This organisation was engaged in falsifying identity papers, mainly *persoonsbewijzen* (abbreviated p.b.'s).

3 *'CS-6'*. This abbreviation means Corellistraat 6, an address in Amsterdam where some of the group members used to live. The principal activities of this organisation consisted of sabotage.

4 *'Vrij Nederland'*, abbreviated VN (The Free Netherlands), an illegal newspaper.

5 *The 'knokploegen' (scrapping teams) of Johannes and Marinus Post.* These teams specialised in raids on public offices to get ration books, identity cards and so on, for people in hiding.

My knowledge of these groups is derived from historical writings, literature, material from archives and from interviews. Because security considerations forced Resistance organisations to leave as few traces as possible, many of the written sources are also based on oral evidence, collected shortly after the war[3]. So, actually, the history of the Dutch Resistance movement is disguised 'oral history'. It is therefore the more striking that the 'official' historiographer of the Netherlands during the Second World War, L. de Jong, uses oral evidence without any discussion of his methodology.

Oral evidence collected after the war was partly given by women. Some of these women were widows of resisters who had been killed, but who were only asked about their former husbands, not about their own experiences.[4] In addition to the interviews which others have done, I use my own interviews too. I have interviewed twelve people, ten women and two men, visiting some of these people several times. Apart from useful information about the role women played, my own interviews gave me a clear insight into certain questions which are hard to get to grips with— like the fact that Resistance organisations overlapped one another to such a large extent, the atmosphere in such groups, the great part played by chance, and so on. In most interviews I did not question the women explicitly about their position as women. By questioning implicitly I expected to get more reliable answers.

To direct my research I worked my initial questions into a hypothesis. When I started my research I was struck that so many women were – and still are – active in illegal organisations like the *Rote Armee Fraktion* (Red Army Fraction). I asked myself whether, in such organisations, traditional role patterns, especially the division of roles between the sexes, are broken. For these illegal organisations, placing themselves outside the 'legal' world with all its rules and norms, tend to create their own rules and norms. Later on I realised that a comparable process did not apply to 'my' Resistance organisations. That is why I formulated the following hypothesis:

Firstly, during the war Dutch women in Resistance organisations did not break the pre-war division of roles between the sexes. So sex remained a criterion for a certain division of roles. Secondly whenever women did take over 'men's work', it was only because they, being women, were not suspected of illegal activities so quickly. So they took advantage of prevalent ideas about what a woman should and should not do. As a female co-operator of the 'PBC' put it:

As a woman, in general you didn't run so much risk, because they rarely stopped you. And a woman may also be a better actress.[5]

First I will deal with my hypothesis in general. In this context it is necessary to make some brief remarks about the division of roles between the sexes in the Netherlands in the years before the war[6].

The thirties were years of depression with unemployment, wage cuts, and other difficulties. Wage-labour by (married) women in those years was seen as taking the bread out of a family's mouth. The government therefore attempted to restrict or prohibit it. At the same time the importance of the tasks of being mother and wife were emphasised. The best place to perform these tasks was home. So men were seen as bread-winners and women as housewives and mothers, responsible for taking care of their families; as figures in the background[7].

So until the spring of 1943, the tasks of women in Resistance organisations were, in the same way, generally tasks in the background; tasks of assisting and serving. Many people thought this situation 'natural': they thought of women as being more emotional and, consequently, more inclined to reckless deeds. For that reason women were considered to be less capable of holding leading positions than the 'rational' men. Moreover, it was thought that 'mother-instinct' was the cause of their inclination to protect, serve and cherish. Finally women, as (future) obedient wives, were supposed to be stimulating, inspiring and morally supportive of men. The biographer of the Resistance hero Gerrit Jan van der Veen characterises the position of women in Resistance organisations in this way:

They are the nameless, perhaps today the trampled-down ground on which the resistance could take a firm stand. Also, he who fell, found his last kisses and soft thoughts there[8].

If women in the Resistance movement came to the fore, it was nearly always in domains considered as 'typically female', for example in the saving of Jewish children. Whenever the former division of roles was broken in an underground organisation, it was only due to the continued existence of traditional role patterns in the 'overground' society. In that society women were not expected to do illegal work. That is why they could sometimes take over 'men's work' quite easily, especially when the *Arbeidsinzet* (forced labour in Germany) for men became obligatory in the spring of 1943. Women could also take advantage of their famous female charms. Of course some women did not restrict themselves to activities in the background: but they were exceptional. These latter women I shall consider further on in this paper[9].

Illegal activities by women have remained anonymous for the most part. Therefore it is hardly possible to know the exact numbers and the socio-political background of the women involved. Nor do we know whether they were usually unmarried or married or to what age group they belonged. Collecting such data through interviews would imply interviewing a sample of some hundreds of women.[10]

It may be of interest to mention that I never came across married women doing illegal work without the knowledge of their husbands. Only one woman told me:

I never said anything to my fiancé, for if something were to go wrong it would be better for him not to know about it [11].

In this case it was not even a husband but only a fiancé. All the other women I know about told their partners in some way about their illegal activities, and the men approved of the things their women did. This approval was even a necessary condition for one of the female cooperators of Groep 2000: ''My husband only had to say yes or no, and then I acted accordingly.'' [12]

In most cases it was not only a question of approval: as far as I know married women always worked *together* with their husbands. Men on the other hand often did illegal work independently of their wives, and often did not say a word about it. This implies that to *them* their wives' approval was not absolutely necessary[13]. Seen against this background, it is understandable that the marriages of some male resisters were wrecked or went through a crisis because of affairs with female resisters, whereas examples of the reverse are not known to me.[14]

I have classified the activities of women according to their function. There are the functions women exercised in cooperation with their husbands or with men in general (in theory these functions could be the same as those of men); there are those of women in Resistance organisations specialising in 'typically female' tasks; there are those undertaken because women were not so easily suspected of illegal activities; and lastly, there are exceptional functions. Let us look at them in turn.[15]

*   *   *   *

Working in cooperation with men, women helped to falsify 'p.b's', to stamp, distribute and edit illegal newspapers, to spy, to distribute ration books, to search out addresses for *onderduikers*, etc. (Later I will turn to their functions in the so-called armed Resistance groups.) They hardly ever held leading positions. For example, they seldom formed part of the editorial staff of an illegal newspaper, whereas there were many female distributors. And the so-called 'secretarial activities' were much more often carried out by women than by men. In many Resistance organisations, especially those where the religious element prevailed, it was thought to be the task of women to provide food, drink, cosiness and moral support:

The girl is always expected to take care of food and drink even though she has been working as hard as anyone else, and moreover she is expected to create a certain homeliness, even though the circumstances are very primitive. Quite often stout resisters consider it a benefit to find in their female companions a sympathetic audience whenever they need to express the problems that trouble their hearts.[16]

On this point, one woman I interviewed said that though she had done a lot of 'courier's work', she spent most of her time taking care of her comrades.[17] To another one, her comrades had said: "You should have been a market woman, you take care of us so well!"[18] The need of the men for service sometimes went so far that they got over their aversion to the presence of women at important conferences for the sake of being able to enjoy perfect service. A female cooperator of Johannes Post said about this:

I was with Johannes at several top conferences. At first the lads did not want the girls to be there, but because they found it so annoying to make coffee and tea while they were discussing, they liked to have a girl around who could play the hostess.[19]

The degree to which the serving task of women was stressed differed from one Resistance organisation to another.[20] It is interesting to study the functions of women in armed Resistance groups, for, of all Resistance groups, the armed ones were, at first sight, no women's business. By armed resistance I mean all Resistance activities in which weapons were used. So I am concerned with Resistance organisations which, for example, were engaged in sabotage, in liquidating dangerous people and in acquiring ration books or 'p.b.'s', by means of force. Women played a part in the background in these kinds of organisations as well. They comforted male resisters in mental and material respects before the men went out for a raid or an act of sabotage, and they did the same after the men had come back. They carried weapons, crowbars and the possible booty; they accompanied the men as the female half of love-couples; and they shadowed people who had been nominated to be killed. They distributed explosives; sewed fake uniforms; provided the men with safe addresses for sleeping; and sometimes, though only very rarely, contributed directly to a raid or liquidation (for these last two activities see also below).

Secondly, in organisations with 'typically female' tasks, like 'Groep 2000' and the group around Gesina van der Molen which saved about 300 Jewish children, women played an important role. To give an idea of these activities, I quote a woman belonging to the second of these groups. She tells here about smuggling Jewish children out of the Jewish crèche which was situated in front of the Hollandsche Schouwburg (Dutch theatre in Amsterdam), the place where the Jews had to wait for further deportation:

Then (in the summer of 1943 – MS) we regularly went to that crèche to get some of the children out. Sometimes I took babies in buttoned up rucksacks, sometimes the children were already dressed to go with us . . . In the moment of action itself I was never afraid. Often I didn't realise what I was doing. I went out to get the children and I said: 'We are going to enjoy ourselves, we are going to Aunt So-and-so, or we are going to make a puppet show, or something like that' . . . and then the children went with me. I was Aunt Julia in the crèche (. . .) Often the children were completely miserable.[21]

In organisations of this kind women were often more numerous than in other Resistance organisations and they were not restricted to functions in the background.

Thirdly, there were those kinds of functions which were considered especially suited to women. From mid-1943 the number of these increased significantly. These women had to do jobs in the public eye, running rather a big risk of unpleasant meetings with the Germans. Women were for example especially suited to accompanying pilots who had been brought down, and liberated prisoners, to safe hiding. Women also checked the safety of addresses by ringing at the doors on a pretext. They stood on the look-out during raids, and illegal periodicals and leaflets were for the most part distributed by them. A doggerel in *Ons Volk* (Our People) of 5th March 1944 illustrates this:

> *Girls*
> Only three kinds of girls we know,
> one is sauntering in front of the barrack gates,
> another is manoevring the men out of the country
> and the third gave you this paper[22].

Most of the activities in question here can be summed up by the term *courier's work*. This work implied carrying all sorts of things: letters, messages, ration books, money, espionage material, arms and so on. A female courier of a *knokploeg* explained:

> The work of a courier consisted of . . . well, looking for addresses for *onderduikers*, going for ration books, taking away ration books when raids had been committed – all things indeed coming from raids – for mostly it was not only ration books but all kinds of things, the whole lot—take it away, get it and take it to a contact address ... and carrying arms of course, you know, going along with the boys, with the men[23].

All these things could be hidden in a pram, in a bag with an innocent piece of needlework hanging out, in a double-layered bicycle coat-protector, in a little linen bag hanging under the clothes, in a suitcase, or under corsets and roll-ons. ('Roll-ons are invaluable and useful articles of dress', the *Centrale Leiding* (Central Management) of VN wrote to a cooperator in 1944.[24]) As long as the trains were still going, couriers often travelled by train:

> And then you thought: God save me if there's a check! And then there was a chap sitting in front of you, looking at you all the time. I thought: Jesus Christ, that chap smells a rat! I'll never forget it. (Laughing). I got out of the station and he followed me. I thought: Oh this is going to go wrong! He comes up to me. Then he says to me: 'What about a cup of coffee?' (laughing). And then I thought: Drop dead, fellow: And I said:' I don't have time for that!'[25]

And another courier speaking of fellow travellers:

> Are you travelling alone? Aren't you scared of all those bombing raids? Yes, but my God, I have to do something, don't I? ... My sister ... just had a child ... (And

then you saw them thinking—MS) 'What are you doing in this train when travelling is so dangerous?' [26]

During the general railway strike from September 1944 to May 1945 the couriers usually went by bicycle. In those days they were the only means by which the various Resistance groups could communicate with each other. But it was not easy: bad roads, bad tyres, the risk of bombing raids, increasing numbers of police checks (because by then the police had started to find out more about their secrets) and hunger and cold caused them a lot of trouble. Nevertheless they succeeded in maintaining the network of communications. Couriers were the liaison between resisters who had to renounce direct contact for the sake of security. That is why couriers knew many addresses; a knowledge that was a heavy burden to them. [27]

So it is clear that female couriers did things which in pre-war society were supposed to be men's work. Yet this phenomenon cannot be considered to have broken the old role patterns, because, as couriers, women only exploited roles which they were traditionally supposed to play.

Finally, the deeds of a few female resisters deviated from the general pattern sketched above. To illustrate this I have chosen some examples at random: [28]

Gesina van der Molen (Aunt Lien), already mentioned as a central figure in the rescue of Jewish children, was successivly one of the editors of *Vrij Nederland* and *Trouw* (Faith).

Mrs. H.H. van Tongeren was the general manager of Groep 2000.

Betty Visser (Karin), a courier of the *knokploeg* of Marinus Post, took an active part in raids on ration offices.

Truus van Lier and *Reina Prinsen Geerligs*, both members of CS-6, are known to have been involved in a number of attempts on Dutch Nazis. [29] One woman who used to be a member of CS-6 herself said about Reina:

She was ... I am inclined to say she was an average girl. Without a striking readiness to fight. She had those ... that ... how do you call that kind of hair-do ... with plaits ... the hair girls have in schoolbooks. Apart from that there was nothing special about her. But that suited her very well, for it was important not to attract attention.

The same CS-6 co-operator told me about Truus van Lier:

Truus van Lier was imprisoned in a cell above mine (laughing) What was she singing all the time? She always sang very patriotic songs, for she was condemned to death, you know, and she knew it. So, sitting in that cell above me, she was singing: 'In the name of Orange open the doors!' So she sang, very loudly.[30]

Finally I want to mention *Hannie Schaft* who was responsible for an unknown number of liquidations together with the sisters *Truus* and *Freddy Oversteegen*.

* * * *

How do these findings look in the light of the hypothesis which I formulated earlier? It would seem that the social and political background of resisters was much more important in determining role patterns in Resistance organisations than the mere fact that these people were members of such organisations. Even before 1940 the principle of equal rights for men and women was upheld, at least in theory, by socialists and liberals. So in organisations like CS-6 and the PBC, which had a relatively large number of people from socialist and liberal settings, the same principle was adhered to. Very often, especially within the PBC, this remained only beautiful theory. But within CS-6 women worked with men on an equal footing and so they actively cooperated in activities like liquidations and sabotage.

Before the war the principle of equal rights for women and men was not generally accepted by the denominational groups of Catholics and Protestants. The degree of acceptance varied from group to group, opinion on the division of roles between the sexes being much more enlightened in more liberal Protestant circles than in Roman Catholic or orthodox Calvinist groups. This is reflected in the corresponding Resistance organisations. In organisations like VN, Groep 2000 – even with a woman as a general leader – and the children's group around Van der Molen, the liberal Protestant element was relatively important. Here role patterns were more flexible than in Johannes Post's *knokploeg*, mostly consisting of orthodox Calvinists. However, the *knokploeg* of his brother Marinus who was also educated as an orthodox Calvinist, deviates from the general pattern: among the members of this group there were socialists as well as Catholics and orthodox Calvinists and here the women participated in raids, just like the women in CS-6. With one exception, comparable activities on the part of women are not to be found in Johannes' *knokploeg*. Thus my provisional conclusion is that there is no question of a breaking-up of old role patterns, with the exceptions of CS-6, Marinus Post's *knokploeg* and Groep 2000.

Let us end by looking at the consequences of illegal activities for these women in terms of punishment and imprisonment.[31] In the course of 1943, when women were getting more and more involved in the illegal activities which I have classified in the third and fourth categories, the risk of their getting caught increased. In April 1943 for example, about three hundred women were imprisoned in a house of detention in Amsterdam. Later on during 1944, when the German police were finding out more and more about the secrets of roll-ons, checks were intensified and the Resistance movement was repeatedly shocked by messages about couriers who had been caught. So even if it is true that women did run less risk of getting caught than men, their work remained dangerous. A courier comments:

As a woman they didn't pick you out so easily, yet once I was on a train and they checked me three times, while I was carrying the weapons: three times! And I could hardly move myself, well, if that man had said: 'Stand up! Get up' ... he would have found out! [32]

In fact she was carrying the weapons under her clothes and there were so many of them that she could not help bending forward.

When a woman was arrested she ran the risk of rough treatment during interrogation just like the male resisters, especially if she had been caught for those activities which I have classified as exceptional. Probably real torture – like putting on thumbscrews, burning with cigarettes, submerging in ice-cold water – did not happen in Holland, in contrast to practices in, for example, Norway and France. Nevertheless, women were beaten up, pushed over, and so on. So the observation in *Onderdrukking en Verzet* [33], that torture occurred only very rarely during interrogation and that, consequently, women needed less courage than men to join the Resistance movement, does not seem altogether right to me.

Executions of women were rare, but they did occur, especially in these exceptional cases. De Jong asserts that until the winter of 1944/1945 no women in Holland were executed. He mentions as exceptions Reina Prinsen Geerlings and Truus van Lier. However, they were not shot in the Netherlands, but in the German concentration camp, Oranienburg [34]. De Jong's assertion must be challenged. Firstly he forgets to mention the fact that Nel van den Brink (belonging to the PBC) was executed together with Reina and Truus. Secondly, apart from these three women, I came across another four executions before the winter of 1944–45. One case De Jong himself mentions elsewhere in his work [35]. Moreover, two other authors make the general statement that women also were executed (they say this without further specification of names and dates [36]).

It is difficult to trace the exact number of female resisters murdered by the Germans, because the Germans did not give these executions publicity by contrast with the executions of male resisters. On the basis of the cases mentioned above, however, I do not consider De Jong's assertion to be completely accurate. Besides, he also fails to give the number of women executed during the winter of 1944−45. I myself found three examples from this period[37].

Usually, women were punished by imprisonment or were sent to concentration camps. In the so-called Oranjehotel at Scheveningen, women made up between 12% to 15% of the total number of prisoners. In the concentration camp at Vught there were 1,900 women. Of these 1,900, some were transported to Ravensbrück in September 1944. Apart from these concentration camps, women were also sent to others and a lot of women did not survive the camps: for example, half of the 800 Dutch women who were in Ravensbrück never came back.

How did women bear imprisonment and concentration camps? De Jong thinks that women were, in general, better able than men to resist the miseries of imprisonment. He explains this statement by saying that women, accustomed as they are to menstruation and giving birth to children, are more used to inconveniences and pain than men. He also thinks that women could bear humiliation of every kind better than men because of their subservient position in society. Moreover, he says, women were in the habit of expressing their feelings: in contrast with men, they did not feel the need to control themselves, and they could have a good cry against the shoulder of comforting fellow prisoners[38].

The first part of De Jong's explanation appears to me as somewhat too biological. The other suppositions look very likely to me. Women who had been imprisoned indeed told me about the warmth, the solidarity and the humour among the female prisoners. One of them had also been in concentration camps and had experienced the same there. About the life in Vught she said for example:

Life in the camp was a very good experience! It was an experience of deep human solidarity![39]

About Ravensbrück another woman told me:

She (a courier of CS-6-MS) in fact saved the life of my sister (the mother of two CS-6 members−MS) with a lipstick she still had. My sister was very ill. And she was called 'Mummy' in the camp because she was always ready to help everybody. One day when the Nazis came to see who were the seriously ill people and who had to be removed from the barracks, she made up my sister with the lipstick.

And she made her up in such a way that she looked healthy, and the Germans just left her alone because she had red cheeks[40].

In conclusion I would like to say this. If women had been executed in Holland instead of being sent to camps to die, and if their executions had been given publicity, then these women would have received the honour they deserve. But today their contribution to the Resistance movement, in this last respect too, remains anonymous.

1   I shall only mention some well-known works, including two titles in English: J.C.H. Blom, 'The Second World War and Dutch society: continuity and change', *Britain and the Netherlands*, Vol. VI, in War and society, Papers delivered to the sixth Anglo-Dutch Historical Conference, The Hague, *Het Grote Gebod*. Gedenkboek van de LO-LKP-stichting. 2 vol. unknown date and place of publication unknown, 1951; L. de Jong, *De geschiedenis van het Koninkrijk der Nederlanden in de Tweede Wereldoorlog*. 8 vol. The Hague, 1969–1978, work in progress; *Onderdrukking en verzet. Nederland in Oorlogstijd*. 4 vol. Arnhem etc., date unknown; H.M. van Randwijk, *In de schaduw van gisteren. Kroniek van het verzet in de jaren 1940–1945*. The Hague etc., 1970; W. Warmbrunn, *The Dutch under German occupation 1940–1945*. Stanford/London, 1963.

2   In my master's thesis, *Het stille verzet, Vrouwen in illegale organisaties, Nederland 1940–1945*, Sua, Amsterdam 1980. I also deal with this question.

3   Of the titles quoted, this is especially true for *Het Grote Gebod*.

4   See, for example, an interview with the wife of Marinus Post: *LO-LKP-collectie* DD 1. This collection is in the Rijksinstituut voor Oorlogsdocumentatie (State Institute for Documentation of the Second World War, abbreviated here: RvO) in Amsterdam.

5   Some of the interviews I have transcribed from tape, others I have only summarised. In cases where the interviewee objected to the use of the tape-recorder, I only have notes. To indicate persons interviewed, I make use of a letter-code. The quotation here is taken from an interview with Mrs. J.IJ.

6   From this point on, this paper is much the same as Chapter 3 of my master's thesis (see note 2.). This third chapter is general in character and is followed by a further chapter, in which I deal more comprehensively with the organisations I have chosen and the part played by women.

7   Historiography on this subject is scarce. I will only mention: *Van Moeder op Dochter. Het aandeel van de vrouw in een veranderende wereld*, O.red.v. W.H. Posthumus-Van der Goot, Leiden, 1948.

8   A. Helman, *Een doodgewone held. De levensgeschiedenis van Gerrit Jan van der Veen 1902–1944* (place of publication unknown, 1946) p. 27.

9   These paragraphs are based on: *D.H. Couvée en A.H. Boswijk, *Vrouwen vooruit! De weg naar de gelijke rechten.* (The Hague, 1962) p. 281; *Opdat wij niet vergeten. De bijdrage van de gereformeerde kerken, van haar voorgangers en leden, in het verzet tegen het Nationaal-Socialisme en de Duitse tyrannie*, Samengest.d. Th. Delleman (Kampen, 1949) pp. 373–376; *'Hulde aan de Nederlandse vrouw' *Vrij Nederland* (Liberation-number); *VN archief* 185a, 1a (RvO); *LO-LKP-collectie* BI 3 and CB 2 (RvO); *Onderdrukking en Verzet*, op. cit, vol. III, pp. 818–827; *Den Vaderland getrouwe. Een boek over oorlog en verzet*, Samengest.d. M. Smedts en geschreven door mensen die beleefd hebben wat zij schreven (Amsterdam, 1962) p. 132.

10   Two students from Amsterdam have done this for their theses. For their conclusions see: Graaff, B. de en L. Marcus, *Kinderwagens en korsetten. Een onderzoek naar de sociale achtergrond en de rol van vrouwen in het verzet 1940–1945*, Amsterdam, 1980.

11   Report of an interview with B. van der Harst-Trompetter, *LO-LKP-collectie* CB 1 (RvO).

12   Truus Wijsmuller-Meijer, *Geen tijd voor tranen* (Amsterdam, date unknown), p. 95.

13   Those women I interviewed who during the War were married or engaged (6 in all) did work together with their partner. Similar examples are to be found in historiography, e.g., L. de Jong, *op. cit*, Vb, 816; VIa, p. 101. One can find an example of a husband's silence in the report of an interview with the widow of Marinus Post: *LO-LKP-collectie* DD 1 (RvO). An example of a man joining a resistance organisation against his wife's will, is the comrade of Hannie Schaft. See Ton Kors, *Hannie Schaft. Het levensverhaal van een vrouw in verzet tegen de Nazi's* (Amsterdam, 1976), pp. 102–103.

14   For example, that marriage of Gerrit Jan van der Veen; see A. Helman, op. cit., p. 110. Or the marriage of Hilbert van Dijk; see *LO-LKP-collectie* CB2.

15   These paragraphs are based on: *Couvée/Boswijk, op. cit., pp. 279–281; *M.R.D. Foot, *Resistance* (Bungay, 1978), pp. 13–14, 99, 267; *M. van Huessen-Pikaar, *Wij en een volk. Belevenissen van een koerierster* (date and place of publication unknown); *interviews with mss. N.R., A.S., L.T., J.IJ., M.I., C.O., N.I.; L. de Jong, op. cit., VIIb; *LO-LKP-collectie* CB2, interview with G. van Dijk etc., CB 1, interview with B. van der Harst-Trompetter etc.; ED 3, interview with R. van Dieden etc., EP 3, interview with K. de Graaf; *Onderdrukking en verzet*, op. cit. III, pp. 793–800, 818–827; *Terug in de tijd. Nederlandse vrouwen in de jaren '40–'45*, interviews en samenst, Dick Walda (Amsterdam, 1974); *Verslag, houdende de uitkomsten van het onderzoek (der) Enquête Commissie Regeringsbeleid 1940–1945* 8 vol, ('s Gravenhage) vol. IV & vol. VII; *VN archief* 185a, 1a, 1b, 8c (RvO); *L.E. Winkel, *De ondergrondse pers 1940–1945*, with an English summary (Den Haag, 1954), p. 40, p. 55; *Wijsmuller-Meijer, op. cit.

16   *Vrouwen van Nederland 1898-1948. De vrouw tijdens de regering van Koningin Wilhelmina*, Samengest. d. M.G. Schenk (Amsterdam, 1948), p. 71.

17   Interview with Ms. A.S..

18   Interview with Mrs. Van Huessen-Pikaar, made by VARA-radio Hilversum, December 1976.

19   Report of an interview with B. van der Harst-Trompetter, *LO-LKP-collectie* CB1.

20   Interview with Ms. J.IJ. She told me that she did not make coffee more often than her male comrades (belonging to the PBC).

21   Interview with Ms. H.C..

22   Quoted in Winkel, op. cit., p. 55.

23   Interview with Ms. M.I..

24   *VN archief* 185a, 1b.

25   Interview with Ms. N.R..

26   Interview with Ms. J.IJ..

27   For example, interviews with Mss. N.R. and N.I..

28   In chapter 4 of my master's thesis (see note 2) all these cases are dealt with extensively. References to the sources are to be found there.

29   Working on my thesis I found 'hard' evidence for four attempts only. After my thesis had been published an ex-member of CS-6 called me and told me that according to him Truus and Reina were responsible for an unknown number of liquidations.

30 Interview with Ms. M.I..
31 This section is based on the following sources: *A. Berendsen, *Vrouwenkamp Ravensbrück* (Utrecht, 1946), pp. 86–87; *Couvée/Boswijk, op. cit., p. 284; *Interviews with Mss. N.R., L.T., C.O.; *J.T. Kuyck, *Partisanen vrouwen* (The Hague, date unknown), *Van Moeder op Dochter*, op. cit., pp. 519, 533–535, 549–551; *Radiobroadcast about Gerhard Badrian (PBC) made by Bob Uschi, December 1978; *M. Smedts, *Waarheid en Leugen in het verzet* (Maasbree, 1978), p. 115; *VN archief 185a, 1a, 1b.
32 Interview with Ms. M.I..
33 *Onderdrukking en verzet*, op. cit., III, p. 822.
34 L. de Jong, op. cit., VIIIa, p. 359.
35 L. de Jong, op. cit., VIIb, p. 1015. The other executions are to be found in Ton Kors, op. cit. and in *LO-LKP-collectie* CB 2 (2 cases).
36 *Den Vaderland getrouwe*, op. cit., p. 133; *Vrouwen van Nederland*, op. cit., p. 71.
37 L.P.J. Braat, *Omkranste hiaten. Levensherinneringen* (Amsterdam, 1966), p. 143; *VN archief* 185a, 1b.
38 L. de Jong, op. cit., VIIIa, pp. 295–296.
39 Interview with Ms. N.R..
40 Interview with Ms. H.C..

Democratic History

The verticle kilns and company housing at Degerhamm Cement Works on the island of Oland in the Baltic, c. 1900; these are mentioned in Sven Lindqvist's article below, p.322.

The Humanistic Tradition and Life Histories in Poland

Paul Thompson

Life histories have a place in Polish culture which is unique. Throughout Eastern Europe the collection of oral folklore flourishes, because of its long-standing association with radical populism, going right back to the 19th century revival of a national cultural resistance to imperial domination by Prussia, Turkey, Russia and Austria. There are a number of anthropologists and sociologists in, for example, Hungary and Bulgaria, who use a life history type of interview for their research studies. In Czechoslovakia there has recently been a quite striking development of filmed life histories for television, while in Hungary there is an independent tradition of popular biography which originated in the 1930s from a radical writers' group urging the need for social change. The best-known of their works was Gyula Illyés' classic, *People of the Puszta* (1936), and its successors may be seen in more recent books like a history, illustrated by photographs, of a family called Mogatu. But all these activities remain essentially separate. Tape recorders have not come into widespread use so that the technical catalyst for an oral history breaking institutional and cross-disciplinary barriers has not been present. There has, all the same, been a remarkable development of the written life history in Poland. Here, as nowhere else, it has won an important place in popular culture, while at the same time providing the central tenet for a significant intellectual influence, the 'humanistic tradition' – as it is called – in Polish sociology.

The intellectual tradition goes back to one of the early masterpieces of the Chicago school of urban sociology, W.I. Thomas and Florian Znaniecki's *The Polish Peasant in Europe and America* (1918). This is well-known among sociologists as a pioneering example of the life history approach. But scarcely anybody is aware of the fruits of Znaniecki's influence in his own country. Znaniecki, who died in 1958, was by origin a landowner, and by training a philosopher. After fighting in the Legion

d'Honneur in the First World War, he found work in helping Polish
emigrants to North America to settle in Chicago. It was here that he met
Thomas, who was looking for a Polish-speaking collaborator for his
research on the city's immigrant districts. There can be no doubt that the
lasting interest of the multi-volume *Polish Peasant* comes from the rich
documentation, especially letters, which Znaniecki provided for it. And
the authors decided to devote one entire volume to an autobiographical
memoir specially written for them by a peasant immigrant, Wladek, who
was out of work and suffering from tuberculosis. With no other means to
support his family, he eagerly took up Znaniecki's offer of five dollars for
writing his memoirs. He proved such an unexpected mine of information
that the five dollars became a monthly wage, until he had eventually produced a text as long as a book. For American sociology, Wladek's memoir
became the founding document of the life history method.

Subsequently life histories were very effectively used by other
American sociologists in research, for example, of criminal sub-cultures
in Chicago, and the method had an important influence on some of the
best studies of race and class in the American south, like the work of John
Dollard. There were the beginnings too of a more sophisticated understanding of how autobiographical evidence could be interpreted, not just
in isolation but also in relation to quantitative information about social
change. In a critical volume published in 1939 – to which Znaniecki also
contributed – Thomas himself argued that their earlier work had not been
sufficiently systematic: 'what is needed is both the continued collection of
the life records . . . and the application of appropriate statistical studies as a
basis for the inferences drawn'.[1] But the promising possibility of such an
integrated approach was never fulfilled in North America, for sociologists
were soon to abandon interest in life histories, lured away by the equally
abstract rival fashions for statistical magic and high theorising. In Poland,
on the other hand, the outcome was to prove very different.

Until 1939 Znaniecki was active as a sociologist in both Poland and
the United States: indeed he failed to return home then only because his
boat was turned back. He had declared in *The Polish Peasant* a burning
faith in his new method – 'We are safe in saying that personal life-records,
as complete as possible, constitute the perfect type of sociological material'[2] – and he established it in Poland through both influence and further
experiment. In particular, from 1921 onwards he instigated the first
Polish memoir competitions, a decisive step forward in technique. Nevertheless it was probably a happy accident which cut off his direct part from
the onset of the Second World War. To the end of his life Znaniecki
remained a political and social conservative and his hostility to statistics

led him into absurd claims for the validity of his own social interpretations. He believed that society should be understood through individual consciousness: this, rather than the 'objective world of science', was the key to social reality.[3] The relative weight of testimony depended not on its representativeness, but on its quality—and of that, he was the judge. In *The Polish Peasant* there had only been a single life story. Similarly when he organised a competition on the attitude of the people of Poznan to their city in 1929, he was not deterred when a mere twenty out of a quarter of a million inhabitants sent him answers. He still regarded this as sufficient basis for a book. At heart his own rather narrow social perspectives did not allow him to see beyond an approach better suited to illuminating the social problem – the 'pathology' of the unknown – than to encompassing ordinary reality. The life history method would never have become so popular in Poland had it not been taken up by more progressive writers, who chose to use it to illuminate the social condition of Poland in the 1930s, exposing through memoirs the deterioration of towns and countryside, drained by emigration, semi-feudal tenures, crowding and lack of work.

Many of these collections proved so successful that they became the start of a series. Thus Ludwick Krzywicki followed his own famous *Memoirs of the Unemployed* (1930) with *Memoirs of Unemployed Peasants* (1939), while his *Memoirs of Peasants* (1935) was echoed first in Jozef Chalasinski's four-volume masterpiece, *The Young Generation of Peasants* (1938), and then in the post-war ten-volume *Young Rural Generation of People's Poland*. Similarly, the *Memoirs of Emigrants* (1939) have been followed by two post-war collections. Equally important, the results were drawn from far larger numbers of memoir-writers. The most prolific pre-war competition, The Young Generation of Peasants, drew over 1500 entrants, but Kryzywicki's competitions for a 'diary' – life history – from the unemployed and from peasants brought just under 800 and 500 responses each. Znaniecki by contrast had never again succeeded as well as in his first memoir competition of 1921, when he received 149 answers. Thus by 1939 both the scale and the social purpose of life history work in sociology had been transformed; and its published results had made a considerable impact in developing public consciousness of the nature of Poland's social problems and the need for change.

At the same time the problems in interpreting memoirs began to be more fully understood. The very volume of material from the 1930s competitions made a purely idiosyncratic conclusion rather less likely. Chalasinski used assistants to sift the entries and pick out those which dealt most fully with the problems which interested him. Later on he tested out his interpretations with the people who wrote the memoirs, and some of these discussions led him to change his views. Nevertheless it remained true that the ideas with which he started, rather than the evidence as a whole, provided the basis for his conclusions. Although at least in his post-war work he showed an awareness of this weakness, he did not find an answer to it; and as early as 1936 a rival rural sociologist, Wladislaw Grabski, criticised his treatment of the material as little more than 'a search for affirmation of his own prejudgements'.[4] Grabski went further to argue that memoir collections in general exaggerated social problems, because they were written largely by unrepresentative social failures, the unemployed lumpenproletariat, or dissolute vodka-drinkers from the peasantry. Chalasinski's approach offered little effective defence to this.

Krzywicki's achievement was in this respect considerably more impressive. Although from a small landowning family, he was the most radical of the life-history sociologists of the 1930s, a materialist strongly influenced by Marxism. (There had been a Marxist current in Polish sociology even before 1900.) Krzywicki was much less concerned with the complexity and psychology of individual lives than with mass phenomena; and he was more anxious to know whether an account was reliable, than to judge its literary merits. He therefore insisted on two safeguards which he applied strictly in each of his published collections. Firstly, the memoirs should be complemented by parallel studies of the same problems, using quantitative methods. Thus for his *Memoirs of Unemployed Peasants* he could refer back to his *Social Structure of the Polish Countryside* published two years earlier, in 1937. Secondly, he tried to assess how far the attitudes of memoir-writers could be taken as more generally representative. Some of his comments on this problem were particularly shrewd, and in fact a good deal closer to the mark than Grabski's criticisms, for Krzywicki recognised that the memoir-writers were normally people brisker and cleverer than the average for their social group.

The truth of this emerged rather unexpectedly after 1945, for undoubtedly several of the memoir-writers picked out by Chalasinski and Krzywicki had been highly class-conscious people, and they subsequently rose to significant political positions with the new Communist government. Paradoxically, writing for the competition had often provided the confidence, and the credentials, for this new career. No doubt this must be in itself one reason why worker-memoirs have become such an established feature of Polish cultural life. But it is also an important expression of a wider democratisation. There never has been a tradition of organised popular participation in, for example, local government in Poland. On the other hand informal open discussion of social problems is highly valued. One vehicle for this today is offered by television; but the memoir-competitions allow still more people to express their views, with some chance of an audience. The published collections are also particularly effective in conveying how life differs for other social groups in the country, especially helping towards understanding between town-dwellers and the peasantry. Memoir-competitions are not just an eccentric aspect of popular Polish culture: they meet real social needs.

Competitions were revived soon after 1945. Even in this delicate political period some memoir-writers were prepared to be remarkably unguarded. Stefan Nowakowski remembers a competition which was sponsored by a magazine in 1947 on 'The Polish Village during the War'. The magazine, unexpectedly inundated with several thousand entries, called him in to assist. He was amazed by how openly people wrote. One entry, complete with name and address, was from a man describing his own activities in a right-wing political organisation, whose membership was officially supposed to have been 'eliminated' by the Communist Party. Nevertheless, the real explosion in memoir-writing came only from the mid-1950s. In 1952 an ambitious project was launched by Polish radio with the publishing house Puf, for memoirs on the Second World War and after. State prizes were offered, and several collected volumes issued. This competition provided a model for others to follow; while the grass-roots pressure for autobiographical expression was proved by the responses met. Chalasinski's post-war new series on the Younger Rural Generation attracted the post-war record—5500 autobiographies. He published 500 of them in his ten volumes. By the 1960s, it had all become part of a regular pattern.

Every year competitions are now organised by the national newspapers and radio, and by local newspapers in every big city. Themes are set, and quite substantial prizes offered, two or three times a year, each competition normally attracting a thousand or more entries. The best results are serialised in the newspapers, and published as collections in book form. These books sell up to 5000 copies each. By now several hundred thousand Poles have entered for competitions. The material collected amounts to millions of typed pages and a special national archive for it has been developed in Rudno. Memoir-writing, in short, has become a recognised part of the national way of life.

Among almost any occupational group in Poland, it seems, enthusiastic memoir-writers can be found: among peasants, professional men and women, domestic workers and factory workers. For the sociologists, this has even become a matter of some concern, for paradoxically it threatens the representativeness of the material collected. Before 1939 part of the prestige won by successful memoir-writers was due to the fact that the majority of peasants were not fully literate. But winning a competition still brings status; and the prizes also offer one way of earning extra money. Consequently every competition attracts entries from people who are almost professional memoir-writers, sometimes even sending round the same autobiography from competition to competition. These semi-professionals are a relatively small group, but there are other ways in which the autobiographies are recognised as tending to be selective. They provide little information, for example, about the lives of the former land-owning aristocracy and business bourgeoisie; or, at the other extreme, of drunkards. And in general, although women enter for all the competitions, they are generally heavily outnumbered by men. There have been themes chosen such as memories of family life which have brought a more even balance, but there have been no competitions specifically focussed on female workers like professional women (a group who have grown dramatically since 1945) or the women textile workers in Lodz (who have recently proved an industrial group of some importance for Polish politics).

The fact that these defects are so fully recognised is, on the other hand, itself noteworthy, and one hopes the first step to filling some of the gaps. In any case, Polish self-criticism must be set against an extraordinary success in generating a truly democratic enthusiasm for history. Perhaps the most remarkable instance of this is the forming of co-operative memoir-writing groups at some of the big factories, coal mines and steel works. In many cases these have been launched through the initiative of one of Chalasinski's most notable pupils, F. Jakubczak, who will call together an initial meeting, suggest some themes, and later assist with the publication of books produced by the group. But the essential dynamic is provided by the commitment of the group members; and where else but in Poland could you find co-operative groups of industrial workers, up to 200 in number, helping to correct and enlarge their own life history drafts through coming together regularly, after work, for two-hour discussion meetings?

In the sociological profession, support for such activities, and indeed for the 'humanistic tradition' as a whole, has been by no means consistent. The prestige of the life history school has ebbed and flowed partly with the turns in national politics, partly with sociological influences from America, and also with the effectiveness with which the school has been able to answer methodological criticism. At present there has been a renewed interest in re-evaluation of its merits, and in particular, in bridging the gap in Polish sociology between the survey statisticians and the life history purists. Part of the difficulty lies in the fact that the tradition has been handed down chiefly through pupils of Chalasinski rather than Krzywicki, who had come closer to solving this problem. There is, however, a small group of sociologists who see themselves as standing between the qualitative and quantitative schools, using both methods together. Probably the best-known of them is Bronislaw Golebiowski, who set the life stories he used in their social context, and tested some of his interpretations by quantifying the distribution of particular attitudes among them. An example is his *Studies of Rural Youth* (1966). Wladyslaw Adamski has developed Golebiowski's approach in the study of the Polish scout movement – still one of the major youth organisations in the country – by combining memoir material with a postal questionnaire and other sources. A long-term study of peasants by economists at the Agricultural Institute is using diaries from a stratified sample of informants, and at Poznan, life history sociologists (Kwilecki and Dulczewski) have attempted some similar selectivity in the memoir-writers for their research.

Perhaps of most general interest is the work of Jan Lutynski and others in exploring the character of memoir-writers and the quality of their evidence. There has been for many years an increasingly subtle understanding of not only the social backgrounds and relative intelligence of their evidence: how far, for example, various types of memoir-writer suppress socially unacceptable truths and try to produce the life story most likely to be approved for a prize. For one recent paper Ilona Przyblowska re-interviewed a random sample of memoir-writers who had entered a 1964 competition on the creation of a new industrial area. She found that while the commonest motive of those who sent in memoirs was to assist in the research study from the competition originated, the most consistently worthwhile memoirs were those from people who above all wanted to express their *own* experience, just for the sake of self-expression. The least successful of all were those whose aim was to win themselves a reputation as writers.[5]

There are certainly differences, as well as similarities, between the problems in interpreting written competition memoirs and tape-recorded spoken life stories. Even so, it would have saved historians here a great deal of wasted time if we had been familiar with Polish life history work ten years ago when arguments about the quality of remembered evidence were first aired. In Poland understanding of these problems has accumulated over more than fifty years and there are sociologists there today whose experience with autobiographical material is probably unequalled.

Stefan Nowakowski, for example, began his work in Upper Silesia soon after 1945, and his active fieldwork continued over twenty years. During this period he watched the creation of a completely new society. The boundaries of Poland had been shifted after the Second World War so that while some of the former eastern provinces were incorporated by Russia, the western frontier was advanced to the Oder-Neisse line. The new western provinces were created from territories which had been absorbed by Germany, or systematically Germanised, through the Prussian advance eastwards from the late middle ages onwards. A massive population movement ensued, with nine million Germans being evacuated to East and West Germany, and replaced by Poles from Russia, western Europe, and from overcrowded Polish cities like Warsaw. They varied from highly traditional small peasants to westernised city-dwellers, bringing different experiences of industrialisation and urbanisation, different attitudes to work, school and church, different regional cultures, and social status.

Nowakowski wanted to see how a new society of Poles evolved out of this frontier melting-pot. Initially, his main technique was participant observation in the style of an anthropologist, returning to the territories for months of watching, interviewing, and talking. At the same time he collected historical and statistical evidence. From 1952 onwards, however, he was also able to make use of memoir competitions for which he was chosen as a jury member. These large-scale competitions gave a particularly good opportunity for comparing the evidence from differing sources. As a whole he found that, even though the competition organisers had given no more guidance than a rather general title, 99% of the problems which had first interested him, or had arisen from his own fieldwork, were covered by at least some of the writers. For example, he had developed a special interest in rural people who travelled daily to industrial work, or lived in workers' hostels returning home only for holidays, so that they were half-workers, half-peasants. How could the social consciousness of such people be understood? He was able to collect an entire volume from the memoirs on this problem alone.

In general the material from memoirs thus paralleled that from observation and interviewing. But there were exceptions: for example, derogatory stereotypes of other social groups were common enough in spoken interviews, but tended to be avoided by the more self-conscious memoir-writers. German-speaking Poles, for example, were referred to in interviews as 'Germans', but not in the memoirs. On the other hand, in contrast to the interviews, the written memoirs were *deeper*, more deliberately reflective in thinking through to explanations of the social processes and phenomena which the writers had experienced. Nowakowski is not categorical about such differences, however. For a sociologist, in his view, the material from written autobiography and informal interviewing is essentially of the same kind.

In contrast to historians, whose interest seems so far to have been limited, Polish sociologists have played a very active part in developing the popular memoir culture in recent years. They devise and judge newspaper competitions. They help form factory groups. They advocate and teach the life history as one of their own research tools. They refine its methodology. But it is important not to exaggerate the influence of academics. The worker-memoir movement is strong enough for competitions to go on continually, whether or not such professionals are involved. No doubt one reason for its strongly independent roots is that during precisely those years after 1945 when it was being popularised, academic sociology had been disbanded as an irredeemably bourgeois activity. It survived from the war only until about 1948, when it was banned. Official sociology was not re-established until after the 1957 revolution which brought Gomulka to power. In the meantime, the humanistic tradition in Polish sociology was only able to survive in an underground way outside formal institutions. The politics of that period are another story. But what seemed a set-back, may have brought a greater gain in the long run, and helped to make the Polish life history into one of the most democratic forms of historical writing anywhere. For ultimately it is the combination of professionalism and popular enthusiasm which gives it such a special quality.

NOTE: The information in this article is derived from a conference on the Biographical Method held by the Institute of Philosophy and Sociology of the Polish Academy of Sciences at the Palac Jablonna outside Warsaw, on 8–10 August 1978. I am particularly indebted to the papers given there by Wladyslaw Adamski and Stefan Nowakowski, and to other assistance from Jan Lutynski, Bronislaw Misztal, Zolton Karpati, Robert Manchin, and Lubomir Faltan.

1 H. Blumer (ed), *An Appraisal of Thomas and Znaniecki's 'The Polish Peasant in Europe and America'*, Social Science Research Critiques, 1, New York 1939, pp. 86–7; see also John Dollard, *Criteria for the Life History, with Analyses of Six Notable Documents*, New York 1935; Clifford R. Shaw, *The Jack-roller; a delinquent boy's own story*, Chicago 1930; and L. Gotschalk, C. Kluckholm and R. Angell, *The Use of Personal Documents in History, Anthropology and Sociology*, New York 1940.
2 *Polish Peasant*, II, pp. 1832–3.
3 e.g. *Polish Peasant*, II, pp. 1846–7.
4 *Roczniki Socjologii Wsi*, I, 1936, p. 42—criticising Chalasinski's earlier *The Ways of Workers' Social Advancement, a Study Based on Worker Autobiographies*, Poznan 1931.
5 *Studia Socjologiczne*, 1974, I.

Dig Where You Stand

Sven Lindqvist

In the mid-60's I was travelling in Latin America investigating multi-national companies for my book *The Shadow*. It struck me then that it was very strange that so little serious independent research had been done about these companies.

You may come across a couple of public relations pamphlets...or one or two books commissioned by a company's directors to celebrate the anniversary of the company.

But where do you find the point of view of those most affected by the activities of the company?

The workers.

The local population.

The inhabitants of the host countries.

Their experiences of the company are never recorded. When I returned to Sweden I went to the catalogue of the Royal Library in Stockholm and found that the situation was almost the same in my own country.

A hundred years ago we used to say that the history of Sweden is the history of its kings. This is now considered old-fashioned. But the history of Swedish industry is still thought of as the history of its owners and directors. Practically every factory history has been written *for them*, by writers *selected by them*, and *paid by them* to produce results that would then be *approved of by them*.

Because my own grandfather had been a cement worker I took a special interest in the cement industry. I read the histories of 11 different companies, written between 1923 and 1973. The wisdom contained in these books could be summarised in five points:

1. Management has never made a mistake.
2. Management has never been morally at fault.

3. The contribution of the shareholders to the production of cement has been vastly more important than that of the workers.

4. The workers' contribution to the development of the cement industry has been mainly to raise unrealistic demands and to receive benefits from the company.

5. In over a hundred years, nothing has ever happened that might give a cement-worker legitimate cause for pride or anger.

This wisdom seemed to me perhaps a trifle lopsided. I felt pretty sure that these books did not present the whole truth about the subject.

And as I continued my study of company histories I gradually formed the opinion that:

NO AREA OF MODERN HISTORY HAS BEEN MORE DISTORTED BY ONE-SIDED TREATMENT THAN THE HISTORY OF BUSINESS.

So, what could be done about it?

At first, I played with the idea that I myself should write a new version of the history of cement production in Sweden. But cement, after all, was only one example. There were thousands of other products and hundreds of other big companies. Even if I spent the rest of my life writing company histories I could hardly hope to cover the ground. This was clearly not a task for one person. Gradually, another solution presented itself.

In order to explain this I must say a few words about the redefinition of the concept of *culture* that has taken place in Sweden during the last decade or so. Ten years ago we used to think of 'culture' as something produced by top artists, writers and musicians, and then *distributed* to the mass of the people who *consumed* it. Today, society instead tries to encourage ordinary people with an interest in the theatre to *take part* in theatrical performance. In the same way we are trying to recognise and encourage other cultural *activities* in the field of music, writing and painting. The emphasis is no longer on the mere *distribution* of culture but rather on active *participation* in the arts.

Now why should this concept of culture as an activity be restricted to the liberal arts? Why, for example, should historical research be looked upon as something carried out by academic specialists for other academic specialists, or at the very best something whose results can be *distributed* to the general public?

People who have got used to the idea that you can make your own music, your own theatre or your own poems will not find it strange that you can carry out your own investigations. Sometimes, the need for such investigations grew directly out of artistic activities. In the old mining community of *Norberg*, for example, several hundred people gathered together to make a play about the big strike in 1891 for which Norberg is famous.

But how were people dressed in those days? What did their homes look like? How did they talk, how did they eat, how did they work? They found that in order to *play* history, you had to *investigate* history. Several such combined theatre and investigation projects are at present being carried out in various parts of Sweden, most notably in *Norrköping*, the former centre of the Swedish textile industry.

In other cases the present *economic crisis* created the impulse for historical investigation. This crisis has caused great changes in most of our major industries. Thousands of people have lost their jobs. Whole communities have been threatened by annihilation. In self-defense these people have turned to their common history. And they have wanted to find out more about it. The small steel community of *Vikmanshyttan* is the best-known example.

The conclusion I drew from this and other examples was:
FACTORY HISTORY COULD AND SHOULD BE WRITTEN FROM A FRESH POINT OF VIEW—BY WORKERS INVESTIGATING THEIR OWN WORKPLACES.

If ordinary people are going to undertake historical research, the history of their own jobs is, I think, a very good place to start. Because that is where they have their competence. They know their jobs. Their working experience is a platform on which they can stand when they are judging what others are doing—or not doing. The experts might each be experts in his or her own field, but when they are talking about your job *you* are the expert. That gives you a measure of self-confidence, and a basis for amateurs and professional researchers to meet on equal footing.

But historical research of course has its own techniques and methods with which the amateur would at least need to have a superficial acquaintance. Above all the amateur must know something about the sources of information about the past. In Sweden – and as far as I know in other countries – there was no guide on how to investigate the history of your own job. So, instead of writing a new history of the Swedish cement industry I decided to write a handbook which would help *others*, especially the workers, to write these factory histories in their own neighbourhoods and their own places of work.

The book is called *Dig Where You Stand: How to Research a Job.*
Using the cement industry as an example it describes in a concrete and practical way how to use thirty different sources of information about the history of one's own job.

The book was four years in the making. Since it came out in March last year I have travelled all over Sweden to take part in trade union meetings, in study groups of the Workers' Educational Association in public libraries, schools and universities, lecturing on the theme of digging where you stand. Most of the people at these meetings are very excited by the idea that there is so much information available about the work they are doing.

They are surprised to hear, for example, that the Patent Registry Office has kept a record of every patent granted since the 1890's and that they are free to use the archives of the Patent Office to trace the technical history of the machine they are working with or the product they are making.

They are surprised to hear the Sweden has had a Factory Inspectorate since 1890 and that the annual reports of the Inspectorate are still available, full of concrete and often critical descriptions of particular workplaces and even of particular industrial accidents.

Very few workers know the history of strikes and industrial disputes at their place of work. It comes as a surprise to them to learn that since 1903, these disputes have been recorded by a public office. And that the archives of the Court of Industrial Disputes contain detailed information about all cases brought before the Court since it was set up in 1929.

Most people don't know that they can find out what the owners and directors of their factory used to earn, simply by looking it up in the Swedish Taxation Calendar, which has been published annually since 1912. And that the corresponding wages of workers in their jobs are just as easily found from the annual wages statistics.

But what do the figures mean? What did people actually buy with these wages? Most Swedes do not realise that the answers to such questions are to be found in the so-called Household Budget Investigations which have covered almost every branch of industry all over Sweden since 1912. Thousands of working class and lower middle class families were asked to keep detailed accounts of their earnings and expenditure over several months. These accounts still exist and tell us precisely how much coffee labourer Karl Malmkvist and his family at the Degerhamm Cement works could afford to buy in 1933, how much milk, how much kerosene, and what presents they gave each other at Christmas.

Documents such as these are interesting in themselves. But I see them, above all, as an excellent starting point for further investigation. When young workers in Degerhamm Cement works today read that Anna Malmkvist bought five pennies' worth of TOOTHWAX or 11 pence worth of CARBIDE they ask themselves: What was Toothwax? What was Carbide used for?

The natural thing for them to do is to take the car and drive into town to visit the old-age clinic at the hospital where Anna Malmkvist was staying in 1977. She was then already very old and weak. When I asked to interview her she sent word that she didn't remember anything and didn't care to talk. But when young people from the factory came along that was something different. She had known them when they were small. And when they brought with them a copy of that old household account book from 1933, with all those things she had bought for her husband and children so long ago all neatly put down in her own familiar handwriting—well, she couldn't help but be interested:

Toothwax?—
Well that was a kind of yellow paste for filling the black holes in your teeth to lessen the pain and to make them look nicer while you were waiting for the district physician to come to the factory every six months to extract black teeth, amongst other things...

And so you get the whole story about the lack of dental care at Degerhamm, at a time when the nearest dentist was 50 miles away, out of reach both geographically and financially for people like the Malmkvists.
And you get that story straight from the toothless mouth of one of those who really suffered from it. 'Carbide', she will muse. 'Well it looked like white gravel and we used it for fuel in Karl's bicycle lamp...' And out comes the whole story of how Karl had the bicycle to get to work, while she had to walk that distance when she went to the factory with his lunch every day.
And then carry on up the hill to the co-operative store to buy all the things which she then had to carry home without a bicycle—and a very long time it took, especially through the snow in winter time, till finally she got home, after dark to the infants she had bound with a piece of rope to the kitchen bench—'You see I used to rope them to the bench with one pillow at the front and one pillow at the back so that they wouldn't hurt themselves while I was away.'
Documents such as the household book – this is the first point I want to make –CAN BE USED AS KEYS TO UNLOCK THE MEMORY OF OLD PEOPLE. In my experience, some old people are very taciturn, while those who like to talk generally have a stock of anecdotes that have been told so many times that it is very difficult to get at the truth behind them. But if you come with a document, like the household book, or a report from the Factory Inspectorate, or a plan of the workplace from the archives of the insurance company, or a collection of photographs, or something else

that captures the interest of the old person, this will awaken their memories and make the interview far more worthwhile for both of you.

My second point is that MOST DOCUMENTS NEED AN ORAL COMPLEMENT TO TELL THEIR WHOLE STORY. This is only natural since most documents have been prepared for purposes other than the historian's. The household budget investigations were undertaken in order to provide information for the price index. The insurance companies' description of the workplace were meant to form a basis for judging the risk of fire. And so on.

Most documents have limitations because of the way they were drawn up to meet their original purpose. And many of them, like police reports, or the description of strikes or accidents, can be quite misleading because the public authority collecting the information did not know the whole truth or did not bother to seek any opinion other than the employer's.

The general reaction of Swedish workers when you tell them about the sources of their own history, is: 'Why have we not been told of this before?' The short answer to that is, of course, that nobody thought of it. But then, again, why did nobody think of it? This question takes us very deep into Swedish class society.

One of the reasons is, I believe, that workers' research into the history of their own jobs could be politically embarrassing to many established institutions in Sweden. History is dangerous.

That was something else that I learnt ten years ago when I was touring Latin America investigating multinational companies. The representatives of these companies spoke willingly enough about present problems and future prospects. But when conversation turned to history they often became uncomfortable.

'We are trying to live down our past', an executive of Bookers told me. Bookers' original capital and Guyana lands were acquired through the slave trade with Africa.

'We are still charged with the sins of the past', said Mr Pilgrim, information officer of Demba, a bauxite company of the same country.

Until the Great War, the land now occupied by Demba belonged to smallholders who had no idea of the riches that the ground contained. It was purchased for a song. And since the ore thus became the private property of the company, they never paid a penny in royalties to the state for the right to mine the land.

Both these gentlemen thought it very unfair that the sins of the past should be held against them today. But the RESULTS of these sins – the land, the buildings, the machinery, in short the Capital – these were of course not willing to surrender. The RESULTS of the past were sacred private property and must not be touched. History is important because the RESULTS of history are still with us. That was what I learnt in Latin America. History is still paying dividends. History is still conferring power on people. In Sweden as well as in Latin America.

The history of the electrostatic dust collector is a case in point, especially for workers in a dusty trade like cement manufacture. The principle of the electrostatic dust collector was discovered in Britain in 1884. But nobody paid attention, until politically powerful Californian orange growers managed to obtain a court order against the Riverside cement works warning that the factory would be shut down if the dust problem was not solved.

Then the problem *was* solved. Cotrell constructed an effective electrostatic dust collector which was installed at the Riverside cement works in 1906. It collected around 98 percent of the dust, or roughly 100 tons a day. About the same time, in 1909, the health hazards of cement dust were, for the first time, statistically proven in the 'Sickness statistics of the Leipzig local sick fund'.

These health hazards, and the methods of preventing them, were both well-known to Swedish cement companies. But when the first electrostatic dust collector was installed in a Swedish cement factory in 1923 the intention was not to protect the health of the workers or the local population. the object was to extract potash from the dust. The operation turned out to be unprofitable and the dust collector was pulled down in 1926.

The years went by. It was not until 1940 that a dust collector was installed for health protection purposes in a Swedish cement factory. And it was only in 1969 that dust collectors were installed in all Swedish cement factories, the last one being Hellekis i Västergötland. By that time the electrostatic dust collector had been in existence for over sixty years. The health hazards had been known for exactly sixty years. Two generations of cement workers had inhaled tons of cement dust. Millions of tons had been spread over the surrounding countryside. But every year that a company could delay installing a dust collector, it saved a few dollars at the expense of the workers and the neighbours. The money has not been lost. It is still there. The money saved in waiting sixty years to install dust collectors today forms part of the capital of the Swedish private cement monopoly, EUROC.

Having come this far in investigating the history of the dust problem, Swedish cement workers tend to ask the question: /
To whom should that part of the capital of EUROC belong? Should it

belong to the shareholders, who never came near the factory? Or should it belong to us, who suffered the dust and the hazards for sixty years?

Such questions are potentially dangerous. The abstract notion of the relation between Capital and Labour suddenly becomes concrete and tangible, almost touchable and breathable, through historical investigation of the particular circumstances in a particular place of work

This is especially so for workers in the asbestos cement factories. The dust they inhaled was the most dangerous of all. These dangers were first discovered in 1907. They were first taken seriously in Britain in the 1930s. They were not acknowledged in Sweden until 1964. And asbestos was still widely used in our country until 1976.

History is important because its results are still with us. This year and next year people will die because of working conditions they suffered from twenty, thirty or even fifty years ago. Towards the end of the 1960s, people were still dying from cancer caused by asbestos fibres buried in their lungs since the time they worked in the gas-mask factories of the Great War.

A 47-year old woman died from cancer caused by asbestos. From two to six years of age, she had been exposed to the dust from the working clothes of her parents who at that time worked in an asbestos factory. A foreman at an asbestos mine sometimes brought pieces of asbestos home for his little daughter to play with. Later in her life, this woman died of mesothelioma. Another little girl used to come to the asbestos factory with her father's food every day for a year. Sixty years later she too died from mesothelioma.

When former asbestos workers gradually discover facts such as these through a combination of interviews and the study of documents, they come to understand that history is still living even in the bodies of those who took part in it. History is lying in wait till finally it kills them. When you open the dead body you will find history in the form of silvery fibres— the last remnants of the air these people had to breathe in the factories and workers' quarters at the beginning of the century.

And when the votes are counted at the shareholders' meetings that same history is still living—the profits from those days still entitle their owners to power and dividends. Just as the workers' children inherited the asbestos fibres, other children have inherited the company shares.

History is not dead. On the contrary, it is living the good life and running the big companies. And that, in the final analysis, is why workers' investigations of factory history are so necessary. Sixty years after the conquest of political democracy, the Swedish workers' movement is now bent on the conquest of economic democracy. In this situation, workers' bent on the conquest of economic democracy. In this situation, workers' investigations of their own jobs will have a definite political significance.

Those who wield economic power have so far also had control over the research dealing with their companies. They have decided what picture should be painted of themselves. They have decided on the picture of the company. That's why many workers do not know their own predecessors. They often know nothing of the history still living in the Capital of the company. That history must first be investigated, concretely and locally, by the combined collection of oral and documentary evidence in company after company.

Those who are to conquer the company must first conquer the picture of the company. A new picture must be created, a picture that puts workers and their work in the foreground. This, I believe, is true not only of Sweden, but of many other countries. My purpose in speaking here today is to try to persuade you that such activities could and should be encouraged. I hope that one of you will soon be writing a *Dig Where You Stand* for the workers of your own country.

Notes on The Contributors

Lutz Niethammer is Professor of Modern History at the University of Essen. One of the leaders of the new social history in Germany, his work has ranged from studies on denazification—*Entnazifizierung in Bayern* (1972) and on anti-fascism, to a comparative study of housing in Britain, France and Germany. Most recently to appear is a collection of essays on oral history edited by him.

Christina Borderias teaches in the Department of Contemporary History at the University of Barcelona. She wrote her master's dissertation on the miners of L'Alt Llobragat in 1977 and is now researching on women's work in and out of the home in 20th-century Spain.

Mercedes Vilanova is Professor of Spanish History at the University of Barcelona. For the last ten years she has been studying the Civil War and the Anarchist movement in the 1930s, combining quantitative and oral sources. Her earlier books include *Espana en Maragall* (1968).

Luisa Passerini teaches contemporary history at the University of Turin, where she took her first degree in philosophy. She carried out research on the history and cultures of southern Africa and published a first book on the liberation struggle in Mozambique and a second on kinship before returning to take up her present subject: the Turin working class under Fascism. Her most recent book is *Storia Orale* (1978), a collection on oral history.

Liliana Lanzardo teaches history at the University of Trieste. She has been studying the Fiat workers of Turin since the 1960s, and her earlier work is published as *Class Operaie e Partito Communista all Fiat ... 1945–68* (1971).

Daniel Bertaux first worked in engineering science and later turned to sociology. He is a full-time researcher at the Centre d'Etudes des Mouvements Sociaux in Paris. His study of social mobility, *Desins personnels et structure de classe* (1977), took him from quantitative statistics to the story of the making of the French working class. He is founder of an international group of sociologists using the life history approach, and editor of *Biography and Society* (1981).

Fañch Elégoët teaches anthropology at the University of Rennes and researches on the recent history of the Breton peasant community from which he himself comes. He edits a local review, *Tud Ha Bro*, and has published two studies of men and women from Léon in north-west Brittany.

Gerhard Wilke was apprenticed as a butcher and worked as a journeyman before studying at Ruskin College in Oxford and King's College Cambridge. He now teaches sociology at a College of Further Education in London. He has published studies of the plays of Samuel Beckett and, with Kurt Wagner, of the German village in which they both grew up.

Dagfinn Slettan is a full-time researcher in history at the University of Trondheim. He worked on an oral history project of the Trøndelag region, which led to his publications on farm workers (*Dreng og taus i Verdal*, 1978) and on small farmers and fishermen (*Kystfolk ser tilbake*, 1979). He is now studying rural social change since the 1930s.

Anna Bravo teaches modern history at the University of Turin. Her continuing research interest in the history of the Italian popular classes has been influenced by personal participation in both the new left and the women's movement. She drew on oral sources in her first book, about a 'liberated zone' under the Piedmontese Resistance, and subsequently used them more systematically in her current work on the Piedmontese peasantry under industrialisation.

Nelleke Bakker is a research assistant in history at the University of Amsterdam. She wrote her doctoral thesis on Dutch women teachers between the wars.

Jaap Talsma teaches history at the University of Amsterdam. In his research he combines 19th century Dutch politics and 20th century social history from oral sources. He is founder of the Dutch oral history society, and organised the 1980 European Oral History Conference in Amsterdam.

Isabelle Bertaux-Wiame trained as a historian in Paris, where she completed her master's dissertation on bakery apprentices (1976). From there she went on to study migration into Paris between the wars, again using oral sources. Now a sociologist at the University of Paris VII, she is researching on the social mobility of women, through family life histories which she is collecting in the Paris region and the north of France.

Lucetta Scaraffia teaches history at the University of Turin. The main focus of her research as well as her first two books have centred on the social history of Italy's underdeveloped regions, particularly Sardinia. She was led to her interest in oral history through the women's movement and the teaching of women's history. In addition, she is currently working on a study of popular religion in the small town of Piassasco outside Turin.

Daniele Jalla studied history at the University of Turin, where he wrote his doctoral dissertation, using oral sources, on the Borgo San Paolo, a working class district of the city. He has subsequently published a study of the town brass band of Piassasco (*La Musica*, 1980) and now works for the Piedmont Regional Council on problems of local history and culture.

Edvard Bull is Professor of History at the University of Trondheim and one of the founders of modern social history in Scandinavia. He moved from a political interest in labour history to an examination of its social roots. He has been collecting and analysing oral history since the 1950s, and has published many books on Norwegian history and labour history, as well as one on the history of East Africa.

Orvar Löfgren is Professor of Ethnology at the University of Lund. His earlier research was on a fishing community in south-west Sweden, as well as on the historical evolution of the Scandinavian peasant family. He now leads a research project on class and culture in Sweden since 1880. His most recent publication, with Jonas Frykman, *Den kultiverad människan* (1980) is a book on the family and changing attitudes to home, nature and sexuality.

Elmer Luchterhand is Professor of Sociology at the Brooklyn College of the City University of New York. An active anti-fascist in the 1930s, his current research interests go back to experience in the American army at the end of the Second World War.

Anna Maria Bruzzone lectures at a teacher training college in Turin. She studied at the university there, specialising in psychology. Besides her two books on women in the resistance and in a concentration camp she has published a third: *Ci chiamavano matti* (1979)—'Voices from Inside a Psychiatric Hospital'.

David Ellwood teaches history at the University of Bologna and has published a book, *L'alleato nemico*, on the British, the Americans and the politics of the war in Italy. He has been associated in oral history work with the Archivo nazionale cinematografico della Resistenza.

Marjan Schwegman teaches modern history at the University of Leiden. Her research interests are in women's history and her publications include *Het Stille Verzet* (1980) and a book on women in the Dutch resistance.

Sven Lindqvist, one of Sweden's most famous contemporary authors, has altogether twenty books of prose, essays and radical social reportage behind him. Internationally he is best known for his work on China and Latin America, including *The Shadow* (1970) and *Land and Power in South America* (1979). The appearance in 1978 in Sweden of his book *Dig Where You Stand* set going a popular movement of research into the history of the workplace.

Paul Thompson is Reader in Social History at the University of Essex. He is editor of *Oral History*, the journal of the Oral History Society, and author of *The Voice of the Past* (1978). His earlier books include *The Work of William Morris* and *The Edwardians*.

Natasha Burchardt is a family planning doctor and psychiatrist in Oxfordshire; she worked on this book while on maternity leave. Esther was born to her and Paul Thompson during the conference of which this book is a record.

ELECTIONS IN DEVELOPING COUNTRIES

ELECTIONS IN
DEVELOPING COUNTRIES

A study of electoral procedures
used in tropical Africa, South-East Asia
and the British Caribbean

BY

T. E. SMITH, O.B.E.

SOMETIME RESEARCH FELLOW OF NUFFIELD COLLEGE, OXFORD
SECRETARY OF THE INSTITUTE OF COMMONWEALTH
STUDIES, LONDON

WITH AN INTRODUCTION BY

B. KEITH-LUCAS

GREENWOOD PRESS, PUBLISHERS
WESTPORT, CONNECTICUT

Library of Congress Cataloging in Publication Data

Smith, Thomas Edward, 1916–
    Elections in developing countries.

    Reprint of the ed. published by St. Martin's
Press, New York.
    Bibliography: p.
    1. Underdeveloped areas—Elections. I. Title.
[JF1001.S63 1973]   324'.24'091724   73-9130
ISBN 0-8371-6987-9

3242
S662e

Reprinted in 1973 by Greenwood Press,
a division of Williamhouse-Regency Inc.

Library of Congress Catalogue Card Number 73-9130

ISBN 0-8371-6987-9   74-1760

Printed in the United States of America

AUTHOR'S PREFACE

MY FIRST real connection with the organisation of elections was in 1954 when, as an officer of the Malayan Civil Service, I was, at rather short notice, given administrative responsibility for the general election held in the Federation of Malaya in 1955. Prior to that, I had seen the first small-scale election of members to the Singapore Legislative Council as a mere spectator, but the admirable Report on the first general elections in India had not been published when the time came for us to make our own arrangements in Malaya and, in 1954, little had been heard about the earlier elections in the various territories of British West Africa. The voluminous reports on elections in Jamaica and other Caribbean territories were of limited help to the administrator on the other side of the globe. So we felt our way, drawing largely on British electoral experience and to some extent experimenting as we went along, just as those responsible for the first elections in many other Commonwealth countries in Africa and Asia have done in the last few years.

Recently a large body of reports and articles on individual elections have been published. This book represents an attempt to collate the electoral experience of tropical Africa, India, South-East Asia and the Caribbean, and thus to provide in one volume a summary of the various electoral methods which have been tried in introducing democracy to developing countries in these parts of the world. It is divided into chapters on a functional basis and I have not hesitated to switch rapidly from one continent to another in order to make a point or serve a warning.

The need for a book of this kind was first seen by Mr Bryan Keith-Lucas, Senior Lecturer in Local Government at Oxford University and Fellow of Nuffield College, before his departure for Sierra Leone in 1954 as Chairman of the Electoral Reform Commission for that territory. Indeed, in that year, both he and I were grappling with electoral problems in different parts of the Commonwealth. It is fitting that Mr Keith-Lucas, as the father of the scheme to produce this book and as my friend, guide and comforter throughout the project, should have written an introduction and I am most grateful to him for doing so.

I am, too, indebted to many others for information, suggestions and assistance. Among the many I must single out Mr C. P. S. Allen, Supervisor of Elections, Uganda, Mr G. W. Y. Hucks, Supervisor of Elections, Tanganyika, and Mr M. V. Smithyman, Acting Senior Commissioner, Zanzibar, who spared no time or effort to make the author's visit to East Africa in the summer of 1958 interesting and profitable; Mr C. A. G. Wallis of the Colonial Office, who has taken a close and friendly interest in my work and provided me with much information; Professor K. E. Robinson, Director of the Institute of Commonwealth Studies in London; Mr N. Nwanodi, whose B.Litt. thesis on West African elections was nearing completion in the autumn of 1957 when I started as a Research Fellow of Nuffield College; and Mr T. W. Gee of the Uganda Civil Service. Above all I must acknowledge my debt to the Warden and Fellows of Nuffield College who have sponsored and financed this project and in whose society I have lived while working on it. Nor can I forget the skilled assistance of Mrs Yates, Mrs Hanna and other members of the clerical staff of the College.

In acknowledging the assistance which I have received from those mentioned above and from many officers in Her Majesty's Overseas Civil Service, I must stress that any errors and omissions are my own. In writing on a subject of this kind, in which fresh developments are taking place every few months, I have tried to ensure that my information is up to date, but readers will, I hope, realise that some changes in electoral procedure and legislation may well take place whilst this book is in the press.

CONTENTS

INTRODUCTION

MUCH of the political history of England in the nineteenth century is closely linked to the struggle for 'Reform' — that is, for a revision of the parliamentary franchise. It is based on the conflict which led, stage by stage, to the ultimate achievement of universal adult suffrage. A similar political development has been going on in many countries, including particularly African colonies and protectorates, in the years since the Second World War. The speed of change has been much greater, but yet the arguments and counter arguments have been to a great extent the same. Much has been spoken and written in these years about the dangers and the advantages of a wide, or a universal suffrage, and a dozen or more territories have been experimenting with a variety of franchises and systems.

Whether these rapid changes be in themselves good or bad, it is clear that they involve many difficult problems of administration. The English code of electoral law is probably far from perfect, but yet it is the model which is being adopted throughout the British territories. Obviously, however, it can not be taken without change or adaption in countries of such widely differing societies and traditions. The administrators of each territory have had to experiment in each case, trying to find satisfactory ways in which to make it fit the local background. In doing so they have to a great extent worked empirically, learning by experience and from their own mistakes.

Those who have been concerned with these problems must often have felt the need for a survey of the experience of other countries which have faced the same or similar questions. There have been available to them the official reports of electoral commissioners and the accounts of observers, official and unofficial. These have been of great value but there has been, and still is, also a need for a more general survey of the practical experience of the countries concerned.

The importance of this survey of administrative experience is hard to exaggerate. In varying ways and at varying speeds all the British territories in Africa are committed to the development of democratic institutions. The final verdict on this policy must depend on how it works; on whether the methods adopted do in fact lead to competent and honest government. In other words, it is not enough merely to introduce the principles of democracy; democracy must be made to work. Franchise systems, whether wide or restricted, can only be justified if they are based on an administration which excludes, so far as can be done, corruption, intimidation, and falsification, and if they result in government which is both just and competent.

The history of democratic government shows numerous examples of how the best intentions of a legislature may be defeated by failure of the administrative machine; of how generously conceived franchise laws have in actual operation become means of political oppression.

It is because of this analysis of the problem that Nuffield College decided to make a survey of the electoral machinery of developing countries, and for that purpose elected Mr T. E. Smith to a Research Fellowship. He already had first hand experience, having served as Supervisor of Elections in Malaya for the general election of 1955.

The intention has been to leave on one side the fundamental questions of whether wide franchises are desirable or not in themselves, of the nature of democratic government, and of the right to self-government. Attention has been concentrated instead on the administration of elections; on the technical questions of how to make them so far as possible free and just, and above all on trying to find out what has actually happened as elections have been introduced in Africa, India, Pakistan, Malaya, and other countries which followed a similar policy; to find out what has worked well and what has not. Such a survey of actual experience serves to show some of the common dangers inherent in introducing an electoral system based broadly on the English pattern; it shows what parts of the machinery are particularly liable to abuse or mistake.

Attention is normally concentrated on the actual process of polling; on the rival merits of separate ballot boxes, 'whispering vote', the French envelope system and the American mechanical voting; but experience in Africa suggests that the prior process of registration is in many ways more important; more important in that trouble more often arises from the deficiencies of the registration procedure than from failure in the actual polling. Not only in

Africa, but also in France, in Ireland and England the same lesson
has been learnt — that an inaccurate register is not only an
inconvenience in itself, but offers the greatest of all opportunities
for personation. The danger lies less in the difficulty of getting
new names onto the register than in that of getting old ones off —
the names of the dead and those who have moved away. Personation almost invariably takes the form of voting in the names of
the dead, and so the removal of their names becomes at least as
important as the inclusion of the names of the newly qualified.

The process of registration can also be open to abuse in another
way. Experience shows that whereas a simple qualification such
as age and residence offers little opportunity for partiality or bias
on the part of officials, this is not true of more complicated and
indefinite qualifications such as literacy. A theoretical case can
undoubtedly be made in some circumstances for limiting the
franchise to the educated part of the population, but a limitation
to those who can read and write entails the testing of each applicant
by an official; the number of such applications generally means
that it is impossible to guarantee that all the officials concerned
are free from all bias, conscious or unconscious, and the granting
of the franchise depends in such cases not upon a simple ascer-
tainable fact but upon the judgment of an official; in practice a
junior official. Donald S. Strong has shown in his *Registration of
Voters in Alabama* how such a qualification has been used in
America to differentiate against the negro; the inquiry into the
conduct of local government elections in Mauritius (1956) also
showed the dangers inherent in applying such a franchise.

The conclusion that may be drawn from this is not that a
literacy test is necessarily undesirable, but that if, for general
reasons, it be decided to adopt it, there are grave risks inherent in
its administration, which would have to be guarded against.

A comparison, such as this book contains, of the working of
electoral codes and regulations, shows many ways in which the
machinery may fail, and in failing, destroy the faith of the public
in the whole conception of democratic government. This faith
depends to a great extent on the details of the administrative
organisation; on whether the polling procedure is truly secret, on
whether there is adequate guarantee that the counting is honest,
and on the machinery of registration. But it also depends very
greatly not on the details of the regulations, but on the men who

operate them; on whether the public has confidence in the impartiality and the honesty of the registration officers, poll clerks, presiding officers and others who work the system. This is not always easy to guarantee.

There are many countries in which this confidence in the working of the system is lacking; where the published figures of the poll are suspect, and political manipulation is thought to be practised. In England, however, public confidence in the honesty of electoral administration appears to be absolute. The suggestion is never heard that the votes have been miscounted for the benefit of a particular party, or that the register was not honestly completed. This confidence is no doubt due primarily to the high standards of our public officials and politicians. But it is significant that we have entrusted the conduct of elections to men who are not under the orders, nor in the pay of, the central government or the party in power. The town clerks and clerks of the county councils manage both local government and central government elections, in accordance with the statutes and under some central control by the Home Office, but they do not depend upon the central government for appointment or promotion. There are several countries in Eastern Europe and South America where confidence in the electoral system has failed because of the mismanagement of elections by officers directly under the orders of party politicians in power at the time.

But if in such cases it may be risky to entrust the conduct of such matters to the central government it does not follow that local government offers any greater security; its officers may be (and often are) worse paid and less capable; they may be just as much subject to political pressure and corruption. But yet the need for independence and freedom from political pressure is of paramount importance, and so a number of countries have looked for some means of establishing an independent non-political authority to manage elections. The model may be that of the Judicial Bench or that of the Government Corporation but in either case the purpose is the same — to put the management of elections beyond the reach of political manipulators. It is as yet too soon to know how far such attempts will succeed. It may be that no such purpose can ever be entirely achieved so long as the politicians wield the ultimate power. But yet in fact such a system may well produce much more nearly just elections than would reliance on any other body of men as administrators.

This question is one which only arises in an acute form in a colonial territory, as a rule, when it is approaching a condition of ministerial responsibility. So long as the administration is in the hands of expatriate officers there is but little danger of their showing serious political bias in the management of elections. They stand outside and aloof from the local party conflicts. But when their places at the head of the ministries are taken by local and inexperienced politicians there is obviously a greater temptation to abuse, and a stronger case for putting control into the hands of an independent commission or commissioner. But it is just at this time of handing over that it is likely to be politically most difficult to make the change.

These questions of administrative technique and the personnel who manage elections can not, however, be divorced from political consideration. There is a temptation in writing on this subject, to try to divorce administration from politics, and to treat the problems of administration as if they could be studied in a politically sterile laboratory. There is much in practice to be said for such a separation, for the problems of elections do fall in general into one or other of these two categories. But yet it must be realised all the time that no such division exists in practice. The form of administrative machinery may profoundly affect the shape of politic life; the nature of politics in a country must influence the choice of administrative methods.

The machinery of elections must first be viewed against the background of the community which it is to serve, and secondly be considered in the light of the effect it may have on political development. Even the smallest of administrative regulations may profoundly affect the organisation of parties or the type of man elected. Thus it is impossible for a legislator or a draftsman to establish a code of electoral law without a preconceived idea of what sort of political structure will result. He is bound, consciously or unconsciously, to answer in his mind such questions as whether independent candidates should be encouraged or discouraged; whether minority groups should be substantially represented, and whether members should be more or less closely identified with their constituents. These, and many other such questions, must be in his mind as he drafts the administrative regulations.

For example, the position of indigenous rulers varies widely. In some countries their power is such that they may be able to exercise a decisive influence on elections, unless they are rigidly excluded. Whether this should or should not be done is a political question outside the scope of this work, but yet the answer must inevitably affect the form of the administrative system. The electoral regulations may be so drafted as to exclude direct intervention by Chiefs, or may recognise and allow the exercise of their power.

So also the delimitation of constituencies can only be done in the light of a decision about the rôle of minority parties. Should the boundaries be so drawn as to make some constituencies predominantly the preserves of minorities, or should these minorities be merged, and perhaps submerged, in the majority? The answer must depend greatly upon whether the object be to achieve a strong and stable majority to govern the country, or to allow the smaller groups a substantial voice in the legislature; and this implies that whoever draws the boundaries of the constituencies must have in his mind some picture of the political structure which is likely to result from his decisions; the whole nature of a nation's politics may depend upon the principles upon which the constituency boundaries are drawn.

Again, devices such as party symbols may serve to help the party candidate at the expense of the independent. If this be so, it would follow that its adoption implies a preconceived picture of a political system in which organised parties play a major part, rather than one in which the independent member is predominant. The method of registration also is no mere administrative question; automatic registration is likely to be more favourable to the independent; voluntary registration to the well-organised party, with a machine capable of bringing its supporters to the registration office, and challenging the claims of its opponents.

These problems of administrative machinery are of the greatest importance, but even with the best of systems for the conduct of registration and polling there is no guarantee of free elections. To assure this one must look outside the mere electoral law and consider whether political and social conditions exist in which the electors can really make an unfettered choice between fairly presented alternatives. Do all parties have an equal opportunity to present their case, in public meetings, through the press and on the wireless? Is political pressure exercised on voters by employers, traditional authorities or secret societies? What restrictions are there on the formation and activities of political parties? To what, if any, extent, is the party in power at the moment able to use the apparatus of government to affect the outcome of an election?

The answers to these questions are more difficult to find than those to the questions concerning the machinery of elections. In the first place they depend more on the peculiar social and political conditions of each individual territory; secondly there is as yet no corpus of experience available in African countries on these matters. The political climate and traditions are only just being formed as these countries reach towards independence. The very nature of the secret societies of Africa and Asia is but little known to the administrators; the part they may come to play in politics is at best conjectural. Moreover, these are fields in which English experience is an inadequate guide. The nature of English politics is formed in part by the knowledge that there is a large uncommitted part of the electorate, whose decision may put either party into power at a general election. This assumption may not be true in a colonial territory, particularly where the population is clearly divided racially. So also English experience gives little guidance to the problems of the relation of party politics to racial divisions or to traditional tribal authorities.

One particularly urgent problem is that of the choice of candidates. In some circumstances, where there is one party with overwhelming support in a constituency, the actual election may be little more than a formality; the representative of the constituency is in reality chosen when the party selects its candidate. In England electoral law has never concerned itself with the question of how the candidate is chosen; indeed, it maintains the formal pretence that there are no political parties, and that candidates are independent individuals. No such attitude is adopted in other countries; in many of the United States the party primaries are regulated by statute, in order to introduce an element of popular choice into the nomination of the candidate; in Russia there is rarely more than one candidate on election day, but there is apparently a lengthy process of discussion and argument by which this one individual is chosen. It may be that the Communist Party plays a great part in directing the choice, but yet the principle is recognised that the selection of the candidate is as important, or more important, than what happens on election day.

This is a question which can not be lightly ignored in the African context. It may happen that, in a number of constituencies, it is a foregone conclusion that one party will win, whoever their representative is. If this be so, one must then ask, who really chooses the member for that constituency? The answer might well imply that some form of regulated primaries is needed. So far as is known, no British territory has yet contemplated this possibility, though they have commonly abandoned the English rule of ignoring the existence of political parties, by allowing elections on the basis of party symbols.

So also the relation of an elected member to his party and to his constituents may not follow the English pattern, but may not necessarily be the worse on that account. Since at least the time of Burke the principle has been generally (but not completely) accepted in England that a member is not to be regarded primarily as a delegate from his constituents or a spokesman for their interests. This view is less firmly held in the United States, and in parts at least of Africa it is contrary to a long established tradition of tribal consultation. The view of a legislator or a draftsman on this matter may be important, for the relation of the member to his constituents will be determined to some extent by the provisions for qualifications. If, for example, candidature is restricted to those born or resident in a constituency based on a tribal area, the member is more likely to be regarded as a delegate from his people than if 'carpet baggers' from the towns, selected by party headquarters, are allowed to stand. Thus the nature of parliamentary representation may be given an impetus in one direction or another.

Such considerations show the need for a much wider study of the development of parliamentary government in Africa, looking at the subject not merely from the point of view of the constitutional lawyer. The man who drafts an electoral code needs to know ideally not only how votes should be recorded, but how parliamentary government is developing, and is going to develop in his country; and how the common pattern of conventions and customs is likely to be adapted to the social conditions of the country.

A parallel problem has been posed by the introduction since 1948 of English local government institutions into a number of

African territories. In some cases, such as Eastern Nigeria, one can see now that the English pattern was adopted too exactly, without fitting it into the social and communal pattern of the country. This too rigid following of the model might be symbolised by the picture of the mayor of a tropical city sweltering in a red flannel robe with fur round his neck, because this is how mayors should be dressed. One may legitimately wonder whether some provisions in electoral codes are not as inappropriate to their local setting as the mayoral robe, and based on the same assumption that what is good in England will be good in Africa.

These however are questions beyond the scope of this book. Mr Smith has wisely accepted limitations to his field. He has restricted himself to a study of the electoral codes which have actually been introduced, and sought to collect and collate the information of how these have been worked in practice. In this he has performed a task which urgently needed doing, but neither he nor anyone else would claim that in doing this he has exhausted the problem. He has not attempted to discuss the wider problem of the nature of democratic government or its place in African society. But he has displayed the facts which are essential for a fuller understanding both by the administrator and the political observer.

B. KEITH-LUCAS

NUFFIELD COLLEGE, OXFORD
1959.

CHAPTER I

INTRODUCTORY

RePRESENTATIVE government is a comparative newcomer to the political scene in tropical Africa and, indeed, in dependent territories and newly independent countries in other parts of the world. The educated and property-owning *élite* were the voters in such elections as were held for a few of the seats in the largely nominated legislatures of British Colonial territories in the years between the two world wars. The ordinary man and woman in these countries had no part to play in the formation of their government until a very few years ago.

The picture has changed rapidly. In 1951-2, after experience of elections on a restricted franchise whilst under British rule, India showed the way to other countries "faced with difficulties in the shape of illiteracy, ignorance and undeveloped communications"[1] in holding parliamentary elections on an adult franchise. Ceylon, too, was one of the pioneers, though there the problems of illiteracy and poor communications were not as great as in India. At much the same time as in India, the first large-scale elections were held in some of the Commonwealth countries of West Africa, usually on an electoral college basis. The British West Indies have a comparatively long experience of holding elections on an ever widening franchise. The successful experiments in India, Ceylon, Ghana and Nigeria were followed by elections in the Sudan, Malaya, Sierra Leone, Kenya, Zanzibar, Uganda, Tanganyika and elsewhere, with methods suited as far as possible to serve local needs and conditions. Simultaneously with and often ahead of these experiments in the British Commonwealth, the French overseas territories have rapidly developed their own electoral systems based on the French model and, under the *loi cadre* of 1956, these countries enjoy a full adult suffrage.

The combined experience of Asia, Africa and the West Indies clearly demonstrates that widespread education and literacy are not essential conditions for the successful working of adult suffrage.

[1] *Report on the first general elections in India, 1951-2*, Vol. I, p. 11.

I

Given a suitable system of voting and elections conducted fairly, the backward peasant in an under-developed country is as capable of casting his vote intelligently in favour of the candidate of his own choice as the working man in the Western democracies. The electoral methods suited to an educated electorate cannot, however, be imposed with much hope of success on a largely illiterate society and it is with the search for electoral techniques suited to the conditions of African and Asian populations that this book is concerned.

A fascinating variety of techniques has been tried at the different stages of the electoral process. Tribal cohesion, minority interests, administrative conservatism in regard to the necessity for preserving undivided various regional and local government units, in addition to population and the size of the electorate, have played a part at different times and in different settings in the delimitation of constituencies. Very considerable differences can be observed in comparing the registration methods used in British African territories, in French overseas territories, in India and in the Caribbean. When it comes to voting, British African territories have now generally adopted the technique of placing unmarked ballot papers in boxes marked with symbols and sometimes colours representing the rival candidates, whilst Malaya, Mauritius and the British West Indies have accepted a system rather like the United Kingdom method of voting, and the French overseas territories have copied metropolitan France. All these techniques are described in detail in the chapters which follow this introductory statement. Whilst most of this book is factual, an attempt has been made to analyse the advantages and disadvantages from the administrative point of view of the more important differences of technique in constituency making, the registration of electors, the nomination of candidates, and in voting and counting the votes.

In so far as the political and administrative aspects of electoral management can be separated, this volume is concerned only with administration. There is, therefore, no discussion of the political morality of a 'fancy franchise' nor has any attempt been made here to inject the author's own views on the respective merits of proportional representation and the 'first past the post' system of voting, and of other forms of electoral engineering. The author has simply taken the electoral systems of developing countries as they are and has attempted to describe how they work in practice.

CHAPTER II

ELECTORAL ADMINISTRATION

THE successful management of a modern election with electors numbering several millions is an administrative undertaking of considerable size, involving a series of operations, the organisation and timing of which must be carefully planned and supervised. For those involved in electoral administration, there are periods of very heavy work and also periods of comparative inactivity; this is true not only of registration officers, who will be busy with electoral duties at the time of the registration of electors, and of returning officers, who will be busy during the period of an actual election, but also, to some extent, of the 'top management' of elections which issues the necessary instructions to registration officers, returning officers and other subordinate authorities. In the development of a genuine electoral administration, then, what is required is an administrative machine, capable of conducting an election with impartiality and without confusion, consisting of a small permanent nucleus and large reinforcements who can be seconded for electoral duties from other work at the periods of peak activity.

In most dependent territories of the British Commonwealth, it has been usual in the initial stages of electoral development to second a civil servant to make the necessary administrative arrangements for elections. This was done for the first general elections in territories such as Uganda, Tanganyika, Sierra Leone, Nigeria and the Federation of Malaya. In all these territories, the 'elections office' for the first elections contained a very small staff and the officer in charge relied upon personnel in provincial, district and local government administrations to carry out extra duties in connection with elections and to follow his circulars and instructions regarding the registration of electors, the nomination of candidates, polling and the counting of votes. The method of appointment and the general nature of the duties of the Supervisor of Elections and of the registration officers and returning officers has usually been specified in the elections legislation of the various territories.[1]

Few of the countries of Asia and Africa have the tradition of an independent civil service and the arrangements for electoral administration therefore require to be reviewed when the Government is in the hands of elected Ministers, as it is now in many of the non-self-governing territories. Newly independent countries such as India and the Federation of Malaya have their permanent election commissions and the commissioners normally have the same security of office as a judge and are not responsible for their actions to the government in power or to a particular minister. Such commissions have powers to require government officers to undertake electoral duties and to give instructions as to how these duties are to be carried out. An electoral commissioner has been appointed for Mauritius under the Representation of the People Ordinance, 1958,[2] to supervise the registration of electors and the conduct of both Legislative Council and local government elections. The Mauritius legislation specifies that the Electoral Commissioner should be a barrister-at-law — a provision which narrows the field for selection. The Western Region of Nigeria has gone part of the way towards copying the example of India, and the Election Commissioner there, though a seconded civil servant rather than a permanent appointee with judicial status, "was not made responsible directly to either the Governor or to any Minister for his actions, although in the final analysis the ultimate responsibility for the efficient conduct of the registration and elections remained with the Governor."[3] The whole purpose of appointing election Commissions is, of course, defeated if the commissioners are not free to perform their duties impartially. The Pakistan Electoral Reforms Commission reported in 1956 that:

[1] Contrary to the general practice, there is no reference to the Supervisor of Elections and his powers and duties anywhere in the Tanganyika Legislative Council Elections Ordinance. In Sierra Leone, too, at the 1957 general election, the officer charged with the responsibility for organising the elections had no statutory powers.

[2] The Ordinance also gives the Governor power to appoint a Deputy Electoral Commissioner; if considered necessary. The Deputy, like the Commissioner, must be a barrister-at-law.

[3] *Report on the Holding of the 1956 Parliamentary Election to the Western House of Assembly*, p. 3.

The Election Commissioners are selected and appointed by the Provincial Governments. . . . Evidently they are at the beck and call of those who made their selection and appointment; they are liable to be lured or brow-beaten to do things which ordinarily they would not do if they felt free and secure.[1]

The Electoral Reforms Commission recommended that the supervision of the elections machinery should be vested in an elections commission headed by a chief elections commissioner who would have the same security of tenure of office as a judge of the High Court.

For the top level of electoral administration, there may well be a growth of permanent election commissions in the near future in British West Africa, and perhaps later on in East Africa. It is, however, difficult to foresee how it will be possible to get away for some time to come from a degree of reliance on the over-burdened District Commissioner to supervise registration and polling arrangements in his own area, though the growth of local government in much of Africa points to the possibility of ultimate development of a system of electoral administration on the lines of the United Kingdom. In the latter country, the supervision of electoral machinery is in the hands of the Home Office, but registration at the local level is the responsibility of town clerks and county clerks, who are servants of autonomous local authorities, and polling is under the control of office-holders such as mayors of boroughs and chairmen of urban district councils, who act as returning officers.[2] It would be foolish to encourage such a development in Africa too quickly, for the officers of local government authorities, even more than locally recruited officers in the civil service, are not as yet committed to established traditions of impartiality in politics, nor is the general standard of the African staff of local government authorities at present of high enough quality to be sure that arrangements for elections, if left entirely to them, would be undertaken efficiently.

The goal of securing fair elections in countries and territories of the British Commonwealth is, then, founded on the development of an electoral administration under governmental authority, staffed with officials, whole-time and part-time, who, whatever

---

[1] Paragraph 6 of the *Report of the Electoral Reforms Commission*.

[2] Town clerks and other officials in similar positions, as deputy returning officers, in fact undertake most of the detailed arrangements for polling.

their private opinions may be, usually succeed not only in exercising their official functions properly but also in impressing the electorate and the rival political parties with their impartiality. The system of electoral administration is, however, in many countries based on a partnership between officialdom and the principal political parties, or may be dependent almost entirely on appointment to electoral posts through political patronage, on the theory that elections will be fair and free if they are the joint responsibility of committees or small groups of persons consisting partly or entirely of the appointees of various rival political parties. Such systems are in use in France and her overseas territories and in Indonesia, to take but two examples.

In France, the 'top management' of elections rests with the Ministry of the Interior just as, in Britain, the Home Office is responsible, but the electoral system has been frequently revised before a general election to suit the government in power and improve its chances of staying in office; once the electoral law has been decided, however, some of the steps to be taken such as the revision of the electoral lists, the distribution of voters' cards and the supervision of polling are undertaken at a local level by multi-party committees. In the overseas French territories, electoral committees of this kind are also used, usually with a civil servant as chairman, and, although administration by committee tends to be slower than direct administration by an individual officer with statutory powers, it seems probable that the more recent elections in French Africa have been administered fairly and run efficiently in contrast with earlier elections at which the French administration is alleged to have brought pressure to bear in support of those political parties which were favoured by the government in power in metropolitan France.

In Indonesia, the first national elections held in 1955 were organised by a pyramid of committees at the national, regional, sub-district and village levels formed of representatives of the main political parties. In most parts of the country, these committees successfully completed a difficult undertaking with a minimum of bickering about trifles, but it must be emphasised that the Indonesian character is particularly well suited to group discussion and group decisions. The Ministers of Justice and of the Interior in Indonesia retained ultimate joint responsibility for the electoral machinery, but wide powers were given to the multi-party Central Electoral Committee which was given the executive task of organising the registration of electors and the polling.

Multi-party electoral commissions or committees are also responsible for the supervision of elections in some countries of the Near and Middle East — in Israel and Turkey, for instance. In Israel, under the Constituent Assembly Elections Ordinance, 1948, a Central Elections Committee was set up, whose chairman was chosen by the Judges of the Supreme Court from amongst their number and whose members consisted of representatives of all the parties in the Provisional Council of State. In Turkey, there is a Supreme Electoral Board in Ankara and electoral boards for each province, district and polling station; the provincial electoral board is presided over by the senior judge of the capital of the province and political parties, selected by lot, may appoint members of the board.[1]

In any country the structure and tradition of government administration, the relationship between political parties and the civil service, the existence or absence of a large corps of experienced administrators, density of population, physical geography and communications are all matters which are likely to enter into decisions regarding the most suitable authority for initiating and maintaining the various facets of electoral administration and regarding the degree of independence and the scope of the responsibility of such an authority. But any electoral administration must be to some extent dependent on the co-operation of central or local government officials placed temporarily at its disposal and, in Asia and Africa, with their comparative lack of educated persons, this dependence on existing central or local government structures will inevitably continue to be most marked.

[1] Articles 63 and 64 of the Election of National Deputies Act, 1950.

CHAPTER III

ELECTORAL GEOGRAPHY

CONSTITUENCIES

MEMBERS of parliaments and of other legislative assemblies are elected by the voters of individual constituencies.[1] A constituency may return one or more members; it is a single-member constituency if it returns one member, a double-member constituency if it returns two members and so on. It is clear that the delimitation of constituencies is a matter of crucial political importance — particularly in countries with a single-member constituency system — as a given political party may stand to gain or lose representation according to the way in which the precise boundaries of constituencies are drawn. If, for instance, *A* and *B* are two neighbouring single-member constituencies, and a certain political party has overwhelming support in *A* but is liable to be defeated in *B* by a narrow margin, it is obvious that a revision of boundaries in which the new constituencies are say, two-thirds of the original *A* for one and *B* plus the remaining one-third of the original *A* for the other is likely to be of considerable benefit to that party.

Because of the obvious political implications of constituency delimitation, the task of recommending the boundaries of constituencies is frequently entrusted to an impartial commission. This has been done in the United Kingdom, India,[2] the Federation of Malaya,[3] Mauritius[4] and Nigeria,[5] to take but a few

[1] With proportional representation, it is possible for the entire area of a general election to be treated as one constituency for the purpose of counting the votes, though for the purposes of electoral administration, the country would be divided into small units. Thus, the Israel Constituent Assembly Elections Ordinance, 1948, provides that, for counting the votes, the entire area of the elections is deemed to be one.

[2] See Ch. VI of the *Report on the first general elections in India, 1951-2*. A new Commission was established in India under the Delimitation Commission Act, 1952.

[3] See *Report of the Constituency Delineation Commission, 1954*. The Election Commission, Federation of Malaya, now has responsibility for delimiting constituencies.

[4] *Report of the Mauritius Electoral Boundary Commission, 1958*.

[5] See *Report of the Constituency Delimitation Commission, 1958*.

8

examples. But an independent commission's recommendations on delimitation are liable to amendment by the elected assembly concerned, where they may be altered as the result of pressure from members or parties who feel that the recommendations may affect entrenched positions adversely; such a commission's findings are seldom legally binding decisions, although they are usually accepted with, at most, minor amendments.

As a preliminary to the delimitation of individual constituencies, it may be necessary to allot seats on a regional basis, particularly in countries with a federal constitution. In the Federation of Nigeria, there was acute controversy and hard political bargaining before agreement was reached on the division of seats in the Federal House of Representatives between the northern, western and eastern regions prior to the first elections to that assembly in 1954. In 1958, the Constituency Delimitation Commission allotted constituencies to the regions on a population basis.[1] In Sierra Leone, one aspect of the political struggle between the Creole population of the Colony and the more backward people of the Protectorate has been the numerical division of elected members as between the Colony and the Protectorate. In the United States of America, the Constitution demands that the membership of the House of Representatives should be apportioned among the States on a population basis and there is a re-apportionment after each decennial census of population. In India, the division of seats in the House of the People amongst the States was a necessary preliminary to the division of each State into territorial constituencies.[2] In the Federation of Malaya, the Constituency Delineation Commission of 1954, having decided that State and Settlement boundaries should not be crossed, used census population statistics to determine the number of constituencies which should be allocated to each State and Settlement, giving a measure of 'weightage' for area in favour of the more rural and less densely populated States to increase or reduce the allocations fractionally.[3]

---

[1] *Report of the Constituency Delimitation Commission, 1958,* pp. 11-12.

[2] The Representation of the People Act, 1950, distributed the seats among the various States. For details see pp. 14-15, Vol. I, of the official *Report on the first general election in India, 1951-2.* The Election Commission made recommendations for the delimitation of constituencies within each State — see pp. 42-8 of the Report.

[3] *Report of the Constituency Delineation Commission,* 1954, pp. 11-13.

Regional allocations of seats are likely to cause most political controversy when there are marked cultural or economic differences between regions or when political parties are regional rather than national, and there can be little doubt but that it is then desirable to incorporate a set formula for dealing with the problem in the constitution as has been done in the United States of America and in Canada. In African territories where this problem arises, however, there is still a marked lack of stability in the composition of legislatures and the number of elected members and it is perhaps too early in countries such as Nigeria and Sierra Leone to expect a permanent solution of the type advocated.

Once regional allocations have, where necessary, been made, the problems involved in delimiting individual constituencies become those of balancing a variety of rival considerations such as the near equality of population between constituencies, the inclusion of complete administrative units in constituencies, and local community interests based on social or economic factors, physical features and communications. In Africa the tendency has been at the time of the first introduction of popular elections to create constituencies (or electoral districts as they are called in many territories) from complete administrative units and to attach rather less importance than in countries such as the United Kingdom and the United States of America to the population factor. Thus, the constituencies used in the first African elections in Kenya and in the first elections in Tanganyika were based on complete provinces or administrative districts. In Sierra Leone, the constituencies used in the 1957 elections were based on the subdivision of administrative districts in the Protectorate along chiefdom boundaries, on existing ward boundaries in Freetown and on local government units in the rest of the Colony. In Kenya, there was a ratio of approximately $5\frac{1}{2}:1$ between the population of the largest and the smallest constituency and in Sierra Leone there were also large variations between the populations and registered electorates of the constituencies (allowing for the fact that some constituencies were two-member constituencies).

In the United Kingdom, the range in the populations of constituencies is far smaller than in Kenya and Sierra Leone. Mackenzie states that "after a thorough reorganisation of constituencies in 1948 the range of size among normal constituencies was of the order of 1:2, if a few unusual constituencies are included it was 1:3".[1] In Malaya, where equality of population was one of the factors which the Constituency Delineation Commission were required to take into consideration, the constituency with the largest population had about two and a half times the population of the smallest constituency.[2] The Constitution of India, as it stood at the time of the first general elections, required that the formation of constituencies for elections to the House of the People should be so determined that there should be not more than one member for every 500,000 of the population nor less than one member for every 750,000 of the population, and, in India, population was the paramount factor in drawing the boundaries of constituencies.

Areas in which there is a community of local interest frequently coincide in African countries with administrative units. It would, indeed, be surprising if this were not so, because the administrative structure of the majority of the territories is of modern creation, and it is only in sectors which have undergone a very rapid social or economic transformation that the administrative units are liable to have ceased to represent, in broad outline, coherent groups based on race, tribe, economic interdependence or some other common interest. The priority which is given to the factor of administrative convenience in African constituency delimitation does therefore go some way towards ensuring that boundaries are drawn in such a way as to take account of local feeling. It must be stressed, however, that the creation of constituencies consisting as far as possible of one or more complete administrative entities inevitably conflicts with the requirement, usually included in the terms of reference of a constituency delimitation commission, that constituencies should contain approximately equal populations or be of approximately equal voting strength.[3]

The tendency to emphasise the factor of administrative convenience in constituency delimitation has had in some territories the result of reversing the 'weightage' for area which is elsewhere given to less densely populated rural districts. In many countries, the average rural constituency has a smaller population

[1] W. J. M. Mackenzie, *Free Elections*, p. 108.

[2] *Report of the Constituency Delineation Commission*, 1954, p. 13.

[3] See, for instance, the comments on this dilemma made on p. 12 and p. 15 of the *Report of the Nigerian Constituency Delimitation Commission*, 1958.

or a smaller electorate than the average urban constituency.[1] But, in parts of West Africa, where it has been decided to create complete parliamentary constituencies from the larger municipalities, some of the urban constituencies are the smallest in population; for instance, Cape Coast, a municipality in Ghana, had at one time the smallest population[2] of all the Ghana constituencies and there has in the past been similar over-representation of the towns (in terms of population) in Nigeria — particularly in the northern region. This reversal of the usual position that the rural areas are entitled to better representation than the towns is understandable in West Africa, where the less developed rural areas tend in some quarters to be regarded more as a hot-bed of illiteracy and ignorance than as the seat of all the political virtues.

Despite Cape Coast, Ghana has gone further than most African countries of the British Commonwealth in delimiting constituencies on the basis of near equality of population. Population replaced community of interest as the primary consideration in the delimitation of constituencies undertaken by the Van Lare Commission in 1953. The Commission divided the Gold Coast into 103 single-member constituencies, seven of which were municipal constituencies and 96 of which were rural constituencies; the number of rural constituencies in each Region had to bear the same ratio to the total number of rural constituencies as the respective populations bore to one another and all rural constituencies were required to have approximately equal populations in so far as geographical and other considerations permitted. The priority given to the population factor led to the splitting of a certain number of local council areas and an attempt to maintain the solidarity of certain linguistic groups resulted in a few rather peculiarly shaped individual constituencies.

At the introduction of an electoral system in an African territory, it is understandable and probably advisable that the boundaries of constituencies should follow those of existing administrative divisions, because the registration of electors and the conduct of elections depend entirely in the initial stages upon local

[1] A smaller population does not necessarily imply a smaller electorate in countries in which an appreciable percentage of the adult population are voteless. For instance, in the Federation of Malaya, the urban constituencies contain larger populations than the rural constituencies but much smaller electorates.

[2] But not the smallest electorate.

administrative personnel, who may find difficulty in enforcing instructions outside the area of their normal administrative competence. But, as elections become more familiar, the factor of administrative convenience should diminish in importance and there would seem to be justification for suggesting that other African territories of the British Commonwealth should gradually follow Ghana's example and gravitate as the result of successive revisions of constituency boundaries in the direction of nearer numerical equality in the size of the electorates of the constituencies.

Normally no area can be within the boundaries of two separate constituencies at the same election. The Somaliland Protectorate is an exception to this rule as "any area may be declared to be within two electoral districts"[1] (i.e. constituencies). The explanation is that there are two types of electoral districts; in Type A electoral districts, the electorate are registered and elections conducted by secret ballot: in Type B electoral districts, the electorate consists of nomadic tribesmen, there is no preliminary registration of electors and voting is by acclamation. In so far as nomadic tribesmen may be temporarily resident in areas with a settled population contained in a Type A electoral district, there is a need to allow the boundaries of the two types of electoral district to overlap.

The gerrymandering[2] of constituencies is a device which has been used to good purpose in some parts of the Commonwealth in an attempt to give as good a guarantee as possible of minority representation in a multi-racial society. Gerrymandering has been adopted in a small way in order to give an effective voice to some of the smaller tribal groups in West Africa and this has occasionally gone to the extent of joining two or more non-contiguous areas inhabited by the same tribe into a single constituency. In Mauritius the Electoral Boundary Commission were instructed to "examine whether it is possible to divide the Colony of Mauritius

[1] Sec. 4, Somaliland Protectorate Legislative Council Elections Ordinance, 1958.

[2] W. J. M. Mackenzie in *Free Elections*, p. 110, has defined gerrymandering as the adjustment of electoral boundaries so as to secure some object other than equal representation. It is a device which can be used to further the interests of particular parties or even individuals (e.g. the old 'rotten boroughs' of England) and some constitutions make special provision to prevent any possibility of gerrymandering by the party in power.

into a series of single-member constituencies up to a maximum of 40 of approximately equal voting strength but with a minimum electorate in any one constituency of 5,000 with the primary objective that:

(a) each main section of the population in Mauritius shall have adequate opportunity to secure representation in the Legislative Council corresponding to its own number in the community as a whole; but providing that

(b) each constituency shall have reasonable geographical boundaries; and that

(c) the boundaries can be expected to endure for a reasonable number of years".[1]

The success of gerrymandering as a measure for giving representation to minorities in a multi-racial society must, of course, depend on the degree of concentration of these minorities in small geographical areas. Gerrymandering has had some success in Ceylon in giving reasonable representation to the Tamil community, but in the cosmopolitan west coast region of Malaya, Malays, Chinese and Indians do not, except on a very local basis, live in separate geographical areas and constituency engineering would have to be carried to absurd lengths in order to give a certainty of adequate representation to the non-Malay element, whose strength in the electorate is at present far below its proportion in the total population.[2] Where the adjustment of electoral boundaries of single member constituencies is unlikely to secure the aim of protecting minorities, a system of multi-member constituencies with reserved seats for minorities (as in India) or with proportional representation may prove to be a more effective alternative. Proportional representation was suggested in 1956 by the Secretary of State for the Colonies as a method of solving the difficulties involved in giving the French, African, Chinese and Muslim communities in Mauritius more adequate representation, but this suggestion was not accepted in the island and it remains to be seen how far the problem will be solved by the methods recommended in the Mauritius Electoral Boundary Commission Report.

[1] *Mauritius Electoral Boundary Commission Report*, p. 3 (Mauritius Legislative Council Sessional Paper No. 1 of 1958).

[2] Because a large percentage of adult Chinese and Indians are not citizens of the Federation of Malaya.

The use of gerrymandering raises the whole question of how desirable it is to cordon off separate communities or separate interests into separate constituencies.[1] Where the aim is to obtain maximum representation for an ethnic or cultural minority whose interests are in many ways quite different from those of the majority, gerrymandering may serve a very useful purpose. But it must be realised that the recognition of communalism in constituency engineering may tend to encourage and perpetuate undesirable division in a population and the promotion of national feeling and pride in an emergent democracy will then be all the more difficult. In the Federation of Malaya, the Committee on Elections to the Federal Legislative Council and the Constituency Delineation Commission both thought that the aim must be to encourage the several racial groups in Malaya in the course of time to form a single community and that, in pursuance of this policy, racial considerations should be wholly ignored in delimiting constituencies. In India, gerrymandering of constituencies either for the House of the People or for any of the legislative assemblies is virtually prohibited by the Constitution. Clearly, although gerrymandering is not necessarily bad in principle, its usefulness and desirability depend upon local factors.

Redistribution of constituencies in Africa and Asia has, so far, been as much a matter of allowing for an increase in the number of elected representatives and for a corresponding decrease in the average size of constituencies as of balancing the rival interests of different communities and ensuring a degree of minority representation. Thus, in the Federation of Malaya, the existing fifty-two constituencies have each been sub-divided into two halves as a temporary measure for the purpose of the 1959 general election in order to allow for a fully elected legislative body of 104 members, and, after these elections, there will be a redistribution of seats based on near equality of registered electorates to permit of a House of Representatives consisting of one hundred elected members.[2] Again, in Nigeria, the constituencies used for the first Federal Elections have been replaced by a larger number of single-member constituencies as recommended in the Delimitation

---

[1] A particularly interesting form of gerrymandering was used in Eritrea at the general election conducted in 1952. There, some of the constituencies were geographical, whilst others were tribal. All constituencies were roughly equal in population.

[2] Article 46 of the Constitution of the Federation of Malaya.

Commission Report in order to provide for an enlarged elected Federal House of Representatives. On a smaller scale, the constituencies for the election of African representatives to the Kenya Legislative Council have recently had to be redrawn as the result of an increase in the number of popularly elected representatives from eight to fourteen. But, even when stability in the number of elected members of a legislative body has been reached, periodic redistribution will be necessary as a result of the internal migration of population, the rapid growth of urban areas or the development of hitherto sparsely populated rural areas. The timing and mechanics of redistribution are therefore of continuing importance. In the United Kingdom, the Electoral Boundary Commissions (of which there are four, one for England, one for Wales, one for Scotland and one for Northern Ireland) are required to consider the position at intervals of not less than three or more than seven years, though the Commission can make reports at any time. In the Federation of Malaya, the Election Commission is required to review the division of the Federation and the States into constituencies at intervals of not more than ten years nor, normally, less than eight years in order to make the changes necessary to comply with the provisions of the new Constitution.[1] The Election Commission in Malaya has unusually wide powers, in so far as the Commission themselves may make changes in the constituencies rather than make recommendations for the approval of the legislature. Where censuses of population are held at regular intervals, a review of the boundaries of constituencies by an independent commission as soon as possible after publication of the first total population figures as ascertained in a census appears to be the obvious procedure.

POLLING DISTRICTS

It is usually considered necessary for the purpose of conducting an election to divide constituencies into smaller units, often known as polling districts or polling areas. The sub-division, unlike the delimitation of constituencies, is not a matter of political controversy. The division of a constituency into polling districts and the provision of one or more polling stations for each polling district has the dual purpose of "giving all electors in the constituency

[1] Article 113 of the Constitution of the Federation of Malaya.

such reasonable facilities for voting as are practicable in the circumstances",[1] and, by the provision of a separate portion of the register for each polling district, easing the task of the polling staff in identifying those persons entitled to vote at a particular polling station. The only kind of dispute likely to arise over the division of a constituency into polling districts and the provision of polling stations occurs where a number of electors regards the arrangements made as insufficient to meet their reasonable requirements for voting, and problems of this kind are obviously more to be expected in rural than in urban areas. In such cases, the cost of increasing the number of polling stations and the provision of more polling staff has to be balanced against the distance and availability of paths or roads from the homes of electors to their allotted polling station.

In Trinidad, a polling 'division' is defined as being one to contain approximately 450 electors. In the Western Region of Nigeria, the electoral regulations require, so far as is practicable, that a polling district should not contain more than 500 electors and that the place of residence of any elector should not be more than three miles by the shortest route from the most convenient building for use as a registration office and polling station.[2] In general, if the polling district is a small enough unit to satisfy both these conditions, the reasonable requirements of electors will have been met and there will be no undue pressure of work on the polling staff on election day. Not all African territories use such small units as polling districts. In Eastern Nigeria, prior to the 1957 House of Assembly elections, the division of constituencies into polling districts was left to the discretion of district commissioners and, in some administrative districts, the polling districts created were very large and contained a number of polling stations; in other administrative districts, the division was more on the lines of the Western Region model. In Tanganyika, where distances are great and the number of registered electors relatively small, it would be quite impracticable to impose a requirement that voters should not ordinarily have to travel more than three miles to reach their polling stations and most polling districts

[1] The wording of part of Section 11 (2) (a) of the U.K. Representation of the People Act, 1949.

[2] Reg. 9 of the Western Region Parliamentary and Local Government Electoral Regulations, 1955.

cover large areas but contain small numbers of electors; in Kenya also voters sometimes have to travel as much as twenty or thirty miles to reach their polling station.

Frequently there is a small administrative unit which in itself forms a suitable polling district. Thus, in Uganda, in practically all the electoral districts (i.e. constituencies), the polling division (i.e. polling district) is the parish. Similarly in the Federation of Malaya many of the polling districts coincide with 'mukims' (small well-defined units used in land registration work). In Sierra Leone, the local government wards were used as the basic units for electoral purposes. In general, it would seem that there are strong arguments for defining polling districts as units small enough in size and containing a sufficiently small electorate to require one polling station only. The main arguments in favour of this course of action are that voters will be in no doubt about their polling station if there is but one for their polling district, whilst the official polling staff are less likely to make errors if all rather than only a proportion of the electorate registered for the polling district are entitled to vote in the station under their command. It is, however, true that, with shifts and growth of population, the boundaries of polling districts will require adjustment more frequently where the standard is one polling station per polling district than would be the case if a district contained a variable number of polling stations; and, in addition, the initial task of defining polling districts will be greater, the smaller the polling district unit in size. Where there is reason to expect an early extension of the franchise and rapidly increasing electorates (as, for instance, in British East Africa), it may prove to be a waste of effort to define small polling district units, but, where something approaching universal adult suffrage has already been established (as in much of West Africa), small polling districts each containing one polling station only are to be encouraged. Initial standards on the lines of the Western Region of Nigeria are to be commended, as electorates will grow slowly with the growth of population given full adult franchise, whilst polling staff, with more experience of elections, will be able to cope with a registered electorate progressively larger than the 500 postulated in the Western Region of Nigeria Electoral Regulations. When both polling staff and electorates are fully experienced in the electoral process, polling stations can be loaded with up to 1,000 electors each in those areas which contain that number of voters living within a reasonable distance of their polling station, and countries such as the Sudan[1] and India already work on this figure when determining the boundaries of polling districts or divisions and the sites for polling stations.

[1] The instructions to registration officers in the Sudan regarding the division of constituencies into electoral divisions (i.e. polling districts) prior to the 1958 elections suggested that "the population of the division be 5 or 6 thousands and that will be equal to about 1,000 qualified voters". Males of twenty-one years of age and of Sudanese nationality can vote in elections for the House of Representatives.

CHAPTER IV

THE REGISTRATION OF ELECTORS

REGISTER of electors is an official list of the persons who are entitled to vote in the election to which the list relates. There is a separate register for each constituency or registration area and there is normally a distinct sub-division of the register for each of the polling districts or other registration units contained in the constituency. It is now fairly generally accepted that large-scale elections must, if they are to be conducted satisfactorily, be based on an up-to-date and accurate register of electors, built and maintained by a team of registration officers whose official actions demonstrate complete impartiality in administering the rules and regulations under which registration is conducted. A register is regarded as essential in a large-scale election because:

(a) Adjudication on the qualifications of electors must be kept separate from the process of polling,

(b) Voters must know before the elections where they have to go to cast their vote,

(c) Political parties and candidates use the registers as a basis for organising their electoral campaign.

The register of electors is, nevertheless, a comparatively recent innovation and, in many countries, the earliest elections took place without such registers. In the United Kingdom, for instance, there was no general system of electoral registration, either for parliamentary or municipal elections, before the Reform Act of 1832, though registration was not unknown before that year in connection with parliamentary elections in some parts of the country[1]. In the absence of registers, each man's right to vote had to be investigated when he arrived at the poll. An election petition was, in such circumstances, an almost certain sequel to a closely fought election. In the state of Trengganu in Malaya, the State Government decided to hold their first state elections in 1954 without undertaking a registration of electors before polling day;

[1] Keith-Lucas, *The English Local Government Franchise*, pp. 131-2.

the results were somewhat chaotic, partly because of the very slow rate of progress of would-be voters through the polling stations and the consequent difficulty in maintaining order with restless crowds outside the stations, and partly because of the obvious difficulties involved in making a series of hasty decisions about each man's right to vote and in preventing persons voting more than once. There might well have been a number of election petitions arising from the Trengganu elections had the results been less one-sided. In the Nigerian (Western Region) elections in 1951 for the Western House of Assembly, the primary elections held at village level for the purpose of choosing members of the 'intermediate' electoral colleges were conducted without registers.[1] Where the primaries were contested, the issue was decided by a show of hands or by asking qualified voters to line up behind candidates; the qualifications of voters were checked at contested elections only at the specific request of one of the candidates. Complaints about the conduct of the primary elections were few. Where such complaints were made, the grounds were usually that some of the supporters of the successful candidate were not qualified or that the defeated candidate claimed to have more supporters than the person declared elected.

The provision of an official register of electors, completed well before polling day, usually[2] implies that the right to vote depends solely on a voter's name being included in the register. In these circumstances it is no longer necessary to investigate in detail each man's right to vote when he comes to the polling station and the whole procedure of polling can be more expeditiously and efficiently conducted. It should not be assumed, however, that an official register of electors is necessarily a good register. Some electoral registers have been and possibly still are padded with the names of mythical electors whose votes can be cast by personators; alternatively the registers can be deliberately or inadvertently purged by the removal of the names of electors who are still alive and fully qualified to have their names retained on

---

[1] See the *Report on the First Elections to the Western House of Assembly, General Election 1951.*

[2] Not, however, always. In the first general election in Zanzibar held in 1957, persons whose names were on the electoral registers were required to take an 'Oath of Qualification' before voting, if their qualifications as electors were challenged in the polling station. Those who refused to take this oath were not permitted to vote and their names were struck off the electoral lists.

the rolls. It is clear that the official guardians of the electoral registers must not only be impartial but they must also be competent to exercise considerable vigilance if electoral frauds are to be kept in check.

ADMINISTRATIVE ARRANGEMENTS FOR THE REGISTRATION OF ELECTORS

The official hierarchy for the registration of electors in general consists of:

(a) A *central authority* which issues instructions and circulars and exercises general supervision of arrangements for the registration of electors. Such an authority may be an election commission or a chief registration officer.

(b) A *registration officer* for each 'registration area'. He receives his instructions direct from the central authority, except in the case of large countries such as India and the Sudan and others formed by the federation of states, where there is usually a state or provincial authority through whom the central authority's instructions are channelled.[1]

(c) *Assistant registration officers* who help the registration officer at a clerical or junior executive level. There may be one or two assistant registration officers assigned to each 'registration unit' in the registration area or a rather smaller number whose duties are not confined to a particular geographical sub-division of the registration area.

There is, inevitably, some confusion in nomenclature in describing both the various grades of officials who bear responsibility for the production of electoral registers and the geographical areas for which these officials are responsible. The registration officer for a registration area may be known locally as a 'registering officer' (Malaya), or as a 'registrar' or member of a 'board of registrars' (United States). The term 'registration officer' may be used for a lower rank of official, as in the Eastern Region of Nigeria, where there is an 'Electoral Officer' for each constituency charged with the responsibility of maintaining a register of

---

[1] In the Sudan the registration officer is responsible to and under the directions of the Chief Election Officer of his Province, who in turn takes his instructions from the Election Commission (Rules 5 and 10(2) of the Parliamentary Elections Rules, 1957).

electors who "shall appoint a registration officer for each polling area".[1] The officials whom we have described as assistant registration officers are thus 'registration officers' in Eastern Nigeria and they are known as 'assistant registering officers' in Malaya and as 'registration assistants' in Zanzibar. For the sake of simplicity we shall throughout this chapter use the term 'registration officer' and 'assistant registration officer' in the sense in which they were introduced in the previous paragraph.

The registration area to which a particular register of electors relates may coincide with a parliamentary constituency or electoral district (if the register relates to central government elections) or with a local government ward (if the register relates to local government elections). If a register is to be framed to serve both central and local government elections, it is usual to define the parliamentary constituency or electoral district as a registration area so that the register for a particular local government ward is a section of the complete register (the area of a local government ward being smaller than that of a parliamentary constituency). The 'registration unit' is the smallest geographical unit for the purposes of electoral administration and it usually coincides with the 'polling district' as defined in Chapter III. Here too different countries have used different terms for these electoral areas. A 'registration area' is known, even for registration purposes, as a 'constituency' in Eastern and Western Nigeria and Zanzibar, as an 'electoral district' in Uganda, and as an 'electoral area' in Kenya. A 'registration unit' is known variously as a 'polling area' (Eastern Nigeria), 'polling division' (Zanzibar), 'electoral unit' (India), 'electoral division' (Sudan) and even as a 'registration area' (Western Nigeria). The terms 'registration area' and 'registration unit' as defined in this paragraph will be used throughout this chapter. It is, then, the duty of the 'registration officer', helped by his 'assistant registration officers', to compile and publish a register for his 'registration area', sub-divided into sections — one section for each 'registration unit'.

The various alternatives which are possible when creating a central authority for the 'top management' of electoral administration (including the registration of electors) have been discussed in Chapter II. As far as the registration officers are concerned, the

[1] The Eastern House of Assembly Electoral Regulations, 1955, Reg. 9(3).

criteria which are normally taken into consideration when deciding on the most suitable persons for appointment are:

(a) The registration officers must have real and obvious independence, so that there is no justification for suspecting political influence and every reason for supposing that they are exercising complete impartiality,

(b) The registration officers must have at their disposal a body of trained clerks who can be transferred from other work at the seasonal peaks of registration work,

(c) If the registers are based on official records of one kind or another — e.g. records of rate payments or poll tax payments — the registration officers must be persons with ready access to these records.

To meet these requirements, regional or local government officers are frequently appointed as registration officers, particularly in British Commonwealth territories. In England and Wales, the registration officer in a county constituency is the Clerk of the County Council and, in borough or urban district constituencies, the Town Clerk or Clerk of the urban district council.[1] The registration officers are thus persons in the employ of autonomous local government authorities, although the general supervision of arrangements for the registration of electors lies with the Home Office, which issues the necessary circulars and instructions. In India, for the registration of electors prior to the first general elections, "Revenue Officers of the Status of Collectors, Deputy Collectors, Tahsildars, etc., were usually appointed as Electoral Registration Officers";[2] these officers worked under the general instructions of the Chief Election Commissioner channelled through the Chief Electoral Officer of each State. In Malaya in 1954, prior to the first general elections in 1955, District Officers or Assistant District Officers were usually appointed as registration officers for the registration areas lying in the district for which they were administratively responsible; clerks from government offices and schoolmasters were appointed as assistant registration officers. Somewhat similar arrangements for using senior government officials as registration officers and for recruiting assistant registration officers from the staffs of local authorities and schools have been a feature of registration arrangements in Ghana.

[1] See A. N. Schofield, *Parliamentary Elections* (1950 edition), pp. 32-3.
[2] *Report on the first general elections in India, 1951-2*, Vol. I, p. 30.

For elections held in the Western Region of Nigeria up to and including 1954, the electoral registers were compiled by Administrative Officers (mostly British expatriates) working under the general supervision of a Chief Electoral Officer. The relevant regulations were, however, revised before the 1956 elections to the Western House of Assembly and, under the revised regulations, central direction and control was intensified as the result of the appointment of an Electoral Commissioner (a seconded civil service officer) whilst the registration officers (all Nigerians) were to be the secretaries of divisional or district councils except where the Commissioner considered the appointment of such officers to be inexpedient. The Administrative Officers — Residents and District Officers — were thus excluded from any mandatory part in the registration machinery, though they remained in the background ready to be consulted on the few occasions when their advice was sought. One of the principal political parties in the Western Region objected unsuccessfully to this arrangement on the grounds that many local government secretaries had party affiliations and suggested that the old system of appointing Administrative Officers (who had or were believed to have no party aspirations or sympathies) as registration officers should be re-established. Ultimately no complaints against registration officers on the grounds of partisanship were substantiated, but difficulties did arise over the intensification of central control of registration owing to inadequate transport and telephonic communications.

Although the fears of bias and unfairness on the part of the registration officers in Western Nigeria proved to be unfounded, there is clearly a danger of partiality in registering electors in countries which lack a long-established tradition of civil service political independence. The Commission on the conduct of Local Government Elections in Mauritius, which submitted its report in January, 1956, found that there were numerous inaccuracies in the register of electors for the Town of Port Louis and were of the opinion that the Town Clerk, as Registration Officer, and the assistant staff employed in registration were working in an atmosphere in which complete impartiality was difficult. This was partly because the Town Clerk regarded the elected Mayor (rather than himself) as the chief executive of the town administration and partly because the house-to-house verification of names on the register and of names of claimants was undertaken entirely by officers acting under the orders of the Mayor.[1] In these circumstances, the Commission recommended the appointment of a permanent independent Registration Officer with legal qualifications, "who would be employed on a part-time basis except when an approaching election made the work too heavy for this". As a result of the Commission's recommendations, new legislation dealing with local government elections was enacted and an independent elections office was opened to conduct these elections. The staff who gave assistance to the registration officer and investigated the validity of applications for registration under the new legislation continued, however, to be drawn largely from the staffs of central and local government departments by the method of temporary secondment. In Mauritius, therefore, considerations of impartiality have been paramount in shifting responsibility for registration of electors at the higher levels from the shoulders of local government authorities, but it has proved necessary to continue to use the staff of these same authorities at lower levels in order to check the qualifications of the electorate.

In a few British Commonwealth territories the existence of records of rate or tax payments has been a paramount consideration in deciding on the appointment of registration officers. In Sierra Leone, for instance, the Electoral Reform Commission recommended in their Report that, in the Colony, clerks of local government councils should be appointed as registration officers because they were ultimately responsible for the rate books, but that, in the Protectorate, town clerks should only be appointed as registration officers in respect of town council elections, as the voters' lists for Legislative Council elections were based on tax assessment lists, to which the town clerks had no access, rather than the rate books.[2]

There are other countries where it has proved desirable on political or administrative grounds to avoid placing responsibility

[1] See *Report of the Commission on the conduct of Local Government Elections in Mauritius* (Mauritius Legislative Council Sessional Paper No. 1 of 1956), pp. 9-11. Under the Mauritius Representation of the People Ordinance, 1958, an Electoral Commissioner is responsible for both central and local government elections.

[2] *Report of the Electoral Reform Commission* (Sierra Leone Sessional Paper No. 2 of 1955), Ch. 13. See also the *Report on the Sierra Leone General Election, 1957*, paragraph 13.

for the registration of electors at the higher levels in the hands of officials in the central or the local government service. The paucity of trained administrative personnel or the fact that the small corps of government administrators is already over-burdened with other duties may make it desirable to entrust the conduct of registration to a body of persons outside the central or local government service. Alternatively a cadre of government officials, whether or not in fact capable of exercising complete impartiality, may be guilty of political bias in the minds of a large section of the population. In some colonial territories approaching self-government or independence it may be thought desirable to use expatriate officers of the colonial Government in electoral adminis-tration on the grounds of their political impartiality and adminis-trative experience, but elsewhere it may be necessary to avoid the use of such personnel, either because local officers must be given responsibility for work which they will in any case have to administer later, or because the expatriates are popularly supposed to support a particular party whose policies are favoured by the metropolitan Government.

A few examples will perhaps clarify the matter. In Indonesia, the lack of trained administrators and the fact that the majority of these administrators were Javanese who knew little of conditions outside Java contributed to the decision to create a pyramid of committees at the national, regional, sub-district and village levels to conduct the registration of electors and to make arrangements for polling.[1] In the State of Alabama in the United States of America, each county has a three-member board of registrars, appointment to which is made for periods of four years at a time by a state board of appointment consisting of popularly elected officials, though "the actual choice of who shall be a registrar is almost always made by the legislative delegation from each county".[2] Similarly in North Carolina the County Boards of Elections select a Registrar for each election precinct from persons recommended by the Chairman of each political party in each county.[3] Thus, in both Indonesia on the one hand and Alabama and North Carolina on the other hand, no attempt has so far been

[1] See Irene Tinker and Mil Walker, *The first General Elections in India and Indonesia*, in *Far Eastern Survey*, July 1956, Vol. XXV No. 7, pp. 105-6.
[2] See Donald S. Strong *Registration of Voters in Alabama*, Ch. 2.
[3] North Carolina Election Laws, Subchapter 1, Art. 5, Section 15.

made to set up a permanent impartial administrative structure for the registration of voters — in Indonesia for the reasons mentioned earlier in this paragraph, and in Alabama and North Carolina partly perhaps for reasons of political patronage and partly because the system used is genuinely thought to be the best way of getting a balanced body of persons to effect the registration of electors.

THE LAYOUT AND CONTENT OF THE REGISTER

Before entering into a discussion of the mechanics of registration, it is necessary to state the form in which a register of electors is usually published. It is a universal practice that, where registration areas have been divided into registration units, there should be a separate section of the register for each of the units. This is normally laid down in the relevant electoral regulations. It is also a common, but not universal, practice[1] to sub-divide the register for each registration unit by headings for each residential locality. If, for instance, a registration unit contains three or four villages or hamlets, there would be a separate sub-section of the register for each of the villages or hamlets; in urban areas there would be a separate sub-section for each street or quarter of a town contained within the boundaries of the registration unit.

In Africa and Asia, where there is frequently no regular system of street numbering even in town areas, it is usual to arrange the names of electors for any sub-section of the register by the alphabetical order of their surnames or other names.[2] Even this, however, can present considerable difficulties owing to various alternative methods of spelling a name or to the fact that aliases are in common use in both Asia and Africa or because of the difficulty in deciding whether to take the first, second or third name as the operative one. In Zanzibar, for instance, the Supervisor of Elections had these comments to make in his report:[3]

> One difficulty initially encountered by Registration Assistants pursued us right through the work of the Listing Office into the

[1] It is the practice to sub-divide the register for each registration unit in the Federation of Malaya and the Western Region of Nigeria, but not in the East African territories.

[2] Some of the Uganda registers are arranged in serial order of number of registration receipt, and some in alphabetical order of the names of electors.

[3] *Report on the Zanzibar elections of 1957*, pp. 9-10. In Zanzibar, a central 'Listing Office' compiled registers for all the registration areas.

final lists of electors. Applicants to register and Public Writers recording their applications insisted on spelling their names in their own way, with the result that the same name appeared in a number of different guises, very often with a different initial letter. This was particularly confusing in the case of Arabic names inaccurately transliterated (e.g. Ismail and Esmail; Abeid, Ebeid and Obeid). If some means can be found of ensuring that names are spelt in future as they are spelt in the 'standard' list, the work of Registration and Listing Officers will be enormously simplified, and over-careful Presiding Officers will be absolved from the labour of administering innumerable unnecessary oaths.

In India, the Chief Election Commissioner had some difficulty over obtaining the names of women voters and the following is an extract from his report:

It came to the notice of the Election Commission during the preparation of the electoral rolls that a large number of women voters had been enrolled in some States not by their own names but by the description of the relationship they bore to their male relations (e.g. A's mother, B's wife, etc.) The reason for this was that according to local custom, women in these areas were averse to disclosing their proper names to strangers. As soon as the matter came to the notice of the Election Commission, instructions were issued that the name of an elector being an essential part of his or her identity, must be included in the electoral rolls and that no elector should be enrolled unless sufficient particulars, including the name, were given. The Electoral Registration Officers were, therefore, instructed to substitute the women voters' proper names for their description in such cases. Directions were also issued to the effect that any woman who refused to give her proper name should not be registered as a voter and if she had already been registered without the name, the entry should be deleted. The Electoral Registration Officers were also instructed to avail of the provisions of the law, wherever possible, for taking the initiative themselves and making application for the substitution of the proper names of women voters if they had been enrolled by description only. The voters were also requested by public appeals to give the necessary particulars to the Electoral Registration Officers. A special extension of one month was given in Bihar for filing such applications so that the number of women voters whose names were liable to be struck off the rolls for this reason might be reduced. This extension was made good use of and the rolls were considerably improved in that State. Although such an extension was given in Rajasthan as well, the response there was poor and a large number of entries relating to women voters had to be deleted for this defect.[1]

The writer has had personal experience of difficulties over names when dealing with Chinese electors. A given name will possess a standard Chinese character or characters but the romanised version of this name will vary among different Chinese communities. There may thus be a different Hokkien, Cantonese and Hakka romanised version of a single Chinese clan name.

In the United Kingdom it is laid down that the electors' names in each registration unit are to be arranged in street order.[2] If, however, the registration officer decides that, for any particular unit, alphabetical order of names is more convenient, then he may arrange accordingly. As mentioned above, however, an arrangement in street order only makes sense when there are recognised street names and there is some sort of systematic street numbering.

The particulars given in the register must as far as possible be sufficient to enable the polling station authorities to identify the elector without difficulty and, if the register serves more than one type of election (e.g. both central and local government elections), the register must indicate for which type of election the voter is qualified. The elector's full name and address appear in electoral registers in almost all countries. In some countries the elector's occupation, sex or tribe is given.[3] In a few countries there are separate parts of the register for male and for female voters. In countries which have a national system of registration, it is usually the practice to include the identity card number and to require the voter to produce his identity card when his name is being found in the register of electors prior to voting.[4] Where a numbered 'registration receipt' or 'voting card' (see below) is given during the registration period to an applicant, the number of the voting card is included in the register if the production of this card is a necessary preliminary to the receipt of a ballot paper by the voter.

[1] *Report on the first general elections in India, 1951-2*, Vol. I, p. 72.
[2] Representation of the People Regulations, 1949, Reg. 2(1).
[3] For instance, the Sudan Parliamentary Elections Rules 1957 require that "the names of voters shall be arranged alphabetically and sufficient particulars shall be included in the entry relating to each voter so as to make his identity readily established, e.g. address, vocation, tribe, etc." (Rule 11(4)).
[4] This is the procedure in Singapore and the Federation of Malaya.

All this sounds simple enough in theory, but there are a number of pitfalls to be avoided in practice. Mention has already been made of possible variations in the spelling of names. The address given by the applicant for registration may give rise to difficulties, particularly in urban areas. In some areas of Kenya, for example, the registration authorities entered a P.O. box number as the address in the registers during the 1956 registration of African electors and during earlier registrations of Asian and European electors; such a box number was frequently a place of work and door-to-door canvassing by candidates and their supporters was often ruled out because the registers did not reveal the domiciliary address of the electors. In a survey[1] conducted in Accra prior to the Gold Coast elections of 1954, it was found that, in a sample of 432 names on the registers, only 340 were traceable at the address given; in respect of the remaining 92 names in the sample, there were errors in the names or addresses given or the address provided could not be located after prolonged search.

Again, it is all too easy for clerical or printing errors to appear in the register of electors. Some of these errors will be eradicated by a series of checks of the draft registers against the application forms or other documents from which the lists have been compiled and other mistakes may be spotted and reported to the registration authorities when the preliminary registers are open to inspection by the general public. In Asia and Africa, it has been a common complaint that registration officers have given inadequate supervision to the detailed compilation of the registers and that more checks should have been carried out by the clerks working under the direction of the registration officers. But registers are never perfect documents and appropriate instructions have to be given to the presiding officers of polling stations as to the latitude which they are to have in identifying voters when it appears that there are mistakes in the register.

It may be appropriate to give illustrations of the forms of registers in two countries of Africa and Asia. In the Gambia, where there is combined registration for the Legislative Council, the Bathurst Town Council and the Kombo Saint Mary Rural Authority, the registers are compiled in a manner specified in the

[1] See W. B. Birmingham and G. Jahoda, 'A pre-election survey in a semi-literate society' in *Public Opinion Quarterly*, Vol. XIX, No. 2, Summer 1955, pp. 140-52.

Colony Elections Ordinance.[1] For each registration area the registration officer is required to compile a list of voters in alphabetical order in a 6-column register of which the headings are:

1. Voter's card number (The registration officer is required to prepare and issue a voting card to every person who is, in his opinion, entitled to be registered and the voter is in turn required to bring the card issued to him to the polling station when the time comes to vote.)
2. Surname
3. Other name or names in full
4. Occupation
5. Sex
6. Voting right.

In the Federation of Malaya, where there is combined registration for Federal and for State elections, each Federal constituency forms a registration area and each polling district a registration unit. There was, prior to the first registration of electors in 1954, a further *de facto* sub-division of rural registration units into villages, hamlets and estates, and of urban registration units into streets and lanes. The Chief Registration Officer was given discretion under the Regulations as to the most appropriate method of arranging the register for each registration unit. For each such unit, the register was compiled in six columns, the headings of which were:

1. Number (Names numbered consecutively, beginning with 1 for each unit.)
2. Electoral qualification (F for Federal elections, S for State elections, FS for both.)
3. Name
4. Address
5. Sex
6. Identity card number.

An extract from the instructions issued in 1954 to the registration officers on the arrangement of the registers read as follows:

Urban Areas
The electors' names in each registration unit in an urban area will normally be arranged in street order. The streets in each registration unit should be arranged in alphabetical order, and each

[1] See Form 7 in the First Schedule, Colony Elections Ordinance, 1954.

street should normally form a sub-heading of the register. House numbers will be given in the 4th column of the register. If, however, the registering officer of a registration area considers, after due consideration, that for any registration unit in an urban area, alphabetical order of names is more convenient than arrangement in street order, then the registering officer may arrange accordingly. In such cases, an identifying address must be given in the 4th column of the register.

Rural Areas

The electors in each registration unit in the rural areas will be arranged by Kampongs,[1] new villages, estate labour lines and other residential localities. These residential localities should normally be arranged in alphabetical order for each registration unit and the names of electors will be arranged alphabetically for each residential locality. The name of the residential locality will be placed at the head of the relevant portion of the register of the registration unit, and the column headed 'address' will be left blank in rural areas except in so far as there is house or street numbering in the residential locality.

In both the countries (the Gambia and the Federation of Malaya) whose registers were described above, the electoral rolls serve more than one type of election. This represents an obvious economy and it would seem desirable to aim at adopting common-user registers except where there is a radically different franchise for the national elections and for regional or local elections and only a small percentage of the electorate qualify for all elections. The Chief Election Commissioner of India in his Report on the first general elections states that it would be an obvious simplification of the law "to do away with the necessity of having separate electoral rolls for Assembly and Parliamentary constituencies".[2] Again the Commission on the conduct of Local Government Elections in Mauritius recommended "that the Registers for local government and for Legislative Council purposes be amalgamated into one general Register, on which electors who are qualified to vote in any area only in local government elections should be marked with a distinctive sign";[3] this recommendation has now

[1] Kampong is the Malay name for village. 'New villages' (the term is now almost defunct) refer to villages formed or greatly enlarged as the result of resettlement during the 'Emergency' in Malaya.

[2] *Report on the first general elections in India, 1951-2*, Vol. I, p. 77.

[3] *Report of the Commission on the conduct of Local Government Elections in Mauritius*, pp. 15-16.

been put into effect. Some countries have achieved a partial economy of effort as a transitional stage by permitting persons already registered for one type of elections to have their names automatically included in a register for another type of elections; in Eastern Nigeria, for instance, the House of Assembly Electoral Regulations, 1955, provided both for voluntary application for registration from entitled persons and for the wholesale incorporation in the new registers of the names of electors in the registers already compiled for the (Federal) House of Representatives Elections in 1954. Somewhat similar provisions were made in the Federation of Malaya for the automatic incorporation in the first 1955 registers of Federal and State electors of those persons who had already registered under State legislation for elections in the two or three States which held their own elections prior to the start of the initial Federal registration period; in Malaya, however, the first nation-wide registers were common-user registers whereas the registers in Nigeria for Federal and Regional elections are still distinct.[1]

VOLUNTARY AND AUTOMATIC REGISTRATION

Registration can be 'voluntary' or 'automatic', as far as the individual elector is concerned. These terms require some explanation and illustration. A 'voluntary' system of registration places the onus of responsibility for registration on the individual citizen who possesses the required qualifications, whilst, in an 'automatic' system, it is the responsibility of the registration officers to do all they can to ensure that every eligible person is registered by the use of records and/or by systematic house to house canvassing.

The arguments in favour of automatic registration can be summarised as follows:

(a) It is only with an automatic system of registration that the number of voters on the electoral rolls approximates to the number of people qualified to register. In a voluntary system there are likely to be a number of people who want to vote but are unable to do so because they have failed to register at the appropriate time.

[1] A decision has now been taken in Nigeria to unify the supervision of Federal and Regional elections under a single chairman, so the registers will probably be combined.

(*b*) In the long run, a well-maintained automatic system of registration will produce a more accurate register of electors, because no reliance is placed on the individual elector to report changes of address or changes of status which may affect the registers (e.g. change of name at marriage, acquisition of the minimum voting age). This matter will be discussed in more detail later in this chapter.

(*c*) An automatic system of registration will be less open to fraud and political party manipulation, assuming that the registration officers exercise impartiality, whereas a voluntary system gives an advantage to a party with an efficient machine and it also makes 'padding' of the register easier in the absence of large-scale verification of the existence and qualifications of applicants for registration.

(*d*) Automatic registration prevents any attempt to make registration instead of voting the primary political arena — for instance by boycotting registration in a voluntary system.

The arguments in favour of voluntary registration are broadly:

(*a*) An automatic system of registration is likely to place an excessive burden on the government administration, particularly in under-developed countries, where the potential electorate is but semi-literate, communications are poor, and senior government officers are already over-burdened with other duties. An automatic system is also likely to be more expensive to the government than a voluntary system, unless the electoral registers can be based on existing official records.

(*b*) A voluntary system of registration assumes that the elector is a responsible citizen, who makes his own decisions as to whether or not to register.

The first argument in favour of automatic registration can be illustrated by the failure of voluntary registration in Singapore. The Rendel Constitutional Commission reported in 1954 that:

> The present system of voluntary registration has proved a failure. Out of a present potential Electorate of some 300,000 for the Legislative Council and some 200,000 for the City Council, only 70,000 and 50,000 respectively have so far registered. It is difficult to see how any means could be devised of inducing a sufficiently large proportion of the potential Electorate to take the initiative of registering, and any substantial increase in the number

of registered electors under the voluntary system must be an unacceptably slow process. We appreciate that a large number of electors registered does not necessarily mean a large number of voters, but we consider that once people are all on the Roll, the task (which is primarily for the Parties) of persuading them to vote will be appreciably easier.[1]

The second argument in favour of automatic registration requires rather more substantiation. All registers are revised from time to time (usually once a year), but a population is never static and a register of electors can never in the nature of things be absolutely accurate. In any system of registration, voluntary or automatic, there is likely to be, to a greater or less extent, some inefficiency in the arrangements for reports of death and reports of changes such as attainment of the qualifying age, change of name at marriage, change of residence, etc., reaching the registration authorities and for the making of appropriate changes in the register of electors. But this inefficiency is likely to be most marked in a voluntary system, where the onus of taking action to report some or all of changes affecting electoral status rests with the individual. In Asian, African and Caribbean countries, it has been a universal experience that, with a voluntary system of registration, the register becomes less and less accurate, despite frequent revisions, as the years pass following initial registration. This theme will be developed in more detail later in this chapter.

The third argument in favour of an automatic system was that such a system is less open than a voluntary system to fraud and party manipulation. Fraud can be kept in check by a thorough investigation of the qualifications of electors by the registration officer and his assistants, but, with a large electorate, a complete check may involve as big an effort in terms of personnel and money as a systematic house-to-house enumeration of persons with the qualifications to become electors. Political party manipulation can be limited by insisting on the delivery of applications for registration in person or by undertaking a very thorough investigation of applications delivered to the registration authorities in bulk by political parties. This subject also will be discussed in more detail later in the chapter.

[1] *Report of the Constitutional Commission*, Singapore, 1954, p. 5. See also paragraph 15 of the *Report on the Sierra Leone General Election, 1957*, regarding the failure to register of a large number of entitled persons in the Protectorate area of Sierra Leone.

It is the argument that an automatic system of registration is likely to place an excessive burden on the administration which has been the paramount factor in the decision of the governments of most African territories to adopt a voluntary system. There are, in African territories, usually no records other than tax or rate payment lists on which an automatic system of registration can be based, and these records do not embrace all the categories of persons eligible to be registered even under a franchise which falls well short of universal adult suffrage. Registration through householders, which operates so successfully in the United Kingdom, is impossible when most of the householders are illiterate, and the only remaining alternative to a system of voluntary registration in African conditions is a census-type enumeration of electors. It might perhaps be straining the administrative resources of the governments of many African territories too severely to undertake such an enumeration more than once every five or ten years. The fact remains, however, that in the French African territories, under the *loi cadre* of 1956, universal adult suffrage has been introduced and registration is a matter of right for adults with the necessary residential and nationality qualifications. Each year, administrative commissions, containing representatives from the political parties as members, are set up at the constituency and local commune levels and it is the duty of these commissions to add to the electoral registers those who are recognised as having acquired the statutory qualifications and those previously incorrectly omitted and to remove from the lists deceased voters and those no longer eligible for other reasons. In other words, registration in the French African territories, as in France, can be classed as automatic rather than voluntary. It is true that, owing to the absence of adequate machinery for recording births and deaths and movements of population, the provisional registers produced by these commissions are frequently far from accurate, but the fact that they are produced at all suggests that some of the arguments used in British Africa in favour of voluntary registration require a searching re-examination.

The majority of British Commonwealth countries in Asia have tended to adopt an automatic method of registration, whilst the voluntary system has been more highly favoured in Africa. In India, the electoral rolls completed prior to the first general elections were prepared on the basis of a house-to-house enquiry in each village or other residential unit followed by a supplementary informal revision and then a period for filing formal claims and objections. The Report on the Indian elections states that, out of a total adult population of 180 millions, the electoral rolls included the names of 173 million persons.[1] In Singapore the electoral rolls are now based on the identity card system and are produced by machine from the office duplicates of identity cards; the errors in the electoral rolls are the errors of the identity card system except in so far as the information contained in the identity cards is insufficient to identify certain categories of electors. The reader is reminded that Singapore started its electoral history with a voluntary system of registration, which was discarded owing to the poor response from the Chinese, who are the majority element in the population. In Kuching, Sarawak, the registers for the first municipal election were based on the assessment registers in the Municipal Offices followed by a house-to-house check.

In the Federation of Malaya, on the other hand, the voluntary system of registration has been used. It would have been impossible to follow the example of Singapore and base the electoral registers on the identity card system, as the identity card does not indicate whether or not the holder is a Federal citizen — and Federal citizenship is a necessary qualification for the franchise. The first electoral registers could have been compiled on the basis of a census-type operation involving a house-to-house investigation of persons with the necessary qualifications, but it was decided that it was preferable to have a voluntary system at least in the early stages of elections because an automatic system would have placed too heavy a strain on State and District administrations.

The voluntary system of registration has been a standard feature in East and Central Africa, although the results of registration among the potential African electorate have been somewhat disappointing except in Zanzibar and Uganda. In West Africa, on the other hand, some of the earlier registers were based on tax records but the system was altered in some territories to a voluntary system of registration when the franchise was extended to include women and other persons whose names did not appear on the tax records.

In East and Central Africa, the complexity of the franchise coupled with poor communications over vast areas and the

[1] *Report on the first general elections in India, 1951-2*, Vol. I, p. 69.

existence of many semi-nomadic communities virtually rules out the possibility of an automatic system of registration. To place on the Government the sole onus of ensuring that the names of all persons qualified to vote were put on the register would, under present conditions, put such a burden on the administrative staff that routine work would come to a complete standstill. Even a voluntary system of registration, coupled with a vigorous official propaganda drive, places a heavy enough burden on the government administration. In most parts of West Africa, with its denser and more settled populations, and somewhat better communications, an automatic system of registration under universal adult suffrage would perhaps be more feasible though burdensome and, in the light of the reasonably successful experience of India and the French African territories, it will probably come sooner or later.

Even in the Western democracies, some countries favour an automatic system of registration whilst others have a voluntary system. In the United Kingdom, the registration officer is under a legal obligation to compile a new register annually by house-to-house canvass or other means;[1] this is usually achieved by sending to householders statutory registration forms which are returnable by post free of charge and sending reminders or visiting those who fail to reply. There is, in fact, a penalty for failure to return the form to the Registration Office, but it is almost unknown for a householder to be fined on such a count. In some European countries with an established system of national registration, the register of electors is compiled (as in Singapore) from the registration records. A national registration system, to be effective for civil purposes, requires a high standard of education and a certain degree of civic consciousness, in order to ensure that the requisite changes are made promptly (e.g. change of address) and it may be doubted whether such a system would successfully form the basis of a register of electors in the present state of social and civic advancement in Africa. In the United States of America,[2] the elector is generally required to take positive action to get his name

[1] Under the newly enacted Mauritius Representation of the People Ordinance, 1958, voluntary registration has been abandoned, and, as in the United Kingdom, the registration officer is to make "a house-to-house or other sufficient inquiry" as to the persons entitled to be registered.

[2] See H. R. Penniman, *Sait's American Parties and Elections*, pp. 605-7, and J. P. Harris, *Registration of Voters in The United States*, Ch. IV.

on the register of electors and this method assumes that it is the duty of a conscientious and responsible citizen to decide whether or not to register; with such systems there is almost inevitably a lower degree of electoral participation among the adult population as apathy or lack of time results in the less energetic and responsible citizens (who might or might not vote if their names were automatically included in the register) failing to take advantage of their opportunities to register. Moreover, interest in elections is high at the time of polling, but not at the time of registration some months before polling. With a voluntary system of registration, there are therefore likely to be a number of people who want to vote but are unable to do so because they have failed to register.

The Mechanics of Registration

Registration of electors consists of some or all of the following processes:

First Stage
The first stage consists of the compilation of a provisional register of electors. In a voluntary system, this may involve:

(a) The receipt and scrutiny of applications for registration from persons not already on the electoral roll.

(b) The receipt and scrutiny of applications for registration from persons wishing to transfer their registration from one area or unit to another (at revisions of the register only).

(c) The checking of the qualifications of new applicants for registration and of the continued eligibility for registration of persons whose names are already on the registers.

(d) The removal of the names of persons no longer qualified to be included in the electoral register (at revisions of the register only).

(e) The completion of the provisional register arranged in accordance with the electoral legislation or with administrative instructions from the chief registration authority.

In an automatic system, the compilation of a provisional register does not involve the receipt and checking of application forms, but rather the listing of persons qualified to be electors from official records or from a house-to-house survey of residents of each registration unit.

Second Stage

The second stage involves the submission and hearing of claims and objections, and consequent revision of the provisional list. This stage may include some or all of the following:

(*a*) A period set aside for public inspection of the provisional list of electors.

(*b*) A procedure for receiving and hearing claims from persons who maintain that they have been wrongly omitted from the provisional list.

(*c*) A procedure for receiving and hearing objections to the inclusion in the final list of persons whose names appear in the provisional list and of claimants whose names do not appear in the provisional list.

(*d*) A revision of the provisional register following the hearing of claims and objections (including appeals against the official decisions on claims and objections).

Third Stage

This stage, the publication of certified registers, will involve:

(*a*) Arrangements for printing or duplicating the revised register.

(*b*) Certification of the revised register.

(*c*) Sale of copies of the certified register.

The mechanics of registration, and particularly of the first stage, will be dependent upon whether the system of registration in force is voluntary or automatic. There will also be differences between the mechanics of initial registration and of revisions of the register; the term 'initial registration' is used here to imply a registration which starts from scratch, either because there has been no previous registration of electors or because changes in the electoral legislation have made it necessary to scrap the old registers or because the system in force involves a periodical complete re-registration or re-identification of electors. The first stage — that is, the compilation of the provisional register — will therefore be discussed under three sub-headings:

(*a*) The compilation of a provisional register at initial registration in a voluntary system.

(*b*) The compilation of a provisional register at revisions of the register in a voluntary system.

(*c*) The compilation of a provisional register in an automatic system.

THE PROVISIONAL REGISTER AT INITIAL
REGISTRATION IN A VOLUNTARY SYSTEM

Initial registration in a voluntary system, to be effective, requires the deployment of a considerable staff. Within each registration area, clerical staff, working under the directions of the registration officer responsible for the area, must be available during the registration period to receive applications to register. This can be done in two or three ways as follows:

(a) If registration areas are small in size (as they may be in urban areas) there may be one or two fixed registration receiving offices in each such area, manned for the whole or for part of each day by assistant registration officers.

(b) If registration areas are large (as they usually are in relation to communications in Africa and Asia), there may be one fixed registration receiving office for each registration unit — usually sited at the prospective polling station for the unit.

(c) If each registration unit contains a few distinct villages or other residential localities, the assistant registration officers may spend one or two days during the registration period in each such locality, their itinerary being publicised well in advance in order that the local inhabitants will know when to register with the minimum of inconvenience.

The first of these three alternatives is, from the administrative point of view, the most economical, but it is likely to be inconvenient for the general public if personal attendance is required at a distant registration centre and if a large percentage of the population is illiterate and requires the help of the assistant registration officers to complete their application forms. With such a system, long queues may develop at the registration centre and registration may then involve both a long and expensive journey and a day off work in order to meet the registration officer or one of his assistants face to face for a very few minutes. The third alternative is the most convenient method of registration for the general public, but it is also the most expensive for the administration owing to the large staff which must be employed and the travelling and subsistence expenses of this staff. In Asian countries, the convenience of the general public has frequently been regarded as the paramount consideration and the third alternative has been adopted; in Africa it has been more usual[1] to strike a compromise and arrange for a fixed registration centre in each unit. In Western Nigeria, the registration officer for each constituency is required to divide his area into a number of units in each of which, as far as is practicable, the number of electors does not exceed five hundred and the place of residence of each and every elector should not be "more than three miles by the shortest route from the most convenient building for use as a registration office and polling station".[2] Similarly in Zanzibar, during the initial 1957 registration, a convenient centre was selected to serve as a registration point, no elector in the division having to travel more than five miles to reach it. "This registration point was designed to serve also in due course as a polling station, so that an elector to whom the registration point was already familiar would require no guidance on polling day as to where he had to go to vote".[3]

Many countries with a voluntary system of registration require the prospective elector to deliver his application to the registration officer or to one of his assistants in person. Personal application is a requirement in countries on both sides of the continent of Africa — particularly in respect of the initial registration — as for instance in the Western Region of Nigeria,[4] Zanzibar[5] and Uganda.[6] Personal attendance and interview by the local Board of Registrars is also a feature of registration in some of the United States.[7] In general, personal attendance tends to be demanded wherever there is a qualitative franchise with qualifications such as literacy or receipt of a certain minimum income and in situations

[1] In British Togoland, however, at the time of the 1956 Plebiscite, many of the registration assistants covering rural areas made several trips to inaccessible villages to provide opportunities for the people to register — *U.N. Plebiscite Commissioner's Report*, p. 142 (U.N. Document A/3173).

[2] The Parliamentary and Local Government Electoral Regulations 1955 (Western Region of Nigeria), Reg. 9(2).

[3] *Report on the 1957 Zanzibar Elections*, p. 6.

[4] See Reg. 18(3)(a) of the Western Region Parliamentary and Local Government Electoral Regulations, 1955.

[5] In Zanzibar, during the first registration of electors in 1957, the registration assistants, acting on instructions from the Supervisor of Elections that applications to register must be handed in personally, refused to accept packets of application forms lodged by party agents on behalf of party members who were not themselves present.

[6] See Section 12 of the Uganda Legislative Council Elections Ordinance, 1957.

[7] In Alabama, each applicant is furnished with a questionnaire which has to be answered in writing by the applicant in the presence of the County Board of Registrars.

where there is a fear that political parties may attempt to 'pad' the register with the names of mythical supporters. If personal application is required, the role of political parties in the compilation of the provisional register is limited to prompting supporters to register, helping illiterate applicants to complete their application forms (in so far as this is permitted), and keeping an eye on the registration officers and their assistants in order to ensure impartiality of treatment of applicants.

The extent to which political parties should be encouraged or permitted to help in the process of getting eligible persons to register is in fact a highly controversial question. It can be argued that the registration of electors should be regarded as above politics and that all possible steps should be taken to ensure that registration does not take place in a tense political atmosphere: the natural corollary to such an argument is to bar the parties from being represented at the registration centres or, at most, to permit them to send observers to the registration centres who, like candidates' agents at polling stations, would not be permitted to interfere with individuals seeking to register. At the other extreme, political parties are actively encouraged to assist in registration work and the onus of securing a good register is thrown on the parties, as was the case in Britain in the nineteenth century and the early years of this century. In the Federation of Malaya, which has a system of voluntary registration and where there is no statutory requirement that the application form should be handed in by the applicant personally, political parties were permitted but not actively encouraged to deliver applications in bulk to the registration authority. Registration officers were instructed to contact the local representatives of political parties before the start of the registration period to inform them of the official arrangements and to attempt to persuade such representatives to arrange that voluntary workers from political parties should work in co-operation with the assistant registration officers rather than independently of them. It was felt that the general public would certainly be confused if, quite independently, they received encouragement and opportunities to register both from agents of political parties and from official assistant registration officers and that co-operation between the registration staff and the political parties was essential to avoid this confusion and a resultant duplication of application forms from many individual applicants for registration. In the event, the political parties played little part in registration and the very great majority of the application forms were handed direct by applicants to assistant registration officers in the course of visits by these officers to each inhabited locality. The few applications which were received from the parties rather than from individuals were subjected to sample checks on the existence and qualifications of the applicants.[1]

In some communities particular difficulties may arise in a voluntary system over the registration of women, many of whom may be entitled to be registered but have objections on the grounds of modesty to appearing at a public registration office. The Commission on the Conduct of Local Government Elections in Mauritius were informed that such difficulties existed and that many women would not come forward unless some special arrangement could be made for them to be registered in private; they accordingly recommended that "provision should be made for women who wish to do so to register at separate offices or in the general offices but at times reserved for women",[2] but this recommendation was not subsequently accepted by the Mauritius Legislative Council.[3] The position of women also exercised the minds of the 1955/56 Pakistan Electoral Reforms Commission, but in relation to voting rather than registration. Mention has already been made of the difficulties of obtaining the correct names of female electors in some parts of India.

The period allowed for the submission of applications at initial registration has varied considerably from one country to another. The writer formed the opinion in Malaya in 1954 that, given an adequate preliminary publicity campaign jointly conducted by the information services and the district administrations, the registration period need not last more than a very few weeks; his

[1] The inaccuracies which can be introduced into the register are well illustrated on pages 5 and 6 of the Keith-Lucas Commission Report on the conduct of local government elections in Mauritius. These inaccuracies were caused primarily by the absence of adequate machinery for checking the qualifications of electors.

[2] *Report of the Commission on the Conduct of Local Government Elections in Mauritius* (Leg. Council Sessional Paper No. 1 of 1956), paragraphs 15, 126-7, and 133 (2).

[3] See Debates Nos. 5 and 6 of 1956, Mauritius Legislative Council. Mauritius has since adopted the United Kingdom system of registration of electors and the question of catering for the requirements of individual applicants at registration offices no longer arises.

experience was that, after the first two weeks of the registration period, the daily total of fresh applications fell sharply and that, after four weeks, the flow had become a mere trickle. In Zanzibar in 1957, as the result of a very intensive preliminary campaign of propaganda supported both by the administration and by the main political parties, the registration was successfully conducted in a period of only six days in each constituency; shortage of staff available for registration purposes made it necessary to stagger registration, the registration staff moving from one constituency to another at the end of each week's work. In Nigeria and Ghana, there have been successful large-scale initial registrations lasting only a few weeks. In Kenya and Tanganyika, on the other hand, the response was rather disappointing, especially in the urban areas. It is not clear to what extent fears of new taxation or the developing Suez crisis at the time of the Kenya registration were responsible for this reluctance to register, how much the indifferent results were due to the lack of active encouragement by political parties or on the part of the administration and how much the lengthy period of several months allotted to registration in the first instance resulted in a psychological tendency on the part of the potential electors to postpone and ultimately fail to submit their registration applications. The author was assured, however, in the course of a visit to Kenya and Tanganyika, that, owing to the sparse population and indifferent roads in the two countries, registration could not have been carried out in a short period of two or three weeks without calling upon the services of a very large number of Government Officers and bringing other Government activities to a standstill.[1]

There have, in most countries in Asia and Africa, been some fears on the part of certain sections of the population that there is a sinister purpose behind the registration of electors. In some parts of Kenya for instance, there were rumours in the closing months of 1956 that registration might ultimately lead to persons being drafted to serve in Egypt. Somewhat similar rumours circulated in West African territories during periods of electoral registration which coincided with the Korean crisis. Again,

[1] The Elections Officer in Sierra Leone, reporting on the 1957 general election, stated that the period of fifteen days allowed for the submission of applications to register was too short, particularly in the more remote parts of the Protectorate where communications are bad, and he recommended that a period of twenty-one days should be allowed in future.

certain sections of the population may fear that registration will lead to an extended system of taxation or even to the appropriation of land. Indeed, the fears and rumours which have to be conquered in a successful registration campaign are very similar to those which have to be dealt with in the course of undertaking a population census. Official publicity must clearly be intense before the start of a first-ever registration of electors if the purpose of registration and the entitlement are to be clearly understood by a semi-literate population. The publicity media used to explain the mechanics and purpose of the registration of electors have included, in various countries:

(a) Visits by mobile units of the Government Information Service to villages.

(b) The publication of official pamphlets and articles on registration.

(c) The distribution of posters exhorting people to register.

(d) The production of short films to explain the purpose of registration.

(e) The use of the local broadcasting services.

In any system of voluntary registration, electors must possess the personal qualifications, which together make up the franchise, either on a fixed 'qualifying date' or at the date of submitting an application for inclusion in the register of electors. There are obviously a number of possibilities for the qualifying date as the following illustrations show:

(a) In the Federation of Malaya, the qualifying date is normally the day before the commencement of the registration period.

(b) In the Western Region of Nigeria, the qualifying date is the first day of the registration period.[1]

(c) In Eastern Nigeria, the qualifying day is the last day of the registration period.[2]

(d) In Uganda and Zanzibar, the elections legislation contains no reference to a qualifying date and qualifications are related to the entitlement of the applicant at the date of application.

In an unsophisticated society whose registration of electors is conducted on a voluntary basis, it is probably simpler for the

[1] See Regs. 10(2) and 26(4) of the Western Region Parliamentary and Local Government Electoral Regulations, 1955.

[2] Reg. 2(1) of the Eastern House of Assembly Electoral Regulations, 1955.

individual applicant to be able to base his claim on his qualifications at the date of submission, and this is likely to be satisfactory if the applicant is required to present his application in person and can at the same time be asked to produce documentary or other evidence of his qualifications, if required to substantiate his claim. In general, however, it is easier for the registration authorities to check an individual's qualifications if the latter relate to a definite qualifying date and it can be argued that it is fairer for the population at large to have a qualifying date laid down by law.

Whether there is a qualifying date or not, the registration officers and their assistants must have clear instructions which reduce to a minimum the margin of doubt in deciding whether applicants satisfy the various qualifications which entitle a person to have his name entered on the register of electors. The franchise is discussed in Chapter V, and all we need to say in this context is that qualifications which prove themselves such as possession of a particular educational certificate are better than qualifications of an uncertain kind such as literacy. In a voluntary system, the registration officers and their assistants will also require guidance as to the extent to which an applicant's affirmation that he possesses the necessary qualifications should be accepted without further investigation. To take a specific example, if local birth is one of the qualifications, should the applicant be required to produce a birth certificate and, if so, what should be done in the many areas of Asia and Africa with incomplete birth registration? If the applicant is required to appear before the registration authorities in person, it may be possible for the officials to use their powers to ask the applicant supplementary questions in order to determine any doubts about his qualifications; this is the procedure in the United States of America. But, in a large-scale initial registration in a semi-literate community, each registration officer will receive many thousands of applications and it may be quite impossible to ensure a complete verification of the qualifications of all applicants before the preliminary lists of electors are drawn up; in such circumstances, there may be some reliance on the second stage — the claims and objections period — for weeding out the names of persons who appear on the preliminary lists but who do not have the minimum qualifications for the vote.

Possible alternative methods of dealing with this problem can be illustrated by giving brief details of the procedure in the

Federation of Malaya, Zanzibar and Mauritius. In the Federation of Malaya, at the initial registration in 1954, an administrative instruction was circulated that "the declaration of an applicant for registration that he or she is a Federal citizen should *normally* be accepted for the first registration period and that further confirmation in the shape of documentation or oral evidence should not be required. Only in those cases where there is good reason to suppose that the applicant has, deliberately or through lack of knowledge, stated that he is a Federal citizen when in fact he is not, should further investigation be made". In the case of applications delivered to the authorities in bulk by the political parties, the registration officers in Malaya were instructed to send a sample (approximately 1 in 20) of such applications to their field staff in order to verify the physical existence and the qualifications of the applicant.

In Zanzibar, the registration assistants were not permitted to question applicants regarding the contents of their applications and the electoral regulations covering initial registration[1] even forbade these officers speaking to an applicant concerning his application form except to point out omissions and illegibility in the application and to return it for completion or rewriting, and to reject and return the application if the entry in respect of the applicant's address showed that he was not entitled "to be registered as an elector in that constituency". Representatives of the political parties were, however, permitted to be present at the registration centre[2] in order to make a note of the name and particulars of persons who appeared to be unqualified, with a view to making objections on the publication of the provisional register. Moreover, the registration officer was permitted to make corrections in the provisional register in order to remove duplicate entries and to expunge the names of persons deceased or subject to any legal incapacity provided that notice and an opportunity of objecting to the correction was given to the person affected. The Zanzibar register did not, therefore, rely in any way for its accuracy on a check on qualifications by the registration assistants,

[1] See Rules 7, 8 and 9 of the Zanzibar Legislative Council (Elections) (Registration) Rules, 1957.

[2] Political parties were also permitted to post representatives to the registration offices in the Western Region of Nigeria in November 1955 at the time of initial registration for House of Assembly elections in order to observe and note details of persons registering and to help applicants complete the forms.

but rather on the submission of objections to names in the provisional lists by political parties based on observation at the registration offices and a scrutiny of these lists.

In Mauritius, on the other hand, the municipal registration of electors in Port Louis in 1956 which followed the enactment of the Local Government Elections Ordinance (No. 1 of 1956) involved a large scale house-to-house verification of applications received in the registration centres. Field investigators were instructed to verify the identity and residence of each elector who based his claim for inclusion on residence and literacy, or residence and military service, or occupation of business premises in the town. All claimants about whose age doubts were entertained had their age checked at the Civil Status Office, and, where satisfactory proof of age was not thus obtained, claimants were summoned to produce evidence of their age during the revision of the provisional list. A check was also made on the nationality of claimants by sending a copy of the provisional register for comparison with the register of aliens.[1] Thus, in Mauritius, as opposed to Zanzibar, the procedure involved a very thorough official verification of the qualifications of applicants both before and immediately after the compilation of the provisional register. The Mauritius registration was, however, on a fairly small scale (there were 26,612 names in the provisional register) and an exhaustive verification of qualifications would be difficult or impossible in some countries at initial registration in a voluntary system when a million or more persons are included for the first time in the registers of electors.[2]

The application for registration in a voluntary system is usually a statutory form in which the applicant is required to provide a statement of his personal particulars and of the qualifications on which he bases his claim for inclusion in the register. Clearly some provision must be made for illiterates if the franchise does not demand literacy as an essential qualification; in Western Nigeria, an illiterate claimant is entitled, when attending before the assistant registration officer, "to be accompanied by a person of

[1] This information was obtained from an unpublished report on the Municipal Elections in Mauritius in 1956.

[2] Mauritius has now abandoned voluntary registration, and under the provisions of the Representation of the People Ordinance 1958, the registration officer is required to prepare a list of all persons who appear to him to be qualified after making "a house-to-house or other sufficient inquiry".

his choice who is literate".[1] In Zanzibar, in 1957, Public Writers, paid by the government, were posted to every registration point for the convenience of illiterate electors. In Malaya in 1954, the bulk of the work of completing the application forms was undertaken by the assistant registration officers on an interview basis. In all cases, the applicant is required to sign or impress his thumbprint on the application form and, in some countries (e.g. the Federation of Malaya) the signature or thumbprint has to be witnessed by a person who knows the applicant personally.

In some countries, a 'registration receipt' or 'voting card' has been given to applicants at the time of registration or to registered electors after the registers have been certified. The system of issuing a voting card at the time of registration and requiring the elector to produce this card at the time of voting is in use in the Gambia, where there is a provision in the Colony Elections Ordinance that "no person shall be entitled to be registered as a voter, or having been registered, to vote unless and until he has been issued with a voter's card".[2] A counterfoil of the voter's card is retained by the registration authorities and both the card and the counterfoil must contain either a photograph or thumbprint of the elector in addition to having the usual particulars such as full name, address, occupation and voting qualifications. It must be pointed out, however, that the number of registered electors in the Gambia is small. A somewhat similar system was used in Kenya in 1956/57. Successful applicants for registration were presented by the assistant registration officer with a card coloured buff, yellow or blue, denoting one, two or three votes, on which was inscribed the applicant's name and number in the register and these cards had to be presented at the polling station on polling day, where they were exchanged for ballots. In Uganda, there is no provision in the legislation for the issue of registration receipts, but receipts were in fact issued at the time of application, and the electors were encouraged, but not compelled, to bring their receipts to the polling station on polling day. In the Western Region of Nigeria, registration receipts were used during the 1955 registration in order to make it easier to connect a given application with the applicant in the event of a claim or objection during the

[1] Regulation 18(3)(b) of the Western Region Parliamentary and Local Government Electoral Regulations, 1955.
[2] Section 14(2) of the Colony Elections Ordinance, 1954.

period of inspection of the registers, but electors were not required to produce these receipts in the polling stations before voting. In the United Kingdom, an official poll card is issued to all electors on the register, but only when a parliamentary election is imminent and not at the time of registration. Where there is a national identity card system in operation, as in Singapore and the Federation of Malaya, the identity card number is entered in the register of electors and the elector is requested or required to produce his identity card in order to verify his identity at the time of polling.

The system of voter's cards, such as that in use in the Gambia, has obvious advantages in assisting in the rapid identification of voters at the polling station and in preventing personation. There are, however, certain disadvantages to their use in African conditions as follows:

(a) The cards are easily lost in a population whose clothing is scanty and who are unused to the custody of documents.[1] The author has been told by a Kenya District Officer of the latter's experience of issuing voting cards to the Masai, a primitive pastoral tribe, whose limited clothing is bare of pockets. The voting cards were often rolled inside pipes for safe custody but had frequently disintegrated when polling day arrived.

(b) Cards which simply give an elector's number in the electoral register without any other means of identification are an open invitation to personation, because they can be illegally bought and sold and yet the polling station staff are liable to accept the card as adequate identification, whatever may be the official instructions on the subject.

(c) On the other hand, cards which identify the elector adequately by means of photographs and thumbprints are expensive and their issue involves special efforts on the part of the electors and the registration officials. Moreover, there may be religious or other scruples against the taking of photographs or thumbprints. For instance the Commission on the Conduct of Local Government Elections in Mauritius were told that a number of people had objections based on religious principle to having their photographs taken.[2]

[1] Many Africans are, however, accustomed to keeping tax receipts over a period of some years.
[2] p. 18 of the Commission's Report.

(d) The purpose of issuing registration receipts or voting cards can easily be misunderstood in a semi-literate society and, in some African territories, political parties have attempted to sequester such cards after their issue in the hope of influencing the way in which electors will ultimately vote. In the Western Region of Nigeria, for instance, the political parties assumed at the time of the registration prior to the 1955 elections to the Western House of Assembly that the registration receipts were intended ultimately to serve as voting cards, particularly since the registration propaganda had stressed the need to keep these cards carefully. The two main parties began to attempt to take custody of the registration receipts as soon as electors left the registration offices after filing their applications and, in this way, the politicians presumably hoped to ensure that their supporters kept faith at the time of the poll; at any rate it would in practice have been possible, even if illegal, for the parties to fail to re-issue the cards to individual electors wherever there was some reason to believe that a former supporter had strayed from the party line and might want to vote for a rival candidate. In the Trust Territory of Togoland under British Administration, as it was in 1956 at the time of the Plebiscite, it is reported[1] that one Chief adopted an attitude of defiance towards the registration officer and collected registration receipts from applicants. As a result the Registration Regulations were amended[2] to make the taking or destruction of receipts and having in possession a receipt issued to some other person punishable offences.

(e) Finally, the provisional register will differ in some respects from the certified register as the result of successful claims and objections. If receipts or cards are issued at the time of registration, attempts will have to be made to withdraw some of the receipts or cards where objections are sustained, but this may not be too easy if the person objected against fails to appear at the hearing of his case. If, on the other hand, cards are issued after the certification of the revised register, reliance must be placed on a distributing agency such as the post office or local headmen. The post office may not, in African conditions, be able to trace the addresses of

[1] Report of the U.N. Plebiscite Commissioner (Document A/3173 of 5th September, 1956).

[2] See Reg. 14, Togoland Plebiscite (Registration) Regulations, 1955, as amended in 1956.

some of the names on the register or may not have facilities for delivery of letters to private addresses; and the headmen are frequently persons with strong political leanings and they cannot always be relied upon to deliver cards to supporters of rival political parties.

There is still too little experience of the use of registration receipts and voters' cards in African and Asian conditions to be able to draw any definite conclusions about the relative merits of their advantages and disadvantages. The author is, however, inclined to the view that voters' cards, if used at all, should be issued as near as possible to polling day through official channels and not as part of the registration procedure. In French Africa,[1] distributing commissions consisting of representatives of the rival political parties carry out the distribution of voters' cards shortly before an election is due to take place. Wherever possible, the commission hands cards direct to voters individually, but, where this is not feasible, small blocks of such cards are handed to the heads of clans or families for individual distribution. Unclaimed cards are available for collection, subject to satisfactory identification, at the polling stations. In general it must be said that there is a trend in favour of the introduction of voting cards in both Asia and Africa. A majority of the Pakistan Electoral Reforms Commission recommended in their Report[2] "that all males qualified to vote at elections should be required to obtain identity cards together with their photographs, both attested by the Registering Officers entrusted with the task of preparing electoral rolls"; one member of the Commission conceded that this recommendation would, if put into effect, be an adequate check against personation at the polls, but felt that the provision of identity cards and photos would involve too much money, labour and time. In Mauritius, the 1956 Commission Report on the Conduct of Local Government Elections made a recommendation that cards should be issued to persons accepted for inclusion in the electoral registers and, after considering various alternatives, the

[1] For a description of the use of voting cards in French West Africa see 'Les Elections aux Assemblées des Territoires d'outre-mer' by Andre Holleaux in *Revue Juridique et Politique de l'Union Francaise*, No. 1, 1956, and the *Report of the U.N. Commissioner for the Supervision of the Elections in Togoland under French Administration*.

[2] *Report of the Electoral Reforms Commission* published in the *Gazette of Pakistan* of April 24th, 1956, paragraph 31.

Commission suggested that the cards should bear the signature of literate voters or the thumbprint of illiterate voters, but should not bear photographs.[1]

Once the period allowed to the public for submitting applications is over, the precise method of compilation of the registers will obviously depend on the type of application form used, the particulars which are to be entered in the provisional registers, and the office machinery and personnel available for the work. In the Federation of Malaya, the original application forms were the only documents used in 1954 in compiling the provisional lists; a small space at the bottom of each application form containing the particulars required for the register was completed by the registration officer after acceptance of the application, and the application forms were sorted by registration units into the order in which the applicant's names were to appear on the register. There was some discussion prior to the registration period on the advisability of requiring the assistant registration officers working in the field to enter brief details of each application, at the time of receipt, in a record book, or index of some kind, as an insurance against the loss of any of the documents, but it was decided that the staff employed as assistant registration officers were sufficiently intelligent and honest to make the preparation of these additional records an unnecessary burden. In Zanzibar, however, in 1957, at initial registration, the registration staff were under a statutory obligation to enter in an 'index book' the names, addresses and occupations of all applicants who appeared to be qualified as electors and to group the names of the electors in the index book according to the initial letters of their first names; the index book and application forms were sent by each registration assistant to his registration officer for forwarding to the central 'listing office' at the end of the six-day period of registration in each area.

In Uganda, the registers for the 1958 elections were compiled on the Kalamazoo binder system, with one strip containing the particulars of each elector. After completion of the period for

[1] *Report of the Commission on the Conduct of Local Government Elections in Mauritius* (Mauritius Legislative Council Sessional Paper No. 1 of 1956), pp. 17-19. Under the provisions of Section 40(3) of the Mauritius Representation of the People Ordinance, 1958 (which covers both Legislative Council and Local Government Elections), elector's cards are to be issued, and each card is to bear either a photograph of the elector or an impression of the elector's thumb or finger.

submitting applications for registration, the strips were typed and, for each registration unit, sorted either in order of registration receipt or in alphabetical order of electors.[1] The provisional register formed by placing the strips in the binder was then photographed, page by page, and a few copies of the register were printed from the plates — the latter being carefully retained in correct order pending the disposal of claims and objections. Where there was no change in a given page of strips after scrutiny of the registers, the same plate was used for producing the corresponding page of the final register: where changes were made in a given page of the provisional register, the necessary amendments were made to the order and content of the strips and the page was photographed anew and reproduced. This system, as used in Uganda, undoubtedly saves a good deal of clerical labour and time in the reproduction of the certified register, provided the number of changes to be made as the result of scrutiny of the provisional register and successful claims and objections are small in number. In the long run, the method will prove its worth if the information contained on the strips is sufficient for the purpose not only of the 1958 elections but also of later elections, and if the 'turnover' in strips is not more than a small percentage of the total register.

The experience of Uganda and the Federation of Malaya suggests that, in a country of any size with an electorate running into several hundreds of thousands, it is desirable to compile the provisional register within each constituency, or at most on a provincial basis for a small group of constituencies, in order to minimize correspondence and delay arising from errors, omissions and illegibility in transferring information from the application forms or index books to the register. In Tanganyika, the arrangements for compiling the register are at present centralised in Dar-es-Salaam, for, despite the size of the country, the electorate is small; but it is open to question whether some decentralisation would not be essential with a wider franchise and a larger electorate. The system of registration at present in use in Tanganyika was in fact copied from the system operating in Southern Rhodesia, where claims for registration as an elector are all sent to the Chief Registering Officer, who files the claims in alphabetical order of name irrespective of constituencies. A card is prepared in respect

[1] The various registration officers were permitted to exercise a choice.

of each accepted claim and such cards are filed in alphabetical order according to the constituency in which the elector resides. Where an elector claims to transfer registration, the original claim is removed and the transfer claim inserted in the file. A fresh card is prepared and filed under the constituency to which the elector has moved and the previous card is destroyed. In the case of death or disqualification of an elector, the last form in respect of that elector is removed from the live file and enclosed in one of a separate group of files marked 'Deaths' or 'Disqualified' as the case may be. Under the electoral legislation of both Southern Rhodesia and Tanganyika there are annual, quarterly and supplementary rolls. The annual roll is closed on a fixed date in each year and it is a consolidation of the previous year's annual roll and the subsequent quarterly and supplementary rolls.

Given the application forms and the index, if any, the provisional registers can be printed (as in the United Kingdom), or typed (as in Malaya), or, if the register is subject to periodic revision, a card index system can be used with the help of which the required number of copies of the register can be obtained by photographic methods or some similar system. The organisation and methods problem involved is in certain respects similar to that of compiling and maintaining the telephone directory of a large town or other area with a considerable number of subscribers. At initial registration there are liable to be a considerable number of alterations which require to be made to the provisional registers as a result of successful claims and objections and the correction of clerical errors and omissions and it may therefore be unwise to plan on the basis of the preliminary register being a printer's proof of the final register; as the number of copies of the provisional register required for purposes of inspection is small, it has usually been the practice in Africa to type a very few copies of these registers.

The elections legislation usually permits the registration authorities to correct clerical or printing errors or unintentional omissions in the registers at any time, even after certification.

THE PROVISIONAL REGISTER AT REVISIONS OF
THE REGISTER IN A VOLUNTARY SYSTEM

Although the periodic revision of the registers of electors may not be such a large-scale operation as the initial registration, planning of the revision needs to be just as careful and detailed as for the original registration. The purpose of periodic revision of the register is to include the names of new applicants, who either did not make use of their earlier opportunities to register or were not eligible to register at a previous stage. At revisions of the register, the authorities must also delete the names of persons who have died or who for some other reason are no longer qualified to vote. Provision must also be made to enable persons previously registered in one registration area to have their names transferred to the register in another area when they move their residence.

The planning of the revision of registers in a voluntary system will depend on a number of factors, including:

(a) The frequency of revision.

(b) Whether the system is 'permanent' or 'periodic'.

(c) The official sources of information available to the registration authorities regarding births and deaths, tax payments, etc.

(d) The extent to which the population can be relied upon to report change of residence and apply for a transfer of registration from one area to another.

By-elections are liable to take place at any time and it is, at least in theory, desirable that the register of electors should be revised not less than once each year, in order to have an up-to-date register available when required. Many registers are for use in both central and local government elections and, in most years, there may be an election of one type or another; it is then almost essential to revise the register annually. On the other hand, when a register is likely to be used for a general election only once every three or four years, it is tempting on administrative and financial grounds to legislate for a less frequent revision of the register.

A population is never static and a register of electors is never absolutely accurate. Reports of deaths and applications for registration as the result of changes such as attainment of the qualifying age, change of residence, etc., may or may not reach the registration authorities. In Asian and African countries, it has been a universal experience that, with a voluntary system of registration, the register becomes less and less accurate, despite frequent revisions, as the years pass following the initial registration. In these circumstances, some countries with a voluntary system of registration demand a periodic re-registration — i.e. an operation essentially the same as an initial registration in which every person with the necessary qualifications, whether previously registered or not, is required to re-register if he wishes to have his name entered or retained on the electoral rolls. The elections legislation in the Gambia provides for an annual revision of the registers (which are used for both central and local government elections) and for a complete re-registration every tenth year. In some states of the U.S.A., an elector is required to renew his registration every two years.

The degree of inaccuracy in the registers will, of course, be to a large extent dependent on the sources of information available to the registration authorities. The elections legislation of some countries in Asia and Africa requires that officers in government service (other than officers of a government department prohibited by law from furnishing information) and local authorities should furnish to the registration officer such information as he may require to enable him to revise the register. The department dealing with the registration of deaths would thus be required to provide the elections registration authorities with a detailed list of deaths.[1] Even with such a list, it may be difficult to connect a name on the death registration records with a name on the registers of electors, particularly in areas where there is no well defined code of spelling of names and where addresses are somewhat haphazard. Again, local authorities would be required to furnish information regarding the payment of rates or other local taxes, if such payments are a necessary qualification for entering or maintaining a name on the register of electors but here too there may be some difficulty in matching the two sets of records. In practice, the governments of under-developed countries have had to make a compromise between administrative convenience and the accuracy of the registers. Consideration of this compromise is clearly illustrated by the following extract from the Van Lare Commission Report on Electoral Reform in the Gold Coast:

> The existing law provides, both for central and local government purposes, that after an initial compilation there shall be an annual revision in order not only to include new names but to remove disqualified ones. We do not, however, consider that the

[1] In the Gambia, for example, the Colony Elections Ordinance requires the Registrar of Births and Deaths to furnish quarterly returns of the names, ages and residences of all persons of full age who have died within any part of an electoral district.

adequate ascertainment of disqualifications, particularly by reason of death, change of residence, or criminal conviction, is within the power of any Registration Officer in the absence of any systematic recording of these facts. We therefore envisage that in the course of time the register will accumulate a considerable number of names of disqualified electors, thus increasing the risk of personation. We believe this objection to be serious, even if, as may be expected, the ascertainment of rate defaulters becomes progressively easier. Accordingly, we recommend that provision be made for the compilation, at regular intervals, of an entirely new register.

In considering what interval should be allowed between the compilation of new registers we took into account both the administrative burden and the expense involved and also the question whether provision should be made between the completion of registers for any form of revision. We appreciate that the larger the interval the greater the need for interim revisions and our problem became one of balancing the administrative and financial burden against the reliability of the annual revision. We also appreciate that, while the normal life of the Legislative Assembly was four years and that of a local government council three years, any sudden dissolution might involve an election on a partially out-of-date register with an interval of more than one year between registrations. Taking all these factors into account, we recommend that an entirely new register be compiled at intervals of four years, combined with an annual revision.

As regards the annual revision we believe that administrative simplicity is the factor of principal importance and we are aware that, in practice, it may be restricted to adding new names and removing those of rate defaulters. With a new register every four years we consider that a revision even thus limited would be adequate but we recommend, nevertheless, that the Registration Officer should be required to remove the name of any person whom he has reason to believe has become disqualified for any reason. This will allow him to remove names of those who are brought to his notice as being disqualified without requiring him to undertake a major enquiry annually.

It may be relevant to discuss at this point the relative degree of accuracy of registration systems in various countries. The British system, which is an automatic system dependent on an annual postal house-to-house canvass, has been estimated at being perhaps 97% or 98% accurate.[1] The Jamaican system, in which

---

[1] W. J. M. Mackenzie, *Free Elections*, p. 118.

there is a quinquennial enumeration of *all* persons qualified to vote coupled with an annual revision, is such that "at the end of the fourth year of the quinquennial period, the lists are approximately 30 to 40 per cent inaccurate",[1] despite relatively elaborate provisions for annual revision. The Report on the 1954 Gold Coast elections suggested that it was doubtful whether the registers compiled at initial registration were more than 60% or 70% accurate and recommended that completely new registers be prepared during the 1955/6 dry season. The Commission on the Conduct of Local Government Elections in Mauritius found that, in all districts, the registers were inaccurate, primarily because the machinery for checking the qualifications of electors was inadequate.[2] D. S. Strong describes the system used in Alabama to 'purge' the registration lists in his *Registration of Voters in Alabama* and states that, in some counties of the State, "the confusion resulting from inadequate purging has led to a throwing up of hands and a determination to start all over from scratch. The procedure seized upon has been that of 're-identification', which means that all registrants must fill out a slip of paper and sign it. The assumption is that the dead and those who have moved out of the county will be unable to do this."[3] It should be mentioned that Alabama, as a State, has a 'permanent' registration system, requiring an elector to register only once in a life time, in contrast to the method of 'periodic' registration used in several of the United States, which requires citizens to register every two years.

Perhaps the evidence in the last paragraph is sufficient to support the contention that permanent registration in a voluntary system will almost certainly lead to progressively more inaccurate registers, and that the inaccuracies are likely to be even greater in an 'under-developed' country with incomplete death registration and low literacy rates than in a country such as the United States of America. A periodical re-registration will to some extent reduce the inaccuracies, but it is suggested that, in the long run, any system which places the main initiative on the elector to secure the accuracy of the lists is unlikely to produce satisfactory results.

[1] *Report of the Committee appointed to examine the existing electoral laws of Jamaica*, 1957, p. 2.

[2] *Report of the Commission on the conduct of Local Government Elections in Mauritius*, p. 6.

[3] Donald S. Strong, *Registration of Voters in Alabama*, Ch. 6.

A survey of the franchise and elections legislation in British African territories suggests that in some areas little consideration has been given at the time of drafting the legislation to its long-term implications from the point of view of maintaining an accurate register of electors. This is understandable enough, as there has almost always been a background of political urgency at the time of introducing a new electoral system and attention is necessarily focussed on first registration and the first elections under the new legislation and not on long-term issues of electoral administration. The position can perhaps best be illustrated by examining in some detail the franchise and registration system in force in Kenya. In that country, the ten or so possible qualifications of voters and the adjudication of one, two or three votes to successful applicants for registration inevitably caused a lot of work for the registration officers at the time of initial registration; and the option of allowing African voters to register in their tribal reserve or 'home district' involved the registration officers in additional work in completing and forwarding applications to other districts (particularly in urban areas such as Mombasa and Nairobi) and in receiving and registering a flood of applications from outside (particularly in the rural districts containing tribal reserves). The system was not in practice as laborious as it might have been if as many people as expected had come forward to register. For the first elections, both during registration and at polling, it proved quite workable. The real complications are, however, likely to arise at revisions of the register which do not involve a complete 're-identification'. A multiple vote franchise will involve continual changes in the register beyond the customary changes caused by movements, deaths and new applications, as electors acquire qualifications which entitle them to additional votes. It will not suffice for a person to register himself as a voter once, as he may subsequently be eligible to increase his voting power. Moreover, if the present system of 'expatriate' voters registration is maintained, the registration officers will be involved in an appalling volume of correspondence if a real attempt is to be made to maintain an accurate register. The existing Kenya legislation provides for permanent registration and an annual revision without periodic re-registration and the author has little doubt in forecasting that the system in its present form will ultimately prove to be unworkable.

The last few paragraphs have been devoted to a rather gloomy appraisal of the difficulties of maintaining an accurate register of electors in a voluntary system in semi-literate societies. Nevertheless the fact has to be faced that, for reasons of administrative convenience or political philosophy or both, voluntary systems will continue to be required for many years in much of Africa and consideration must therefore be given to steps which can be taken to reduce the inaccuracies in the registers to a minimum. In the first place, it seems clear that a complete re-registration is desirable every few years; this has been recognised in the legislation of territories such as the Gambia and Jamaica[1] and has been recommended for introduction elsewhere. Secondly it is desirable that there should be specific legislative provision for quarterly or periodical returns, however incomplete these returns may be, to the registration officers from Heads of Government Departments such as Registrars of Births and Deaths (who can provide lists of the names and addresses of adults whose deaths have been registered), Commissioners of Police or Prisons (who can provide lists of the names and addresses of adults who have received sentences for offences involving voting disqualifications), Tax or Rate Collectors (where payment of a tax or rate is a franchise qualification) and others. Thirdly, local government authorities, village elders and other local notables can be asked to co-operate in scrutinising the registers, encouraging persons who have changed their residence to apply for a transfer of registration if already registered and persons qualified but not yet registered to submit an application for registration. They can also point to the names of persons on the existing registers who appear to have ceased to possess the qualifications of electors. Fourthly, although it may not be feasible to check the continued eligibility of all persons already registered as electors, small random samples can be and should be checked in order to give the registration authorities an idea of the accuracy of the registers.

In a few African territories with a voluntary system of registration, revision of the registers is continuous and applications for registration can be submitted at any time of the year. This system

---

[1] The 1957 Report of the Committee appointed to examine the electoral laws of Jamaica in fact recommended that, despite the cost, there should be a house to house check of the electoral registers by enumerators either once or twice a year. The existing legislation provides for a quinquennial enumeration of all persons qualified to vote and for annual revisions.

has been adopted for use in Tanganyika, where there is to be an annual roll, arranged in alphabetical order, of voters registered not later than 31st March in each year, and, in addition, supplementary quarterly rolls of voters registered in each constituency during each period of three months.[1] It should be noted that there is no 'qualifying date' for registration in Tanganyika and that the prospective elector is required to hold the requisite qualifications at the time of making his application to register. In the majority of African territories, however, the applications for registration must be submitted during a definite period, usually of about one month's duration, each year; thus, in Western Nigeria, claims can be submitted at any time during the month of January[2] and, in the Gambia, claims may be submitted during a period of not less than one month starting at some date between the middle of April and the middle of May — the starting date and length of the period being specified by the Registration Officer by public notice.[3] Both the Western Region of Nigeria and the Gambia have a qualifying date in respect of an elector's qualifications (the qualifying date in the Gambia relates only to the residential qualification and not, oddly enough, to the other qualifications) and, in general, wherever there is a qualifying date for some or all of the elector's qualifications, applications for new registration or for the transfer of registration have to be submitted during a prescribed period in each year.

In the United Kingdom, the provisional register is framed in three parts for each registration unit — lists *A*, *B* and *C*. List *A* is the register in force, list *B* consists of the newly qualified electors of the registration unit, and list *C* is a list of those who have ceased to be qualified as electors, or whose qualification has been altered.

The arrangements for compiling the preliminary register in British African territories are not always so clearly defined. There is provision in the Gambia Colony Elections Ordinance for the publication of provisional registers in separate lists on the general lines of the United Kingdom system.[4] In the Western Region of

---

[1] Sections 30 and 31 of the Tanganyika Legislative Council Elections Ordinance, 1957.

[2] Regulation 26(4) of the Western Region Parliamentary and Local Government Electoral Regulations, 1955.

[3] Section 7(2) of the Gambia Colony Elections Ordinance, 1954.

[4] See Section 7(2) of the Colony Elections Ordinance, 1954.

Nigeria, the 'Preliminary List' consists of two parts — the register of electors for the time being in force (List A in the U.K. system) and an amending list consisting of persons whose claims for registration or transfer have been accepted (List B in the U.K. system).[1] There is no list corresponding to the United Kingdom List C, but the registration officer has power to make such corrections in the Preliminary List as are required for "the expunging of the names of persons who are dead or disqualified", and "shall also make such corrections as he thinks necessary and as are practicable to secure that no person is entered on the list who will be registered in any other constituency", provided that due notice is given to the person affected, who is to be given a reasonable opportunity of objecting to the proposed correction.[2] In Eastern Nigeria, where there is no prescribed period for the submission of claims for registration, the register is closed and made available for inspection as soon as a date for a general election or by-election has been appointed but the Regulations do not provide detailed instructions as to the methods to be adopted in compiling the provisional register and making corrections as the result of death, disqualification and transfer of residence.[3] Again, in the Uganda Legislative Council Elections Ordinance (where revision is to take place "not more than three years after the last general compilation of registers") there is no section specifically devoted to the revision of the registers of electors (as opposed to initial registration) and there may well have to be later amendments to the ordinance to cover, if only in outline, the methods to be adopted in 'purging' the register and in compiling the provisional register at each revision.[4]

[1] Regulation 27 of the Western Region Parliamentary and Local Government Electoral Regulations, 1955.
[2] Regulation 24 of the Western Region Parliamentary and Local Government Electoral Regulations, 1955.
[3] The fact that the registration authorities are not given detailed instructions in the relevant legislation as to the methods to be adopted in order to maintain the registers does not necessarily imply inefficiency in electoral administration. Indeed there is a school of thought, with which the author has some sympathy, which considers that, in the early stages of the development of democratic institutions, the elections legislation should not be too rigid and that the officials responsible for electoral administration should have considerable freedom to adapt administrative methods to the needs of the immediate situation.
[4] Part II of the Uganda Legislative Council Elections Ordinance, 1957, covers the registration of electors.

Enough has been said to suggest that the maintenance of a reasonably accurate register of electors is likely in the long run to prove one of the most intractable problems in African electoral administration, and, now that most territories have held elections of some sort, it is to the hitherto somewhat neglected field of registration rather than to the problems of polling that attention will have to be turned.

THE PROVISIONAL REGISTER AT REVISIONS OF THE REGISTER IN AN AUTOMATIC SYSTEM

In an automatic system of registration the onus of responsibility for registration lies on the registration officers rather than on the individual citizen. It is assumed that it is the business of the government administration to ensure that its elections are properly conducted and that, as far as possible, all eligible electors are registered. The individual is not, in such a system, required to apply for registration, although some of the prospective electors — e.g. householders in the United Kingdom — may be under an obligation to supply certain particulars to enable the registration officers to compile a provisional register efficiently.

The methods employed in compiling the provisional register will necessarily depend on the nature of the franchise and the availability of relevant records. To illustrate the various possibilities, the registration systems in use in seven countries of the British Commonwealth will be briefly described. They are India, Sierra Leone, Sarawak (Municipal elections only), Singapore, the United Kingdom, Canada and Trinidad.

In India, for the first general elections of 1951-2, there was full adult suffrage. There were no records in existence from which the electoral register could be compiled and registration of voters was conducted in respect of each village or other residential unit on the basis of a house-to-house enquiry. This enumeration of potential electors was started before the first part of the electoral law had been approved and a supplementary enumeration had to be conducted after the enactment of the Representation of the People Act, 1950, because of changes in the qualifying date and the more liberal provisions regarding residential qualification. As the boundaries of constituencies had not been defined when the provisional registers were ready for publication, these preliminary rolls were published according to administrative units and not by constituencies.[1] From the methodological point of view, the important point to note is that, despite the magnitude of the task, the electoral registers were drawn up largely on the basis of a house-to-house enquiry. A somewhat similar method of compiling the registers, with suitable modifications to serve local conditions, was used in Indonesia (prior to the elections held in 1955) and in parts of the Sudan (prior to the elections held in 1953). Such a system appears to be particularly well suited to an under-developed country with universal adult franchise. An operation of this kind can, of course, be suitably and economically combined with a census of population, although possibly at the expense of some amendments to census legislation (which usually demands that information obtained in a census should be used solely for the purpose of compiling statistics) and, more important, at the risk of possible inaccuracies in census age statistics (because persons who are just below the age for registration as electors may be tempted to overstate their age in order to be entered on the electoral rolls).

In Sierra Leone, for the first general elections held on a wide franchise in 1957, the arrangements for registration followed closely the recommendations of the Keith-Lucas Commission[2] and involved a combination of automatic and voluntary registration. The franchise was somewhat complicated and different for the Colony and the Protectorate; but, for present purposes, it is sufficient to say that one of the alternative qualifications in the Colony and the town of Bo in the Protectorate was the ownership or occupation of rateable premises of at least £2 annual assessed value, whilst in the Protectorate the vote was given to men of twenty-one years and over liable to pay tax and to certain categories of women, one category of which consisted of those few women of twenty-one years of age and over who in fact paid tax. In the Protectorate, the tax assessment lists gave in theory a list of the great majority of the persons entitled to vote and no application was required from taxpayers; in practice, however, the tax lists were by no means complete or accurate in recording the names

[1] A full description of the preparation and publication of electoral rolls is to be found in Chapter VII of the first volume of the *Report on the first general elections in India, 1951-2.*
[2] See *Report of the Electoral Reform Commission,* Sierra Leone, 1954.

of taxpayers and the electoral registers produced from the tax lists suffered in accuracy accordingly. In the Colony, only a minority of the potential electorate could be registered automatically, as the assessment registers listed the names of owners but not the names of occupiers of property.[1] The moral to be drawn from the Sierra Leone experience and from earlier experiments in automatic registration in other West African territories is that tax and rate assessment registers may not prove to be entirely satisfactory basic documents for drawing up electoral registers, particularly if these documents were originally designed without the franchise in view.

This conclusion would appear to be supported by the experience gained at the first Municipal Elections in Kuching, Sarawak.[2] The report on these elections indicates that one of the franchise qualifications was the occupation of the whole or part of premises within the municipal area assessed at a certain minimum annual value or for which a certain minimum monthly rental was being paid. The electoral rolls were drawn up from the assessment registers in the Municipal Office and the names on the rolls were then checked by means of a house-to-house enquiry before inspection by the public. The fact that, with an electorate of rather over 4,500, no fewer than 237 persons came forward when the registers were open for public inspection and submitted claims stating that they had either been missed off the registers altogether or had been missed by the assistant registration officers in the course of the house-to-house enquiry suggests that the assessment registers were a far from accurate basis for electoral purposes. Nevertheless, in both Kuching, Sarawak, and in Sierra Leone, the final registers in all probability contained more electors and were in general better documents than would have been the case had registration been entirely voluntary.

In Singapore, where there is an identity card system in use, the particulars on the counterfoils of the identity cards are transferred to punched cards and statistical sorting and printing machines produce the provisional registers of electors, sorted by registration units and street addresses. When a person moves his

[1] See paragraphs 13-16 of the *Report on the Sierra Leone General Election, 1957.*

[2] See pages 3-4 and 9 of the *Report on the Kuching Municipal Council Elections held on 4th November, 1956.*

residence, he is legally required to report his change of address to the identity card registration authorities and corresponding changes are then made in the counterfoil; the statistical office is duly informed of the changes and the old punched card relating to the elector is cancelled and replaced with a new card. In practice, many persons change their address without informing the identity card registration authorities; in other respects the system is by no means foolproof, as many people leave the Colony permanently without surrendering their identity card. A new issue of identity cards has been under consideration in both Singapore and the Federation of Malaya for some years in view of the known inaccuracies in the existing identity card system. Despite these inaccuracies, however, the present arrangements are the best that can be devised for Singapore, where, it will be remembered, the original system of voluntary registration for elections proved to be an abject failure. It must be stressed, however, that a national registration system can only be maintained efficiently with a literate, civic-minded population and that electoral registration systems of the type in use in Singapore are in general better suited to conditions in Europe than to conditions in Africa or Asia.

In the United Kingdom, the registration officers are required each year to make a "house-to-house or other sufficient enquiry" "as to the persons entitled to be registered (excluding persons entitled to be registered in pursuance of a service declaration)".[1] In practice in most registration areas the enquiry is conducted by despatching a statutory form to each householder, and requiring him, under penalty for failure, to return the form with a statement of residents who possess the electoral qualifications on the qualifying date. The form is a simple one and is postal franked both outwardly and inwardly, so that the householder is put to no expense and but little trouble to supply the information required of him. But this method of conducting registration, like the method based on identity cards, is best suited to a literate and civic minded population.

In Canada there is no standing list of electors and, instead, new lists of electors are compiled for each and every election and by-election by enumerators.[2] The Canadian experience over eighty

[1] The Representation of the People Act, 1949, Sec. 9(1).
[2] The procedure for enumerating electors in Trinidad is similar to that of Canada, and the Trinidad Legislative Council Elections Ordinance is based on the Canadian Dominion Elections Act.

years suggests, according to an expert commentator, that any scheme of 'standing lists', kept up-to-date by regular revisions, cannot be operated satisfactorily in a country which has considerable internal movements of population and that any system which puts "the ultimate burden of compiling accurate lists not on the state, but on interested individuals and organisations . . . is certain to produce inaccurate and unsatisfactory lists".[1] Under present legislation, following the issue of a writ, enumerators are appointed by the returning officer after consultation with the party organisations which ran first and second at the last election; enumerators in urban areas work in pairs and bring to the returning officer lists compiled by going from door to door in the constituency, whilst, in the rural areas, enumerators work singly and door-to-door visitation can be replaced by other sources of information.

In Trinidad, as in Canada, there is an enumeration of electors before every general election.[2] One enumerator is appointed for each polling division (i.e. registration unit); each enumerator must be qualified as an elector in his own electoral district (i.e. registration area) and he should preferably be a resident of the polling division which he is enumerating. Ten days are allowed for the enumeration which seems ample in view of the fact that a polling division is defined as being one to contain approximately 450 electors only. The enumeration prior to the 1946 general election was conducted immediately after a census enumeration and, as far as possible, the same staff were used for the two operations. The enumeration prior to the 1950 general election was not quite so satisfactory, and the following extract from the Report on the 1950 general election is of considerable interest:

> Judging from the number of complaints received about enumeration, the actual listing of names was not as well done as it was in 1946 and this in spite of the fact that many of the enumerators had done the work before. In a few cases complainants were good enough to provide lists of their own showing names left out by the enumerators. It was possible to check these lists and it was found that they were, in large measure, accurate. Various reasons were adduced at the time for the inaccuracy of the lists. Among these were:
> (a) That many of the persons were labourers who were out in the fields for long hours of the day and were not easy to contact.

[1] Norman Ward, *The Canadian House of Commons — Representation*, p. 204.
[2] Reports on the 1946 and 1950 General Elections in Trinidad.

(b) That the amount paid to enumerators was not sufficient to induce them to do a proper job.

(c) That numerous persons refused to give the necessary information either from prejudice or fear of reprisals or on account of the mistaken belief they had already registered when interviewed by candidates and their helpers[1] and

(d) That enumerators were induced by certain persons interested in elections to enumerate only persons of a certain political leaning or of a certain race.[2]

Despite these inaccuracies in the Trinidad enumeration, however, the registration experience of Jamaica, as summarised in the 1957 Report of the Committee appointed to examine the existing electoral laws of Jamaica, suggests that in under-developed countries an enumeration of electors shortly before a general election is likely to prove to be one of the most effective methods of ensuring a reasonably good register at the election.

Arrangements for automatic registration of voters in France and her overseas territories are based on administrative commissions set up annually to revise the registers. The following brief description of registration in Togoland under French administration, extracted from the Report[3] of the United Nations Commissioner for the supervision of the 1958 general election in that territory, can be regarded as typical of the French system, in so far as the electoral system originally designed for Metropolitan France has been extended with minor alterations to the overseas territories. Within each constituency several administrative commissions are set up each year to revise the electoral registers. Both on the constituency commissions and the local commune commissions, there is included a representative of each political group as member, who is usually required to be a registered voter of the constituency and must be able to read and write. The commissions, which sit for a period of about six weeks each year, are required to register all those who have the statutory qualifications but are not already registered and to remove from the lists the names of deceased voters, of persons ordered by the courts to

---

[1] There is also a reference to the confusion caused by private enumeration on a party basis before the official enumeration in the Report on the 1957 General Election in St. Lucia. Some electors refused to give names 'a second time'.

[2] *Report on the 1950 General Election in Trinidad*, p. 10.

[3] U.N. Document T/1392 of 30 June, 1958.

be struck off and of persons who are wrongfully registered or no longer hold the qualifications. After the work of these commissions has been completed, the provisional registers are available for inspection and applications for deletion or inclusion of names can be made to adjudicating commissions. Finally, an appeal can be lodged to a magistrate against the decision of an adjudicating commission and, right up to the day of voting, the magistrates can deal directly and decide on applications for registration from persons claiming to have been omitted from the electoral lists owing to errors of a purely technical nature or to have been removed from the lists in disregard of the statutory formalities. This 'emergency registration' procedure by application to a magistrate has been of considerable importance in some of the overseas French territories; the United Nations Commissioner in French Togoland has commented:

> This provision, enacted in France shortly after the war, was intended to enable individual voters to have themselves registered on the electoral lists by the magistrates, after an individual inquiry. Omission for technical reasons meant omission because of errors arising, for example, out of an oversight during the copying of the lists, but the provision seems always to have been broadly interpreted, particularly in Togoland. This procedure — known as 'emergency registration' — was certainly not intended to cope with the flood of requests received by the Administration and the courts. Eighty thousand requests had to be examined by seven to nine magistrates in a period of two months.[1]

These applications represented about 20% of the number of persons on the registers produced by the administrative commissions and the large number clearly indicates that, in the conditions of an under-developed territory such as Togoland, there is no small difficulty in putting into practice the principal that registration is a matter of right and that it is the responsibility of the electoral administrative machinery to produce accurate registers.

THE SECOND STAGE — CLAIMS AND OBJECTIONS
AND REVISION OF THE PROVISIONAL REGISTER

When the first stage of registration has been completed, it is the practice to publish a provisional register containing the names

[1] *Report of the U.N. Commissioner for the Supervision of the Elections in Togoland under French Administration* (Document T/1392), p. 44.

and particulars of the electors. There is some variation in the elections legislation regarding the way in which these lists should be published. In the Federation of Malaya, the registration officer is under a legal obligation to have available for inspection in his own office a complete list of electors for the registration area; in 1955, after the initial registration period, the registration officers were also given instructions to have available for inspection the register for each registration unit at some suitable place within the boundaries of the unit, but this was an administrative rather than a legal requirement.

In the Western Region of Nigeria, the position is somewhat similar to the Federation of Malaya; in the Region, the manner of publication of the preliminary register "shall be by displaying the whole or part thereof in such places in the constituency as the Registration Officer thinks fit".[1] In some other countries, such as the Eastern Region of Nigeria and Zanzibar, however, the statutory requirement is to display a preliminary register of electors for each registration unit within the boundaries of the unit — in other words the emphasis is on the smaller registration unit rather than the larger registration area. As an example, the relevant regulation in the Zanzibar Legislative Council (Elections) Rules, 1957, reads as follows:

> Not later than the day after the receipt by him of the certified copies of the preliminary lists for his constituency the registration officer shall cause a certified copy of the preliminary list for a polling division to be affixed to one or more public buildings in each polling division in that constituency, or if there are no public buildings in such polling division, to a building in such polling division, having first obtained permission from the occupants, or shall otherwise cause a certified copy of the preliminary list to be exhibited in such a manner that it may be easily read by the public in a place of public resort in such polling division and such copies of the preliminary list shall remain posted up for not less than twenty days.[2]

The regulations lay down a period during which the lists must be available for inspection and during which claims and objections may be lodged. During this period, in a voluntary system of

[1] Reg. 19(2) of the Western Region Parliamentary and Local Government Electoral Regulations, 1955.

[2] Rule 17, Zanzibar Legislative Council (Elections) (Registration) Rules, 1957.

registration, any person whose name does not appear on the preliminary list and who submitted an application during the registration period may file a claim stating that his name has been omitted from the register; in an automatic system any person qualified to be an elector may submit a claim if his name is not on the register. An objection may be lodged by a person whose name appears on the preliminary register of electors against the inclusion either of his own name or the name of some other person in the list on the grounds that he or that other person is not qualified to be an elector.[1] In Western Nigeria the period during which claims and objections may be lodged lasts for fifteen days. The corresponding period in Uganda is twenty days. In the Federation of Malaya, the period is fourteen days. A period of two or three weeks appears to be fairly uniform. At the end of this period, lists of claims and objections are published locally prior to hearing and an opportunity is given for the making of objections to the registration of any person whose name is included in the list of claimants.

In countries in which initial registration has coincided with the emergence or existence of two strong political parties, considerable interest has been taken in the preliminary lists and large numbers of claims and objections have been lodged. In Zanzibar, for instance, in those constituencies in which rivalry between the Nationalist Party and the Afro-Shirazi Union was keenest in 1957, successful objections were raised against about one-quarter of the names on the preliminary list.[2] Again, in those parts of Western Nigeria in which the political conflict was most bitter, such as

[1] Usually any person on the electoral roll of a complete registration area (constituency) can object to the inclusion of a name on the same roll, irrespective of whether that name is in the register of the same registration unit as the objector or another registration unit. In Uganda, however, an objector can only object to a name appearing in the register of the same polling division (i.e. registration unit) where he himself is registered (Sec. 13(3) of the Uganda Legislative Council Elections Ordinance).

[2] The highest percentage was in the Ngambo constituency where, on a preliminary list of 6,622 persons there were 1,363 deletions as a result of objections made by representatives of political parties and 756 deletions as a result of investigations made on the initiative of the registration authorities. On the other hand, in Pemba South where there was little political rivalry, there were no deletions on objections made by political parties but about 10% of the names on the preliminary list were deleted as the result of investigation made on the initiative of the authorities. For more details see the *Report on the Elections in Zanzibar*, 1957, pp. 12-15.

THE REGISTRATION OF ELECTORS

75

Warri and Ibadan, the rival parties showed great zeal early in 1956
in "attending to the register" and making claims and objections;
in the Western Region as a whole, however, objections were not
numerous. In Sierra Leone, after publication of the provisional
registers prior to the 1957 elections, objections were not numerous
except in Freetown and one of the rural colony constituencies
neighbouring Freetown; in Freetown most of the objections were
the result of rivalry between the Creoles of Freetown and its
neighbourhood and residents of Protectorate origin, most of whom
had a legitimate claim to vote. On the other hand, in the Federation
of Malaya in 1955, there was only one party — the Alliance —
with a widespread branch organisation and this party would have
been cutting its own throat had it registered objections in bulk
on racial or other grounds, as was done in Zanzibar; partly for this
reason and partly because all parties knew that the assistant
registration officers had already investigated the validity of a fair
sample of the applications for registration, there were very few
objections in Malaya.

In an effort to keep the number of objections within bounds,
some countries have imposed a deposit, which must be paid by
the objector at the time of making an objection. In Mauritius,
for instance, a deposit of ten rupees has to be paid with each
objection; this deposit is returned to the objector if the objection
made is successful and is awarded to the person objected
against or forfeited to the Crown if the objection is unsuccessful.[1]
In Uganda, an objector has to pay a small deposit of two
shillings, which is refunded if the objection is upheld. If an
objection is overruled by the officer conducting the enquiry,
that officer has power not only to forfeit the deposit but, in
addition, to order the objector to pay up to five pounds to the
persons objected to as compensation if it is considered that the
objection was made without reasonable cause.[2] Similarly in
Tanganyika, an objection has to be accompanied by the
sum of twenty shillings as a deposit "which shall be liable to
be forfeited to the Government if the objection is disallowed
and the Resident Magistrate holds that the grounds of objection
were not reasonable".[3] There is, however, no provision for

[1] Section 14 of the Mauritius Local Government Elections Ordinance, 1956.
[2] Sec. 13(13) of the Uganda Legislative Council Elections Ordinance.
[3] Section 51 of the Tanganyika Legislative Council Elections Ordinance, 1956.

the payment of a deposit of this kind in Zanzibar,[1] Eastern Nigeria, Western Nigeria, the Gambia or the Federation of Malaya. The trouble about a deposit is that it is likely to be a deterrent to an individual elector objecting to the inclusion of another name in the list even if the former feels quite certain of his facts.

Another method of restricting the number of objections is to require that an objector can only object to a name appearing in the register of the registration unit where he himself is registered and not to names appearing on the register of other registration units in the same registration area. This restriction is incorporated in the present legislation dealing with Legislative Council Elections[2] in Uganda and has been recommended by the Supervisor of the 1957 Elections in Zanzibar[3] as a desirable amendment to the existing legislation in the latter territory. In the author's opinion, however, such a restriction is undesirable as there are likely to be small local pockets of the electorate who unanimously support a particular political party. If objections are restricted to electors of the same registration unit, it would be theoretically possible for the register relating to a particular unit to be padded with the names of unqualified persons who support the party or candidate universally popular within the unit and for electors elsewhere in the registration area to be powerless to object.

The usual procedure for disposing of claims and objections is for the registration officer to call the parties concerned to his office, where he hears evidence at a public enquiry on a fairly informal basis and makes his decision, against which there is an appeal to a 'Revising Officer' or to the Courts. Where claims and objections have amounted to an appreciable percentage of the names on the preliminary register, it has been necessary to make provision for the employment of 'registration advisers' to assist the registration officers to dispose of claims and objections with reasonable rapidity. In the Western Region of Nigeria, in 1956, the Electoral Commissioner made use of the powers given him in the Electoral Regulations[4] to nominate a number of barristers

[1] The Supervisor of the 1957 Elections in Zanzibar considers that it would have been desirable to have had a deposit payable on making an objection, see the Report, p. 51.

[2] Sec. 13(3).

[3] *Report on the Elections in Zanzibar, 1957*, pp. 51-2.

[4] Reg. 23(6) of the Western Region Parliamentary and Local Government Electoral Regulations, 1955.

from Ibadan to conduct hearings in the Warri area, where objections were particularly numerous. Similarly in Zanzibar in 1957 the Supervisor of Elections made use of the powers given to him in the Legislative Council Elections Decree (Section 8(2)) to appoint registration advisers to hear claims and objections and "to advise the registration officer as to his decision on such claims and objections". There is a similar provision in the Mauritius Local Government Ordinance, 1956.[1]

In the Eastern Region of Nigeria, there is no appeal against the decision of the Electoral Officer (i.e. registration officer) on a claim or objection.[2] In the Gambia, Northern Ireland and in Tanganyika, the registration officer does not hear claims and objections; instead they go direct to the Revising Officer (in the Gambia and Northern Ireland) and the Resident Magistrate (in Tanganyika) for hearing. In Great Britain, Uganda and the Federa- of Malaya, the procedure is as outlined in the first sentence of the preceding paragraph.

The kind of difficulties which may arise in the claims and objections period are clearly illustrated by the course of events prior to the 1957 elections in Zanzibar, described in the following extracts from the report of the Supervisor of Elections:

> The Elections Decree envisaged objections being lodged by individual electors, but from the very first it was evident that no individual elector was prepared to incur the odium of 'denouncing his neighbour', and the lodging of objections was left entirely to party agents. Long lists of persons objected to, containing often several hundred names, were now being handed in to Registration Officers by a single objector. Our original intention was that the Registration Officer should distribute the objections to be con- sidered amongst his Registration Advisers, who, sitting separately and simultaneously, would be able to deal with from fifty to a hundred cases in a single session. When only a single objector appeared only one objection could be dealt with at a time. Our proposed arrangement had accordingly for the time being to be abandoned, and although in due course we managed to persuade the Nationalist Party to appoint additional objectors, the latter were so comparatively few in number that proceedings were still seriously delayed.

[1] Section 23.
[2] Regulation 12(3) of the Eastern House of Assembly Electoral Regulations, 1955.

The system of package objections provoked a series of protests from the Afro-Shirazi Union. Nationalist Party objectors, they claimed, were committing wholesale perjury in swearing away qualifications of scores of electors of whose origin and personal histories they could know nothing. Many of their objections, indeed, were lodged upon what seemed to be very inadequate grounds. Their packages were carelessly made up, and a good many persons were included merely because their names in the pre-liminary lists of electors indicated the possibility of a mainland origin.

A good deal of trouble was caused by the difficulty, in an urban area with a shifting population, of finding persons against whom objections had been lodged, and who had no recognisable address. It was clearly right that they should be given every reasonable chance of appearing to substantiate their claims. Extra process servers were accordingly engaged to assist Headmen to look for them; a senior Elections Officer was drafted in from another constituency to organise the service of summonses; and nightly lists of 'wanted' persons were read out on the Zanzibar radio. Even so hundreds of these persons were never traced. Many of them were unknown even to the party agent who lodged objections against them.

Very similar difficulties occurred in the Warri area of the Western Region of Nigeria in 1956. A large number of names on the preliminary register were objected to by a member of one or other of the tribes, simply because they appeared to belong to members of the opposite tribe and blocks of a hundred or so names were objected to by the same person. Although every effort was made to expedite the hearings, the proceedings took so long and there was such noise among the milling crowds outside the rooms in which the cases were being heard that many people had lost heart and gone home by the time their cases came up for hearing. As a result some 8,200 names on the preliminary registers in Warri were struck off, in many cases because the persons objected to did not appear when they were called.[1]

In Eastern Nigeria at the initial registration prior to the elections to the Eastern House of Assembly in 1957, a large number of block objections were lodged. If an objector did not appear at

---

[1] In Freetown, Sierra Leone, too, in 1957, the revising officers' courts did not announce in advance the cases to be considered at each session and a number of persons were struck off the registers because they were not present when their names were called.

the proper time, the objection was over-ruled; if, on the other hand, the person whose name was objected to did not appear, his name was deleted if it appeared to the Electoral Officer that the objection had some foundation.[1]

There has not, however, invariably been such enthusiasm for 'attending to the register' even at initial registration. In the Federation of Malaya in 1955, few electors bothered to inspect the provisional registers and claims and objections were negligible in number. In India, the number of claims and objections was small in relation to the total electorate; with an electorate of 173 million persons, there were rather over one and a half million claims and rather under three-quarters of a million objections, the great majority of which were allowed.[2] Indeed, the problem has usually been to devise methods of persuading the adult members of a peasant society to take steps to ensure that their own names are correctly entered on the registers.

The confusion which existed in parts of Zanzibar and the Western and Eastern Regions of Nigeria during the claims and objections period at initial registration is unlikely to be so marked at revisions of the register, when the additions to the register will only be a fairly small proportion of the total electorate. Indeed, in the long run, the re-drafting of legislation and the issue of suitable administrative instructions to registration staff regarding the claims and objections period are likely to depend on policy decisions as to where to strike a balance between, on the one hand, encouraging the individual elector to overcome apathy and ignorance and to take an interest in the provisional register and, on the other hand, discouraging the political party with an axe to grind from making wholesale objections based on narrow racial or tribal grounds without any detailed knowledge of the individuals to whom objection is taken. Some of the specific problems on which policy decisions will be required are:

(a) whether to impose the payment of a deposit as a condition for making an objection;

(b) whether to publish the provisional registers as lavishly as possible — both for the registration area as a whole and

[1] See J. H. Price 'The Eastern Nigerian General Election of 1957' in W. J. M. Mackenzie and K. E. Robinson (eds.), *Five Elections in Africa*.

[2] See pp. 68-9 of the *Report on the first general elections in India, 1951-2*, Vol. I.

separately for each registration unit — or whether to restrict publication for each unit to the geographical boundaries of the unit, on the theory that only local residents are likely to have detailed knowledge of the personal particulars of their neighbours;

(c) how to ensure that notices to interested parties regarding the hearing of claims and objections reach their proper destinations.

The Third Stage — The Publication of Certified Registers

After all claims and objections have been disposed of, the register is corrected and sent to be duplicated or printed. In many countries of Asia and Africa the registers have been printed apparently because the electoral regulations demand that this must be done. However, it is unlikely that more than a hundred or so copies of the final register will be required in under-developed countries, particularly where there is to be a frequent revision of the register, and printing of the register may, with limited printing resources, be unnecessarily expensive and time consuming.[1] The Western Region of Nigeria is an example of a country which had considerable difficulty with the printing of the registers.[2] Part of the registers had to be printed in Europe in order to have them available in time for the elections and the fact that the printers and the elections authority were some thousands of miles apart inevitably led to a number of errors. In India, where an average of about 200 copies of the electoral rolls were printed, the Chief Election Commissioner records that the State Government had to distribute the work of printing amongst a large number of private and government presses and that "comparatively high charges had to be paid for printing on account of the shortness of the period within which the work was required to be completed".[3]

[1] The Electoral Commissioner responsible for Municipal Elections in Mauritius has estimated that the cost of a printed register is three to four times greater than the cost of a cyclostyled register, and that duplication involves an appreciable saving in time as compared with printing.

[2] See the *Report on the holding of the 1956 parliamentary election to the Western House of Assembly*, Nigeria, p. 6.

[3] P. 75 of the *Report on the first general elections in India, 1951-2*, Vol. I.

In the Federation of Malaya, in 1955, the electoral registers containing the names of one and a quarter million electors were duplicated with the assistance of typists seconded temporarily from other Government Departments over a period of about two months. The possibility of introducing a card index system and compiling the registers by photography after ordering the cards by pages was considered by an organisation and methods committee, but was rejected, partly because of the possibility that there would be numerous corrections and additions to be made to the rolls after the first elections and the first revision of the registers. A card index system combined with some form of automatic reproduction in bulk is, however, well suited to a settled system of registration in which the annual turnover is only a small proportion of the total number of names on the register.

In the Eastern Region of Nigeria in 1957, the House of Assembly Electoral Regulations did not prescribe the form which the registers were to take nor were the registration officials under a statutory obligation to produce a sufficient number of copies of the registers to make them available for sale, or even for issue, to validly nominated candidates. As a result of this lack of direction, each Electoral Officer (the Eastern Nigerian equivalent of registration officer) relied upon his own ingenuity in producing the final registers. Some of the final registers were typed or cyclostyled, whilst other registers in their final form were written in pencil in school exercise books, duplicate copies having been made by putting carbon paper between the leaves.

In Zanzibar, the regulations covering initial registration in 1957 required that the registers, revised in the light of successful claims and objections, should be sent to the Supervisor of Elections and printed and returned to the registration officers, for posting in the polling division, within nine days of the last date for their receipt by the Supervisor. This allowed only seven days for printing and the job was beyond the capacity of the local press. The printers therefore printed proofs on the basis of the preliminary register, removed names after successful objections and added a supplementary list on the basis of successful claims. The final lists were thus printed in two parts. Not very surprisingly, the final lists were not free from errors and, owing to a lack of effective supervision by some of the registration officers, the names of a number of electors, against whom objections had been successfully taken, had not been struck off, and the names of a number of successful claimants had not been included. The moral to be drawn from this is that a registration officer employing inexperienced clerks on registration work must exercise personal supervision over every stage in the registration process, however obvious and routine the steps in the process may appear to him to be.

The registration officer is usually required to certify the register before publication and a copy of his certificate is frequently printed as part of the register. The newly certified and published register comes into force on a date specified either in the legislation or (if the date varies each year) by public notice, and the old register (if any), which it displaces, ceases to have effect. The timing of the coming into force of the new registers is sometimes a matter of political significance, as one party may prefer to fight an election on an old register and another party may view the new register with more favour; and for this reason it is probably preferable to have a statutory date for bringing new registers into force if revision of the register takes place each year.

In most British Commonwealth countries in Asia and Africa, the electoral authority is required to make available a reasonable number of copies of the register for sale to the public and is given power to prescribe the price to be paid for such copies. This is the practice, in, for instance, the Western Region of Nigeria, Zanzibar, Mauritius and the Federation of Malaya. In the Gambia, the Colony Elections Ordinance, 1954, requires that the registers of voters should be printed and published[1] but there is not apparently a statutory requirement that the registers should be made available for sale to the public. In the United Kingdom, the price charged for copies of the register is just about sufficient to cover the cost of paper and printing without taking into consideration the work put into the preparation of the register by the registration officer and his assistants. Some large commercial firms purchase complete copies of the electoral registers, presumably as a basis for advertising, and this raises the questions of whether the price charged for the register should be a commercial rather than a bare cost price and of whether sales of the electoral registers should be restricted to persons who can prove that they are making the purchase for political ends.

[1] Section 30.

THE PERIOD REQUIRED FOR REGISTRATION

The total period required from the beginning of the registration period to the publication of the final registers during large-scale initial registration in a voluntary system has varied from three to six months where there has been pressure on the election administration to have the stage set for early elections. The period has been much longer where pressures have not been so great. In Zanzibar in 1957, when a total of just under 40,000 persons were registered as electors, eighty-eight days were required in any given constituency from the commencement of registration to the publication of the register for that constituency; only one week was given for application for registration in each constituency and the preliminary lists were compiled in the central election office in the following two weeks; the period allowed for the inspection of the registers by the electorate, the hearing of claims and objections and the consequent revision of the preliminary lists consumed fifty-eight days. In Western Nigeria, registration of nearly two million electors prior to the 1957 elections to the Western House of Assembly started at the beginning of November, 1955, and the final registers were ready for publication on 1st May, 1956 — a total of six months. One month was allowed for submission of registration applications and one month for the completion of preliminary registers; the inspection of the registers and the settlement of claims and objections took rather less time than in Zanzibar, but a number of weeks were required for the printing of the final registers in Nigeria, the Gold Coast, the United Kingdom, and Holland. In the Federation of Malaya in 1954/55, when one and a quarter million electors were registered, the total period required was six and a half months; the period for submission of applications was extended from four weeks to one and a half months as the result of political pressure; nearly two months were given for the preparation of preliminary registers, though this period could have been reduced if necessary to four or five weeks; there were few claims and objections and the revision of the preliminary lists was not therefore a time consuming process; the final registers were duplicated in two and a half months, but the period could again have been reduced by employing a larger staff for a shorter period had this been absolutely necessary. Where elections have been on a rather smaller scale — e.g. municipal elections — the time required to produce a certified register of electors has normally been of the order of three months. In Port Louis, Mauritius, in 1956, a completely new register of local government electors containing the names of 24,000 persons was prepared following the revision of the relevant legislation and the work occupied a total of three months divided as follows:

Registration of applications	23 days
Preparation of preliminary lists	16 days
Inspection of registers and consideration of claims and objections	45 days
Preparation of final registers	11 days

Where revisions of the register are undertaken annually according to a set timetable, the period allowed from the beginning of the revision to the certification of new registers is usually of the order of four or five months. In Great Britain, the registration officers send out forms to householders for completion in September or early October, and the new register comes into force in the following February. In the Western Region of Nigeria, the period for applying for registration begins on the first day of January each year and the new registers come into force on the first day of May. In Mauritius, under the new Local Government Elections Ordinance, 1956, a rather lengthy period of three and a half months (from the beginning of April to the middle of July) is allowed for submitting applications for new registration or for changes in existing registration and the new registers are required to be published at some date between 15th November and 20th November — the whole interval between the commencement of registration and the publication of the rolls being in this case as much as seven and a half months.

CHAPTER V

THE FRANCHISE

ADULTS who live in the United Kingdom are now accustomed to regard the vote as a right. Only middle-aged and old people have any clear personal recollection of the sometimes dramatic fight for votes for women,[1] and it comes as a surprise to visitors from England and North America to find that women are still denied the vote in Switzerland[2] and in most Muslim countries. The system of universal and equal adult suffrage, whether for both men and women or for men only, is, however, in most countries, a fairly recent introduction; thus, in England, the concept of votes for all adults displaced a system of voting restricted, in broad outline, to holders of property, as the result of a series of amendments to the law starting with the Reform Act of 1832. Universal adult franchise was in fact only introduced in English Local Government Elections as recently as 1948.

Even in the England of to-day, universal adult franchise is subject to some limitations. For instance, aliens resident in the United Kingdom are not entitled to be registered as electors. The law prescribes certain incapacities. Peers have no right to vote at parliamentary elections and persons certified as being of unsound mind are disqualified; there are other disqualifications based on criminal convictions and corrupt or illegal electoral practices. Nevertheless, the present English electoral system is founded on the idea that voting is essentially a right to which all adult British subjects resident in the country are entitled rather than a privilege to be based on property, income, education or status.

The British Commonwealth countries in Asia which have gained independence since the Second World War are, in general, firmly wedded to the concept of universal adult suffrage. The Federation of Malaya gives the vote to all adult Federal citizens

---

[1] Women in Japan were enfranchised in 1946, less than twenty years after British and American women had won the right to vote.

[2] The (male) voters of Switzerland have voted against the enfranchisement of women in a nation-wide referendum held in January, 1959.

resident in the country subject to the standard list of disqualifications based on mental incapacity, criminal convictions, etc.; in Malaya the pressure exerted by the Chinese and Indian communities to widen the constitutional provisions on citizenship is in effect a struggle to extend the franchise to give more voting power to the Chinese and the Indians. The Government of independent India adopted the principle of adult suffrage despite the difficulties involved in putting this principle into practice.

It is pre-eminently in Africa that the idea of the vote as a privilege still holds sway. Qualifications for the franchise based on literacy, educational qualifications, income, or the ownership or occupation of property can be found in the Rhodesias, Nyasaland, Kenya, Tanganyika, Uganda, Zanzibar, Sierra Leone and the Gambia, to take but a few examples. Reports such as the Coutts Commission Report on African elections in Kenya[1] and the Tredgold Commission Report on elections in Southern Rhodesia[2] stress that qualitative tests for the franchise are a necessary feature of electoral arrangements in countries whose peoples are far from homogeneous and where there is a high percentage of illiteracy.

The qualifications and disqualifications of electors in Tanganyika, Uganda, Kenya, the Gambia, Western Nigeria and Eastern Nigeria illustrate the range of variation in the franchise schemes adopted. In Tanganyika, voters for Legislative Council elections must be at least twenty-one years old, possess the requisite residential qualifications and have an educational, income or office holder qualification; disqualifications relate to unsoundness of mind and criminal lunacy, conviction and sentence to death or imprisonment, and conviction for electoral offences.[3] In Uganda, African voters in Legislative Council elections must be at least twenty-one years old, be resident in the electoral district in which they are registered and be the owner or occupier of land or possess a literacy qualification or a public service or agricultural employment qualification or have a certain minimum income; the disqualifications are similar to those of Tanganyika, with the addition that non-Africans are, of course, not entitled to vote in

---

[1] *Report of the Commissioner appointed to Enquire into Methods for the Selection of African Representatives to the Legislative Council*, 1955.

[2] *Report of the Franchise Commission*, 1957.

[3] Tanganyika Legislative Council Elections Ordinance, 1957, Sections 5-12.

African elections.[1] The most complicated franchise is that of
Kenya, where African Legislative Council electors must all be
British subjects or British protected persons and have attained the
age of twenty-one years, must be members of an African tribe
indigenous to East Africa and must have been born in Kenya or
been resident there for ten years. Voters are awarded one, two or
three votes according to their possession of one, two, or three or
more qualifications which are under the broad heads of education,
property or income, service in the armed forces or in the police
or prisons service, seniority through having reached the grade of
elder or the age of forty-five years (men only), higher education,
past or present membership of the central legislature or a local
government authority, and meritorious service rewarded with a
civil or military decoration. There are additional qualifications
relating only to certain tribes (Kikuyu, Embu and Meru) which
were involved in the Mau-Mau rebellion and some of the disqualifications are a reflection of the emergency in Kenya.[2] In the
Gambia, Legislative Council electors must be British subjects or
British protected persons of the age of twenty-five years or over
and are required to possess a residential qualification; disqualifications are somewhat similar to those of Tanganyika but there
are differences in detail.[3] In Western Nigeria, for election to the
Western House of Assembly, the qualifications of electors, all of
whom must be British subjects or British protected persons, are
based on either residence in the constituency and payment of
taxes for a prescribed period of two years, or birth in the constituency coupled with being either twenty-one years of age or over or
payment of taxes for one year; disqualifications are very similar to
those of the Gambia.[4] Finally, in Eastern Nigeria for election to
the Eastern House of Assembly, electors must be British subjects
or British protected persons of the age of twenty-one years or over
and satisfy either birth or residential qualifications.

This indigestible list of qualifications and disqualifications
could be extended indefinitely by a description of the franchise in

[1] Uganda Legislative Council Elections Ordinance, 1957, Sections 9 and 10.
[2] Kenya Legislative Council (African Representation) Ordinance, 1956,
Sections 12 and 13.
[3] The Gambia Colony Elections Ordinance, 1954, Section 3. Elections in
the Gambia at present cover only a small part of the Colony.
[4] The Western Region Parliamentary and Local Government Electoral
Regulations, 1955, Regs. 10 and 11.

other territories and by the provision of more details of the peculiar features of each territory. It seems preferable, however, to consider the qualifications and disqualifications on a functional rather than a territorial basis, particularly with a view to drawing conclusions, where possible, regarding the implications from the point of view of those charged with the task of administering the electoral system. We shall start by considering qualifications which are in fairly general use.

AGE

The minimum age for electors varies from eighteen upwards.[1] In Africa and Asia, the registration of births is incomplete and age has frequently to be estimated, because individuals may not know their correct age. Experience of the results of population censuses in under-developed territories shows a strong tendency for people, particularly adults, to state ages in round figures. Moreover, some cultural communities, for instance many Muslim communities, reckon age in lunar rather than solar years; again the Chinese method of reckoning age gives a child the age of one during the first Chinese calendar year of its existence, two during its second Chinese calendar year, and so on. A minimum age for the registration of electors is thus liable to be less accurate in practice than in theory and appropriate instructions have to be given to the registration officials to enable them to make decisions on doubtful cases. If the minimum age for electors is twenty-one, it may be possible to get over the difficulty if some event of local historical importance took place approximately twenty-one years prior to the registration period; all persons born prior to that event would be eligible for registration. In the Sudan, where an elector must be not less than twenty-one years of age on the date of application for registration for voting in House of Representatives elections and not less than thirty years of age for voting in Senate elections, registration officers were given the following notes of guidance:

> If there is a dispute as to the age of a person you can draw some help from his physical appearance. You can also ask him questions about the year in which he left the Kuttab or the year in which he left the Intermediate school. Usually people leave the Kuttab at

[1] Countries in which the minimum age for voting is less than twenty-one include the Soviet Union, Indonesia, Iraq and Syria.

the age of twelve or eleven and the Intermediate school at the age of 16 or 17. Of course he may not tell you the truth.

You may also try to get a birth certificate if you can. You may rely but not much on the words of the father as to the age of his son. However, if in your opinion the applicant is less than twenty-one years of age in the case of the House of Representatives or less than 30 years in the case of the Senate you must then reject his application straight away. He may go to the court and appeal against your decision.

In Indonesia, where the less educated section of the population marry at a fairly early age, the qualification is the attainment of eighteen years of age or the status of having a wife or husband. In this way, difficulties over the determination of age have, for the most part, been neatly side-tracked. In parts of Africa, the African population are liable to pay an adult poll-tax on reaching a given age and the determination of age for electoral purposes can be made to hinge on the number of payments of poll-tax so far made; this would not, of course, necessarily result in a strictly accurate register, because some persons may have started to pay tax at an age above or below the statutory age. It is reported for instance, that in the Sierra Leone elections of 1957 persons applied to vote and had their names traced in the registers who were obviously well below not merely the minimum voting age of twenty-one but also the minimum taxpaying age of eighteen.

There are some particularly illuminating comments contained in the United Nations Reports on the referendum in British Togoland in 1956 and the general election in French Togoland in 1958 on the subject of evidence of age. In British Togoland, registration assistants were instructed to ask male applicants when payment of taxes had begun, if in doubt about an applicant having reached the minimum voting age; the obligation to pay tax begins at the age of eighteen. As regards women who do not pay taxes, the registration assistants were asked to bear in mind that "a woman who has had two children is probably over twenty-one. In this criterion the Administration has not merely wished to uphold the sound consideration that a mother of two children has surely come of age. An important native custom is observed for this conclusion. It is usual that girls marry around the age of seventeen or eighteen and would have their first child within the following year, but after this first childbirth the young wife retires to her mother's home and remains with her, caring for her child, for two or three years, after which she joins her husband and then probably has a second child, which may be safely calculated to be born when the mother is over twenty-one".[1] The Report goes on to say that "physical features of young persons have been considered, and chiefs and elders have been able to offer considerable assistance to ascertain the age of applicants. Questioning has been strongly based on custom. Men have been asked in many places not how many years they are old but how many crops they have helped collect, or how tall they were when a given event took place". In French Togoland, too, women who had at least two children were presumed to be twenty-one years of age; there, as in British Togoland, "physical appearance, particularly the hair style, or the shape or firmness of the breasts, often served as a criterion. Where the applicant appeared in person before the magistrate, even if the latter worked rapidly, there was at least a minimum of assurance; where the inquiry was made by the Administration and the judge relied on documentary evidence, that element of assurance tended to disappear. This explains such oddities as the case where a woman was ruled not to be of the required age although her son was registered as an elector".[2]

Zanzibar and Kenya have provided, in addition to a minimum age of twenty-five and twenty-one respectively for all voters irrespective of other qualifications, for the age of forty and forty-five respectively as an alternative to other qualifications in a qualitative franchise. In Zanzibar, every elector has, inter alia, to be able to read English or Arabic or Swahili or to be of the age of forty or over.[3] In Kenya, the attainment of the age of forty-five was one of the alternative qualifications which determined the voting power of each elector. It is not clear what criteria were adopted to estimate the ages of forty or forty-five in these two territories, but the results must in any case have been rather approximate.

In the Gambia, where the minimum age for electors is twenty-five, the Colony Commissioner in charge of the initial registration under the 1954 Colony Elections Ordinance commented:

[1] *Report of the United Nations Plebiscite Commissioner for the Trust Territory of Togoland under British Administration* (Document A/3173), p. 145.
[2] *Report of the United Nations Commissioner for the Supervision of the Elections in Togoland under French Administration* (Document T/1392), p. 63.
[3] Section 4(c) of the Zanzibar Legislative Council Elections Decree.

We had great difficulty in determining the ages of some claimants as they cannot all produce birth certificates. In some cases we referred to school records in which the ages of pupils are entered but these ages are very often understated. In the end the political parties realised that it was very difficult to prove that a claimant had not reached a particular age and they came to a working agreement not to dispute entries in the list of voters on grounds of age in the Revising Officer's Court.

It has undoubtedly been necessary to come to some practical working arrangement in respect of age determination in most African territories.

SEX

A few countries do not accept women as electors. Examples are Zanzibar, Northern Nigeria, Iraq, Transjordan and the Sudan,[1] where most of the population is Muslim, the Bahamas[2] and Switzerland. In African territories with a qualitative franchise, the minimum qualifications required of electors are sometimes such that very few women succeed in getting their names on the electoral rolls. Thus, in Kenya, less than 1% of the electorate registered for the first African elections were women; similarly in the Protectorate area of Sierra Leone only a very small proportion of the electorate consisted of women.[3] Again, in Syria under the Electoral Law of 1949 every Syrian, male and female, who is eighteen years old or over, has the right of suffrage, but there is a proviso that women must have at least a certificate of primary education in order to be allowed to vote. On the other hand, in some West African and Asian countries, there are about as many or more female voters registered than males — e.g. the Western Region of Nigeria.[4] Where there is a full adult franchise, the number of female voters will normally exceed the number of male voters, owing to higher male mortality in the pre-adult age groups.

[1] Women (fifteen in number) were enrolled as voters in the Graduates' Constituency in the Sudan at the first general elections.
[2] Sec. 15 of the Bahamas General Assembly Act, 1946.
[3] In Sierra Leone very few Protectorate women pay tax, and payment of tax is one of the franchise qualifications.
[4] The 1956 figures for the Western Region were 1,009,716 female electors in a total 1,947,152 (Appendix I of the Report on the 1956 Parliamentary Election).

Residence

The residential qualification required of electors varies very considerably from one country to another. In the United Kingdom, the qualification for parliamentary electors is based on a person's residence on a particular qualifying date and length of past residence is not a factor in the determination of any question as to a person's residence on the qualifying date. The residential qualification in many countries of Africa is, however, based not only on actual residence either on a particular date or at the time of application for registration as an elector but also on length of past residence either in the country or in the constituency in which the applicant desires to be registered.

The United Kingdom franchise is unusually generous to British subjects who have recently taken up residence in the country, as newcomers who possess the other qualifications are eligible to be registered as electors at the first revision of the registers after their arrival. A British subject from the United Kingdom taking up residence in some of the African territories or countries of the Commonwealth would not be in such a favourable position; in the Gambia, for instance, he would have to have been ordinarily resident for at least a year prior to the beginning of the registration period in the constituency in which he wished to be registered and to vote;[1] in Tanganyika he would have either to have been ordinarily resident in the territory for a period of not less than three years out of the five years immediately preceding his application to register or, at the time of application to register, to be in possession of a valid 'certificate of permanent residence'.[2] In the Federation of Rhodesia and Nyasaland, an applicant for registration must be resident in the constituency at the date of his application and must have been so resident for a continuous period of three months immediately preceding that date *and* must have been resident in the Federation for a continuous period of two years.[3]

It is, of course, natural that a prospective elector should be required to show some identification with the country in whose elections he wishes to take part, and where, as in many British African territories, there is no local citizenship, it is understandable

---

[1] The Colony Elections Ordinance, Section 3(1)(c).
[2] The Tanganyika Legislative Council Elections Ordinance, Sec. 6.
[3] The Electoral Act, 1958, Sec. 16.

that the residential qualification should be used as a means of establishing this identification. But those Governments which require a prospective elector to identify himself by possessing a residential qualification over a period of time in a particular constituency are, perhaps, more open to criticism; it is difficult to see why a person whose work requires him to transfer his residence at frequent intervals from one constituency to another should be penalised through failure to satisfy the residential qualification in any one constituency. Electors in the Western Region of Nigeria, for instance, are either residents of two years' standing in or are natives of the Division in which the constituency is situated.[1] As application for registration as an elector must be made in person and there are no provisions for postal or proxy voting in Nigeria, it would appear that a native of one Division of the Region whose work involves residence in another Division will be at some practical disadvantage for the first two years or so of his residence; the position in the Eastern Region of Nigeria is similar, save that the qualifying period of residence for persons who are not 'natives' of the constituency is twelve months rather than two years.[2] The residential qualification in Sierra Leone is identical with that of Eastern Nigeria. In these three territories, there seems to be no very good reason why length of residence should not relate to the territory as a whole, with actual residence on the qualifying date deciding the constituency in which the applicant should be registered, and a residential qualification of this kind has been adopted in, for instance, Tanganyika and Zanzibar.

There may be, in special circumstances, very good reasons for enforcing a length of residence qualification for registration in a constituency. Mackenzie states that ". . . an Act of 1949 restored a qualifying period of three months' residence for registration in any constituency in Northern Ireland; this was done because there was a slight risk that the balance in some marginal constituencies there might be upset if additional voters could be brought across the vexed Border in large numbers to establish residence with friends for a day or two at the time of registration."[3] But, barring special circumstances of this nature, the requirement of a period

---

[1] 'Native' in relation to a Division means a person who was born in, or whose father was born in that Division. See Reg. 10 of the Western Region Parliamentary and Local Government Electoral Regulations, 1955.

[2] Reg. 7 of the Eastern House of Assembly Electoral Regulations, 1955.

[3] W. J. M. Mackenzie, *Free Elections*, p. 28.

of residence in a constituency rather than in a country simply has the effect of disfranchising a number of people who are, for one reason or another, internal migrants in their own country.

In Kenya, where there is a good deal of movement of the African population between the tribal areas on the one hand and the towns and the 'white highlands' on the other hand, Africans are permitted to register either in the electoral area (constituency) containing their own 'native land unit' or in "the electoral area in which such African resides, carries on business or is employed".[1] Non-Africans in Kenya can register for an electoral area in which the applicant resides, carries on a business or is employed.[2] It is, in the author's opinion, difficult to justify permitting applicants for registration such a choice of electoral area, for many people may work in one such area and live in another. In the first place, there may well be people registered in more than one electoral area, despite the provision of the law forbidding it, unless there is sufficient liaison between the various registration officers to prevent it. Secondly, a register in a marginal constituency can be packed at the instigation of a particular party or candidate by the employees of a large factory or business, though very few of them live there.

CITIZENSHIP OR NATIONALITY

Where a self-governing country (e.g. India, Indonesia, the Federation of Malaya) or a non self-governing territory (e.g. Zanzibar) has its own citizenship, electors must usually be citizens to obtain a parliamentary vote or even a local government elections vote. Many non self-governing territories do not, however, possess a citizenship of their own, and, in some British Commonwealth territories in Africa, the requirement is, instead, that the elector should be either a British subject or a British protected person. A qualification of this kind can be found throughout the non self-governing territories of British West Africa, but, in the Gold Coast prior to independence, the franchise was also extended to persons other than British subjects or British protected persons who were serving in the armed forces of the Crown or in the Gold Coast Police Force. The position has changed since the attainment of independence and the substitution of the name 'Ghana' for

[1] Sec. 14, The Legislative Council (African Representation) Ordinance, 1956.
[2] Sec. 9(1)(i) The Legislative Council Ordinance.

'Gold Coast', and electors must now be, *inter alia*, citizens of Ghana.

There has been less uniformity in East and Central Africa in imposing a nationality or citizenship qualification in the franchise. In Northern Rhodesia and Nyasaland, electors have in the past had to be British subjects and, as the vast majority of Africans are British protected persons rather than British subjects, the great majority of the voters in those two countries have been European. Southern Rhodesia has its own citizenship, but it is the literacy qualification and means test which preserve a European majority on the electoral roll and not the African's citizenship status, which is acquired by birth within the territory. Further north, in East Africa, Uganda has not imposed any nationality qualification for voters in the first African elections held in 1958 under the Uganda Legislative Council Elections Ordinance of 1957, nor has Tanganyika done so for voters in the first elections held under the Tanganyika Legislative Council Elections Ordinance. Kenya requires of African electors that they should be British subjects or British protected persons and, in addition, members of an African tribe indigenous to East Africa. Elections in East Africa are in fact organised on the basis of a franchise restricted by means of qualifications other than a nationality qualification; in any country, variables such as birth and length of residence can of course be used in addition to, or instead of nationality, in order to define the group of people who are to be regarded as the genuine inhabitants of a country to whom voting power should be given.

Where the vote is regarded as the right of adult citizens, a combination of age, sex, residential and nationality qualifications (or of some of these qualifications) determine the franchise. Where the vote is regarded as a privilege, additional qualifications may be enforced based on literacy, education, income, or the ownership or occupation of property. Qualifications of this latter kind will now be discussed.

LITERACY

Describing the extension of the Ceylon franchise by the Donoughmore Commission of 1928, Sir Ivor Jennings suggested that the illiterate villager may be, in practice, shrewder and wiser than a town-dweller who is just able to read and write.[1] This faith

---

[1] Sir Ivor Jennings, *The Approach to Self-Government*, p. 68.

in the practical common sense of illiterate peasants was also shown by the Constituent Assembly of India when, in drafting the country's Constitution, the principle of full adult suffrage was adopted. In many territories of Africa, however, the view has been accepted that, in general, only an electorate of literate and educated persons can make democracy work. The border-line between literacy and illiteracy is hazy as persons who have been concerned with census-taking in under-developed territories know well, and it is in practice a matter of the greatest difficulty to adopt a literacy test capable of being administered with uniform fairness by a large and scattered group of registration officers. Those whose ability to write is limited to scrawling their signature and whose ability to read is limited to the painful deciphering of one word out of every three or four in a newspaper article would be generally classed as illiterate; but how much further does a semi-literate person have to go to cross the shadowy border-line between literacy and illiteracy? However carefully drafted the administrative instructions may be, registration officers and assistant registration officers will inevitably find it difficult to make decisions in doubtful cases.

Moreover, simple literacy tests are open to political or racial pressure. In some of the States of the U.S.A., literacy tests are carried out in a way which effectively disfranchises a section of the negro population. The applicant for registration as an elector is required to complete an application form or pass some other literacy test in the presence of the Board of Registrars, and, in some States, the arbitrary fashion in which decisions are given by the Boards on these literacy tests suggests a bias against the admission of the negro to the electorate.[1] Alternatively political parties may seek to control the administration of literacy tests so as to reduce to a minimum the voting strength of their opponents. Both on grounds of ease of administration and in order to avoid undesirable political pressure in the process of the registration of electors, it seems preferable to introduce, where necessary, an educational qualification based on a standard reached or a certificate given by the education authorities rather than to rely upon a literacy test. Where, however, educational systems are new and expanding, or have been subject to periodic revision, it may prove difficult to devise tests of formal education which do not penalise one section

[1] See D. S. Strong *Registration of Voters in Alabama*, and J. P. Harris, *Registration of Electors in the United States*, p. 203.

(e.g. the older section) of the population. It would, for instance, have been difficult to devise a suitable educational qualification (had such a qualification been wanted) for the franchise in Malaya which would have been fair to all sections of the population, old and young, Malay, Chinese, Indian and others.

There has been little use of literacy as a qualification for the franchise in modern Asia, but it has been and still is in common use in Africa. Literacy is usually not an obligatory qualification but rather one of the alternative qualifications in much of East Africa. In Zanzibar, for instance, electors must either be literate (in English, Arabic or Swahili) or be of forty-five years of age or over.[1] In Kenya, literacy is one of the alternative qualifications for African voters. In Tanganyika, however, the relevant qualification is a certain standard of education rather than literacy. In Southern Rhodesia, the position is more akin to that pertaining in some of the United States; the voter must have an adequate knowledge of the English language and be able, unassisted, to fill in the claim for enrolment as a voter. The registration officer is responsible for the test of literacy in English. On the West Coast of Africa, the literacy qualification has almost disappeared; it survives, no doubt temporarily, in the Protectorate sector of Sierra Leone, where women voters must either be literate or own property.

EDUCATIONAL QUALIFICATIONS OTHER THAN LITERACY

It has been suggested above that, both on the grounds of administrative convenience and in order to limit undesirable political pressure, an educational test involving the possession of a certificate or the attainment of a standard is to be preferred to a literacy test. Voters in Tanganyika are required to possess an educational qualification and Section 7 of the Legislative Council Elections Ordinance which deals with this qualification, reads as follows:

(1) In order to have the requisite educational qualification to be registered as a voter, a claimant must have completed satisfactorily the course of general education known as Standard VIII in the schools established by the Government, or a course of general education or training equal to or higher than that standard.

[1] The Zanzibar Legislative Council Elections Decree, Section 4(c).

(2) A certificate purporting to be under the hand of the Director of Education, or any officer of the Department of Education authorised in that behalf by the Director of Education, that a course of general education or training is or is not of a standard equal to or greater than the course of general education known as Standard VIII in the schools established by the Government shall be prima facie evidence of that fact.

(3) A certificate purporting to be under the hand of the principal of any school or other educational or training institution or establishment that a claimant has or has not completed satisfactorily the course of general education or training therein specified (being a course of general education or training provided by the school or educational training institution or establishment of which the person issuing the certificate is the principal) shall be prima facie evidence of that fact.

This Section has been quoted in full because its text illustrates the possible difficulties in the use of such a qualification. If the Government decides that voters must have reached a certain minimum standard of education, the precise definition of this standard will be easy if there is an established uniform educational system within the country, and but little fresh immigration. But if the registration authorities have to decide on the relative standing of an education obtained in another country or if standards vary for the different races in a multi-racial community, the registration officers may have to deal with a number of difficult cases and there would be a margin of doubt about the interpretation of the educational qualification.

QUALIFICATIONS BASED ON INCOME, THE OWNERSHIP OR OCCUPATION OF PROPERTY, OR TAXATION

Many of the earlier, and, indeed, a few of the present franchises in Africa are based on the payment or liability to payment of taxes or rates or the ownership of property. In African conditions, a franchise based on taxation may well achieve something approaching adult male suffrage, but it often does little to provide a basis for the inclusion of female electors, only a small number of whom are under an obligation to pay taxes. In a homogeneous monogamous society it would be possible to give the vote to the wives of electors who qualify by the payment of taxes or rates, but such a solution is fraught with difficulties in those parts of

Africa where polygamy and legal complexities in the determination of marital status under native law and custom are encountered. Moreover, problems will arise if the tax lists or tax receipts fail to give full and sufficient particulars of the various individuals who have made payments; difficulties of this nature will obviously arise if assessments are made on a communal rather than an individual basis.

The level set for taxation, property or income qualifications has necessarily been a matter for local decision in each territory. In parts of West Africa, the franchise has been founded on the theory that the payment of 'basic' taxes is a proof of civic responsibility and entitles the taxpayer to apply for a vote. Thus, in Western Nigeria, a qualification for the franchise is the payment of 'direct tax' or 'income tax' or exemption from the payment of taxes, or the payment of a rate to the prescribed authority;[1] in the Gold Coast, at the time of the 1954 elections, the qualifications of electors included the requirements that he or she, at the time of registration and voting,

. . . .

(c) either owns immovable property within, or has, for a period of not less than six months out of the twelve months immediately preceding the date of his application to register, resided within, the ward in respect of which the application is made; and

(d) being or having been by virtue of Sec. 93 of the Local Governments Ordinance or of Sec. 98 of the Municipal Councils Ordinance 1953 under a duty to pay the basic rate for the current or previous year, has, at the date of his application to register paid to the appropriate Council the basic rate in respect of either the current year or the previous year.

Again, in Sierra Leone, the franchise in the Protectorate is based on the liability to payment of taxes (with literacy or owner-ship of property as alternatives in the case of women who do not pay taxes) and in the Colony it is based on the occupation of rateable premises of a certain minimum assessed value or the possession of a certain minimum yearly income. In Eastern Nigeria and the Gambia (for Legislative Council Elections), there is no taxation or property or income qualification. It will be seen that, nowhere in West Africa, is this kind of qualification set at

[1] The Western Region Parliamentary and Local Government Electoral Regulations, 1955, Reg. 10.

such a high level as to exclude a large section of the population, save in the Protectorate area of Sierra Leone, where the qualifications are such that women are virtually voteless.

In East and Central Africa, on the other hand, property and income qualifications are frequently used as one of the means of limiting the electorate. At one extreme is the example of Southern Rhodesia, where the franchise is one of the root causes of current political controversy; there the means qualification, as it is called, stipulates the occupation of property valued at £500 for the three months before registration, ownership of a registered mining location or an income of not less than £240 per annum. At the other end of the scale is Zanzibar, where each elector has to satisfy one of the following five qualifications:

(a) ownership of immovable property valued at £150 or more.

(b) an annual income of £75 per annum or more.

(c) ownership of immovable property which, when added to annual income, amounts to £150 or more.

(d) membership of the Legislative Council or (for a total of five years or upwards) of a local government authority.

(e) possession of a civil or military decoration or award.

It would appear that these alternative qualifications probably had rather little effect in limiting the franchise in the 1957 elections as it was calculated that a man "who was earning his living as a settled member of a village community, was supporting a wife and family, was contributing to the upkeep of the village mosque and otherwise discharging his local debts and obligations must have, and until the contrary was proved, might reasonably claim to have an average daily income of not less than four shillings and fifty cents. The minimum annual income that qualifies a man to vote is £75, the equivalent of a daily income of four shillings and twenty-five cents."[1] Had the qualifications been set rather higher, however, great difficulties would have ensued, as "claims based on the possession of immovable property, small shops, clove or coconut trees, etc., could be worked out and checked with reasonable accuracy against known current values, but fishermen, squatter farmers, coconut tree climbers, clove pickers, and other persons casually or seasonally employed were totally unable to calculate their intermittent earnings in terms either of an annual

[1] Extract from the *Report of the Supervisor of Elections, Zanzibar, on the 1957 elections*, p. 11.

or of a daily average income". Another difficulty which arose in Zanzibar was that "a few applicants in the propertied class, who were determined that they saw the hand of the tax collector in the registration questionnaire, deliberately disqualified themselves by declaring a daily income of only two or three shillings in spite of being assured that, whatever their total incomes might be, all that they had to do was to disclose the minimum qualifying sum and that the application forms were filed confidentially, for electoral purposes only, in the Elections Office".[1] Difficulties in assessing income and fears of new taxation in a semi-literate society have been experienced elsewhere and it is for consideration in the local circumstances of each territory whether some easier method of assessing "the fitness of the applicant to be an elector" could be devised. In Uganda, possession of a cash income of Shs.2,000 or more a year or ownership of property worth Shs.8,000 or more are alternatives to ownership of land, occupation of land for agricultural or pastoral purposes, regular paid employment in agriculture, commerce, industry, or in the public service, or literacy as qualifications for the franchise and, for this reason, the difficulties which arose in Zanzibar did not bother the registration authorities in Uganda to the same degree. Most of the difficulties experienced in Uganda at the time of the registration related to the qualification of an elector in occupying land on his or her own account for agricultural or pastoral purposes. In the first instance, the news that one of the alternative qualifications related to land occupation led to rumours that the Government intended to register the occupants for sinister purposes of its own. Secondly the position of wives living with their husbands presented some difficulty and it had to be left to the discretion of assistant registration officers with knowledge of local tribal custom to decide whether a woman applying for registration was in fact cultivating "on her own account". In most Bantu areas of Uganda, women do not have their own plots of land, but in other parts of the country, especially among the tribes of the Northern Province, the women have their own plots, separate from their husbands', for which they are entirely responsible. In the latter cases the women qualified for the vote, and, in the result, the percentage of women registering as electors varied from one area to another according to the interpretation of the local tribal custom. In general, "property or

[1] Extracts from the *Report by the Supervisor of Elections, Zanzibar*, p. 11.

income qualifications can only be expected to work easily if they are related to some assessment made independently of the process of elections. Registration Officers cannot be expected to act as valuers, except in a situation (like that under the Kenya African elections law of 1956) in which no one expects serious pressure from voters to get their names on the roll".[1]

A property qualification in the franchise inevitably raises the question of how an owner or tenant of property should be treated when the owner or tenant is a company rather than an individual. In the Bahamas, when the owner or tenant is a company, one of the officers or directors of the company, if otherwise qualified, is permitted to become a registered voter in respect of such property if nominated for the purpose by the directors of the company.[2] In general, however, a 'company vote' of this kind is not permitted by the elections legislation of those countries with a qualitative franchise including a property qualification.[3]

Finally a word must be said about the effect of inflation on an income qualification. In the Colony area of Sierra Leone, at the 1957 elections, a yearly income of at least £60 was an alternative qualification to the occupation of rateable premises of at least £2 annual assessed value, in accordance with the recommendations of the Keith-Lucas Commission of 1954.[4] But inflation and rising wages between 1954 and registration in 1957 resulted in nearly everyone being able to claim an income of £60. A similar situation arose in Zanzibar in 1957. In the Federation of Rhodesia and Nyasaland, the legislation governing Federal elections includes a complicated section[5] on the subject of the variation of the means qualification, under which a statutory committee conducts inquiries into the 'purchasing power of money'; variations are made to the means qualification by set formulae according to the increase or decrease in the purchasing power of money reported by the committee. The experience of Sierra Leone and Zanzibar

[1] W. J. M. Mackenzie, *Free Elections*, p. 28.
[2] The Bahamas General Assembly Elections Act, 1946, Sec. 17. It is understood that the company vote in the Bahamas is about to be abolished.
[3] There is provision for the 'company vote' in nineteenth-century English local government legislation — see Keith-Lucas, *The English Local Government Franchise*, p. 28 — and the Representation of the People Act, 1928, of Northern Ireland, gives a vote to companies for local government elections.
[4] Report of the Commission for Electoral Reform, 1954.
[5] Sec. 20, The Electoral Act, 1958.

and the legislation mentioned in the last sentence appear to emphasise the artificial nature of an income qualification.

SERVICE OR STATUS QUALIFICATIONS

As a postscript to the above description of the general categories of qualifications for the franchise, it must be mentioned that a few African territories with a qualitative franchise attempt to avoid anomalies and ensure the inclusion in the registers of all those who are regarded as 'fit' for the vote by providing qualifications such as membership of a local council or holding the office of chief or tribal elder as an alternative to qualifications based on literacy, education, income or property. Qualifications of this kind are likely to be purely temporary expedients adopted in an effort to maintain a balance between traditional leadership and the educated section of the population in a time of rapid social and economic change.

DISQUALIFICATIONS

Disqualification for voting can be discussed under five heads:
(1) Disqualification of convicted criminals serving prison sentences or under sentence of death.
(2) Disqualification for corrupt or illegal electoral offences.
(3) Disqualification of persons of unsound mind.
(4) Disqualification of persons under an acknowledgement of allegiance to a foreign power.
(5) Special local disqualifications.

Although it is usual to disfranchise certain categories of convicted criminals serving sentences, the details of the disqualification are the subject of considerable variation as between one country and its neighbours. The disqualification may be defined by length of sentence, by the name of the offence, or by a combination of the two. Moreover, the disqualification may be limited to the period of confinement in prison, to a specified time interval after release, or it may be a permanent disqualification. In Great Britain, persons convicted of treason or felony and sentenced to death or imprisonment exceeding twelve months are disqualified, though only whilst they are in prison, but persons convicted and serving a sentence for a misdemeanour have the right to vote in British elections, unless their punishments prevent them from so doing.[1] In Ghana persons who are sentenced to a term exceeding twelve months are not permitted to vote until five years after their release. Those convicted for dishonesty whether sentenced to imprisonment or not are made to suffer the same loss of civic rights. Throughout Nigeria those sentenced to more than six months' imprisonment are barred during their imprisonment from voting in general elections.[2] In the Gambia a sentence in excess of six months disqualifies for ten years after completion of the sentence.[3] The British precedent of a term of twelve months' imprisonment or more has been adopted in Kenya together with disfranchisement for two years after expiry of sentence. In addition, disqualification for certain serious offences continues at the Governor's pleasure. Zanzibar has also taken twelve months' imprisonment as a minimum for disqualification, the disqualification extending for a two year period from date of discharge.[4] All convicts in Southern Rhodesia are disfranchised for five years after release from prison. In the dependent territories of the British Commonwealth, the disqualification usually relates to conviction in any part of Her Majesty's dominions or in any territory under Her Majesty's protection.

From the administrative point of view, it is simplest to exclude from registration or, having registered, from voting, all persons currently serving prison sentences and this is the system which has been adopted for use in Tanganyika[5] and Uganda.[6] Where, however, postal or proxy voting is permitted, as in Great Britain, arrangements can be made for prisoners to vote. The reports on elections in West African territories do not indicate whether prisoners serving short sentences not amounting to disqualification have been permitted to vote on polling day, but it is clear that, with police forces extended to their limits in order to ensure law and order at polling stations, it is rather unlikely that special arrangements could be made for prisoners to be taken to polling stations, save at the risk of dislocating security arrangements generally. Whether or not prisoners convicted of minor offences

[1] Schofield, *Parliamentary Elections* (1950 edition), p. 21.
[2] See, for instance, Reg. 11(b) of the Western Region Parliamentary and Local Government Electoral Regulations, 1955.
[3] The Gambia Colony Elections Ordinance, Section 3(2)(b).
[4] Zanzibar Legislative Council Elections Decree, Section 5(a).
[5] Section 10 of the Tanganyika Legislative Council Elections Ordinance, 1957.
[6] Section 10 of the Uganda Legislative Council Ordinance, 1957.

and serving short prison sentences should be allowed to vote is, however, only partially a question of administrative convenience; clearly the moral question of whether such a sentence ought to involve the temporary loss of civic rights is also a factor to be taken into consideration. Similarly, the question of whether it is correct to continue disfranchisement for a period after completion of a prison sentence is a matter of political morality, and both questions are beyond the scope of discussion of this book.

There is rather less local variation in the fairly common provision that temporary disqualification for voting should be a consequence of conviction for corrupt or illegal electoral offences, but it should be noted that Asian and African countries have little experience to date of this disqualification in practice. In Western Nigeria, persons convicted of bribery, treating, undue influence or personation are disqualified as electors for fifteen years, whilst those convicted of certain minor electoral offences are disqualified for three years from date of conviction.[1] In the Federation of Malaya, persons convicted of corrupt or illegal practices under the Election Offences Ordinance become "incapable of being registered or listed as an elector or of voting at any election . . ." for five years from date of conviction or (in the case of corrupt practices) release from imprisonment, whichever is the later.[2] In Eastern Nigeria, the period of disqualification from voting is five years from the date of conviction for certain corrupt or illegal practices.[3] In the Gambia, disqualification is for a period of ten years on conviction for bribery, treating, undue influence or personation and for five years for certain lesser electoral offences.[4]

There is little scope for variety in the disqualification of lunatics and of persons adjudged to be of unsound mind, and this category of disqualification does not call for comment.[5]

[1] Regs. 95 and 101 of the Western Region Parliamentary and Local Government Electoral Regulations, 1955.

[2] Sections 11 and 27 of the Federation of Malaya Election Offences Ordinance.

[3] Regs. 63 and 66 of the Eastern House of Assembly Electoral Regulations, 1955.

[4] Sections 49 and 52 of the Gambia Colony Elections Ordinance, 1954.

[5] Registration officers in the Sudan were given the following instructions on this matter prior to the 1958 elections:

"The voter must be of sound mind. In ordinary language he must not be mad. Registration Officers are advised to consider every person of sound mind unless his madness is so obvious that it is stupid to ignore it. In such cases of 'raving madness' the Registration Officer must reject the application straight away. The applicant will have his remedy in the Courts of Justice".

The disqualification as electors of persons who are under an acknowledgement of allegiance, obedience or adherence to a foreign power or state is of some importance in areas which receive, or have received in the not too distant past, large numbers of migrants. In the Federation of Malaya, for instance, it would be inconceivable to give the vote to persons, otherwise qualified, who consider that they owe allegiance to the Republic of China. But such a disqualification has rarely to be used, because allegiance can be covered positively by the citizenship or nationality category of qualification, and some territories (e.g. Tanganyika and Uganda) find it unnecessary to legislate for a disqualification of this category at all.

Special disqualifications are usually a product of local circumstances. In Kenya, for instance, the franchise under which African elections were held in 1956 disqualified members of certain tribes[1] which had been associated with the Mau-Mau rebellion, except for individuals who could satisfy their District Commissioner that they had aided the administration during the emergency. The legislation covering non-African elections in Kenya disqualifies persons who have, since the publication of the last register, received relief from Government funds or the funds of any local authority, and also persons who have been declared bankrupt and have not received a discharge.[2] The Gambia prohibits from voting (but not from registering as an elector) at Legislative Council and local government elections any person "who has been retained or employed for reward by or on behalf of a candidate at an election, for all or any of the purposes of such election, as an agent, clerk, messenger or in any other capacity",[3] presumably in an effort to prohibit concealed bribery of electors. Peers are prohibited from voting in parliamentary elections in Great Britain. In Sierra Leone, paramount chiefs are not permitted to vote as special provisions are made for their representation in the legislature. A few countries[4] do not allow persons serving in the armed forces and police officers to vote.

The categories of disqualifications which have been discussed in the above paragraphs are those which are essentially negative

[1] Kikuyu, Embu, and Meru.
[2] The Kenya Legislative Council Ordinance, Sec. 9(1)(e) and (f).
[3] The Gambia Colony Elections Ordinance, Sections 3(3), 4(3) and 5(3).
[4] e.g. Turkey (Art. 9 of the Election of National Deputies Act, 1950), and Syria (Art. 10 of the Electoral Law of Syria, 1949).

in character. In so far as every qualification also implies a dis-qualification, qualifications and disqualifications must necessarily be considered in conjunction. Indeed, in the legislation of British Colonial territories, it is not uncommon to find a qualification doubly emphasised by being listed both positively as a qualification and, by the addition of a simple negative, as a disqualification. Alternatively, something which is essentially a positive qualification is instead listed negatively as a disqualification — for instance, in the Uganda Legislative Council Elections Ordinance, 1957, being a non-African is listed as a disqualification when it would perhaps have been more appropriate to enter being an African as a positive qualification.

Franchise Weighting

If the Government of a country accepts the view that the vote is a privilege to be limited to persons qualified by education, status or experience, it is merely an extension of this doctrine to grade electors according to their qualifications and to give the more highly qualified electors more than one vote.[1] If plural voting is permitted, the more fortunate group of electors either have several votes in one and the same constituency or they may have one vote in each of two or more constituencies. Kenya is a current example of the first alternative whilst Northern Ireland is a current example and Sudan and Great Britain are past examples of the second alternative. In Kenya, each African elector is awarded one, two or three votes according to his qualifications, and he must cast all his votes in the constituency in which he is registered. There is an important body of opinion in East and Central Africa which regards a multiple vote system of this nature as an ultimate method of eliminating communal electorates and substituting a common roll of electors with a method of weighting votes by criteria other than race or colour, and a form of 'weightage' has been recommended by the Tredgold Commission for use in Southern Rhodesia. In the Sudan at the first elections, and also in Great Britain until 1948, there were special constituencies for persons who had completed a higher education — the three

[1] An English nineteenth-century example of franchise weighting is to be found in the Poor Law Amendment Act of 1834, see B. Keith-Lucas, *The English Local Government Franchise*, p. 35.

graduates' constituencies of the Sudan and the university constituencies of Great Britain — and a graduate had one vote in his territorial constituency and one vote in his graduate constituency (Sudan) or university constituency (Great Britain).

The advantages of a system of franchise weightage are as follows:

(a) It may make the introduction of an electoral system more acceptable in tribal communities whose social systems do not accept human equality. For instance, a tribe may consider it most appropriate to give the elders a higher voting power than the younger adults.

(b) A wide differentiation between the highest and lowest levels of suffrage may serve as a step towards the introduction of a common electoral roll in a plural society.

(c) The system represents a simple way of giving extra weight to electors whom the State wishes to favour without excluding the lower level of voters from the franchise altogether.

The disadvantages of the system are as follows:

(a) There is a progressively stronger sentiment in favour of equal universal suffrage and the history of the development of the franchise in widely scattered parts of the world suggests that fancy franchises and systems of weighting the franchise can have but a limited tenure.

(b) Systems of this kind are bound to cause some popular dissatisfaction.

(c) Plural voting involves a more complicated electoral organisation.

CHAPTER VI

MINORITIES AND THE ELECTORAL SYSTEM

OST people who live outside the Communist countries would agree that the best system for the government of a people is democracy based upon a universal adult franchise. In most of Western Europe and North America, this tenet is taken for granted. Nevertheless, such a system operates much more satisfactorily in countries containing a homogeneous electorate than in countries in which divisions of race, colour or culture confuse the political issues. In fact, a very high proportion of those countries of Asia and Africa in which electoral systems have recently been introduced contain mixed populations with different cultures and frequently at vastly different stages of development.

Sometimes, as in most of the countries of East and Central Africa, the more advanced communities are, numerically, a small minority of the total population. Elsewhere, as in India and New Zealand, the minorities to whom the electoral system gives some protection are the least advanced elements in the population. Again, there are countries whose populations are split by race or culture in which no one part of the electorate can be described as more or less advanced than the other sections; in Ceylon, for instance, there are divisions between Sinhalese on the one hand and Tamils and other minority communities on the other hand, but it would not be correct to state categorically that one or other of these Ceylonese communities has reached a very much higher stage of material and cultural development than the rest.

The methods which have been adopted in an effort to protect the interests of minorities include the following:

(a) Limitation of the franchise;
(b) Communal representation;
(c) 'Gerrymandering' of constituencies; and
(d) The adoption of a method of voting which gives minorities a reasonable chance of some representation.

In those countries in which the most advanced communities form only a small minority in the population, the limitation of the franchise and communal representation are the two methods which have been most generally adopted to protect the interests of the dominant minority. Limitation of the franchise, by demanding certain minimum educational, income or property owning qualifications of the electorate, is a feature of the electoral systems in the Rhodesias, Kenya and Tanganyika, in all of which there is a small but vocal European population. But there has also been some pressure to limit the franchise in other parts of Africa where there is no European political element; in Sierra Leone, for instance, the Creoles are more advanced than the inhabitants of the Protectorate and there has been some pressure to postpone the introduction of a full adult franchise. In East and Central Africa considerations of political philosophy advanced to justify a 'fancy' (i.e. limited) franchise range from theories of racial superiority at one extreme to the more liberal arguments used in the Tredgold Franchise Commission report in Southern Rhodesia in 1957. The Tredgold Commission argued that, in a young country with a mixed population at vastly different stages of development, democracy could not survive if large numbers of Africans, mostly illiterate, were given the vote on a common roll with a minority of Europeans of much higher education and with different cultural values. The solution recommended by the Commission to the franchise problem was not communal representation which the Commission regarded as wrong in principle, but rather a common roll with minimum qualifications for voters which would ensure that the electorate consisted of "civilised and responsible" persons only.[1] Among the solutions considered and rejected in whole or in part by the Commission were:

(a) A common roll with adult suffrage (which would mean that the overwhelming majority of the voters would be African).

(b) A common roll with qualifications for the franchise fixed so high that the African would be virtually excluded.

(c) A common roll with a 'multiple' vote, under which the qualifications for a single vote would be placed fairly low but additional votes would be given to those regarded as possessing more than the minimum qualifications.

[1] *Report of the Franchise Commission*, 1957, pp. 2-9.

(d) A common roll electing two members for each constituency, one an African and the other European.

In Tanganyika, where there is a substantial Asian community, in addition to the Africans and the Europeans, the solution adopted on an experimental scale in 1958 was a common electoral roll based on a limited franchise electing three members for each constituency, one African, one Asian and one European. Every elector, in order to cast a valid vote, had to choose one African, one Asian and one European candidate assuming that all three seats in his constituency were contested; there might perhaps have been less controversy had the elector the option of casting a vote for candidates of races other than his own, but it has been argued that the system adopted was more likely to lead to the creation of political parties and platforms which cross racial boundaries.

In Kenya, there are both communal rolls and a limited franchise. The qualifications for the franchise differ for electors of the various communities, and for African electors the 'multiple' vote system on a communal roll has been adopted.

It will be seen that the common element in the electoral systems of Southern Rhodesia (and also the other territories forming the Central African Federation), Tanganyika and Kenya is the adoption of a limited franchise. The qualifications for electors have been discussed in some detail in Chapter V. Where these countries differ is in their attitude towards communal representation, which has been as frankly accepted in Kenya as it has been rejected in Southern Rhodesia. The system adopted in Tanganyika can be described as a variant of communal representation with some ameliorative features.

It is beyond the scope of this book to enter into a detailed discussion of the political advantages and disadvantages of communal representation, but it is appropriate to suggest here that communal representation, once established, will tend (although it will not necessarily have this result) to lead to the establishment and strengthening of pressure groups and entrenched interests desirous of perpetuating communalism. Nevertheless, however undesirable in theory communal representation may be, the problem in practice in such situations is to attempt to reconcile existing communal sentiment with majority rule, and communal representation, as a temporary expedient, may be the only means of introducing an element of parliamentary democracy.

Communal representation is not restricted to countries like Kenya, in which the minority communities are politically dominant. It was used before partition in India to provide separate electorates for Hindus, Muslims and various minorities under successive Acts of 1909, 1919 and 1935, and on a much smaller scale and in a very much modified form, is still used in India to assist in ensuring some degree of representation for the Scheduled Castes and the Scheduled Tribes. Where there is a sufficiently large concentration of the Scheduled Tribes population, seats are reserved for them in single member constituencies. Where there are considerable numbers of persons belonging to the Scheduled Castes or Tribes, but not in sufficient concentration to justify the reservation of a single-member constituency for either, one or two seats are reserved in two or three member constituencies.[1] The number of reserved seats is, however, small in relation to the total number of seats in the Indian House of the People and the present Indian system of elections is but little affected by the existence of these reserved seats. Similarly in New Zealand, where franchise limitation was once used as a weapon to ensure political control for the European minority, the four seats out of a total of eighty which are now reserved for the Maori minority do little to affect the electoral system as a whole; it should be noted that, in India, the reserved seats are filled by common roll elections whereas in New Zealand the four reserved seats are filled by the votes of Maoris only. In both India and New Zealand, it is possible for a member of the minority community to gain election either in a reserved seat or in a non-reserved seat.

Communal electorates have also been in use in Cyprus (from 1878 to 1931), in Burma prior to independence under pre-Second World War legislation (in order to give some protection to Europeans and Indians) and in Ceylon, up to 1931 (in order to protect Tamils and Muslims). In Ceylon, sections of the minority communities advocated 'balanced representation' involving communal electorates on the lines of the system in use prior to 1931 when the constitution was being revised immediately before the attainment of independence in 1947, but such a scheme would not have been acceptable to the State Council and, instead, a scheme

[1] See pp. 49-52 of the official *Report on the first general elections in India, 1951-2*, Vol. I, for a detailed description of the method of reserving seats for the Scheduled Castes and Tribes.

for providing 'weightage' for sparsely populated areas was adopted. As the minorities were strongest in the sparsely populated areas, the Constituency Delimitation Commission was able to form constituencies which were comparatively homogeneous without making them specifically communal.[1] Ceylon thus adopted the system of 'gerrymandering' to give its minority communities reasonable representation and the results were amply vindicated in the first two post-war Ceylon general elections.[2] Gerrymandering has also been adopted in recognition of the existence of strong tribal cohesion in parts of West Africa, where two or more separated areas have sometimes been combined to form one constituency because of the concentration of members of some tribe; its use has also been the subject of recommendations by a commission in Mauritius,[3] in which recent elections have failed to give adequate representation to minority communities. The interest of minorities in electoral geography is discussed further in Chapter III.

In Malaya, where there are three major communities — the Malays, the Chinese and the Indians — and a number of minor communities such as Eurasians, Ceylonese and Aborigines — consideration was given to the desirability of drawing up communal rolls of electors for the election of communal candidates, but such a system was decisively rejected, as the following extract from the relevant Committee's Report shows:

> The Committee is of the opinion that to adopt such a system would not be in keeping with the agreed object of promoting national unity amongst the peoples of Malaya and might arrest the process of assimilation and co-operation which is so essential if the country is to have a single united people. We, therefore, agreed that elections should not take place on a communal basis, but that all communities should participate together in voting on a common basis and that candidates should be elected by individual territorial constituencies and not by individual communities.[4]

[1] See *The Constitution of Ceylon* by Sir Ivor Jennings, p. 39 *et seq.*

[2] The communal riots in Ceylon in 1958 do not invalidate the conclusion that, under the existing electoral arrangements, the minority communities are able to gain reasonable representation.

[3] *Report of the Mauritius Electoral Boundary Commission* (Legislative Council Sessional Paper No. 1 of 1958).

[4] *Report of the Committee appointed to examine the question of elections to the Federal Legislative Council*, 1954, p. 13.

114 ELECTIONS IN DEVELOPING COUNTRIES

The Committee felt, however, that some temporary provision was necessary to give representation to racial minorities which might not otherwise secure any representation at all through the electoral process, and concluded that the High Commissioner for the Federation of Malaya should be empowered to nominate one member each to represent the Eurasians, the Ceylonese and the Aborigines.[1] Representation of minorities by nomination is not, however, possible in a fully elected legislative assembly.

Before discussing methods of voting which in themselves give minorities a reasonable chance of representation, it should be mentioned that the limitation of the franchise and the delimitation of constituencies are weapons which can be used as easily against minorities as in their interests. Negroes in some of the United States of America have in the past been effectively disfranchised by the operation of State laws and, even to-day, the *de facto* operation of arrangements for the registration of electors in parts of the Deep South reduces negro participation in elections to a level far below their percentage representation in the population.[2] In other countries containing cultural minorities, constituency delimitation has ignored communal divisions and thus, intentionally or otherwise, given a flying start as it were to the dominant majority. In Malaya, for instance, where the Malays form a large majority of the total electorate (because most adult Federal citizens are Malays), the Constituency Commission in 1954 ignored the somewhat nebulous boundaries between localities in which Malays formed the majority of the local residents and those in which Chinese and Indians formed the majority and drew up their constituencies on the basis of population and existing administrative divisions, with a weightage in favour of rural areas. It would have been theoretically possible (though far more difficult than in Ceylon) to define a number of constituencies, some of which would probably have had to contain two or more geographically separated areas, in which Chinese or Indians or both together would have formed the majority of the electorate; in fact there were only two such constituencies out of a total of fifty-two. Rather to the surprise of the critics, however, voting

[1] *Report of the Committee appointed to examine the question of Elections to the Federal Legislative Council*, 1954, pp. 5-6.
[2] See 'Negro Registration in Louisiana', by Fenton and Vines in the *American Political Science Quarterly*, September 1957.

was not entirely on a communal basis and, in a number of constituencies containing largely Malay electorates, Chinese and Indian candidates backed by the Alliance on a non-communal platform defeated with some ease Malay candidates backed by communally minded parties.

The method of voting, too, can be adapted in order to give some protection to minorities. Proportional representation, which, in one form or another, is a system of awarding seats proportionately to the votes cast for each group of candidates, is in use in a number of countries on the continent of Europe and elsewhere. Some of the methods of voting based on proportional representation are, however, unsuited for adoption in a semi-literate society. The single transferable vote, for instance, requires an electorate with the ability to indicate by the use of a ballot a first and second preference and, perhaps, further choices among the candidates. The list systems of voting based on proportional representation are more easily adapted for use in semi-literate communities and some of the possibilities are described below. The discussion is, however, necessarily limited to methods of voting which are suited to conditions in Africa, Asia and other under-developed areas, and the reader is referred to books such as Mackenzie's *Free Elections*[1] and Miss Lakeman and Lambert's *Voting in Democracies*[2] for a more general and fuller description.

The majority of the countries of the British Commonwealth have in fact adopted one or other of the 'first past the post' systems of voting, partly because simple plurality voting is in use in the United Kingdom (in all 'Empires' dependent or formerly dependent countries have tended to adopt the parliamentary institutions of the mother country), and partly because there has been a desire to create a stable parliamentary system with a small number of parties — and this is quite likely to be achieved under a simple plurality system of voting. In India, most constituencies electing members to the House of the People are single-member constituencies and the exceptions are constituencies in which, as described above, there are special arrangements for ensuring the representation of the Scheduled Castes and the Scheduled Tribes. In the Federation of Malaya, Singapore and Ghana, all the constituencies electing members to the Legislative Councils are

---

[1] W. J. M. Mackenzie, *Free Elections*, Chs. VII, VIII, IX.
[2] Enid Lakeman and J. D. Lambert, *Voting in Democracies*.

single-member constituencies. But it is clear that, given a number of candidates in a single-member constituency, the successful candidate may be elected with considerably less than half of the votes cast; similarly, under a system of simple plurality voting, all the seats in a multi-member constituency are likely to go to the party with most backing in the constituency, even though the rival parties can together muster more supporters than the successful party.

The easiest way of giving organised minorities in under-developed countries some chance at the polls without adopting a form of proportional representation is the system of the single non-transferable vote. Under this system, each elector can give one vote only in a multi-member constituency. If voting is largely on communal lines, a minority of about one quarter of the electorate would, with proper organisation, stand to gain one seat in a four-member constituency and would have a very good chance of gaining one seat in a three-member constituency. A system of this kind is as easy for the illiterate voter to understand as simple plurality voting in a single member constituency. There has, however, been little use of the single non-transferable vote in parliamentary elections.

Another method of helping organised minorities to gain some representation is to permit 'plumping' in multi-member constituencies. Each elector is given as many votes as there are seats to be filled in a multi-member constituency and he is permitted to cast all his votes for one candidate if he so wishes. The practical effect of this method is very much the same as the single non-transferable vote. The main disadvantage of both methods is that they put too much of a premium on organisation of the minority community[1] and this tends to enhance rather than to soften the differences between the majority and the minority. But both methods are perfectly practicable for use by illiterates.

List systems of voting appear to offer more hopeful possibilities for use in under-developed countries than the single transferable vote. In a list system, the voter is required to choose between lists of candidates, each of which has the backing of a political party.

[1] Some of the English School Board Elections in the nineteenth century illustrate the importance of careful party control when there are a number of candidates to be elected and 'plumping' is permitted — see Keith-Lucas, *The English Local Government Franchise*, pp. 216-17.

One of the many variations of the list system was used in the first general elections held in Indonesia in 1955, mainly perhaps because of the pressure exercised by a large number of small parties, many of which thought that a list system was the only method likely to give them some degree of representation. The system used — the d'Hondt system — allowed for the elector voting for an individual candidate on the list if he so desired and, in addition, it permitted individuals as well as organised parties to contest the elections. But, partly because the counting procedure under the system adopted is complicated, the official results were not announced until some months after the elections, and the Indonesian experience suggests that it is essential in backward communities to keep the system of voting reasonably simple so that the outlines of the scheme at least can be readily understood by the electorate and the results announced within a few days of polling.

The extent to which it proves necessary to adopt one or more of the various devices outlined in this Chapter to protect the interests of minorities must inevitably be answered by the interplay of political forces within each country containing minorities. Limitation of the franchise and communal representation have, however, usually been adopted as temporary expedients only for the purpose of reconciling communal feeling with democratic forms of government and it is in terms of constituency delimitation and methods of voting that long-term solutions of communal problems are more likely to be found.

CHAPTER VII

THE ELIGIBILITY, NOMINATION, PRIVILEGES AND EXPENSES OF CANDIDATES

CANDIDATES for election to legislatures, like the electors who vote for them or for their rivals, are restricted by qualifications and disqualifications imposed by the law. The possible variants in determining the qualifications and disqualifications of candidates are as numerous as has been shown to be the case in the determination of the franchise. Candidature usually bears a fairly close relationship to the franchise, however, and, as a preliminary comment, it may be mentioned that "There is no inevitable rule that all those entitled to vote should also be allowed to stand as candidates. It may be desirable to restrict candidature within narrower limits, or alternatively, to allow a wider choice".[1]

The residential qualification is frequently widened to permit a choice of candidates for a constituency from persons, otherwise qualified, living anywhere in the country. Electors must be resident in their constituency either on a qualifying date or for a given period before the qualifying date or before registration; many electoral systems deliberately omit this residential qualification for candidates in order to permit political parties to make the best use of their country's available talent, which, in underdeveloped countries, tends to be highly concentrated in the capital city and the other major urban centres. On the other hand, qualifications relating to age, education and property or income are sometimes higher for candidates than for electors. For instance, in the Federation of Malaya at the time of the 1954 elections, candidates for election to the Legislative Council were required to possess the ability to read and write the English or Malay languages with a degree of proficiency sufficient to enable them to take an active part in the proceedings of the Council, if elected; there were

[1] Paragraph 62 of the *Report of the Electoral Reform Commission*, Sierra Leone, 1954.

no literacy or educational qualifications for electors, however. On the other hand, the residential qualification for candidates for election was confined to a requirement that the candidate should have been ordinarily resident in the Federation of Malaya during the twelve months prior to nomination, but there was no requirement for local residence in the constituency.

Some electoral systems demand that a candidate should be a registered elector. The electoral law of India as it stood at the time of the general elections of 1951-2 required that "the candidate must himself be registered as a voter in some constituency or other of the House to which he seeks election and the proposer and seconder must be voters enrolled in the particular constituency in respect of which the nomination is made".[1] Uganda requires that the prospective candidate should be already registered "as an elector in the administrative area in which the electoral district for which he is standing as a candidate is situated".[2] Some other countries require that a candidate should possess the qualifications to vote, without going so far as to demand that he should be already registered at the time of nomination; this is the position in Ghana, for instance.

Specific Qualifications of Candidates

Age

The minimum age for candidates in elections to Parliaments or other Legislative Assemblies is frequently higher than for electors. As far as the author is aware, the minimum age for candidates is nowhere lower than that for electors. When adult universal suffrage has been introduced it is often the practice to fix the minimum ages for candidates and electors at the same level; this is the position in the United Kingdom, the Federation of Malaya and Ceylon (for elections to the lower House but not for the Senate). In India and Ghana, however, the minimum age[3] for candidature at the last general elections was twenty-five years — in India for election to the House of the People and in Ghana for election in 1956 to what was then known as the Gold Coast Legislative Assembly. An age limit of twenty-five years or even

---

[1] *Report on the first general elections in India, 1951-2*, Vol. I, p. 112.

[2] Uganda Legislative Council Elections Ordinance, Section 17(1)(c).

[3] The minimum age for candidates to the Diet in Japan is also twenty-five years.

higher is frequently adopted in territories with a limited or 'fancy' franchise, for instance in Uganda (27 years), Tanganyika (25 years) and Kenya (25 years).

Sex

In general, women are eligible as candidates on equal terms with men, save in predominantly Muslim territories such as Zanzibar and the Northern Region of Nigeria. In practice, however, few women have offered themselves as candidates for election to African legislatures, partly because the qualifications for candidature are in fact such that few women possess them and partly because the existing social order is an unfavourable climate for such an innovation.

Residence

It has been stated above that candidates are frequently not under any obligation to identify themselves through residence with the constituency in which they are standing for election. Thus, in Great Britain, any British subject of full age resident in the country may be elected to Parliament, irrespective of residence in a particular constituency, if he or she is not otherwise disqualified. In Tanganyika, the electoral law requires that candidates should have been ordinarily resident in the territory for a period of not less than four years out of the six years immediately preceding nomination or should be in possession of valid certificates of permanent residence, but residence within the constituency is not required.[1] Nor is residence within the constituency a requirement in British West Africa, India, or the Federation of Malaya. In Zanzibar, however, a rather closer identification of the candidate with his constituency is required; one of the qualifications is residence "in the island in which is situated the constituency for which he seeks to be elected for a period of twelve months immediately preceding his nomination as a candidate".[2] And, as has been mentioned, in Uganda the candidate is required to be registered as an elector and therefore resident in the administrative area in which the electoral district for which he is standing as a candidate is situated.[3] For African

---

[1] The Tanganyika Legislative Council Elections Ordinance, Sec. 15.
[2] The Zanzibar Legislative Council Elections Decree, Sec. 82(b).
[3] The Uganda Legislative Council Elections Ordinance, Sec. 17(1)(c).

electors in Kenya, a candidate must have a place of residence in the electoral area in which he is standing.[1]

If it is considered desirable to identify the member with his constituency very closely and to regard him as a delegate of his constituents, one obvious means of doing this is to require that the candidate should reside in his constituency. But to stress the importance of locality in this way may not only prevent political parties from using the best available candidates but also may well retard the growth of truly national parties and a national public opinion. In under-developed countries, more than in industrial countries of Western Europe, the 'local' candidate starts with a big initial advantage over outsiders and it would appear to be unnecessary to reinforce this advantage by prohibiting by law the candidature of persons resident in other constituencies. In the Protectorate area of Sierra Leone at the first elections of 1957, local birth was in practice considered to be an essential requirement for success and a number of candidates stood in their home districts rather than in the constituencies in which they were currently resident.

Citizenship or Nationality

Qualifications for candidature in relation to citizenship or nationality are usually parallel with the corresponding qualifications for electors. Thus in Great Britain candidates, like electors, must be British subjects; in Zanzibar, both candidates and electors must be Zanzibar subjects; and in the Federation of Malaya, both candidates and electors must be Federal citizens. Where there is no local citizenship, the qualifications are still usually to be found in parallel; for instance those British Commonwealth territories which limit the franchise to British subjects and British protected persons also restrict candidature in the same way. Where, as in the Gold Coast before independence was achieved, persons other than British subjects or British protected persons have been admitted to the franchise, nationality requirements may be somewhat more restrictive for candidates than for electors.[2] In

---

[1] The Kenya Legislative Council (African Representation) Ordinance, Sec. 16(2)(e).

[2] The Gold Coast (Constitution) Order-in-Council, 1954, Section 29, restricted membership of the Legislative Assembly to British Subjects and British Protected Persons, although certain categories of aliens had the right to register as electors.

Uganda and Tanganyika, which have not imposed any nationality qualification for voters in the first elections held in 1958, candidature also is unrestricted by virtue of nationality, but it should be noted that successful candidates are usually required to take an oath of allegiance before occupying seats in the legislature; Tanganyika includes the specific qualification that a candidate should be "both willing and able to take the oath of allegiance specified in Clause X of the Order in Council".[1] Candidates at African elections in Kenya are required to take "the prescribed oath of allegiance to Her Majesty" at the time of nomination.[2]

Literacy and Education

The value of successful candidates as members of a legislature will be severely limited if they do not possess an adequate knowledge of the language in which the legislature conducts its business. The qualifications for candidates therefore often include a simple requirement that the candidate should be literate or the slightly more complex requirement that the candidate should be able to read and write the required language with a degree of proficiency sufficient to enable him to take an active part in the proceedings of the legislature. Zanzibar has adopted the simple literacy qualification but, more usually, a minimum degree of proficiency is required — Kenya, Uganda, Tanganyika, Ghana and the Federation of Malaya, to take but a few examples, make this stipulation. The author knows of no case in which the possession of the required literacy qualification has been questioned in respect of a successful candidate in central government elections though this qualification was questioned in respect of two candidates in the 1957 Municipal elections in Malacca in the Federation of Malaya. Tanganyika has taken the wise precaution of including in its electoral laws a statement of the way in which prospective candidates are, where necessary, to be tested, as follows:

> For the purpose of satisfying himself that a prospective candidate has or has not the requisite literacy qualification the Speaker, or any person duly authorised in that behalf by the Speaker, may make such enquiries as he deems fit and may test a prospective

[1] The Tanganyika Legislative Council Elections Ordinance, Sec. 14(2)(h).
[2] The Kenya Legislative Council (African Representation) Ordinance, Sec. 16(2)(f).

candidate as to his ability to read and understand documents normally considered by the Council and as to his fluency in either the English or Swahili language.[1]

Kenya requires that a candidate should be able to read, write and converse in fluent English, and his ability to do so and his general education is tested in an examination conducted by a committee consisting of members of the Education Department sitting with African assessors appointed by the Provincial Commissioner.[2]

The literacy qualification is sometimes waived for blind or handicapped persons. The Ghana qualification is that a candidate must be able to speak and, unless incapacitated by blindness or other physical cause, to read the English language sufficiently well to enable him to take an active part in the proceedings of the Legislative Assembly. Similarly Uganda requires all candidates to be able to speak the English language proficiently but the electoral law specifically exempts persons incapacitated by blindness from the requirement of being able to read and write the English language proficiently.[3] No special exemptions of this nature are, however, made in the electoral laws of Tanganyika, Zanzibar and Kenya.

Qualifications for candidature relating to literacy and education are nowhere lower than for the franchise and sometimes the minimum educational level set for candidates is well above that for the electorate. Tanganyika requires candidates, like electors, to hold either an educational qualification or an income qualification or an office holder qualification and the educational qualification for candidates (Standard XII) is higher than that for electors (Standard VIII). Kenya requires all candidates in African elections to hold at least the Kenya African Preliminary Certificate, issued on successful completion of the Junior Secondary School course, whereas the educational qualification for electors is lower and is one of the alternative point-earning qualifications, so that an elector need not have undergone a formal education at all. The elimination of the inexperienced and the irresponsible candidate by qualifications of this nature appears,

---

[1] The Tanganyika Legislative Council Elections Ordinance, Sec. 16(3)
[2] The Kenya Legislative Council (African Representation) Ordinance, Sec. 16(3).
[3] The Uganda Legislative Council Elections Ordinance, Section 17(1)(b).

in general, to be in accord with African opinion, for the feeling has been expressed on numerous occasions in different territories that the African electorate can best be represented by the more highly educated from among themselves.[1] Many territories[2] which impose a literacy qualification for candidates have no literacy or educational qualification for electors.

The desirability of imposing an educational qualification on candidates seeking election to the various legislative bodies in Pakistan was discussed by the Electoral Reforms Commission for that country. The majority opinion of the Commission rejected the idea of prescribing an educational qualification, saying that:

> It is up to the electors to choose whomsoever they think fit to represent them in an Assembly. . . . Similarly it is for the political parties to select such persons as they think would succeed in elections and properly represent and advocate their points of view in an Assembly. Apart from these considerations, it cannot be reasonably said in all cases that the mere passing of a Matriculation Examination or any other equivalent examination is a 'sine qua non' of political sagacity or even of worldly wisdom.[3]

Income or the Ownership of Property

Where there is a 'means' qualification for electors, there is usually a similar or stiffer qualification based on income or the ownership of property for candidates. Zanzibar requires candidates for election to the Legislative Council to be in possession of a yearly income of £150 per annum or alternatively in possession of immovable property or a business to the value of £300, whereas the corresponding figures in the alternative qualifications for electors are a yearly income of £75 per annum or the ownership of immovable property of a capital value of £150.[4] In Tanganyika, the income qualification for candidates is one-third higher than the income qualification for voters.[5] In Uganda, the income qualification for candidates is twice as high as that for voters.[6] In general, the electoral laws of East African territories effectively

---

[1] See, for instance, paragraph 51 of the Kenya Coutts Commission Report.

[2] e.g. The Federation of Malaya and Ghana.

[3] Paragraph 19 of the Report of the Electoral Reforms Commission.

[4] Sections 4 and 82 of the Zanzibar Legislative Council Elections Decree.

[5] Sections 8 and 18 of the Tanganyika Legislative Council Elections Ordinance. The reader is reminded that educational, income and office-holder qualifications are alternatives for both voters and candidates.

[6] Sections 9 and 17 of the Uganda Legislative Council Elections Ordinance.

confine membership of the local legislative assemblies to persons of some substance by African standards.

In West Africa, the means qualification is less exacting and, indeed, in some territories, there is no such qualification. In Ghana electors must possess the modest qualification of owning immovable property within, or, for a period of not less than six out of the twelve months immediately preceding the date of application to register, residing within the ward in respect of which the application is made; candidates are required to be qualified to be registered as Assembly electors, but need not in fact have their names on the rolls, and, if so registered, it is immaterial whether the candidate is registered in the constituency in which he is seeking election or elsewhere. There is currently a property qualification for candidates for the Legislative Council in Sierra Leone, but this may well prove to be a transitional requirement, as the Electoral Reform Commission recommended in 1954 that there should ultimately be no such qualification.[1] In Nigeria, there is no income or property qualification for candidates to the Regional Houses of Assembly or to the Nigeria House of Representatives.

Other Qualifications

As has been seen to be the case in the franchise, a few African territories attempt to ensure the inclusion in the list of possible candidates of all those who are regarded as 'fit' for election by prescribing special status qualifications as alternatives to other qualifications. Tanganyika, for instance, has ensured the eligibility for election to the Legislative Council of previous members of the Council by providing previous membership as an alternative to the educational and income qualifications for candidates. Special qualifications of this kind are, however, of purely transitional significance.

DISQUALIFICATION OF CANDIDATES

General

Disqualifications are of greater significance for candidates than for electors. Any of the local disqualifications for electors in a territory normally also apply to candidates. But, in addition, candidates are liable to disqualification for candidature on grounds

[1] Paragraph 68 of the *Report of the Electoral Reform Commission*, 1954.

such as bankruptcy, the holding of a public office of emolument, the possession of a current government contract, or because of professional misconduct. Moreover, persons who have been found guilty of criminal offences may be more severely restricted for candidature than for the franchise. Persons of unsound mind and persons under an acknowledgement of allegiance to a foreign power are disqualified uniformly both from being registered as electors and from candidature, and these two categories of disqualification will not be discussed in this chapter.

Bankruptcy

Bankrupts are not normally permitted to seek election to or to sit in legislatures. The receipt of relief from public funds is, occasionally, also a disqualification.[1] In Southern Rhodesia receipt of poor relief or of relief under the Farmers' Debt Adjustment Act disqualifies for a period of five years. The 1951 Sierra Leone constitution disqualified as candidates those who had received poor relief within five years of seeking election. Disqualification for bankruptcy is usually (particularly in self-governing countries) limited to bankruptcy under the local law, but in non-self-governing territories it may extend to bankruptcy in the metropolitan country or even, as in Kenya, to undischarged bankrupts declared insolvent by any competent court in the colony "or elsewhere".

Holders of Public Office

The exclusion of some or all of those holding public offices of emolument from candidature has been a controversial debating point in many countries of the world. Controversy has been particularly acute in countries of Asia and Africa where many of the best potential candidates are civil servants. In the Federation of Malaya, only a small majority of the forty-four members of the Committee appointed in 1953 to examine the question of elections to the Federal Legislative Council were in favour of debarring government servants from election to the Council; the large minority felt that there would be a dearth of suitable

[1] In England, the Representation of the People Act, 1918, abolished the disfranchisement of paupers, which had continued throughout the nineteenth century. It was not until 1948, however, that the National Assistance Act abolished the legal status of a pauper and thus ended his disqualification from membership of local authorities.

candidates for election, particularly among the Malays, unless some facilities were given to civil servants to withdraw temporarily from their office in order to become electoral candidates. Ultimately a compromise was struck and civil servants were permitted to retire prematurely with pension if they wished to stand for election; in addition, certain of the lower ranks of government employees (e.g. messengers, telephone operators and storekeepers) were deemed not to be holders of offices of emolument and were thus permitted to stand as candidates for election.

The issue of where to draw the border-line of incompatibility of office between the civil servant and the politician was also the subject of some debate in Kenya when methods for the selection of African Representatives to the Legislative Council were under consideration. The Commissioner charged with the task of recommending electoral methods stated that:

> Most Africans take the view at the present time that those who serve the Government either directly as civil servants or in local government, through municipalities, etc., are probably some of their best potential candidates. There was a very strong plea, therefore, that such people should be allowed to stand for election and if they were successful then they should resign. If they were unsuccessful, they would then be allowed to return to work. In this I have considerable sympathy, as I feel that to insist upon a civil servant resigning before taking part in any African election is putting such a financial risk upon him as virtually to debar him from standing. In the circumstances I do feel therefore that the holding or acting in any public office should not be a disqualification for a candidate and that Government should seriously consider allowing civil servants to stand and giving them leave, with or without pay, if they wish to contest an election. Once again, as the Colony as a whole moves towards a greater freedom of choice, I feel that this point might be reconsidered, but certainly for the first election and possibly for one or two to come the Government should concede this point.[1]

This recommendation was not accepted without some reservations by the Kenya Government, but, for the first elections, government servants other than members of Her Majesty's Overseas Civil Service, members of the uniformed disciplined services, and officials actively concerned with the direction of polling were

---

[1] *Report of the Commissioner appointed to enquire into methods for the selection of African Representatives to the Legislative Council,* 1955, p. 24.

permitted to take leave in order to stand as candidates and were required to resign only if elected.

The disqualification of holders of public office tends to affect local government employees less than the civil service. Many African territories, Kenya included, leave local government authorities to decide for themselves whether to permit their officers to stand for election to the central government legislature; the extent to which such permission has been requested and granted is not, however, apparent in the reports on African elections.

In Uganda, teachers, whether employed in government schools or grant-aided schools, were among the classes of persons considered as not holding office in the public service and therefore eligible for election to the Legislative Council. Paid officers or employees of a Municipal Council or Township Authority and of certain quasi-government organisations in Uganda were, however, excluded under the 'office-holding' rules. As a result of the interpretation of 'holding office in the public service', a considerable percentage — well over one-third — of the candidates in the 1958 Uganda elections were school teachers.

In addition to including persons holding or acting in an office of profit in the public service, some electoral laws specifically include among the categories of disqualified those who hold or act in any office the functions of which involve any responsibility for the conduct of elections or for the compilation or revision of the register of electors.[1] Where all the work of registration and the conduct of elections is undertaken by regular civil servants, the exclusion of electoral officers is implied in the disqualification of persons holding an office of emolument in the public service.

Government Contractors

In some of the older colonial constitutions, persons financially interested in any subsisting contract with the Government were frequently disqualified from membership of the legislature, though this disqualification would in a few colonial territories be waived if full details of such interests were described to the Governor (or High Commissioner, as the case may be) and the latter's approval to membership obtained. With the growth of partially or fully elected legislatures, disqualifications of this

[1] See, for instance, Sec. 18(d) of the Uganda Legislative Council Elections Ordinance.

kind have tended to be amended or even dropped altogether. Typical of the 'older' type of disqualification is the provision in the Zanzibar Legislative Council Elections Decree that no person shall be a candidate for election to the Legislative Council who —

> is a party to, or a partner in a firm or a director or manager of a company which is a party to, any contract with the Government for or on account of the public service and has not disclosed to the British Resident the nature of that contract and his interest, or the interest of the firm or company, therein.[1]

Ghana has a somewhat similar disqualification, except that the particulars of the contract have to be published in the Government Gazette (rather than disclosed to a senior official) one month before the day of the election.

The constitution of the Federation of Malaya does not, however, include a disqualification of this kind for candidature. The Committee which considered in 1953/54 the type of electoral system to be introduced had this to say on the subject:

> Although we would see considerable disadvantage in permitting any member to enter into such a contract after he had been elected, unless the nature of the contract is disclosed to the High Commissioner and his permission obtained, we see very little disadvantage in a man who has already obtained such a contract presenting himself as a candidate. Since the contract will have been made already, its terms can owe nothing to his subsequent success at the polls nor is he likely to gain any advantage at the latter from his possession of the contract. However appropriate this disqualification might have been in older constitutions when Government's activities were comparatively limited, we feel that with the immense expansion in Government activity and the extent to which it now participates in all aspects of the life of the community, the disability imposed by this disqualification is unnecessarily wide. It is accordingly in our opinion both unnecessary and undesirable to continue this particular disqualification for candidates; but if retained in its present very broad terms it should at least be modified so as not to affect those who merely subscribe to Government loans or are minority shareholders in a company which has a contract with the Government.[2]

[1] Section 83(e), Zanzibar Legislative Council Elections Decree.
[2] *Report of the Committee appointed to examine the question of elections to the Federal Legislative Council*, 1954, p. 11.

The 1946 Constitution disqualified parties to contracts with the Nigerian Government, particulars of which had not been disclosed, from membership of the legislature, but this disqualification was omitted from the two succeeding constitutions of 1951 and 1954. In Sierra Leone, the Electoral Reform Commission of 1954 recommended that contractors should be disqualified from candidature even if details of their interest in public contracts had been disclosed; this recommendation was not, however, accepted *in toto* and the law provides a disqualification somewhat similar to that of Ghana.

Professional Misconduct

Some electoral laws provide for disqualification from candidature and membership of the legislature for persons disciplinarily disqualified from the practice of the professions. Thus, lawyers and medical practitioners disqualified from practice were excluded from candidature under the 1946 Nigerian Constitution, but, in later Constitutions, this disqualification has been omitted. Under the Gambia Order in Council of 1954, persons disqualified from the practice of their professions are also excluded from candidature for the legislature until they have been reinstated professionally. Again, in the Gold Coast at the time of the 1956 election no person possessed of professional qualifications disqualified in any part of the British Commonwealth from practising his profession by the order of any competent authority could stand for election to the Legislative Assembly unless five years had elapsed since his disqualification. Disqualifications of this nature have been, in the main, confined to West Africa and there is no similar disqualification in the electoral laws of territories such as Zanzibar, Uganda and Kenya.

Disqualification on the grounds of professional misconduct was the subject of great controversy in Sierra Leone prior to the 1957 elections, but there the argument had a very practical bearing on local politics, as exclusion on professional grounds affected the position of one of the political party leaders. The Electoral Reform Commission of 1954 had expressed doubts in their Report whether professional misconduct necessarily implied unfitness to serve on the Legislative Council and pointed out that such a disqualification might give to professional bodies an excessive power to exclude individual members from the Council and might also import a political flavour into the judicial deliberations of such bodies. The Commission therefore did not recommend the inclusion of such a disqualification in the law relating to elections to the Legislative Council, nor its retention for local government elections.[1] When, however, in 1956 a Bill for the amendment of the Freetown Municipal Ordinance was debated in a Select Committee of the Legislative Council, the Commission's recommendation for removal of the disqualification for municipal elections was not only rejected, but the disqualification itself was made even more severe, by omitting the previous limitation of disqualification to a ten year period; the electoral disqualification thus remained even when the period of disqualification from professional practice had expired. Similar amendments were later copied into the legislation dealing with central government elections but were repealed shortly after the first general election of 1957.

Quite apart from the suggestion that excessive powers are given to professional bodies by an electoral disqualification of this nature, it can be argued that the electorate should be allowed to exercise its own discretion at the polls in deciding whether a candidate found guilty of professional misconduct is fitted for election to the legislature. It is suggested that disqualifications on the grounds of professional misconduct become progressively less necessary as the membership of legislatures becomes to an ever greater degree elected under a system approaching universal adult suffrage.

Criminal or electoral offences

It has been mentioned above that persons who have been found guilty of criminal or electoral offences may be more severely restricted for candidature than for the franchise. The extreme example is, once again, to be found in the laws of Sierra Leone; there persons who have been convicted of treason or felony or any offence involving dishonesty are permanently disqualified for membership of the House of Representatives. In Kenya, the Commissioner appointed to examine methods for the selection of African representatives to the Legislative Council went so far as to recommend that a candidate for election should never have been imprisoned but the Government modified this proposal to exclude only those candidates who had been convicted of a criminal offence

[1] *Report of the Electoral Reform Commission*, 1954, para. 73.

and had been sentenced to imprisonment for a term of six months or more and had not received a pardon; moreover, powers exist to remove this disqualification in particular cases.[1] In Ghana, however, the disqualification for criminal offences is the same for candidates as for electors, and five years or more must elapse after the termination of imprisonment or conviction (in the case of conviction for dishonesty not punished with imprisonment) before a person can either register as an elector or stand as a candidate.

In the United Kingdom persons convicted of a felony and sentenced to death or penal servitude or imprisonment for more than twelve months are excluded from seeking election to or from sitting in either House of Parliament until the sentence has been served or a pardon granted, but there is no disqualification until conviction or after the serving of a sentence.[2] In some Commonwealth territories, for instance Zanzibar, disqualification ends, as in the United Kingdom, on completion of sentence;[3] elsewhere the disqualification continues for a defined period — three years in Uganda[4] and five years in Ghana — or permanently as in Sierra Leone.

As regards electoral offences, the length of period of disqualification on conviction for corrupt and illegal practices is usually the same for both potential electors and potential candidates. Thus, Uganda disqualifies persons convicted of a corrupt practice for a period of seven years from the date of conviction "from being registered as an elector or from voting at any election under this ordinance"[5] or from being elected a Representative Member. The Eastern Region of Nigeria disqualifies both electors and candidates for five years in respect of corrupt practices; it would appear that conviction for an illegal practice disqualifies electors from voting for five years, and is also a bar to standing for election to the Eastern House of Assembly for a similar period.[6] The Federation of Malaya disqualifies persons convicted of corrupt or illegal practices under the Election Offences Ordinance for five

[1] Kenya Legislative Council Sessional Paper No. 39 of 1955/56, pp. 9-10 and 21.

[2] A. Norman Schofield, *Parliamentary Elections* (1950), pp. 88-9.

[3] Sec. 83(c) of the Zanzibar Legislative Council Elections Decree.

[4] Sec. 18(c) of the Uganda Legislative Council Elections Ordinance.

[5] The Uganda Legislative Council Elections Ordinance, Sec. 55.

[6] Regs. 63 and 66 of the Eastern House of Assembly Electoral Regulations, 1955.

years from date of conviction or (in the case of corrupt practice punished with imprisonment) from release from prison, both from being registered as an elector or from being elected at any election.[1]

Disqualification of persons convicted of offences may well have important political implications in some of the emergent countries in which a number of the leading members of the nationalist parties have been sentenced to varying terms of imprisonment during the struggle for independence. In the overseas French territories, disqualification on conviction is permanent in the case of some offences and only temporary in others and, in sentencing an offender to a penalty normally involving temporary electoral disqualifications, the court may order that the temporary deprivation of the right to vote and be elected should not apply. Conversely the courts are authorised under certain legislation, when sentencing offenders for other offences, to suspend the right to vote and to be elected for the period stipulated in the sentence. It has been alleged that a number of the leading members of opposition parties in French Togoland have been placed under an electoral disqualification in consequence of 'repressive measures' taken against them and have thus been prevented from standing for election.[2]

Special Disqualifications

For candidates, as for electors, there may be additional disqualifications of local and often of temporary significance. Thus for the elections held in Singapore in May 1959, no person was permitted to stand as a candidate if he or she had been the subject of a detention order made under the Emergency Regulations. There is a somewhat similar disqualification for both electors and candidates in African elections in Kenya.[3] In Trinidad, ministers of religion are disqualified from sitting as elected members of the Legislative Council. There is a similar disqualification in Britain in so far as no priest or deacon of the Church of England and no minister of the Church of Scotland can be elected to the House of Commons.[4]

[1] Sections 11 and 27 of the Federation of Malaya Election Offences Ordinance.
[2] *Report of the U.N. Commissioner for the Supervision of the Elections in Togoland under French Administration*, pp. 82-3.
[3] See the Kenya Legislative Council (African Representation) Ordinance, Sec. 13(e) and Sec. 16(1).
[4] See A. N. Schofield *Parliamentary Elections*, pp. 83-4.

THE NOMINATION OF CANDIDATES

The choice of candidates by political parties

The procedure for selecting party candidates for nomination prior to an election is not, in most British Commonwealth countries, the subject of regulation by law and the methods by means of which persons are selected are not the concern of the electoral authority. In Britain the local branches of the Conservative Party generally wield more power than their counterparts in the Labour Party in the selection process, but neither party is bound by law or by practice to maintain the open procedure for the choice of party nominees which is in use in the U.S.A., where the rival candidates for office belonging to one party have to direct their appeal in primary elections to the whole enrolled membership of that party. The candidate who gets to the head of the poll is the nominee of the party at the second stage when the electorate has to choose between the Democrat and the Republican nominees.[1]

In theory the direct primary destroys the power of the party convention which, in the U.S.A. before the introduction of primaries, had unbridled power to decide which persons should be the party candidates for office. In practice it is a mixed blessing. On the one hand sectional interests within a party can bring the internal problems of the party to the notice of the public and this is obviously to the good. The disadvantages of the system, judging by American experience, are that the direct primary consolidates the domination of individual states by one political party and that the party bosses can still in practice exercise considerable influence on primary elections for minor offices.

Where there is no open procedure for the choice of party nominees, interest is centred on the relative importance of central party headquarters and local constituency party branches in the choice of candidates for election. In Britain, as has been mentioned, the local branches of the Conservative Party tend to have more freedom of choice than the local branches of the Labour Party. In the new democracies of Asia and Africa, the views of the central headquarters of the main political parties have usually been decisive. It would, however, be out of place to attempt a more

[1] See *The American Political System* by D. W. Brogan, Part Two, Ch. IV, 'Party Sections and the Direct Primary.'

detailed analysis of the procedures for selecting candidates, as this is not a problem of electoral administration.

Deposits

In most large-scale elections, candidates are required to pay deposits as a condition of nomination. The deposit is usually returnable if the candidate obtains more than a fixed minimum percentage of the votes cast in the constituency in which he is standing for election. The deposit serves to discourage frivolous candidature and candidates who support a cause which has very little appeal to the electors at large.

The legislation dealing with deposits does not always make adequate allowance for the position of candidates standing in multi-member constituencies in which each voter has as many votes as there are vacant seats. Thus, in Eastern Nigeria,[1] under the Eastern House of Assembly Electoral Regulations, 1955, the deposit is returnable to a candidate or his personal representative in a contested election if the candidate is actually elected or if he obtains votes equal in number to not less than one-eighth of the total number of votes cast in his constituency (it is also returnable if the candidate dies before the date of the election or if he withdraws his nomination before the date of publication of the list of candidates).[2] But all of the constituencies in Eastern Nigeria for the 1957 elections to the Eastern House of Assembly were multi-member constituencies, and, in a three-member constituency, a defeated candidate would lose his deposit if he did not secure votes from three-eighths of those voting. In fact the very great majority of the defeated candidates in this election lost their deposits, including all the defeated candidates in the only six-member constituency and twenty-two out of the twenty-three defeated candidates in the three five-member constituencies. Even in the eight three-member constituencies, all but one of the defeated candidates lost their deposits![3] It is the intention of the Government of the Eastern Region to introduce legislation enabling future elections to the Eastern House of Assembly to be

[1] There is a similar flaw in the electoral law of the Bahamas in relation to multi-member constituencies — see Sec. 36(7) of the General Assembly Elections Act, 1946.
[2] Reg. 23.
[3] See Appendix C of the official Report on the General Election to the Eastern House of Assembly, 1957.

held on the basis of single member constituencies, and this situation is not therefore likely to recur. There is, of course, no objection to a regulation providing for the forfeiture of the deposit if a defeated candidate obtains less than a prescribed proportion of the total number of votes cast if all the constituencies return single members to the legislature; but adjustments must be made possible in the regulations if the constituencies return a varying number of members.[1]

A somewhat more realistic provision regarding the forfeiture of deposits is to be found in the Tanganyika Legislative Council Elections Ordinance.[2] In Tanganyika each constituency is to return three Members, one African, one Asian and one European and the voter, in order to cast a valid vote, is required to vote for one candidate for each contested seat in his constituency. The deposit of a candidate in a Tanganyika Legislative Council constituency is forfeited if he obtains less than one-eighth, or one-sixteenth or one twenty-fourth of the total number of votes cast, according to whether one or two or three of the seats in the constituency are being contested. Another possible type of provision in a territory containing multi-member constituencies is that of the Gambia where, for Legislative Council Elections, the candidate's deposit is returned after a contested election if he obtains one hundred votes or votes equivalent to not less than one-fifth of the votes cast for the elected candidate to whom the least number of votes is given, whichever is the least.[3]

The 'one-eighth' rule is fairly common in the British Commonwealth and is in use in the United Kingdom, Uganda, Tanganyika and the Federation of Malaya, to take but a few examples. In India, however, deposits were forfeited by candidates in the 1951-52 elections who failed to secure votes "(a) exceeding one-sixth of the total number of votes polled in the case of a single-member constituency, or (b) in the case of a constituency returning more than one member, one-sixth of the total votes polled divided by the number of members to be elected";[4] with forfeiture at the one-sixth level, well over one-third of the total number of

---

[1] The harshest provision of all is the forfeiture of the deposit if the candidate withdraws or is unsuccessful in the election. Such a provision appears in the Jordan Council of Representatives Electoral Law, 1947.

[2] See Sec. 73 of the Ordinance.

[3] The Gambia Legislative Council (Election) Rules 1954, Rule 6(5).

[4] *Report on the first general elections in India, 1951-2*, Vol. I, p. 143.

candidates for election to the various legislatures forfeited their deposits. Ghana and the Bahamas also require candidates to obtain at least one-sixth of the votes cast to avoid forfeiting the deposit. In the Western Region of Nigeria the fraction is one-fifth;[1] in the 1956 elections to the Western Region House of Assembly, 71 out of a total of 229 validly nominated candidates lost their deposits. The percentage of candidates losing their deposits can, of course, be just as high as in India and Western Nigeria with a 'one-eighth' rule if the elections are one-sided; for instance in the Federation of Malaya in 1955, 43 of the 128 candidates who contested 51 seats (one of the 52 seats was uncontested) lost their deposits, but at these Malayan elections one party almost swept the board.[2] Given a sizeable deposit, one-eighth of the total votes cast is perhaps a large enough fraction to require a candidate to obtain in order to avoid the forfeiture of his deposit.

The size of the deposit naturally varies according to the wealth of the community providing the candidates and the amount which is considered to be required to guard against the nomination of frivolous candidates. Candidates for election to the British Parliament are required to deposit the sum of one hundred and fifty pounds. In the Bahamas the deposit is as high as one hundred pounds. In Canada, the deposit is somewhat smaller — two hundred Canadian dollars. The deposit required of candidates to the Federal Legislature in the Federation of Malaya is slightly lower than the Canadian deposit — five hundred Malayan dollars, which is equivalent to a little under sixty pounds sterling. The deposits required of candidates in central government elections in Africa have tended to be somewhat lower still — £50 for the Eastern House of Assembly (Nigeria), £50 for the Ghana Legislative Assembly, £25 for the Gambia Legislative Council, £25 for the Western House of Assembly (Nigeria), £25 for the Zanzibar Legislative Council, £25 for the Tanganyika Legislative Council and £25 for the Uganda Legislative Council. Deposits are usually much lower for local government elections — for instance, in the Western Region of Nigeria, the deposit in the case

[1] In Japan, too, the fraction is one-fifth. The deposit "is returned if the candidate for the House of Representatives polls at least one-fifth of the total number of votes cast divided by the number of seats to be filled in the electoral district". (Yanaga, *Japanese People and Politics*, p. 286).

[2] See paragraph 68 of the *Report on the First Election of Members to the Legislative Council of the Federation of Malaya, 1955*.

of a local government election is only five pounds as compared with the twenty-five pounds required for candidature in a parliamentary election.[1]

There is an interesting discussion about the size of the deposit in the U.N. Commissioner's Report on the 1958 general election in French Togoland.[2] The law required a deposit of 50,000 francs, which is very considerably higher than the deposit required of candidates in other countries of French and British West Africa or even of candidates in France itself. The Commissioner suggested that, while a deposit was necessary to prevent abuses, the amount required was too high in view of the country's standard of living and he suggested that consideration be given to lowering it. This suggestion was rejected by the Togoland Government who regarded the deposit as security for the costs incurred on behalf of the candidates by the local Treasury, the actual amount of which were estimated as averaging 50,000 francs. The Commissioner countered with the comment that a lower deposit would suffice to discourage splinter groups and frivolous candidates, but the law was not in fact amended.

Subscription of the nomination paper

As an additional safeguard against frivolous candidature, most electoral systems require the nomination of a candidate for election to be subscribed by a number of the registered electors of the constituency in which the candidate proposes to stand. The first two of these electors are the candidate's proposer and seconder, and a certain amount of additional support is usually required — the precise number of electors required to assent to a nomination depends, of course, on the electoral law. In the United Kingdom the assent of a total of ten electors is required for the valid nomination of a candidate, — a proposer, a seconder and eight other electors;[3] in Canada, the number of signatures required for a valid nomination was at one time as high as twenty-five, but the figure was reduced to ten in 1920;[4] in the Federation of Malaya,

[1] The Western Region Parliamentary and Local Government Electoral Regulations, 1955, Reg. 36(4).
[2] *Report of the United Nations Commissioner for the Supervision of the Elections in Togoland under French Administration* (T/1392), pp. 90-94.
[3] The Parliamentary Election Rules, Rule 7(4). See also A. Norman Schofield, *Parliamentary Elections*, p. 129 et seq.
[4] See Norman Ward, *The Canadian House of Commons — Representation*, p. 156.

a proposer, seconder and four other persons, all of whom must be registered electors of the constituency in which the candidate seeks election, are required for a valid nomination of a candidate for election to the Federal Legislature. In the Sudan, a candidate has to be proposed by only two persons whose names are on the constituency roll.[1]

In the British Commonwealth territories of West Africa, a smaller amount of support is required as a condition for nomination. Thus in the Gambia (for Legislative Council Elections), every candidate has to be "nominated by at least three voters whose names appear in the register of voters for the electoral district for which he seeks to be elected",[2] and in Eastern and Western Nigeria, for election to the respective Houses of Assembly, it is sufficient for the candidate to be nominated by two electors registered in the constituency. Candidates for the Ghana Parliament require three nominators. In East Africa, however, the requirements are as great or greater than in the United Kingdom; the Tanganyika Legislative Council Elections Ordinance requires a candidate to be "nominated in writing by not less than twenty-five voters in the constituency for which he is a candidate",[3] and of these twenty-five, fifteen must be members of his own community — e.g., in the case of a candidate who is an African, at least fifteen of the nominators must be Africans. Requirements in the other East African territories are not quite so high as in Tanganyika, but candidates for the Legislative Council in Uganda require the support of ten registered electors,[4] in addition to their proposer and seconder, and candidates for the Legislative Council in Zanzibar and for the Legislative Council in Kenya must be nominated by not less than nine registered electors.[5] In the Federation of Rhodesia and Nyasaland, not less than ten voters are required to support a nomination. In some countries outside the British Commonwealth, a considerable amount of support is required for a valid nomination. Thus, in Indonesia (where each constituency returns a considerable number of representatives to Parliament and to the Constituent Assembly), each list of candidates has to be "supported by the signatures of

[1] The Sudan Parliamentary Election Rules, 1957, Rule 22(2).
[2] The Gambia Legislative Council (Elections) Rules, 1954, Rule 6(2).
[3] Sec. 71(1).
[4] The Uganda Legislative Council Elections Ordinance, Sec. 20(2).
[5] The Zanzibar Legislative Council Elections Decree, Sec. 27(2).

registered voters, 200 signatures for the first candidate of a list
and 25 for every other candidate".[1] In some States of the U.S.A.,
a valid nomination has in the past required the signature of
hundreds or even thousands of electors.[2]

The position in Tanganyika is of particular interest, as the
procedure for subscription of a nomination paper is designed to
ensure that a successful candidate is acceptable in some degree
both to his own ethnic group and at the same time to all sections
of the community. A candidate with ideas of racial superiority of
the Hitler type might find the required support for nomination
from members of his own community but would find some
difficulty in obtaining votes from members of the other communities; equally, a prospective candidate whose words or actions
indicated a complete lack of sympathy for the views of other
members of his own community would experience difficulties in
completing his nomination papers.

Time and Place for receiving nominations

The official designated as Returning Officer for the constituency
receives the nomination papers of candidates. The electoral law
usually prescribes the exact period during which candidates or
their proposers may tender nominations. This period is sometimes
confined to a few hours on one day and sometimes to a few hours
on each of a number of successive days.

The nomination papers have usually to be delivered at the
office of the returning officer by the candidate himself or by one
of the persons nominating him. It is often sufficient if the papers
are handed to a member of the returning officer's staff, but
sometimes personal delivery to the returning officer is required.
In the Western Region of Nigeria, in the case of a parliamentary
election, the electoral authority is permitted to appoint more than
one place for the delivery of nomination papers and "any place
appointed shall not be required to be within the constituency".[3]
The provision of more than one place for the delivery of nomination papers for a given constituency appears to be somewhat
unusual, but the place appointed for the receipt of nomination
papers is frequently outside the boundaries of the constituency;

[1] Herbert Feith, *The Indonesian Elections of 1955*, p. 4.
[2] See H. R. Penniman, *Sait's American Parties and Elections*, pp. 411-12.
[3] The Parliamentary and Local Government Electoral Regulations, Reg. 33(3).

in the Colony of Singapore, for instance, it has been the practice to receive nomination papers for all constituencies in elections to the legislature in one central public building.

The allocation of symbols

Although there are some differences in detail, as has been noted above, in the size of deposit, in the circumstances under which the deposit is forfeited and in the amount of support a potential candidate requires from the electorate in order to be validly nominated, the general outline of nomination procedure is comparatively uniform throughout the British Commonwealth. The political parties or their local branches choose their prospective candidates, the candidates are proposed and assented to by a certain number of registered electors, some or all of whom are likely in fact to be party members, the required deposit is paid and the nomination papers are completed and submitted to the proper authority at the correct time and place. In Britain, there is no legal recognition of the part played by political parties in elections and the candidate is in law an individual rather than the representative put forward for election by a given party; an attitude of legal detachment to parties may however be impossible in territories with a semi-literate electorate who rely on the use of symbols to identify the candidate for whom they wish to vote. Symbols, if used, must be allotted at the time of nomination to enable the candidates to educate the electorate in the recognition of the symbols as part of their election campaigns and to permit the electoral authorities to print notices listing the candidates and ballot papers (where the latter show names and symbols of candidates) in time for the election.

It is obvious that symbols must be familiar to and recognisable by illiterate and ignorant voters. Moreover, symbols must be easily distinguishable one from another and should have no religious, political or racial associations.[1] These basic principles have found ready acceptance wherever symbols have been used. Nevertheless, problems have arisen in deciding:

   (a) whether all symbols should be chosen by the administration and distributed by lot or by some other method to candidates.

---

[1] For instance, the National Flag would be unacceptable as a symbol. So too would a cow in India or among the pastoral tribes of Africa.

(*b*) whether political parties should be permitted to register symbols for the use of party-sponsored candidates and, if so, what criteria the returning officers are to adopt in deciding whether in fact a particular candidate is so sponsored. The term 'political party' itself has to be defined for this purpose.

(*c*) If political party symbols are permitted, how one candidate should be differentiated from another belonging to the same party in a multi-member constituency.

It can be argued that, if symbols are to be of neutral design and without religious, racial, political or sentimental significance, they should be distributed by lot to the validly nominated candidates in a particular constituency at the time of nomination. It can further be argued that, if political party symbols are permitted, the personal qualities of the candidate are given less consideration by a semi-literate electorate than would be the case if a symbol had no party significance. On the other hand, it is confusing for the electorate and maddening for political party machines if a given symbol represents a candidate belonging to a certain party in one constituency and a candidate of a rival party in another constituency at the same general election; moreover, it can be argued that it is only if symbols are approved and allocated well before nomination day that there is sufficient time to print and distribute party election propaganda.

Among the countries which have used symbols and permitted recognised political parties to register party symbols for the use of their candidates are India, the Federation of Malaya, Ghana, Nigeria, Sierra Leone, Indonesia and the French African territories. Territories which have in the past not permitted the use of party symbols are in a small minority — they include Singapore, Zanzibar, Uganda and most of the British West Indies.[1]

In India, for the first national elections, the Election Commission gave 'recognition' to fourteen parties on an *ad hoc* basis as national parties which, in the Commission's estimate, had

---

[1] In the general election of 1953 in British Guiana, a political party was allowed a common symbol for all the candidates it sponsored. The Representation of the People Ordinance of 1957, however, reversed the position and provided for the allocation of symbols to each candidate, the symbols being prescribed in numerical order in Regulations made under the Ordinance, and the order of allocation of the symbols being based on the alphabetical order of the candidate's name on the ballot paper.

sufficient standing or following in the country to merit such recognition. Only parties given recognition had symbols reserved for them in the general elections. A further fifteen parties demanded but were refused this recognition. After the first general election, the position was reviewed and the Commission fixed the minimum standard for recognition at the figure of 3% of the valid votes polled in the elections; this had the effect of reducing the number of parties recognised as national parties from fourteen to four.[1] In order that the names of the official candidates sponsored by a party could be ascertained by the electoral authority, each 'recognised' party was required to inform the authorities of the names of persons authorised to convey party decisions regarding the adoption of candidates and to forward specimen signatures of such persons. For the purpose of assigning symbols to independent candidates and to candidates sponsored by parties which had not achieved recognition, each candidate was permitted to indicate his first, and, if necessary, subsequent choices from the list of officially approved symbols (other than the symbols reserved for recognised parties). The first choice of a candidate was accepted if it did not clash with the first choice of any other candidate. If there was any such clash, the returning officer was required to decide the matter by drawing lots and the unlucky candidate would then be allotted his second choice if available.

In the Federation of Malaya, the elections legislation provides that political parties intending to contest more than one seat at general elections are permitted to register a party symbol for the use of candidates, and party candidates were required at the first general elections in 1955 to produce to the returning officer on Nomination Day a written authority signed by a responsible official of their party authorising the candidate to use the party symbol. Independent candidates were assigned a symbol by lot conducted by the returning officer on Nomination Day from among a selection of officially approved symbols; these candidates were shown the list of approved symbols and given the opportunity to request the removal of any symbols to which they objected.

In Ghana, for purposes of the 1956 Assembly elections, candidates of the seven political parties which contested the elections were allocated their party symbol on production of an authority from the National Headquarters of their parties. Independent

[1] *Report on the first general elections in India, 1951-2*, Vol. I, Ch. IX.

candidates were allowed to choose one of the approved 'independent' symbols. Returning officers were instructed that, if a candidate claimed to be a party candidate but could produce no authority from the National Headquarters of the Party to which he claimed to belong, he should be treated as an independent candidate and given an 'independent' symbol. In both Ghana and the Federation of Malaya, it was easier for a party to qualify for a party symbol than in India, as, in both the former countries, parties which were confined to regions and were not national in character were permitted to use party symbols in the national elections.[1]

In Sierra Leone, experience of the use of symbols was gained in district council elections held a few months before the general elections of 1957. At the district council elections, the fact that symbols were merely distinguishing marks was fairly generally understood, although it is reputed that in one area candidates using the symbol of a paramount chief's staff of office were thought to be harbouring ambitions to be chiefs whilst those who used the symbol of a cooking pot were regarded as having pledged themselves to feed their supporters![2] At the general election, party discipline was such that there was a possibility of several candidates from one of the principal political parties[3] offering themselves for election in some of the constituencies and the procedure used elsewhere of allocating party symbols only to candidates in possession of letters of appointment from their parties was put into operation. In the double member constituencies, the party symbols were produced in two colours to differentiate one candidate from another of the same party.

In Zanzibar, for purposes of the first general elections held in 1957, symbols were allocated to all candidates, including party candidates, on nomination day from an officially selected list of symbols, copies of each of which had been printed before nomination day and were made available for sale to the candidate to whom a particular symbol had been allocated. The political parties in Zanzibar were not, at the time of the 1957 elections, regarded as sufficiently 'fixed' in their identities to justify the allocation of

[1] For instance, the Togoland Congress and the Wassaw Youth Association in Ghana and the Perak Progressive Party and the Perak Malay League in Malaya.
[2] See D. Scott on 'The Sierra Leone Election of 1957' in W. J. M. Mackenzie and K. E. Robinson (eds.), *Five Elections in Africa.*
[3] The Sierra Leone People's Party.

party symbols.[1] Under the provisions of the Zanzibar Legislative Council Elections Decree,[2] every candidate or his agent is required, at the time of delivery of the nomination papers, to choose a symbol from the prescribed list. As in India, in the event of two or more candidates choosing the same symbol, the returning officer decides the matter by lot and the candidate who has not succeeded in gaining his first choice of symbol is asked to choose another symbol from the prescribed list. Requests were received from more than one candidate for the allocation of a symbol at a much earlier date than nomination day, or alternatively for approval of a symbol designed by himself, but such requests were turned down.[3]

In French Africa, the symbol system is in use and there is a separate list or ballot paper at the polls for each party or independent candidate contesting a constituency; the rival papers usually being in different colours. The voter selects from the various lists or ballot papers the one which he prefers, recognising it by its colour if he is illiterate, and places it in the official envelope which he shows, closed, to the polling officer before dropping it into the ballot-box. The French system has the merit of simplifying voting procedure (which is discussed in detail in Chapter VIII) and of avoiding the necessity of differentiating the symbol or colour of one candidate from another of the same party in a contest in a multi-member constituency.

The acceptance and scrutiny of nominations by the returning officer
The returning officer has the duty of receiving nomination papers and, within the limits imposed by the electoral law, of deciding on the validity of the nominations. The content and lay-out of the nomination paper and of any documents which must accompany the nomination (such as a statutory declaration of qualifications or a candidate's assent to nomination) are usually prescribed in the electoral legislation and the returning officer is generally bound to accept completed nomination papers if tendered at the correct time and place. There is, however, some variation in the powers which a returning officer possesses to adjudicate on

---

[1] See the *Report on the Elections in Zanzibar, 1957*, p. 17.
[2] Section 27.
[3] In Uganda, however, there was a provisional allocation of symbols to prospective candidates well before the official nomination day for the 1958 general election.

the validity of nominations and, in order to illustrate the position, the powers and duties of the returning officer in respect of nominations in Ghana, Malaya, Nigeria, India and Zanzibar will be compared briefly.

In Ghana, the nomination paper for Assembly elections is a single document in which the candidate assents to nomination, states that he is qualified and gives brief personal particulars, and the three nominators state that they are electors of the electoral district (i.e. constituency) for which the candidate seeks election and give their own personal particulars (name, occupation and address). The returning officer has no authority to refuse to accept a nomination paper provided it is properly completed, submitted at the correct time and place and accompanied by a deposit. A decision whether or not a particular candidate is qualified or disqualified for election can only be made by a Court on an election petition. On receipt of a nomination paper, the returning officer or a responsible person deputed by him is required to make a note of the date and time of receipt and to allocate a symbol and colour to the candidate. Withdrawal of nomination is permitted for a period of twelve days after the closing date for the receipt of nomination papers.[1]

In the Federation of Malaya, for elections to the Legislative Council, nomination papers in triplicate and one copy of a candidate's statutory declaration of qualifications must be handed to the returning officer simultaneously. If the Statutory Declaration is not delivered with the nomination papers, the latter cannot be accepted by the returning officer. The deposit must be paid before the closing time for the receipt of nominations, but it need not be paid at the same time as the submission of the papers and arrangements are made in most constituencies for the local branch of the Treasury to receive the deposit on behalf of the returning officer. One copy of every accepted nomination paper is posted in a conspicuous position outside the place of nomination. It is not necessary for the returning officer to wait until the deposit has been paid before posting the nomination paper, but the

---

[1] The Electoral Regulations provided that, in a general election, nomination papers are receivable up to 4 p.m. of the day falling twenty-one days before the first day appointed for the election and withdrawal is permitted up to 4 p.m. on the tenth day before the first day appointed for the election. 'A recent amendment to the regulations has made withdrawal impossible'.

candidate is deemed to have withdrawn his candidature if the deposit is not paid by twelve noon on Nomination Day. It is not the returning officer's duty to decide whether or not any given candidate is qualified to be elected a member of the Legislative Council unless it is apparent from the contents of the nomination paper that he is not capable of being elected or unless the returning officer has good reason to believe that the candidate is unable to read and write the Malay or English languages with a degree of proficiency sufficient to enable him to take an active part in the proceedings of the Council. Thus, although undischarged bankrupts are disqualified from election to the Council, the fact that a given candidate was an undischarged bankrupt would not be apparent to either the returning officer or a rival candidate from the contents of the nomination paper, and any objection taken to the candidate on the grounds of his bankruptcy would not be valid. Any person whose name appears in the register of electors for the constituency being contested and any candidate for the constituency has the right to object to the validity of any nomination paper for a short period immediately after the closure of nominations, but objections may only be made by such persons on all or any of the following four grounds:

(*a*) That the description of the candidate in the nomination paper is insufficient to identify the candidate (e.g. if the only name given for the candidate in the nomination paper is an alias not commonly known).

(*b*) That the nomination paper does not comply with or was not delivered in accordance with the provisions of the electoral regulations (e.g. nomination papers handed to the returning officer by anyone who is not the candidate or his proposer or seconder).

(*c*) That it is apparent from the contents of the nomination paper that the candidate is not capable of being elected a member of the Council (e.g. if the place of residence given in the description of the candidate in the nomination paper is an address outside the Federation).

(*d*) That the required deposit of $500 was not paid within the time limits laid down by the electoral regulations.

It is the returning officer's duty to give his decision on any objection to a nomination paper as soon as is practicable after the objection has been made. In the Federation of Malaya, a candidate may not withdraw his candidature after the closure of nominations but he is entitled to do so by written notice of withdrawal up to the hour of closure.

In the Western Region of Nigeria, the nomination paper is rather similar in form to that used in Ghana and has to be subscribed by the candidate and by two registered electors nominating him. The following particulars are required in the paper:

(*a*) The name, address and occupation of the candidate.

(*b*) The names, addresses and occupations of the nominators of the candidate.

(*c*) A certification by the candidate that he is willing and qualified to stand for election.

(*d*) A statement by the candidate as to his choice of symbol for the purpose of a contested election.[1]

The Electoral Officer (i.e. returning officer) in the Western Region has no powers to adjudicate on the qualifications of a candidate and is only entitled to hold a nomination invalid if:

(*a*) The particulars of the candidate or of his nominators are not shown on the nomination paper as required by the relevant regulations.

(*b*) The nomination paper is not subscribed as required by the relevant regulations.

(*c*) The nominators or any one of them are not persons whose names appear on the relevant register of electors.

(*d*) The deposit is not paid to the appropriate treasury and the official receipt produced to the Electoral Officer with the nomination paper.

Nominations close at one o'clock on the fourteenth day before a parliamentary election and withdrawal is permitted up to one o'clock in the afternoon of the eighth day before the election.

At the time of the first general election in India, the nomination procedure was as follows:

> A proposer and a seconder have to subscribe to the nomination paper and the candidate must also agree in writing to the nomination. The nomination paper has to be delivered to the Returning Officer at the place notified by him between the hours of 11 a.m. and 3 p.m. on or before the last date fixed for the filing of nominations.

[1] Reg. 34(2) of the Parliamentary and Local Government Electoral Regulations, 1955.

Only the candidate in person or his proposer or seconder is competent to deliver the nomination paper to the Returning Officer. The candidate must himself be registered as a voter in some constituency or other of the House to which he seeks election and his proposer and seconder must be voters enrolled in the particular constituency in respect of which the nomination is made. The proposer and seconder are entitled to subscribe as many nomination papers as there are vacancies to be filled and no more.

The nomination paper of every candidate is required to be accompanied by:

1. A declaration in writing appointing an election agent;
2. A receipt showing the necessary deposit has been made for the candidature;
3. A declaration making the choice of a symbol.

In the case of a candidate desiring election to a seat reserved for the Scheduled Castes or for the Scheduled Tribes, his nomination paper must, in addition, be accompanied by a declaration verified by a Magistrate that he belongs to a Scheduled Caste or a Scheduled Tribe.[1]

At these elections, considerable difficulty was experienced by the average returning officer at the time of scrutiny of nomination papers, and, despite a provision in the law which laid down that no nomination paper should be rejected on technical grounds, there were in fact several instances of such rejection. Out of a total of 338 election petitions arising out of the general elections, 116 contained allegations regarding improper rejection of nomination papers, and 64 of these rejections were held to be improper by the Election Tribunals. As a result of the experience gained in the first elections, the Indian Election Commission recommended a considerable simplification of the laws relating to nomination procedure.

Provision for the scrutiny of nominations was omitted from the Elections Decree of 1957, under which the first general elections of Zanzibar were held. All that a returning officer was empowered to do was to satisfy himself that a candidate's supporters to the required number were duly registered electors in the constituency in which he proposed to stand; that he had paid his deposit, and that the candidate's Statutory Declaration had been duly completed, signed and attested. The returning officer and the rival candidates were thus powerless to intervene even if there

[1] *Report on the first general elections in India, 1951-2*, Vol. I, p. 112.

was reason to believe that the Statutory Declaration contained statements which were false. The Supervisor of the 1957 Zanzibar elections has suggested that, although it is desirable to keep nomination procedure as simple as possible, it may nevertheless be desirable to make some provision for the scrutiny of nominations before the next general election.[1] The difficulties experienced in India in connection with the scrutiny of nomination papers suggest, however, that an extension of the powers of returning officers might very well lead to the improper rejection of nomination papers. It is, in fact, a matter of opinion whether it is preferable to give the returning officer powers to scrutinise nomination papers and prevent an apparently unqualified candidate from contesting a constituency or to limit his powers drastically and rely on the deterrents of the deposit, the expense of election campaigning and the likelihood that an election petition will be submitted if a successful candidate has not complied with the electoral legislation.

Some other British African territories such as Uganda[2] and the Gambia[3] follow the example of the Western Region of Nigeria and limit the powers of the returning officer to hold a nomination paper invalid to much the same grounds as in Nigeria; in neither of these two territories is there provision for objections to nomination by rival candidates. In Tanganyika,[4] the position is much more akin to that pertaining in the Federation of Malaya. Kenya is the one territory in British Africa which demands positive proof of certain of the candidate's qualifications; all prospective candidates in the African elections, other than those in possession of a university degree, or a Makerere diploma or who have already served on the Legislative Council are required to appear before a Languages Board which, if satisfied, will issue a certificate of proficiency in reading, writing and speaking English. Moreover, candidates are required to take an oath of allegiance to Her Majesty and to make a statutory declaration. Nomination procedure is also stiffer in Kenya than elsewhere insofar as the signatures of the candidate's proposer, seconder, and other supporters must be witnessed by a magistrate, justice of the peace, commissioner for oaths or public notary, and the nomination

---

[1] *Report on the Elections in Zanzibar, 1957*, p. 49.
[2] Sec. 21 of the Uganda Legislative Council Elections Ordinance, 1957.
[3] Rule 7 of the Gambia Legislative Council Elections Rules, 1954.
[4] Sec. 81 of the Tanganyika Legislative Council Elections Ordinance, 1957.

paper has to be stamped with a 2s. revenue stamp in respect of every signature so witnessed.

The withdrawal of candidates is permitted in many African territories and in the Caribbean for a period of some days after nominations have closed. In this respect, the procedure in most of British Africa and the West Indies differs from the procedure in countries such as Britain, Uganda and the Federation of Malaya, where candidates are not permitted to withdraw after the close of nominations. But the present electoral laws of Nigeria, Tanganyika, the Gambia, Zanzibar, Jamaica and British Guiana all permit the withdrawal of candidature for a period of a few days after the close of nominations. In Jamaica,[1] a candidate may withdraw at any time after being officially nominated up to seven days before polling day, whilst in British Guiana[2] withdrawal is permitted up to the day before polling day. In both these territories voters mark the ballot papers, and, if there has been a late withdrawal after the ballot papers have been printed, some voters are liable to cast their votes for candidates who have withdrawn. In Jamaica, whenever a candidate withdraws after the ballot papers have been printed, it is the duty of the returning officer to advise every presiding officer in his constituency of such withdrawal and the presiding officer is required to post up a notice of withdrawal in a conspicuous place in the polling station during the whole of polling day; if, nevertheless, some voters cast their votes for a candidate who has withdrawn, such votes are null and void. In British Guiana, the presiding officer is required not only to post a notice of withdrawal as in Jamaica, but he is also required to inform each elector of the withdrawal when delivering a ballot-paper; these safeguards are presumably regarded as sufficient, as there is no special provision in British Guiana's electoral laws for treating as null and void at the count any ballot-papers marked in favour of a candidate who has withdrawn. The circumstances in which candidates in various territories have withdrawn their nominations has not been well enough documented to make it possible for the author to hazard an opinion on the respective merits of the two systems; but it is obvious that, even if corrupt withdrawal from candidature is an election offence (as it usually is), the possibility of corrupt practices are greater in the system

[1] Sec. 22, Jamaica Representation of the People Law, 1944.
[2] Sec. 23, British Guiana Representation of the People Ordinance, 1957.

adopted in most of the African territories than in Britain and Malaya. In Ghana, at the time of the 1956 general election, there were numerous allegations that some of the twenty candidates who withdrew between nomination day and the last day for withdrawal had accepted sums of money as a consideration for withdrawal. Whether there was any basis of truth for these allegations is not known, but it is perhaps significant that it was recommended after the election that consideration should be given to the amendment of the relevant regulation.

<h2 style="text-align:center">STATE ASSISTANCE TO VALIDLY NOMINATED CANDIDATES</h2>

Having been validly nominated, the candidate is often entitled to some measure of State assistance during his election campaign. In France, the amount of assistance given to candidates is considerable; the cost of paper for posters, election addresses and ballot papers is met by the State, in addition to the cost of envelopes, printing and despatch. Each party contesting a constituency has the right to put up on any official 'emplacement' three posters, which are restricted as to format. Each party is also entitled to print and despatch at State expense two election addresses to registered electors and ballot papers (responsibility for providing ballot papers is left to the parties) may be enclosed with the election addresses. There are similar concessions to candidates in the French overseas territories.[1] In addition to the free provision of propaganda material, there is in France a free issue of petrol to candidates. The amount of this issue is determined by law and depends on the size of the constituency. Candidates are not, of course, debarred from using more petrol than the free issue in pursuing their campaign, but the cost of any excess must be met from their own pockets.[2] Some of these privileges are lost if the party fails to obtain a certain minimum percentage of the votes cast.

In Japan, the government makes certain facilities available to candidates without charge. Each candidate is permitted a certain

[1] See pp. 146-7 of the *U.N. Commissioner's Report on the 1958 elections in French Togoland.*

[2] For a more detailed description of the provisions of French electoral law in regard to State assistance to candidates, see H. G. Nicholas on French electoral law and machinery in *Political Studies*, Vol. IV, No. 2 (1956).

number of short broadcasts. All candidates are required to participate in joint meetings held under the supervision of the local election supervision commission, but the number of individual campaign speeches which may be made is limited to sixty. Each candidate is permitted to have a 1500-word statement of his views and personal particulars published and distributed to all the electors in his constituency by the supervising commission and is entitled to certain advertising facilities provided at the expense of the government.[1]

The provisions relating to State assistance are not so generous in the electoral laws of countries of the British Commonwealth. In Britain candidates have the right to the use of halls and schools for the purpose of holding election meetings and the candidate in parliamentary elections also has the right to send his election address through the post free of charge to registered electors. But there are no privileges such as free printing or free advertising space on official notice boards for British parliamentary candidates, nor is there any provision for the issue of free petrol. In Commonwealth countries of Asia and Africa, the legal provisions for State assistance to candidates tend to be even more limited than in Britain. In Ghana which has, perhaps, a longer history of large-scale elections than any of the dependent territories of British West, East and Central Africa, there are no special provisions in the legislation covering State assistance to candidates. The most liberal provisions appear to be those of the Federation of Malaya where a candidate at Federal elections is permitted to send one election communication free of postal charges to all registered electors in the constituency which he is contesting and where, given reasonable notice on written application, candidates are given conditional permission to use schools in their constituencies for political meetings;[2] the State assistance given to candidates in the Federation of Malaya thus compares closely with the position in Britain. The Western Region of Nigeria provides for the use of schools and public buildings by candidates holding public meetings in furtherance of their candidature,[3] but not for the distribution of election addresses without cost to the candidates.

[1] See Yanaga, *Japanese People and Politics*, pp. 288-9.
[2] *Report on the first election of members to the Legislative Council of the Federation of Malaya*, 1955, pp. 22-3.
[3] The Parliamentary and Local Government Electoral Regulations, 1955, Reg. 122.

In Britain, the Representation of the People Regulations provide for the issue of free copies of the register of electors to parliamentary and local government candidates (or prospective candidates). Such provision does not usually appear in the electoral legislation of Commonwealth countries and territories of Africa and Asia.

It is, then, clear that, in law, candidates in Commonwealth countries of Asia and Africa are not granted very many privileges. In fact, however, a considerable amount of State assistance is given in a few of these countries. Thus, in Uganda prior to the 1958 elections, the Government printed in the officially sponsored vernacular newspapers the names of the nominated candidates, their photographs and symbols, and the message which each was invited to write for publication. In addition, each candidate was given a chance to make a ten-minute broadcast over the Uganda Broadcasting system. Moreover, persons intending to stand as candidates in Uganda were permitted to draw their symbols long before the nomination day to enable them to have adequate time to prepare their election campaigns. In the Federation of Malaya in 1955, each validly nominated candidate was supplied with two free copies of the elections legislation and two free copies of the register of electors in addition to the privileges covered by the law relating to election communications and the use of schools and other buildings for meetings; moreover the political parties (but not individual candidates) were given the chance to make broadcasts and take part in broadcast discussions over Radio Malaya.

There can be little doubt but that, in under-developed countries, it is desirable that the Government should do more than is strictly necessary in law to publicise the candidates and their views and to make known the arrangements for holding the elections and the very meaning of elections in order to make democracy in 'new' countries work as well as possible. But just how far to go in giving assistance to candidates raises a number of problems, as is shown by the example of the radio. It is an obvious requirement in the United Kingdom that the Conservative Party should have as much time but no more on the air over the B.B.C. as the Labour Party, but it is far less obvious how to allocate broadcasting time between rival candidates and rival parties in countries which are holding elections for the first or second time, where these parties are often in an early stage of development and independent candidates are numerous. The discussion earlier in this chapter has illustrated the somewhat arbitrary fashion in which political parties are recognised for purposes of the use of party symbols and much the same considerations apply to the minimum requirements which entitle a political party to broadcast.

For the 1958 elections in Uganda, where candidates were not too numerous and parties were in an embryo stage, this difficulty was surmounted, as we have seen, by treating each candidate, whether standing as an independent or a party candidate, as an individual and allocating broadcasting time accordingly. In Malaya, at the first election in 1955, candidates were more numerous than in Uganda, and independent candidates were not given broadcasting time, whilst political parties were awarded time on the air which bore some relation to the number of seats which the various parties were contesting. In Sierra Leone, prior to the 1957 elections, two short periods a week were made available to four political parties over a period of four months, time being given equally to each party in turn and not in proportion to the number of candidates or prospective candidates (the broadcasts began well before nominations were submitted). In Western Nigeria, prior to the 1956 elections to the Western House of Assembly, it was decided that a party would be allowed broadcasting time if it put forward candidates numbering at least one-fifth of the number of seats being contested and, in fact, only the two major parties qualified for this concession. In Eastern Nigeria, prior to the 1957 House of Assembly elections, the party controlling the Government (the N.C.N.C.) took half the period allotted for political broadcasts, while the two main opposition parties shared the other half.

THE ELECTION EXPENSES OF CANDIDATES

Candidates at parliamentary elections in Britain are restricted in respect of their personal and other expenses in connection with the conduct of their election campaigns, and the maximum amounts which may be spent are laid down in the Representation of the People Act.[1] No statutory time has been fixed in Britain for the commencement of election expenses, and the general principle to be deduced from a number of court judgments cited in Schofield[2] is that, before as well as after formal nomination,

[1] Section 64.
[2] See Schofield, *Parliamentary Elections*, pp. 168-76.

expenses incurred in promoting a person's candidature in a constituency are election expenses.

Some other countries of the British Commonwealth have followed Britain's example in restricting the election expenses of candidates. There is, for instance, legislation which regulates the election expenses of candidates for the Canadian House of Commons, though it is reported that the provisions of the law in this respect have been uniformly disobeyed.[1] In India, every candidate is required by law to submit a return of his electoral expenses in the prescribed form and signed by him or his election agent, within forty-five days from the date of publication of the result of the election to which the expenses relate; the maximum scale of expenses is laid down in the Indian Representation of the People Rules and these maxima vary, both for Parliamentary and for Assembly constituencies, according to whether the constituency returns one, two or three members.[2] At the first general elections in India, there were a large number of defaults in lodging the returns of election expenses within the time and in the manner required by the law, but most of these defaults were ascribed to "the technical and intricate nature of the law and the ignorance of the same on the part of the candidates and agents".[3] A lenient view was taken of these defaults by the Election Commission, who considered that there would be progressively less justification for extending the same measure of leniency in the future after the law had become familiar. In the Federation of Malaya, as in India, some candidates and their agents experienced difficulties in submitting properly completed returns and, at the general election of 1955, some of the defeated candidates defaulted in failing to submit returns, as the law requires, within thirty-one days after the date of publication of the results of the election in the official gazette.

On the West Coast of Africa, there has so far been no provision for the limitation of the electoral expenses of candidates and for the submission of a return of such expenses. In British East Africa, Tanganyika is unique in having included in its electoral legislation provisions in regard to election expenses,[4] and it is premature to

---

[1] *The Canadian House of Commons — Representation* by Norman Ward, Ch. XV.

[2] *Report on the first general elections in India, 1951-2,* Vol. I, Ch. XX.

[3] *Report on the first general elections in India, 1951-2,* Vol. I, p. 172.

[4] The Tanganyika Legislative Council Elections Ordinance, 1957, Part VIII.

pronounce on the merits of including clauses of this nature in the electoral law.

The fact that British African territories have, in general, dispensed with provisions relating to the election expenses of candidates is probably to be explained by the poverty of African political parties and of the great majority of the candidates. So far, control of expenditure through the submission of accounts has been superfluous as a weapon in the battle against corrupt practices in elections. Moreover, we have seen that, in India, many of the candidates and their agents found difficulty in complying with the intricate law relating to election expenses and it is certain that members of unsophisticated African societies would be even more confused by a system of control of expenditure based on the British model.[1]

Even in those countries in which accounts must be submitted in accordance with the electoral law, there is no guarantee that the accounts are in fact an accurate statement of candidates' expenses.[2] It is true that the accounts are checked and published, that it is an offence for anyone to spend money in support of a particular candidate except through the candidate's election agent who, in turn, commits an offence if he spends any money for which he does not account or if he spends money above the legal maximum. But the system is better adapted for use in an advanced society with modern methods of accounting than in the countries of Africa, although the time will no doubt come when, even in Africa, control of expenditure will be introduced in order to make more effective the repression of corruption.

Where control over a candidate's expenses has been introduced, as in Britain, India, Malaya and Tanganyika, the candidate is required to appoint an election agent at nomination or very shortly thereafter, and, in the event of failure to make such an appointment, the candidate is deemed to have named himself as election agent.[3] The main duty of an election agent is to keep election expense accounts properly and he is the only person

[1] In Japan, too, the provisions relating to election expenditure are considered to be the most difficult and least effectively regulated part of the election laws. See Yanaga, *Japanese People and Politics*, pp. 292-3.

[2] Particularly in view of the practical difficulties involved in defining election expenses.

[3] See, for instance, Sections 127 and 128 of the Tanganyika Legislative Council Elections Ordinance, 1957.

permitted to make payments or contracts (other than the candidate's personal expenses) in furtherance of candidature. In India,
many of the election agents had no clear understanding of their
duties at the first general elections, and a considerable number of
them incurred disqualifications both for voting and for membership of the Legislatures as a result of default in lodging the returns
of election expenses within the time and in the manner required
by law.[1]

It may be noted in connection with election expenses that
corruption in connection with elections is less likely to occur when
the franchise is wide and the electorate large than when the
franchise is limited and the number of electors small. English
literature of the early nineteenth century is full of stories of
bribery and corruption.[2] Once electioneering becomes a mass
operation, the cost and the risk of bribing the electors tends to
become too great for even the most unprincipled candidate. The
Corrupt Practices Act of 1883 simply put the finishing touches to
the process of making elections fairer and drabber, which had
started with the enlargement of the electorate by successive
Reform Bills.

ELECTION OF UNOPPOSED CANDIDATES

Where, on completion of the nomination proceedings, the
number of candidates remaining validly nominated in any
constituency does not exceed the number of vacant seats in the
legislature for that constituency, the returning officer declares the
unopposed candidates to have been elected and no poll is taken.
The arrangements for contested elections are discussed in Chapter
VIII.

PROCEDURE IN CASE OF DEATH OF A CANDIDATE
AFTER NOMINATION

In most British Commonwealth countries, the returning officer
is required to countermand notice of the poll and start all proceedings in connection with the election in his constituency afresh
if, after publication of the statement of persons nominated and
before the poll, he is given proof of the death of one of the

[1] *Report on the first general elections in India, 1951-2*, Vol. I, p. 171.
[2] See *To the Hustings — election scenes from English Fiction*, selected by H. G.
Nicholas.

candidates.[1] In Mauritius, however, if one of the candidates dies, the election is not started afresh and, if only one surviving candidate remains nominated, he is declared elected.[2] In Metropolitan France, Algeria and the Sahara, a candidate must when registering his candidature name a person who would replace him if, after being elected, he vacated his seat. If a candidate dies during the election campaign, his substitute becomes candidate and nominates a new substitute; if a substitute dies during the campaign his candidate nominates a new substitute.[3]

[1] See A. N. Schofield, *Parliamentary Elections*, pp. 166-8 for the effect of death of a candidate on elections in Britain.

[2] Regs. 9 and 11, Mauritius Legislative Council Elections Regulations, 1958.

[3] Peter Campbell and Brian Chapman, *The Constitution of the Fifth Republic*, p. 59.

CHAPTER VIII

POLLING PROCEDURE AT
CONTESTED ELECTIONS

IN a contested election, it is the duty of the returning officer in each constituency to make suitable arrangements to enable the registered electorate to cast their votes. The execution of this duty involves a considerable amount of organisation, particularly in a country with a largely illiterate population and indifferent communications. The returning officer has to find and train the staff to man the polling stations, ensure the supply of the equipment required for the stations, and, particularly when elections are something of a novelty, assist in teaching the electorate the method of voting. In accomplishing these tasks, he may have the help of various government departments, but the responsibility for the success or failure of the polling arrangements rests primarily with him.

The detailed work of the returning officer will, of course, be dependent in part on the types of voting in use. Thus, if all voting is to be in person at polling stations, his job is more straightforward than would be the case if certain categories of electors are permitted to vote by post or by proxy. Postal and proxy voting is discussed in Chapter IX, and this chapter is confined to a description of the arrangements for personal voting at polling stations.

Some of the earliest popular elections in West Africa were conducted on an electoral college basis. As an example, the arrangements for the 1951 elections to the West Nigerian House of Assembly were as follows.[1] Each of the twenty-five electoral districts or constituencies returned two members to the House; every electoral district was divided into a number of "intermediate electoral areas", which were usually subordinate native authority areas; and every "intermediate electoral area" was divided into a number of "primary electoral areas", each of which consisted of a

[1] For a more detailed description see *Report on the first elections to the Western House of Assembly*.

160

village, a quarter of a town or a group of hamlets. Inside each primary electoral area, election meetings were called to elect the requisite number of persons to represent the area in the intermediate electoral college. Attendance at these election meetings was often poor and, very frequently, a decision had been taken by a village at a palaver held before the day appointed for the meeting. Where elections were contested, the issue was decided by a show of hands or by asking qualified voters to line up behind the rival candidates. The person in charge of these meetings was usually the traditional head of the area and he was helped, if necessary, by clerks. The few complaints about the conduct of the elections were on the grounds that the supporters of one candidate were not qualified or that the defeated candidate had more supporters than the person declared elected.

At the intermediate electoral area level, the electoral college consisted of the native authority members together with an equal or greater number of persons elected in the primary electoral areas. There was considerable variation in the size of the intermediate electoral college and in the number of representatives which the intermediate colleges were required to elect to go forward to the final college of each electoral district or constituency. Polling in the intermediate electoral colleges took place on the same day as or on the day following nominations and the small number of ballot papers required were either printed or cyclostyled. Administrative officers usually presided over the meeting of the intermediate electoral college and illiterate members of the college were permitted to whisper their choice of candidate to the presiding officer and get him to mark the ballot paper.

The representatives chosen by each intermediate electoral college took part in the final elections held at the electoral district or constituency levels. These final elections were a little more formal than the intermediate elections in so far as nominations closed five days before polling day, proper ballot papers were prepared, and deposits were required of candidates. Even at the final electoral college level there was a degree of illiteracy amongst members and illiterate voters were permitted to whisper their votes to the presiding officer.

The total cost of the elections, conducted without registers or ballot papers at the primary electoral area level, was a mere £750. There were no election petitions and everyone appears to have been reasonably happy with the way in which the elections were conducted. Elections on an electoral college basis have been conducted in other countries — and particularly in Africa — with equally happy results. Why then, it may be asked, should the expensive, complicated and formal procedures used in the western democracies be imposed on poor countries with largely illiterate populations?

There are a number of objections which can be made against the system of voting used in the 1951 elections in the Western Region of Nigeria. In the first place, there were no registers of electors in the primary electoral areas, and some unqualified persons might have voted and, indeed, probably did vote at the elections. Secondly, voting in the primary electoral areas was not secret — and the secrecy of the vote is one of the most highly prized features of elections to the legislatures of most democratic countries. Thirdly, the voters in the primary electoral areas had no voice in the final election of the two representatives for their electoral district; instead the final election was the result of voting by a very small number of persons in the final electoral college and there is in this system a very real danger of nepotism and corruption. Fourthly, a non-elected element (the native authority members) had a direct right of entry to the first rung of the electoral ladder.

The desirability of having a register of electors prepared well before polling takes place has been discussed in Chapter IV. The remaining objections listed in the last paragraph to the system of voting used in Western Nigeria in 1951 indicate the desirability of a brief discussion on the relative merits of open and secret voting and on the relative merits of direct and indirect elections.

Open voting is commonly used in committee work and in small societies for the election of officials and for decisions on matters of policy. Not only is open voting a cheap and expeditious form of taking group decisions, but the open group discussion which usually precedes the voting assists in the process of forming views and consolidating standpoints. But, as soon as it is no longer contained within the boundaries of a small cohesive unit, open voting can easily lead to very serious abuses, such as intimidation and corruption. With a large electorate, the only hope of getting people to vote according to their own conscience and wishes is to make voting secret. The fact that open voting is nearly obsolete in elections to legislative assemblies is a clear indication of the advantages of voting by secret ballot. It must be stressed, however, that the general acceptance of the secrecy of the ballot is of recent origin; voting by acclamation followed, if necessary, by the voters filing past the presiding officer and stating their choice, was the practice in British parliamentary elections for most of the nineteenth century, and, as we have seen, some West African territories have retained a system of open voting until very recently. At the elections to be held under the new Somaliland Protectorate Legislative Council Elections Ordinance, voting is to be open in some constituencies. The voters are to meet for the election and the presiding officer is to assemble the electors in a group and explain to them the method of voting. Each elector then records his vote by entering one or other of the voting areas demarcated — one voting area for each candidate — and remaining there until the conclusion of the election. The presiding officer has to count each voting area, refusing to count the vote of any person not entitled to vote, and the results of the count are recorded and forwarded to the returning officer as soon as counting is completed.[1]

Open voting is not, of course, a necessary counterpart of the first stage or any other stage of indirect elections. At the primary elections in Western Nigeria in 1951, the voters could quite well have indicated by token ballot papers used in secrecy which candidate they wished to elect, although such an operation would have taken longer than the method used. There can be little doubt but that the indirect elections held in Nigeria and other African countries have been most useful in preparing backward peoples for later direct elections. Once the process of political education has gone beyond the first few steps, however, indirect elections have served their purpose and most countries have substituted direct elections.[2] The reasons are fairly obvious; with indirect elections the elector merely chooses a representative to vote for him and can have no real feeling of personal participation in the creation of a government; moreover, the electoral colleges created

[1] Sec. 55, Somaliland Protectorate Legislative Council Elections Ordinance, 1958.

[2] The French Senate is, however, elected by indirect suffrage through local government units. The deputies of the National Assembly are, of course, elected by direct suffrage in single-member constituencies — see Art. 24 of the Constitution of the Fifth Republic. The Iraq Electoral Law of 1946 provides for the indirect election of members of the Chamber of Deputies.

by a system of indirect elections are liable to degenerate as the result of intrigue and nepotism.[1] African countries and territories which have used indirect elections as a step in preparing for direct elections include the Sudan (for the most backward parts of the country at the first general elections of 1953), the Gold Coast (1951 elections), the Western Region of Nigeria (1951 elections) and the Northern Region of Nigeria (up to 1956).

The emphasis now is, however, on direct elections conducted in conjunction with secret voting and it is on the procedures used at the polling stations with this system of elections that the rest of this chapter is devoted. Once again we must go back to our returning officer and examine his preparations for an election, on the assumption that his constituency has been divided into polling districts, that there is a certified register of electors for each such polling district and that candidates have been validly nominated in sufficient number to make a contested election.

PROVISION OF POLLING STATIONS

Within each polling district or polling area, one or more polling stations have to be provided. The number and situation of the polling stations will depend on the size and geographical distribution of the electorate within the polling district, and frequently a polling district will contain but one station. The site for the station must suit the convenience of the electors, and it is usual to utilise a school or some other public building for the purpose where such a building is available; elsewhere, it may be necessary to build a temporary, inexpensive structure to give adequate protection from sun and rain to polling station staff and the voters.

In India, for the first general elections, the Election Commission directed that the following considerations should be kept in view in selecting the location of polling stations:

(a) There should not, ordinarily, be more than 1,000 voters for a polling booth.

(b) A polling station should serve a geographically well-defined area.

[1] See the *Report of the Sierra Leone Electoral Reform Commission*, p. 15, for a discussion of the objections to indirect elections through electoral colleges. There is also a long discussion of the reasons for rejecting a system of indirect elections in the Somaliland Protectorate in the *Report of the Commission of Inquiry into Unofficial Representation on the Legislative Council*, June, 1958.

(c) Where absolutely necessary, separate polling booths should be provided for women voters.

(d) A voter should not, ordinarily, be required to travel more than three miles to reach his polling station.

(e) Polling stations should not be located in places of religious worship.

Public buildings were preferred for use, where available, but private buildings were used where necessary, with the consent of the owners and sometimes on payment. Owing to the absence or shortage of suitable buildings, inexpensive temporary structures were erected in some places to serve as polling stations, the cheapest materials available being used for such structures. The Election Commission also defined the manner in which lists of polling stations were to be published, so that voters could, without difficulty, know at which polling station they were to cast their votes.[1]

In the Federation of Malaya, the boundaries of polling districts were defined prior to the first registration of electors in 1954, and, after registration and before the first general elections, decisions had to be taken in respect of each polling district on the number of polling stations required, bearing in mind the requirements that all electors should have reasonably easy access to their polling station and that the polling staff would not be able to deal with a flow of more than about 1,000 electors during the polling hours. Where all electors had reasonable access to a single suitable building in a polling district, but the number of registered electors was too great for one set of polling staff, dual facilities were provided at the polling station, the voters being divided into two groups either by sex[2] or by residential neighbourhoods or by the alphabetical order of the first letter of the principal name (e.g. the A — M's polling in one room of the building and the N — Z's in another room). In some densely populated rural areas, where boundaries of polling districts were particularly difficult to define owing to the absence of suitable natural or man-made boundaries, some of the districts contained a sufficiently large electorate scattered over a wide area to make it necessary to provide a number

---

[1] *Report on the first general elections in India, 1951-2*, Vol. I, p. 123.

[2] The electoral laws of some Muslim countries require that separate polling stations or polling booths should be established for women voters — e.g. Art. 7, Electoral Law of Syria, 1949.

of separately situated polling stations; most of the polling districts, however, contained but one polling station.[1]

In the Western Region of Nigeria, polling stations were provided for the 1956 Parliamentary Elections to the Western House of Assembly on the basis of "a formula of no voter having to travel more than three miles by the most direct route to reach his/her polling station, and not more than 500 registered electors being allocated to a polling station".[2] With the use of this formula, about 5,000 polling stations had to be provided for a registered electorate of about 1,947,000. The majority of the buildings used as polling stations were local schools. Each polling station was clearly marked by a poster upon which was depicted a large blue ballot box upon a white background, and posted up outside each polling station was a copy of the section of the register of electors with the names of the persons eligible to vote there. As far as possible, the polling stations were in the buildings which had previously been used as offices for the registration of electors.

The provision of polling stations for the 1957 general elections in Sierra Leone was somewhat uneven. In Freetown, the capital, the number of polling stations required was under-estimated and the average number of registered electors per polling station was over 2,000, a figure well above the safe maximum for any one polling station when the electorate and the polling staff are inexperienced. In the rural areas of the Colony and the Protectorate, the number of registered electors per polling station was considerably lower, but voters were apparently reluctant to travel more than about two miles to get to their polling station, and the low poll in some constituencies suggests that, in the rural areas too, the number of polling stations provided may have been insufficient because of the factor of distance from the station to the residential localities served by it.

In Ghana, the returning officers are given no precise instructions about the provision of polling stations, but the relevant regulation requires the returning officer to "provide a sufficient number of

[1] There were 1,679 polling stations in 1,504 polling districts for a registered electorate of just over 1,280,000 persons.

[2] *Report on the Holding of the 1956 Parliamentary Elections to the Western House of Assembly, Nigeria*, p. 7. At the plebiscite conducted in British Togoland in 1956, each polling station catered for a maximum of 500 voters, and no voter was required to walk more than *seven* miles to the station and as many back to his house, "a distance which is considered there entirely within reason".

polling stations in each ward[1] and allot the electors within the ward to the polling stations in such manner as he thinks most convenient"[2] — a general provision which is copied in the legislation of some of the other African territories of the Commonwealth. The Ministry of Local Government directed the returning officers prior to the general elections held in 1956 to bear the following points in mind:

(a) Geographical convenience. The Polling Station should be convenient to the electors it serves, easily accessible, situated on ground that will not become swamped if it rains on or near Polling Day, etc., etc.;

(b) Construction. The Polling Station should if possible be of permanent or semi-permanent construction, strong enough to withstand the elements and the pressure of large crowds;

(c) Supervision. The Polling Station should be sited with a view to facilitating Police supervision if required and the control of crowds;

(d) The Polling Station should either be in a building large enough to shelter the queue or near to a building which could be so used;

(e) The manner in which the Returning Officer allots the electors to a Polling Station will be determined partly by the manner in which the registers have been prepared. If electors are divided between Polling Stations on an alphabetical basis, the Polling Stations should be within easy reach of one another, so that e.g. Mr. Cobbina does not have far to go if he finds that his name is not registered under C, but under K;

(f) Polling Stations should not be sited in Chiefs' houses or State Council buildings. Generally, if a School is available, it should be used, otherwise Local Authority Offices may be used or Native Court houses, if they are separate from the Chief's house.

At the 1956 elections, it is reported that polling had virtually ended in many districts about three hours before the close of polling and at only two or three polling stations had any electors to be turned away at the closure. The percentage poll was, however, on the low side and it is not clear how much this is to be attributed to apathy on the part of electors and to what extent the provision of more polling stations would have increased the poll. In the light of the result of the 1956 elections, it was recommended that wards

[1] i.e. polling district.
[2] Reg. 14(a) of the Electoral Provisions (Assembly Elections) Regulations, 1954.

which contained excessive numbers of electors should be divided into sub-wards containing not more than 500 electors so that, as far as possible, no elector would have to walk more than three miles to vote.

In Zanzibar, at the first 1957 elections, polling stations were provided for every 400 registered electors in the rural constituencies and for every 300 electors in the towns. These figures are rather low, but it should be remembered that the Zanzibar Legislative Council Elections Decree of 1957[1] provides opportunities for intervention by candidates or their agents at the polling stations which, if abused, could seriously slow down the rate of voting; candidates or their agents were permitted to challenge the qualifications as well as the identity of registered electors as they made their appearance at the polling station and those challenged were not permitted to vote without taking an oath of qualification or an oath of identity, as the case may be. The decision to provide polling stations on the basis of the above formula involved the provision of two or more polling stations in the same or adjoining buildings at the original registration point in a number of polling districts and voters were split among the polling stations according to the initial letters of their first names. The Supervisor of Elections reports that:

> This proved a workable, though unsatisfactory, arrangement. It was unsatisfactory because the two or more polling stations in question had to be sited so close together than an elector who had evaded the Direction Clerks and had gone to the wrong polling station, would, on re-direction, have no more than a few yards to go to reach the right one, and the consequent concentration of all the electors in one place complicated the situation from the control point of view. It is highly desirable that every polling station should have its own separate list of electors with the names entered alphabetically from A to Z. It thus becomes an independent unit; the names of the people who are to vote there can be given the necessary publicity before polling day; and it can be sited at any point in the polling division, approved by the administrative and police authorities, which is convenient for the electors.[2]

In the Sudan, returning officers at the second general election in 1958 were instructed by the Election Commission to bear the following principles in mind in preparing polling stations:

[1] Sections 44 and 45.
[2] *Report on the Election in Zanzibar, 1957*, pp. 7-8.

(a) That the average number of voters for each polling station must not be more than 1,000 registered voters. Of course it may be less according to the influence of the factors next following.

(b) That the station must be at a reasonable distance from the dwelling places of voters. It is suggested that in rural areas a distance of 20-25 miles may be reasonable.

(c) That the station must not be situated in a building belonging to a political party or to a party man. Government buildings, e.g. schools, dispensaries, etc., are always preferable.

(d) That the secrecy of voting can easily be maintained within the site selected.

(e) That discipline and order can easily be maintained.[1]

In French Togoland, "the law provides that a polling station, for a maximum of 1,500 voters, shall be set up in each commune and in each administrative 'circonscription'. The list of polling stations must be drawn up, published and posted fourteen days before the opening of the polls."[2] For the 1958 elections in Togoland, the Government gave instructions that chiefs' houses should not be used as polling stations where there was a feasible alternative and that buildings for polling stations were to be selected, bearing in mind the need for a sound watertight roof, ready access and clear approaches, and adequate size, in the following order of preference: schools, dispensaries, indigenous court-houses, indigenous council houses and, lastly, village court-houses situated outside the chief's concession. The desire to avoid the use of chiefs' houses was motivated by the belief that some chiefs might attempt to take advantage of their position to influence voters.

Some rather tentative conclusions can be drawn from the experience of these countries in providing polling stations for their voters. As regards the number of voters who can be passed through a single polling station, it is probably wise in an unsophisticated society to whom voting is still something of a novelty to work on a maximum figure of 100 persons voting per hour[3] in a

---

[1] Extract from instructions to returning officers supplied to the author by courtesy of the Secretary of the Sudan Election Commission.

[2] *Report of the U.N. Commissioner on the 1958 elections in Togoland under French Administration* — p. 115.

[3] Returning officers at the first general election in Uganda reported that polling stations coped with a flow of 75 to 100 voters per hour and that some of the better organised stations dealt with 200 voters per hour.

given polling station, and on a rather smaller figure if it is anticipated that any large-scale difficulties are likely to be experienced in the identification of electors, or, if (as in Zanzibar), there are special provisions in the electoral legislation which could lead to delays in the speed of voting. In the second place, it seems likely that voters in general are unwilling to travel very far to reach their polling station, and, in rural areas with scattered populations, a compromise has to be struck in the provision of polling stations between the convenience of the electors and the necessity for economy in the conduct of polling. Every additional polling station costs money because the polling staff have to be paid and, in some cases, buildings have to be hired or special structures erected; moreover, as will be seen below, many countries of Africa and Asia experience the greatest difficulty in finding suitable staff to man the polling stations. But the rather low polls in some of the recent general elections in West Africa suggest that, in so far as staff and funds permit, a better turn-out might be achieved if more polling stations are provided.

STAFF FOR POLLING STATIONS

The provision of an adequate number and grade of staff to man the polling stations and the training of such staff for their polling duties is far from easy at general elections in under-developed countries. Sometimes staff considerations alone necessitate the 'staggering' of polling — the same staff manning one station on the first day of polling and other stations on the subsequent days. And the electoral authorities are frequently empowered to commandeer the services of employees of other government departments on polling day in order to meet staffing requirements. A 'presiding officer' is in charge of each polling station and he is assisted by a small number of clerks, called 'poll clerks' or 'polling assistants' or by some similar title. The number of clerks required in any polling station will depend on the number of electors entitled to vote at the station and on the instructions which the presiding officers receive from the returning officers on the distribution of duties of the polling staff.

In the Federation of Malaya, at the 1955 general elections, the number of clerks appointed to assist the presiding officer varied from a minimum of one to a maximum of four, according to the size of the registered electorate entitled to vote at the polling station. One of the first problems relating to polling which had to be settled prior to these Malayan elections was whether it would be possible to find and train a sufficient number of suitable persons to hold elections throughout the country on the same day. After a careful review of the situation, it was decided that it was in fact feasible to hold the elections simultaneously throughout the country, but this did involve the dispersal of a number of government officers from the towns to outlying rural areas and the use of the Federal Police Reserve to reinforce police contingents with an inadequate strength for ensuring the security of the polling stations. The task of selecting suitable presiding officers and polling assistants was begun six months before the elections; the majority of those chosen were government officers, but there were some others such as business men and planters who offered their services for the occasion.

In India, the poll at the first general elections had to be taken at over 132,000 polling stations and the search for the vast army of polling personnel of the standard required for the purpose involved the maximum possible utilisation of the resources of the State Governments in man-power and, in addition, recourse to the employees of local bodies and Government-aided institutions. Only in the State of Delhi did it prove possible to complete the poll in all the constituencies of a State in a single day and, in some States, lack of adequate polling personnel and difficulties created by the absence of transport facilities made it difficult to complete polling even in a single Assembly constituency in one day.

In States in which polling was spread over a number of days, each polling party was assigned a number of polling stations, and the programme was so arranged that the party went on its beat, completing polling at the stations assigned to it, one after another, on the dates notified for those areas. In order to ensure that the polling parties reached their destinations in time and took preliminary steps for the setting up of polling stations, an interval of a day or more was allowed between the dates fixed for the taking of the poll. Thus only was it possible for one polling party to take the poll at a number of stations on different dates and the difficulty arising from the shortage of polling personnel was solved.[1]

[1] *Report on the first general elections in India, 1951-2*, Vol. I, p. 126.

In some of the African territories of the British Commonwealth, it has been necessary to 'stagger' polling for the same reasons as in India. Thus, there were two polling days (12th July and 17th July) in the Northern Territories of the Gold Coast (now Ghana) at the 1956 general elections; in the Zanzibar elections of 1957, polling in one of the six constituencies, Pemba South, was held over until two days after polling in the remaining five constituencies, and some of the staff employed in Pemba North constituency on the first polling day were transferred to Pemba South during the intervening twenty-four hours; similarly in the Sierra Leone elections of 1957, the small supply of suitable personnel for the polling stations was such that polling had to be held on several days, with the staff moving about, and, even in these circumstances, there was probably little or no talent to spare. It has been mentioned above that the number of polling stations established in both Freetown and in the rural areas of the Protectorate of Sierra Leone was inadequate; most returning officers recognised this inadequacy, but were unable to establish more stations because they could not obtain the staff to man them.

Where general elections have had to be staggered on the grounds of shortage of suitable staff, it can be argued that it is desirable to organise this staggering in such a way that no results are announced before polling has been completed. The effect on polling in one constituency of the premature announcement of the result in another constituency is, of course, a matter of surmise, but there can be little doubt but that polling is influenced to some extent if the election results of other constituencies are known at the time of voting. One possible arrangement (which is not necessarily a practicable arrangement) is to have two polling days, where necessary, the first for the more inaccessible constituencies and for the more distant polling districts of otherwise accessible constituencies and the second day for the balance, so that all results are available very shortly after, but never before, the conclusion of polling. A good alternative is the method used at the 1958 elections in Uganda where voting took place on three days in each electoral district, about one third of the electorate polling on each day. The voters in any given polling division (i.e. polling district) were allotted one day only and many of the polling officials travelled from one part of the electoral district (i.e. constituency) to another and officiated on two or even on all three of the polling days. There was a gap of one day between each polling day to enable the polling officials to travel and make the necessary preparations for voting.

In France and French Africa, each polling station is run by a polling committee composed of a chairman and a representative of each list or candidate (unless some parties or candidates fail to appoint or refrain from appointing such representatives within the prescribed time-limits). In French Africa, the chairmen of the polling committees have usually been people such as teachers, health service workers or other government officers of clerical or executive grade. The candidates' representatives have to be chosen from among voters who are able to read and write and are registered as voters in the electoral list of the 'circonscription', and, in some parts of the overseas French territories, candidates have found difficulty in obtaining a sufficient number of representatives to satisfy both these conditions.[1] It should be explained that provision is made in the French electoral law for every party list or candidate to be represented in two ways at each polling station, firstly by the appointment of a representative to serve on the polling committee which is officially responsible for voting operations and the subsequent counting of the votes, and secondly by the appointment of a polling agent on the general lines of the system adopted in the British Commonwealth.

The reports on African elections are often silent on the sources of recruitment of staff for the polling stations and on the rates of pay offered to them. It would appear, however, that, in most territories, a very high percentage of the presiding officers and poll clerks are volunteers from various government departments and teachers from schools. In some territories students have been enrolled as poll clerks — for instance, students from teacher training colleges are reported as having assisted at both the Zanzibar and the Sierra Leone elections in 1957. Some territories[2] pay a flat rate to presiding officers and poll clerks for the job, including time required for training purposes, whilst others differentiate between government officers and others or between the higher paid government officers and others; thus, for the Gold Coast Assembly Elections of 1956, there were three categories of

[1] See pp. 117-21 of the U.N. Commissioner's Report on the 1958 elections in French Togoland.
[2] For instance, Zanzibar and the Federation of Malaya.

polling staff for the purposes of pay and allowances, the first consisting of the more senior government officers who received no extra pay for undertaking duties but were entitled to the standard government allowances, the second consisting of the lower paid government officers, who were given a small honorarium in respect of their duties on polling day plus standard government allowances and the third category consisting of private persons whose remuneration was at a rather higher rate.

TRAINING OF POLLING STATION STAFF

Where elections are new or of recent introduction and there are but few people who know the polling procedure well, some form of training is essential. Most countries issue small booklets of instructions[1] to presiding officers, with the help of which they should be able to find the answers to any problems which arise during polling, but, in addition to this, visual aids assist the polling staff to understand the new techniques. Some countries[2] have made training films for this purpose, whilst the electoral authorities of other countries have contented themselves with election rehearsals and with discussion and lecture groups.

THE LAYOUT OF POLLING STATIONS

The electoral laws of most territories provide that the presiding officer in charge of a polling station has power to maintain order and ensure the correct polling procedure within the limits of the polling station; some electoral systems also provide that persons already inside the polling station at the prescribed hour for the closing of the poll should be permitted to vote. For both these reasons, it is important that the outer limits of the polling station should be clearly defined. In Eastern Nigeria, where persons inside the polling station at the close of voting are permitted to vote, the law requires that the electoral authority should cause each polling station to be fenced.[3] In the Federation of Malaya, wherever

---

[1] India, Malaya, Uganda and Ghana, for instance, issue booklets of instructions to presiding officers of polling stations.

[2] e.g. the Malayan Film Unit's production 'A Model Polling Station'.

[3] Reg. 30(b) of the Eastern House of Assembly Electoral Regulations, 1955.

necessary, a small area surrounding the building used as a polling station was included within the limits at the 1955 elections to enable the presiding officer and the police to exercise proper crowd control; temporary fences were frequently erected where necessary for this purpose.[1] The electoral law sometimes [2] provides that no canvassing is permitted within a specified distance of the polling station and this, too, requires that the limits of a polling station should be clearly defined.

It has often been found desirable to have separate entrances and exits for the polling stations wherever the buildings used for the purpose permit. Thus, the rough layout plans of polling stations suggested by the Indian Election Commission to all returning officers prior to the first general elections in India and by the Supervisor of Elections in Uganda in his handbook for presiding officers show a separate entrance and exit. Where, however, the forces available for controlling crowds at polling stations are barely adequate, it may be desirable to use one entrance only for voters going in and out of polling stations.

Where an adequate number of polling assistants are available, one assistant is frequently stationed immediately outside the entrance to the polling station as a kind of receptionist, identifying voters and finding the electoral numbers of persons queueing up to vote outside the entrance. Inside the polling station, the polling clerk or assistant in charge of the register is responsible for the formal identification of the voter, for the checking of his particulars and for calling out his name and electoral number prior to the issue of a ballot. Seated next to him is the presiding officer or an assistant who marks the electoral number of the voter on the counterfoil of the ballot paper, perforates or stamps the ballot paper and hands it to the voter. The candidates' polling agents are usually situated well away both from the polling compartments and from the table at which the ballot papers are issued in order to ensure that they have no chance of ascertaining the number of the ballot paper issued to any voter or the way in which the latter has cast his vote.

[1] See, for instance, the photographs on pages 20-1 of the *Report on the First Election of Members to the Legislative Council of the Federation of Malaya*.

[2] For instance, Reg. 63 of the Gold Coast Electoral Provisions (Assembly Elections) Regulations, 1954 and Sec. 26(3) of the Federation of Malaya Election Offences Ordinance, 1954, as amended by the Election Offences (Amendment) Ordinance, 1955.

HOURS FOR OPENING THE POLLING STATIONS

The following are the prescribed hours for the opening of polling stations in various countries:

Ghana	7 a.m. to 5 p.m.[1]
Western Region of Nigeria and Eastern Region of Nigeria	Hours fixed for the poll to be specified by the electoral officer, with the proviso that there shall be a continuous period of not less than 8 hours.[2]
Zanzibar	8 a.m. to 6 p.m.[3]
Tanganyika	9 a.m. to 6 p.m.[4]
Uganda	8 a.m. to 6 p.m. unless the returning officer orders otherwise.[5]
The Gambia (Legislative Council Elections)	7 a.m. to 7 p.m.[6]
Sierra Leone	8 a.m. to 6 p.m.[7]
Malaya	Polling stations normally open for 12 hours but the elections authority has discretion to open particular polling stations for a shorter period when the circumstances demand it.[8]
India	Hours of poll fixed by the Governments concerned, varying in first general elections from 8 hours to 10 hours.[9]

[1] Reg. 17 of the Electoral Provisions (Assembly Elections) Regulations, 1954.

[2] Reg. 47 of the Western Region Parliamentary and Local Government Electoral Regulations, 1955, and Reg. 29(2) of the Eastern House of Assembly Electoral Regulations, 1955.

[3] Sec. 37 of the Zanzibar Legislative Council Elections Decree in fact specifies a continuous period of not less than ten hours beginning at a time to be fixed by the Supervisor of Elections.

[4] Sec. 84(2) of the Tanganyika Legislative Council Elections Ordinance, 1957.

[5] Sec. 30(2) of the Uganda Legislative Council (Elections) Ordinance, 1957.

[6] Rule 17 of the Gambia Legislative Council (Elections) Rules, 1954.

[7] Reg. 24 of the Sierra Leone House of Representatives (Elections) Regulations contains a proviso for the extension of the hours of polling over the statutory ten hours in case of emergency.

[8] *Report on the First Election of Members to the Legislative Council of the Federation of Malaya*, p. 26.

[9] *Report on the first general elections in India, 1951-2*, Vol. I, p. 130.

Britain	7 a.m. to 9 p.m.[1]
France	8 a.m. to 6 p.m. with powers
	to fix an earlier opening and
	to permit an extension to
	8 p.m. where necessary.[2]

This rather lengthy list has been given in order to give a full illustration of the diversity in provisions for determining the hours for opening the polling stations. It is, of course, essential to fix the hours of opening for each polling station before polling day and to give due notice of the hours to the electors involved but, if that is done, the author's experience has tended to sway him in favour of the kind of flexibility which is permitted in the electoral laws of Nigeria, Malaya and France. Some polling stations in isolated rural areas with small populations are provided to cater for a very few voters only and, if these voters are given due notice of the hours at which their polling station will be open, it may be quite unnecessary to keep the station open throughout the day. Moreover, even in more densely populated areas, the hours which are best suited for opening polling stations in a rural agricultural area may differ from the best times for use in the towns.

There is a rather unusual feature in the 1949 Electoral Law of Syria regarding the hours for opening polling stations. Voting is ordinarily from 7 a.m. to 7 p.m., but can be extended to 10 p.m. if voters continue to arrive at 7 p.m. If 60% of the electorate have voted at the close, voting is deemed to be completed, but if a smaller percentage of the electorate have voted, polling continues on the following day from 7 a.m. to 4 p.m.

THE APPOINTMENT OF POLLING AGENTS

The law relating to the appointment of polling agents is comparatively uniform. In general, each candidate is permitted before polling starts to appoint polling agents to attend at the polling stations as his representatives to detect personation. There is sometimes no limit to the number of polling agents who may be appointed for this purpose, but normally only one or at most two such agents for a given candidate are permitted to be inside the polling station at any one time. These agents, like the official

[1] Rule 1 of the Parliamentary Election Rules.
[2] H. G. Nicholas on French Electoral Law and Machinery in *Political Studies*, Vol. IV, No. 2.

polling station staff, are required to take oaths of secrecy before the commencement of polling and they are not permitted to interfere in any way with the voters or try to find out how the voters intend to vote or have voted. Any challenge of voters on the ground of personation is made through the presiding officer rather than as a direct interrogation of the challenged voter by a polling agent, and the form of questions which may be put to a person applying to vote by the presiding officer is frequently laid down in the relevant legislation. The polling agent is permitted to mark in his copy of the register those registered electors who have applied to vote, but the marked copy of the register must not normally be taken from the polling station until after polling has ended. Where ballot papers are numbered, the polling agent is not permitted under any circumstances to know the number of the ballot-paper issued to a voter. Before the poll commences, the polling agent, if present, is invited to inspect the ballot box or boxes to ascertain that they are empty, and, at the close of polling, he is usually at liberty to add his seal to that of the presiding officer in sealing the ballot box. The above description is a very brief outline of the normal position of polling agents and it is only necessary to mention deviations from this norm.

It may first be mentioned that, when elections are something of a novelty, polling agents frequently have no more than a very hazy idea of their duties and responsibilities. This was the case in Malaya at the first general election in 1955, in Uganda at the first general election of 1958, and was also true of India at its first general election. The Indian Election Commission reports of polling agents that:

> Out of 17,500 contesting candidates, as many as 4,194 did not appoint any polling agents at all. This was unfortunate inasmuch as polling agents who represent the candidates at the polling stations are expected to play an important part in enforcing the precautionary checks which the law has laid down to ensure that polling takes place in a fair and honest manner and that the ballot boxes are handled and sealed properly. It has been reported that most of the polling agents were ignorant of their duties and functions and were very often mere passive spectators of the proceedings. The Presiding Officers of course helped the polling agents to acquire a working knowledge of their duties and responsibilities in course of the proceedings, but even then they were a poor substitute for what the law had intended them to be, namely,

a body of intelligent and alert persons who could, by properly carrying out their duties, materially enhance public confidence in the verdict of the ballot box. Although the best use was not made of the system of polling agents a good beginning has been made and polling agents may be expected to play a more and more important role in future.[1]

In Malaya, the presiding officer can be notified in writing at any time before the commencement of polling by the candidate's election agents of the names of the polling agents assigned to attend at his polling station and, in practice, the polling agents brought their letters of appointment and presented them shortly before polling started. The presiding officer was required to inspect the agent's oath of secrecy and was instructed to refuse admission to any agent who could not produce both an oath of secrecy and a letter of appointment.[2] In Nigeria, the appointments of polling agents are notified to the returning officer rather than to the presiding officer and each candidate may appoint two persons per polling station; in the Western Region, these appointments must be notified "not later than three days before the day fixed for the election",[3] and, in the Eastern Region, the requisite notice must be given as much as seven days before the election.[4] Tanganyika has followed the example of the Western Region and requires three days' notice,[5] whilst Uganda has copied the Eastern Region and requires seven days' notice;[6] in each case the notice is given to the returning officer.

There is, in the British African territories, a fairly common provision[7] relating to the procedure to be adopted on a polling agent's objection to a voter on the grounds of attempted personation. He is required to make his objection to the presiding officer and the latter then ascertains whether the polling agent is prepared to undertake to substantiate the charge in a Court of Law. Only if the polling agent is prepared to make such an undertaking is the

---

[1] *Report on the first general elections in India, 1951-2*, Vol. I, p. 129.

[2] *Report on the First Election of Members to the Legislative Council of the Federation of Malaya*, p. 57.

[3] Reg. 46(2) of the Western Region Parliamentary and Local Government Electoral Regulations, 1955.

[4] Reg. 32(2) of the Eastern House of Assembly Electoral Regulations, 1955.

[5] Sec. 86 of the Tanganyika Legislative Council Elections Ordinance, 1957.

[6] Sec. 36(2) of the Uganda Legislative Council Elections Ordinance, 1957.

[7] This provision appears, for instance, in the legislation of Ghana, Nigeria and Tanganyika.

presiding officer under an obligation to take any further action, and such action is discussed below.

OUTLINE OF ALTERNATIVE METHODS OF VOTING BY BALLOT

Before proceeding to discuss in detail the equipment of polling stations, and the activities in the polling station of the voters, the polling station staff, the polling agents and others, it is necessary to give an outline of how the individual voter casts his vote. Before polling day, the elector will have been informed by public notice, or by political party agents, or by receipt of an official polling card or by some other method of the location of the polling station at which he is entitled to vote. After arrival at the polling station on polling day, he takes his place in the queue of electors waiting to vote and, when his turn comes, his identification is checked and the electoral register is examined to ascertain his voting entitlement. If and when the presiding officer is satisfied of his identity and his right to vote, he is given a ballot paper and his name is marked in the register as having received a ballot: he proceeds to cast his vote either by:

(a) marking the official ballot paper given to him in the secrecy of a polling booth or compartment in such a way as to indicate the candidate or candidates for whom he wishes to vote, and placing the marked ballot paper in the ballot box which is in the charge of the presiding officer, or

(b) placing the official ballot paper (or ballot papers in a multi-member constituency), unmarked, in the ballot box marked with the name or symbol of the candidate for whom he wishes to vote, each candidate having a separate ballot box, and all ballot boxes being screened from view to enable the voter to make his choice in secret, or

(c) enclosing the party list for which he wishes to vote in an officially provided voting envelope in the secrecy of a polling compartment and then placing the envelope in the ballot box under the eyes of the presiding officer, or

(d) The 'Whispering vote' — informing the presiding officer by whispering how he wishes to vote, the presiding officer then marking a ballot paper or making an appropriate entry in a ballot book, or

(e) entering a screened compartment and voting by the use of a voting machine (no ballot papers are issued when voting machines are used).

Having used one of these five methods to cast his vote, the voter has done his job and he proceeds to leave the polling station.

THE EQUIPMENT OF A POLLING STATION

The equipment required at a polling station depends on the method of voting employed and on the number of voters for whom the polling station has to cater. The list of polling materials to be provided by the electoral authorities will include some (but not all) of the following:

1. Furniture.
2. Lighting.
3. Polling booths or compartments.
4. Copies of the electoral register and of lists of special voters (e.g. lists of postal voters).
5. Ballot boxes.
6. Ballot papers and tendered ballot papers.
7. Voting machines.
8. Indelible ink or indelible ink pads, ordinary ink, pens, pencils, rubbers, paper, envelopes.
9. Various printed forms.
10. Perforator.
11. Presiding officer's seal.
12. Sealing wax, candles, matches, tape, scissors, gum.
13. Labels bearing the symbols of candidates.
14. Notices listing the names and symbols of all candidates.

Supplies of many of these articles can only be obtained some months after placing orders and, for such articles, the electoral authorities must ensure adequate stocks and make arrangement for storage. Examples of such articles are ballot boxes, perforators, seals and polling booths.

Suitable furniture, such as chairs and tables or desks, is not always available *in situ* in many of the buildings used as polling stations in under-developed countries, and it is usually necessary in such circumstances to improvise either by local temporary removal of furniture or by some other method. Such buildings are also frequently without any form of lighting and lamps must be provided if polling starts at or before dawn or if it continues until dusk.[1]

Where the system of marking the ballot paper in the secrecy of an individual polling compartment is in use, as, for instance, in the United Kingdom and the Federation of Malaya, collapsible cubicles are provided and, in these, the voter can mark his ballot paper without the risk of being overlooked.[2] In Britain and the British Caribbean, these compartments are provided at the rate of one for every one hundred and fifty electors allotted to the polling station. At the first general elections in Indonesia in 1955 the regulations provided that the cubicles should have no rear walls and the members of the polling station committee were "able to see from behind whether a voter put his hole on the right, the left or in the centre of his very large ballot paper".[3] The regulations were amended before the Constituent Assembly elections later in the year and closed voting cubicles were used which offered a better guarantee of the secrecy of the ballot.[4] Where there is a separate ballot box for each candidate and the voter is not required to mark his ballot paper but merely to drop it in the box marked with the symbol of the candidate of his choice, it is usual to screen off a corner of the polling station and place within this screened area a table or bench on which are placed the ballot boxes.[5]

The official polling station staff require at least one and preferably more than one copy of the portion of the electoral register which contains the names and particulars of the electors who are entitled to vote at the polling station. One of these copies is used throughout polling to mark the names of voters who have received a ballot paper and any additional copies are used to speed up the process of identification of voters.[6] In addition, if

[1] The absence of any form of lighting is obviously a factor to be taken into consideration in determining the hours of polling.

[2] A photograph of the type of polling booth used in Malaya appears on page 27 of the *Report on the First Election of Members to the Legislative Council of the Federation of Malaya.*

[3] Herbert Feith, *The Indonesian Elections of 1955*, p. 43.

[4] *Ibid*, p. 54.

[5] A diagram showing the rough layout plan of polling stations in India appears on page 125 of Vol. I of the *Report on the first general elections in India.* See also the diagram contained in the handbook for presiding officers in the 1958 Uganda elections and reproduced in *The Times* of 21st October, 1958.

[6] In British Guiana, five copies of the register are issued to the presiding officer, one for his own use, one for the assistant presiding officer, one for the poll clerk, one for posting up outside the polling station and the fifth as spare.

postal voting or proxy voting is permissible, the polling station staff require to have lists of voters who are entitled to vote by post or by proxy. Special arrangements for postal and proxy voting are discussed in Chapter IX.

Most countries use metal ballot boxes. Boxes are usually made to standard specifications, but they are sometimes made in three or four sizes in order to cater for polling stations with small, medium and large registered electorates. All ballot boxes are provided with strong locks to secure the lids to the boxes and the lid contains a slit[1] for the insertion of ballot papers. There is a removable cover for the slit so that the slit can be left open at the time of polling and can later be effectively closed and sealed once polling is over. The general construction of ballot boxes must obviously be such as to make the box proof against fraud of any sort. In order to minimise fraud, there is a requirement in the Electoral Law of Thailand which requires that one side of the ballot box should be transparent; this provision is regarded as a safeguard against the "stuffing" of ballot boxes. In some of the African territories, wooden ballot boxes have been used; for instance in Sierra Leone wooden boxes with detachable lids were used for the 1957 elections. The lids of the boxes were screwed down but it was found that a large number of boxes were badly damaged when opened for counting because of the impatience of counting assistants who frequently levered the lid from the box without taking out the screws.[2] In view of the likelihood of rapid deterioration of wooden boxes in tropical climates, it seems possible that metal boxes are more economical in the long run and there can be little doubt but that metal ballot boxes also represent a gain in security over wooden boxes. Metal ballot boxes have been manufactured for the purpose of national elections in countries such as India and Malaya. Where separate ballot boxes are provided for each candidate at every polling station, it is particularly important that there should be some uniform system of numbering or labelling the boxes and every box has to be marked with the candidate's name and symbol or colour. In order to guard against the fraudulent removal of symbols pasted to the outside

[1] Some of the returning officers in the Uganda General Election of 1958, where wooden boxes were used, reported that the slits were too large and that it was possible to remove ballot papers by turning the boxes upside down.

[2] Unpublished report of the Supervisor of Elections on the Sierra Leone elections of 1957.

of boxes, some countries[1] take the precaution of pasting one copy of the symbol on the inside of the box.

Where the candidates' names (and symbols where used) are to appear on the ballot papers, printing of ballot papers cannot commence until after nomination day. In a country with limited printing resources, the length of time between the closure of nominations and polling may in such circumstances be determined by the time taken for the printing and distribution of ballot papers rather than by other considerations.[2] Where, however, the ballot paper is not to be marked by the voters and separate ballot boxes are provided for each candidate, the ballot papers can be printed as soon as the size of the electorate of each constituency is known, and printing ceases to be a factor in the determination of the interval between nomination and polling.

In the latter case (where a voter is not required to mark his ballot) it is more than ever necessary to take precautions for the printing of the ballot papers under security conditions in order to prevent forgeries. Thus, in Zanzibar prior to the first 1957 elections, the ballot papers were set up in a special type not found in the Protectorate except in the Government Printer's office.[3] In Ghana, prior to the 1956 general elections, the papers were full of rumours that it was intended to forge ballot papers for use in the election and, in order to ensure that no unauthorised printing took place, the presses used were placed in a separate room in the Government Printing Office, screened with expanded metal. In India, watermarked paper was used for all ballot papers, which were printed centrally for the first general elections;[4] the ballot paper contained only a serial number with a prefix consisting of two letters which denoted the State in which the ballot paper was to be used. In the Western Region of Nigeria, the ballot papers used for the Parliamentary elections of 1956 were printed outside Nigeria and contained secret marks in the design known only to the Electoral Commissioner and the printers.[5] Most of the ballot

[1] e.g. The Sudan, Uganda, and Zanzibar.

[2] As, for instance, in the Federation of Malaya in 1955, when there was an interval of six weeks between nomination day and polling day in order to provide time for 'security' printing of the ballot papers by the Government Printer.

[3] *Report on the 1957 elections in Zanzibar*, p. 18.

[4] *Report on the first general elections in India, 1951-2*, Vol. I, p. 102.

[5] At the 1956 Municipal elections in Port Louis, Mauritius, where the ballot paper was headed "Election for the Electoral Area of ——", arrangements were

papers used at the first general election in Sierra Leone in 1957 were printed in the United Kingdom and the minority printed in Sierra Leone were produced by the Government Printer under security conditions.

PREPARATIONS BEFORE THE COMMENCEMENT OF POLLING

Before polling begins on election day, the presiding officer and his staff must arrange tables, chairs and polling booths in the most suitable positions, post up statutory and other notices outside the polling stations and in the polling booths, ensure that the seats for the polling agents are conveniently arranged so that the latter can perform their duties without being in a position to communicate with voters, mark out suitable limits for the polling station bearing in mind the necessity for secrecy of voting and maintenance of law and order, inspect the credentials of polling agents, check the equipment provided for polling and show the ballot box empty before locking and sealing it. Obviously these preparations take time. As it is essential that everything should be in readiness for opening the poll at the appointed time, presiding officers and their polling assistants are usually instructed to be at their polling stations half an hour to an hour before polling is due to commence. In the United Kingdom, Schofield suggests that the presiding officer should arrive at 6.30 to 6.40 for a 7 a.m. opening of the poll at parliamentary elections,[1] whilst Gillings suggests that, for local government elections, the presiding officer and poll clerks must be at the station at least a quarter of an hour before the time appointed for the opening.[2] In Malaya, on the occasion of the first general elections in 1955, polling station staff were instructed to be at their posts at least half an hour before the time appointed for the opening of the poll, and, where it had not been possible to arrange the polling station and post up the necessary notices on the previous day, at least one hour before the opening.

made with the Government Printer for one of the letters in this heading to be omitted as if by accident, and this measure was kept secret until the morning of the election.

[1] A. Norman Schofield, *Parliamentary Elections*, p. 294.

[2] W. G. Gillings, *Handbook for the Conduct of Polls at Local Government Elections*, p. 10.

The ceremony of opening the ballot boxes and showing them empty to those present prior to the commencement of polling is a standard statutory requirement and is obviously necessary if the rival candidates are to be satisfied that there has been 'fair play'. The presiding officer is not, however, bound to await the arrival of a polling agent of a candidate who has no representative present at the prescribed hour for opening the poll. The ballot box, having been shown empty, is locked and sealed (or screwed down and sealed in the case of some ballot-boxes made of wood) and must not on any account be opened again until polling has been completed and the returning officer or someone authorised by him opens it at the place for counting the votes.

Admission to the Polling Station

The electoral law usually places restrictions on admission to polling stations. Thus, in Britain, the presiding officer has power to regulate the number of voters to be admitted to the polling station at one and the same time and is required to exclude all other persons except the candidates and their election agents, the polling agents appointed to attend at the polling station, the clerks appointed to attend at the polling station, the constables on duty and the companions of blind voters.[1] The law in Malaya is similar to that of Britain. In the Western Region of Nigeria, the presiding officer is to exclude all persons other than voters, candidates, polling agents, polling officers, "and any other person who in his opinion has lawful reason to be admitted".[2] The Uganda Legislative Council Elections Ordinance requires the presiding officer to regulate the number of persons to be admitted to vote at one time, and to exclude "all other persons except the candidates, the polling agent of each candidate, the returning officer and persons authorised in writing by the returning officer, the police officers on duty, and other persons officially employed at the polling station".[3] The wording of these clauses is of some importance, as the possibility of admitting such persons as V.I.P.'s, official observers from foreign countries, newspaper reporters, etc., will

[1] Representation of the People Act, 1949, Parliamentary Election Rules (Rule 33(1)).
[2] Reg. 51(2) of the Western Region Parliamentary and Local Government Electoral Regulations, 1955.
[3] Sec. 40(3) of the Uganda Legislative Council Elections Ordinance, 1957.

depend on the phraseology used, and, perhaps, as in Uganda, on the discretion given to the returning officer to issue authorisations. In Ghana, at the time of the 1956 general elections, presiding officers were instructed to allow entry to journalists who produced an identity card from their newspapers. The Zanzibar Legislative Council Elections Decree is unusual in that it permits the presiding officer to give admittance to "not more than three electors whom he may select from those who have voted at that polling station" and these electors, like the polling agents, are to be "posted in such a place that they can see each person who presents himself as an elector and hear his name as given in by him but so that they cannot see how any elector votes"[1] — in other words not more than three electors who have voted are selected to assist the polling agents in ensuring fair play and preventing personation.

The law does not usually prescribe how the presiding officer is to regulate the number of voters to be admitted to the polling station at any one time, and the precise number who can be safely admitted will obviously depend on the method of voting employed and the number of polling booths available. It is usual not to admit more than three or four voters at a time and to require other voters waiting for admittance to form an orderly queue[2] outside the entrance to the polling station under the charge of a police constable, if one is available. When the method of voting involves the use of a separate ballot box for each candidate, and the ballot boxes are screened from view in the polling compartment, it is obvious that only one elector can cast his vote at a time if secrecy is to be preserved and admission of voters is then limited to two or three at a time, one person voting whilst the identification of the next in the queue is being checked. Where ballot papers are marked, and two or three polling booths are provided in each polling station, the rate of admission of voters will normally depend on the speed at which they can be identified and checked in the register.

In Asia and Africa, it has usually been found that there are large queues of voters waiting for admission during the first few hours

[1] Sec. 49 of the Zanzibar Legislative Council (Elections) Decree, 1957.

[2] In this connection it may be mentioned that the provision in the Turkish electoral law (Art. 95, Election of National Deputies Act, 1950) to the effect that votes are to be cast in order of arrival except for pregnant women, the disabled and the aged could well be incorporated in the electoral laws of other countries.

of polling and that a large percentage of those who intend to cast a vote will have done so by the middle of the day. This phenomenon has been noted, for instance, in the Federation of Malaya,[1] Zanzibar,[2] Nigeria[3] and Ghana.[4] In India, on the other hand, it is reported that, at the first general elections, "polling was heavier in the morning and afternoon hours as compared to the middle of the day",[5] and, in this respect, the experience of India is more akin to that of the Western industrial countries than to that of the other Asian and African countries. In the Western democracies, pressure to vote is usually greatest when people are on their way to work or to shop and when they return from work. Another contrast between the first Indian general elections and those of a country like Malaya is that, in India, heavier polling was experienced in the urban areas than in the rural areas, whereas, in Malaya, polling was very much lighter in the urban areas.

THE IDENTIFICATION OF VOTERS

It is obvious that the correct identification of those persons who are entitled to vote at a particular polling station is one of the most crucial aspects of an election and that the electoral system will have but a poor reputation if personation is attempted on a large scale with any degree of success or if ways of casting votes over and above an elector's entitlement can be practised without detection. It is therefore of great importance that the official polling staff should be quite clear which electors listed in a constituency register are entitled to vote at the polling station at which they are officiating and that care should be exercised in establishing the identity of a person claiming to be an elector and in marking the register clearly to show which electors have exercised their right to vote.

The need for an accurate register of electors containing sufficient detail for the purposes of identification has been stressed in Chapter IV. Given a good register, there are still a number of

[1] *Report on the First Election of Members to the Legislative Council of the Federation of Malaya*, p. 26.

[2] *Report by the Supervisor of Elections on the 1957 Zanzibar Elections*, p. 19.

[3] *Report on the holding of the 1956 Parliamentary Election to the Western House of Assembly*, p. 9.

[4] *Report on the 1956 General Election in the Gold Coast* (now Ghana).

[5] *Report on the first general elections in India, 1951-2*, Vol. I, p. 130.

possible measures which can be taken to ease the task of rapid identification and to ensure that electors vote but once. The first possibility, which has been discussed to some extent in connection with registration, is the issue of voters' cards, either at the time of registration or shortly prior to an election; if a card can be issued to each elector showing his or her name, address and position in the register shortly before an election and if a check is made at the time of polling to ensure that the person bringing such a card to the polling station is in fact the elector entitled to its possession, the voter's identification and electoral number are likely, in most cases, to be established quickly and efficiently. The dangers involved in the use of such cards are that the cards may not be distributed in the first instance to the right people; that, even if correctly distributed, they may be corruptly bought or sold or withdrawn by a political party or interested individual; and that the polling assistants are likely to rely on the cards produced at the polling station without ensuring that the persons producing the cards are in fact the electors entitled to the vote. Even where distributing commissions composed of representatives of the rival political parties are appointed to distribute voters' cards shortly before an election, as in France and her overseas territories, it is often necessary to rely on village and family heads to complete the distribution and this may lead to unlawful retention of the cards or to the use of undue influence in completing the distribution.[1] There are similar possibilities of corrupt or unlawful practices if the cards are distributed at the time of registration, for there have been frequent attempts by political parties in West Africa to corner 'registration receipts'; moreover, in the absence of periodic re-registration or distribution of fresh cards, there is the possibility that cards issued in the first instance to persons who have since died or moved to another area or who have for some other reason ceased to be eligible to vote in a particular constituency may be unlawfully used by personators. Finally, whenever the cards are distributed, and however much the instructions to polling staff stress the great care which must be exercised in the identification of voters, there is a real danger,

[1] Voting cards were also distributed to registered electors prior to the first Indonesian elections of 1955 and there were some instances of intimidation in the course of distribution and a few cases of the use of voting cards at polling stations by persons other than those for whom they were intended. See Herbert Feith, *The Indonesian Elections of 1955*, p. 43.

which the author has noted on a number of occasions in Malaya, of the poll clerks, conscious of a large queue of electors impatiently waiting for admission to the polling station, relying entirely on the card produced as establishing identity without even bothering to inquire of the applicant his or her name and address. In British territories in Africa, registration receipts have usually been issued and these must sometimes but not always be produced at the polling station before the elector can be issued with a ballot paper.[1] Experience suggests that, in general, the advantages of the registration receipts or voters' cards in speeding up the poll outweigh the dangers discussed above, but the author is of the opinion that, in order to minimise unlawful practices, the production of a card should be voluntary rather than obligatory at the time of polling and that, where conditions permit, the issue of cards a week or two before polling is to be preferred to the issue of registration receipts which, as the years go by, will grow more and more out-of-date in the absence of complete re-registration and the issue of fresh receipts.

As an alternative to the issue of official poll cards, it is possible to permit the candidates to issue cards to electors giving electoral numbers and other details such as the symbol of the candidates, and, in countries where there are two or more well developed rival political parties which can keep a check on one another's activities, this may well be the best method of dealing with the problem.[2]

Some account of the distribution of registration receipts in certain British African territories has been given in Chapter IV; it is now necessary to supplement that account with a brief description of the procedure in two countries in which some form of poll card is used but no registration receipt. In French Africa, the distribution of electors' cards is commenced some two weeks before polling; in the municipalities, cards are usually delivered

---

[1] Production of a registration receipt before issue of a ballot paper is a statutory requirement in Kenya and 'a voter who fails or neglects to produce his voter's card shall not be supplied with a ballot paper' (Rule 21(5) of the Legislative Council (African Representation) (Election of Members) Rules, 1956).

[2] It should be noted, however, that in British parliamentary elections since 1948, the returning officer has been required by law to issue official poll-cards and it is an offence for any person to issue imitation poll-cards "so closely resembling an official poll-card as to be calculated to deceive" (Sec. 81, Representation of the People Act, 1949).

to individuals at their home address but this is not often possible in the villages and the rural areas, and, in such areas, distribution points are sometimes set up under the supervision of the distribution committees in each of the main villages and people are encouraged to collect their cards individually; alternatively, bundles of cards are distributed to electors through village headmen, though this practice is generally regarded as unsatisfactory owing to the possibility that some of the cards may not reach the correct destination.[1] There are likely to be a certain number of cards left undistributed by election day and these can be claimed at the polling stations. In Britain, the returning officer is required to send or deliver official poll cards to each elector at his qualifying address prior to a parliamentary election and these cards, which must be in a prescribed form, state the name of the constituency, the date and hours of polling and the situation of the elector's polling station, and the elector's name, qualifying address and number on the electoral register. The elector is not, however, obliged to produce his official poll card at the time of voting and the card serves more as a reminder of the date of the election and of the whereabouts of the polling station than as a means of identification in the polling station.

A method adopted in India, West Africa and Jamaica to prevent persons from voting more than once — and hence in some measure to prevent personation — is the marking of a part of the thumb or of the finger with indelible ink or paint. If the mark is carefully made and cannot be erased for a day or so, it should be possible to detect persons attempting to vote a second time without too much difficulty. In India, an elector on entering a polling station is required to allow his left forefinger to be inspected by a polling officer for the purpose of ascertaining whether he already has any mark of indelible ink on the finger. If there is no such mark, the polling officer in charge of the electoral roll proceeds to ascertain the elector's name and address and other particulars and the elector is required to submit to an indelible ink mark being put on his left forefinger before being given a ballot paper. If a person enters a polling station and applies for a ballot paper and is found to have such a mark already on his left

---

[1] A very full description of the French method of distribution of voters' cards is given in pp. 103-14 of the *U.N. Commissioner's Report on the 1958 elections in French Togoland* (U.N. Document T/1392).

forefinger, he is liable to be arrested and prosecuted for personation.[1] In Ghana, the voter is required to press his left thumb on an ink pad on being given a ballot paper; polling assistants are required to report to the presiding officer any applicant for a ballot paper whose left thumb has got a violet mark and the presiding officer then has the responsibility of questioning the applicant in the presence of the polling agents to decide whether there is reasonable cause to believe that the offence of personation has been committed. It must be emphasised, however, that the use of indelible ink will not help in preventing a person not registered as an elector from voting once and it seems to follow that marking with ink is more likely to be an effective deterrent against personation in a country like India with a full adult franchise than in a territory with a 'fancy' franchise. It should also be stated that, although the Indian authorities appear to be satisfied with the indelibility of the ink used for marking purposes, the author has been told by persons with West African experience that the ink or dye used there can be erased without too much difficulty.

Indelible ink was used, apparently for the first time in a French territory, to mark the left thumb of voters at the 1958 general election in Togoland under French administration.[2] Tests undertaken before polling day indicated that the method of inking the thumb by pressing it on an ink pad was unsatisfactory (this method has been used in the past in parts of British West Africa). Several samples of ink were tried, and it was finally decided that the voter's left thumb should be dipped in a container of the indelible ink selected for use. The United Nations Commissioner reports that the measure was effective in general, though there were complaints that the ink was not sufficiently indelible, and, at some polling stations, the observers reported that the operation of inking was not carried out or not applied systematically and in accordance with the instructions. During this election, a number of people were found removing the traces of ink from their thumbs with detergents, and several people came to the polling stations and applied to vote when they had traces of ink at the base of the thumbnail.

[1] The Indian Representation of the People (Conduct of Elections and Election Petitions) Rules, 1951, Rules 22 and 23.

[2] See pp. 148-9 and p. 171 of the *U.N. Commissioner's Report*.

In the Sudan, it was the intention that a silver nitrate pencil should be used for marking the finger of voters at the 1958 general election. The Election Commission's plans had to be abandoned at the last moment as the mark of the pencil does not appear immediately unless treated with a developer solution, and the right chemical formula for this solution is still the subject of experiments in the Khartoum laboratories. The Government of Trinidad is also examining the possibility of using silver nitrate pencils, as indelible ink can be removed too easily.

The use of poll cards and indelible ink as a means of preventing personation and multiple voting is in fact no substitute for vigilance and intelligence on the part of the official polling staff and the candidates' polling agents. The electoral legislation of some countries lays down statutory questions to be put by the presiding officer to an applicant for a ballot paper when there is doubt about identity or any suggestion that the applicant has already voted. If required by a candidate or his election or polling agent, the presiding officer is bound to put the statutory questions to a person applying as an elector. In Britain, if a person is asked one or both of the statutory questions[1] by the presiding officer, a ballot paper must not be delivered to him unless he has answered the question or questions satisfactorily. No inquiry is permitted into the right of any person to vote save through these questions, but, if at the time a person applies for a ballot paper for the purpose of voting in person, or after he has applied for a ballot paper for that purpose and before he has left the polling station, a candidate or his election or polling agent declares to the presiding officer that he has reasonable cause to believe that the applicant has committed an offence of personation and undertakes to substantiate the charge in a court of law, the presiding officer may order a constable to arrest the applicant, and the order of the presiding officer is sufficient authority for the constable to carry out the arrest.[2] A person in respect of whom a challenge of this

[1] The statutory questions, in the case of a person applying for a ballot paper as an elector, are:
    (i) Are you the person registered in the register of parliamentary electors for this election as follows (read the whole entry from the register)?
    (ii) Have you already voted, here or elsewhere, at this election, otherwise than as proxy for some other person?
[2] Rule 37, Parliamentary Elections Rules.

nature has been made is not, however, to be prevented from voting merely by virtue of the challenge.

Somewhat similar statutory questions which may, and if required by a candidate or a polling agent, must be put to a person applying for a ballot paper appear in the elections legislation of Ghana, Tanganyika and Nigeria.[1] The laws of these countries also contain a provision similar to that of the British Parliamentary Elections Rules regarding the power of a presiding officer to order the arrest of a person whom a candidate or his polling agent challenges on the ground that an offence of personation has been committed. In Malaya, however, there are no statutory questions, but, as an alternative, the presiding officer at any polling station may in his discretion require any voter, before he is given a ballot paper, to furnish such evidence of his identity as the presiding officer may deem necessary and to make and subscribe to one or more of certain statutory declarations, the first of which is a declaration of identity and the second and third of which are declarations that the person concerned has not already voted at the current election.[2] The effect of the statutory declarations, if subscribed, is, of course, the same as that of the statutory questions and they can be regarded as alternative means to the same end. Uganda has followed Malaya's example in using declarations by voters in lieu of statutory questions. In both Malaya and Uganda, the presiding officer may refuse to give a ballot paper to any person who fails to furnish evidence of identity or refuses to make a declaration when called upon to do so.

In most countries of the British Commonwealth, if a person representing himself to be an elector named in the register of electors applies for a ballot paper after that elector has been marked in the register as having already voted, and the applicant gives satisfactory answers to the statutory questions (or subscribes to a suitable statutory declaration where declarations rather than questions are used), he is entitled to receive a ballot paper in the same way as any other elector save that the ballot paper he receives — a "tendered ballot paper" — is normally of a colour

[1] See, for instance, Regs. 18 and 21 of the Ghana Electoral Provisions (Assembly Elections) Regulations, 1954, and Sections 89 and 91 of the Tanganyika Legislative Council Elections Ordinance.

[2] Reg. 22 of the Federation of Malaya Legislative Council Election Regulations, 1954.

different from the ordinary ballot papers. The use of tendered ballot papers is discussed in more detail later in this Chapter.

The Marking of the Register

When a person applying for a ballot paper has been satisfactorily identified as a registered elector who has not already voted he is given his ballot and his name is marked on the register as having received it. This can be done in a variety of ways. In the Federation of Rhodesia and Nyasaland, the presiding officer, after handing the ballot paper to the person claiming to vote, is required to "draw a line through the number and surname of the voter on the roll as evidence that the voter has received the ballot paper or papers to which he is entitled".[1] In Zanzibar, at the 1957 elections, the presiding officer ticked off the elector's name on his official list of electors prior to issuing the ballot paper.[2] In Uganda, at the 1958 elections, the presiding officer was instructed to "put a clear firm horizontal line with the red pencil" against the name or number of a voter before marking the counterfoil of the ballot paper.[3] In French Togoland, at the 1958 elections, the Chairman of the Polling Committee in charge of a polling station or one of the members of the Committee signed or initialled in the margin of the electoral register next to the voter's name when each voter had voted.[4] In Turkey, the voter is required to sign the electoral register opposite his own name; a thumb-print is used in lieu of a signature in the case of voters who cannot sign their own names. The net effect of all these methods is the same, save that it is possible that some methods of marking a register may be more liable than others to lead to error.

Use of Poll Books

In Jamaica, Trinidad and Zanzibar, poll books are used. In these islands, polling assistants make entries in a poll book when voters have been issued with their ballot papers in addition to the marking of the electoral registers. In Jamaica,[5] when the identity

[1] The Electoral Act, 1958, Sec. 71(1)(c).
[2] Information obtained from *Notes for the guidance of Presiding Officers*, supplied by courtesy of the Zanzibar Government.
[3] Uganda *Handbook for Presiding Officers*.
[4] *Report of the U.N. Commissioner* (Document T/1392), p. 161.
[5] See pp. 178 and 242 of the *Report on the 1949 general election in Jamaica*.

of an elector has been ascertained and a check has been made to ensure that the name of such elector appears on the register, the poll clerk enters the name, address and occupation of the elector in the poll book for the polling station, giving the first elector to vote the number '1', the second the number '2', and so on. The number of the elector in the electoral register is also entered in the poll book in the appropriate column, but it is the number given to the elector in the poll book rather than the number in the electoral register that is entered on the counterfoil of the ballot paper. When the elector has inserted his ballot in the ballot box, the poll clerk is required to write the word 'Voted' in the proper column of the poll book. There are additional columns of the poll book for use when any elector is required to swear an oath before voting, when a person applies for a ballot paper after another person has voted in his name, and when objections are made on behalf of any of the candidates. The presiding officer is required to check off the name of each voter on the list of electors when he hands the voter his ballot.

In Zanzibar, the procedure for using the poll book is very similar to that of Jamaica, and, indeed, the forms[1] of poll book are virtually identical. The existence of poll books of this kind undoubtedly provides a useful record of the action taken in respect of each individual voter and affords an opportunity of checking on the possibility of mistakes made by presiding officers and polling assistants. The necessity to write particulars of each voter reduces the average rate of polling, however, and makes it necessary to provide for a lower maximum of registered voters for each polling station. It is suggested that poll books are an unnecessary burden on the official polling officers, once the latter are fully trained and reasonably experienced in the work demanded of them, although it is useful to have a record of action taken in respect of voters against whom protests or challenges have been entered and of any complaints or observations made by candidates or their agents. A record of this kind is kept in polling stations in France and the overseas French territories and entries are made in the poll books used in British Guiana only in respect of such voters.[2]

[1] Form 10 of the Zanzibar Legislative Council (Elections) (Prescribed Forms) Rules, 1957, and Form 25 in the Second Schedule of the Jamaica Representation of the People Law, 1944.
[2] See 'Specimen Poll Book' on pages 102 and 103 of Appendix V Book A of the *Report on the 1957 General Election in British Guiana*. Whenever one of

BALLOT PAPERS AND THEIR ISSUE

In the United Kingdom, at the time of issue of a ballot paper to a voter, the voter's number on the electoral register is entered on the counterfoil of the ballot paper. The counterfoil and the ballot paper bear the same number, consecutive ballot papers having consecutive numbers. The numbering of ballot papers and the use of the counterfoil together go far to eliminate attempts to use forged ballot papers and to provide a method of identifying a particular ballot paper with an elector in the event of election petitions or other legal proceedings. The register is marked at the time of issue of a ballot paper to an elector and, at an election. there is thus a running record in each polling station not only of those who have the right to vote but also of those who have exercised this right.

Throughout the Commonwealth countries of Africa, the statutory prescription for ballot papers for central government elections requires that each ballot paper should have a counterfoil and that the same number should be printed or written on the counterfoil and on the corresponding ballot paper. Everywhere in British Africa, as in Britain, the number of the elector in the register of electors has to be marked on the counterfoil at the time of issue of a ballot paper. In India, however, counterfoils are not used: instead the serial number on the ballot paper is recorded at the time of issue on the electoral roll against the name of the voter to whom the ballot paper is issued; the effect of this arrangement is the same as with the use of counterfoils, as a record is available of the number of the ballot paper issued to each voter if required by an Election Tribunal investigating charges of electoral offences. At the time of the first general elections in India, there were charges that the recording of the ballot paper number on the electoral roll violated the secrecy of the ballot, but it does not, of course, do so any more than the recording of electoral numbers on the counterfoils of ballot papers.[1]

the statutory oaths is administered, an appropriate entry must be made in the poll book. No entry is made however for ordinary voters who are not required to subscribe to oaths before voting.

[1] The marked copy of the electoral roll and the counterfoils of the ballot papers are put in sealed packets and locked up. These packets are opened only on the instructions of a Court and their contents are ultimately destroyed by the returning officer.

There is usually a prescribed form for the ballot paper, but the actual content varies considerably from one country to another. Where the ballot paper is a mere token and there are separate ballot boxes for each candidate, the content of the ballot is usually restricted to a statement of the country or territory in which the election is taking place, the date or year of the election and the serial number. The name of the constituency is sometimes printed on the ballot paper, but, more frequently, the constituency is coded in the serial numbering of the ballot papers. In order to prevent forgeries, the design and numbering of ballot papers are usually kept secret until polling day. The possibilities of fraud or misconduct when ballot papers are not numbered and attached to counterfoils are illustrated by the allegations investigated by the Commission on the Conduct of Local Government Elections in Mauritius.[1] The ballot papers used for the 1953 Municipal Elections in Port Louis were printed by a local firm of printers and were delivered in bundles. They were not attached to counterfoils and were not serially numbered. The paper on which the ballot papers were printed was of a type used for general purposes in the Municipality and had no watermark. No exact account was kept of the amount of paper sent to the printers, or of the amount used by them. Each ballot paper, on being issued to a voter, was stamped with an inked stamp bearing the name and device of the Municipality and the number of the polling station, but the Commission thought that it would have been possible for unauthorised copies of the stamp to be made. In these circumstances, it is not very surprising that the Commission found that the method of preparing and the form of the ballot papers and the arrangements for manufacturing and using the stamps left the door wide open to abuse, even though there was no evidence to support the view that fraud had actually taken place.

When ballot papers are to be marked, as in Malaya, the British West Indies, Tanganyika, and the United Kingdom, there are several points of some importance which arise. In the first instance, the paper used for printing the ballot papers should be opaque in order to minimise the risk of polling station staff and polling agents being able to see through the folded ballot paper and discover how an elector has voted. Secondly, experience in Malaya and, probably, elsewhere has shown the importance of using thick,

[1] Mauritius Leg. Co. Sessional Paper No. 1 of 1956, pp. 11-13.

prominent lines to divide the ballot paper into its various compartments; if thin lines are used, there is a greater likelihood of a voter spoiling his ballot paper by placing his mark in a way which does not make his voting intention completely unambiguous. Thirdly, Malayan experience indicates the desirability of printing the ballot paper in such a way that the names and symbols (where used) of the candidates and the spaces for marking the ballot paper occupy virtually the whole of the face of the ballot paper; the more empty space there is outside the blank spaces designed for marking the ballot, the greater the likelihood that a voter will mark his ballot in the wrong place or write comments leading to the rejection of his vote at the count. Usually, where ballot papers are to be marked, the content of the ballot paper is restricted to the names of the candidates (usually arranged alphabetically), symbols (where used), spaces for marking and the serial number; in Tanganyika, however, where every voter is required to vote simultaneously for each vacant contested seat in his constituency, the ballot paper has a distinct section for the candidates of each race,[1] and each section is to contain "the full names, addresses and descriptions of the candidates for that seat, as shown in their respective nomination papers, arranged alphabetically and, where applicable, their symbols or identification colours".[2] In Jamaica, too, the addresses and occupations as well as the names and symbols of the candidates appear on the ballot paper.[3]

It has already been mentioned that, in most Commonwealth countries, the electoral number of a voter is entered on the counterfoil at the time of issue of a ballot paper. It is also immediately prior to the issue that the ballot paper is stamped or perforated with the official mark or initialed or signed by the presiding officer. The purpose of the stamp or perforation or signature is to assist the counting staff to recognise forgeries and any ballot paper which has not been stamped or perforated or signed is normally rejected at the count. The stamp or perforation mark is, of course, kept a closely guarded secret prior to the poll. It is arguable whether the likelihood of the introduction of forged ballot papers is great enough to counterbalance the ballot papers which, at

[1] In each constituency, there is one seat for an African Member of the Legislative Council, one for an Asian Member and one for a European Member.
[2] Section 88(a) of the Tanganyika Legislative Council Elections Ordinance.
[3] Section 30(2) Representation of the People Law, 1944.

many elections in under-developed territories in the British Commonwealth, are rejected through failure of the polling station staff to stamp or perforate or sign ballot papers as required by the electoral law. The Supervisor of Elections in Sierra Leone at the first 1957 elections reported that "the necessity of marking ballot papers with an official mark proved to be a stumbling block at several polling stations" and cited the failure to stamp ballot papers as the cause of rejection of a large number of otherwise valid votes; he, together with most of his returning officers, recommended the deletion of the regulation[1] which provides for the marking of ballot papers. In this connection it is perhaps significant that, prior to the 1956 general elections in Ghana, the requirement that the ballot paper be marked with the official stamp was deleted from the electoral regulations — and Ghana has perhaps had more electoral experience than any other West African territory in the Commonwealth. In British Guiana, too, a feature of the 1957 electoral act was the adoption of initialling of the back of the ballot paper by the presiding officer in lieu of the rubber-stamping of an official mark previously used.

In marked contrast to the arrangements for the issue of ballot papers in the British Commonwealth is the procedure used in France and her overseas territories, where counterfoils are not used, ballot papers are not numbered, nor are they perforated or embossed prior to an elector voting. In France and French Africa, after a voter has been identified and his name checked in the register, he takes an envelope and chooses a ballot paper; there are a series of ballot papers — each containing the list of candidates representing one party or one associated group of parties in a multi-member constituency whilst there is a separate ballot paper for each candidate in a single member constituency. The voter chooses between the various ballot papers and places the ballot of his choice in the envelope in the secrecy of the voting compartment; he then satisfies the chairman[2] that he is carrying only one envelope and deposits the envelope in the ballot box. With the French method of polling the likelihood of an otherwise valid vote being rejected on account of an error on the part of the polling

---

[1] Reg. 25(b)(1) of the Sierra Leone House of Representatives (Elections) Regulations.

[2] The Chairman of the Polling Committee in French territories corresponds to the presiding officer in British territories.

station staff is discounted; with the system used in British Africa, votes have frequently been disallowed because the presiding officer or his assistant has marked the ballot paper rather than the counterfoil with the electoral number or because the ballot paper has not been properly embossed, perforated, initialed or signed before issue.

REFUSAL OF A BALLOT PAPER

The contents of the register of electors are normally conclusive as to the right of the persons named therein to vote. Indeed the machinery of registration exists precisely for the purpose of avoiding the raising at the poll of any question as to why a particular name appears in the register and whether a given registered elector has the required qualifications. The presiding officer is therefore normally required to deliver a ballot paper to any person who is shown on the register and who succeeds in establishing his or her identity as a registered elector.[1] In Zanzibar, however, under the electoral law at present in force, electors can, before receiving their ballot paper, be challenged not only in respect of their identity, but also in respect of their qualifications;[2] and, at the 1957 elections, a number of electors were challenged in the polling station by candidates' agents, mostly on grounds of status, but others too on grounds of age, income, or literacy and those who refused to take the "oath of qualification" were not permitted to vote and had their names struck off the electoral lists.

Outside Zanzibar, the register is normally conclusive as to the right of the electors to vote, and the presiding officer can only refuse a vote to a person claiming to be a registered elector on grounds such as that:

(a) The applicant is apparently not the person whose name is on the register, or

(b) The presiding officer has reason to believe that the applicant has previously voted at the same election, or

(c) The applicant refuses to answer the statutory questions when requested to do so by the presiding officer, or

[1] Even when the register is conclusive, it is normally an offence for a person to vote when registered as an elector but not legally qualified to vote. See, for instance, Sections 39(4) and 48(1)(a) of the British Representation of the People Act, 1949.

[2] Section 45(1) of the Zanzibar Legislative Council Elections Decree, 1957.

(d) The elector is marked on the register as being on the list of postal or proxy voters (where postal or proxy voting is in use).

If the presiding officer is doubtful about the identity of an applicant for a ballot paper who claims to be a registered elector, he would normally put the relevant statutory questions to the claimant or request him to subscribe to the relevant statutory declaration. The presiding officer would usually take similar action if he had reason to believe that the applicant for a ballot paper had previously voted at the same election. The first two grounds for refusing a ballot are therefore to some extent covered by the third.

RECORDING THE VOTE

One ballot box for each candidate

Polling by means of the provision of one ballot box for each candidate and ballot papers which do not have to be marked by voters has a wide appeal in under-developed countries for the very obvious reason that it is perhaps easier for illiterate electors to vote by this method than by any other. When this method of recording votes is used, the ballot boxes are usually placed behind screens or in a separate room and the voters enter the screened compartment or separate room one by one to cast their votes in secret, all previous proceedings in connection with identification and receipt of ballot papers having taken place in the open part of the polling station in the presence of the official polling staff and the polling agents.

Where this method of voting has been adopted, the following difficulties have arisen:

(a) The screened compartment has sometimes been designed in such a way that, although no-one can see the ballot box into which the voter is putting his ballot paper, an intelligent guess can be made by the position of his feet or some other part of his body regarding the way in which he is voting.

(b) The siting of the ballot boxes may play an important part in determining voting behaviour.

(c) As the ballot paper does not in itself indicate how an elector has voted, any carelessness on the part of presiding officers in ensuring that ballot boxes remain properly marked or on the part of counting staff in mixing votes from one ballot box with votes from another will ruin an election.

(*d*) As the ballot boxes are hidden from view, it is difficult to ensure that an elector does in fact put his ballot paper in one or other of the ballot boxes and does not emerge from the polling station and sell his ballot paper to the highest bidder.

(*e*) As the ballot boxes are hidden from view, the presiding officer can never be certain that a voter does not spend part of his time behind the screen in tampering with the ballot boxes.

The last item in the above list — the possibility of dishonest tampering with ballot boxes — indicates the desirability of keeping the elector as much as possible within view of the polling officers while he is casting his vote. For a ballot box must have a slit, and, if there is a slit, it is possible to 'stuff' a ballot box with forged or purchased ballot papers or to force in ink or acid or sand or glue in the ballot box of one or more of one's rivals. On the other hand, as the first item in the list suggests, if the elector is not entirely screened from view, the polling officers and the polling agents may be able to tell how the elector is voting. The problem of how to arrange the screened compartment and the ballot boxes within it in order both to prevent dishonesty and maintain the secrecy of the vote has in fact exercised the minds of election officials in many of the countries of Africa and Asia in which this method of voting is used and no entirely satisfactory solution appears to have been found as yet.[1]

Some territories arrange for the searching of electors on entering or leaving the polling station, and it is usually an offence under the electoral law for a ballot paper to be taken out of a polling station, or for a voter to insert into a ballot box any paper which he is not authorised by law to put in.[2] Power to search voters is probably indispensable if the unlawful taking of ballot papers into and out of polling stations and trading in ballot papers is to be avoided, and the procedure adopted in the Gold Coast elections of 1956 is worth a detailed description. The Gold Coast Electoral Provisions (Assembly Elections) Regulations, 1954, as

[1] There are some interesting comments on arrangements for secrecy in the *Report of the U.N. Commissioner on the British Togoland Plebiscite of 1956* (U.N. Document A/3173, pp. 174 and 175). A considerable variety of polling booths were erected, and, after testing them, the Commissioner was satisfied that "the element of secrecy was scrupulously safeguarded".

[2] See, for instance, Reg. 96(1) of the Western Region of Nigeria Parliamentary and Local Government Electoral Regulations, 1955.

amended prior to the 1956 elections, made it an offence to take into or out of any polling station any ballot paper without the authority of the presiding officer. All presiding officers were appointed special constables for the purpose of the election. A presiding officer, on hearing a complaint that an elector at a polling station had a ballot paper concealed on his person, was required to hand the complainant a form to complete on which the grounds for the complaint had to be stated. If the written complaint showed that the complainant was relying on hearsay or rumour, he was to be asked to produce a person with first-hand knowledge of the concealment and, if this evidence was not produced in a reasonable time, the presiding officer would be justified in disregarding the complaint. If, however, the presiding officer was satisfied that the grounds of the complaint were reasonable, he was to instruct the police officer at the polling station to arrest and search the person, or, in the case of females, to have the person searched by a female searcher. In the absence of a police officer, the presiding officer could himself carry out the arrest and search of a suspect by virtue of his position as a special constable. Before a search, the presiding officer was required to inform the elector that he was suspected of having ballot papers concealed on his person and that he was liable to be arrested and searched on this ground. After a search, the presiding officer would have to decide that an offence had apparently been committed, in which case the elector was to be detained until he could be taken to a police station, or that the complaint was apparently unfounded, in which case the presiding officer would immediately effect the release of the suspect. Presiding officers were warned that they might be held responsible if they wrongfully arrested innocent persons and that they should therefore investigate complaints very carefully before deciding to arrest and search a person against whom a complaint had been lodged. They were also instructed to ensure that the expeditious conduct of voting was not impeded by searching and for this reason that, when in any polling station the polling agents of a candidate had made four unfounded complaints against electors, the presiding officer should report to the assistant returning officer or returning officer who could direct that no further complaints were to be entertained from the polling agents concerned. A commentator on electoral procedure in West Africa has stated that:

In the Western Nigerian election of 1956 voters were searched for ballot papers as a matter of routine, and apparently without any serious exception being taken to the practice, but in the Gold Coast realisation of the inadvisability of so proceeding where there were no grounds to suspect an offence produced regulations for searching so hedged about with conditions as not to be applicable in practice. In Sierra Leone fears of this particular form of malpractice were not pronounced, and no power of search was provided or demanded.[1]

In this connection, it is of some interest to record that, in Hungary in the nineteenth century, the danger of electors removing the ballots and selling them outside was avoided by the use of rods from four to six feet in length, instead of ballot papers.[2] This presumably necessitated rather large ballot boxes!

Attempts may be made to alter the position of the ballot boxes or to erase or to exchange the symbols attached to them. In some territories, the boxes are secured to the tables or benches by nailing.[3] Again, the precaution has been adopted in some countries of pasting the candidate's symbol inside as well as outside the ballot box.

Another problem has been that presented by the voter who enters the polling booth and shows no inclination to come out again.[4] The electoral law usually prescribes that every elector should vote without undue delay and should leave the polling station as soon as he has voted; on the other hand the law also states that the elector shall record his vote in secret. There is therefore no clear-cut procedure for dealing with voters who delay the proceedings by staring in bewilderment at a large array of ballot boxes unable to make up their minds what to do with their ballot papers nor, for that matter, for dealing with those who, with dishonest intent, investigate the possibility of tampering

[1] 'Problems of West African elections' by D. J. R. Scott in *What are the problems of Parliamentary Government in West Africa* (Hansard Society, 1958), p. 67.

[2] On the nineteenth century experience of a number of countries in polling methods, see *Encyclopaedia Brittanica*, 9th edn., Vol. III, pp. 288-92.

[3] For instance in Western Nigeria — see the *Report on the holding of the 1956 Parliamentary Election to the Western House of Assembly*, p. 6.

[4] This problem can arise with other methods of voting. In Turkey where the 'envelope' system of voting (similar to that of France) is in use, there is a provision in the electoral law (Art. 97 of the Election of National Deputies Act, 1950) that, if the voter remains in the polling booth for an undue length of time, he shall first be warned and, if he continues to remain, removed.

with the boxes and damaging the electoral chances of some of the candidates. Usually this situation has been remedied by the presiding officer or some other official looking into the screened compartment. But the powers given to the presiding officer to accompany voters into the polling compartment and assist persons to cast their votes are normally limited to those which enable him to help the blind and other voters who, by reason of physical disability, are unable to vote themselves; he is not normally permitted to assist those who are illiterate or stupid or even those who are experiencing difficulty in getting their ballot papers through the slit provided in the lid of the ballot box. The electoral law does, however, usually require the presiding officer to inspect the ballot boxes together with the polling agents at stated intervals and, at each such inspection, the presiding officer would clear the booth of ballot papers left outside the ballot boxes (and therefore invalid)[1] and also deal with any jamming of the slits in the lids of the boxes.

The use of a separate ballot box for each candidate can cause some complications in multi-member constituencies in which the voter is eligible to cast more than one vote. If 'plumping' is not permitted and each vote has to be cast for a different candidate, the voter is given as many ballot papers as there are votes to be cast and some check must be devised to ensure that no voter has in fact cast all his votes for one candidate. In the Eastern Region of Nigeria and in India, where this problem has arisen, a necessary preliminary to the counting of votes in multi-member constituencies was the arrangement of the ballot papers from each ballot box in serial order and the rejection of ballot papers wherever more ballot papers than one with the same serial number were found in the same box. The report[2] on the first elections in India indicates that the counting of votes in two-member constituencies took three or four times as long as the counting of votes in single-member constituencies. In the Eastern Region of Nigeria, all the constituencies used for the return of members in 1957 to the House

[1] In Ghana and Sierra Leone, the Electoral Regulations provide that, when the presiding officer makes his periodic inspection of the ballot boxes, "any ballot papers found upon or in contact with a ballot box shall be placed in that box by the presiding officer and any other ballot papers found near a ballot box shall be treated as spoilt ballot papers".

[2] See pp. 138-9, Vol. I of the *Report on the first general elections in India, 1951-2.*

of Assembly were multi-member and it is reported that counting the votes within a reasonable time was the biggest single undertaking from the administrative point of view of the whole election period — because of the necessity for checking to ensure that two or more papers bearing the same serial number had not found their way into the same ballot box. This difficulty does not, of course, arise if 'plumping' is permitted and a voter is allowed to cast all the votes to which he is entitled for one and the same candidate.

This fairly formidable account of difficulties and problems which have arisen in connection with polling by providing a separate ballot box for each candidate must not, however, be permitted to mask the fact that the method has proved reasonably successful with a simple, largely illiterate, and fairly honest electorate. The system is in use in India, throughout British West Africa, in Uganda, Zanzibar, Kenya (for African elections), and in parts of the Sudan. It is, perhaps, of some significance that, for the 1958 Sudan elections, the method of voting now under review was used only in the less developed parts of the country and that ballot papers were marked and a single ballot box used in the more sophisticated areas. The author has discussed the multiple ballot box method of voting with a number of persons who have had responsibilities in connection with African elections and the impression which he has gained is that this method of voting has proved its value in present circumstances but that it might well be replaced by some other system of voting as literacy grows.

The marking of ballot papers

Were it not for illiteracy, the British method of marking the ballot paper against the name of the candidate or candidates chosen by the voter would present little difficulty, particularly where a simple plurality system of voting in single member constituencies is in use. It is because it was argued that an illiterate voter would not be able to put a cross or some other mark opposite the name of the candidate of his own choice that the method of recording the votes by providing one ballot box for each candidate in each polling station was introduced. The validity of this argument requires some examination.

The electorate numbering about one and a quarter million at the time of the 1955 general elections in the Federation of Malaya were probably in the region of 50% literate. The ballot papers showed the name and symbol of each candidate and the voter was required to mark a cross against the candidate of his choice. Before polling day, mock elections were organised by district officers and information officers all over the country and instruction in the correct method of marking the ballot paper was also given by the canvassers representing political parties or individual candidates. As a result of this electoral education, the percentage of rejected ballot papers was low, amounting to about 2½% of the total number of votes cast.[1] The Malayan experience suggests that, given adequate preparation, a partially illiterate electorate can in fact succeed in marking ballot papers, even without going to the length of adopting the 'whispering vote', which requires that voters unable to read, as well as those incapacitated by blindness or other physical cause, should call the presiding officer aside and tell him the name or names of the favoured candidates and the presiding officer must then mark the ballot paper accordingly. It is emphasised that, at the 1955 general elections in Malaya, the whispering vote was used only on the application of a voter incapacitated by blindness or other physical cause from voting in the normal manner and presiding officers were reminded that the electoral law did not empower them to assist voters to mark their ballot papers merely on the grounds of illiteracy.

The marking of ballot papers by voters, literate and illiterate, has also been a feature of elections in the West Indies. The percentage of rejected votes at general elections in Jamaica, Trinidad, Barbados and British Guiana between 1955 and 1957 ranged from 1.2 to 2.6;[2] in the smaller islands, the percentage of rejected votes has been higher, however, and as many as 10.41% of the votes cast in the 1957 elections in St Vincent were rejected. But the figures for the larger territories are much more significant and they confirm the experience of Malaya. One of the most interesting features of the 1957 elections in British Guiana was the return to the old method, last used at the General Election of 1947, of casting the vote by marking the ballot paper after the introduction in 1953 of the separate ballot box for each candidate system. The percentage of rejected votes at the count in the 1957 elections was but 1.4.

[1] *Report on the First Election of Members to the Legislative Council of the Federation of Malaya*, p. 27.
[2] See Appendix I of the *Report on the 1957 general election in British Guiana.*

A system of marking of ballot papers was also utilised at the first general elections in Indonesia in 1955. There the electors, most of whom were illiterate, marked their ballots, not by attempting to inscribe a cross or some other simple written indication of their choice but, instead, by driving a pointed prong through the symbol of their choice on the ballot paper. Only a very small minority of the electors adopted the permitted alternative method of voting for an individual candidate by writing the individual's name on the ballot paper. Before emerging from the voting cubicle, the voter was required to fold his ballot paper and he then took it to the ballot box showing the back of the ballot paper to a member of the polling station committee to indicate that the object which he was proposing to put in the box was in fact a single ballot paper on which the chairman and two other members of the polling committee had signed their names at the time of issue. The percentage of rejected votes in these first Indonesian elections was about 4.[1]

In a number of countries, all voters are required to write on the official ballot the name of the candidate or candidates for whom they wish to vote. Thus in Japan, where the single non-transferable vote is used in conjunction with multi-member constituencies, the voter writes in the name of the single candidate of his choice; the physically disabled and the blind are given assistance in voting. Ballots cast in the names of persons who are not candidates and those which are illegible are rejected at the count.[2] In Turkey, the voter is free to fill out a blank ballot slip by writing the name of the candidate of his choice or he may delete a name from among those on the printed ballot and substitute the name of another candidate.[3]

The majority of the members of the Pakistan Electoral Reforms Commission, which reported in 1956, came to the conclusion that it was possible for the ordinary voter in Pakistan to mark a ballot paper by putting "any mark such as an ordinary line opposite the name and symbol of the candidate of his choice in the column specified for the purpose in the ballot paper".[4] The system of voting in use in Pakistan prior to the Electoral Reforms Commission's

[1] Herbert Feith, *The Indonesian Elections of 1955*, pp. 40-50.
[2] Yanaga, *Japanese People and Politics*, p. 291.
[3] Art. 89, Turkish Election of National Deputies Act, 1950.
[4] The Report was published in the *Gazette of Pakistan*, dated 24th April, 1956, see particularly pp. 933-4.

Report involved the use of assigning colours to different candidates at elections and of painting ballot boxes in different
colours. This system had not worked satisfactorily, partly because
some voters were colour blind or at least unable to distinguish
between two fairly similar colours, and partly because "in the
case of allotment of a separate ballot box to each candidate there
are greater chances of tampering; it also does not ensure the
secrecy of the ballot. An elector at the instance of the interested
party may pour ink and even acid through the slit in the ballot
box and thus damage or destroy the ballot papers already inserted
in the box". One of the members of the Commission thought that
the ordinary voter would not be able to mark his ballot paper even
by drawing an ordinary line but the majority found it difficult to
subscribe to that view and thought that the advantages of the
proposed system far outweighed the disadvantages.

The marking of ballot papers, combined with the 'whispering
vote' for illiterates, was used in Tanganyika at the first Legislative
Council Elections held in 1958[1] and in the first municipal elections
held in Kuching, Sarawak, in 1956.[2] The whispering vote has in
the past been used in West Africa — for instance in the 1951
elections in the Gold Coast, but there are two important objections
to it in practice. In the first place, the presiding officer, whom the
voter asks to mark his ballot paper, necessarily knows how the
illiterate elector has voted. Secondly, the integrity of the presiding
officer is of even more crucial importance than would otherwise
be the case, and there will be no public confidence in the election
machinery unless the electorate are completely satisfied in the
honesty of the presiding officers. These objections to the
whispering vote have led the West African territories to adopt the
multiple ballot box method of voting in preference to the marking
of ballot papers in secrecy, as modified by the whispering vote.
But throughout West Africa, and for that matter in India, there
has been an untested assumption, which Malayan experience
suggests may be unwarranted, that a person who cannot read and
write is incapable, even with tuition, of marking his ballot paper
with a simple mark in the correct space. It would be interesting and
instructive if some of the governments of the African territories

[1] See Sec. 89(h) of the Tanganyika Legislative Council Elections Ordinance,
1957.
[2] *Report on the Kuching Municipal Council Elections.*

were to undertake pilot experiments to determine the minimum degree of literacy and education which would warrant the introduction of voting by marking ballot papers — and there may here be a lesson to be learnt from the 1958 Sudan elections, as well as from Malaya and the West Indies.

Whatever method of voting is adopted, there is usually a clause in the electoral legislation which states that a voter shall not place on the ballot paper any writing or mark by which he may be identified and any ballot paper, on which any such writing or mark appears by which a voter can be identified (other than the printed number on the ballot paper), is not counted.[1] Indeed, in the Federation of Rhodesia and Nyasaland, the legislation governing elections to the Federal Assembly goes even further and requires the returning officer to reject any ballot paper "on which there is any writing or mark other than the official mark of a presiding officer or of the returning officer and one cross in a rectangle opposite the name of a candidate"[2] irrespective of whether the writing or mark is such that a voter can be identified from it. Rejection of ballot papers at the count is, obviously, more likely to happen when the voter is required to mark his ballot paper — not only because of the possibility that he will sign his name or write something on the ballot paper which could lead to his being identified, but also because of the possibility that the voter will have failed to indicate with certainty the candidate or candidates for whom he wishes to vote or that he will have voted for more candidates than there are seats to be filled. But it should not be forgotten that the $2\frac{1}{2}\%$ rejection rate of ballot papers in Malaya at the time of the 1955 elections included not only those ballots which were not counted because of an error on the part of the voter but also the ballots which were rejected because of errors on the part of the presiding officer and his staff, and this latter type of error is just as likely to occur with the multiple ballot box method of voting as with the method adopted in Malaya.

The advantages which the system of marking the ballot papers has over the multiple ballot-box system are as follows:

(a) Only one ballot box is required for each polling station and the cost of equipment is therefore less.

[1] See for instance, Sections 89(f) and 101 of the Tanganyika Legislative Council Elections Ordinance.
[2] Section 90(2)(d) of the Federation of Rhodesia and Nyasaland Electoral Act, 1958.

(*b*) The ballot box is, throughout polling, in view of the polling officials and polling agents and cannot be tampered with, and the voter puts his folded ballot paper into the ballot box under the eyes of the presiding officer.

(*c*) Counting is easier, in so far as there is no risk of the votes for one candidate being irredeemably mixed up with the votes for another candidate.

(*d*) Voting is not held up by the voter who takes his time to decide how to vote provided that there are a number of polling compartments for marking the ballot paper. Voting can however be seriously retarded by the slow voter if the ballot paper is a mere token and there are separate ballot boxes for each candidate.

The disadvantages of the system of marking ballot papers are:

(*a*) A certain minimum level of literacy and 'know-how' is required of an electorate to operate the system successfully.

(*b*) The percentage of rejected papers is likely to be somewhat higher than under the separate ballot box for each candidate method of voting.

The system of marking ballot papers is, from the administrative point of view, rather simpler than the separate ballot box for each candidate method of voting in multi-member constituencies. Mention has been made of the time consumed at the counting of votes under the latter system to check that not more than one ballot paper bearing a given serial number has found its way into the same ballot box. When ballot papers are marked, a single ballot paper can be used to enable a voter to cast all his entitlement of votes in a multi-member constituency and, at the counting of votes, it will be obvious from a perusal of each individual ballot paper whether the voter has kept to his entitlement or exceeded it.

The use of party list ballot papers

In France and, in general, in the French overseas territories, there is a separate ballot paper for each candidate in a single-member constituency or for each associated group of candidates in a multi-member constituency. A typical associated group of candidates in a multi-member constituency would be either all the candidates representing one political party or all the candidates representing a group of parties which are fighting the particular constituency (but not necessarily other constituencies) in league.

In French Africa, each party or group of parties is allotted a distinct colour in order to assist the illiterate voter, and the ballots are printed on correspondingly coloured paper. These party ballot papers are frequently distributed by the parties to voters before election day and many voters bring their ballot paper to the polling station. But the complete selection of ballot papers is also available in the polling station. An elector, after entering the polling station, presenting his identity papers and voting card and having his identity satisfactorily checked, takes an officially supplied envelope and goes into the screened compartment and there places the ballot paper of his choice in the envelope. After sealing the envelope, he places it in the ballot box, of which there is but one and which is placed where the polling officials can observe the voter as he puts his envelope into the box.

A voter can cast his vote for one party list only. If he places two or more different ballot papers into his envelope, his vote is rejected at the count. If he places two or more identical ballot papers in his envelope, his vote is counted but once. In France the voter used to be permitted to amend the party ballot paper by striking out a particular candidate from the list and substituting the name of another candidate, or by altering the order of priority of the candidates as shown on the party list. The possibility of amending ballot papers in this way does not of course arise in single-member constituencies, into which France was divided for the 1958 elections.

There have been reports from at least one of the French African territories to the effect that this voting procedure leads to delays and also does not guarantee the secrecy of the vote. The United Nations Commissioner responsible for the supervision of the 1958 elections in French Togoland reports that ". . . there were difficulties, because some electors, having little skill in handling a balloting paper and an envelope, remained in the voting booth for three or four minutes or else emerged from the booth without having managed to place the paper in the envelope".[1] As regards the secrecy of voting, the various ballot papers in French Togoland were laid on a 'voting table' in the polling station and "the voter was free either to take a single ballot paper, that

[1] Extract from the U.N. Commissioner's Report (U.N. Document T/1392), p. 166.

of the candidate for whom he was voting, or papers bearing the names of each of the candidates. The voter very often took only one paper, which naturally showed how he was voting and made his retirement to the booth useless".[1] In his Report, the Commissioner recommended that[2] "steps be taken to help illiterate persons to vote while ensuring the secrecy of the ballot. One way might be to place a number of ballot boxes clearly marked with the candidates' colours or emblems in the polling booth; each voter would then be given a single official ballot paper which he would drop in whichever box he chose". In other words, the Commissioner preferred the system of casting the vote used in British West Africa and India to the French system for use by illiterates.

It should be noted, too, that the French method of casting a vote may perhaps render the voter more open to intimidation than other methods. It was reported from French Togoland that some of the chiefs ordered their people to take only the ballot paper of the candidate who they themselves favoured and that, in many cases, "the traditional chiefs installed themselves in the polling stations in order to influence voters and to observe the progress of operations."

One of the political parties in the part of Togoland under British administration at the time of the plebiscite of 1956 suggested that the French system of voting be used, each voter being provided with two ballot papers, one in black for one of the alternatives proposed for the future of the territory, another in white for the other alternative, plus an envelope. The United Nations Plebiscite Commissioner, in rejecting this request, drew attention to the handicaps which had made the system the subject of criticism in plebiscites after the First World War and said "it was slow, counting of the votes imposed on the counting officer the meticulous task of opening and destroying thousands of envelopes without destroying the ballot paper contained in them. Attention was drawn especially to the possibility of intimidation, it being obvious that a chieftain could prevail on his associates not to destroy the unused ballot but to produce it as evidence that they had voted right. In one plebiscite in Europe it is believed

[1] Extract from the U.N. Commissioner's Report (U.N. Document T/1392), pp. 172-3.
[2] Ibid, p. 186.

that armed bands kept near some of the polling centres and requested that voters show the unused ballot papers."[1]

The use of Voting Machines

There has been a steadily increasing use of voting machines in elections in America. On a voting machine the voter indicates his choice simply by turning voting levers over the names of the candidates of his choice. The machines are arranged so that the voting levers cannot be turned in the wrong way and it is impossible for the elector to vote for more than the proper number of candidates.[2] One of the companies manufacturing voting machines in America compares the use of voting machines with the use of ballot papers as follows:

> The cumbersome paper ballot is out of place in this age of adding machines, cash registers and other calculating devices. The printed ballot has made voting slow and laborious. It has given us void votes, lost or destroyed votes, and mistakes in count. It has invited tampering with the totals. It has caused delays in getting returns. It has led to protested elections and costly recounts."

"The automatic voting machine makes voting easy, and quick. Every vote is recorded automatically and counted with mechanical precision. Steel-enclosed counters give the exact totals when the polls close — a permanent record that cannot be altered. Recounts, if requested, are a matter of a few hours only.

The election of a large number of representatives and officials usually takes place simultaneously in the United States of America and the voting machines have been constructed with this in mind. A single master lever usually makes it possible for an elector who wishes to vote the straight party ticket to do so with the minimum of time and effort. As far as the author is aware, voting machines are not in use in any largely illiterate community and there is insufficient experience available to forecast:

(a) Whether a largely illiterate community would be able to deal with a simple voting machine; and

(b) Whether the capital value and maintenance of such machines would be cheaper or dearer than the use of polling officers for issuing ballot papers and clerks for counting the votes.

[1] *Report of the U.N. Plebiscite Commissioner for the Trust Territory of Togoland under British Administration* (Document A/3173), p. 170.

[2] See H. R. Penniman, *Sait's American Parties and Elections*, pp. 635-641.

The indications are that it would be difficult to interest industrial corporations in the possibility of manufacturing a new kind of voting machine for use in under-developed countries when the market for the product would be rather uncertain and there appears therefore to be little likelihood of these machines being used in the near future for elections in Asia and Africa.

TENDERED BALLOT PAPERS

It has been stated earlier that, in most countries of the British Commonwealth, a tendered ballot paper can be issued to a person representing himself to be a registered elector who applies for a ballot paper after that elector has been marked as having already voted. These tendered ballot papers are frequently not put into the ballot box or boxes but are instead given to the presiding officer for custody. If the system of marking ballot papers is in use, all tendered ballot papers used at one polling station are kept in one envelope; if the ballot papers are mere tokens, there is a separate packet for the tendered ballot papers for each candidate, the voter informing the presiding officer of his wishes. Tendered ballot papers are not normally included in the constituency count. To clarify the position, the procedure regarding the use of tendered ballot papers in the Western Region of Nigeria, Uganda and the Federation of Malaya will be described.

In the Western Region of Nigeria,[1] the ballot papers are tokens and there is a separate ballot box for each candidate. Tendered ballot papers are of a different colour from ordinary ballot papers, but are otherwise identical. If a person claims the vote as a registered elector and answers the statutory questions satisfactorily, he is given a tendered ballot paper and the presiding officer endorses it with the voter's name and electoral number and then puts it according to the voter's wishes into one of the separate packets of tendered ballot papers, each packet being marked with a candidate's symbol and there being one packet for each candidate. The name of the elector and of his number in the register of electors is entered on a list called the 'tendered votes list', and this list is admissible in any legal proceedings arising out of the election. The sealed packets of tendered ballot papers are not opened and

[1] See Reg. 53 of the Western Region Parliamentary and Local Government Electoral Regulations, 1955.

counted by the returning officer at the count but are retained in safe custody together with other documents relating to the election.

In Uganda, as in the Western Region of Nigeria, there is a separate ballot box for each candidate and tendered ballot papers are of a different colour from ordinary ballot papers, but are otherwise identical. Procedure in Uganda differs from that of Western Nigeria in that the presiding officer, after endorsing the tendered ballot paper with the name and electoral number of the voter, hands it to the voter to cast his vote in precisely the same manner as any other elector. The tendered ballot papers are therefore put into the ballot boxes. At the count the procedure is:

> The returning officer shall not count the tendered ballot papers but shall place them in separate packets according to the candidate whom they support and shall mark each such packet with the name of such candidate and shall seal the packet and retain it unless it is required for the purposes of an election petition.[1]

The outstanding difference between the two systems is that, in the Western Region of Nigeria, the presiding officer of the polling station will inevitably know how the recipient of a tendered ballot paper has voted and it may be difficult to prevent other persons in the polling station acquiring this information. In Uganda, on the other hand, the returning officer and his counting staff could easily find out how recipients of tendered ballot papers have voted, by inspection of the names and electoral numbers on the reverse of the ballot papers, but this is not in fact likely to happen. The Uganda system is perhaps more consistent with the idea of secret voting.

In the Federation of Malaya,[2] voters mark their ballot papers against the name and symbol of the candidate of their choice. A person representing himself to be a particular elector who has been recorded in the register as having already voted is, on application for a ballot paper, required to take an oath of identity in statutory form administered by the presiding officer, before being issued with a tendered ballot paper which, as in Uganda and Nigeria, is coloured differently from other ballot papers and

---

[1] Sec. 45(6) of the Uganda Legislative Council Elections Ordinance. See also Sec. 41.

[2] Reg. 24 of the Federation of Malaya Legislative Council Elections Regulations, 1954.

which has to be endorsed by the presiding officer with the name
of the voter and his number in the register. A 'tendered votes list'
is kept as in Nigeria. Tendered ballot papers, after being endorsed
by the presiding officer and marked by the voter, are placed in
the ballot box. The procedure for dealing with tendered ballot
papers at the count is identical with that of Uganda.

In Ghana, tendered ballot papers are not used, but the presiding
officer is required to keep a tendered votes list in which the name,
number in the register of electors, and choice of candidates are
entered by the presiding officer, in conditions of secrecy, in
respect of any person who would, in Nigeria, Uganda and Malaya,
be given a tendered ballot paper — i.e. any person who, representing himself to be an elector named in the register of electors,
applies for a ballot paper after another person has voted as such
elector and gives satisfactory answers to the statutory questions
put to him by the presiding officer.[1]

Tanganyika, the Eastern Region of Nigeria, Sierra Leone,
Zanzibar and India all use tendered ballot papers. In the first two
territories, the presiding officer takes custody of tendered ballot
papers, which are not therefore placed in ballot boxes.

Tendered ballot papers are not, however, used in Jamaica nor
were they used at the first African elections in Kenya. In the
latter country, the procedure is that:

> If a person representing himself to be a particular voter applies
> for a ballot paper after some other person has already voted in the
> name of such voter, and if he further produces satisfactory evidence
> of his identity as such voter, together with a voter's card purporting
> to have been issued to such voter, the presiding officer shall allow
> such person to vote. The presiding officer shall record a statement
> of the particulars of each such case.[2]

In Jamaica, when a personator has voted in the name of an
elector before the elector himself appears to vote, the elector is
required to take an oath of identity and, by answering questions
or producing witnesses, to satisfy the presiding officer of his
identity. On the back of the ballot paper then given to the elector
are entered, in addition to the presiding officer's initials, the number
given to the elector in the poll book and, in the remarks column

---

[1] Reg. 22 of the Electoral Provisions (Assembly Elections) Regulations, 1954.

[2] Rule 24, Kenya Legislative Council (African Representation) (Election of
Members) Rules, 1956.

of the poll book are inserted the words "second ballot: see consecutive No. . . .", mentioning the consecutive number given to such elector in the poll book when it was entered at the instance of the personator.

In both Kenya and Jamaica, then, there may be more than one ballot paper counted in respect of a given registered elector. Given good registers and competent polling station staff, it seems preferable to adopt the tendered ballot paper system, as in most other Commonwealth countries. A tendered vote has a value, despite the fact that it is not included in the count, because, on a scrutiny, the vote of the personator will be struck off and the tendered vote will be counted.

The number of tendered ballot papers used is, of course, only a tiny fraction of the number of ordinary ballot papers utilised. Sometimes, however, the number has been inflated owing to the erroneous issue of tendered ballot papers instead of ordinary ballot papers. Errors of this nature occurred at one polling station in the first general election in Malaya in 1955 and also in one polling station in the first general election in Sierra Leone in 1957.

SPOILT BALLOT PAPERS

In British Commonwealth countries, provision is usually made for the possibility that a voter may accidentally spoil his ballot paper after issue to him and before placing it in the ballot box. Where such provision is made, the spoilt ballot is returnable to the presiding officer and another ballot paper can be issued to the voter. Provisions of this nature appear in the electoral legislation of countries and territories such as Kenya, Tanganyika, Uganda, Malaya, Nigeria, and Jamaica.

ASSISTANCE TO BLIND AND PHYSICALLY HANDICAPPED VOTERS

Electoral law generally makes some special provision for assistance in voting to physically incapacitated voters. Normally the presiding officer is permitted to assist such voters to mark their ballot papers in secrecy or, where there is a separate ballot box for each candidate, to insert their ballot paper in the correct box. As an example, the Uganda Legislative Council Elections Ordinance[1] states that:

> If an elector is incapacitated by blindness or other cause he shall call the presiding officer aside, and shall tell him, no other person being present or within hearing, the name of the candidate for whom he wishes to vote, and the presiding officer shall then go immediately into the screened compartment in the polling station with the elector and place the elector's ballot paper into the ballot box bearing the name and symbol, if any, of the candidate for whom the elector wishes to vote.

There are some variations in this procedure in so far as:

(a) In some territories — e.g. Jamaica[2] and Zanzibar[3] — a blind elector is permitted the choice of receiving assistance from the presiding officer or from a friend brought by the blind elector to the polling station. In Zanzibar the helpmate must be another elector in the polling division, but this is not a requirement in Jamaica. In both territories, the presiding officer only is permitted to record the vote on the application of an elector who is incapacitated by some physical cause other than blindness. In the Gambia, a voter incapacitated by blindness or other physical cause can take one person selected by him into the screened compartment, such person not being a candidate or candidate's agent.

(b) In Jamaica, Trinidad and the Bahamas,[4] the presiding officer asks the elector for which candidate he desires to have his ballot marked and then marks the ballot in the presence of the poll clerks and the agents of the candidates at the polling station, and the presiding officer does not therefore share the secrecy of the vote with the disabled elector only.

(c) In a few territories — e.g. Tanganyika,[5] Kenya,[6] and the Bahamas — the presiding officer is required to afford the same assistance on request to persons who cannot read that he gives to disabled electors. This is in fact the 'whispering

[1] Section 38(d).
[2] Sec. 33(3) (4) and (5) of the Jamaica Representation of the People Law, 1944.
[3] Sec. 48(3) (4) and (5) of the Zanzibar Legislative Council (Elections) Decree, 1957.
[4] Sec. 57 of the Bahamas General Assembly Elections Act, 1946.
[5] Sec. 89(h) of the Tanganyika Legislative Council Elections Ordinance, 1957.
[6] Rules 23 and 24 of the Kenya Legislative Council (African Representation) (Election of Members) Rules, 1956.

vote' which has already been discussed earlier in this chapter.

(d) In British Guiana, the blind or otherwise incapacitated elector has three alternative methods of voting. He can ask the presiding officer to mark his ballot paper "in the manner directed by such elector in the presence of the elector alone, no other person being within hearing"[1] or he can be accompanied by a friend in the voting compartment or he can vote by proxy.[2]

TRANSFER OF ELECTORS IN SPECIAL CASES

There is often a provision in the electoral legislation of British Commonwealth territories providing for the transfer of the name of any person, who is a registered elector and has been appointed to officiate as a presiding officer or in some other capacity in a polling district other than his own, to the register of the polling district in which he is to officiate. A provision of this kind appears, for example, in the legislation of Zanzibar,[3] the Federation of Malaya,[4] Uganda[5] and British Guiana.[6] In Zanzibar, this transfer can be made not only from one polling district to another in the same constituency but also to a polling district in another constituency. In the other three territories, however, the latitude of the returning officer is restricted to authorising the transfer of persons employed in an official capacity at an election to vote at a polling station other than their own but within their own constituency. In British Guiana, those employed on electoral duties have the alternative of applying for a transfer from one polling station to another in the same constituency or of applying to vote by proxy. Special provisions of this kind do not appear in the legislation of the British West African territories.

One of a number of unusual features of the first Kenya African elections was that although, in general, no elector could vote at

[1] Sec. 35(3) and (4) of the British Guiana Representation of the People Ordinance, 1957.
[2] Sec. 28(4) of the British Guiana Representation of the People Ordinance, 1957.
[3] Sec. 41 of the Zanzibar Legislative Council Elections Decree, 1957.
[4] Reg. 18(1) of the Federation of Malaya Legislative Council Elections Regulations, 1954.
[5] Sec. 40(1) of the Uganda Legislative Council Elections Ordinance, 1957.
[6] Sec. 29(1) of the British Guiana Representation of the People Ordinance, 1957.

any polling station except the one allotted to him, there was a proviso that:

> Any person, who shall satisfy the presiding officer that he has good and sufficient reason for inability to present himself at the polling station appointed for the portion of the electoral area in which he resides, shall be permitted to vote in any other polling station within such electoral area.[1]

The facts that any voter who failed to produce his voter's card was not supplied with a ballot paper and that the presiding officer was required to detach and retain a part of the card prior to the issue of a ballot paper were together some guarantee against abuse of this provision of the law, but voting cards can be forged and it seems possible that attempts of this kind to help electors who find themselves far away from their own polling stations on polling day could lead to fraudulent voting. The main purpose of an electoral register is to provide an undisputed list of names of those entitled to vote at each polling station and, in territories of British Africa other than Kenya, the rule that no person shall be admitted to vote at any polling station except the one allotted to him is rigidly enforced.

THE CLOSING OF THE POLL

The presiding officer is not usually permitted to issue a ballot paper to a voter after the hour fixed for the closing of the poll, though any voter to whom a ballot paper has been issued is allowed to record his vote. This is the legal position in, for instance, the Federation of Malaya[2] and Uganda.[3] In Nigeria,[4] Zanzibar[5] and Jamaica,[6] the presiding officer is required to allow those persons already inside the polling station to vote, irrespective of whether or not a ballot paper has already been issued, when the hour for closing the poll has been reached. The electoral law of

---

[1] The Kenya Legislative Council (African Representation) (Election of Members) Rules, 1956, Rule 16.

[2] Reg. 25, Federation of Malaya Legislative Council Elections Regulations, 1954.

[3] Sec. 43, Uganda Legislative Council Elections Ordinance, 1957.

[4] Reg. 39, Eastern House of Assembly Electoral Regulations, 1955, and Reg. 56, Western Region Parliamentary and Local Government Electoral Regulations, 1955.

[5] Sec. 47(b), Zanzibar Legislative Council Elections Decree, 1957.

[6] Sec. 32(b), Jamaica Representation of the People Law, 1944.

the Federation of Rhodesia and Nyasaland requires the presiding
officer to permit every voter who at the time of closing the poll:

(a) is inside the room in which the ballot box is placed; or
(b) in his opinion was in the immediate precincts of the polling
     station before the close of the poll and was prevented from
     entering the room in which the ballot box is placed owing to
     congestion in that room;
to record his vote before closing the poll.[1]

In Ghana, however, no ballot paper may be placed in the ballot
box outside the hours of voting,[2] so that the elector who joins the
queue outside the polling station but fails to cast his vote during
voting hours is unlucky.

The system adopted in Nigeria, Zanzibar and Jamaica is
perhaps less likely than that of Ghana to lead to angry dissatisfaction and, perhaps, to rioting outside the polling station, but the
most important requirement is that the presiding officer should
have clear-cut instructions as to whom he is to permit to vote at
the closing of the poll. In this respect, there was some confusion
at the recent elections in French Togoland, where the chairmen
of polling committees had received instructions to announce that
the polls were about to be closed a few minutes before the closing
time but, at the hour of closure (5 p.m.), to permit voters arriving
at the polls before that time to cast their ballots even after 5 p.m.
The United Nations Commissioner reports[3] that:

   The authors of these instructions (to Chairmen of polling
   committees) obviously had in mind the few late-comers and not
   a crowd of voters awaiting admission to the polling station, often
   for hours. The chairman's exhortation to 'lose no time in casting
   their ballots' (given at the time of announcing that the polls were
   about to be closed) must have struck them as ironical. Moreover,
   as they thronged outside the premises where the ballots were cast,
   they would not even hear that exhortation in the general uproar.
   Different chairmen seemed to have adopted widely varying
   attitudes in these circumstances. In some cases, at Lomé for
   example, they simply continued the electoral operation until all
   the voters had cast their ballots. In other cases, they would admit
   only the voters who had been able to get inside the waiting room

[1] Sec. 66(3), Federation of Rhodesia and Nyasaland Electoral Act, 1958.
[2] Reg. 17, Electoral Provisions (Assembly Elections) Regulations, 1954.
[3] *Report of the United Nations Commissioner for the Supervision of the Elections
in Togoland under French Administration* (U.N. Document T/1392), p. 169.

before 5 p.m. Sometimes the chairman asked the Chief Sub-divisional officer or the 'commandant de cercle' what he should do. These officials also made a variety of decisions.

In Sierra Leone, there was at the time of the 1957 general election a provision in the electoral regulations[1] which made it possible to extend the hours of polling by postponing the closure from 6 p.m. to 10 p.m. This provision was invoked in Freetown, where the number of polling stations was inadequate and crowds thronged the stations throughout the day. With the help of this extension of polling hours, voting had ceased at all except one polling station in Freetown by 10 p.m. when the doors were closed. At this one polling station,

> . . . there were not more than twenty persons still in the queue. The Presiding Officer had some difficulty in dealing with these persons as they had been admitted into the polling station and objected to being turned away without being able to vote. Since, however, Regulation 24 . . . clearly states that no ballot paper may be placed in any ballot box outside the hours of voting, there was no option but to turn them away.[2]

After the completion of polling, the presiding officer's duties are far from finished. If counting of votes is to take place centrally for the whole constituency, he has the task of sealing his ballot box or boxes, completing his ballot paper account, sealing up various documents such as the counterfoils of used ballot papers, the marked copy of the register, the unused ballot papers, the tendered votes list etc., and supervising the removal of the ballot boxes and documents from the polling station to the place of count, where they are handed over to the returning officer. If counting of votes is to take place separately for each polling station (as in France and the overseas French territories, Jamaica and the Bahamas), the count is the next task for the presiding officer. Methods of counting of votes are discussed in Chapter X.

LAW AND ORDER AT POLLING STATIONS

If elections are to be fair and free, the voter must be in a position to make his choice among the candidates in peace and

[1] Reg. 24 of the House of Representatives (Elections) Regulations.
[2] Extract from unpublished report on the Sierra Leone General Elections, 1957.

without fear of intimidation. It is for this reason that the vote is secret and that polling agents are not permitted to talk to or otherwise interfere with voters in the polling station or to get to know the serial number of a ballot paper issued to a voter. The protection of the voter goes a good deal further than this, however. In the first place, there are usually some restrictions on political propaganda on polling day. Secondly, it may be an offence to give information regarding the names of those who have and those who have not voted whilst polling is in progress. Thirdly, most countries list a number of corrupt and illegal electoral practices punishable on conviction by fine or imprisonment and deprivation of voting rights.

As regards restrictions on political propaganda on polling day, it is usual to prohibit the display of party posters or emblems inside the polling station or within a stated distance of a polling station and to bar any public address by a party agent either within a stated distance of a polling station or anywhere at all on polling day. Thus the notes for polling agents at the 1956 elections in Ghana reminded them that it would be an offence:[1]

(a) To display in the polling station or within 50 yards of it any emblem (such as a button, tie or rosette), symbol or card which shows support for any political party or for a particular candidate;

(b) To make any public address within 200 yards of the polling station, showing support for any party or for a particular candidate;

(c) To try to find out how someone is going to vote, or how he has voted;

(d) To tell anyone the number on the ballot paper issued to a voter.

The limitation of political propaganda on polling day in the Federation of Malaya takes a rather different form.[2] There is a complete prohibition on canvassing and on the display of any party material within a distance of fifty yards of a polling station, save that individuals are permitted to wear small rosettes or favours within these limits, and the use of musical instruments and loudspeakers on vehicles is barred everywhere on polling day.

---

[1] Except for candidates, who alone are permitted to wear their symbols and colours anywhere at any time on polling day.

[2] Sec. 26, Federation of Malaya Election Offences (Amendment) Ordinance, 1955.

There are, also, in Malaya as in Britain,[1] limitations on the number of motor vehicles which can be used by a candidate to take voters to the poll. The Jamaican and the Malayan Electoral Laws limit the use of animals, as well as vehicles, for the purpose of conveying electors to and from the polls.

In Uganda the prohibitions[2] on the use of loudspeakers, on flags, and on the wearing of badges and favours apply to the whole area in which polling is taking place, and not merely to a limited area around each polling station.

It can be seen from these three examples that countries and territories of the British Commonwealth go to varying lengths to impose an atmosphere of restraint on polling day. Somewhat similar restraints are enforced in many countries outside the Commonwealth. In the U.S.A. for instance, no loitering or 'electioneering' is permitted within a polling station or within a defined distance of the station, nor are any political banners, posters, or placards permitted on polling day in or around the polling stations; in addition, to ensure a sober atmosphere for voting, no liquor may be sold at any place within a prescribed distance of a polling station during the voting or immediately before or after the election. Liquor stores and taverns are also kept closed during polling in British Guiana,[3] Trinidad and Mauritius.

Another method of protecting the voter from harassment is the provision demanding a declaration of secrecy from polling agents. Candidates, election agents and polling agents are, in Britain, prohibited from communicating to any person before the poll is closed any information as to the name or number on the register of electors of any elector who has or has not applied for a ballot paper or voted at a polling station,[4] and this implies that a polling agent should leave in the polling station his own marked copy of the register whenever he departs. There are similar provisions covering the requirement of secrecy in the legislation of other countries and territories of the Commonwealth.[5]

[1] There is, at the time of writing, a Bill before Parliament to repeal the provisions in force in Britain.
[2] Sec. 57, Uganda Legislative Council Elections Ordinance.
[3] Sec. 40(1), British Guiana Representation of the People Ordinance, 1957.
[4] Sec. 53(1)(b), Representation of the People Act, 1949.
[5] For example, Reg. 89(2) of the Western Region of Nigeria Parliamentary and Local Government Electoral Regulations, 1955, and Sec. 77(1) of the

Finally, it has been mentioned that most countries list a number of corrupt and illegal practices punishable on conviction by fine or imprisonment and deprivation of voting rights. It is not possible here to embark on a comparative study of the law of election offences of various countries. All that need be said is that provisions providing punishments for bribery, treating, exerting undue influence on and interfering with electors are standard features of electoral law and that these provisions, if observed in practice, help to ensure that the elections are freely and fairly conducted. The law is, however, ineffective if the electorate are in general prepared to tolerate offences such as treating. There is, without doubt, much corruption in elections in Asia and Africa,[1] and it can be argued that a healthy democracy cannot thrive unless persons guilty of such offences are fairly certain to be exposed and convicted.

It is difficult to provide any satisfactory answer to the question of just how freely the individual voter has in fact been permitted to exercise his choice at elections in Asia and Africa. It seems fairly clear that secret societies in Singapore have been effective in the past in ensuring that some electors go to the polling stations and cast their votes according to instructions whilst effective measures have been taken to prevent other electors from voting.[2] At the first elections in Indonesia in 1955, there were a number of electoral offences and abuses such as intimidation, personation and misuse of powers by polling station committees; reports of intimidation practised on or immediately prior to election day came from all parts of the country and the polling station committees, in theory always of multi-party composition but in practice often quite unrepresentative, were not always able or willing to prevent intimidation.[3] The Report of the Electoral

Zanzibar Legislative Council Elections Decree, 1957. The Committee appointed to examine the electoral laws of Jamaica considered however that this restriction was unnecessarily rigid and recommended that the relevant provision in the Jamaican law be amended so as to permit a candidate's agent to disclose either to the candidate or someone acting on his behalf the names and numbers of persons who have voted or not voted before the close of the poll.

[1] See, for instance, the *Report of the Pakistan Electoral Reforms Commission* and the *Report on the problems of parliamentary government in West Africa* (Hansard Society, 1958) particularly pp. 72-3.

[2] See *Report of the Commission of Inquiry into corrupt, illegal or undesirable practices at elections*, p. 12 et seq. (Sessional Paper No. Cmd. 7 of 1958, Singapore).

[3] Herbert Feith, *The Indonesian Elections of 1955*, pp. 43-7.

Reforms Commission in Pakistan suggests that there has been a great deal of malpractice at past elections in various parts of the country, that intimidation has been exercised and that persons with wealth and power have been able to use the electoral machine to their own advantage; indeed it has been suggested to the author that it will not be possible to hold free and fair elections in Pakistan until there has been a measure of land reform and tenants no longer feel obliged to vote in accordance with their landowner's instructions. It would be surprising, however, if electoral systems could be introduced in developing countries without some abuses of this kind and it would certainly be wrong to assume that intimidation, corruption and other abuses are a permanent part of the electoral scene in Asia and Africa.

The Turn-out at Elections and the Use of Compulsory Voting

At the first few general elections in Commonwealth countries of Asia and Africa there has often been a very high percentage poll. In the first elections held in Uganda in 1958, the poll was 86% and in the first elections in the Federation of Malaya in 1955 the turn-out was over 80%. In the six constituencies contested at the first Zanzibar elections of 1957 the average percentage of voters to registered electors was as high as 90. In these three elections, registration was voluntary so that most of those without any interest in the formation of a government of their country would not have bothered to become electors. Moreover, the novelty of the occasion and the holiday atmosphere, even more than interest in the outcome, were probably responsible for the high turn-out in these three countries.

There was a very high turn-out of voters at the first general election in Indonesia held in 1955. Despite the fact that registration of voters took place a full year before voting, with a consequent loss of registered voters through deaths and other causes, over 91% of the electorate voted and over 87% cast valid votes.[1] This high poll has been attributed to the general sense of community obligation and urge to conformity which villagers in Indonesia felt and to the sense of importance which voting gave to the villager.

[1] See Herbert Feith, *The Indonesian Elections of 1955*, p. 50.

Inevitably, the poll is not so high if poor communications and a sparse distribution of the population make it necessary for the average voter to take quite a lot of time and trouble to reach his polling station. Thus, at the first Sierra Leone elections of 1957, only about a third of the registered electorate cast votes.[1] The difficulty of reaching the polling stations was undoubtedly a contributing factor to this low poll. But other factors entered into the picture too, among them lack of information and knowledge in the rural areas of the Protectorate of what was really going on, and also the system of registration, which resulted in the automatic inclusion of those whose names were on the tax-lists. Indeed, if the system in use involves the registration of qualified, yet uninterested, persons as electors, the poll can hardly fail to be lower than would be the case where registration is voluntary and requires a positive act of application from each elector. Thus, the poll of about 51% at the first general elections in India was officially regarded as "by no means unsatisfactory".[2]

Climatic and crop considerations play an important part in determining the most suitable time of year for voting and, therefore, the size of the poll. It is reported that, in Sierra Leone, "only the dry season, from November to June, is suitable for the holding of elections"[3] and the Indian Election Commission reported that "January and February appear to be the best months for polling, taking the country as a whole", and recommended that, apart from the premature dissolution of a legislature due to extraordinary circumstances, all future general elections should be so timed that polling took place in those months.[4]

The size of the poll is significant, not only because it gives some indication of the political interest or apathy of the electorate, but also for the reason that, in some countries[5] at any rate, a high poll is believed to be favourable to one political party and a medium or low poll to a rival party. This relationship between size of poll and political party advantage suggests that, where

[1] Appendix 'E' of unpublished Report on the 1957 Sierra Leone General Election.
[2] *Report on the first general elections in India, 1951-2*, Vol. I, p. 131.
[3] *What are the problems of parliamentary government in West Africa?* (Hansard Society, 1958), p. 71.
[4] *Report on the first general elections in India, 1951-2*, Vol. I, p. 111.
[5] For instance in the U.K. and U.S.A.

compulsory voting[1] is under consideration, a decision is at least as likely to be reached on purely political grounds as on the moral ground that the vote is a duty or, alternatively, that a fundamental liberty is violated if people are not free to decline to vote. Australia is the most often quoted example of a country with compulsory voting and, there, a fine is imposed on all electors who have failed to vote at an election and cannot produce a valid excuse such as ill health. The recommendation that compulsory voting should be introduced in Singapore elections came from the Commission of Inquiry into corrupt, illegal or undesirable practices at elections; they considered that the use of compulsory voting, coupled with a prohibition on the provision of private transport to take voters to the polling stations and a prohibition on any form of canvassing for votes on polling day, might counter the influence of secret societies on voting which had been exercised through the intimidation of electors to vote for the candidate supported by the secret society and through preventing electors likely to favour another candidate from voting.[2] Compulsory voting was used for the first time in Singapore at the elections held in May 1959.

[1] In this connection, it was reported from the West Nile District of Uganda that those who had registered as electors thought that voting was compulsory and did not realise that they need not vote if they did not wish.

[2] *Report of the Commission of Inquiry into corrupt, illegal or undesirable practices at elections* (No. Cmd. 7 of 1958), pp. 13-14 and 39-40.

CHAPTER IX

POSTAL AND PROXY VOTING
AND OTHER SPECIAL
VOTING ARRANGEMENTS

A T ANY large scale election there must inevitably be a number of registered electors who, for reasons of illness, absence on business or on holiday, or some other cause, are unable to vote in person at the assigned polling station. Some countries make special provision for such voters and others do not.

Postal voting is perhaps the most common method of providing special facilities for voters who cannot attend their own polling station in person. It is, however, not always easy to decide who should be entitled to vote by post. Moreover, postal voting obviously demands efficient postal services and the procedure involved, particularly in relation to the preparation of postal ballot papers for the count, is somewhat intricate. Common sense and expediency demand that the categories of persons permitted to vote by post should be strictly limited and, in under-developed countries where postal delivery service is uncertain and the returning officers have enough problems on their hands without the addition of special arrangements for absentee voting, administrative considerations may rule out postal voting altogether.

Countries which allow postal voting for certain categories of electors include Britain, the U.S.A., the Federation of Rhodesia and Nyasaland and the Federation of Malaya, and a brief description of postal voting in each of these countries will illustrate great variation in entitlement to vote by post coupled with near uniformity in procedure once entitlement has been decided.

Those permitted to vote by post in British parliamentary elections include persons registered as service voters; persons unable or likely to be unable to go in person to the polling station by virtue of the general nature of their employment or, in some cases, the particular circumstances of their employment on polling day; persons unable or likely to be unable, through illness or blindness, to go to the polling station or, if able to go, to vote unaided; persons who would have to make a journey by air or sea in order to vote; and persons no longer residing at their qualifying address.[1] Such persons can only vote by post if they apply to be treated as absent voters before the last but one day for the delivery of nomination papers and supply an address in the United Kingdom to which a ballot paper can be sent. The returning officer sends postal ballot papers to persons on his list of postal voters as soon as possible after the receipt of the ballot papers from the printers; the ballot paper sent to postal voters is in the same form as ballot papers used at polling stations and it is accompanied by a declaration of identity in a prescribed form and an envelope for the return of the documents. The returning officer places envelopes returned before the close of the poll in a postal voters' ballot box and opens this box in the presence of the candidates' agents before the time for counting of votes. There is a rather involved procedure for checking the declarations of identity and ballot paper envelopes after which postal ballot papers accepted for the count are mixed with the ballot papers of those voting in person and the general counting of votes proceeds.

In the State of North Carolina in the U.S.A.[2] "any qualified voter of the State who finds that he will be absent from the county in which he is entitled to vote during the day of the holding of any general election, or who by reason of sickness or other physical disability will be unable to travel from his home, or place of confinement, to the voting place in his precinct, may vote" as an absentee voter.[3] In general, such voters have to apply for an absentee ballot to the Chairman of the County Board of Elections not more than thirty or less than two days prior to the date of the election and the ballot can be issued either by delivery in person to the voter or a member of his family or by mail. The ballot together with an affidavit must be back in the hands of the Chairman of the County Board of Elections by 3 p.m. on election day and, if the documents are in order and received within the time limit, the ballot is delivered to the officials of the precinct for inclusion in the precinct count.

In the Federation of Rhodesia and Nyasaland, any voter who is on the roll of an electoral district (constituency) in which an

---

[1] Sec. 12(1), Representation of the People Act, 1949.

[2] There is, of course, a separate set of election laws for each State and there are differences between the laws of one State and another.

[3] Sec. 54, North Carolina Election Laws.

election is to take place and "who is resident therein or was, within twelve months of the polling day, resident therein and:

(a) has good reason to believe that on the polling day he will not be in the electoral district during polling hours; or

(b) has good reason to believe that on account of ill health or infirmity he will be prevented from attending at a polling station on polling day; or

(c) resides more than ten miles from the nearest polling station for that electoral district;

may apply to the returning officer"[1] for a postal ballot paper. The application, which must be signed in the presence of a competent witness, must reach the returning officer not later than noon of the day before polling day. Once the application has been accepted, the procedure for the issue, return and disposal of postal ballot papers is the same as that of the United Kingdom.

In the Federation of Malaya, at the time of the 1955 elections, postal voting was restricted to members of the armed forces and the police force and to election officials liable for duty on polling day outside their own constituencies. The postal voting regulations[2] provided for the addition of other categories of electors from time to time. Postal voting was introduced at these elections solely in order to make it possible for members of the armed forces on operational duty against the terrorists and members of the police force on operational or security duty to cast their votes. As in the Federation of Rhodesia and Nyasaland, the procedure for the issue, return and disposal of postal ballot papers is similar to that of Britain.

In all four of these countries, postal voting is carried out by means of official forms (application forms and declarations of identity). A tight procedure is essential in postal voting in order to avoid abuses and the necessity of using forms and reading official directions suggests that postal voting should ordinarily be restricted to educated voters. It is, therefore, not surprising to find that postal voting has not as yet made an appearance in countries such as Nigeria and Uganda where the rate of illiteracy is high. In India, where illiteracy is also prevalent, only members

[1] Sec. 77, Federation of Rhodesia and Nyasaland Electoral Act, 1958.

[2] Reg. 3, Federation of Malaya Legislative Council Elections (Postal Voting) Regulations, 1955.

of the Armed Forces and persons holding certain government offices were permitted to vote by post at the first general elections, so that India, like Malaya, prescribes voting in person at the polling station for ordinary voters and, unlike the U.S.A. and the Federation of Rhodesia and Nyasaland, does not permit a postal ballot to ordinary voters who are away from their constituencies or bed-ridden on polling day. It should be noted that all voters (both in the general and special categories) in the Federation of Rhodesia and Nyasaland must possess an educational qualification so that the fairly generous provisions for postal voting there and the very limited provisions in Malaya and India do support the contention that postal voting must in practice be confined to educated voters.[1]

It will have been noted that, whereas in Britain applications to be treated as absent voters must be made before the last but one day for the delivery of nomination papers, in America and the Federation of Rhodesia and Nyasaland applications can be received until a day or so before the election. In Kenya, where postal voting is permitted in non-African elections to electors who can show genuine cause, the returning officer is obliged to issue postal ballot papers right up to the time of the close of the poll. The returning officer is required *if possible*[2] to notify the presiding officer of the fact of issue of a postal ballot paper to an elector whose name is on the latter's polling station register of electors but, under the existing rules, it is clearly not possible for the returning officer to inform the appropriate presiding officers in time of the names of all the people who have been issued with postal ballot papers and the door is therefore open to unscrupulous electors voting by post as well as in person. In a country like Kenya, with limited telecommunications and postal services, it would appear that applications to vote by post should be received by the returning officer several days before the commencement of the poll if all postal voters are to be marked on the registers used in polling stations and adequate safeguards thus created to prevent electors who are given postal ballot papers from voting in person as well.

[1] There is postal voting for persons engaged on election duties in Sierra Leone under Reg. 25(1) of the House of Representatives (Elections) Regulations, 1957.

[2] Rule 4(2) of Schedule IV, Kenya Legislative Council Ordinance.

An alternative to postal voting is proxy voting, but it is very doubtful whether any form of proxy voting is desirable in countries without long traditions of parliamentary democracy. One can visualise the old and feeble voters — and illiterate voters too — in under-developed countries being subjected to undue influence in order to agree to apply for a proxy vote which some other person will cast on their behalf. In general, the scope of proxy voting in central government elections is limited to those voters who are necessarily absent from the poll and cannot easily vote by post. Thus in British parliamentary elections, service voters and other electors who, because of the general nature of their employment, are likely to be at sea or out of the country at the time of an election are entitled to vote by proxy. Many countries which make provision for postal voting do not allow proxy voting at all — examples are the Federation of Rhodesia and Nyasaland and the Federation of Malaya. Where proxy voting is permitted, there are often restrictions on the number of proxy votes which any given person can exercise and on the type of person who can be appointed as proxy. Thus, in British Guiana, as in Britain, persons appointed as proxy must be British subjects of full age and not subject to any legal incapacity to vote and they are not entitled to vote as proxy at the same election in any constituency on behalf of more than two electors outside the immediate family.[1]

If, as has been suggested, postal voting is best suited to a literate electorate and proxy voting is undesirable in emergent countries without established standards of parliamentary democracy, it is necessary to consider whether any other methods can be employed to assist persons who find difficulty in reaching their polling station on election day. Experiments with the aim of giving this assistance to certain categories of electors have been made in Kenya, British Guiana and Jamaica. In Kenya, there are a large number of migrant African labourers whose normal place of residence is their own tribal area but who are often temporarily resident in the towns or in the 'white highlands' for periods of some months at a time. At the time of initial registration of African voters in 1956, Africans living temporarily outside their own tribal area were permitted to register as electors in their home

[1] Sec. 31(2), British Guiana Representation of the People Act, 1957 and Sec. 14(2), U.K. Representation of the People Act, 1949.

constituency. These absent voters were permitted to vote on polling day at the polling station nearest to their place of temporary residence for candidates in their constituency of permanent residence, and their votes were sent to their home constituency for counting.[1] This system of absentee voting in person at a polling station in another constituency worked reasonably satisfactorily at the first 1957 elections, despite the complexities of the system both at the time of registration and at the time of polling. In the long run, however, it seems possible that this novel system of absent voting may involve considerable difficulties if attempts are to be made to maintain an accurate absent voters' list for use at future elections. Moreover, the system does not permit of the normal safeguards against personation, for candidates in one constituency are unlikely to be able to appoint polling agents to attend polling stations in other constituencies nor are polling officials in the towns and other labour inflow areas likely to have any personal knowledge of persons temporarily resident there for a few months. The Kenya system of absent voting[2] would appear, then, to be a praiseworthy and successful experiment as far as the first elections are concerned, but some modifications and special measures to check personation may be required if the system is to continue in operation. Quite apart from absent voting, it has been mentioned in Chapter VIII that Kenya permits electors, who can satisfy the presiding officer that they have good and sufficient reason for being unable to present themselves at their own polling station, to vote at any other polling station within their constituency and it was suggested that this might well lead to multiple voting. In short, Kenya has gone further than any other British Commonwealth territory — and, perhaps, rather too far — to be kind and helpful to the African voters.

In British Guiana there is, as has been mentioned, provision for proxy voting, but only those electors who are members of the police forces or are engaged in running trains or vessels as employees of the Transport and Harbours Department or are employed in an official capacity by the returning officer and are likely to be unable to go in person to the polling station and those electors unable to vote in person by reason of blindness or physical

---

[1] Rules 27-32 and Rule 35 of the Kenya Legislative Council (African Representation) (Election of Members) Rules, 1956.
[2] More commonly described in Kenya as 'expatriate voting'.

incapacity are permitted to appoint proxies.[1] There are therefore other electors who, by reason of distance from their polling station or through absence from their constituencies, may be unable to vote in person but are not permitted to appoint proxies. The British Guiana legislation makes an exception to the rule that all persons voting at an election should do so in person at the allotted polling station by making provision for the framing of regulations which allow special arrangements in respect of those whose names appear on the official list of electors for any electoral district or for any polling division or group of polling divisions specified in the Regulations. Use was made of regulations to authorise special arrangements for certain 'interior' electoral districts, where communications are poor, and, as an example, at the 1957 general election, voters in the North West constituency were permitted to vote at any polling station within the constituency.[2] In this particular constituency, covering an area of 7,621 square miles, there were only 3,481 registered electors.

In Jamaica, special arrangements[3] are made for electors in the police forces and the Jamaica Battalion to vote before polling day. Ballot papers are supplied to the Commissioner of Police and the Garrison Commander and the votes cast are sent to the Chief Electoral Officer for distribution to the various constituencies. There are no provisions for postal or proxy voting in Jamaica. Some of the other territories of the British Caribbean have made similar arrangements for the police to vote before polling day. It had been found that, when the police were on duty on polling day and were therefore unable to vote, they came in for a lot of unjustified criticism during the election campaign. When, however, arrangements were made for the police to vote separately and on a previous day, they had to be wooed by candidates as potential supporters. This silenced criticism of the police and improved their morale.

[1] Sec. 28, Representation of the People Ordinance, 1957.
[2] See Appendix V of the *Report on the British Guiana General Election, 1957*, p. 12.
[3] Under Jamaican Law No. 64 of 1949.

CHAPTER X

COUNTING THE VOTES

THE counting of votes and declaration of the result is the final major administrative exercise in the course of an election. The detailed steps to be taken will, of course, depend in the first instance on the method of voting used and on whether the contest is for the election of a single member for the constituency or for the election of two or more members. As a preliminary to a discussion of methods of counting votes, it may be useful to differentiate between:

(a) The group of countries in which the counting of votes is undertaken centrally for the whole constituency, and

(b) The group of countries in which the counting of votes is undertaken in each polling station on the conclusion of polling.

Britain and most of the countries of the British Commonwealth fall into the first category. In Britain, the Federation of Malaya, the Federation of Rhodesia and Nyasaland, and Tanganyika, in all of which countries voters mark their ballot papers, the returning officer opens each ballot box one by one, counts and records the total number of ballot papers in each box, and then mixes together all the papers contained in the various ballot boxes so that "it is impossible to determine from which ballot box any particular ballot paper was taken".[1] During the counting and recording of the total number of ballot papers in each ballot box, the votes given to each candidate are not separated and there is thus no record of the support given to each candidate at a particular polling station, but only for the constituency as a whole. In the West African countries and territories of the British Commonwealth, however, where voting is conducted by providing a separate ballot box for each candidate at each polling station, the individual ballot papers are mere tokens, and it is necessary for the returning officer to count the ballot papers in each box separately and to record the total number in each box as the

[1] Federation of Rhodesia and Nyasaland Electoral Act, 1958, Sec. 89(5).

number of votes cast in favour of the candidate whose symbol is
marked on the ballot box concerned.[1] The preservation of secrecy
regarding the way in which the group of electors polling at a
particular station have voted is thus more feasible when ballot
papers are marked than when they are mere tokens. In all the
Commonwealth countries of West Africa, however, counting of
votes is undertaken centrally for the whole constituency.

The picture is a little different in the British West Indies. In
Jamaica, there is a preliminary count of the votes within each
polling station at the conclusion of polling.[2] The presiding officer
empties his ballot box, unfolds the ballot papers one by one,
examines each and verifies his initials upon it (ballot papers in
Jamaica are initialed rather than perforated or stamped) and calls
out the name of the candidate for whom each ballot paper has
been marked so as to permit any person present to keep his own
score — the presiding officer or his assistant keeps the score
whether others do or not. This preliminary count gives the
presiding officer an opportunity to correct some of the errors
which he and his assistants may have made; he is instructed, for
instance, to detach the counterfoil of any ballot paper which he
forgot to detach at the time of issue to the voter and to initial any
ballot paper which he omitted to initial at the time of issue, with
the proviso that before initialing he must satisfy himself that the
ballot paper really is one that has been supplied by him to an
elector. The presiding officer also rejects any irregular or invalid
ballot, the validity of each paper being determined before another
is considered. At the conclusion of this preliminary count, the
presiding officer places the ballots cast for each candidate in
separate envelopes, which are then sealed, places the rejected
ballots in a separate envelope and makes out a preliminary
statement of the poll, the purpose of which is to enable the
returning officer to ascertain the result of the poll on receipt of
each ballot box and to make a preliminary compilation of the
number of votes polled for each candidate in his constituency.
When the returning officer has received the preliminary statements
of the poll from all polling stations, he communicates the result
of the preliminary compilation to the Chief Electoral Officer and

[1] See, for instance, Reg. 61 of the Western Region of Nigeria Parliamentary
and Local Government Electoral Regulations, 1955.
[2] Sec. 37, Jamaican Representation of the People Law, 1944.

the tentative results are announced within a few hours of the closing of the poll. There is, however, an official count of the ballots by the returning officer commencing on the day after polling and the returning officer does not declare elected the candidate who has received the most votes until this final addition of votes has taken place. The results of the election are published polling station by polling station,[1] so that there is an official record of the votes cast for each candidate for local groups of electors, numbering two or three hundred to a group.

In British Guiana, as in Jamaica, the results of polling are published for each constituency, polling station by polling station, but there is no preliminary count in British Guiana. Instead, as in Britain, the presiding officer's first duty after the close of the poll is to seal the ballot box so as to prevent the introduction of any additional ballot papers and the ballot box, as originally sealed, is handed over to the returning officer for the count. The important difference between counting procedure in British Guiana and Britain is that, in the former territory, the Chief Electoral Officer is required by law[2] to publish a report on each election "including *inter alia*, by polling places, the number of votes polled for each candidate, the number of rejected ballots, the number of names on the lists of electors . . ." and this rules out the possibility of mixing all the papers contained in the various ballot boxes before the counting of votes for each candidate commences.

In France and the French African territories, the chairman and members of the polling committee supervise the counting of votes for their own polling station, assisted if necessary by additional tellers. After excluding ballot papers such as those on which voters have identified themselves and those which must be rejected on other grounds, and annexing a note indicating the reason for rejection in each case, the votes for each candidate or for each list of candidates are counted and the result of the poll for the individual polling station is recorded and signed by the polling committee and delivered for tabulation of the total votes for the whole constituency and announcement of the result. In France and the French African territories, as in the British West Indies, the results for each individual polling station are made public

[1] See, for instance, pp. 23-117 of the *Report on the 1949 Jamaican General Election*.

[2] Sec. 44(4), British Guiana Representation of the People Ordinance, 1957.

and, indeed, the voters are permitted to move around the tables at which the votes are being counted.[1]

In the United States of America, as in France, the ballots are counted separately for each precinct (the American equivalent of polling district). Where voting machines are used, the poll for each candidate is automatically recorded. Where voting machines are not in use, the Registrar (equivalent to the presiding officer) and the 'judges' who assist him (equivalent to the members of the polling committee in the French system) inspect each ballot paper, decide how the ballot is to be counted (or mark it as a disputed ballot if unanimous agreement on a particular ballot paper cannot be reached), and, when counting has been completed, the results are certified by the Registrar and his judges and sent to the Chairman of the County Board of Elections, where the votes cast in the county are tabulated and the necessary abstracts prepared. The County Boards usually have powers to decide on the legality of any ballots transmitted to them from the precincts as disputed ballots. In Canada, too, the ballots are counted separately in each polling station. "When polling closes at six p.m., each of the thirty-six thousand deputy returning officers,[2] attended by a candidate or his agents and anybody else invited, counts the ballots in his box. He packages them, adds to the pile various statements concerning the day's polling, puts the lot in the ballot box, seals this and despatches it to the returning officer. The votes cast in the constituency are in due course totalled; but as candidates and their agents receive statements from each deputy returning officer of the results in the several polling stations, the unofficial result is known well before the final count."[3]

It will be recalled that, in the first paragraph of this chapter, countries were put into two groups according to whether counting was undertaken centrally for the constituency or separately for each polling station. It has been seen that there is a fair representation of countries in each group and that a few countries such as Canada and Jamaica undertake a preliminary count at the polling station followed by a constituency count on a central basis. In all

---

[1] The rules for counting votes in French elections are contained in Articles 28-32 of the General Decree of 2nd February, 1852 and in Articles 8 and 9 of Decree of 3rd January, 1914.

[2] i.e. presiding officers.

[3] *The Canadian House of Commons — Representation* by Norman Ward, pp. 208-9.

countries of the second group (those in which counting takes place in the polling station) and in some of those of the first group (particularly those countries in which voting is by token with a separate ballot box for each candidate), the results of the poll are published or at least made known to the candidates or their agents for each individual polling station. It must be pointed out that this means that there is a separate record of the poll for each of a series of local groups of electors of an average size of a few hundred persons. In a few polling districts, it might in these circumstances be possible to make a shrewd guess as to how individual electors have voted; it is certainly possible, in theory at least, for a successful candidate to shower the favours of political patronage on those areas which have supported him and to turn the cold shoulder to other areas in which the majority have voted against him. In practice, the broad political affiliations of small geographical areas may be fairly well known whatever the method of counting the votes adopted, partly because the results of local government elections are necessarily announced for each ward — and this is usually a fairly small geographical unit — and partly because party canvassing, if carried out at all efficiently, usually results in a reasonably detailed picture of the areas in which a given candidate can expect to find his main support. Nevertheless, when the method of voting permits, the British method of mixing the ballots from all polling stations before the count would appear to give the individual voter the maximum possible assurance of secrecy.

In all countries in which elections are free, each candidate is entitled to appoint a number of counting agents to attend the counting of votes. In the United Kingdom, the Parliamentary Election Rules authorise the returning officer to limit the number of counting agents, provided that the number allowed to each candidate is the same and is not less than "the number obtained by dividing the number of clerks employed on the counting by the number of candidates".[1] Use of this formula in determining the number of counting agents makes for equality in the number of officially employed counting clerks and the total number of counting agents, and makes it possible to seat clerks on one side of a long table and the counting agents opposite them. A similar formula for determining the number of counting agents for each

[1] Rule 31(1) of the Parliamentary Election Rules.

candidate is in use in the Federation of Malaya.[1] In many other countries of the Commonwealth and outside it, however, in which counting of votes is undertaken centrally for the constituency as a whole, each candidate is permitted to appoint but one counting agent; this is the position in Tanganyika,[2] Ghana,[3] the Eastern Region of Nigeria,[4] the Sudan[5] and Uganda.[6] Each candidate is permitted to appoint two agents to attend the count in the Western Region of Nigeria[7] and Zanzibar.[8] Whether or not one counting agent, in addition to the candidate and his election agent, if any, can be regarded as sufficient to look after a candidate's interests will, of course, depend on the size of the poll and the number of counting clerks engaged by the returning officer. It is suggested that a larger number of counting agents could usefully be employed in watching the counting and inspecting doubtful ballot papers in countries such as Uganda and the Eastern Region of Nigeria, where each constituency contains a fairly large electorate.

When counting takes place separately at each polling station, the officials who supervise polling also undertake the counting of votes and those agents who have represented the candidate as polling agents continue as counting agents. Thus, at the preliminary counting of votes in the polling stations in Jamaica, "Any candidate is entitled to be present as well as the agents or electors representing them, and if no candidate is represented it is the duty of the presiding officer to secure the attendance of at least two electors. He may permit as many more as he desires to be present."[9] In the French territories, each list of candidates or, in single-member constituencies, each candidate is entitled to appoint an agent to attend each polling station and this agent is in turn entitled to appoint tellers not later than an hour before the closing of the poll and the latter help to count the votes in the polling

---

[1] Sec. 14(1) of the Federation of Malaya Election Offences Ordinance, 1954, as amended by the Election Offences (Amendment) Ordinance, 1955.

[2] Sec. 96(1) of the Tanganyika Legislative Council Elections Ordinance.

[3] Reg. 25(1) of the Electoral Provisions (Assembly Elections) Regulations, 1954.

[4] Reg. 41(1) of the Eastern House of Assembly Electoral Regulations, 1955.

[5] Rule 31(1) of the Sudan Parliamentary Election Rules, 1957.

[6] Sec. 45(2) of the Uganda Legislative Council Elections Ordinance, 1957.

[7] Reg. 58(1) of the Western Region Parliamentary and Local Government Electoral Regulations, 1955.

[8] Sec. 51(3) of the Zanzibar Legislative Council Elections Decree, 1957

[9] *Report on the Jamaican General Election, 1949*, p. 183. See also Sec. 37 of the Representation of the People Law, 1944.

stations as soon as voting has ended. If there are no agents present, the chairman of the polling committee chooses the tellers from among the voters present. The chairman and members of the committee supervise the counting and, in polling stations attended by fewer than 300 voters, the committee may itself count the votes without the assistance of additional tellers. It should be remembered that on each committee there is a representative of each candidate or of each party list.

Essentially the duties of the counting agent consist of watching to see that no irregularities take place and drawing the attention of the returning officer or his assistants to any ballot papers of the rival candidates which should, in his opinion, be rejected. The counting agent frequently is entitled to copy the returning officer's statement of rejected ballot papers and the statement of verification of the presiding officers' ballot paper accounts with the number of ballot papers actually found in each ballot box.[1]

COUNTING PROCEDURE WHEN BALLOT PAPERS HAVE BEEN MARKED BY VOTERS

It was stated at the beginning of this chapter that in Britain, the Federation of Malaya, the Federation of Rhodesia and Nyasaland, and Tanganyika, the returning officer opens each ballot box one by one, counts and records the total number of ballot papers in each box and then mixes together all the papers contained in the various ballot boxes, so that it is impossible to determine from which ballot box any particular ballot paper has been taken. In the British West Indies there is no mixing of the papers from the different ballot boxes and a separate record is kept of the number of votes for each candidate cast at each polling station.

The main difficulty over counting is usually experienced in connection with the rejection of ballot papers. A counting agent has the right to draw the attention of the returning officer or his assistants to any ballot papers of the rival candidates which should, in his opinion, be rejected; he is also usually entitled to object to the rejection of a ballot paper containing a vote apparently cast for his own candidate and to require the returning officer to record

[1] See Chapter VI of Schofield's *Parliamentary Elections* for a full account of the duties of counting agents in Britain.

the objection. The legislation governing elections always details the circumstances under which a ballot paper should be rejected and, in Britain, there is a considerable volume of case law to assist the returning officer to make decisions in doubtful cases. It should be noted that the returning officer's decision on whether or not to reject a ballot paper, after he has heard representations from counting agents, is final. In Britain a returning officer must reject a ballot paper at a parliamentary election if:

(a) the ballot paper does not bear the official mark; or

(b) votes have been given for more than one candidate on the ballot paper (all parliamentary constituencies in Britain now return single members); or

(c) anything is written or marked on the ballot paper (other than the printed number on the back) by which the voter can be identified; or

(d) the ballot paper is not marked or void for uncertainty.

The first of these four reasons for rejecting a ballot paper in Britain applies to any voting system in which the ballot paper must be perforated or stamped or initialed by the presiding officer at the time of issue. In most British West African territories, for instance, ballot papers are not marked by the voter, but they are or should be marked with the official mark before issue and failure to apply the official mark has, as we have seen in Chapter VIII, led to the rejection at the count of a number of otherwise valid ballot papers. In order to mitigate the undesirable effects of rejection of ballot papers due to thoughtless errors by polling officials, Ghana abolished the official mark for its 1956 election "without any disastrous consequences, though in view of the currency of rumours of intended forgery of ballot papers, the authorities felt obliged to involve themselves in the most elaborate security precautions in their printing and distribution",[1] whilst the Western Region of Nigeria, though continuing to provide for the official mark, allows the returning officer to count a ballot paper notwithstanding the absence of the mark, provided he is satisfied that the ballot paper was in fact issued from a book of ballot papers furnished to the presiding officer of the polling station in which the vote was cast.[2] The requirement of an official mark on the

[1] D. J. R. Scott on 'Problems of West African elections' in *What are the problems of Parliamentary Government in West Africa?* (Hansard Society, 1958), p. 72.

[2] Reg. 62 of the Western Region Parliamentary and Local Government Electoral Regulations, 1955.

ballot paper is, of course, a substantial guarantee against the introduction of forged ballot papers provided that the nature of the mark is kept a closely guarded secret before the poll takes place, and the special provision in the West Nigerian Regulations appears to be a sensible attempt to strike a compromise.

The second of the four reasons for rejecting a ballot paper in British parliamentary elections, namely that votes have been given for more than one candidate on the ballot paper, applies in that form only to the election of members in single member constituencies where the voter marks his ballot paper. A minor modification of the rule makes it applicable to multi-member constituencies where the voter marks his ballot paper — the ballot would then stand to be rejected if more votes have been given than there are candidates to be returned.[1] There is no analagous rule when there is a separate ballot box for each candidate, as the individual voter is given but one ballot for each vote he is entitled to cast. The corresponding rule in the French system of voting involves the rejection of a vote when the envelope contains two different ballot papers and the counting of the vote but once when the envelope contains more than one of the same series of ballot papers.

Rejection of a ballot paper when anything has been written or marked on it by which the voter can be identified is of near universal application. Provision for such rejection appears in the legislation of all British Commonwealth countries which the author has examined as well as in the laws of France and the overseas French territories. An exception is, however, sometimes made when a technical error has been made by the polling station officials; for instance, the British Guiana Representation of the People Ordinance, 1957, provides that no ballot paper shall be rejected on account of any "writing, number or mark placed thereon by any presiding officer"[2] and this implies that, if a presiding officer has inadvertently written the number of the elector (as shown in the register of electors) on the ballot paper instead of on the counterfoil of the ballot paper, the ballot is not on that account rejected. Where there is no specific exemption from rejection of a ballot paper which has become identifiable

[1] See, for instance, Reg. 28(1)(b) of the Federation of Malaya Legislative Council Elections Regulations, 1954.

[2] Sec. 42(2)(d) of the British Guiana Representation of the People Ordinance, 1957.

owing to an error on the part of the presiding officer or his assistants, it is reasonable to assume that any mark on the ballot paper indicating the identity of the voter invalidates, whether the mark was placed there by the voter or not. The law in Britain on this point is subject to some doubt owing to conflicting court decisions.[1] In Malaya, a number of ballot papers emanating from one polling station were rejected at the first general elections in 1955 owing to the presiding officer's error in entering the voters' electoral numbers on the ballot paper instead of on the counterfoil.

Just what is required to make a ballot paper identifiable is a matter of opinion. At the 1949 General Election in Jamaica, presiding officers (who undertook the preliminary counting of votes immediately after the close of the poll) were instructed not to accept:[2]

> Ballots upon which the voter has made any mark of writing by which he could be identified. Thus any ballot marked for a candidate otherwise than with a cross, e.g. with a circle, a single line or any other figure which is not a cross, should be rejected. So a ballot should be rejected if, although the voter has made a proper cross, he has added anywhere on the ballot any additional voluntary mark or any writing whether initials, names or words. Finally, as a pencil has been provided, ballots marked in ink or coloured pencil should be rejected.

These instructions would probably not be an acceptable definition of "anything written or marked by which the voter can be identified" in Britain or in the Federation of Malaya.

The last of the four reasons for rejecting a ballot paper in Britain — because the ballot paper is not marked or is void for uncertainty — is the one which is intrinsically the most likely to lead to arguments at the counting of votes. The British Parliamentary Elections Rules[3] provide that a ballot paper on which the vote is marked elsewhere than in the proper place, or otherwise than by means of a cross, or by more than one mark, shall not be rejected as void if the ballot indicates a clear intention to vote for one or other of the candidates and the way the paper is marked does not of itself identify the voter. But even with these qualifications, some ballot papers present problems because there is a

---

[1] Schofield, *Parliamentary Elections*, pp. 368-9.
[2] *Report on the General Election, 1949*, p. 185.
[3] Rule 48(2).

difficult border-line between those ballot papers which are void for uncertainty and those which are deemed to indicate the intention of the voter. Some countries of the Commonwealth have taken steps to define the border-line more closely. In the Federation of Rhodesia and Nyasaland, the returning officer is required to reject and not to count, *inter alia*, any ballot paper:

(*d*) on which there is any writing or mark other than the official mark of a presiding officer or of the returning officer and one cross in a rectangle opposite the name of a candidate; or

(*e*) on which the cross has been placed elsewhere than in a rectangle opposite the name of a candidate; or

(*f*) on which more than one cross appears.[1]

It will be seen that sharper definition of the border line has been achieved only at the expense of increasing the scope for rejection of ballot papers.

One aspect of counting procedure in which there is some variation in the practice adopted is in relation to the verification of the presiding officer's ballot paper account. When counting of votes takes place centrally for the constituency, the presiding officer seals his ballot box, makes up and seals various packages and completes a ballot paper account, in which he states the number of ballot papers entrusted to him in the first instance and accounts for them under the heads of used ballot papers (excluding spoilt and tendered ballot papers), unused, spoilt and tendered ballot papers. At the count it is usually the returning officer's duty to compare the total number of ballot papers found in each ballot box with the corresponding presiding officer's ballot paper account and to record the results of this comparison.[2] In Britain, the returning officer has no authority to open any of the sealed packets of documents sent in by the presiding officer to assist in this verification, if there is a discrepancy between the number of ballot papers found in each ballot box and the figure of used ballot papers entered in the presiding officer's account. The discrepancy simply appears in the record, of which the candidate or his counting agent is permitted to make a copy. In some territories of the British Commonwealth, however, the returning officer is permitted to open certain of the sealed packets of documents when verifying

---

[1] Sec. 90(2), Federation of Rhodesia and Nyasaland Electoral Act, 1958.

[2] See, for instance, Rules 46(1)(a) and 55(2) of the British Parliamentary Election Rules.

the ballot paper account; in the Federation of Rhodesia and Nyasaland, for instance, the returning officer verifies the ballot paper account "by comparing with it the number of ballot papers in the ballot box and the unused and spoilt ballot papers and the tendered votes list"[1] after having opened the sealed packets containing the latter documents, and then makes a report of the result of such verification, allowing any candidate or agent of a candidate to copy the report on request. In the event of a very closely fought election, a defeated candidate might, of course, base an election petition on a discrepancy between the ballot paper account and the number of ballot papers found in each ballot box, and there would seem to be some grounds for permitting the opening of documents which can assist in the detection of obvious errors provided that this does not lessen in any way the public feeling of security in the secrecy of the vote. The Western Region of Nigeria is another territory which permits the inspection of certain of the presiding officer's documents at the time of verification of the ballot paper account.[2]

In this discussion of certain aspects of counting procedure when ballot papers are marked by voters, it has been assumed that a simple plurality system of voting is in use. In countries such as Britain, the Federation of Malaya, and the Federation of Rhodesia and Nyasaland, in whose parliamentary constituencies the candidate who gets the most votes is declared elected, the essentials of counting procedure consist of the examination of all ballot papers, the setting aside of rejected ballot papers, and the sorting of accepted ballot papers on the basis of the candidate for whom the vote has been cast or, particularly in the case of multi-member constituencies, the use of tally sheets to count the score for each candidate. There are, of course, certain rules to be followed and these relate particularly to the preservation of secrecy. There is, indeed, some variation in the actual methods adopted to safeguard the secrecy of the vote; for instance in many countries (but not all) the serial numbers are printed on the back of the ballot papers and the law requires that all ballot papers should be placed face upward before the count in order to ensure that a vote for a particular candidate cannot be connected with a given serial

---

[1] Federation of Rhodesia and Nyasaland Electoral Act, 1958, Sec. 89(4).

[2] Reg. 66(1) of the Western Region Parliamentary and Local Government Electoral Regulations, 1955.

number; again in some countries admission to the place in which the votes are being counted is strictly limited to those officially engaged in counting and to candidates and their agents, whilst elsewhere the returning officer is empowered to admit a limited number of members of the public.[1] These, however, are mere variations of the details of procedure. More fundamental are the complications in counting which are implied in any system of voting — e.g. the alternative vote, the single transferable vote — which enables the elector to indicate his order of preference by putting numbers against the names of the various candidates. Where such systems of voting are in use, the second and sometimes the subsequent preferences of the voters are taken into account in a series of counts involving the gradual elimination of the least favoured candidates. Such systems of voting are not, however, used in developing countries containing largely illiterate populations, if only for the very good reason that a voter who cannot read and write would have the greatest difficulty in indicating his order of preference, and a discussion of counting procedure in connection with such methods of voting would appear to be unnecessary in this context.

COUNTING PROCEDURE WHEN THERE IS A SEPARATE BALLOT BOX FOR EACH CANDIDATE

When the voters do not mark ballot papers and there is a separate ballot box for each candidate, very strict precautions must necessarily be taken to ensure that there is no possibility of confusing the ballot papers belonging to the various candidates. It is, under these circumstances, more than ever essential that arrangements for counting should be most carefully organised. On the other hand, there is less likelihood of disputes over the rejection of votes because the voter has merely to drop his ballot paper token into one or other of the boxes and he is unlikely to have written anything on the ballot paper which would reveal his identity nor can there be any doubt about his voting intention if his ballot paper is found inside one of the ballot boxes.

[1] The author has been told that, in Mauritius, the public is admitted to the count and the local press reports the progress of the count like a Test Match! Again, in Turkey, the law requires that the votes should be counted and sorted publicly. (Art. 1 of the Election of National Deputies Act, 1950).

Variations in counting procedure from one country to another thus largely relate to matters of organisation and methods. For instance, in Uganda at the time of the 1958 elections, returning officers were instructed to start the operation by sorting the ballot boxes into separate piles, one pile containing all the ballot boxes of one candidate, and to proceed to count and dispose of all the ballot papers for one candidate before the papers of the next candidate were removed from any ballot box. On the other hand, in the Sudan for the 1958 elections, all the boxes for a given polling station were brought to the counters, their contents counted and recorded box by box, and the polling station ballot paper account checked before a start was made on opening the boxes of the next polling station. In Sierra Leone, too, at the 1957 elections, the instructions to returning officers were that not more than one box was to be opened at each counting table at a time and that all boxes from one polling station were to be counted before another was started.

Rejection of ballot papers with this method of voting is in practice likely to be confined to cases of thoughtless errors on the part of polling station officials, usually through failure to inscribe the official mark on the ballot paper or to stupidity on the part of voters by signing their names on the ballot paper or otherwise indicating their identity.

As has been mentioned in Chapter VIII, voting by token involves a tedious check on the serial numbers of the ballot papers during the counting of votes in multi-member constituencies when each voter has as many ballots to cast (each with the same serial number) as there are seats to be filled and 'plumping' is not permitted. In these circumstances, the returning officer and his assistants, after taking the ballot papers from each ballot box, are required to "examine the serial numbers thereof to ensure that no two papers bear identical numbers".[1] In the Eastern Region of Nigeria and in India, where there has been practical experience of counting of token votes in multi-member constituencies, the need for this check of serial numbers has caused considerable delays.[2] In both countries, the legislation requires that, if more ballot papers than one with the same serial number are found in the same box, all

[1] The wording of part of Reg. 44(1) of the Eastern Region of Nigeria House of Assembly Electoral Regulations, 1955.
[2] *Report on the first general elections in India, 1951-2*, Vol. I, pp. 138-9.

but one of them has to be rejected. In order to ensure the exclusion of cumulative votes, therefore, the ballot papers in each box have to be arranged in serial number for a check on plumping before the count proper can begin.

With the system of voting by token, it is possible (though the author knows of no recorded instances) that when the ballot boxes are opened, the candidate's label found stuck to the inside of a particular box may be different from the label on the outside. This could be caused either by an error of the presiding officer in the polling station before the start of voting or by interference with the labels during or after polling. Such a situation is not covered by the electoral law; the returning officers in Uganda were advised by the Supervisor of Elections that the commonsense action to take in the circumstances would be to reject the ballot papers found in the box and put them aside with the other rejected papers. This problem is far from academic; in Sierra Leone there were rumours that the ballot boxes might be tampered with between polling and counting, especially in places where the carriage of boxes from the polling stations to the count took some days, and there is an obvious danger of stuffing of boxes and switching of labels unless regulations dealing with the sealing not only of the boxes but also of the labels on the boxes are rigidly observed.

As was mentioned at the beginning of this chapter, the fact that the number of ballot papers found in each ballot box must be recorded as a step in the counting procedure necessarily means that the political inclination of the small group of voters attending each polling station must necessarily become known and there is no possibility of mixing the ballot papers from different polling stations as is the practice in Britain. The results of elections in British West Africa, Uganda, Zanzibar and India, where the system of voting by token is used, are however published, not by giving the score for each candidate in each polling district, but only the total vote for each candidate in the constituency.

COUNTING PROCEDURE WHEN THERE ARE SEPARATE
BALLOT PAPERS FOR EACH CANDIDATE OR PARTY LIST

In France and the overseas French territories, the counting of the ballot papers and the tabulation of the returns takes place at each polling station immediately after the closing of the polls. The chairman and members of the polling committee supervise the counting and they are assisted at the larger polling stations by tellers, who are chosen from among the voters registered in the constituency electoral lists. The counting procedure is as follows.[1] The ballot box is opened and the number of envelopes contained in each box is ascertained. If the number of envelopes is greater or less than the number of marginal checks in the electoral list, that fact is noted in the record. In the meantime the tellers are divided into groups of not less than four, and, when checking of the number of envelopes has been completed, the chairman divides the envelopes among the groups of tellers. At each table, one teller extracts the ballot paper from each envelope, unfolds it and passes it to another teller, who in turn reads aloud the names of the candidate or candidates on the ballot paper; these names are recorded by at least two tellers on lists prepared for the purpose. If an envelope contains more than one ballot paper and the ballots are for different lists or names, the vote is rejected as invalid; if the ballot papers contained in the one envelope name the same list or candidate, they count as one vote. Blank ballot papers, ballot papers which are insufficiently marked or on which voters have identified themselves, ballot papers found in the ballot box without an envelope or enclosed in a non-official envelope, ballots written on paper of a colour other than that chosen by the candidate or list, envelopes bearing identifying marks on the inside or outside, and ballot papers or envelopes bearing words insulting to candidates or to third parties are not included in the count but are instead annexed to the record with a note attached indicating the reason for rejection. Immediately after the votes have been counted, the result of the poll is announced publicly and ballot papers, other than those rejected and annexed to the record, are burned in the presence of the voters. The result of the voting is recorded and signed by the polling committee and forwarded for tabulation of the total votes in the constituency and announcement of the names of the successful candidates.

The French system of counting the votes places a very heavy responsibility on the polling committee in charge of each polling station, but it should be remembered that each candidate or party

[1] Articles 8 and 9 of Decree of 3 January, 1914. See also pp. 24-5 of Annex 1 of the *Report of the U.N. Commissioner on the French Togoland Elections, 1958* (T/1392).

contesting the election in the constituency is entitled to be represented on the polling committee and this representative is entitled to make observations, protests and challenges and to insist that an entry be made of all such events in the polling station record. There is, therefore, a reasonable assurance of fair dealing in the polling station and there are full records of the conduct of polling and counting on the basis of which election petitions can be judged. Moreover, the counting of votes immediately after the closure of the polls rules out the possibility of tampering with the ballot box *en route* from the polling station to the count and it contributes to the speedy announcement of the result of the election.

PROCEDURE IN CASE OF AN EQUALITY OF VOTES

In Britain[1] and in many of the other countries of the British Commonwealth, for instance in Uganda[2] and in the Western Region of Nigeria,[3] the winning candidate (or candidates) in case of an equality of votes is determined by or in the presence of the returning officer by casting lots. In the Federation of Rhodesia and Nyasaland, however, the proceedings in case of equality are more formal; the returning officer is required to report the fact of equality at the count to the Minister of Home Affairs, who then proceeds to arrange for the determination of the winning candidate by the casting of lots in the presence of a judge.[4] In Jamaica, under the Representation of the People Law, 1944,[5] the returning officer has a casting vote. In Tanganyika[6] and the Eastern Region of Nigeria,[7] there is a fresh election if, after a re-count, there is found to be an equality of votes.

[1] Rule 50, Parliamentary Elections Rules.
[2] Sec. 45(9), Uganda Legislative Council Elections Ordinance, 1957.
[3] Reg. 68, Western Region Parliamentary and Local Government Electoral Regulations, 1955.
[4] Sec. 90(5), Federation of Rhodesia and Nyasaland Electoral Act, 1958.
[5] Sec. 38(8).
[6] Sec. 104, Tanganyika Legislative Council Elections Ordinance, 1957.
[7] Reg. 50, Eastern House of Assembly Electoral Regulations, 1955.

CHAPTER XI

CONCLUSIONS

W HEN the author was given responsibility for making arrangements for the first general election in the Federation of Malaya, he was confronted with prophecies of chaos and disaster from some of the 'older hands'. These prophecies gained some support when, shortly after his appointment, one of the States forming the Federation decided to ignore advice from Federal Headquarters and to hold elections to their own State Council without the precaution of making an electoral register as a preliminary. The results were unfortunate.[1] Luckily for the author's reputation, the Federal elections in 1955 took place in a calm and peaceful atmosphere, and this first general election in Malaya and similar first elections in other parts of Asia and Africa during the past few years must have dispelled any lingering doubts on the suitability of the ballot box for use by semi-literate societies. It is now quite clear that, given proper backing and competent staff, an administrator can with careful preparation go through all the motions of organising a large-scale election when the electorate is drawn from the ranks of such societies and it is equally evident that most of the voters in these elections have realised that they are in fact making a choice of some kind when they take part in the polling. More research is required, however, before any general pronouncements can be made regarding the interpretation of the meaning of elections by large groups of illiterate and materially backward voters — particularly in respect of central as opposed to local government elections. Nor has the impact of the new equalitarian system of representative government on the traditional social system and forms of leadership of peasant populations as yet been the subject of adequate study with a wide geographical spread.

Returning to the mechanics of elections, it seems likely that in the long run any trouble which may occur in operating the

[1] Those who are interested in reading about the commotion which these elections caused are advised to refer to the Malayan newspapers of 30th October. 1954, and the next few days.

electoral system is more likely to arise from deficiencies in the registration procedure than from failure to organise actual polling efficiently. This does not imply that there may not be a number of improvements which could usefully be made to the methods of nominating candidates, voting and counting the votes at present in use in some of the developing countries mentioned in this book. But the discussion in Chapter IV did indicate that rather little thought has so far been given to the maintenance of registers of electors — particularly in British dependent territories in Africa — and the experience of some advanced countries such as the United States of America does appear to lend support to the suggestion that accuracy of registration is likely to be the most difficult long-term problem in connection with elections. Unfortunately there has been a tendency to breathe a sigh of relief and forget about elections as soon as they are over and to fail to make maximum use of the experience gained to improve procedure and remove anomalies and absurdities from the relevant legislation.

The system of voting, the delimitation of constituencies, the franchise and the method of registering electors are all, of course, of crucial importance in determining the political shape of national elections. We have seen that some countries, for example India and Ghana, pay a great deal of attention to having constituencies as nearly as possible equal in population, but that this factor has been regarded as of comparatively small importance in a good many of the non-self-governing territories of the Commonwealth in Africa, where the emphasis has been very much more on the identification of constituency boundaries with the boundaries of administrative districts or even with whole provinces. But there is a tendency, already discernible in West Africa, to give more and more weight to the population factor in constituency delimitation and, with it, has gone a movement in the direction of having a larger number of single member constituencies and fewer multi-member constituencies. It has been mentioned that, in West Africa in particular, the political quarrels at the time of deciding on constituencies have generally arisen over the allocation of the number of constituencies to regions rather than over the boundaries of individual constituencies.

Whereas the simple plurality system of voting has been adopted widely within the tropical countries of the British Commonwealth and also by a number of emergent countries outside the

Commonwealth, the franchise varies widely. At one extreme, as in India, Malaya and the overseas French territories there is universal adult franchise for all resident nationals; at the other extreme, in East and Central Africa, there are various forms of franchise with qualifications based not only on age and nationality but also on education, literacy, income, ownership of property and the like; in between these two extremes, but much nearer to India than to East Africa, lie the Commonwealth countries of West Africa, where the right to vote has been extended in the last few years in most territories to include women, who were largely excluded in the first instance because the earlier electoral rolls were based on tax lists and few women pay taxes. History suggests and political pressure is likely to demand a continuous movement in the direction of universal adult franchise throughout tropical Africa.

Having settled on the franchise, most of the African territories have placed the onus of registration as an elector on the individual rather than on the government. If registration is voluntary, the elector has to take positive action to get his name on the register and many people with the necessary qualifications in fact fail to do so. Where there is a limited franchise with alternative qualifications based on education, income and so on, as in East and Central Africa, there is probably no alternative to voluntary registration as it would be very difficult indeed for the government to sort out which of the individuals in the population possess the required qualifications. But it has, so far, been an almost universal experience that, with a voluntary system of registration, the register becomes less and less accurate, despite frequent revisions, as the years pass following the initial registration. It can therefore be argued that, if there is something approaching universal adult franchise, it is the government's job to see that elections are properly conducted and, hence, that it is the responsibility of officials of the government or of properly constituted committees set up by the government to ensure as far as possible that all eligible electors are duly registered. In British West Africa there has, no doubt, hitherto been a sound case for voluntary registration on administrative and financial grounds, but consideration of the degree of responsibility for registration now accepted by the Governments of India, Indonesia, the French overseas territories and some of the British West Indies suggests that, in

British West Africa too, more of the onus of responsibility for full and accurate registers could be accepted by the various Governments. As a minimum, a periodic enumeration or re-identification of electors is desirable.

With regard to standing for election to legislatures, where there is a limited franchise there also tend in general to be high minimum qualifications placed on candidature. Conversely, where there is something approaching adult franchise as in India, Malaya and much of West Africa, the qualifications for candidates are less stringent. As a result rather higher qualifications are demanded of candidates in East Africa than in West Africa, despite the fact that there is a wider choice of well educated and well qualified Africans in the latter region.

Voting by acclamation is virtually a thing of the past — at any rate for the purpose of central government elections. The days of the whispering vote are also nearly over — but not quite, as the voters in the recent Tanganyika elections were permitted to whisper in the ear of the presiding officer and get him to mark their ballot papers if they couldn't cope with it themselves. The days of electoral colleges are numbered too, though there are still traces of this method of election in parts of Africa. If we concentrate on direct elections conducted in secrecy, there are three standard methods of voting if part of the electorate is illiterate and symbols are used. The first method is the most popular and is used in India, throughout British West Africa, in part of East Africa and part of the Sudan — it is the method of using a separate ballot box for each candidate. It has the advantage that the voter doesn't have to mark his ballot paper in any way and the disadvantage that one can't be too sure what tricks an evil-minded voter may be up to when he gets behind the screen and is alone with the ballot boxes. The second method is the one used in Malaya, in the West Indies, in part of the Sudan and in Tanganyika — there the voter has to mark his ballot paper (and he may perhaps spoil it), but there is only one ballot box and he can't play any tricks with it nor can he very easily take his ballot paper outside and sell it. Experience shows that this method is not so difficult for the illiterate voter as has been sometimes suggested. The third method is the one used in the French territories; there the voter is issued with an official envelope and there is a separate ballot paper for each candidate or each party list of candidates;

he selects the paper with the name of the candidate or candidates for whom he wishes to vote, recognising it by colour or by symbol if he is illiterate, and puts the envelope containing the paper of his choice into the ballot box. All these methods of voting have their advantages and disadvantages and the author's own feeling is that the first method — the multiple ballot box method — may lose its present popularity as the degree of literacy grows and knowledge of how to perpetrate electoral frauds grows with it.

We have seen that in most dependent territories of the British Commonwealth a civil servant is seconded to make the necessary administrative arrangements for elections. Newly independent countries such as India and Malaya and the Sudan have their permanent Election Commissions and the Commissioners normally have the same security of office as a judge and are not responsible to the government in power or to a particular minister.[1] The Commissioners have powers to require government officers to undertake electoral duties and to give instructions as to how these duties are to be carried out. The Western Region of Nigeria has already gone some way towards copying the example of India in appointing an Electoral Commissioner and there may well be a growth of permanent Election Commissions in the near future in West Africa and perhaps later on in East Africa. But it is difficult to see how, on a local basis, it will be possible to dispense with a considerable degree of reliance on the overburdened District Commissioner and his staff to supervise electoral arrangements in his own area.

The first one or two general elections held in the Commonwealth countries of Asia, Africa and the Caribbean have usually been rather one-sided affairs. Sometimes, as in Sierra Leone, Zanzibar, Mauritius and the three regions of Nigeria, this has been mainly due to the fact that voting has been on communal lines and the strong party has been associated with the ethnic majority and its weaker rivals with ethnic or cultural minorities; sometimes, as in India, Malaya, Ghana and some of the territories of the Caribbean, the successful party has been more closely associated than its rivals with the drive for self-government. A high voter turn-out has been a feature at most of these early elections.

[1] The Sudan Election Commission is apparently disbanded after each general election and formed anew for the next election.

Probably some details of the procedures now in use in Commonwealth countries of Africa are too faithful a reproduction of practice in the United Kingdom, just as methods in French African territories may in some respects be too close a replica of the French system. In polling procedure, India and Ghana have perhaps gone further than other tropical Commonwealth countries and territories in adaptation of the electoral system to suit local conditions. For instance, India has dispensed with ballot paper counterfoils whilst Ghana has simplified procedure by abolishing the official marking of ballot papers and doing without tendered ballot papers. Turning to registration procedure, the most interesting experiments are perhaps to be found in some of the Caribbean territories and in the Gambia. Simplification of the rules of the game is desirable provided only that disastrous consequences can be avoided, for many of the staff as well as most of the electorate in developing countries find some of these rules somewhat baffling and often unfair. Why, for instance, should an elector have to vote on a differently coloured ballot paper because an inefficient clerk has marked off the wrong name on the register? Why should a perfectly good vote be rejected at the count because the same foolish clerk has failed to put the official mark on the ballot paper? And what about those illiterates who, with assistance, have completed applications to register as electors and then find themselves omitted from the register through no fault of their own? To those conversant with United Kingdom practice, the answers to these questions may be obvious. But the issues are not nearly so clear cut in the minds of African and Asian peasants and indeed it is by no means certain that the answers should in fact be identical in the varying background of different countries.

This book will have served its purpose if it gives a lead to administrators and others interested in electoral procedure in emergent countries by suggesting possible lines of new development and ways of improvement of method. But the subject matter is very far from exhausted. Studies of electoral procedure in the countries of South and Central America, in Japan, Thailand and the Middle East are required. Japan has used the single non-transferable vote in her elections. Thailand has used ballot boxes with a transparent side to prevent malpractices. The author understands that Bolivia in South America has experience of some of the disadvantages of the French envelope system of voting.

Obviously much can be learnt from studies of the electoral methods of these countries. There is, however, as this book has shown, sufficient diversity of procedure in the British Commonwealth alone to indicate clearly that there is no single right way of conducting elections and the administrator required to make decisions on the subject can only take note of practice elsewhere and then introduce or amend the system in his own country as local conditions seem to dictate.

BIBLIOGRAPHY

PART I: BOOKS, REPORTS, ARTICLES, ETC.

General

W. J. M. Mackenzie, *Free Elections*, (London, 1958).

Sir Ivor Jennings, *The Approach to Self-Government*, (London, 1956).

D. J. R. Scott, 'Problems of West African Elections', in *What are the Problems of Parliamentary Government in West Africa?*, (London, 1958).

W. J. M. Mackenzie and K. E. Robinson (eds.), *Five Elections in Africa*, (Oxford, 1960).

Enid Lakeman and J. D. Lambert, *Voting in Democracies*, (London, 1955).

G. van den Bergh, *Unity in Diversity, a systematic critical analysis of all election systems*, (London, 1957).

Helen Davis, *Constitutions, Electoral Laws, Treaties of States in the Near and Middle East*, (Durham, N. Carolina, 1953).

B. Keith-Lucas, 'Electoral Procedure in Africa' in *Zaire*, Vol. XI, No. 5, May, 1957.

J. A. Laponce, 'The Protection of Minorities by the Electoral System' in *Western Political Quarterly*, Vol. X, No. 2, July, 1957.

Irene Tinker, 'Electoral patterns for plural societies' in *Western Political Quarterly*, Vol. IX, No. 2, June, 1956.

O. M. Bird, 'Administrative Problems of Elections in Developing Countries' in *Journal of African Administration*, Vol. IX, No. 4, October, 1957.

Encyclopaedia Britannica, Articles on 'Ballot' and on 'Voting'.

Africa

Belgian Congo

W. J. Camhof van der Meersch and F. Perin, *Le Droit Electoral au Congo Belge*, (Brussels, 1958).

Article, 'Elections in Ruanda-Urundi' in *The Belgian Congo To-Day*, Vol. VI, No. 2, April, 1957.

Federation of Rhodesia and Nyasaland

Southern Rhodesia

Report, *Report of the Franchise Commission* (Tredgold), (Salisbury, 1957).

Northern Rhodesia
R. S. Burles, 'The Katengo Council elections' in *Journal of African Administration*, Vol. IV, No. 1, January, 1952.

Nyasaland
Colin Leys, 'An election in Nyasaland' in *Political Studies*, Vol. V, No. 3, October, 1957.

France and the overseas French Territories in Africa

H. G. Nicholas, 'French electoral law and machinery' in *Political Studies*, Vol. IV, No. 2, June, 1956.
André Holleaux, 'Les Elections aux Assemblées des Territoires d'Outre-mer' in *Revue Juridique et Politique de l'Union Française*, Vol. X, 1956.
K. E. Robinson, 'Political Development in French West Africa' in Calvin Stillman (ed.), *Africa in the Modern World*, (Chicago, 1955).

Togoland
Report, *Report on Togoland under French Administration*, (U.N. Visiting Mission, 1955), T/1238, April, 1956. Ch. 1, 'Political advancement, containing description of 1955 Assembly elections'.
Report, *Report of the U.N. Commissioner for the Supervision of the Elections in Togoland under French Administration*, T/1392, June, 1958.

Ivory Coast
Michel Vignaud, 'Les élections du 2 janvier 1956 en Côte d'Ivoire' in *Revue Française de Science Politique*, Vol. VI, No. 3, July-September, 1956.

Senegal
K. E. Robinson, 'Polling Day in Senegal' in *West Africa*, 27th April, 4th, 18th May, 1957.

The Gambia

Report, *Revision of Electoral Machinery Committee Report*, Sessional Paper No. 4, 1953.

Ghana (formerly Gold Coast)

Report, *Report of the Select Committee of the Legislative Council on the questions of Elections and Constituencies* (Ewart), (Sessional Paper No. 5 of 1950), (Accra, 1950).
J. H. Price, 'The Gold Coast General Election of 1951' in *West African Affairs*, No. 11.

A. C. Russell and others, 'The Gold Coast Election, 1951
   I. The delimitation of the electoral areas, the registration of
    electors and the conduct of the elections.
   II. The election itself in two areas of Ashanti — the munici-
    pality of Kumasi and the rural electoral district of Kumasi
    South.'
  in *Journal of African Administration*, Vol. III, No. 2, April, 1951.

Article, 'Aspects of the Elections' in *West Africa*, 24th February,
  3rd, 10th March, 17th April, 1951.

Asa Briggs, 'People and Constitution in the Gold Coast' in *West
  Africa*, 8th, 15th, 29th March, 5th, 26th April, 3rd, 10th, 17th,
  May, 1952.

W. Peters, 'Tradition and change in the Saltpond sub-district of the
  Gold Coast Colony' in *Journal of African Administration*, Vol.
  VI, No. 1, January, 1954.

Report, *Report of the Commission of Enquiry into Representational and
  Electoral Reform* (Van Lare), (Sessional paper No. 1 of 1953),
  (Accra, 1953).

P. H. Canham, *Report on the Gold Coast general election, 1954*, (Cape
  Coast, 1954).

George Bennett, 'The Gold Coast general election of 1954' in
  Parliamentary Affairs, Vol. VII, No. 4, Autumn, 1954.

W. B. Birmingham and G. Jahoda, 'A pre-election survey in a semi-
  literate society' in *Public Opinion Quarterly*, Vol. XIX, No. 2,
  Summer, 1955.

1956 Plebiscite in Togoland

Report, *Report of the United Nations Plebiscite Commissioner for the
  Trust Territory of Togoland under British Administration*
  (Espinosa), T/1258 and T/1258/Add. 1, (19th and 29th June,
  1956).

Report, *Report by the Plebiscite Administrator on the Plebiscite held in
  Togoland under U.K. Administration on 9 May, 1956* (Sir John
  Dring), T/1269, (6th July, 1956).

Kenya

Report, *Report of the Commissioner appointed to Enquire into the
  Methods for the Selection of African Representatives to the Legislative Council* (Coutts Report), (Nairobi, 1955).

Sessional Paper, Kenya Government Sessional Paper, No. 39,
  1955/1956. (Contains the Government's Views on the Coutts'
  Report).

G. F. Engholm, 'Kenya's first direct elections for Africans' in
  Parliamentary Affairs, Vol. X, No. 4, Autumn, 1957.

Report, *Report of Mr. Justice Forbes on Irregularities in conduct of General Election in Kiambu*, January, 1957.

Mauritius

Report, *Report of the Commission on the conduct of Local Government Elections in Mauritius* (Keith-Lucas), (Sessional Paper No. 1 of 1956), (Port Louis, 1956).
Report, *Mauritius Electoral Boundary Commission Report*, (Sessional Paper No. 1 of 1958), (Port Louis, 1958).

Nigeria

Federal
Report, *Report of the Constituency Delimitation Commission, 1958*, (Lagos, 1958).

Eastern Region
Report, *Report on the General Election to the Eastern House of Assembly, 1957*, (Enugu, 1957).
J. M. Price, 'Eastern Region Election, 1957' in *West Africa*, 23rd March, 1957.

Northern Region
C. R. Niven, 'Elections in Northern Nigeria' in *Corona*, Vol. IV, No. 5, 1952.
H. G. Jelf, 'The Northerner goes to the Polls' in *Corona*, Vol. V, Nos. 5-7, 1953.
Report, *Report on Electoral Reform in the Northern Region*, (Nigeria, 1953).
J. G. Wallace, 'The Tiv System of Election' in *Journal of African Administration*, Vol. X, No. 2, April, 1958.

Western Region
Report, *Report on the first elections to the Western House of Assembly: General Election 1951*, (Ibadan, 1952).
P. C. Lloyd, 'Some comments on the elections in Nigeria' in *Journal of African Administration*, Vol. IV, No. 3, July, 1952.
Philip Whittaker, 'The preparation of the register of electors in the Western region of Nigeria, 1955-6' in *Journal of African Administration*, Vol. IX, No. 1, January, 1957.
P. H. Balmer, *Report on the holding of the 1956 parliamentary election to the Western House of Assembly*, (Ibadan, 1957).
Report, *Report on Local Government Elections in Western Region of Nigeria, 1958*, (W. R. Sessional Paper No. 7/1958).

Sierra Leone

Report, *Report of the Electoral Reform Commission* (Keith-Lucas), (Freetown, 1954).

Sessional Paper, *Statement of the Government of Sierra Leone on the Report of the Electoral Reform Commission*, (Sessional Paper No. 2, 1955).

B. Keith-Lucas, 'Electoral reform in Sierra Leone' in *Political Studies*, Vol. III, No. 2, June, 1955.

D. Scott, Articles on the General Election in *West Africa*, April/May, 1957.

D. Kirby, 'Ballots in the Bush' in *Journal of African Administration*, Vol. IX, No. 4, 1957.

Somaliland Protectorate

Report, *Report of the Commission of Inquiry into Unofficial Representation in the Legislative Council*, (1958).

Somalia

Report, *Le Prime Elezioni Politiche in Somalia, 1956*, (Stamperia del Governo Mogadiscio).

Sudan

1953 Election

Report, *Report of the Sudan Electoral Commission*, (13th December, 1953). Cmd. 9058. (H.M.S.O. 1954.)

Sukumar Sen, 'The General Election in the Sudan' in *Foreign Affairs Reports*, (New Delhi), Vol. III, No. 2, February, 1954.

Sukumar Sen and Mekki Abbas, 'The general election in the Sudan' in *Parliamentary Affairs*, Vol. VII, No. 3, Summer, 1954.

1958 Election

Report, *Election Commission's Final Report, Parliamentary Elections 1957/8*, (Khartoum, 1958).

Tanganyika

Report, *Report of the Committee on Constitutional Development*, Part IX — Elections, (Dar-es-Salaam, 1951).

Report, *Report of the Special Commissioner appointed to examine matters arising out of the Report of the Constitutional Development Commission* (MacKenzie), (Dar-es-Salaam, 1953).

Report, *Report of the Committee appointed to study Government's proposals regarding the qualifications of voters and candidates for Elections to Legislative Council*, (Govt. Paper No. 1 of 1957), (Dar-es-Salaam, 1957).

K. G. Mather, 'A Note on African Councils in the Rungwe District of Tanganyika and their Election' in *Journal of African Administration*, Vol. IX, No. 4, October, 1957.

Uganda

Sessional Paper, *Elections to Legislative Council*, (Sessional Paper No. 4 of 1957/58), (Entebbe, 1957).
C.P.S. Allen, *A Report on the First Direct Elections to the Legislative Council of the Uganda Protectorate*, (Entebbe, 1959).

Zanzibar

Report, *Methods of choosing unofficial members of the Legislative Council* (Coutts), (Zanzibar, 1956).
J. C. Penney, *Report of the Supervisor of Elections on the Elections in Zanzibar, 1957*, (Zanzibar, 1958).

Asia

Ceylon

Report, *Report of the Commission on Constitutional Reform* (Soulbury), 1945, Cmd. 6677. (H.M.S.O.), Ch. X, 'Franchise.'
1947 Election Report, *Report of the First Parliamentary General Election, 1947*, (Ceylon Sessional Paper VI, 1948).
I. D. S. Weerawardana, 'The General Elections in Ceylon, 1952' in *Ceylon Historical Journal*, Vol. 2, Nos. 1 and 2, July and October, 1952.
Sir Ivor Jennings, 'Additional notes on the General Election of 1952' in *Ceylon Historical Journal*, Vol. 2, Nos. 3 and 4, January and April, 1953.
S. Namasivayam, 'Ceylon's General Election, 1952' in *Parliamentary Affairs*, Vol. V, No. 4, Autumn, 1952.
Pierre Meile, 'Les Elections de Ceylan' in *Revue Française de Science Politique*, Vol. VI, No. 2, April-June, 1956.
S. Namasivayam, 'The General Election in Ceylon in 1956' in *Parliamentary Affairs*, Vol. IX, No. 3, Summer, 1956.

India

Report, *Report on the first general elections in India, 1951-2*, by the Election Commission. 2 Vols, (Government of India, 1955).
Ela Sen, 'Free India faces her first elections' in *Parliamentary Affairs*, Vol. V, No. 2, Spring, 1952.
Ed. S. V. Kogekar and Richard L. Park, *Reports on the Indian general elections, 1951-2*, (Popular Press, Bombay, 1956).

W. H. Morris-Jones, 'The Indian Elections' in *Political Quarterly*, Vol. XXIII, No. 3, 1952.

Ela Sen, 'The Indian general election and after' in *Asiatic Review*, April, 1952.

M. Venkatarangaya, *The General Election in the City of Bombay*, (Bombay, 1953).

Irene Tinker and Mil Walker, 'The first General Elections in India and Indonesia' in *Far Eastern Survey*, Vol. XXV, No. 7, July, 1956.

W. H. Morris-Jones, *Parliament in India*, (London, 1957).

W. H. Morris-Jones, 'Indian Voting Behaviour' in *Pacific Affairs*, Vol. XXX, No. 3, September, 1957.

Indonesia

H. Feith, 'Towards Elections in Indonesia' in *Pacific Affairs*, Vol. XXVII, No. 1, March, 1954.

B. R. Compton, 'The Indonesian Electoral Law' in *Far Eastern Survey*, April-May, 1954.

Robert C. Bone, 'Organisation of the Indonesian Elections' in *The American Political Science Review*, Vol. XLIX, No. 4, December, 1955.

Irene Tinker and Mil Walker, 'The First General Elections in India and Indonesia' in *Far Eastern Survey*, Vol. XXV, No. 7, July, 1956.

Herbert Feith, *The Indonesian Elections of 1955*, (Cornell 1957).

Japan

Chitoshi Yanaga, *Japanese People and Politics*, (New York, 1956), Ch. 12, 'Electing the Policy Makers'.

Hessell Tiltman, 'A Japanese General Election' in *Parliamentary Affairs*, Vol. VIII, No. 3, Summer, 1955.

Harold S. Quigley and John E. Turner, *The New Japan*, (Minnesota, 1956), Ch. 18, 'Elections'.

Malaya

Report, *Report on the introduction of elections in the municipality of George Town, Penang, 1951*, (Kuala Lumpur, 1953).

Report, *Report of the Committee appointed to examine the question of elections to the Federal Legislative Council*, (Kuala Lumpur, 1954).

Report, *Report of the Constituency Delineation Commission*, (Kuala Lumpur, 1954).

F. G. Carnell, 'Constitutional Reform and Elections in Malaya' in *Pacific Affairs*, Vol. XXVII, No. 3, September, 1954.

T. E. Smith, *Report on the first election to the Legislative Council of the Federation of Malaya*, (Kuala Lumpur, 1955).

F. G. Carnell, 'The Malayan Elections' in *Pacific Affairs*, Vol. XXVIII, No. 4, December, 1955.

Irene Tinker, 'Malayan Elections: Electoral pattern for plural Societies' in *Western Political Quarterly*, Vol. IX, No. 2, June, 1956.

Report, *Report of the Federation of Malaya Constitutional Commission* (Reid), Col. 330, 1957.

Report, *Report of the Election Commission on the Delimitation of Constituencies, 1958*, (Kuala Lumpur, 1958).

Pakistan

Report, *Report of the Electoral Reforms Commission*, (The Gazette of Pakistan, No. S.1033, 24th April, 1956).

Sarawak

J. C. B. Fisher, *Report on the Kuching Municipal Council Elections, 1956*, (Kuching, Sarawak, 1957).

Singapore

Report, *Report of the Constitutional Commission*, (Singapore, 1954).

Report, *Report of the Electoral Boundaries Delimitation Committee*, (Singapore, 1954).

Report, *Report of the Commission of Inquiry into corrupt, illegal or undesirable practices at elections*, (Singapore, 1958).

Caribbean

Barbados

Report, *Report on Local Government* by Sir John Maude, (Bridgetown, 1949), Qualifications for voting, pp. 7-9; also pp. 42-3.

British Guiana

Report, *Report of the Constitutional Commission, 1950-51*, (Waddington), Col. 280, (H.M.S.O.), Ch. IV, 'Franchise'.

Colin A. Hughes, 'The British Guiana general election, 1953' in *Parliamentary Affairs*, Vol. VII, No. 2, Spring, 1954.

Report, *Report on Local Government in British Guiana, 1955* (Marshall) Ch. XI, 'Universal Franchise for Local Government'.

Report, *Report on the General Election 1957*, (includes instructions to returning officers, polling officers and counting assistants).

Dominica

Report, *Report on the Legislative Council general elections, 1954*.

Report, *Report on the Legislative Council general elections 1957*, (St Lucia, 1957).

Grenada

Report, *Report on the Legislative Council general elections, 1954*, (St George's, 1955).

Jamaica

Report, *Report of the Chief Electoral Officer on the 1944 General Election*, (Kingston, 1945).

Colin A. Hughes, 'Adult suffrage in Jamaica, 1944-55' in *Parliamentary Affairs*, Vol. VIII, No. 3, Summer, 1955.

Report, *Report of the Chief Electoral Officer on the 1949 General Election*, with appendices listing instructions to registration, revising, returning, and presiding officers, and specimen forms, (Kingston, 1950).

Report, *Report of the Committee appointed to examine the existing electoral laws of Jamaica*, (Kingston, 1957).

St Lucia

Report, *Report on general election, 1954.*

Report, *Report on Legislative Council general election, 1957.*

St Vincent

Report, *Report on general election, 1954*, (Kingstown, 1954).

Trinidad and Tobago

Report, *Report of the Franchise Committee, 1944.*

Report, *Report on the Legislative Council general election, 1946*, (Port of Spain, 1947).

Report, *Report on the Legislative Council general election, 1950*, (Trinidad, 1954).

Other Countries

Australia

L. F. Crisp, 'Compulsory Voting in Australia' in *Parliamentary Government in the Commonwealth*, (Hansard Society).

Canada and the U.S.A.

Norman Ward, *The Canadian House of Commons — Representation*, (Toronto, 1950).

J. P. Harris, *Registration of Voters in the United States*, (Washington, 1929).

B. M. Bernard, *Election Laws of the 48 States*, (New York, 1950).

Donald S. Strong, *Registration of Voters in Alabama*, (Alabama, 1956).

D. W. Brogan, *The American Political System*, (London, 1943).

H. R. Penniman (ed.), *Sait's 'American Parties and Elections'*, (New York, 1948).
John H. Fenton and Kenneth N. Vines, 'Negro Registration in Louisiana' in *The American Political Science Review*, Vol. LI, No. 3, September, 1957.

Germany

James K. Pollock, 'The West German Electoral Law of 1953' in *The American Political Science Review*, Vol. XLIX, No. 1, March, 1955.

Jugoslavia

Thomas T. Hammond, 'Jugoslav elections: Democracy in Small Doses' in *Political Science Quarterly*, Vol. LXX, No. 1, March, 1955.

Malta

Report, *Report on the general elections 26th - 28th February, 1955*, (Malta Government Gazette, No. LXXXI, 28th June, 1955).

United Kingdom

Report, *Report of the Royal Commission on Electoral Systems in the United Kingdom*, Cd. 5163, 1910, H.M.S.O.
A. N. Schofield, *Parliamentary Elections*, (London, 1955).
B. Keith-Lucas, *The English Local Government Franchise*, (Oxford, 1952).
A. N. Schofield, *Local Government Elections*, (London, 1954).
D. E. Butler, *The Electoral System in Britain 1918-1951*, (Oxford, 1953).
H. G. Nicholas, *To the Hustings — election scenes from English fiction*, (London, 1956).
W. G. Gillings, *Handbook for the Conduct of Polls at Local Government Elections*, (London, 1952).

PART II: LEGISLATION DEALING WITH CENTRAL GOVERNMENT ELECTION PROCEDURE IN TROPICAL AFRICAN TERRITORIES AND COUNTRIES OF THE BRITISH COMMONWEALTH

Federation of Rhodesia and Nyasaland
The Electoral Act, 1958.

The Gambia
The Colony Elections Ordinance, 1954.
The Legislative Council (Elections) Rules, 1954.

Ghana
The Electoral Provisions Ordinance, 1953.
The Electoral Provisions (Assembly Elections) Regulations, 1954, (as amended).

Kenya
The Legislative Council Ordinance.
The Legislative Council (African Representation) Ordinance, 1956, as amended, and rules made under this Ordinance including The Legislative Council (African Representation) (Registration of Voters) Rules, 1956, (as amended).

Mauritius
Representation of the People Ordinance, 1958.

Nigeria
Eastern Region: The Eastern House of Assembly Electoral Regulations, 1955, (as amended).
Northern Region: The Northern House of Assembly (Elected Members) Electoral Regulations, 1956.
Western Region: The Parliamentary and Local Government Electoral Regulations, 1955.

Sierra Leone
The House of Representatives (Registration of Electors) Regulations, 1956, (as amended).
The House of Representatives (Elections) Regulations, 1957, (as amended).

Somaliland Protectorate
The Legislative Council (Elections) Ordinance, 1958.

Tanganyika
The Legislative Council (Elections) Ordinance, 1957.

Uganda
The Legislative Council (Elections) Ordinance, 1957.

Zanzibar
The Legislative Council (Elections) Decree, 1957.
The Legislative Council (Elections) (Registration) Rules, 1957.

INDEX

273